Custom Edition for
Prince George's Community College

# Foundations for College Writing

Compiled by
Marci Dawson
&
Anthony DeBartolomeo

Taken from:

*Writing for Life: Sentences and Paragraphs*
by D.J. Henry

*Writing for Life: Paragraphs and Essays*
by D.J. Henry

*Along These Lines: Writing Sentences and Paragraphs,* Fourth Edition
by John Sheridan Biays and Carol Wershoven

*Pathways Writing Scenarios: Sentences and Paragraphs*
by Kathleen T. McWhorter

*Writing with Confidence: Writing Effective Sentences and Paragraphs,* Ninth Edition
by Alan Meyers

Revision material (pages 84-107)
by Anthony DeBartolomeo at Prince George's Community College

**Learning Solutions**

New York   Boston   San Francisco
London   Toronto   Sydney   Tokyo   Singapore   Madrid
Mexico City   Munich   Paris   Cape Town   Hong Kong   Montreal

Cover Art: Courtsey of Photodisc/Getty Images

Taken from:

*Writing for Life: Sentences and Paragraphs*
by D. J. Henry
Copyright © 2011 by Pearson Education, Inc.
Published by Longman
New York, New York 10036

*Writing for Life: Paragraphs and Essays*
by D. J. Henry
Copyright © 2011 by Pearson Education, Inc.
Published by Longman

*Along These Lines: Writing Sentences and Paragraphs,*
Fourth Edition
by John Sheridan Biays and Carol Wershoven
Copyright © 2010, 2007, 2004, 2001 by
John Sheridan Biays and Carol Wershoven
Published by Prentice Hall
Upper Saddle River, New Jersey 07458

*Pathways Writing Scenarios: Sentences and Paragraphs*
by Kathleen T. McWhorter
Copyright © 2010 by Pearson Education, Inc.
Published by Longman

*Writing with Confidence: Writing Effective Sentences and
Paragraphs,* Ninth Edition
by Alan Meyers
Copyright © 2009 by Pearson Education, Inc.
Published by VangoBooks
Boston, MA 02116

This special edition published in cooperation with Pearson Learning Solutions.

All trademarks, service marks, registered trademarks, and registered service marks are the property of their respective
owners and are used herein for identification purposes only.

Pearson Learning Solutions, 501 Boylston Street, Suite 900, Boston, MA 02116
A Pearson Education Company
www.pearsoned.com

Printed in the United States of America

11 12 V092 17 16 15


000200010270645533

JL

ISBN 10: 0-558-87228-X
ISBN 13: 978-0-558-87228-1

# Detailed Contents

## Foundations for College Writing

Taken from: *Writing for Life: Sentences and Paragraphs* by D.J. Henry

Taken from: *Pathways Writing Scenarios: Sentences and Paragraphs* by Kathleen T. McWhorter

Taken from: *Writing for Life: Paragraphs and Essays* by D.J. Henry

# Preface and Course Objectives for DVE-0011

The *Foundations for Writing* text is a collaborative effort and was designed with the unique needs of the students in Developmental Composition at Prince George's Community College. Students in developmental classes tend to be a unique and diverse blend of various ages, backgrounds, experiences, and cultures. Additionally, many developmental students have already been in the workforce, raised a family, or sought other interests, and are now returning to school for enrichment, professional training, or further education. While these students may need some review to assist them in returning to academia, these same students also offer insights and experiences invaluable to the class.

This textbook draws material from five previously published texts (Henry's *Writing for Life: Sentences and Paragraphs*, Henry's *Writing for Life: Paragraphs and Essays*, McWhorter's *Pathways Writing Scenarios: Sentences and Paragraphs*, Biays's *Along These Lines: Writing Sentences and Paragraphs*, and Meyer's *Writing with Confidence*). There is also a section included in the text authored by Anthony DeBartolomeo, Assistant Professor of Developmental English at Prince George's Community College. We have tried to organize this textbook in as logical a manner as possible to address the fundamental basics of writing, while providing practical applications for these concepts in a clearly organized form that students and instructors can follow. The various chapters are arranged into the following sections:

♦ The basics of writing a paragraph, from the idea, through the prewriting stages, into outlining, creating a topic sentence, creating the first draft, and revising the entire paragraph for content, organization, wording, and grammar.
♦ Rhetorical strategies, their definitions, purposes, and methods.

- ◆ Sentence structures, such as sentence types, variety, and uses; the several parts of a sentence, such as subjects and verbs; and how to avoid common sentence errors.
- ◆ Mechanics, such as grammar and punctuation.
- ◆ Reading selections that illustrate each of the rhetorical strategies and are chosen to be of interest to the student, from professional writers and others with whom the students would be familiar.

This textbook is further designed to help students meet the course outcomes of DVE-0011, so that, upon successful completion of the course, the student should be able to:

- ◆ identify subjects and verbs,
- ◆ identify correct forms of nouns, pronouns, adjectives and adverbs,
- ◆ identify sentences according to structure,
- ◆ make the subject and verb agree,
- ◆ make the pronoun and antecedent agree,
- ◆ write the correct tense and forms of verbs,
- ◆ punctuate phrases, clauses, and sentences according to conventional rules; use standard forms of verbs, nouns, pronouns, adjectives, and adverbs; and write a sentence that is not a fragment, comma splice or run-on,
- ◆ write an effective topic sentence,
- ◆ select appropriate illustrations, details, or examples to develop the topic sentence,
- ◆ organize the illustrations, details, or examples in paragraph form,
- ◆ include transitional devices to achieve coherence within the paragraph,
- ◆ proofread a paragraph to eliminate common errors in usage and mechanics, (e.g., fragments, comma splices, run-on sentences, and/or misspellings),
- ◆ compose original paragraphs that demonstrate critical thinking based on an assigned reading/writing task.

Finally, regardless of a person's profession, aspirations, or hobbies, that individual will be expected to express him or herself effectively in writing throughout his or her life. In fact, a primary requirement for most jobs today is "good communication skills;" that is, critical thinking, cogent writing, and good work ethics. Whether in a job application, a workplace report, or a letter to a child's teacher, one's writing tells a great deal about that person – who he or she is, what he or she wants, how he or she feels, and even how intelligent he or she is perceived to be. Students who enter the classroom are filled with ideas, opinions, and creativity, and though they are often struggling to be heard, these individuals are unable to clearly express their thoughts in written form. This textbook is designed not only to help the student prepare for the writing tasks expected of college-level courses, but also the writing tasks he or she will undoubtedly face in the workplace, at home, and in everyday life. We hope we have provided both instructors and students alike with the tools necessary to prepare students for future courses and enrich them with a sense of accomplishment and satisfaction that they can express themselves competently in writing.

Anthony DeBartolomeo and Marcia Dawson

# Foundations *for* College Writing

# 1 Preparing to Learn about Writing

In countless situations in life, preparation is essential to success. Even a trip to the grocery store requires some planning in order to get all the items needed to feed a family and run a household in the most economical way. A wise shopper thinks about the health and well-being of those who will consume the goods. He takes steps to buy the best products and foods at the cheapest prices. A careful shopper may create a menu, check the pantry and make a list of what is needed, read the ads for sale items, or clip coupons. In short, an effective shopper thinks about the outcome or goal of each shopping trip before he goes shopping.

Writing is an essential life skill, and learning to write well allows you to express yourself, influence others, succeed in college, and compete in the job market. By starting your academic career with this writing course, you are preparing for success. You are laying a sturdy foundation for writing for life. If you are like many others, you may have a few qualms about writing, but take heart! With the right attitude, a study plan, and clear goals, you can count on having good outcomes. You *can* learn to write well. So get ready to learn about writing!

# What's the Point of Preparing to Learn about Writing?

Like any other worthwhile endeavor, learning requires preparation. Preparation usually involves setting a goal, adopting an attitude for success, setting aside time to accomplish the task, gathering tools or supplies, and planning a course of action.

## PHOTOGRAPHIC ORGANIZER: PREPARING TO LEARN ABOUT WRITING

The following pictures represent one student's effort to prepare to learn about writing. Write a caption for each photograph that identifies her efforts to prepare to learn.

What is this?

What is this?

What is this?

What is this?

What's the point?

# Making a Point about Preparing to Learn about Writing: One Student Writer's Response

The following paragraph records one student's efforts to prepare to learn about writing. As you read the paragraph, underline specific steps he took that you might use as well.

## My Plan for Success

(1) I am very nervous about taking this English course! (2) Our professor Mrs. Hawkins gave the whole class advice about getting ready to learn about writing. (3) I am going to take her advice and create a study space and a study plan. (4) I have set up a study area in my bedroom with a table, chair, desk lamp, and computer. (5) On my desk are a dictionary, thesaurus, paper, pens, pencils, pencil sharpener, stapler, and hole-puncher. (6) The next step is to make a study schedule based on the list of assignments in the course syllabus. (7) I will study for this class every Monday, Tuesday, and Thursday evening from 5:00 p.m. until 7:00 p.m. (8) Also, I will study with Sherri, Jamal, and Anton every Wednesday for an hour after our class. (9) Our study group is going to be great! (10) If one of us has to miss class, we can get class notes and assignments from someone in the group. (11) I am also going to ask questions in class or see my teacher for help. (12) For example, Mrs. Hawkins makes notes on our papers about what needs more work. (13) I am going to make a list of the things I don't understand and ask her to explain them. (14) I am going to do my best.

# Preparing Yourself to Learn about Writing

As you prepare to learn about writing, take some time to evaluate yourself as a student writer. Think about your attitude, ways you can become an active learner, your relationship with your teacher, your study plan, and how you will track your growing writing abilities. The more you reflect and the more you prepare, the more likely you are to learn about writing and to become an effective writer.

## The Attitude of Learning

### Use Positive Self-Talk

Many people have negative thoughts going through their minds that constantly repeat "I can't" phrases: "I can't write. . . . I can't spell." Often these negative attitudes are the result of a prior negative event. A basic step to success is changing that script in your head. Replace "I can't" thoughts with "I can." Then, take steps to prove that you can. For example, instead of believing "I just can't spell," think, "I can use a spell checker," or "I can make a list of words I often misspell and memorize their correct spellings." Success begins in your mind!

## Be an Active Learner

Come to class. Be on time. Sit where you can see—and be seen. Take notes. Ask questions. Do your work—on time! Make connections between assignments and learning outcomes. Apply what you learn. Seek help. Find a study partner. Take responsibility for your own learning. The more you do, the more you learn!

## Trust Your Teacher

One of the toughest tasks in a writing class is getting and accepting feedback on your writing. Many of us take the teacher's feedback as a personal rejection. Some of us become defensive. Think of feedback as a form of coaching from a personal trainer. A personal trainer assesses your strengths and needs, creates an exercise program, and corrects your form to ensure that you make progress. Likewise, your teacher is your writing coach who offers expert advice. So accept feedback as helpful advice. Take note of those errors, study the rules, and revise your work. Turn feedback into an opportunity to learn!

---

**THE ATTITUDE OF LEARNING**

Read the following reflection written by a student that records how she feels about writing and why. On a separate sheet of paper, write a letter to her, giving her advice to help her overcome her anxiety.

I have some bad memories about writing. I will never forget one teacher; I call him "Mr. Gotcha." My papers were never good enough for him. At first, I spent a lot of time coming up with something to write about. It didn't matter how much time I spent, he always put red marks all over my papers, and he always gave me Ds. I never read his comments. I mean what was the point? I think he didn't like me because I was quiet and sat in the back of the class. On one day, I didn't hear the page number he told us to turn to, so I asked "where are we at?" And instead of answering my question, he said, "At? At? You are nowhere when you end a sentence with a preposition!" I had no idea what he was talking about. I still avoid writing as much as I can.

# Create a Study Plan

A vital part of preparing to learn about writing is creating a study plan.

## Gather Your Tools

Foster success by creating a place to study that is equipped with all the tools you will need: reference materials such as your textbook, a dictionary, and a thesaurus; pens (blue or black ink), pencils, and paper; a stapler and 3-hole punch. Optional items include a computer and a printer. In addition, you will need a 3-ring binder to file the teacher's syllabus, handouts, assignments, class notes, textbook notes, and lab work. Be sure that you bring your textbook, binder, pens, and pencils to class every day.

## Set Goals

Students who set goals reduce stress, improve concentration, and increase self-confidence. Use the following general guidelines to set effective goals. Aim high: Demand your best effort. Write goals down: Recording goals makes them clear and important. Be specific: Instead of writing, "Stop procrastinating," write, "Study English on Monday, Tuesday, and Wednesday evenings between 7 and 9 o'clock." Be positive: Instead of writing, "Don't make stupid errors," write, "Use commas properly." Set priorities: Rank goals based on need so you can pace your work. Set daily goals based on larger goals: Break a larger goal such as "Understand how to use semicolons" into a series of steps such as "Study the rule, take notes, and do the exercises; then proofread my paper for proper use of semicolons."

## Take Action

Turn your goals into action steps by setting up a time schedule for your study. The following study plan is easy to use, flexible, and will help you set long-term, intermediate, and short-term goals.

| SAMPLE STUDY PLAN | |
|---|---|
| **Long-Term Schedule:** | Record ongoing weekly commitments such as job hours, class meetings, church, and so on, for the entire semester. |
| **Intermediate Schedule:** | Make a short list of the events taking place and the tasks to be completed in your class (or classes) this week. Make a fresh list each week, as these activities will change from week to week: Writing assignment Tuesday; Math quiz Tuesday; Chapter 3 in English by Wednesday. |
| **Short-Term Schedule:** | List your daily schedule. Be specific! Then, cross off each goal as you accomplish it. Monday: 9:00–9:30 Revise writing assignment; 12:00–12:30 Review math for quiz; 3:30 Return books to library. |

## CREATE A STUDY PLAN

Complete the following chart to create your own study plan. Discuss your plan with your class or in a small group. How will your plan change throughout the semester?

| MY STUDY PLAN | |
|---|---|
| **Long-Term Schedule:** | |
| **Intermediate Schedule:** | |
| **Short-Term Schedule:** | |

## ATTITUDE AND BEHAVIORS OF LEARNING

Complete the survey.

| WRITING ATTITUDE AND BEHAVIOR SURVEY | Strongly Agree | Agree | Disagree | Strongly Disagree |
|---|---|---|---|---|
| **1.** I enjoy writing. | | | | |
| **2.** Teacher feedback is discouraging. | | | | |
| **3.** I enjoy sharing what I write with peers. | | | | |
| **4.** I want to improve my writing. | | | | |
| **5.** I have a quiet, well-equipped study place. | | | | |
| **6.** I always come to class prepared. | | | | |
| **7.** I complete assignments on time. | | | | |
| **8.** I read and study to improve my writing. | | | | |
| **9.** I manage my time wisely. | | | | |
| **10.** I need to improve my writing attitude or behavior. | | | | |

# Learning Outcomes for Student Writers

A **learning outcome** states what a student writer should know or be able to do as the result of a lesson or course of study. The following chart outlines four major learning outcomes (goals) for student writers. Each major learning outcome is built upon its listed block of skills and concepts. If you think about these learning outcomes as you study, your writing will improve more quickly. Notice that the learning outcomes are stated as actions. Every assignment is an opportunity to prove mastery of one or more of these learning outcomes.

## Learning Outcomes—Connect Reading and Writing

***Read to Write*; Think Critically**
- Analyze/respond to a piece of writing
- Write a summary
- Study/apply rules of writing

## Learning Outcomes—Structure

**Identify/Apply the *Structure* of a paragraph and an essay**
- Introduction
- Main Idea
- Body: Major, Minor Supporting Details
- Conclusion

## Learning Outcomes—Writing Process

**Identify/Apply the phases of the *Writing Process***

**PREWRITE**
- Analyze the three aspects of the writing situation
  - Topic
  - Purpose
  - Audience
- Brainstorm, Map, Outline

**DRAFT** paragraphs and essays
- Compose a main idea: topic sentence, thesis sentence
- Generate adequate and relevant details
- Use logical order of ideas

**REVISE** drafts for effective expression
- Control sentence structure
- Use words appropriately

**PROOFREAD** drafts for effective expression
- Identify and correct errors in grammar

## Learning Outcome—Self-Evaluation

***Self-evaluate*; Think Critically**
- Reflect on writing progress
- Reflect on writing process

# Using Learning Outcomes to Improve Your Writing

You will achieve these learning outcomes as you study *Writing for Life*. To help you make the most of your studies, the icons for these learning outcomes appear in the margins throughout this textbook. Use these icons to connect a lesson to its learning outcome.

---

**LEARNING OUTCOMES: CREATE A STUDY PLAN**

To begin your learning process about writing, identify what you already know about writing and what you need to learn. Answer the following questions.

Which three learning outcomes pose the greatest challenge? Why?

_____

_____

_____

Which three learning outcomes have you already mastered? How could you prove mastery?

_____

_____

_____

---

**LEARNING OUTCOMES: CREATE A STUDY PLAN**

Compare these learning outcomes to your course syllabus. Then answer the questions below.

Which learning outcomes are also on your syllabus?

_____

_____

_____

Skim the textbook and locate two lessons that have challenging learning outcomes. What are the outcomes? What are the page numbers for the lessons? How did you locate these lessons?

_____

_____

_____

Practice 5

Practice 6

# Create a Portfolio of Your Work

To ensure that you learn about writing and to develop writing skills, you need to track your strengths, your needs, and your growth. A portfolio enables you to organize your work and think about what you are learning.

## What Is a Portfolio?

A portfolio is a collection of all the work you do as a writer organized in a notebook or in an electronic folder. Your portfolio shows how much time and effort you put into studying and practicing your writing. A portfolio allows you to assess your own strengths and needs, and to prove your learning outcomes. In your portfolio, you can show which learning outcomes you are working toward. You can also display the learning outcomes you have achieved. Your portfolio shows what you know and what you are able to do as a student writer.

## What Should I Include in My Portfolio?

Your portfolio may include class notes and activities, textbook notes and exercises, grammar tests, lab activities, reflective journal entries, prewrites, drafts, revisions, edited drafts, and polished copies of your writing. By collecting and organizing your work, you are better able to reflect upon your strengths and needs. As a result, you are able to achieve the learning outcomes you need to as a writer. For example, one learning outcome is to "identify and apply the phases of the writing process." (See page 8.) Thus, you will keep in your portfolio all the prewrites, drafts, and final copies of your writings. In addition, each of the lessons, practices, workshops, and learning logs in this textbook is tied to one or more learning outcomes. An icon is placed next to each activity to identify which learning outcome you are working on. So the learning activities in *Writing for Life* are excellent entries for your portfolio. The pages of this textbook are tear-outs. So tear out the pages and organize them in your portfolio to prove your progress based on learning outcomes.

## What Is a Reflective Journal Entry?

A reflective journal entry is an informal piece of writing. When you reflect, you self-evaluate your work as a student writer. For example, you may write a journal entry that lists and responds to the feedback that your teacher gave on a piece of your writing. Reflective journal entries are tied to the learning outcome "Self-evaluation." In this type of journal entry, you reflect upon both your "writing process" and your "writing progress." (See page 8.)

# Reflective Journals: Self-Evaluation

## Critical Thinking Questions

To deepen your critical thinking about the feedback you have received, your reflective journal entry should answer the following questions:

- [ ] What steps did I take to write this piece? Did I prewrite, write, revise, and proofread? Do I need to spend more time on any one step?

- [ ] Which of my errors are proofreading errors? What steps will I take to catch these proofreading errors on my next piece of writing?

- [ ] Which of these errors results from the need to study a certain rule? Where in my textbook is this rule found? How much time do I need to learn this rule? How will I study this rule (take notes, complete exercises)?

# What Is the Best Way to Set Up My Portfolio?

Many students purchase a 3-ring binder and tabbed dividers to section off different types of study and writing tasks. Be sure to date and label all work.

All work that is turned in for feedback should include the following information: At the top of the first page and flush with the left margin, place your name, your professor's name, the course name or number (include the section number if the course has multiple sections), and the date you're turning in the paper, each on a separate line with double-spacing throughout.

Iama Writer

Dr. Richards

ENC 001: Section 32

September 24, 2010

All independent work that is created for your notebook or portfolio should be labeled with the date and the type of work or learning outcome:

Oct. 9, 2010
Reflective Journal Entry for Narrative Paragraph

Oct. 10, 2010
Comma Splices, Chapter 18, pp. 330–345

Oct. 12, 2010
The Process Paragraph, Class notes

The point of labeling is to help you see and discuss your strengths and needs as they occur in real time.

## CONNECTING LEARNING OUTCOMES TO LESSONS IN *WRITING FOR LIFE*

To get the best use of this textbook, learn more about the connection between the learning outcomes on page 8 and the lessons in *Writing for Life*. Answer the following questions.

**1.** Go to page 51 in Chapter 3 "Understanding the Paragraph." What is the learning outcome for the section "What's the Point of a Paragraph"? ........................................................

**2.** Go to page 58 in Chapter 3. What is the learning outcome for the section "Developing Your Point Using a Paragraph"? ........................................................

**3.** Go to page 69 in Chapter 4 "The Descriptive Paragraph." What is the learning outcome for Practice 1? ........................................................

**4.** Go to page 72 in Chapter 4. List the learning outcome for the section "Workshop: Description Graphic Organizer and Writer's Journal"? ........................................................

**5.** Go to page 182 in Chapter 10 "Sentence Variety." What is the learning outcome for the Writing Assignments? ........................................................

**6.** Go to page 183 in Chapter 10. What is the learning outcome for the Academic Learning Log? ........................................................

## THE PORTFOLIO

Write an e-mail to a classmate who missed class. Explain the portfolio process. Explain how portfolio assessment will improve critical thinking.

........................................................

........................................................

........................................................

........................................................

........................................................

........................................................

To test and track your understanding of what you have studied, answer the following questions.

**1.** What are some of the materials and supplies needed by a writing student?

------------------------------------------------------------

**2.** What are the three attitudes of learning discussed in this chapter?

------------------------------------------------------------

**3.** What three general steps can you take to create a study plan?

------------------------------------------------------------

**4.** What is a learning outcome?

------------------------------------------------------------

------------------------------------------------------------

**5.** What are the four major learning outcomes?

------------------------------------------------------------

**6.** What is a portfolio?

------------------------------------------------------------

**7.** What is included in a portfolio?

------------------------------------------------------------

------------------------------------------------------------

**8.** What is a reflective journal entry?

------------------------------------------------------------

------------------------------------------------------------

*Academic Learning Log*

**mywritinglab**

**WANT A BETTER GRADE?**
For more practice with preparing to learn about writing, go to **www.mywritinglab.com** <http://www.mywritinglab.com/> > Getting Ready to Write > **Prepare to Learn about Writing.**

# 2 Thinking Through the Writing Process

The writing process has four stages: prewriting, drafting, revising, and proofreading.

Writing develops, records, and communicates your thoughts to other people. Careful writers rely on the writing process to discover, organize, and record information in response to a specific writing situation.

# What's the Point of the Writing Process?

The following photographs document some of the situations in which we use writing in our everyday, college, and working lives. Write a caption for each picture that includes a reason for writing well in that situation. Then, state the point of writing well.

PHOTOGRAPHIC ORGANIZER: REASONS TO WRITE

What's the point of writing well?

---

## My First Thoughts: A Prewriting Activity

Set a time limit, such as five minutes, and jot down in your notebook your thoughts about the importance of writing. Do not let your pen or pencil stop, even if you must repeat ideas. Keep writing until the time limit is up.

# Making a Point about the Writing Process: One Student Writer's Response

The following paragraph is one writer's response to the question "What's the point of writing?"

> Writing is a necessary skill for success in college, everyday, and working life. Everyone knows that writing essays and reports is expected in the college classroom; however, writing is also important in other situations. For example, last week I got an e-mail from my cousin thanking me for the money I loaned him. His note meant so much to me that I printed it out and put it on the refrigerator as a daily reminder that I can make a difference in someone else's life. His note hangs right next to the newspaper clipping of a letter I wrote to the editor. A friend of mine was hurt in an accident due to a drunk driver, so I wrote a letter warning people against driving while under the influence. Finally, good writing is key to a successful career, too. An effective cover letter or resume can make a big difference in getting a job or promotion. Overall, writing helps me to learn and share ideas.

# Understanding the Point: Assessing the Writing Situation

When you write, you develop a point about a topic to fulfill a purpose for a specific audience. To develop your point, you need to think about two aspects of writing: the writing situation and the writing process.

A piece of writing develops in response to a specific **writing situation** that is composed of the **topic** (your subject), the **purpose** for writing (your goal), and the **audience** (your reader).

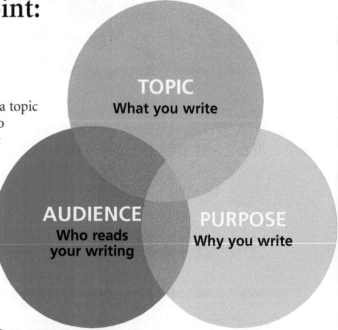

## The Topic: What You Write

When writing about situations in our personal lives, we may choose to compose a letter of complaint to a business or an e-mail to a friend. Often in these circumstances, the topic of our writing naturally emerges from our need to communicate. However, when writing for college, many of us face writer's block in our search for a topic. You can break through writer's block by building a topic bank for college writing.

The following thinking guide can help you generate a bank of topics.

## The Writing Situation Step by Step:

### Topic

Build a bank of topics by listing ideas in a special section in your notebook. Use the following prompts to create several lists:

☐ Write down the major topics of importance in a specific course (such as biology, psychology, history).

☐ Find interesting or important current events.

    ☐ Topics most often covered in magazines and newspapers

    ☐ Controversial topics from television (such as news and talk shows)

    ☐ Topics about which you want to learn more

    ☐ Topics about which you feel deeply

    ☐ Hobbies and personal interests

☐ Share your lists with your classmates; use class discussion to generate more ideas.

☐ Review and expand your list on a regular basis.

As you continue to build your bank of general topics, read, read, and read some more. Read newspapers, magazines, and textbooks for additional topics. Many textbooks provide writing topics at the end of sections or chapters; in addition, headings and subheadings of chapters or sections are excellent sources of topics for your writing.

---

**TOPIC**

Rank the following topics **1** through **5** to reflect your interest in each one, with **1** representing the least interesting topic and **5** representing the most interesting topic. Then, write a few sentences that explain the reasons for your ranking.

...... Reasons to raise minimum wage

...... Causes and effects of global warming

...... Ways to overcome stress

...... Icons of popular entertainment

...... A hard-to-learn lesson in life

Practice 2

Skim a newspaper, a magazine, and a textbook and write a list of five topics from each one. Then, share your list with your class or in a small group.

TOPICS FROM A NEWSPAPER: ........................................................................................................

........................................................................................................................................................

TOPICS FROM A MAGAZINE: ........................................................................................................

........................................................................................................................................................

TOPICS FROM A TEXTBOOK: ........................................................................................................

........................................................................................................................................................

# The Purpose: Why You Write

Good writing focuses on a goal or purpose. Your writing will flow much more easily when you write with purpose. The following chart presents four basic purposes for writing.

| | | | |
|---|---|---|---|
| **Informative**<br>When writing informatively, your purpose is to share, explain, or demonstrate information.<br><br>**EXAMPLE:**<br>An **informative essay** that explains the cycles of grief to your reader; a paragraph that answers an exam question about the major causes of global warming. |  | **Persuasive**<br>When writing persuasively, your purpose is to change your reader's opinion or call your reader to take action.<br><br>**EXAMPLE:**<br>An **argumentative essay** that defends graffiti as an art form; a letter to the editor that argues for a midnight curfew for teenagers. |  |
| **Expressive**<br>When writing expressively, your purpose is to share with the reader your personal opinions, feelings, or reactions to a topic.<br><br>**EXAMPLE:**<br>An **expressive piece** that expresses an emotion or insight about a particular topic in the form of a poem, short story, or personal essay. |  | **Reflective**<br>When writing reflectively, your purpose is to record your understanding about what you have experienced or learned.<br><br>**EXAMPLE:**<br>An **informal essay** that explores what you think is significant about a current event; a journal entry that discusses the strengths of a paper written by you or a peer. |  |

The following thinking guide can help you identify your purpose in writing.

## The Writing Situation Step by Step:

### Purpose

- [ ] Annotate the lists of topics in your topic bank to indicate possible purposes for each topic: Beside each topic write **I** for informative, **P** for persuasive, **E** for expressive, or **R** for reflective.

- [ ] Generate four sets of topics based on different purposes for writing, using "The Writing Situation: Step by Step: Topic" box on page 17 to guide your thinking.

- [ ] Select one topic for each of the four purposes and complete the following statements:

  - [ ] This topic will inform the reader about...

  - [ ] This topic will persuade the reader to...

  - [ ] This topic will express...

  - [ ] This topic will reflect upon...

---

**PURPOSE**

State the purpose of each of the following topic sentences. Discuss with your class or in a small group how a writer's purposes may be combined in certain situations.

**1**. After examining the results of this week's quiz, I need to review the following topics.

**2**. Love forgives even when it can't forget.

**3**. Drug companies should not use animals to research or test products.

**4**. A few reasons for obesity include poor diet choices, inactivity, and increased stress levels that are linked with overeating.

**5**. The government must fund improvements for the nation's aging roads and bridges.

Practice 4

**PURPOSE**

For each of the following topics, write a sentence that states a purpose you may have for writing about this subject. Discuss your answers with your class or in a small group.

**1**. Identity theft

......................................................................................................................

**2**. Responsible use of cell phones

......................................................................................................................

**3**. Steroids and athletes

......................................................................................................................

**4**. How to earn an "A"

......................................................................................................................

# The Audience: Who Reads Your Writing

When we take part in a conversation, we know exactly to whom we are speaking, and we adjust our tone, word choice, and examples to match the situation. For example, contrast how you talk with a friend with the way you talk to the dean of your college. Audience has the same impact in the writing situation.

Assume that you have chosen to write about the topic of alcohol abuse. What main points do you want each of the following audiences to consider about alcohol abuse? Use the blanks below each picture to record your ideas.

.........................................................    .........................................................

.........................................................    .........................................................

.........................................................    .........................................................

The following thinking guide can help you identify your audience.

# The Writing Situation Step by Step:

## Audience

- [ ] Choose a specific topic and purpose for writing.
- [ ] List the traits of your audience that are relevant to your topic and purpose:
  - [ ] Age
  - [ ] Gender
  - [ ] Education level
- [ ] If you are writing for a general audience of mixed traits, identify the main traits most relevant to your topic and purpose.
- [ ] Identify three or four points about the topic of most interest to a specific audience.
- [ ] Choose several key words to describe your topic and hook the interest of a specific audience. Use a thesaurus to find the words best suited for your audience.

## AUDIENCE

Based on your first thoughts about the audiences represented by the four pictures on pages 20–21, write a brief response to the following questions. Then, discuss your answers with your class or in a small group.

*Answers may vary.*

- What are the most important traits of each audience represented by the pictures?

- Did your main points differ based on the audience? Why or why not?

- Will your word choice or examples differ based on the audience? Why or why not?

## AUDIENCE

Each of the following four pieces of writing appeals to one of the audiences depicted by the photos on pages 20–21. Write the letter of the piece of writing in the picture that shows its audience.

**A**. Research indicates that alcohol abuse among youth can be reduced by initiating strong intervention policies. Therefore, the legal drinking age should not be lowered to 18, but must remain at 21.

**B**. By the time you become a teenager, you will most likely also become a binge drinker. You probably already know a teenager who abuses alcohol because 92% of American teenagers binge drink on a regular basis.

**C**. Did you know that binge drinking contributes to the three leading causes of death among young people: unintentional injury, homicide, and suicide? If you are a girl and drink more than three drinks in two hours, you are a binge drinker. If you are a guy and drink more than four drinks in two hours, you are a binge drinker. Now you know. So if you are a binge drinker, stop now! Save your life!

**D**. The well-being of our youth is the responsibility of the entire community. You, as a member of the business community, can help reduce binge drinking by being aware of the problem and being a part of the solution.

When student writers are asked "Who is your audience?" most reply, "The teacher." Of course, the teacher is your immediate audience, and you must carefully consider his or her expectations. However, many teachers understand the value of writing to a real-life audience. College is preparing you for success in life. You are learning to write for life.

## TOPIC AND AUDIENCE

The following writing prompts apply an academic topic to a real audience.

Write the name of the college course(s) for each prompt and describe the traits of each audience. Discuss your answers with your class or in a small group. Talk about how each audience affects the writer's choice of words and details.

**1**. Write a report for a bank to convince investors to finance your business plan.

COURSE(S): ..................................................................................................................

AUDIENCE: ....................................................................................................................

....................................................................................................................................

**2**. Write a letter to the editor of a newspaper to convince readers to "Go Green" by buying hybrid cars.

COURSE(S): ..................................................................................................................

AUDIENCE: ....................................................................................................................

....................................................................................................................................

....................................................................................................................................

**3**. Write a memo that explains the company's sexual harassment policies to a new, young sales clerk who works part time at a retail clothing store.

COURSE(S): ..................................................................................................................

AUDIENCE: ....................................................................................................................

....................................................................................................................................

**4**. Write an e-mail to a friend who is a victim of identity theft that explains the steps he needs to take to protect himself.

COURSE(S): ..................................................................................................................

AUDIENCE: ....................................................................................................................

....................................................................................................................................

# Understanding the Point: Using the Writing Process

Writing is a process that comprises a series of phases or steps. The process approach focuses on the writer, the way writing is produced, and how the writer can improve his or her personal writing process. The process approach is recursive; the writer may loop or combine any of the stages at any point during the writing process. The key outcome at the end of the process is a published piece of writing. Throughout each stage, think about the relationships among your topic, purpose, and audience.

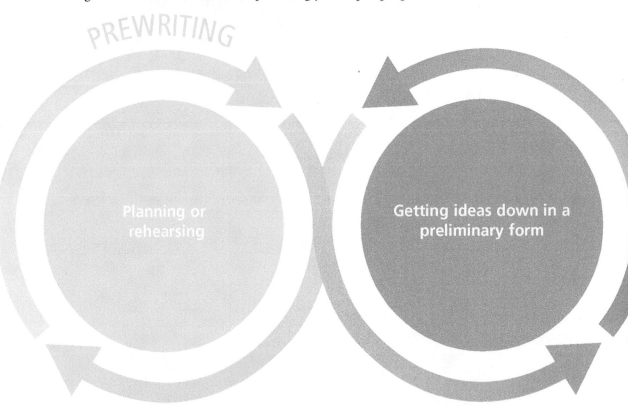

PREWRITING

Planning or rehearsing

Getting ideas down in a preliminary form

DRAFTING

## PREWRITING

During the prewriting stage, you create a plan for your piece of writing.

This phase of writing is made up of the following steps:

- Decide on a topic.
- Determine your purpose for writing.
- Gather information.
- Generate details by using clusters, lists, and freewrites.
- Organize the details into an outline.

The rest of this chapter covers specific prewriting techniques.

## DRAFTING

During the drafting stage, you create a draft of your writing.

This phase may include the following steps:

- Decide on an audience.
- Choose a format (such as an essay or a letter).
- Create an introduction, body, and conclusion for longer pieces.

Chapters 3–4 guide you through the entire writing process as you learn how to write paragraphs.

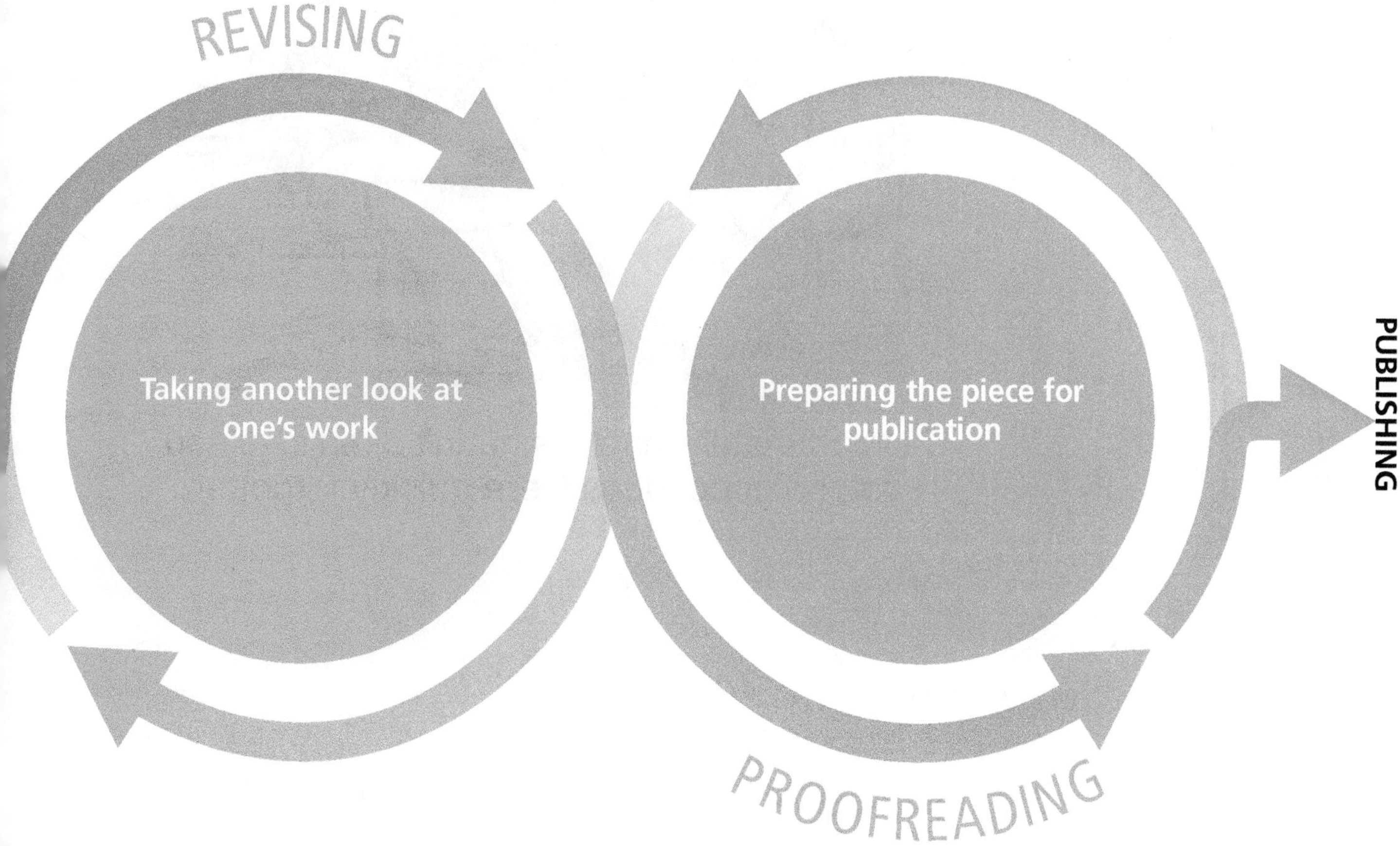

REVISING

Taking another look at one's work

Preparing the piece for publication

PROOFREADING

PUBLISHING

## REVISING

During the revision phase, you fine tune the ideas in your essay. After you have written a draft, allow some time to pass so that you can examine your writing with fresh eyes.

This phase includes the following steps:
- Delete details that are not relevant.
- Add details to ideas that need more support.
- Reorder ideas for clarity.
- Insert transitions between details for a smooth flow of ideas.
- Replace vague or weak words with vivid, strong words.
- Write a new draft if necessary.

Part 5 covers specific skills to consider while revising.

## PROOFREADING

During the editing phase of the writing process, you polish your draft so your reader will not be distracted or confused by careless errors.

This phase includes correcting errors such as:

- Fragments
- Fused sentences
- Shift in tenses
- Spelling
- Punctuation

Part 6 covers the skills to consider during editing.

# Prewriting

Carefully examine the cartoon. Then, in the space provided, write a few sentences explaining your understanding of what prewriting is.

© Mike Baldwin / Cornered

www.CartoonStock.com

Unfortunately, napkins hadn't been invented yet, so good ideas were quickly forgotten.

What is prewriting?

_____

_____

_____

_____

_____

_____

In general, writing occurs long before you pick up your pen or your fingers touch the keyboard. **Prewriting** includes reading, listening, discussing, and thinking about your topic before you write a rough draft that captures your prewriting thoughts on paper. It allows you to explore ideas and plan your strategies without worrying about polishing them.

Have you ever stared at a blank piece of paper with a blank mind, unable to think of how to start a writing task? Or, have you ever had so many ideas that they jumble up in chaos so that you can't even begin to write? Finding those first few words to put on paper can grind a writer's thinking process to a complete halt.

If you face these problems, take heart, you are not alone! Even the best writers face writer's block now and then. Although no cure-all for writer's block exists, prewriting fuels thinking, triggers the writing process, and fires past the block. Experienced writers have learned to spend time thinking about what they are going to write before they begin drafting.

---

**Prewriting** is the act of generating, exploring, developing, and roughly organizing ideas. Prewriting can help you choose a topic, narrow a topic, and put details related to a topic in logical order.

---

The rest of this section guides you through six prewriting techniques:

- Asking Questions:
    The Reporter's Questions
    Reflective Questions

- Freewriting
- Keeping a Journal
- Listing
- Concept Mapping
- Outlining

As you write for life, try out each one. Combine a few to stretch your thinking. Experiment with all of them. Discover which one(s) best suit you as a writer or in a particular writing situation.

## Asking Questions

Asking questions helps you identify a topic and develop details about it based on thoughtful insights. Asking and answering questions helps you discover both what you already know and what you need to learn about the topic. Your goal as a writer is to share a point or main idea about a topic. Usually, a main idea or point is made up of the topic and the writer's opinion about the topic. Two types of questions enable you to explore topics and your opinions about those topics: the reporter's questions and reflective questions.

### THE REPORTER'S QUESTIONS

To describe a newsworthy event, effective reporters gather the facts by asking six basic questions:

- Who?
- What?
- When?
- Where?
- Why?
- How?

At first, the answers to these questions may help you identify and narrow a topic that grabs your interest; once you have narrowed your topic, these questions also yield many details of support for your topic.

**TOPIC AND AUDIENCE**

Assume you are preparing an informative speech for your college speech class on the issue of binge drinking among college students. You have decided to use a photograph as a visual aid to help you make your point. Use this photo and the reporter's questions to brainstorm your first thoughts for your speech.

What is binge drinking?

Why is binge drinking a problem?

How should colleges deal with binge drinking?

## REFLECTIVE QUESTIONS

Reflective questions also help you discover your purpose for writing by revealing your attitude toward a topic. By using these questions to reflect, identify, and add your opinion about a topic to your writing, you can also narrow a writing topic that is too general. For example, binge drinking is a controversial topic about which many disagree. For the purposes of narrowing this particular general topic, the following questions might help you identify your opinions about it:

- When, if ever, should parents be notified about a student's binge drinking?
- Who supports binge drinking? Why? Who opposes binge drinking? Why?
- In what ways do I agree or disagree with these opinions?
- How can I best express my point about binge drinking to someone with whom I disagree?

Answering these questions before writing will also guide you to make logical decisions about which details to select and highlight when you do begin to write.

When you are ready to explore ideas about a topic on paper, the following thinking guide can help you use questions as a prewriting technique.

# The Writing Process Step by Step:

## Prewriting by Asking Questions

Use the reporter's questions to identify a topic, purpose, and audience.

☐ What?

☐ Why?

☐ Who?

Use the reporter's questions to generate details about the topic.

☐ When?

☐ Where?

☐ How?

Use reflective questions to identify attitudes and generate additional details about the topic.

☐ What are my attitudes or feelings about this topic?

☐ What are my audience's attitudes or feelings about this topic?

☐ Why is this topic important?

☐ How will my audience respond to my point?

☐ How can I make this topic interesting and relevant to my audience?

---

**QUESTIONING**

Assume you are reporting on the influence of Hollywood on society. Using the box "The Writing Process Step by Step: Prewriting by Asking Questions," write a list of questions to identify your point and generate details. Share your ideas with the class or in a small group.

---

**QUESTIONING**

Ask questions to brainstorm your first thoughts about one of the following topics:

- Underage Drinking
- Tattoos
- Obesity
- Managing Stress
- Minimum Wage

## Freewriting

During **freewriting**, you record your thoughts as they stream through your head. The key to this brainstorming strategy, like all prewriting activities, is to turn off the critic inside your head. At this point, no thought is wrong, off base, or silly. The idea is to warm up your thinking muscles, flex your creativity, and set your ideas free. The following thinking guide can help you use freewriting as a prewriting technique.

---

# The Writing Process Step by Step:

## Prewriting by Freewriting

☐ Set a time limit, such as ten minutes, and write whatever comes to mind as fast as you can, without stopping at all.

☐ If you get stuck, write the same word or phrase until a new idea comes along. Do not stop writing. Do not worry about wording, organization, or grammar. Later in the writing process, you will organize and polish your ideas—tell that critic inside your head to pipe down for now.

☐ When the time limit is up, read what you wrote and underline interesting ideas.

☐ Use one of the ideas you underlined as a starting point for a focused freewrite. A **focused freewrite** occurs when you freewrite about a specific topic you have chosen or been assigned.

---

**FREEWRITING**

Read the following two freewrites. Discuss with your class or in a small group how ideas develop using freewriting and focused freewriting. What are the advantages of freewriting? What are the disadvantages?

> Our next writing assignment is due in a couple of days, and I still don't know what to write about. It's a lot easier to get started when the teacher assigns a topic, but usually assigned topics don't interest me. If only I could think of a topic. Right now the only thing I can think about is my growling stomach. Gosh, what I wouldn't give right now for one of Aunt Kay's biscuits. No one makes biscuits like my Aunt Kay. When we were growing up, my mom took us back to Ripley, Mississippi, her hometown for two weeks every summer. Every morning, we would get up to a big breakfast of eggs, bacon, ham, gravy, biscuits, and homemade blueberry jelly. My mouth is watering at the memory. Aunt Kay made two kinds of biscuits—fluffy and flat. First, we pulled the tall, fluffy ones apart into two generous halves that sopped up the spoonfuls of thick'n gravy we heaped on them. Then we sliced the thin, brown-bottomed biscuits into crispy wafers that we slathered with butter and blueberry jelly. Um, um, good! Everything about my grandfather's farm was like those biscuits—really special, really satisfying.

**Focused Freewrite**

Everything about my grandfather's farm was special and satisfying. What seemed like work to my uncles and cousins seemed like a game to us. My brother, sister, and I would race to see who could find the most eggs from the hens' nests in the barn. We would fight over who got to milk the cow. We even wanted to hoe the weeds in the garden patch. I do believe we probably chopped down more corn stalks than we did weeds, but everyone was always very patient as they tried to teach us the ways of farming. The best memories I have are of the day's end when all the chores were done and our stomachs were full after a Southern feast. I can still see Dad, Grandfather, and my brother standing near the old barn—shadow figures against the fiery sunset.

## FOCUSED FREEWRITING

**Step 1**: Choose one of the following topics and freewrite for five minutes. Ask and answer the reporter's and reflective questions before you begin freewriting.

- Peer Pressure

- Useful Technology

- Eating Disorders

- A Role Model

**Step 2**: Read your freewrite and highlight ideas. Write a focused freewrite for an additional five minutes using the idea(s) you highlighted.

## Keeping a Journal

Many people keep a **journal** to record how they feel about the events of their daily lives, current events, or life in general. A journal allows the writer to explore experiences in a personal way and store them in a private place. Some writers use a spiral notebook; others use a diary or a pre-made journal. The point is to create a specific place where you can record and review your private thoughts and personal experiences. Journal entries are often freewrites, with your main purpose being to get ideas on paper, but they may take on different creative forms, such as a letter or a poem. Many writers use journals as a place to practice their writing and experiment with language. The key to keeping a journal is to write on a regular basis. Writing and reflecting on what you have written on a consistent basis leads to a deeper understanding of yourself and your world—and improves your writing!

The following thinking guide can help you use journaling as a prewriting technique.

# The Writing Process Step by Step:

## Prewriting by Journaling

- ☐ Create a section in your notebook for journal entries or buy a spiral notebook, diary, or pre-made journal that you will use only for journal writing.

- ☐ Commit to writing in your journal on a regular basis for the next two weeks. Select a time of day that you can write in your journal, such as during your lunch break or at the end of the day. Set a time limit, such as fifteen minutes for each journal entry.

- ☐ Ask and answer the reporter's questions and reflective questions to stimulate your thinking.

Use the following topics to get started:

- ☐ Record events, images, or scenes of interest to you; write as many details as you can.

- ☐ Record a favorite memory; explore why that memory is so important.

- ☐ Write a brief autobiography.

- ☐ Recount a news event and your reactions to it.

- ☐ Write a letter to yourself or to someone else, giving advice about a particular matter.

- ☐ Vent about something that really bothers you.

- ☐ Reread a previously written journal entry and develop an idea in greater detail.

Read the following journal entry. Identify the academic courses that are relevant to the personal experiences recorded in the journal. Discuss with your class or in a small group the ways in which the ideas in the journal entry might be developed into an essay in each course.

April 6: 9:00 p.m.: Okay, it happened again. I lost my temper and said something I wish I could take back. It happened at the gym right after I finished a grueling forty-five minute workout session. The session was really hard because I have chronic obstructive pulmonary disorder (COPD), and the Spring pollen makes it hard for me to breathe even when I am not exercising. I always hang my keys on the pegboard by the front door, but today they were missing. Someone had picked up my keys by mistake. After waiting for a few minutes, hoping whoever had my keys would realize their mistake and bring them back, I became upset and complained in a loud, sarcastic voice, "How much intelligence does it take to pick up your own keys." As soon as the words were out of my mouth, Mr. Bennett, an 80-year-old who is loved by all, tapped my shoulder. He was so apologetic and embarrassed, saying "Sometimes, I get confused." He kept saying how sorry he was as he handed me my keys. Everyone knows that Mr. Bennett suffers from the early stages of Alzheimer's disease. I felt ashamed of myself. I always thought exercise was supposed to help control stress. I need advice about anger management.

Academic topics related to journal entry:

_____

_____

_____

## Listing

A common way to brainstorm ideas is to **create a list**. If you have a free choice of topics, then create a topic bank: List ideas you want to learn more about or topics you already know something about and that you enjoy discussing. To create a list of topics for an academic course, look at the table of contents, the index, and the glossary of your textbook. Use these resources to create a list of topics based on what you will be studying throughout the semester. If you already have a topic, then create a list of everything that comes to mind as you think about your topic. Write your list as quickly as you can. Just as in freewriting, quiet your inner critic. Once you make a thorough list, then you can organize your ideas.

The following thinking guide can help you use listing as a prewriting technique.

# The Writing Process Step by Step:

## Prewriting by Listing

- [ ] Write a topic at the top of your page.
- [ ] List ideas as quickly as possible in the order that they occur to you.
- [ ] Use words or short phrases.
- [ ] List all ideas that occur to you; reject nothing.
- [ ] If you run out of ideas, choose one idea you have already recorded and begin a new list about that idea.
- [ ] Review your list and group ideas into logical relationships.
- [ ] Label each group of ideas as possible points of development for a piece of writing.

**LISTING: PREWRITING FOR AN ACADEMIC COURSE**

The following lists are based on the table of contents of two textbooks. Identify the academic courses to which each list is related. Then, brainstorm a list of additional writing topics based on an idea from each list.

COURSES: _____

COURSES: _____

### List 1

The Great Depression
  Causes of the Crisis
  "We Are Not Bums"
  Surviving Hard Times
  The Dust Bowl
Presidential Responses to the Depression
  Herbert Hoover
  Franklin Delano Roosevelt
  "Nothing to Fear but Fear Itself"

**New Lists of Additional Ideas**

### List 2

Finding the Right Balance
  Promoting Healthy Behavior Change
  Mental, Emotional, Spiritual Wellness
  Managing Stress
  Violence and Abuse
Building Healthy Lifestyles
  Eating for Health
  Managing Your Weight
  Exercising for Personal Fitness

**New Lists of Additional Ideas**

Assume you are applying for a position as a loan officer at a local bank. You need to write a cover letter for your application. Read the description of the job and complete the prewriting activity. (Hint: If you prefer to find a different position to write about, go to the Department of Labor's Occupational Outlook Handbook and browse the A-Z index for additional job descriptions: http://www.bls.gov/oco/)

**Education and Training:** The position of loan officer requires a bachelor's degree in finance, economics, or a related field, or several years of work in another related occupation, such as teller or customer service representative.

**Other Qualifications:** An applicant should be good at working with others, confident, and highly motivated. Loan officers must be willing to attend community events as representatives of their employer. Sales ability, good interpersonal and communication skills, and a strong desire to succeed also are important qualities. Familiarity with computers and their applications in banking is preferred.

**Step 1**: Based on the job description, write a list of the skills you already possess that qualify you for the job.

**Step 2**: Choose three skills that are your strengths and list one example of how you learned or used each skill.

**Step 3**: List the skills you need to acquire or improve to qualify for the job.

**Step 4**: List the steps you will take to acquire or improve each skill you listed in Step 3.

## Concept Mapping

**Concept mapping**, also known as **clustering** or **webbing**, creates a visual picture of the relationships among the ideas you generate. Think of what you already know about a map. Someone can tell you how to get somewhere, but it is much easier to understand the directions when you can study a map and see how each road connects to other roads. Likewise, a concept map shows how a topic connects to supporting details—how each idea connects to another idea and how the main idea connects to supporting details. Sometimes, as you use a concept map, the idea that first occurred to you might be a great example for a supporting detail. Rarely do ideas occur to us in a logical order. Concept mapping helps a writer figure out the logical order of ideas. Chapters 3–4 will show you how to adapt concept maps to specific writing situations and thought patterns.

The following thinking guide can help you use concept mapping as a prewriting technique.

## The Writing Process Step by Step:

### Prewriting by Concept Mapping

- ☐ Draw a circle in the middle of your page and write your topic in the circle.
- ☐ Write a word that relates to the topic, circle the word, and connect it to the topic circle with a line.
- ☐ Repeat this process so that a set of major supports radiates out from the topic circle.
- ☐ Write a word that relates to one of the major supports, circle it, and connect it to that major support circle.
- ☐ Repeat this process for each of the major supports to create clusters of minor supports.

**MAPPING**

The writer of the following paragraph used a concept map to brainstorm ideas. Read the paragraph. Then, recreate her concept map by filling in the appropriate blanks with ideas from her paragraph. Discuss how the concept map differs from her final draft.

To Whom It May Concern:

It is with great pleasure that I recommend Monica Surrency as a Worldwide Online Support Specialist for the Center for Instructional Design. I had the opportunity to work with Ms. Surrency for five years as we trained faculty in the use of technology to design and deliver traditional and online courses. During our work together, Ms. Surrency's technical skills proved invaluable. Team members consistently sought out her expertise in Web design and development, the online course management system, the Microsoft Office Suite, Flash programming, and much more. In addition to her technical skills, Ms. Surrency possesses strong interpersonal skills that make her an ideal team member. For example, as a good listener, she guided teachers toward realistic goals and appropriate resources. As an excellent speaker and writer, she delivered effective instruction on a wide range of topics such as the use of hardware and software. One of the key reasons for Ms. Surrency's success is her ability to research. The relevant questions she posed enabled her to identify problems. Then, she diligently searched for solutions by reviewing the literature and market for best practices. She willingly educates herself so that she remains abreast of current technology. Rarely have I had the opportunity to work with someone as dedicated and skilled as Monica Surrency. She will be an asset to your team.

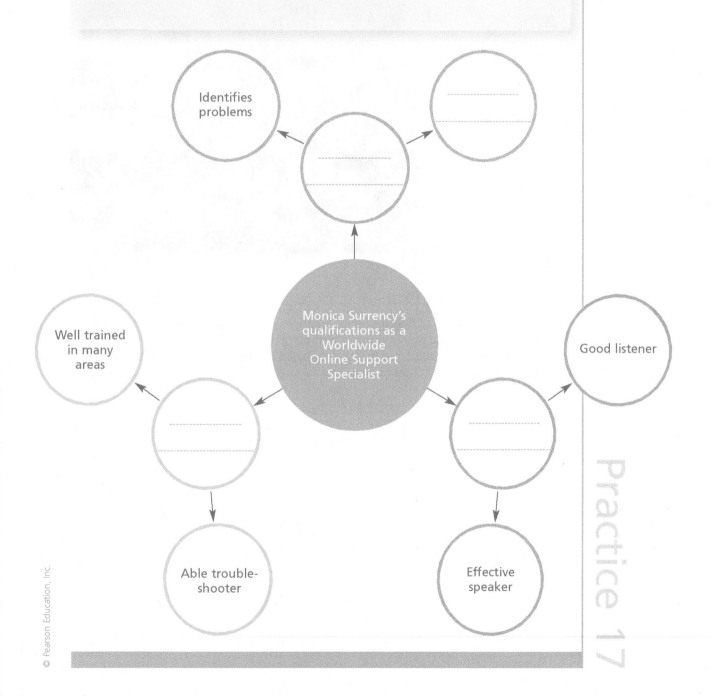

**MAPPING**

Using your own sheet of paper, create a concept map to brainstorm ideas for one of the following topics. Use circles and arrows to show your flow of ideas. Or feel free to use ideas generated in a freewrite during Practices 11 and 13.

- Shocking Celebrity Behavior
- Minimum Wage
- Prescription Drug Abuse
- A Natural Disaster
- Balancing Work and School
- Gun Control
- Dieting
- College Stress

## Outlining: A Writing Plan

In addition to brainstorming first thoughts, a prewrite also organizes ideas into a writing plan. A concept map is one way to create a writing plan because it shows the flow of ideas among the topic, major details, and minor details. An outline is another way to create a writing plan. An **outline** lists ideas in blocks of thought, as shown in the following outline for a paragraph.

> *Main Idea Statement: Topic Sentence*
>
> A. *Major supporting detail*
>    1. *Minor detail*
>    2. *Minor detail*
>
> B. *Major supporting detail*
>    1. *Minor detail*
>    2. *Minor detail*
>
> C. *Major supporting detail*
>    1. *Minor detail*
>    2. *Minor detail*

The following thinking guide can help you use outlining as a prewriting technique.

# The Writing Process Step by Step:

## Prewriting by Outlining

☐ Create an outline from other prewriting activities such as freewrites, lists, and concept maps.

☐ List and identify each item with Roman numerals, capital letters, Arabic numerals, and lowercase letters, in that order, to show the flow of ideas, as illustrated below:

I. Main Idea

    A. Major supporting detail

        1. Minor supporting detail
          a. Subpoint

☐ Place a period after each numeral or letter.

☐ Capitalize each item.

☐ For topic outlines, state each item with a word or phrase.

☐ For sentence outlines, state each item as a complete thought.

---

**OUTLINING**

The following reflection and concept map was created by a student during the prewriting phase of an assignment. Complete the outline with ideas from the concept map.

**Tamika's First Thoughts:**

*I am going to write about the topic "Our Differences," and my classmates are my audience. I am going to focus my topic by discussing three ways my sister and I are different from each other. My purpose is to show my readers how we differ.*

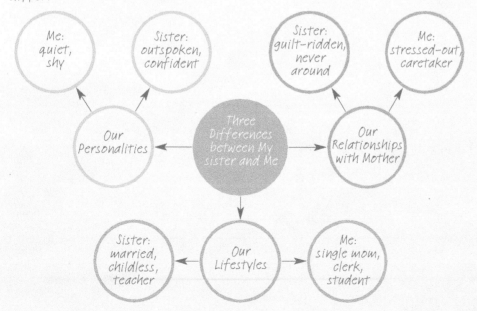

Practice 19

Main Idea Statement:  My sister and I are different in three ways.

**A.** _____

    **1.** My sister is outspoken and confident.

    **2.** _____

**B.** Our lifestyles are complete opposites.

    **1.** _____

    **2.** I am a single mother, a clerk, and a student.

**C.** We have very different relationships with our mother.

    **1.** _____

    **2.** I am my mother's caregiver, and I am often stressed out by my responsibilities.

## CREATING A WRITING PLAN

Choose your own topic or select one of the following topics. Identify your audience and purpose. Then, generate major and supporting details using the outline.
Use the reporter's questions *Who? What? When? Where? Why?* and *How?*
to produce details.

- An important life lesson everyone needs to know

- Stem cell research

TOPIC: _____

AUDIENCE: _____

PURPOSE: _____

_____

_____

_____

TOPIC SENTENCE: _____

_____

_____

**A.** _____

    **1.** _____

    **2.** _____

**B.** _____

  **1.** _____

  **2.** _____

**C.** _____

  **1.** _____

  **2.** _____

# Drafting

The **drafting** stage of the writing process may include several tasks depending on the writing situation. An essay or letter may require the drafting of an introduction, a main idea, supporting details, and conclusion. A stand-alone paragraph may require only a main idea and supporting details.

> **Drafting** is putting your ideas into sentences and paragraphs.

## Compose a Main Idea

The **main idea statement** for an essay is called a **thesis statement**. The main idea statement for a paragraph is called a **topic sentence**. Drafting an effective main idea statement requires several steps. Since the focus of this chapter is the writing process, the steps for writing a topic sentence are explained, illustrated, and reinforced with in-depth practice activities on page 60. Likewise, the steps for writing a thesis statement are covered on page 108. The following discussion and activities introduce the concept of topic sentences and thesis statements to show when they are created during the writing process.

See the following for more information about Introductions: page 128, Conclusions: page 129, Topic Sentences: page 60, Thesis Statements: pages 107-109

In general, the main idea sentence presents a topic and the point you are making about the topic, as in the following example:

*TOPIC*

Guitars are versatile instruments that range in type of sounds such as acoustic, classical, and electric. ◄——*WRITER'S POINT*

The writer's point focuses the general topic "Guitars" into a narrow topic for a discussion about three types of guitars. This main idea statement gives an overview of the paragraph or essay. The writer narrowed the topic "guitars" by stating the opinion "versatile" and by identifying three "types of sounds such as acoustic, classical, and electric."

The following thinking guide can help you draft a piece of writing.

# The Writing Process Step by Step:

## Drafting

- [ ] Write your main idea in a complete sentence. Make a specific statement rather than a vague, general statement.
- [ ] As you write a thesis statement or topic sentence, assert an idea instead of announcing your topic. Avoid the following announcements:
    - "I am going to write about…"
    - "My paragraph (or essay) is about…"
    - "My topic is…."
- [ ] As you write your first draft, do not worry about issues such as spelling and grammar.
- [ ] Generate major and minor details to support your main idea.
- [ ] As you write, include new ideas as they occur to you without self-criticism or editing before you have a complete draft; this first draft does not need to be perfect. You will use the revision process to evaluate details for logic and relevance once your draft is complete.
- [ ] Use the first draft to discover how your ideas flow and fit together.
- [ ] Resolve to write multiple drafts to produce your best work.

Practice 21

### STATING THE MAIN IDEA

Complete the following set of exercises about main idea statements. Discuss your work with your class or in a small group.

**A.** Read the following main idea statements. Underline the subject once and underline the writer's point twice.

**1.** Road rage is a mental disorder that can be treated.

**2.** The twentieth century was a time of great scientific progress.

**3.** Dr. Martin Luther King had hope, strength, and courage.

**4.** *American Idol* remains popular for three reasons.

**B.** Revise the following main idea statements so they are more effectively expressed. Identify the hint you used to revise each one.

**5.** I am going to write about how regular exercise relieves stress and improves health.

.................................................................................................

.................................................................................................

Hint: .........................................................................................

.................................................................................................

**6.** The benefits and responsibilities of owning a home.

_____

_____

**Hint:** _____

_____

**7.** Many people participate in binge drinking.

_____

_____

**Hint:** _____

_____

## Write a Draft of Your Paragraph

A draft of a paragraph or essay is the result of careful thought based on prewriting activities. Creating a first or rough draft allows you to get a working copy of your ideas that can be improved upon during the revision process.

### COMPOSE A TOPIC SENTENCE AND A DRAFT

**Step 1.** Choose a topic from a previous practice exercise and compose a main idea statement. (Remember that your **main idea statement** is also called a **topic sentence** if you are writing a paragraph. If you are writing an essay, your main idea statement is also called a **thesis statement**.)

**Step 2.** Write a draft using your own paper.

AUDIENCE AND PURPOSE: _____

_____

TOPIC: _____

_____

WRITER'S POINT: _____

_____

MAIN IDEA STATEMENT (topic sentence or thesis statement): _____

_____

# Revising

Now that you have gotten your ideas on paper, you can review your work to make sure your paragraph offers a focused, unified, well-supported, and coherent chunk of information. As you revise your draft, review and apply what you have learned.

> **Revising** is re-seeing your work through the eyes of your reader. Revising is reworking your draft for clarity, logic, interest, and credibility.

The following thinking guide can help you revise a piece of writing.

## The Writing Process Step by Step:

### Revising

- [ ] Read your draft out loud (either on your own or to a peer). This is an easy way to identify parts of your draft that may be unclear or awkward.

- [ ] Make sure your main idea is stated clearly in a topic sentence or thesis statement.

- [ ] Make sure that the details in the body of your paragraph or essay fully support your topic sentence or thesis statement.

- [ ] Make sure every sentence in a paragraph relates to your main idea so that a reader can easily follow the logic of your ideas.

- [ ] Move information as needed into the most logical order.

- [ ] Add transitions as needed to clarify the relationship between ideas.

- [ ] Add details and examples as needed to strengthen or clarify the main idea and supporting points.

- [ ] Replace vague words and details with vivid and precise expressions.

- [ ] Delete irrelevant details.

- [ ] If your paragraph or essay draft seems to end abruptly, add a concluding sentence (or paragraph, if you are writing an essay), restating and summing up your main points.

Read Tamika's first draft of her paragraph "Our Differences." Then complete the activity that follows. Share your work and thoughts with a small group of your peers.

## Our Differences

(1) My sister and I are different in three ways. (2) Our personalities are very different. (3) My sister is outspoken and confident; she always says what is on her mind and means what she says. (4) I am more quiet and shy. (5) I often put the desires of others before my own and try to offer helpful advice even when someone asks for my opinion. (6) Second, our lifestyles are complete opposites. (7) On the one hand, my sister is married with no children, a college graduate, and a high school biology teacher. (8) On the other hand, I am a single parent with two children, a college student, and a night clerk in a retail store. (9) ~~My~~ sister and I have different relationships with our mother. (10) My sister lives out of state and sees our mother only when she "has time," which means not very often. (11) When my sister does visit, she is very guilt-ridden and wishes she was more involved with our mother. (12) As my mother's caregiver, I am always with her. (13) Unlike my sister, I am stressed out by my responsibilities to my mother and how tied I am to her. (14) Despite our differences, my sister and I have a strong bond. (15) Like me, my sister loves our mother.     --Tamika Grayson, English Student

1. Locate the topic sentence by underlining the topic once and the writer's point about that topic twice.
2. Cross out any details that are not related to the topic sentence.
3. Circle any ideas that need more examples to fully support the main idea.
4. Choose three words to revise; cross out the words you chose and above them, write stronger, more vivid words. Use a thesaurus.
5. Insert the following transitions where they best show the logical flow of ideas: First, In contrast, Finally.

Review a draft you have written. Annotate or mark your paragraph with the changes you need to make, and write a journal entry about your revision. Do you need to brainstorm more details for certain ideas? Identify those ideas and describe or explain the kinds of details you need. Do you need to use a thesaurus to improve word choice? List and discuss the words that need to be replaced. Based on your review, revise to create a new draft of your work.

# Proofreading

Once you have revised your paragraph, take time to carefully proofread your work. Publishing a clean, error-free draft proves you are committed to excellence and that you take pride in your work. Many student writers struggle with common errors, and every writer has her or his own pattern or habit of careless errors. To create a polished draft, a writer masters the rules of writing and edits to eliminate careless errors.

> **Proofreading** is preparing your work for publication.
> Proofreading is correcting errors in punctuation, capitalization, mechanics, grammar, and spelling.

The following thinking guide can help you proofread a piece of writing.

# The Writing Process Step by Step:

## Proofreading

- ☐ Allow some time to pass between revising and proofreading.
- ☐ Read your work one sentence at a time from the *end* to the *beginning*. Reading your work from the end to the beginning allows you to focus on each sentence.
- ☐ Read again from the beginning with a cover that you slide down the page as you read so you focus on one sentence at a time.
- ☐ Use a highlighter to mark mistakes.
- ☐ Proofread more than once; focus on one type of error at a time.
- ☐ Proofread for the types of errors you commonly make.
- ☐ Use word processing spell checkers carefully (they don't know the difference between words such as *there, their,* or *they're*).
- ☐ Use a dictionary to double check your spelling.
- ☐ Have someone else read over your work.

The following draft by a student writer reveals her struggle with a common error: subject-verb agreement. The box below sums up the rules for subject-verb agreement and includes sentence examples that are correct. Read the rule and examples in the box, and then use them as a guide to correct three errors in subject-verb agreement in the student's draft.

---

### Subject-Verb Agreement

If the subject of a sentence is singular, then the verb and object of the verb must be singular. If the subject of a sentence is plural, then the verb and object of the verb must be plural.

CORRECT: *SINGULAR SUBJECT*

The lead driver rams his race car into the wall.

*THIRD PERSON SINGULAR VERB (ADD "–S")*

CORRECT: *PLURAL SUBJECT*

Four other drivers lose control of their cars.

*THIRD PERSON PLURAL VERB*

---

**Student draft**

## Learning the Value of Money

(1) When I lived with my mother, I didn't appreciate the value of money. (2) I never thought about how much food I was eating or how much it cost. (3) While shopping with her, I never looked at the prices. (4) I just threw items into the basket and never gave a thought about paying bills. (5) Now, being on my own, I watch what I spend. (6) My roommate and I shops for sale items. (7) We mostly buys Wal-Mart products. (8) Bills is another issue. (9) It's hard to keep up with all the due dates for bills, and there is no one to tell me when to pay them. (10) We've learned to pay our bills early to avoid late fees. (11) Now that I pay my own way, I appreciate the value of money.

PORTFOLIO

**THINKING THROUGH THE WRITING PROCESS**

To test and track your understanding of what you have studied, answer the following questions.

1. A piece of writing develops in response to a specific situation that is composed of the

   ........................, the ........................ for writing, and the ........................

2. The four basic purposes for writing are ........................,

   ........................, ........................, and ........................

3. The four phases of the writing process are ........................,

   ........................, ........................, and ........................

4. The writing process is ........................: any step can be repeated as necessary.

5. Several prewriting techniques are ........................, ........................,

   ........................, ........................, and ........................

6. Drafting is putting your ideas into ........................ and ........................

7. Revising is ........................ your work through the eyes of your reader.

8. Revising is reworking your draft for ........................, ........................,

   ........................, and ........................

9. Proofreading is preparing your work for ........................

10. Proofreading is correcting errors in ........................, ........................,

    ........................, ........................, and ........................

**11.** What did I learn based on my study of Chapters 1 and 2? What did I learn about "getting ready to write," and what did I learn about "the writing process"?

----------------------------------------

----------------------------------------

----------------------------------------

----------------------------------------

----------------------------------------

----------------------------------------

----------------------------------------

----------------------------------------

**12.** Based on my study of Chapters 1 and 2, what about "getting ready to write" do I need to continue studying or practicing? What about "thinking through the writing process" do I need to continue studying or practicing?

----------------------------------------

----------------------------------------

----------------------------------------

----------------------------------------

----------------------------------------

----------------------------------------

----------------------------------------

----------------------------------------

Academic Learning Log

# 3

## Understanding the Paragraph

A paragraph is a well-planned sequence of sentences joined together to support a narrowed topic.

All of us have had some experience reading, writing, or studying paragraphs. What do you already know about paragraphs? What are the traits of a paragraph?

A paragraph allows a writer to express clearly and powerfully one main idea about a narrowed subject. A well-written paragraph can express a valid consumer complaint, a compelling reason to be hired, a sincere apology to a loved one, or a concept tested by a written exam in a college course.

# What's the Point of a Paragraph?

A paragraph is a well-thought out chunk of information. A writer narrows a topic into a focused main idea, selects enough relevant details to support the main idea, and organizes these supporting details in a logical flow of information.

## Three Levels of Information in a Paragraph

The following flow chart shows the three levels of information within a paragraph.

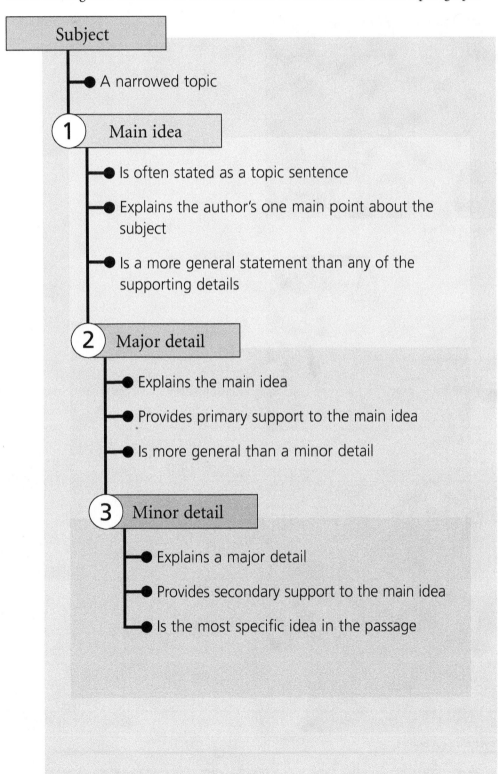

Subject

● A narrowed topic

**1** Main idea

● Is often stated as a topic sentence

● Explains the author's one main point about the subject

● Is a more general statement than any of the supporting details

**2** Major detail

● Explains the main idea

● Provides primary support to the main idea

● Is more general than a minor detail

**3** Minor detail

● Explains a major detail

● Provides secondary support to the main idea

● Is the most specific idea in the passage

Study the following outline based on information in an article about bullying that was published online by the *American Academy of Child & Adolescent Psychiatry*. In the blanks, identify each piece of information as the narrowed topic, main idea, major supporting detail, or minor supporting detail.

Traits of Bullying Behavior _____

Bullying behavior can be physical, verbal, and psychological. _____

**A.** Physical bullies.

_____

**1.** use physical threats

_____

**2.** attack victims regardless of the sex of their victims

_____

▲ **Physical bullies**

**B.** Verbal bullies

_____

**1.** send cruel instant or e-mail messages

_____

**2.** post insults about a person on a website

_____

▲ **Verbal bullies**

**C.** Psychological bullies

_____

**1.** exclude or gossip about victims

_____

**2.** cause mental health problems

_____

▲ **Psychological bullies**

Read the paragraph developed from the previous outline. Circle the main idea. Underline the three sentences that state the major supports.

## Traits of Bullying Behavior

(1) Bullying occurs when a person is picked on over and over again by an individual or group with more power, either in terms of physical strength or social standing. (2) Bullying behavior can be physical, verbal, and psychological. (3) Some bullies attack their targets physically, which can mean anything from shoving or tripping to punching or hitting, or even sexual assault. (4) For example, boys tend to use physical threats. (5) These bullies attack victims regardless of the sex of their victims. (6) Other bullies use verbal insults to put themselves in charge. (7) For example, cyber-bullies send cruel instant or e-mail messages. (8) They may also post insults about a person on a website. (9) Finally, most bullies use psychological attacks to control their victims. (10) For instance, people in popular groups or cliques often bully people they see as different by excluding them or gossiping about them. (11) Victims of bullies are at risk for mental health problems, such as low self-esteem, stress, depression, or anxiety.

Adapted from "Bullying." *Facts for Families.* American Academy of Child & Adolescent Psychiatry. May 2008. http://www.aacap.org/cs/root/facts_for_families/bullying

Read the following paragraph that gives advice to a young person about how to respond to bullies. Then fill in the sentence outline with the main idea and missing supporting details.

## Dealing with the Bullies

(1) Here are some things you can do to combat psychological and verbal bullying. (2) Ignore the bully and walk away. (3) It's definitely not a coward's response—sometimes it can be harder than losing your temper. (4) Bullies thrive on the reaction they get, and if you walk away, or ignore hurtful e-mails or instant messages, you're telling the bully that you just don't care. (5) Sooner or later the bully will probably get bored with trying to bother you. (6) Take charge of your life. (7) Think about ways to feel your best—and your strongest—so that other kids may give up the teasing. (8) Exercise is one way to feel strong and powerful; learn a martial art, or take a class like yoga. (9) Another way to gain confidence is to hone your skills in something like chess, art, music, computers, or writing. (10) Joining a class, club, or gym is a great way to make new friends and feel great about yourself. (11) Talk about it. (12) It may help to talk to a guidance counselor, teacher, or friend—anyone who can give you the support you need. (13) Talking can be a good outlet for the fears and frustrations that can build when you're being bullied.

–Adapted from "Dealing with Bullying."
*TeensHealth.* Nemours Foundation. May 2008.
<http://kidshealth.org/teen/school_jobs/bullying/
bullies.html>.

▲ **Ignore it**

▲ **Take charge of your life**

▲ **Talk about it**

Practice 3

Main idea (Topic Sentence): ..................................................................................................
...........................................................................................................................................

**A.** Major support: ..........................................................................................................

...........................................................................................................................................

    **1.** Minor support: It's definitely not a coward's response—sometimes it can be harder than losing your temper.

    **2.** Minor support: Bullies thrive on the reaction they get, and if you walk away, or ignore hurtful e-mails or instant messages, you're telling the bully that you just don't care.

    **3.** Minor support: ..................................................................................................

**B.** Major support: Take charge of your life.

    **1.** Minor support: Think about ways to feel your best—and your strongest—so that other kids may give up the teasing.

    **2.** Minor support: ..................................................................................................

    ...........................................................................................................................

    **3.** Minor support: Another way to gain confidence is to hone your skills in something like chess, art, music, computers, or writing.

    **4.** Minor support: Joining a class, club, or gym is a great way to make new friends and feel great about yourself.

**C.** Major support: ..........................................................................................................

    **1.** Minor support: It may help to talk to a guidance counselor, teacher, or friend—anyone who can give you the support you need.

    **2.** Minor support: Talking can be a good outlet for the fears and frustrations that can build when you're being bullied.

Practice 3

# The Parts of a Paragraph

A paragraph is a series of closely related sentences that develop and support the writer's point about a narrowed subject. Often, the paragraph serves as a building block for a longer piece of writing such as an essay, since an essay is composed of two, three, or more paragraphs. In many situations a writer can make a point through one well-developed paragraph. Sometimes, a writer provides a stand-alone paragraph with a title. In addition to a title, a paragraph has three basic parts:

**A Beginning:**
**An introduction of one or more sentences: A topic sentence that states the author's purpose and main point**

**A Middle:**
**A body of major and minor details that supports the topic sentence**

**An Ending:**
**A conclusion of one or more sentences that reinforces the author's purpose and main point**

The following graphic describes the function of each part of a paragraph and shows the general format of a paragraph.

**Title:**
Use Key Words or a Phrase to Vividly Describe the Point of Your Paragraph

**Introduction:**
An introduction is usually one or more sentences that explain the importance of the topic or give necessary background information about the topic.
<u>Your topic sentence states your narrowed subject and your point about the subject.</u>

**Body:**
The body of a paragraph is made up of a series of sentences that offer major details in support of your topic sentence. If needed, provide minor details that support the major details. Link sentences within the paragraph with clear transitions so your reader can easily follow your thoughts.

**Conclusion:**
The conclusion restates or sums up your paragraph's main idea in one or more sentences.

The following student essay by Michaelle Gilson illustrates the use of a title and the three parts of a paragraph. Underline the topic sentence. Circle each of the three parts of the paragraph: Introduction, Body, and Conclusion. Provide a title for the paragraph.

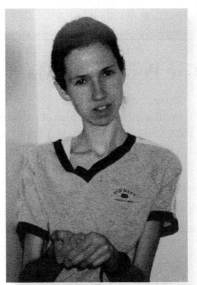

▲ **Anorexia Nervosa**

▲ **Bulimia Nervosa**

▲ **Compulsive Overeating**

(1) Most people, regardless of race, age, or gender compare themselves to others, and some become obsessive about their looks. (2) This obsession can lead to three types of eating disorders. (3) One of the most common eating disorders, Anorexia Nervosa, occurs when people severely restrict their food intake; sometimes they stop eating altogether. (4) Also, anorexics often exercise excessively to control their weight. (5) Another common eating disorder is Bulimia Nervosa. (6) Bulimia can be described as self-induced vomiting after eating large amounts of food to avoid weight gain. (7) In addition, bulimics often use laxatives and enemas as part of their efforts to control their weight. (8) Anorexia and bulimia lead to unhealthy weight loss and even death without proper treatment and counseling. (9) A third common eating disorder, Compulsive Overeating is marked by uncontrollable eating and weight gain. (10) Compulsive eaters take in large amounts of food in a very short period of time. (11) This disorder leads to obesity; and obesity increases the risk of heart disease and cancer. (12) Ultimately, all three of these eating disorders can be cured with the proper treatment.

Find more information and practice on each part of the paragraph in the following sections: Introductions— page 128. Conclusions— page 129.

# Developing Your Point Using a Paragraph

An effective paragraph is *focused*, *detailed*, *logical*, and *well expressed*. A writer (1) narrows a topic into a focused main idea; (2) offers only those details that are relevant to the main idea; (3) provides adequate details to support the main idea; (4) organizes these supporting details in a logical flow of information; and (5) uses effective expression through the purposeful choice of words, sentence structure, and grammar.

## The Point: The Main Idea

A focused main idea presents a narrowed subject and the writer's controlling point about the narrowed subject. The controlling point often indicates both the writer's opinion and a pattern of organization. A topic sentence states the focused main idea in a complete sentence.

### Narrow the Topic

Use the following suggestions to guide your thinking as you focus a general topic into a narrowed subject or topic.

- Narrow the topic based on your **opinion**. An opinion is expressed by using words such as *amazing, alarming, beautiful, best, likely, should*, or any other word that states personal values, judgments, or interpretations. Use questions, freewriting, mapping, listing, or another brainstorming technique to discover your opinion about a topic.

  | Example: | General Topic | Narrowed Subject |
  |---|---|---|
  | | Dieting | A healthful diet |
  | | | Dangerous diets |

- Narrow the topic based on a **pattern of organization**. A writer may use a pattern of organization to narrow a subject and generate details. Patterns of organization are also used to develop, organize, and express a main idea, major details, and minor details in a logical order. The following list provides a few examples of patterns of organization and signal words for each one.

  | Pattern of Organization | Signal Words |
  |---|---|
  | Space Order | *above, below, next to, underneath, scene* |
  | Time Order | *first, now, then, before, after, process, use* |
  | Example | *for example, exemplify, includes, such as* |
  | Classification | *types, kinds, levels* |
  | Compare/Contrast | *similar, likewise, just as / however, in contrast* |
  | Cause/Effect | *source, origin / results, impact* |

  | Example: | General Topic | Narrowed Subject |
  |---|---|---|
  | | Exercise | The effect of exercise |
  | | | The types of exercise |

- Combine topic, opinion, and pattern of organization to generate a narrowed subject.

  | Example: | General Topic | Narrowed Subject |
  |---|---|---|
  | | Dieting | Three steps to a healthful diet |
  | | | Dangerous types of diets |
  | | Exercise | The benefits of weightlifting |
  | | | The difference between aerobic and anaerobic exercise |

## FOCUS A TOPIC INTO A NARROWED SUBJECT

Combine the topic with an opinion and pattern of organization signal words to narrow the topic.

1. GENERAL TOPIC: Health Issue: Walking

   OPINION: positive    SIGNAL WORD: effects

   NARROWED SUBJECT:

2. GENERAL TOPIC: A Public Figure: Barack Obama

   OPINION: admirable    SIGNAL WORD: traits

   NARROWED SUBJECT:

3. GENERAL TOPIC: Vacation destination: Blue Springs State Park

   OPINION: beautiful and peaceful    SIGNAL WORD: scene

   NARROWED SUBJECT:

4. GENERAL TOPIC: Business: Opening a bank account

   OPINION: easy    SIGNAL WORD: steps to

   NARROWED SUBJECT:

5. GENERAL TOPIC: Digital cable

   OPINION: efficient and clear signal    SIGNAL WORD: characteristics

   NARROWED SUBJECT:

6. GENERAL TOPIC: organic food

   OPINION: better    SIGNAL WORD: leads to

   NARROWED SUBJECT:

# Write the Topic Sentence

Once you have focused a topic into a narrowed subject with your opinion and a pattern of organization, you are ready to write a complete sentence to state the main idea. Each of the following topic sentences offers a subject and a controlling point: a **topic** narrowed by the writer's **opinion** and a suggested **pattern of organization**.

WRITER'S OPINION      TOPIC      PATTERN OF ORGANIZATION

Create a healthful diet in three steps.

PATTERN OF ORGANIZATION    TOPIC      WRITER'S OPINION

Three types of diets are dangerous.

TOPIC      PATTERN OF ORGANIZATION      WRITER'S OPINION

Weightlifting offers several benefits.

WRITER'S OPINION      PATTERN OF ORGANIZATION      TOPIC

Important differences exist between aerobic and anaerobic exercise.

---

## WRITE A TOPIC SENTENCE

Write topic sentences for each of the following narrowed subjects.

1. Narrowed Subject: Benefits of walking

TOPIC SENTENCE: _____

_____

2. Narrowed Subject:  The admirable traits of Barack Obama

TOPIC SENTENCE: _____

_____

3. Narrowed Subject: Blue Springs State Park, a beautiful and peaceful scene

TOPIC SENTENCE: _____

_____

4. Narrowed Subject: Easy steps to opening a bank account

TOPIC SENTENCE: _____

_____

# Writing

## Revising Ineffective Topic Sentences

Your topic sentence is the most important sentence in the paragraph. It promises what the remainder of the paragraph will deliver. A weak topic sentence usually produces a weak paragraph. Your topic sentence will be weak if it (1) lacks a viewpoint or attitude, (2) is too broad, or (3) is too narrow.

## Topic Sentences That Lack a Point of View

A topic sentence should identify your topic *and* express an attitude or viewpoint. It must make a point about the topic.

   If your topic is the old roller coaster at Starland Park, it is not enough to make a general statement of fact in your topic sentence.

| | |
|---|---|
| **LACKS POINT OF VIEW** | There is an old roller coaster at Starland Park. |

Your reader would rightly ask in this case, "So what?" A topic sentence needs to tell the reader what is important or interesting about your topic. It should state the point you are going to make in the rest of the paragraph. For every topic, you can find many points to make in a topic sentence. For example:

| | |
|---|---|
| **EXPRESSES POINT OF VIEW** | The old roller coaster at Starland Park is unsafe and should be torn down. |
| | The old roller coaster at Starland Park no longer seems as frightening as it did when I was young. |
| | Three types of people go on the old roller coaster at Starland Park: the brave, the scared, and the stupid. |

   If you write a topic sentence that does not express a viewpoint, you will find you have very little or nothing to write about in the remainder of the paragraph. Look at these topic sentences:

| | |
|---|---|
| **LACKS POINT OF VIEW** | Pete works at the YMCA. |
| **EXPRESSES POINT OF VIEW** | Pete got over his shyness by working at the YMCA. |

If you used the first topic sentence, "Pete works at the YMCA," what else could you include in your paragraph? If you instead used the second topic sentence, you would have something to write about. You could describe Pete before and after he began working at the YMCA, discuss positive aspects of the job, or give examples of friends Pete has made through his work.

Notice how the following topic sentences have been revised to express a point of view.

| | |
|---|---|
| **LACKS POINT OF VIEW** | Mark plays soccer. |
| **REVISED** | Mark's true personality comes out when he plays soccer. [Details can explain Mark's personality as revealed by his soccer game.] |
| **LACKS POINT OF VIEW** | Professor Cooke teaches accounting. |
| **REVISED** | Professor Cooke makes accounting practical. [Details can describe how Professor Cooke makes accounting skills relevant to everyday life.] |
| **LACKS POINT OF VIEW** | I read newspapers. |
| **REVISED** | I recommend reading newspapers from back to front. [Details can give reasons why this method is best.] |

The following suggestions will help you revise your topic sentence if you discover that it lacks a point of view:

1. **Use brainstorming, freewriting, or branching.** Try to generate more ideas about your topic. Study your results to discover a way to approach your topic.

2. **Ask yourself questions about your topic sentence.** Specifically, ask "Why?" "How?" "So what?" or "Why is this important?" Answering your own questions will give you ideas for revising your topic sentence.

**TOPIC SENTENCES THAT LACK A POINT OF VIEW**

**Directions:** The following topic sentences lack a point of view. Revise each to express an interesting view on the topic.

SENTENCE   I took a biology exam today.

REVISED   The biology exam that I took today contained a number of surprises.

**1**. I am taking a math course this semester.

REVISED:   ..........................................................................................................................................

..........................................................................................................................................

**2**. I purchased a video camera last week.

REVISED: _____

_____

**3**. Soft rock was playing in the dentist's office.

REVISED: _____

_____

**4**. Sam has three televisions and four radios in his household.

REVISED: _____

_____

**5**. There is one tree on the street where I live.

REVISED: _____

_____

**6**. Many people wear headphones on their way to work.

REVISED: _____

_____

**7**. Our sociology professor will give us three exams.

REVISED: _____

_____

**8**. The first hurricane of the season is predicted to strike land tomorrow.

REVISED: _____

_____

**9**. My four-year-old son has learned the alphabet.

REVISED: _____

_____

**10**. Juanita enrolled her son in a day-care center.

REVISED: _____

_____

# Topic Sentences That Are Too Broad

Some topic sentences express a point of view, but they are too broad in scope.

| | |
|---|---|
| **TOO BROAD** | The death penalty is a crime against humanity. |

This statement cannot be supported in a single paragraph. Lengthy essays, even entire books, have been written to argue this opinion.

A broad topic sentence promises more than you can reasonably deliver in a single paragraph. It leads to writing that is vague and rambling. With a broad topic sentence, you will end up with too many facts and ideas to cover or too many generalities (general statements) that do not sufficiently explain your topic sentence. In the following example, note the broad topic sentence and its effects on paragraph development.

---

**Sample Paragraph**

All kinds of violent crimes in the world today seem to be getting worse. Sometimes I wonder how people could possibly bring themselves to do such horrible things. One problem may be the violent acts shown on television programs. Some people think crime has a lot to do with horror movies and television programs. We have no heroes to identify with other than criminals. News reporting of crimes is too "real"; it shows too much. Kids watch these programs without their parents and don't know what to make of them. Parents should spend time with their children and supervise their play.

---

The topic sentence above promises more than a good paragraph can reasonably deliver: to discuss all violent crimes in the world today and their worsening nature. If you reread the paragraph, you will see that in the supporting sentences the author wanders from topic to topic. She first mentions violence on television, then moves to lack of heroes. Next she discusses news reporting that is too graphic, then switches to children watching programs alone. Finally, she ends with parental supervision of children. Each point about possible causes of violence or ways to prevent it seems underdeveloped.

An effective topic sentence needs to be more focused. For example, the topic sentence for a paragraph about crime might focus on one type of crime in one city and one reason for its increase.

| | |
|---|---|
| **FOCUSED** | Home burglaries are increasing in Owensville because of increased drug usage. |

Another effective topic sentence for a paragraph on crime could focus on one possible cause of rising violence in the workplace.

| FOCUSED | The mass layoffs in the past few years have led to more criminal acts by desperate, unemployed workers. |
|---------|---------|

The topic sentence of the following paragraph is also too broad.

## Sample Paragraph

People often forget the spirit and value of life and concentrate on worldly goods. These people buy things for show—nice cars, nice clothes, nice houses. These people are scraping their pennies together just to live well. They do not realize that things not from the store are just as nice. Their health, their families, and the people they care about are far more important than money. You can be rich and poor at the same time.

Because the topic was too broad, the writer continued to use general statements throughout the paragraph and to repeat the same or similar ideas. A more effective approach might be to select one worldly good and show how it affects one person.

| FOCUSED | My sister is so concerned with dressing stylishly that she ignores everyone around her. |
|---------|---------|

Now the writer can explain how an emphasis on clothing detracts from her sister's relationship with others.

Another effective topic sentence might focus the paragraph on not taking good health for granted:

| FOCUSED | I used to think I could buy my way to happiness, but that was before I lost my good health. |
|---------|---------|

The following suggestions will help you revise your topic sentence if you discover that it is too broad:

1. **Narrow your topic.** A topic that is too broad often produces a topic sentence that is too broad. Narrow your topic by subdividing it into smaller topics. Continue subdividing until you produce a topic that is manageable in a single paragraph.

2. **Rewrite your topic sentence to focus on one aspect or part of your topic.** Ask yourself, "What is the part of this topic that really interests me or that I care most about? What do I know most about the topic and have the most to say about?" Then focus on that aspect of the topic.

3. **Apply your topic sentence to a specific time and place.** Ask yourself, "How does this broad topic that I'd like to write about relate to some particular time and place that I know about? How can I make the general topic come alive by using a well-defined example?"

**4. Consider using one of your supporting sentences as a topic sentence.** Reread your paragraph; look for a detail that could be developed or expanded.

### TOPIC SENTENCES THAT ARE TOO BROAD

**Directions:** Turn each of the following broad topic sentences into a well-focused topic sentence that could lead to an effective paragraph. Remember that your topic sentence must also include a point of view. Then compare your answers with your classmates' answers to see the variety of effective topic sentences that can come from a broad one.

TOO BROAD   Hunting is a worthwhile and beneficial sport.

REVISED   Hunting deer in overpopulated areas is beneficial to the herd.

**1**. I would like to become more creative.

REVISED: .................................................................................................

.................................................................................................

**2**. Brazil is a beautiful country.

REVISED: .................................................................................................

.................................................................................................

**3**. Pollution is a big problem.

REVISED: .................................................................................................

.................................................................................................

**4**. The space program is amazing.

REVISED: .................................................................................................

.................................................................................................

**5**. It is very important to learn Japanese.

REVISED: .................................................................................................

.................................................................................................

**6**. We must protect the environment.

REVISED: .................................................................................................

.................................................................................................

**7**. Lani is a good mother.

REVISED: .................................................................................................

.................................................................................................

**8**. The book was interesting.

REVISED: ..............................................................................................

..............................................................................................

**9**. Lots of magazines are published.

REVISED: ..............................................................................................

..............................................................................................

**10**. Honesty is important.

REVISED: ..............................................................................................

..............................................................................................

# Topic Sentences That Are Too Narrow

If your topic sentence is too narrow, you will realize it right away because you won't have enough to write about to complete your paragraph. Topic sentences that are too narrow also frequently lack a point of view.

| | |
|---|---|
| **TOO NARROW** | My birdfeeder attracts yellow songbirds |
| **REVISED** | Watching the different birds at our feeder is a pleasant diversion enjoyed by our entire family, including our cat. |
| **TOO NARROW** | My math instructors look at his watch frequently. |
| **REVISED** | My math instructor has a number of nervous habits that detract from his lecture presentations. |

The following suggestions will help you revise your topic sentence when it is too narrow:

1.  **Broaden your topic to include a wider group or range of items or ideas.** For example, do not write about one nervous habit; write about several. Look for patterns and trends that could form the basis of a new, broader topic sentence.

2.  **Broaden your topic so that it takes in both causes and effects or makes comparisons or contrasts.** For example, do not write only about how fast an instructor lectures. Also write about the effect of his lecture speed on students trying to take notes, or contrast that instructor with others who have different lecture styles.

3. **Brainstorm and research; try to develop a more general point from your narrower one.** Ask yourself, "What does this narrow point mean? What are its larger implications?" Suppose you've written the following topic sentence:

I wanted to buy a CD this week, but it was not in my budget.

You could expand this idea to discuss the importance or value of making and following a weekly budget.

## Need to Know

### Topic Sentences

Ineffective paragraphs may frustrate, confuse, or bore your reader.
**A weak topic sentence may**

- Lack a point of view or attitude toward the topic.
- Be too broad.
- Does the detail support the main idea?
- Be too narrow.

**To revise a topic sentence that lacks a point of view**

- Use brainstorming, freewriting, or branching.
- Ask yourself questions about your topic sentence to focus on a particular viewpoint.

**To narrow a topic sentence that is too broad, consider**

- Narrowing your topic.
- Rewriting your topic sentence to focus on one aspect of your topic.
- Applying your topic sentence to a specific time and place.
- Using one of your supporting sentences as a topic sentence.

**To broaden a topic sentence that is too narrow, consider**

- Broadening your topic to make it more inclusive.
- Broadening your topic to consider causes and effects or to make comparisons or contrasts.
- Brainstorming and researching to develop a more general point.

**TOPIC SENTENCES THAT ARE TOO NARROW**

**Directions:** Turn each of the following narrow topic sentences into a broader, well-focused topic sentence that could lead to an effective paragraph. Remember that your topic sentence must also include a point of view. Then compare your answers with your classmates' answers to see the variety of effective topic sentences that can come from a narrow one.

TOO NARROW   Football players wear protective helmets.

REVISED   Football players wear several types of protective equipment to guard against injuries.

**1**. I planted a tomato plant in my garden.

REVISED: ...............................................................................

...............................................................................

**2.** The cafeteria served hot dogs and beans for lunch.

REVISED: ........................................................................

........................................................................

**3.** Orlando sings in a low key.

REVISED: ........................................................................

........................................................................

**4.** Suzanne bought a stapler for her desk.

REVISED: ........................................................................

........................................................................

**5.** Koala bears are really marsupials, not bears.

REVISED: ........................................................................

........................................................................

**6.** On our vacation, we stopped at a small town called Boothbay Harbor.

REVISED: ........................................................................

........................................................................

**7.** Homemade bread contains no preservatives.

REVISED: ........................................................................

........................................................................

**8.** At Halloween, the girl dressed as a witch.

REVISED: ........................................................................

........................................................................

**9.** The comedian told a joke about dental floss.

REVISED: ........................................................................

........................................................................

**10.** We had a family portrait taken for Christmas.

REVISED: ........................................................................

........................................................................

# Revising Paragraphs to Add Supporting Details

The details in a paragraph should give your reader sufficient information to make your topic sentence believable. Paragraphs that lack necessary detail are called underdeveloped paragraphs. **Underdeveloped paragraphs** lack supporting sentences to prove or explain the point made in the topic sentence. As you read the following student paragraph, keep the topic sentence in mind and consider whether the rest of the sentences support it.

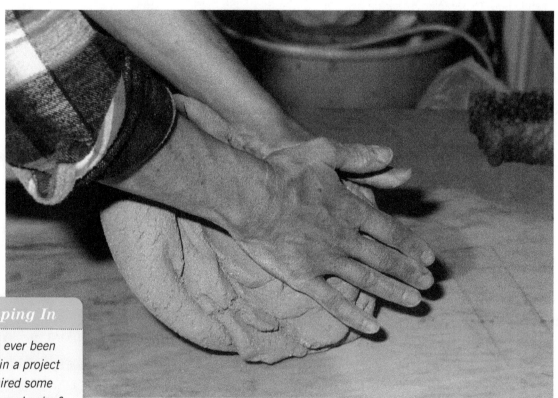

### Jumping In

*Have you ever been involved in a project that required some planning or shaping? For example, have you ever painted a room? Worked with clay? Designed a Web page? Writers often begin with a range of ideas and details. Later, they find a way to sort, shape, and focus them. Part of the planning and shaping process involves devising a **topic sentence and an outline**.*

# Writing a Paragraph: Planning—Devising a Plan

Once you have a topic sentence, you can begin working on an *outline* for your paragraph. The outline is a *plan* that helps you stay focused in your writing. The outline begins to form when you write your topic sentence and the details beneath it.

## Checking Your Details

You can now look at your list and ask yourself an important question: "Do I have enough details to support my topic sentence?" Remember, your goal is to write a paragraph of seven to twelve sentences.

Consider this topic sentence and list of details:

---

**TOPIC SENTENCE:** Fresh fruit is a good dessert.

**DETAILS:** tastes good
healthy
easy

---

Does the list contain enough details for a paragraph of seven to twelve sentences? Probably not.

## Adding Details When There Are Not Enough

To add details, try brainstorming. Ask yourself some questions:

What fruit tastes good?
What makes fruit a healthy dessert?
Why is it easy? How can you serve it?

By brainstorming, you may come up with these details:

---

**TOPIC SENTENCE:** Fresh fruit is a good dessert.

**DETAILS:** tastes good
a ripe peach or a juicy pineapple tastes delicious
crunchy apples are always available and satisfying
plump strawberries are great in summer
healthy
low in calories
rich in vitamins and fiber
easy
served as it is
in a fruit salad
mixed with ice cream or sherbet
no cooking necessary

---

Keep brainstorming until you feel you have enough details for a paragraph with seven to twelve sentences. Remember, it is better to have too many details than to have too few, for you can always edit the extra details later.

---

ADDING DETAILS TO SUPPORT A TOPIC SENTENCE

Do this exercise with a partner or group. The following topic sentences have some—but not enough—details. Write sentences to add details to each list.

**1.** TOPIC SENTENCE: Renting a movie on a DVD has many advantages over seeing a movie in a theater.

DETAILS: **1.** You don't have to get dressed up to see a DVD at home.

**2.** You can stop the DVD to get a snack or answer the phone.

**3.** _____

_____

**4.** _____

_____

**5.** _____

_____

**6.** _____

_____

**2.** TOPIC SENTENCE: I find amazing objects in the pockets of my jeans and jackets.

    DETAILS: **1.** Once I found a wrinkled apple in my raincoat.

          **2.** There was a toothbrush in my hoodie.

          **3.** _____

_____

          **4.** _____

_____

          **5.** _____

_____

          **6.** _____

_____

**3.** TOPIC SENTENCE: People hold garage sales for a number of reasons.

    DETAILS: **1.** Some people want to clear the clutter out of their house.

          **2.** Others want to make a little money.

          **3.** _____

_____

**4.**

_____

_____

**5.**

_____

_____

**6.**

_____

_____

_____

**4.** TOPIC SENTENCE: I listen to some kind of music nearly all day.

   DETAILS: **1.** I hear soft background music at the supermarket.

   **2.** I jog with an iPod that plays my favorite music.

   **3.** When I wake up, my son is singing a song that he learned in first grade.

   **4.** _____

   _____

   **5.** _____

   _____

   **6.** _____

   _____

   _____

**5.** TOPIC SENTENCE: Not all fast-food restaurants offer the same kinds of food.

   DETAILS: **1.** Some offer pizza.

   **2.** Others sell deli subs.

   **3.** _____

   _____

   **4.** _____

   _____

5. _____

6. _____

# Eliminating Details That Do Not Relate to the Topic Sentence

Sometimes, what you thought were good details don't relate to the topic sentence because they don't fit or support your point. Eliminate details that don't relate to the topic sentence. For example, the following list contains details that don't relate to the topic sentence. Those details are crossed out.

---

**TOPIC SENTENCE:** My neighbors are making my home life unbearable.

**DETAILS:** play their music loud at 3:00 a.m.
I can't sleep
leave garbage all over the sidewalk
~~come from Philadelphia~~
sidewalk is a mess
insects crawl all over their garbage
~~I carefully bag my garbage~~
they argue loudly and bang on the walls
my privacy is invaded
park their van in my parking space

---

### ELIMINATING DETAILS THAT DO NOT FIT

Following are topic sentences and lists of details. Cross out the details that do not fit the topic sentence.

**1**. TOPIC SENTENCE: Some professional athletes set a bad example for the children who admire them.

DETAILS: One basketball player choked a coach.
I think basketball has become more of a business than a sport.
A baseball player spit at an umpire.
Several football players have been charged with spousal abuse.
I used to collect autographs of famous players.
Some hockey players are notorious for fighting on the ice.
Children see this behavior and think it is acceptable.

**2**. TOPIC SENTENCE: Caps are worn by all kinds of people in all kinds of places.

DETAILS: Truckers wear caps when they drive.
Men on tractors wear caps with the name of the tractor company.
Caps are inexpensive.
Children in Little League wear baseball caps.
There are caps to protect fishermen from the sun.
Servers in some restaurants have to wear caps.
Some ladies wear baseball caps covered in sequins to match their fancy clothes.
College bookstores sell caps printed with the name of the college, for students.
Years ago, businessmen used to wear hats to work.
Teens wear caps when they're having a bad hair day.

**3**. TOPIC SENTENCE: Daniella is known for bringing something whenever she visits.

DETAILS: If she visits someone in the hospital, she always brings flowers.
Fresh flowers are really expensive.
Daniella brings dessert when you invite her for dinner.
She brings me candy when she stops by.
When Celeste had a baby, Daniella brought the baby a knitted blanket.
I invited her to a picnic, and she came with an extra bag of ice.
Daniella always takes an extra pencil to class for the person who forgot one.

**4**. TOPIC SENTENCE: For a number of reasons, most children enjoy teasing their siblings.

DETAILS: Bored children can find teasing exciting.
Teasing a brother or sister makes a child feel powerful.
By teasing, a child can release a little anger or envy.
Some adults enjoy teasing other adults and children.
A child enjoys getting a reaction from a sister or brother.
Teasing a sibling can also win a parent's attention.
Nothing is worse than children fighting in a car.

**5**. TOPIC SENTENCE: The new movie theater was very glamorous.

DETAILS: The exterior was made to look like a rock-and-roll drive-in restaurant.
Neon lights were shaped like guitars and musical notes.
Rock music blasted outside the ticket booths.
The ticket prices were reasonable.
The movies showing were the same as the ones at the theater down the block.
The concessions area sold gourmet pizza as well as popcorn and candy.
It also had a coffee bar with cappuccino.

# From List to Outline

Take another look at the topic sentence and list of details on the topic of My Mother:

---

**TOPIC SENTENCE:**  My mother survived difficult times to become a good parent and worker.

**DETAILS:**  She's a good mom.
Always takes care of me.
She works hard.
She cooks, cleans.
makes a great chicken casserole
She has a job.
She's a nurse.
She had a rough life.
lost her husband
went to school at night

---

After you scan the list, you will be ready to develop the outline of a paragraph.

The outline is a plan for writing, and it can be a kind of draft in list form. It sketches what you want to write and the order in which you want to present it. An organized, logical list will make your writing unified because each item on the list will relate to your topic sentence.

When you plan, keep your topic sentence in mind:

*My mother <u>survived difficult times</u> to become <u>a good parent</u> and <u>worker.</u>*

Notice that the key words are underlined and lead to key phrases:

*survived difficult times*
*a good parent*
*a good worker*

Can you put the details together so that they connect to one of these key phrases?

**survived difficult times**
*She had a rough life, lost her husband, went to school at night*
**a good parent**
*She's a good mom, Always takes care of me, She cooks, cleans, makes a great chicken casserole*
**a good worker**
*She works hard, She has a job, She's a nurse*

With this kind of grouping, you have a clearer idea of how to organize a paragraph. You may have noticed that the details grouped under each phrase explain or give examples that are connected to the topic sentence. You may also have noticed that the detail "She works hard" is placed under the phrase "a good worker." It could also be placed under "a good parent," so it would be your decision where to place it.

Now that you have grouped your ideas with key phrases and examples, you can write an outline:

## An Outline for a Paragraph on My Mother

| | |
|---|---|
| **topic sentence:** | My mother survived difficult times to become a good parent and worker. |
| **details:** **difficult times** | She had a rough life. She lost her husband. She went to school at night. |
| **a good parent** | She's a good mom and always takes care of me. She cooks and cleans. She makes a great chicken casserole. |
| **a good worker** | She works hard at her job. She's a nurse. |

As you can see, the outline combines some details from the list. Even with these combinations, the details are very rough in style. As you reread the list of details, you may notice places that need more combining, places where ideas need more explaining, and places that are repetitive. Keep in mind that an outline is merely a rough organization of your paragraph.

As you work through the steps of devising an outline, you can check for the following:

## Checklist: A Checklist for an Outline

✓ **Unity:** Do all the details relate to the topic sentence? If they do, the paragraph will be unified.

✓ **Support:** Do I have enough supporting ideas? Can I add to those ideas with more specific details?

✓ **Coherence:** Are the ideas listed in the right order? If the order of the points is logical, the paragraph will be coherent.

# Coherence

Check the sample outline again; you'll notice that the details are grouped in the same order as in the topic sentence: first, details about your mother's difficult life; next, details about your mother as a parent; finally, details about your mother as a worker. Putting details in an order that matches the topic sentence is logical for this paragraph. It makes the paragraph *coherent*.

# Determining the Order of Details

Putting the details in a logical order makes the ideas in the paragraph easier to follow. The most logical order for a paragraph depends on the subject of the paragraph. If you are writing about an event, you might use **time order** (such as telling what happened first, second, and so forth); if you are arguing some point, you might use **emphatic order** (such as saving your most convincing idea for last); if you are describing a room, you might use **space order** (such as describing from left to right or from top to bottom).

## COHERENCE: PUTTING DETAILS IN THE RIGHT ORDER

These outlines have details that are in the wrong order. In the space provided, number the sentences so that they are in the proper order: *1* would be the number for the first sentence, and so on. (Put the sentences in time order, from first to last.)

**1**. TOPIC SENTENCE: My last day at my job was sadder than I had expected.

............... Everyone went through the morning routine as usual.

............... I spent my afternoon feeling hurt and insulted.

............... At lunchtime, no one even asked me out for a farewell lunch.

............... When I first came in, no one acted as if he or she remembered it

was my last day.

............... Just as we were closing the store, my boss and coworkers

surprised me with a big cake and other treats.

............... I left feeling grateful for their thoughtfulness.

............... I was also sad to leave these kind people.


**2**. TOPIC SENTENCE: As a result of the car accident, David suffered multiple injuries. (Put the sentences in space order, from top to bottom.)

............... His eye sockets were black and blue.

............... David had cracked several ribs.

............... Broken glass from the windshield had cut his neck.

............... His jaw was dislocated.

............... He suffered a broken ankle.

............... His nose was broken.


**3**. TOPIC SENTENCE: Driving while texting is foolish and dangerous. (Put the sentences in emphatic order, from the least important reason to the most important.)

............... You can be killed.

............... In some states, you can be ticketed.

............... You can be bumped and bruised in a minor fender bender.

............... You can be severely hurt in a more serious accident.


**4**. TOPIC SENTENCE: The speech was long, boring, and confusing. (Put the sentences in the same order as in the topic sentence.)

............... The speaker jumped from topic to topic.

............... One minute he was talking about pollution; then he was telling a joke.

............... He spoke in a monotone.

............... He was putting me to sleep.

............... I checked my watch after thirty minutes.

............... He went on for another forty minutes.

# Logical Order

Use a writing plan to establish a logical order for details and a clear flow of ideas. A writing plan includes one or more of the following elements:

**A Pattern of Organization** As discussed on page 58, a writer uses a pattern of organization to arrange major details and minor details in a logical order. The following chart provides a few examples of patterns of organization and signal words for each one (see pages 68–105 for in-depth instruction about patterns of organization and signal words):

| PATTERNS OF ORGANIZATION | SIGNAL WORDS |
| --- | --- |
| Description (Space order) | above, below, next to, underneath, scene |
| Narrative/Process (Time order) | first, now, then, before, after, next, stage |
| Example | for example, exemplify, includes, such as |
| Classification | types, kinds, levels |
| Compare/Contrast | similar, likewise/however, in contrast |
| Cause/Effect | source, origin/results, impact, reasons |

**Order of Importance** Often, a writer decides upon and arranges details according to his or her opinion about the importance of the details, known as **climactic order**. Usually, climactic order moves from the least important point and builds to the paragraph's climax, the most important point.

**Order of Topic Sentence** Often the controlling point of the topic sentence divides the subject into chunks of information. The order of the ideas in the topic sentence often reflects a pattern of organization or an order of importance for details.

---

**LOGICAL ORDER**

The following paragraph from a college textbook demonstrates a writing plan based on the logical order of a topic sentence and pattern of organization. Underline the topic sentence. Circle the pattern of organization's signal words.

(1) In play, children learn to take the role of the other, that is, to understand how someone else feels and thinks and to anticipate how that person will act. (2) Learning to take the role of another goes through three stages. (3) The first stage is imitation. (4) During this stage, children under 3 mimic the words and gestures of others. (5) The second stage is play. (6) From the age of 3 to 6, children pretend to take on the roles of others; they pretend to be a firefighter, nurse, or super hero. (7) The third stage focuses on games. (8) During the early school years, children join in organized play; team games teach children to take on the roles of all the other players.

–Adapted from Henslin, James. *Essentials of Sociology:* A Down-To-Earth Approach, 7th ed., p.64

Study the following list of ideas. Label the major supports in each group A, B, and C to achieve the most logical order. Discuss the reasons for your choices with a small group of peers.

1. Writing for Everyday Life

Dear Kenesha, thank you for the surprise birthday party you organized for me.

.............. the weeks of secret planning

.............. the beautiful decorations and lovely gifts

.............. the surprise of walking through the door

2. Writing for Working Life

To: Heather Brady. From: Nicolas Wienders, Supervisor. You are to be highly praised for your outstanding contributions to the team's project.

..............Ultimately, you suggested the best solution possible.

.............. Throughout the project, you researched ways to solve the problem.

.............. You identified a problem early on in the project.

3. Writing for College Life

Although not identical, weather and climate have much in common.

.............. Thus, climate is the total of all statistical weather information that helps describe a place or region.

.............. On the other hand, climate is often described as "average weather."

.............. On the one hand, weather is the state of the atmosphere at a given time and place.

# Relevant and Adequate Details

Relevant and adequate details support and develop the main idea. As you narrow a topic, usually you generate many ideas before you decide on one main point. You must evaluate each detail based on its relationship to the point you want to make.

*Relevant details* explain and support only the writer's point. Once you narrow a subject into a focused main idea, you then include only those details that relate to your opinion and pattern of organization.

## Check for Relevant Details

Apply the following questions to each detail to see if it is relevant to a main idea. If the answers are "no" to these questions, then the detail is most likely irrelevant and should not be included as a support.

- Does the detail reinforce the writer's opinion?
- Does the detail carry out the pattern of organization?
- Does the detail support the main idea?
- Does the detail support a major detail?

**RELEVANT DETAILS**

The following prewrite list includes a focused main idea and a set of details. Use the "Check for Relevant Details" questions given on page 62 to identify the irrelevant detail, and cross it out.

Main Idea: Follow these three steps to open a bank account.

Step 1: Choose type of account
- Savings to build interest
- Checking to record transactions
- Cash transactions

Step 2: Choose services
- ATM
- Internet banking
- 24-hour service

Step 3: Choose your bank
- Convenient location
- Federally insured
- Fees for services
- Apply and deposit money

*Adequate details* offer in-depth explanations and supports for the writer's opinion and pattern of organization. In-depth support of a main idea often requires both major and minor details. Major details directly support the main idea. Minor details support and explain the major details (review the chart on page 51 of this chapter).

## Check for Adequate Details

Apply the following questions to see if you have adequate details to support your main idea. If the answer is "yes" to these questions, then additional details are most likely needed to fully support the main idea.

- Is more information needed to explain the writer's opinion?
- Is more information needed to carry out the pattern of organization?
- Does a major detail need a minor detail of support or explanation?

**ADEQUATE DETAILS**

The following list includes a main idea statement, three major supporting details, and minor details that support each major detail. Circle the major detail that needs more support. Add another minor detail of support for the idea you circled.

Main Idea: Blue Springs State Park is a beautiful and peaceful place.

Major Details:  Beautiful  Peaceful

Minor Details:
- Lush tropical plants
- Plentiful wildlife

- Shady and cool
- Soothing sound of water
- Fragrant smell of earth

Many writers use concept maps and other brainstorming techniques to generate enough relevant details to convincingly support a point.

Read the following rough draft of a paragraph. Cross out the irrelevant detail. Underline the point that needs more information to adequately support the main idea.

▲ **Hip-hop Mural**

▲ **Gang graffiti**

## The Various Shades of Graffiti

(1) Graffiti is made up of the words, colors, and shapes drawn or scratched on buildings, overpasses, train cars, desks, and other public surfaces. (2) It is done without permission; it is against the law, it is vandalism. (3) However, not all graffiti is the same. (4) Graffiti varies based on its purpose and style. (5) For example, the goal of Hip-hop graffiti is to gain fame for the individual style of the graffiti artist. (6) Hip-hop graffiti offers colorful and often artistic designs that range from simple tags, or signatures, to more complex pieces, such as murals. (7) In contrast, the purpose of gang graffiti is to build recognition, create fear, and mark the gang's turf or area. (8) Gang graffiti may list members, offer drugs for sale, or send warnings to rivals. (9) Gang graffiti differs from Hip-hop graffiti not only in its purpose, but also in its style. (10) Both Hip-hop graffiti and gang graffiti are statements of rebellion against authority.

# Effective Expression

Effective expression enhances the writer's purpose through the precise choice and use of words, sentence structure, and grammar.

## Word Choice

Precise word choice communicates exact meaning. Writers choose words that effectively communicate tone, purpose, and order. For example, strong transitions and signal words clue the audience into the logical order of the writer's thoughts. Another example of effective expression is the use of action verbs. In addition, words chosen for their emotional or visual impact create strong mental images in the reader's mind and carry out the writer's purpose.

**Ineffective Expression**

NON–ACTION VERBS

Leigh was glad when the race was over.

**Effective Expression**     ACTION VERBS

Leigh shouted in triumph when the race ended.

## Sentence Structure

Four types of sentences serve as the basis for all sentences in the English language: simple, compound, complex, and compound-complex sentences. Effective expression uses a variety of sentence types to express ideas in clear and interesting statements. (You will learn more about sentence structure in Chapters 8–12.)

**Simple sentence:**

Jerome struggles with test anxiety.

**Compound sentence:**

Jerome knows the material, but he freezes up during an exam.

**Complex sentence:**

Because Jerome does not test well, he has created a test-taking plan to improve his test scores.

**Compound-Complex sentence:**

For example, Jerome reads through the entire exam; then he answers all the easy questions so that he can build points and gain confidence.

## Grammar

Grammar is a tool of effective expression. Writers use grammar to clarify and polish ideas. Grammar includes a wide variety of language rules such as the following: tense, agreement, and punctuation. (You will learn more about grammar throughout your studies in this text.) During the revision process, many writers focus on one element of expression at a time.

---

EFFECTIVE EXPRESSION

Revise the following paragraph for effective expression through word choice. With a small group of your peers, revise the underlined verbs of the following paragraph. Discuss how your revision improves the effectiveness of the paragraph.

### A Survivor's Account

(1) The tornado tore through the neighborhood. (2) The funnel cloud was huge and roared like a train. (3) The wind was blowing so hard that the trees were touching the ground. (4) All around us, houses were splintering, and debris was flying through the air. (5) We barely made it out of our car and into the roadside ditch where we were flat on our stomachs. (6) We were praying for our lives.

# Analyzing the Effectiveness of a Paragraph

Many student writers benefit from the study of a scoring guide. A scoring guide identifies and describes levels of writing effectiveness. The following scoring guide describes the traits of an effective paragraph as discussed in this chapter: A score of "5" indicates a highly effective paragraph. In a small group of your peers, discuss the differences between a "5" paragraph and a "3" level paragraph.

## Scoring Guide for a Paragraph

5   A focused main idea presents the narrowed subject and the writer's point, and suggests a pattern of organization. Relevant and in-depth details convincingly support and develop the main idea. Strong transitions indicate careful ordering of details based on a logical pattern of organization. Effective expression enhances the writer's purpose through the precise choice and use of words, sentence structure, and grammar.

4   A focused main idea presents the narrowed subject and the writer's opinion, and suggests a pattern of organization. Relevant and adequate details support and develop the main idea. Clear transitions indicate an order of details based on a logical pattern of organization. Effective expression carries out the writer's purpose through the competent use and choice of words, sentence structure, and grammar.

3   A focused main idea presents the narrowed subject and the writer's opinion or a pattern of organization. Relevant details offer enough support to develop the main idea. Occasional transitions indicate the use of a pattern of organization, but details are not always logically ordered. Expression does not interfere with the writer's purpose, even though occasional errors in use and choice of words, sentence structure, and grammar occur.

2   The main idea presents a general subject or a broad opinion. Details are generalized statements or lists that do not offer enough information to support the main idea. Weak or misused transitions and confused order of details indicate little use of a pattern of organization. Weak expression interferes with the writer's purpose through frequent errors in use and choice of words, sentence structure, and grammar.

1   The main idea presents a vague, weakly worded opinion about a general subject. Details are missing, superficial, or rambling. Lack of transitions and illogical order of details indicate no use of a pattern of organization. Confused expression interferes with the writer's purpose through pervasive errors in choice and use of words, sentence structure, and grammar.

# Revision

## Revise my draft:  What does that mean?

A writer, teacher, or student may all have different definitions for this word. The word comes from a Latin word which means "to look at again, visit again" (*Online Etymology Dictionary*).

Indeed, revising a written work is like visiting it once again, just as one might stop by the home of a friend for dinner and conversation.

So, what's new?

When we revise something we have written, we are, in fact, looking at it again with the intention of improving it - changing those aspects we find objectionable, incomplete, or in need of better expression; correcting errors or omissions in phrasing, word usage, sentences structure; filling in the blanks in our evidence, analysis, or reasoning; and making our writing more relevant, precise, and exciting. Revision means looking at the purpose and audience of our writing and determining whether or not what we have written is most effective in saying precisely what we want it to say. Revision involves reviewing, evaluating, correcting, and improving: content, organization, words and sentences, and mechanics (that pesky grammar, spelling, and punctuation stuff). So, how do we methodically revise a written draft for maximum impact?

The following are a set of steps that will enable you, the student writer, to revise your draft into a well-developed, refined, and polished piece of writing that effectively communicates your message.

Once you have completed the draft, look it over briefly for any obvious problems, mistakes, or changes; then, "put it to bed." Go eat dinner, do some other homework, watch a good movie, talk to your family or friends.  If you have the opportunity to wait until the next day, this is even better.  The idea is to get away from what you have written long enough to clear your mind.  You know what you want to say.  The idea is to communicate that to your reader.  If you start revising your composition right away, there is the possibility that you will "read into it" exactly what you want it to say, rather than reading what it actually says – and you won't really be saying what you want to say. That sentence was as clear as mud, right?  By taking a break, you can come back to your composition, thinking more clearly.  You might read something and ask: "What am I saying here?" or "Why did I say it that way; let me fix it!"

Return to your draft after you have been away from it for at least a few hours. Begin re-reading what you've written and change what you think needs revision.  This is the point at which you determine if your paragraph's topic sentence (or your essay's thesis statement) is clearly presented to the reader, your subpoints are presented in an organized manner and relate to the topic sentence (or thesis statement), you have supported every point you have made, and you have written a conclusion that effectively summarizes your paragraph (or essay) and refers back to the topic sentence (or thesis statement) without repeating it. This is the point at which you open the Thesaurus to find the "right" words for the ones you circled or left blank. This is the point at which you check your spelling and grammar meticulously.

*Understand that revising is generally done in a particular order, to avoid needless revision and redoubling one's efforts. The preferred order of revision is:*

1. **content/organizational issues (topic and main point, support points, organization, unity, coherence, transitions),**

2. **stylistic issues (word choice and missing or improperly used words; sentence structure and sentence variety),**

3. **mechanics (grammar, such as proper tenses, pronouns preference, and number agreement; spelling; and punctuation).**

# Revising a Paragraph

As you revise, constantly ask yourself: Did I say what I wanted to say in this paragraph? Did I get my message across in the clearest, briefest, most exciting possible way? Do my words, sentences, paragraphs, conclusion – all have sufficient details, examples, evidence to help readers see, hear, taste, or smell my point? When choosing points to raise or evidence to use to support these points, have I taken into account the purpose of my paper and the audience it is intended for? **Let's look…**

## 1. Revise for Content:

- **Topic sentence:**

  - Is my narrowed or focused topic specific enough to be adequately explained in a paragraph?

---

### *For example:*

If I chose to write about the time I received an award for a ninth grade science project, that might fit into a paragraph. If I decided to write about the 2009-10 economic crisis and its effect on unemployment, that would be too broad a topic for even an essay; I would need to narrow it down – by location, job field, age group, time frame, or some other focus that could be adequate explained in a paragraph or essay.

---

- Do I have a clearly stated topic sentence that includes my topic <u>and</u> the main point that I wish to make to the reader, so that the reader has a clear idea of what my paragraph is about?

> ### *For example:*
>
> Too broad and vague: **Some people are not ready for college.**
>
> Specific: **Many young people who attend college for the first time are not emotionally or intellectually ready for the challenges that college presents.**
>
> Specific, listing the three points to be talked about (a three point topic sentence): **Although many young people believe college to be simply grade thirteen, they soon discover that the challenges of college require more focus, discipline, and diligence than they had employed in high school.**

- Did I consider the purpose of my paragraph?

> ### *For example:*
>
> If I am writing a comparison and contrast paragraph, do I mention the two items I am comparing and let the reader know that I am discussing similarities, differences, or both?
>
> ### *OR:*
>
> If I am writing an argument (persuasive) paragraph, do I clearly state my position and why I feel that way, so the reader clearly understands what I plan on proving in my paragraph?

- If I use an introductory sentence, do I have a clear, engaging introduction that catches the reader's attention? Does my introductory sentence lead logically to my topic sentence?

- **Detail & Support:**

  - Unity: Do my major details (the individual aspects of my topic which I present) relate to and support my main point? Sometimes we are tempted to "detour" from the main point. A detail or a story about the topic may seem interesting to include, but it may have little to do with the actual main point we are making. That is, do I have extraneous information: details or ideas that do not need to be part of the paragraph?

> ### *For example:*
>
> In the sample topic sentence above
>
> **Although many young people believe college to be simply grade thirteen, they soon discover that the challenges of**

**college require more focus, discipline, and diligence than they had employed in high school)**

the specific major details that would be presented in your paragraph would be

(1) focus,

(2) discipline, and

(3) diligence.

These are the points you write about, in the same order in which you presented them in your topic sentence. You do not talk about college social life, or finances, or even the cafeteria, all of which are off topic. Concentrate only on those aspects of college which relate directly to focus, discipline, and diligence.

- Are my major details specific, and are they clearly and individually explained?

---

*For example:*

Using the sample topic sentence above, you might write the following sentence as your first major detail:

**Students should make sure that they are focused on the course material when in class.**

---

- Is each major detail backed up with supporting evidence - such as facts, statistics, examples, observations or experiences, descriptions, illustrations, definitions, analyses, comparisons or analogies, expert or authoritative testimony, etc. - that proves or explains it in enough detail to make this point clear and understandable to the reader? If not, is there information that needs to be added to make my meaning clearer, strengthen my argument, or support my subpoints? Too often students believe that simply by raising an issue they have adequately explained it. Raising an issue merely presents it to the reader, usually along with your opinion about it.

---

*For example:*

Again, look at the major detail above:

**Students should make sure that they are focused on the course material when in class.**

That sentence is the major detail, but the sentence does not explain what you mean by focus, why students should be *focused*, or even how students can *focus*. Those minor details must follow the major detail you raised, thus adding support to the major detail, and ultimately supporting the main point of your paragraph.

- Have I made sure that I don't have contradictions within my paper, especially due to improper phrasing or missing words? Look especially for use of negative words (e.g., This is not the proper way to study. Leaving out the word not would change the meaning entirely) or words of degree (e.g., most important. Only one point can be most important).

- **Conclusion:**

  - Do I have a strong conclusion that summarizes my paragraph and reminds the reader of my main point without actually repeating my topic sentence?
  - Does my conclusion give the reader a sense of completeness, making the reader feel that the writer is done, the paragraph is over, and the reader feels satisfied that the writer's points are "complete"?

# 2. Revise for Organization:

**Logical order: Is my paragraph organized in some logical order? The most common are:**

- Chronological (time order),
- Spatial (space order; that is, from left to right, front to back, etc.),
- Order of importance (either most important to least important **or** least important to most important).

- **Coherence: connecting all dots to form a picture.**

  - Do all my points, details, and sentences flow logically from one idea to the next, rather than seeming choppy or unrelated? Could the average person follow your progression of ideas?
  - Do I use transitional words, phrases, and clauses to relate information, eliminate redundancy, combine choppy simple sentences for better flow, and help the reader move from one idea to another? *OR:* Do I need to change the order of my ideas, add or change transitional words or phrases, or repeat key words or concepts to make my point more clearly or cogently?

---

### *For example:*

Original: **Your writing needs to be precise; a Thesaurus is a good way to find more specific words.**

Revised: **Because your writing needs to be precise, a Thesaurus is a good way to find more specific words.**

Original: **Samantha is my sister and dances exceedingly well.**

Revised: **Samantha, who is my sister, dances exceedingly well.**

---

# 3. Revise for Words and Sentences:

This is the part of revision which many writers enjoy the most. It is the time to create truly exciting writing, replacing old tired expressions (words, phrases, sentences) with new vibrant ones – words and phrases that don't just convey your message, but sing it, shout it, proclaim it to the reader in clear, precise, unmistakable language.

This is also a good time to read what you've written out loud (you'd be surprised at the mistakes you can catch by reading your composition orally). If possible, ask someone else to read what you've written to see if he or she understands it. (I use "he" or "she" for a reason: when I was writing feature articles some years ago, I would often ask my female friends to read my articles on women's issues to determine if I, as a male, were properly informative and sensitive to these issues.) Having someone else read what you've written is a good way to determine if you've communicated your ideas clearly. Having someone read your writing out loud to you also often alerts you to errors as the person reading may stumble or pause in parts that are in need of revision. In a persuasive essay, asking someone else to read what you've written is also a good way to see if you've made your point clearly, factually, and logically.

## • <u>WORDS (see "Revising for Effective Expression")</u>:

Choose words to reflect your writing style and the specific style or format you have chosen to use (e.g., informative, persuasive, humorous). Most writers, even if writing basic informational essays, use vivid writing that conveys their thoughts to the reader in "image-filled" ways. In addition, revision is the time in which you replace the words you were unsure of in your draft. This is the time you reach for the Thesaurus. But make sure you keep the dictionary handy: if you do not know the exact meaning of a new word, confirm it with the dictionary before actually using it.

- Pick words that describe exactly what you want to say. Eliminate and replace vague, ambiguous, general words (e.g., *interesting, good, pretty*). Look instead for precise, specific, vibrant words and expressions: vivid imagery that conveys the feelings, the urgency, the excitement of your message to the reader.

---

### *For example:*

Original: **Not many Americans like the IRS.**

Revised: **To most Americans, the IRS is as popular as leprosy.**

Original: **Her eyes were dark brown, and she wore a fluffy white hat. She had a nice figure and looked like a woman, but she still acted a little like a tomboy.**

Revised: **Her deep brown eyes contrasted with her fluffy white fur hat, which surrounded her face and made those dark eyes seem all the more mysterious and seductive. Yet, while the young lass's physical charms spoke richly of womanhood, her demeanor was more that of an unbroken colt just released from its stall.**

---

Avoid common overused words whenever possible, and try not to use the same word to describe the same or similar thing too many times in your writing. Find more exciting words.

---

### *For example:*

Replace common overused words like look with more precise dynamic words like: *glanced, peered, stared, jeered, gazed,* etc.

The same could be said for another common word, said. *He said..., she said..., we all said...* could be replaced with expressions like: *he asked..., she answered..., we declared...,* etc.

---

**HINT:** Look over the words you've used. Underline commonly overused words like: <u>*it, there, their, they, this, that, do, go, has/have, just, all, mostly*</u>. You can even use the <Edit-Find> function in WORD to find these words. Ask yourself: "What are these words referring to?" Then ask: "Can I use another, more precise word for any of them?"

- <u>Use adjectives, adverbs, prepositional phrases, and other modifiers, such as participial and other verbal phrases.</u>
- <u>Use precise strong verbs to say what it would take several words with a weak verb to say,</u> and avoid overuse of simple verbs (e.g., is, has, goes).

---

### *For example:*

Replace phrases like run away quickly with more dynamic verbs like *flee, dash, fly.*

---

- <u>Make note of the connotations of a word.</u>

---

### *For example:*

The words odor and aroma both mean smell; but word you rather have an odor or an aroma about you?

---

This includes words that have sexual, racial, or other connotations.

---

### *For example:*

*babysitter* vs. *day care provider, flight attendant* vs. *stewardess,* etc.

---

This also includes emotionally charged words, especially in persuasive writing. After all, if you are trying to convince someone to agree with your viewpoint, does it make sense to insult or demean that person. How inclined would you be to agree with someone who has just put you down?

> ### For example:
>
> In writing a paper on the abortion issue, a person arguing the right to life position will not gain any followers by calling the opposition *baby killers;* neither will those arguing for a woman's right to choose win the argument by calling the opposition *bigoted woman haters.*

- Avoid redundancy and extraneous language. Eliminate:
  - words or phrases that say or mean the same thing:

> ### For example:
> *the large multitude* (a multitude by definition is large)
>
> *He repeated things over and over* (the word repeated implies over and over)
>
> *I thought to myself* (can you think to anyone else?)
>
> *totally awesome* (can something be partially awesome?)
>
> *Too many young people waste time playing computer games. One computer game they waste time playing is Halo.* Why not simply say:
>
> *Too many young people waste time playing computer games, such as Halo.*

  - vague, trite, trivial words.

> ### For example:
> *due to the fact that* (why not simply say because?)
>
> *being as* (why not simply say since?)
>
> *In the article it talks about…* (why not simply say: The article talks about…?)

  - obvious statements

> ### For example:
>
> *to be honest* (were you dishonest previously?),
>
> *in my opinion* (your name is on the paper; the reader knows it's your opinion)

- superlatives or redundant words

> ### For example:
>
> *back in the past* (can something be back in the future?)

Repetition should be used only to emphasize a point to the reader, not simply because the writer could not think of a better way to say something.

> ### For example:
>
> In Rev. Dr. Martin Luther King's famous "I Have a Dream" speech, he effectively repeats the phrase *I have a dream* to emphasize his main message to his audience.

- talking about your writing in your writing.

> ### For example:
>
> *This paragraph is about...* (Tell us what it is about; don't tell us that you're going to tell us.)
>
> *In this paragraph I am going to compare two different styles of learning.* (Don't tell us what you're going to do; just do it.)
> *There are two different styles of learning that most students engage in when attending college.* (That sentence clearly states your intention – that you intend to compare two different types of learning - without referring to your writing.)

- Eliminate jargon, clichés, colloquial, conversational, or slang expressions, and euphemisms.

> ### For example:
>
> Original: **I spent many a leisurely afternoon hanging out with my friends at the shopping mall.**
>
> Revised: **I spend many a leisurely afternoon getting together with my friends at the shopping mall.**

In rare cases in which you feel that such expressions are the best way to convey your message, then make them clear to the reader by:

- placing them within quotation marks to show that the word or phrase is being used differently from its literal meaning.

---

### *For example:*

**Many adolescents think that missing classes to joy ride with their friends is "cool."**

---

- defining less familiar expressions to the reader (with additional phrases or within parentheses).

---

### *For example:*

**Too often, employees call out (i.e., call into work to take a sick day) simply because they feel like taking a day off.**

---

- Eliminate unnecessary use of the conversational *you.*

Most scholarly and collegiate writing uses the third person almost exclusively. The first person is used in rare occasions when the writer is recounting a person experience or reflection to provide support for the main idea or a major detail. The second person is virtually never used, except sometimes in Process writing (a set of instructions explaining to the reader how to do something), or in textbooks like this one, in which the author is speaking directly to *you* the students, as if in the classroom. Unfortunately, most speaking is replete with the conversational *you* – that informal *you* which all of us use regularly in conversation.

---

### *For example:*

A typical sentence used in conversation might be:

**You know how you get hungry late in the afternoon if you haven't eaten anything for lunch.**

That sentence has no place in formal college writing. If you wish to refer to the same topic, rephrase the sentence and use the third person, for example:

**A person often gets hungry late in the afternoon if he or she has not eaten anything for lunch.**

Similarly, we often shift "persons" when speaking. Usually the listener understands what we mean, and can even ask us if he or she does not. This is not so in writing; you must make your meaning clear to the reader the first time.

Original: **When someone was hired at that company, training was irrelevant to what you were doing.**

---

This sentence is incorrect, even though it might be typical in conversation, because the person being talked about shifts from third, *someone*, to second, *you*.

Revised: **When someone was hired at that company, training was irrelevant to what he or she was doing.**

This sentence is correct, because the person being talked about remains the same; *someone* and *he* or *she* are both third person.

Original: **When he was a young boy, he would often see small shops lining the streets, unlike the large shopping centers you might see today in your town.**

Revised: **When he was a young boy, he would see small shops lining the streets, unlike what someone might see today.**

• **SENTENCES:**

Look for variety, clarity, and proper meaning. Correct structural problems, redundancy, and trite expressions. Vary sentences for a smoother style, limiting your simple sentences and use compound and complex sentences whenever possible, saving simple sentences for emphasis or brief thoughts.

- Use repetition to emphasize or to make a point more forcefully.

---

*For example:*

**The enemy fired at our troops, but they stood their ground.**

**The enemy fired cannons at our troops, but they stood their ground.**

**The enemy sent tanks against our troops, but they still stood their ground.**

---

Otherwise, eliminate unnecessary repetition (especially of nouns), and combine similar ideas into single sent to avoid redundancy. Either use coordinating conjunctions to combine two simple sentences into one compound sentence, or use subordinate conjunctions (dependent words) to create complex sentences which subordinate lesser dependent ideas to main ones.

---

*For example:*

Original: **I often waste time playing computer games. One computer game I waste time playing is Halo.**

Revised: **I often waste time by playing computer games, such as Halo.**

---

- Correct fragments and run-ons (**see the chapters on "Fragments" and "Run-ons"**).

- Check for sentences that are confusing, unclear, vague, and awkward (often marked by instructors with the letters AWK), especially looking at those sentences with long, complex modifiers, or other complicated phrasing

- Check for misplaced or dangling modifiers (**see "Misplaced and Dangling Modifiers"**).

- Check for sentences that lack parallelism, particularly when listing items or concepts in words, phrases, or clauses. A proper sentences uses the same construction in a list; that is, if one item is a noun, all items should be nouns; if one item is a subject-verb combination, all should be subject-verb combinations(reference chapter on parallelism).

---

### *For example:*

Original: **On my way home from school, I stopped at the store, then stopping by the Post Office, and I drove over to where Michael lived.**

Revised: **Revised: On my way home from school, I <u>stopped</u> at the store, <u>went</u> to the Post Office, and <u>drove</u> to Michael's house.** (The underlined words are all verbs in perfect parallelism.)

Other examples of correct parallelism include:

**I came, I saw, I conquered.** (There is a subject-verb combination for each clause.)

**I saluted him back, we turned around, and we went our separate ways.** (There is a subject-verb combination for each clause.)

---

- Vary sentence structures: length, composition (simple, compound, complex, compound-complex), and word arrangement for clarity, meaning, and flow. Remember: simple sentences stand out; if you use too many simple sentences, they become commonplace, thus losing their effectiveness. Note the following types of sentence composition:

  - **Simple sentences.** Check for choppy, simple sentences. Simple sentences stand out; therefore, they should be used sparingly for emphasis and poignancy. If you use too many simple sentences, nothing stands out and you lose the emphasis. Instead, your paragraph or essay sounds choppy and "elementary." "I do not like green eggs and ham. I do not like them; Sam I am" might make sense for a Dr. Seuss children's story, but not for collegiate writing.

    <u>HINT</u>: you can flavor your simple sentences with modifiers, participial phrases, and descriptive adjectives, which make them not seem quite so "simple."

> ### For example:
> **Writing feverously, <u>Susan sat at the desk</u>, ideas pouring into her head, through her pen, and onto the paper.** (The underlined portion is the simple sentence, while the remaining words are modifiers, adding description and sentence variety).

- **Compound sentences** tie two related ideas together, using coordinating conjunctions (remember the seven coordinating conjunctions?). First, make sure that the ideas are indeed related. Then, be sure not to use too many clauses connected by *and* or *but*. Otherwise, you run the risk of creating run-on sentences.

- **Complex sentences** subordinate one idea to another, making the one dependent upon the main idea by using subordinate conjunctions (i.e., dependent words). Complex sentences are used for such relationships as:

  - conditional clauses (clauses which suggest possibility or condition):

> ### For example:
> **If a person wants to succeed at anything, that person must have a vision and the determination to reach his or her goal.**
>
> ### OR:
> **If I had more money, I could afford a better car.**

<u>HINT:</u> this seems like a good time to remember that, when using conditional clauses, you must use conditional words, like *could, would, should*; not *can* or *will*. The conditional clause expressions just that – a condition, a possibility, not a definite. You cannot say for sure that you *will* go, only that you *would* go if…

  - less important related ideas:

> ### For example:
> **Although he is old, he still works out.**

  - cause & effect ideas:

> ### For example:
> **When the whistle blows, it's time to leave.**

- contradictory ideas:

> ### *For example:*
> **Even though we have little disposable income, we still make sure we go out to dinner at least once a month.**

- time clauses:

> ### *For example:*
> **While we were waiting for the train, we decided to eat lunch.**
>
> ### *OR:*
> **He had to leave during the play.**

- or general subordinate clauses (which often answer the question "why?":

> ### *For example:*
> **I attended college because I wanted to become more productive in my life.**

- **Compound/Complex sentences**: combine a compound sentence (using a coordinating conjunction) with a complex sentence (using a subordinating conjunction, i.e., dependent word). These should be used occasionally, intermingled with the other types of sentences, to add variety, without making one's writing sound cumbersome.

- Watch your use of passive voice, which stresses the person or thing acted upon, rather than the person or thing doing the acting. Passive voice is usually used when the writer is being tactful or the person or thing doing the acting is unknown.

> ### *For example:*
> Original: **Many votes were cast by us that day.**
> Revised: **We cast many votes that day.**

Be aware that positive construction is often more convincing than negative construction:

---

### *For example:*

Original: **He was not late.**

Revised: **He was on time.**

---

**A few words of caution, especially when using word processors in this electronic age:**

---

**Spell-checker:** A spell checker is just that: it checks for spelling – not meaning. It will recognize misspelled words, but ignore correctly spelled words that are not the ones you intended. It will ignore typographical errors (e.g., "or" for "of," and commonly confused words (e.g., "it's" for "its"). A spell-checker is no substitute for knowing how to spell, nor for proofreading for meaning, as well as spelling.

**Grammar checker:** Grammar checkers are, in a word, terrible. They miss as many grammatical problems as they find, giving a false sense of security. Furthermore, the more complex the writing, the more problems grammar checkers will purport to have found, leaving you with more confusion over the supposed mistake than certainty. If you must use them, be sure to proofread also.

**Thesaurus:** A Thesaurus is indispensable when trying to use precise wording in a paper or finding new words to take the place of tired, overused words or expressions. Keep in mind, however, that, although both a print & electronic thesaurus lists vocabulary options, neither indicates which word is more appropriate in the circumstances. For example, both *odor* and *fragrance* are synonyms for the word *smell*; but which one of the two would you rather have? Check new-found words against their dictionary definitions.

---

## 4. Revise for Mechanics (grammar, spelling, and punctuation:

This part of revision is sometimes referred to as "editing." Once you have revised your content, organized your thoughts and points logically, revised for the most precise, vibrant, exciting wording and sentence structure, you should look at the mechanical elements of writing: grammar, spelling, and punctuation.

Just as the most well written musical composition, whether classical, rock, or rap, loses its appeal if the wrong notes are played or sung, so too the most carefully written paragraph or essay loses its effectiveness if the mechanics are flawed. The reader, unable to discern what the writer is saying among all the misspelled words and atrocious grammar, finally abandons reading the paragraph altogether, just as a listener eventually reaches his or her fill of wrong notes and selects another song. Therefore, proper grammar, spelling, and punctuation in your writing make a difference in your ability to effectively convey your meaning to your reader.

So what does one look for in revising the mechanics of your paragraph? Let's look at each of the three areas – grammar, spelling, and punctuation.

- **<u>Grammar:</u>**

  Where does one begin? Unlike the liberties most of us take in conversational English, formal writing requires adherence to a set of rules regarding the use of the parts of speech and their placement in a sentence and paragraph. The following pages list the most common mechanics problems most college students face, but it is by no means an exhaustive list. You should refer to the several chapters on parts of speech for a better understanding of grammar **<u>(see chapters on:</u>**

  **<u>"Nouns and Pronouns"</u>**

  **<u>"Subject-Verb Agreement"</u>**

  **<u>"The Past Tense of Verbs"</u>**

  **<u>"The Past Participle"</u>**

  **<u>Adjectives and Adverbs")</u>**

Then, review your writing with a clear understanding of the rules set forth in these chapters.

- Subject-verb-pronoun agreement:

  In every sentence, the subject and the main verb much agree in number. That is, if the subject is singular, the verb must be singular; if the subject is plural,  the verb must be plural. Fairly straightforward, right?

---

### *For example:*

**John is a new student.** (*John* = singular subject; *is* = singular verb.)

**The girls are new students.** (*girls* = plural subject; *are* = plural verb.)

---

Yet, few of our sentences are that simple. Well-expressed writing often includes words or phrases that modify (help describe or explain) the subject. It is easy to be fooled, especially when prepositional phrases modify the subject. are introduced in the sentence.

<u>HINT:</u> the subject of a sentence can never be in the prepositional phrase. So, if you are unsure of the subject, mentally eliminate the prepositional phrase, and the subject should become clearer.

---

### *For example:*

Original: **Each of the committee members <u>are</u> expected to be there on time.**
(The sentence is incorrect because the subject is *Each*,

not *members*, which is part of the prepositional phrase.)

Revised: **Each of the committee members is expected to be there on time.**

In addition, any pronouns which refer to the subject must also agree in number with the subject. As simple as that sounds, the English language often times fools us, as well as our own propensity for simplifying conversational English.

---

### *For example:*

Original: **Every student must bring their textbooks to class tomorrow.** (This sentence may work well in conversation, but it is grammatically incorrect. The subject *student* is singular, but the pronoun referring to *every student* is plural, *their*.)

Revised: **Every student must bring his or her textbook to class tomorrow.** (Making the pronoun singular makes the pronoun agree with the subject it refers to.)

Revised: **All students must bring their textbooks to class tomorrow.** (Making the subject plural allows the pronoun to remain as *their*, eliminating the need for *his* and *her*. However, you will notice that the word *textbook* becomes the plural *textbooks* to agree with the now plural subject *students*.)

---

<u>HINT:</u> any pronoun ending in the word *–one*, *-thing*, or *–body* is grammatically singular, regardless of its meaning. That is, pronouns like *everyone* may mean more than one person, but grammatically they must always use a singular verb in a sentence.

- Pronoun reference <u>(see "Nouns and Pronouns")</u>:

  Make sure that the pronoun reference (also called the pronoun *antecedent*) is clear. A pronoun can help prevent monotony and repetition of the same person, place or thing. But a pronoun can cause more confusion than clarity if not used properly. A pronoun usually refers to the noun most logically preceding it. If what you are using to reference the pronoun is not close enough or logical enough, your reader could be confused.

---

### *For example:*

In the sentence:

**John wanted to become an Air Force pilot, so his father offered to help John apply. He went to the local Air Force recruiter.**

who is *he*? Is the pronoun referring to *John* or his *father*?

Correct the pronoun reference by using the noun instead of the pronoun, for example:

**John wanted to become an Air Force pilot, so his father offered to help John apply. So his father went to the local Air Force recruiter.**

In the sentence:

**Jane, Sharon, and Elisa went shopping.  She bought a pair of slacks.**

who is *she*? Which woman are you referring to? Correct the pronoun reference by using the name of the woman instead of the pronoun, for example:

**Jane, Sharon, and Elisa went shopping. Elisa bought a pair of slacks.**

In the sentence:

**John, Sherman, David, and Elisa went shopping. She bought a pair of slacks.**

the reader might be able to determine who *she* is, since Elisa is the only *she* in your previous sentence and the noun closest to the pronoun; considering that many names can refer to either gender, the sentence would still be clearer if you used the name of the person instead of the pronoun, for example:

**John, Sherman, David, and Elisa went shopping. Elisa bought a pair of slacks.**

- Pronoun case (**see "Nouns and Pronouns"**):

  Be sure that you are using the right form of the pronoun, whether as subject, object, or even possessive.

  **HINT:** don't confuse *its* and *it's*: *its* is a possessive pronoun; *it's* is a contraction of *it is*.

- Check your verb tenses and correct any unnecessary tense shifts (moving from past to present, present to past, past to future, etc. without any logical reason). (**see "The Past Tense of Verbs" and "The Past Participle"**).

- **Spelling:**

Modern inventions can be very helpful, but they can also make us lazy and sloppy. Just as calculators can be helpful and yet allow us to forget how to perform simple math calculations in our heads, so too computer spell-check software has allowed us to become sloppy and lazy with our spelling. This sloppiness has no place in formal writing. Imagine submitting an employment application or a letter for admission to a four year college filled with spelling errors. As insignificant as such errors may seem, employers and deans of admissions alike look at such errors as signs that the applicant is not diligent, careful, and serious enough to be part of their organizations.

Additionally, spelling errors can change the meaning of your sentences, and even your paragraph.

---

#### *For example:*

In the sentence:

**He definitely played basketball during school.** (implying certainly)

Has a very different meaning from:

**He defiantly played basketball during school.** (implying rebellion or defiance)

---

When proofreading to correct spelling errors, look especially for:

• Commonly misused or misspelled words, including sound-alike words:

---

#### *For example:*

*than* and *then* (*than* = comparison, *then* = time)

*accept* and *except* (*accept* = receive, *except* = exclude)

*affect* and *effect* (when used as verbs) (*affect* = cause, *effect* = result)

---

• Look-alike or sound-alike words: as with commonly misused words, sometimes words sound correct or even look correct, but are not.

---

#### *For example:*

*break* and *brake* sound the same but have entirely different meaning, as do such words as:

*roll* and *role,*

*to, too, two*

*their, there, they're* (do you really need an explanation for these?)

---

• Plurals and possessives: the plural form of a word usually includes a "s" at the end, but not an apostrophe, whereas the possessive form (showing ownership) usually includes both.

> ### *For example:*
>
> *I am a <u>student.</u>* = singular (no "s" and no apostrophe)
>
> *We are all <u>students.</u> (as in many students)* = "s" at the end of the noun, but no apostrophe
>
> *The <u>student's</u> book is on the desk.* = ownership of one student and uses an apostrophe + "s"
>
> *The students' tests are ready.* = ownership of many students and uses an "s" + apostrophe.

<u>**HINT:**</u> One of the most common spelling mistakes students make is forgetting to put an "s" at the ends of a plural noun and a singular verb. Always check for the "s."

- ## Punctuation:

Punctuation can be considered the writer's equivalent as the inflection we use during face to face conversation. For instance, when speaking we pause briefly at the end of sentences, raise the pitch of our voices when asking a question, speak more loudly and distinctly when emphasizing something, and even raise our eyebrows when shocked or surprised. Writers have similar ways of conveying such messages; it is called punctuation.  **(see chapters on:**

    **"The Comma"**

    **"The Apostrophe"**

    **"Quotation Marks"**

    **"End Punctuation: Period, Question Mark, and Exclamation Point"**

    **"Capitalization"**

Just as a speaker's inflection can clarify or obscure his or her meaning, so too punctuation can either make your meaning clearer, confuse the reader about what you are saying, or even change the meaning of your words if you are not careful.

> ### *For example:*
>
> A teacher supposedly asked his students to punctuate the following sentence:
>
> **A woman without her man is nothing.**
>
> The men punctuated it like this:
>
> **A woman, without her man, is nothing.** (This suggests that a woman was entirely dependent upon her man for her worth.)
>
> The women, however, punctuated it different, like this:
>
> **A woman: without her, man is nothing.** (This suggests that man was worthless without his woman.)
>
> Do you see how a few changes in punctuation can change the entire meaning of the sentence?

Proofread your writing to ensure that you have used the correct punctuation to make your meaning unmistakably clear.

**HINT:** one way to check for proper punctuation is to read your sentence slowly, out loud - exactly as you have written it, such as pausing at each comma or period, but not pausing where there is no punctuation. You will actually find yourself wanting to change your inflection in places where your should change your punctuation.

---

### One final word about "Text-Speak":

Along with computers, cellphones, iPods, and all the other wonders of the modern electronic age has come "text-speak," the language by which words, numbers, and symbols can relay messages. These are words and expressions used most often in text messaging, internet chats ("IM"), and personal emails. They are abbreviations for ease and convenience and have no place in formal writing. What seems appropriate when "texting" one's "bff" is inappropriate for college writing and should never be used. For example:

*I*, referring to the person speaking or writing, is **always** capitalized. The lower case *i* used in text messaging is never acceptable in formal writing.

*u*, referring to the person spoken or written to, is a letter, not a word, and should never be used in formal writing.

Other abbreviations, such as: **smthg** for **something, ppl** for **people,** the letter **r** for the word **are**, numbers for words (e.g., **2** for the word **to, 4** for the word **for**), are not acceptable in formal English or any scholarly writing.

Be sure to proofread your writing to eliminate **all** "text-speak" and use proper words and spelling.

---

# Using a Checklist for Revising

An effective means of revising your writing is to use a checklist to confirm that you have carefully reviewed each aspect of your writing. Effective formal writing consists of adequate and accurate content, that is:

- clearly presented and supported with sufficient credible evidence,
- organized in a logical order, in which ideas flow clearly from one to another with transitions,
- written in clear precise language, with complete well-connected sentences,
- and grammatically correct, with proper spelling and punctuation,

Therefore, it makes sense to check each of the above to ensure that your writing is as clear, concise, and cogent as possible. On the following page is a sample checklist for paragraphs developed at the request of students who said they would revise their writing if they knew what to look for. Using this checklist when revising your writing will thus help you determine exactly what you should be looking for and thus enable you to correct any errors, omissions, or other issues in your writing.

## A Checklist for Content and Support, Organization, Style (words and sentences), and Mechanics

### Content & Organization:

—Do I have a clear topic sentence that includes my narrowed topic and my main point, idea, or message?

—Do I have specific major details which support my topic sentence (main point)?

—Does each major detail have enough supporting minor details, examples, or facts? Does this support answer the question "Why" to the major details?

—Is my paragraph focused on the main idea and its associated major details? (That is, I do not include any information which is not important or relevant to the main idea.)

—Does my paragraph flow logically from one idea to another?

—Do I provide transitions (signal words or phrases) between sentences and ideas to aid this logical flow?

—Do I have a strong conclusion that summarizes my paragraph and retains the essence of the topic sentence (main idea), without repeating it word for word?

### Style (Words & Sentences):

—Do I avoid unnecessary or trite phrases like "This paragraph is about…," "I am writing about…," "To me, personally…," "I thought to myself…," "My reasons for…," "In my opinion…"?

—Did I eliminate colloquial, conversational, or slang words or phrases, **especially the conversational** *you*?

—Have I used precise wording whenever possible and made sure that I have no missing words?

—Is the meaning of each sentence clear, with no confusing or awkward phrasing?

—Do I vary my sentence structure – simple, compound, complex, beginning w/modifiers, etc.?

—Are my sentences complete AND correct (i.e., no fragments and run-ons)?
  **Suggestion: starting at the end of your paper, read every word group that begins with a capital. Is each a complete sentence?**

## Mechanics (Grammar, Spelling, Punctuation):

——Did I proofread for grammar mistakes, especially subject/verb/pronoun agreement?

——Are all my verb tenses correct?

——Did I make sure each pronoun has a reference (antecedent)?

——Do all my modifiers make sense (no "I found a penny walking across the road.")?

——Did I use correct punctuation, especially after introductory phrases, subordinate clauses, before coordinating conjunctions, and in any lists?

——Did I use correct upper and lower case letters (i.e., capitalization) as appropriate?

——Did I proofread for spelling, especially sound-alike words such as "they're," "there," and "their"?

## Finally:

——Did I make my overall point as clearly & completely as possible?

Works Cited (MLA format).

"revise." *Online Etymology Dictionary*. Douglas Harper, Historian. 14 Apr. 2010. <Dictionary.com http://dictionary.reference.com/browse/revise>.

# 4

# The Descriptive Paragraph

A description is an account that creates a vivid mental image.

The ability to describe people, places, or objects accurately is a useful life skill. Whether you are talking with a stylist about the exact hairstyle you want, sharing a funny or startling scene from your day with a friend in an e-mail, or reporting on the structure of a plant cell for a biology class, you will use description to make your point.

"Snow blows across the highway before me as I walk—little, wavering trails of it swept along like a people dispersed. The snow people—where are they going? Some great danger must pursue them. They hurry and fall, the wind gives them a push, they get up and go on again."

JOHN HAINES, FROM "SNOW"

# What's the Point of Description?

In a descriptive paragraph, the writer uses sensory details such as sights, sounds, smells, tastes, feelings, and textures to create vivid images in the reader's mind. An experienced writer relies on sense memories of a specific experience to evoke these details. In addition, the writer often uses spatial order to create a clear visual image of a person, place, object, or scene: the location or arrangement in space from top to bottom, bottom to top, right to left, left to right, near to far, far to near, inside to outside, or outside to inside.

Every day, we experience rich sensory details from television, movies, music DVDs, and daily life. Think of a scene that grabbed your attention recently. What is your main impression of the scene? What are several details that make this impression so vivid or memorable?

Description also may include or suggest time order because a person, place, or object usually appears in a situation, or an incident usually occurs or suggests a scene.

Descriptive transition words signal that the details follow a logical order based on one or more of the following elements:

1. The arrangement in space of a person, place, object, or scene

2. The starting point from which the writer chooses to begin the description

3. The time frame as relevant to the description (see Chapter 5 for information about time order)

Getting a mental picture of the person, place, object, scene, or situation helps a writer discover his or her point about the subject being described. Study the following photograph of a popular destination for travelers: the Riverwalk in San Antonio, Texas. Use your sense memory of this or similar scenes to call up sensory details. Fill in the graphic with captions that capture the particular details of specific locations on the Riverwalk. Then answer the question "What's the point or impression you are trying to make?" with a one-sentence statement of the overall main idea.

PHOTOGRAPHIC ORGANIZER: DESCRIPTION

*Practice 1*

*WRITING FROM LIFE*

**A** Where is this detail in the scene?

......................................................................

What are the sensory details?

SIGHT: ......................................................................

SOUND: ......................................................................

SMELL: ......................................................................

TASTE: ......................................................................

TOUCH: ......................................................................

**B** Where is this detail in the scene?

......................................................................

What are the sensory details?

SIGHT: ......................................................................

SOUND: ......................................................................

SMELL: ......................................................................

TASTE: ......................................................................

TOUCH: ......................................................................

**C** Where is this detail in the scene?

......................................................................

What are the sensory details?

SIGHT: ......................................................................

SOUND: ......................................................................

SMELL: ......................................................................

TASTE: ......................................................................

TOUCH: ......................................................................

**D** Where is this detail in the scene?

.................................................................

What are the sensory details?

SIGHT: ...........................................................

SOUND: .........................................................

SMELL: ...........................................................

TASTE: ...........................................................

TOUCH: ...........................................................

**E** Where is this detail in the scene?

.................................................................

What are the sensory details?

SIGHT: ...........................................................

SOUND: .........................................................

SMELL: ...........................................................

TASTE: ...........................................................

TOUCH: ...........................................................

**What's the point?**

.................................................................

.................................................................

.................................................................

Practice 1

## My First Thoughts: A Prewriting Activity

Brainstorm about the images you just studied. Set a time limit, such as five minutes, and write in your notebook about the images you just studied and the details you generated. Write as quickly as you can without stopping. Getting your first thoughts about a topic on paper is an excellent way to overcome writer's block and set your mind to thinking.

PREWRITING

# Making a Point Using Description: One Student Writer's Response

The following descriptive paragraph, written as an online review for tourists, offers one writer's point about the Riverwalk in San Antonio. Read this description and the explanations; complete the activities in **bold type** in the annotations. Then read the writer's journal entry about her experience writing the paragraph.

**Main Idea:**
The main idea is the point the author is making. The topic is "Paseo Del Rio, the San Antonio Riverwalk." **Underline the author's point.**

**Spatial Order:**
The phrase "left bank" establishes spatial order. **Circle four more words or phrases that indicate spatial order.**

## Paseo Del Rio: A Festival of Color and Light

(1) The Texas spirit of fun and hospitality lights up Paseo Del Rio, the San Antonio Riverwalk. (2) This festive and popular travel destination shimmers with color and light. (3) Along the left bank, two lines of brightly colored café umbrellas—tropical red, Cancun blue, emerald green, lemon yellow—shelter outdoor diners and adorn the cobblestone walk. (4) Above the rainbow rows of umbrellas, white lights strung between oak trees along the walking path glimmer softly in the dusk. (5) Miniature white lights rim the eaves and roofs of the buildings behind the diners and illuminate the graceful drape of the oak branches bending over them. (6) Diners can stay warm on cool, damp evenings with spicy fajitas and salty margaritas as they watch the lights of the Riverwalk and the sunset glimmer upon the water. (7) As they watch, a steady flow of purple trimmed boats putter to midstream from under the bridge on the right side of the river. (8) On this side of the river, the rock walls and the footbridge showcase the rough beauty of the area's natural elements and earth tones. (9) Colorful lights trace the arch under the footbridge. (10) Luminaries sit atop both sides of the bridge's stone-grey railings. (11) At the far side of the bridge, more luminaries light the path along the water's edge. (12) People fill the path with laughter and conversation as they stroll beneath trees shimmering with countless tiny lights. (13) All along the river, this canopy of lights buffers the Riverwalk from the buildings rising in the distance. (14) The lights, the good food, the water, the spectacle of color, the festive atmosphere provide a luscious retreat—Texas style!

**Relevant Details:**
Relevant details describe elements of the scene to support the point "shimmers with color and light." **Draw a box around three additional details that support this point.**

**Effective Expression:**
Sensory details such as "cool, damp evenings," "spicy fajitas," "salty margaritas," "lights" and "sunset glimmer" create a vivid mental picture. **Double underline 3 more sensory details.**

# Writer's Journal

The student writer of "Paseo Del Rio: A Festival of Color and Light" completed the following reflection to record her thinking about her use of details. Read her writer's journal that describes a few key choices she made as she wrote. Then, in the given space, answer her questions about her use of details in her paragraph. Work with a peer or a small group of classmates.

RELEVANT DETAILS: During one revision, I discovered that my sentence about the boats wasn't relevant to my point. I had included the boats because they were in the picture, not because they supported the point I wanted to make. So I revised that sentence to include the color of the boats, which does add to the festive atmosphere of the Riverwalk and directly supports my point.

RELEVANT DETAILS: Did I use too many details to support my main idea? Should I leave out any details? Which ones and why? Which details are the most effective? Why?

# Developing Your Point Using Description

Writers use descriptive paragraphs to make a point through the vivid details they observe and share about a person, place, object, scene, or situation. To make a point by describing details, a writer often relies on spatial order transitions and sensory details. At times, a writer also uses time order to describe an experience.

## The Point: The Main Idea

When you write a description, you limit your topic to concrete details based on sight, sound, smell, taste, and touch. Your opinion or attitude about the subject you are describing is your point or main idea. In a description, your main idea may also include logical order signal words; other times, the logical order is implied without including the signal words.

For example, the first of the following two topic sentences includes (1) the topic, (2) the writer's opinion about the topic, and (3) spatial order signal words. The second topic sentence only includes (1) the topic and (2) the writer's attitude about the topic.

PATTERN OF ORGANIZATION:     THE TOPIC
SPATIAL ORDER

**From head to toe, Latoya dressed to appear professional and confident.**

THE WRITER'S OPINION

**Miguel's office reveals his careful attention to organization.**

THE TOPIC              THE WRITER'S OPINION

---

### TOPIC SENTENCES

Practice creating topic sentences. The first two items present a topic, an opinion, and logical order signal word(s). Combine the ideas in each group to create a topic sentence for a descriptive paragraph. Then complete the practice by composing your own topic sentences.

**1.** TOPIC: (a favorite place) *Grandmother's kitchen*

OPINION: *offered a haven of old-fashioned country warmth*

LOGICAL ORDER SIGNAL WORDS: *A small room at the rear of the house*

TOPIC SENTENCE: ................................................................

................................................................

................................................................

*Practice 2*

**2.** TOPIC: (a treasured possession) _The handmade well-pump lamp_

OPINION: _is an eye-catching and whimsical family treasure_

LOGICAL ORDER SIGNAL WORDS: _implied: such as in top to bottom_

TOPIC SENTENCE: _____

_____

**3.** TOPIC: (a useful product) _____

OPINION: _sleek, lightweight, flexible, easy to use_

LOGICAL ORDER SIGNAL WORDS (as needed): _____

_____

TOPIC SENTENCE: _____

_____

**4.** TOPIC: (a person of character) My mother (or father, brother, sister, friend, etc.)

OPINION: _kindness_

LOGICAL ORDER SIGNAL WORDS (as needed): _____

_____

TOPIC SENTENCE: _____

**5.** TOPIC: _____

OPINION: _____

LOGICAL ORDER SIGNAL WORDS (as needed): _____

_____

TOPIC SENTENCE: _____

_____

# Logical Order

Once you have chosen a topic and focused on a main idea, you are ready to generate and organize details. To organize visual details, spatial order transition words are helpful during the prewriting phase as well as during the drafting part of the writing process. During prewriting, spatial signal words such as *top*, *middle*, or *bottom* can be used as headings to list details. During the drafting stage, explicitly stating spatial transition words creates a picture in your reader's mind of how your subject is arranged in space. Strong transition words establish coherence, a clear and easy-to-follow flow of ideas.

## Transition Words Used to Signal Visual Description

| | | | | | |
|---|---|---|---|---|---|
| above | at the top | beyond | farther | left | right |
| across | back | by | front | middle | there |
| adjacent | behind | center | here | nearby | under |
| around | below | close to | in | next to | underneath |
| at the bottom | beneath | down | inside | outside | within |
| at the side | beside | far away | | | |

Practice 3

**SPATIAL ORDER DETAILS**

Determine the logical order of the following details taken from Maya Angelou's autobiography *I Know Why the Caged Bird Sings*. *Hint:* Underline the words that signal spatial order. Complete the exercise by answering the question "What's the point?"

_____ And when they put their hands on their hips in a show of jauntiness, the palms slipped the thighs as if the pants were waxed.

_____ When they tried to smile to carry off their tiredness as if it was nothing, the body did nothing to help the mind's attempt at disguise.

_____ In the store the men's faces were the most painful to watch, but I seemed to have no choice.

_____ Their shoulders drooped even as they laughed.

What's the point Maya Angelou makes with her use of spatial details?

_____

# Relevant Details

A writer narrows a topic into a focused main idea by generating descriptive details that answer questions such as *who, what,* and *where.* As a writer brainstorms, the thinking process brings to mind many sensory as well as spatial details. A writer evaluates the relevance of each detail and uses only those that illustrate the main idea. Some relevant details describe the appearance of a person, object, place, or scene; other relevant details explain the author's opinion about the topic. Many descriptive details appeal to sight, sound, smell, taste, and touch. A **concept map**, or **graphic organizer**, helps in several ways. First, the graphic can prompt your thinking, memory, and creativity. In addition, the graphic helps to order ideas as they occur to you. A graphic organizer also allows you to visualize the details and determine if you have enough to make your point. Irrelevant details do not explain, support, or illustrate the focused point of the paragraph. In addition to the graphic organizer, writers use the revision process to double check details for relevance and to eliminate irrelevant ones.

During the prewriting phase, a writer naturally generates irrelevant details. In fact, an effective writer evaluates the details and uses only the details that support the main idea. All descriptive details should work together to create a strong, unified impression, a mental image of the author's main point.

| Concept Chart: Description | | | | | |
| --- | --- | --- | --- | --- | --- |
| TOPIC: *Latoya and professional attire for a job interview* | | | | | |
| WHERE | SIGHT | SMELL | SOUND | TASTE | TOUCH |
| Top: Hair | *hair gathered and smoothed into a neat and stylish twist* | | | | |
| Face | *light touch of blush and lip gloss; small gold earrings* | | *calm, assured tone of voice* | | |
| Middle: Blouse and Jacket | *white dress cotton button-up collared shirt; dark blue jacket with a rich pin stripe* | | | | *firm handshake* |
| Skirt | *below the knee; dark blue, A-line* | | | | |
| Bottom: Shoes | *dark blue, polished, low heels, attractive* | | | | |

**RELEVANT DETAILS**

The following paragraph develops the ideas recorded in the graphic organizer about Latoya and her professional attire. Circle the main idea. Underline the spatial signal words and the sensory details. Cross out the two details that are not relevant to the main idea.

### Dressed to Impress

(1) Latoya Bond had been job hunting for months; finally, she landed an interview with a company that she was eager to join. (2) Latoya felt confident that she was well qualified for the position. (3) After all, she was one of the three final candidates chosen from over 100 applications, yet she also knew the importance of making a good impression. (4) From head to toe, Latoya dressed to appear professional and confident. (5) Latoya gathered her hard-to-manage curls into a neat and stylish twist. (6) To complement her no-nonsense hairstyle, Latoya used makeup sparingly but effectively. (7) A little black mascara on her lashes, a touch of blush across her cheeks, and bit of tinted lip balm brought attention to her interested eyes and her earnest smile. (8) She would also be sure to speak with a calm and assured voice. (9) The neatly pressed collar of a white cotton shirt contrasted nicely with her tailored blue pinstriped jacket. (10) Her dark blue A-line skirt reached to just below her knees. (11) Latoya finished her outfit with a flattering pair of blue low-heeled pumps that matched her briefcase and purse. (12) She would offer her prospective employer a firm handshake. (13) Latoya looked as professional and confident as she felt.

Practice 4

# Effective Expression: Concrete Word Choice

Precise word choice communicates exact meaning. Words chosen for a specific emotional or visual impact create strong images in the reader's mind and carry out the writer's purpose. As you move through the writing process, think about the impact you want to have on your reader. For the greatest impact, choose concrete and precise words and phrases instead of general or vague expressions. Choose words that *show* instead of *tell*. Consider the following examples.

**General or vague words that tell:**

This property has curb appeal.

**Concrete words that show:**

This beachfront cottage charms potential buyers with its colorful garden, wrap-around porch, and ocean view.

### CONCRETE WORD CHOICE

Each item below presents a general sentence using vague words. The phrase in parentheses before each sentence— (A customer to a mechanic) in item 1, for example—describes the speaker of the sentence and the person hearing it. Revise each sentence to eliminate vague wording. Consider the point of the writing situation; express ideas with words that have concrete and precise meanings for a specific impact. Discuss your revisions with your class or with a small group of peers.

**1.** (A customer to a mechanic):  My car makes a funny sound sometimes.

**2.** (A student commenting to his or her companion): The restaurant was disappointing.

**3.** (A weather reporter to a commuter):  The weather is nice (or horrible).

**4.** (A staff assistant to Technology Support):  The printer is broken.

# Using Description in Your Academic Courses

Many college courses in subjects such as literature, composition, history, psychology, ecology, and biology use description. As you study these subjects, you will read descriptions of historical places, influential people, natural elements, and scientific experiments. In addition, you will write descriptions to learn or demonstrate what you have learned.

## USING DESCRIPTION IN A HISTORY ASSIGNMENT

Student writer Jean Powell composed the following descriptive paragraph of an important historical site for a report in her American History course. Complete the following activities: (1) Insert appropriate transition words in the blanks; (2) underline the words or phrases used to create sensory details; (3) discuss the point of her report with a small group of peers or with your class.

The Vietnam Memorial is made up of two black granite walls joined in a wide-angled V shape. A study of just one of the walls reveals the significance of the memorial. A polished black granite slab stretches hundreds of feet long. At its highest tip, it stands 10 feet tall and then tapers to a height of 8 inches at its end point. Its low tip points _____ the Lincoln Memorial. _____ its polished face are the carved names of service men and women who gave their lives during the Vietnam War. Starting at the highest point on the first panel, thousands of names are listed in chronological order. The high polish of the black granite reflects the image of the world _____ the wall. The reflection of earth, sky, and visitors are seen along with the inscribed names. On the wall, the present and the past mingle. A path runs _____ the base of the wall so visitors can walk the path to read the names. Many create pencil rubbings or leave tokens such as flowers, flags, and personal notes. To the side of the path, a wide grassy park adds to the sense of serenity. The memorial is a quiet place where one can come to terms with loss and grief. Its tranquility is a fitting memorial to a controversial war that cost so many their lives.

▲ The Vietnam Memorial

# Workshop: Writing a Descriptive Paragraph Step by Step

## Prewrite Your Paragraph

The various activities below will walk you through the steps of the prewriting stage of the writing process: choosing a topic, focusing your point, and generating and organizing relevant details.

### Choose Your Topic

The following activities are designed to help you choose a topic.

**1.** Create a bank of topics. Use the following headings and brainstorm or list as many topics as you possibly can. Don't analyze your thoughts; just jot down topics as quickly as they occur to you. Compare your bank of topics with those of your classmates.

- The Scene of an Accident
- A Nature Scene
- A Pop Icon
- An Advertisement
- Emotions (such as fear)

**2.** Reread the freewrite you composed based on the photograph of the San Antonio Riverwalk. Underline ideas that could be used for a descriptive paragraph. Map out the logical order of details.

**3.** Select a photograph of a special place. Write captions, brainstorm sensory details, and freewrite about the photograph. Remember to ask "What are the sensory details and how are the details arranged in space?" and "What's the point?" as you generate ideas.

### Focus Your Point

Think about a prewrite you have generated for a descriptive topic. Underline or generate words that suggest your values, opinions, or attitudes about what you described. Think about what strikes you as important about your subject. Consider your audience. Who would be interested in this information and why? Choose a purpose. Write a list of adjectives and sensory details that relate the essence of what you are describing. Use a thesaurus and choose several vivid words to express your thoughts. State in one sentence the point of your description.

AUDIENCE: _____

PURPOSE: _____

SENSORY DETAILS: _____

WHAT'S THE POINT? _____

## Generate and Organize Relevant Details

Using the ideas you have already recorded and the concept chart for a description, generate and organize sensory and spatial details that support your point. (*Hint*: Fill in the "Where" column with spatial signal words such as *left, right, near, far, above.*)

| Concept Chart: Description | | | | | |
|---|---|---|---|---|---|
| TOPIC: | | | | | |
| WHAT'S THE POINT? | | | | | |
| WHERE | SIGHT | SMELL | SOUND | TASTE | TOUCH |
| | | | | | |
| | | | | | |
| | | | | | |
| | | | | | |
| | | | | | |

# Write a Draft of Your Paragraph

Using ideas you generated during the prewriting phase, compose a draft of your paragraph. Return to the prewriting process at any time to generate additional details as needed. Use your own paper.

# Revise Your Draft

Once you have drafted a description, read the draft and answer the questions in the "Questions for Revising a Descriptive Paragraph" box that follows on the next page. Indicate your answers by annotating your paper. If you answer "yes" to a question, underline, check, or circle examples. If you answer "no" to a question, write needed information in the margins and draw lines to indicate placement of additional details. Revise your paragraph as necessary based on your reflection. (*Hint*: Experienced writers create several drafts as they focus on one or two questions per draft.)

# Questions for Revising a Descriptive Paragraph:

☐ Have I stated or implied a focused main idea? Have I created a strong impression? Can I state my point in one sentence?

☐ Is the logical order of the details clear? Have I used strong transitions to indicate spatial order? Time order?

☐ Have I created a vivid mental image through the use of sensory details?

☐ Have I made my point with adequate details?

☐ Do all the details support my point?

☐ Have I chosen concrete words to make my point?

# Proofread Your Draft

Once you have made any revisions to your paragraph that may be needed, proofread your paper to eliminate unnecessary errors, such as dangling or misplaced modifiers.

### Grammar in Action: Eliminate Dangling or Misplaced Modifiers

Modifiers are words and phrases that describe other words. A **dangling modifier** occurs when a writer uses a modifier without including the word that the modifier describes.

- **Dangling modifier:**

  **INCORRECT:** Entering the museum of shrunken heads, my stomach lurched with queasiness.

  *(The missing word is "I": It was I, not my stomach, that entered the museum.)*

- **Revised sentence:**

  **CORRECT:** As I entered the museum of shrunken heads, my stomach lurched with queasiness.

A **misplaced modifier** occurs when a writer separates the modifier from the word it is describing.

- **Misplaced modifier:**

  **INCORRECT:** Scattering in a million directions, Tyrone hustled to scoop up the spilled ball bearings.

  *(The ball bearings scattered, not Tyrone)*

- **Revised sentence:**

  **CORRECT:** Tyrone hustled to scoop up the spilled ball bearings scattering in a million directions.

PORTFOLIO Workshop

Edit the following student paragraph to eliminate one dangling modifier and two misplaced modifiers.

## The Amazing Ruby Falls

(1) The caves at Ruby Falls are one of the wonders of the world, eerie yet intriguing. (2) Our tour group was a small one of about ten people. (3) We all piled onto an elevator, stuffy from all the bodies and stinking like a dirty sock, to sink 250 feet underground. (4) We exited the elevator, gasping for air because of the lack of oxygen and the dampness of the cave. (5) The cave was dark with barely any light. (6) We wore helmets mounted with lights. (7) I looked like a real spelunker. (8) We saw stalactites hanging from the ceiling and stalagmites growing up from the ground. (9) The columns, drapes, and flow stone were phenomenal. (10) We walked through an onyx jungle flowing with layers of limestone. (11) The massive monuments were smooth and damp. (12) Some were slimy like a snail. (13) Water trickled from the ceiling in my hair and down my face, a kiss from the cave. (14) We squeezed through stone pathways littered with rock shapes resembling everything from bacon, to a dragon foot, to a form that looked like New York City, all natural. (15) We came across a huge formation; that appeared to be lifelike; the ice sickle stalactites looked like they could break free and assault us. (16) A breathtaking formation that appeared to be lifelike. (17) The caves are amazing.

# Review

**MY WRITER'S JOURNAL**

Work with a classmate to give and receive feedback about your descriptive paragraphs. Use the following form to record your thinking about your writing process for your descriptive paragraph. Use the writer's journal on page 77 as a model for your own journal. Discuss the decisions you made as you wrote, and describe what you have learned by writing. Also, ask for advice about how to improve your paragraph.

MAIN IDEA: ..................................................................................................................

..........................................................................................................................................

..........................................................................................................................................

..........................................................................................................................................

LOGICAL ORDER: ...........................................................................................................

..........................................................................................................................................

..........................................................................................................................................

..........................................................................................................................................

RELEVANT DETAILS: .......................................................................................................

..........................................................................................................................................

..........................................................................................................................................

..........................................................................................................................................

EFFECTIVE EXPRESSION: ...............................................................................................

..........................................................................................................................................

..........................................................................................................................................

..........................................................................................................................................

# Writing Assignments

## Considering Audience and Purpose

Study the photographs at the beginning of the chapter. Assume you are a member of the Riverwalk business community, and the community leaders have asked you and other interested parties for needed safety improvements along the Riverwalk. Suggest and describe one or more specific safety improvements.

## Writing for Everyday Life

Assume you are separated from your family or loved ones during a holiday or a special occasion. Write a letter in which you describe a significant element of the event. For example, describe the decorations of the season or event, a bride's dress, a favorite birthday gift, or the spread of food at a party or dinner. Choose words that reflect one of the following: (1) approval and enjoyment or (2) disapproval and disappointment.

## Writing for College Life

Assume you are writing a report in your psychology class about how a person's mood is reflected in the clothes he or she chooses on any given day. Describe an outfit that reflects an individual's mood.

## Writing for Working Life

Assume you have invented a product that will make life much easier; also assume that the Small Business Association finances the production and marketing of useful new inventions. Write a paragraph describing your product to submit your idea to the Small Business Association.

PEARSON
**mywritinglab**
**WANT A
BETTER GRADE?**
For more practice with description, go to
**www.mywritinglab.com >
Using Patterns of
Organization to Develop
Paragraphs > The
Descriptive Paragraph.**

# 5

## The Narrative Paragraph

Narration is an account of events told in chronological order to make a specific point.

All of us love a good story. Think of a good story that you have heard, read, or watched on TV or in a theater.

A good story is about personalities or characters, whether real or imagined. A good story is full of vivid action and details. A good story makes a point.

A writer uses narration to tell a story to make a specific point. Often we tell stories to warn about dangers, to teach important lessons, to record important historical events, or to amuse and entertain each other. Narration is a chain of events. These events unfold in chronological order—the order in which they occur. Thus, details follow a logical order based on time. The writer presents an event and then shows when and how each of the subsequent events flows from the first event. In addition to relaying an event, a writer also uses vivid actions and details to show the point of the story. Vivid details may include specific sights, sounds, smells, tastes, textures, feelings, and actions.

# What's the Point of Narration?

Getting a mental picture of an event helps a writer to discover the point he or she wishes to make. The following sequence of photographs documents a series of events that took place in the life of Jennifer Hudson over the course of several years. Study each photograph in the timeline. Write a caption that states the topic of each picture. Then answer the question "What's the point?" with a one-sentence statement of the overall main idea.

**PHOTOGRAPHIC ORGANIZER: NARRATION**

FIRST EVENT

What happened?

_____

_____

_____

▲ *American Idol, 2004*

SECOND EVENT

What happened?

_____

_____

_____

◄ *Oscar ceremony, 2007*

THIRD EVENT

What happened?

_____

_____

_____

◄ October 24, 2008, a memorial for Hudson's mother and brother

**What's the point?**

TOPIC SENTENCE: _____

_____

WRITING FROM LIFE

Practice 1

## My First Thoughts: A Prewriting Activity

Set a time limit, such as five minutes, and write in your notebook about the images you just studied. Do not let your pen or pencil stop. Even if you must repeat ideas, keep writing until the time limit is up. Let the ideas flow freely. Getting your first thoughts about a topic on paper is one excellent way to kick-start your writing process.

PREWRITING

# Making a Point Using Narration: One Student Writer's Response

The following paragraph offers one writer's narrative inspired by photographs of Jennifer Hudson. Read the narrative paragraph and the explanations; complete the activities in **bold type** in the annotations. Then, read the writer's journal that describes a few key choices she made as she wrote.

**Chronological Order:**
Chronological order is established with the phrase "in the moment." Circle four more words or phrases that indicate time order.

**Main Idea:**
The main idea is the point of the narration. Notice the topic is Jennifer Hudson. Underline the author's point.

**Vivid Verbs:**
Vivid verbs such as "exploded" creates a mental image and emphasizes action. Double underline three more vivid verbs.

**Relevant Details:**
Relevant details describe events to support the point about Hudson's faith and determination.

## Jennifer Hudson's Faith and Determination

(1) All of us, at some point in our lives, face great disappointment or loss. (2) Often, in the moment of such challenges, we want to give up or give in to hopelessness. (3) Jennifer Hudson's story shows us how to overcome loss with faith and determination. (4) In 2004, fans booted Hudson off of the third season of *American Idol*. (5) Many critics following the show that season had expected her to win. (6) Suddenly, however, she sank to seventh place and was sent home. (7) For the most part, the general public forgot about her. (8) However, losing did not stop Hudson. (9) She hoped and watched and worked for her next big break. (10) Then in 2006, Hudson exploded back onto the national stage with the release of the smash-hit movie *Dreamgirls*. (11) By 2007, her show-stopping performance as Effie White in *Dreamgirls* had won her an Academy Award, a British Academy of Film and Television Award, a Golden Globe Award, and a Screen Actors Guild Award. (12) In 2008, she snagged a Grammy as Outstanding New Artist; she had achieved her own dreams. (13) At the height of her success, Jennifer Hudson endured a horrible tragedy. (14) On October 24, 2008, Hudson's mother, Darnell Donerson, and her brother Jason Hudson were found shot to death in Donerson's home. (15) Three days later, Hudson's nephew, 7-year-old Julian King, was also found shot and killed in a sport-utility vehicle belonging to Jason Hudson. (16) Even in the middle of her own suffering, Hudson revealed her faith and determination. (17) Immediately, she and her family created *The Hudson-King Foundation for Families of Slain Victims* in honor of her mother, brother, and nephew.

# Writer's Journal

## PEER EDITING

The student writer of "Jennifer Hudson's Faith and Determination" completed the following reflection to record her thinking through the writing process. Read her writer's journal that describes a few key choices she made as she wrote. Then, in the given space, answer her questions about her use of details in her paragraph. Work with a peer or a small group of classmates.

LOGICAL ORDER: When I read over my first draft, I noticed that the paragraph didn't really flow smoothly. I had used contrast and addition transition words instead of time order words. So I revised to include chronological transitions because this is a narrative. For example, the signal word "suddenly" replaced the contrast signal word "however," and the signal word "immediately" replaced the addition signal word "and."

LOGICAL ORDER: Does the paragraph flow smoothly now? Which transitions are most effective? Are more time order transition words needed? Where and why?

# Developing Your Point Using Narration

A narrative tells a story. The story illustrates the writer's point or main idea. To make a point by telling a story, a writer relies on the use of time order transitions, relevant sensory details, and vivid word choice.

## The Point: The Main Idea

When you choose to write a narrative, you limit your topic to the details of a specific event based on time order. Most likely, you also have an opinion or point of view about the event. Your opinion or attitude about the event is your point or main idea. Many writers of narrative paragraphs create topic sentences to state the points illustrated by the events.

For example, the following topic sentence contains (1) the topic, (2) the writer's opinion about the topic, and (3) the pattern of organization used to organize details.

Aaron Ralston  bravely  survived  a five-day ordeal.

*TOPIC IS AARON RALSTON*

*WRITER'S OPINION IS STATED WITH THE WORDS "BRAVELY" AND "ORDEAL"*

*PATTERN OF ORGANIZATION: NARRATION TIME ORDER IS ESTABLISHED WITH THE PHRASE "FIVE-DAY ORDEAL"*

This example illustrates the relationships of the topic, the author's opinion, and the pattern of organization in this particular topic sentence. Note that the word "ordeal" suggests both time order and the writer's opinion.

**Practice 2**

**TOPIC SENTENCES**

Practice creating topic sentences. The following items present a topic, an opinion, and time order signal word(s). Combine the ideas in each group to create a topic sentence for a narrative.

**1.** TOPIC: *Jeff Gordon*

OPINION: *squeaked to narrow victory*

TIME ORDER SIGNAL WORDS: *during the last few laps of the Daytona 500*

TOPIC SENTENCE: _____

_____

**2.** TOPIC: *honesty*

OPINION: *I learned the value of*

TIME ORDER SIGNAL WORDS: *during my first job interview*

TOPIC SENTENCE: _____

_____

# Logical Order

Once you have selected your topic and focused on a main idea, you are ready to generate additional details and organize your ideas into a logical sequence based on time order. Each event in a narrative is developed by describing the individual actions and details that make up that event. Just as time order words in the topic sentence signal a narrative, time order transition words also show the flow of events as they unfold in the narrative. Strong transitions establish coherence, a clear and understandable flow of ideas.

## Transition Words Used to Show Time Order

| | | | | |
|---|---|---|---|---|
| after | during | later | previously | ultimately |
| afterward | eventually | meanwhile | second | until |
| as | finally | next | since | when |
| before | first | now | soon | while |
| currently | last | often | then | |

---

**TIME ORDER SIGNAL WORDS**

The following paragraph was first published by Linda M. Hasselstrom in *High Country News* to explain her choice for self-defense. Fill in the four blanks with appropriate time order signal words based on the logical order of ideas.

### A Peaceful Woman Explains
### Why She Carries a Gun

(1) As I drove home one night, a car followed me. (2) It passed me on a narrow bridge .......... a passenger flashed a blinding spotlight in my face. (3) I braked sharply. (4) The car stopped, angled across the bridge, and four men jumped out. (5) I realized the locked doors were useless if they broke the windows of my pickup. (6) I started forward, hoping to knock their car aside so I could pass. (7) Just .......... another car appeared, and the men hastily got back into their car. (8) They continued to follow me, passing and repassing. (9) I dared not go home because no one else was there. (10) I passed no lighted houses. (11) .............. they pulled over onto the roadside, and I decided to use their tactic: fear. (12) Speeding, the pickup horn blaring, I swerved as close to them as I could .......... I roared past. (13) It worked: they turned off the highway. (14) But I was frightened and angry. (15) Even in my vehicle I was too vulnerable.

© Pearson Education, Inc.

# Relevant Details

A writer narrows a topic into a focused main idea by generating details that answer questions such as *who, what, when, where, why,* and *how.* A writer evaluates the relevance of each detail and uses only those that illustrate the main idea. Some relevant details show the action of the event; other details explain the author's opinion about the event. Relevant details also often include sensory details, which appeal to sight, sound, smell, taste, and touch. These vivid details work together to create a mental image of the author's main point. During the prewriting phase, a timeline can help a writer organize ideas as they are generated. Study the following concept map that was used to generate details about the topic "Aaron Ralston's Ordeal."

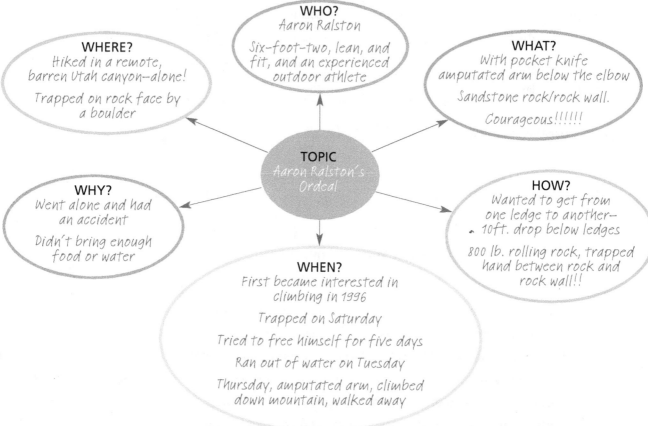

**WHO?**
Aaron Ralston
Six-foot-two, lean, and fit, and an experienced outdoor athlete

**WHERE?**
Hiked in a remote, barren Utah canyon—alone!
Trapped on rock face by a boulder

**WHAT?**
With pocket knife amputated arm below the elbow
Sandstone rock/rock wall.
Courageous!!!!!!

**TOPIC**
Aaron Ralston's Ordeal

**WHY?**
Went alone and had an accident
Didn't bring enough food or water

**HOW?**
Wanted to get from one ledge to another—10ft. drop below ledges
800 lb. rolling rock, trapped hand between rock and rock wall!!

**WHEN?**
First became interested in climbing in 1996
Trapped on Saturday
Tried to free himself for five days
Ran out of water on Tuesday
Thursday, amputated arm, climbed down mountain, walked away

---

**RELEVANT DETAILS**

Using the details in the concept map above about the topic "Aaron Ralston's Ordeal," complete the timeline below to show the proper time order of events.

1 ------------------------------------------------------------

2 ------------------------------------------------------------

3 ------------------------------------------------------------

4 ------------------------------------------------------------

5 ------------------------------------------------------------

Practice 4

During the prewriting phase, a writer naturally generates irrelevant details. In fact, an effective writer often produces far more details than can be used to make a specific point. Irrelevant details do not explain, support, or illustrate the focused point of the paragraph. Often, writers use the revision process to double check details for relevance and to eliminate irrelevant details.

### RELEVANT DETAILS

The following paragraph develops the ideas recorded in the brainstorming list about Aaron Ralston. Circle the main idea. Underline the relevant sensory details. Cross out the two details that are not relevant to the main idea.

### The Courage to Survive

(1) Aaron Ralston courageously survived a five-day ordeal.

(2) Ralston began his ordeal Saturday morning when he made an attempt to climb over a ten-foot drop between two ledges.

(3) Suddenly, an 800-pound rock roared down upon him from above. (4) He quickly scrambled to get out of its path in time.

(5) In the next second, the mammoth stone trapped him on the barren rock face. (6) The boulder had smashed and pinned his right hand between it and a sandstone wall. (7) Six-foot-two, lean, and fit, Ralston is an experienced outdoor athlete. (8) He first became interested in climbing in 1996. (9) For five days, Ralston chipped away at the boulder with a pocket knife.

(10) Finally, on Tuesday, he ran out of his meager ration of food and water. (11) By Thursday rescue seemed unlikely, so Ralston, parched with thirst, made the gutsy decision to amputate his own hand. (12) Knowing his flimsy pocket knife would not cut through bone, he used the force of the rock to snap his bones just below the elbow. (13) Then after applying a tourniquet, Ralston cut through his own muscles, veins, and arteries. (14) Once he completed the hour-long amputation, he rappelled down the mountain. (15) At last, a haggard Ralston hiked out of the canyon.

# Effective Expression: Vivid Verbs

Show, don't tell! Some of the verbs most commonly used by student writers belong to the *to be* family of verbs. However, *to be* verbs such as *am, is, are, was,* and *were* are vague and lifeless. They *tell* instead of *show* action, as in the following sentence: *Ivan was angry.* This sentence tells us about Ivan's emotion, but it doesn't show how he acts when he is angry or how his anger fits into the flow of events.

A writer draws a mental picture for the main idea through the use of vivid verbs.

**Vivid verbs show the action that is taking place:**

Ivan stomped to the trash can and hurled the report into it.

*The verbs "stomped" and "hurled" are biased words. Another witness may have chosen objective language to describe Ivan's actions:*

**Vivid verbs reflect the author's opinion:**

Ivan walked to the trash can and tossed the report into it.

**Vivid verbs express sensory details:**

Ivan snorted with contempt.

Many writers dedicate one full revision to focus on word choices.

---

## VIVID VERBS

Revise each of the following sentences by using vivid verbs to replace *to be* verbs such as *am, is, are, was,* and *were.*

**1.** The coffee was hot.

_____

**2.** Ryanne was injured during the race.

_____

**3.** Lance Armstrong was the winner of Tour De France six times.

_____

**4.** We were so excited; we were screaming and jumping all around like lunatics.

_____

**5.** I am afraid of my next door neighbor's pit bull.

_____

# Using Narration in Your Academic Courses

Many college courses in subjects such as history, psychology, composition, and literature use narration. As you study these subjects, you will read narrations of historical events, case studies, short stories, and novels. In addition, you will write narratives to demonstrate what you have learned. For example, an essay exam may ask you to relate the key events of a major war or the important events in the life of an influential person. Some college writing assignments ask you to draw upon your personal experience and relate it to what you are learning.

## USING NARRATION IN AN INTERPERSONAL COMMUNICATION ASSIGNMENT

Read the following information from a college communications textbook. On a separate sheet of paper, write a response to the writing assignment, given in the last sentence of the text.

### Ethics in Interpersonal Communication

Because communication has consequences, interpersonal communication involves ethics, a moral aspect of right or wrong. It is believed that there are certain universal ethical principles: you should tell the truth, have respect for another's dignity, and not harm the innocent.

In the U.S. legal system, you have the right to remain silent and to refuse to incriminate yourself. But you don't have the right to refuse to reveal information about the criminal activities of others that you may have witnessed. Psychiatrists and lawyers are often exempt from this general rule. Similarly a wife can't be forced to testify against her husband nor a husband against his wife. In interpersonal situations, however, there aren't any written rules so it's not always clear if or when silence is ethical.

What would you do? While at the supermarket, you witness a mother verbally abusing her three-year-old child. You worry that the mother might psychologically harm the child, and your first impulse is to speak up and tell this woman that verbal abuse can have lasting effects on the child and often leads to physical abuse. At the same time, you don't want to interfere with a mother's right to say what she wants to her child. Nor do you want to aggravate a mother who may later take out her frustration on the child. Write a short narrative that illustrates what you would do in this situation.

# Workshop: Writing a Narrative Paragraph Step by Step

## Prewriting for Your Paragraph

The various activities that follow will walk you through the steps of the prewriting stage of the writing process: choosing a topic, focusing your point, and generating and organizing relevant details.

### Choose Your Topic

The following activities are designed to help you choose a topic.

**1.** Create a bank of topics. Use the following headings and either brainstorm or list as many topics as you possibly can. Don't be critical of what you write; just get as many topics written down as quickly as possible. As you think of new topics, add them to the list. Compare your bank of topics with those of your classmates.

- Heroes
- Health
- Pop Culture
- Memories

**2.** Generate ideas with a freewrite. Choose one of the topics from your topic bank and think of an event related to the topic. Write about the event for ten minutes without stopping. Include sensory details: sight, sound, smell, taste, and touch.

**3.** Select a photograph of a special event. Write a caption, brainstorm topics, and freewrite about the photograph. Remember to ask "What happened?" and "What's the point?" as you generate ideas.

### Focus Your Point

Read a freewrite you have generated for a narrative. Underline words that suggest your values, opinions, or attitudes about the event. Think about what interests you about the event. Use a thesaurus and choose several vivid words to express your thoughts. Identify your audience and purpose. Write a list of vivid verbs that show the actions that occur during the event. State in one sentence the point of the story you are going to tell.

AUDIENCE: ....................................................................................

....................................................................................

PURPOSE: ....................................................................................

....................................................................................

VIVID VERBS: ....................................................................................

....................................................................................

WHAT'S THE POINT? ....................................................................................

....................................................................................

## Generate and Organize Relevant Details

Using ideas you have recorded so far and the timeline graphic, generate and organize details that support your point.

**What's the point?**

TOPIC SENTENCE: ......................................................................................................................

......................................................................................................................

......................................................................................................................

**What happened?**

| 1 |
|---|

↓

| 2 |
|---|

↓

| 3 |
|---|

↓

| 4 |
|---|

↓

| 5 |
|---|

# Write a Draft of Your Paragraph

Using the ideas you generated during the prewriting phase, compose a draft of your paragraph. Return to the prewriting process at any time to generate additional details as needed. Use your own paper.

# Revise Your Draft

Once you have created a draft of a narrative, read the draft and answer the questions in the "Questions for Revising a Narrative Paragraph" box that follows. Indicate your answers by annotating your paper. If you answer "yes" to a question, underline, check, or circle examples. If you answer "no" to a question, write additional details in the margins and draw lines to indicate their placement. Revise your paragraph based on your reflection. (*Hint:* Experienced writers create several drafts as they focus on one or two questions per draft.)

## Questions for Revising a Narrative Paragraph:

☐ Have I stated or implied a focused main idea? Have I created a strong impression? Can I state my point in one sentence?

☐ Is the logical order of the events clear? Have I used strong transitions to indicate time? And space?

☐ Have I made my point with adequate details?

☐ Do all the details support my point?

☐ Have I used vivid verbs to keep my readers interested in what I am saying? Have I used sensory details to make my point?

☐ What impact will my paragraph make on my reader?

## Proofread Your Draft

Once you have made any revisions to your paragraph that may be needed, proofread your paragraph to eliminate careless errors such as shifts in verb tense.

### Grammar in Action: Unnecessary Shifts in Verb Tense

Verb tense tells your reader when an event occurred. "Sandra laughed" is past tense. "Sandra laughs" is present tense. "Sandra will laugh" is future tense. A shift in tense for no logical reason is confusing to the reader.

- **A Shift in Verb Tense:**

  **INCORRECT:** Monica sighed loudly, rolled her eyes, and stomps off angrily.

- **Consistent Use of Tense:**

  **CORRECT:** Monica sighs loudly, rolls her eyes, and stomps off angrily.

---

**TENSE SHIFTS**

Edit these sentences for unnecessary shifts in tense.

**1.** Raul works two jobs and attends a community college. He wanted to become a registered nurse and join the Peace Corps.

**2.** Hurricane Ivan destroyed property along the coast in Pensacola, Florida. The hurricane force winds and waves would batter hotels to pieces and rip roofs off restaurants and homes.

**3.** Vitali and Carl had fun at the Daytona 500 race. They always pay to sit in the infield. They will grill hamburgers and hot dogs. As they ate, they watched the cars zoom around them.

**4.** Joe and Jarvonna had a wonderful first date. Joe makes reservations at the Japanese Steak House. After dinner, he surprises her with tickets to watch her favorite team, the Orlando Magic, play the Miami Heat. On the way home, Jarvonna suggested stopping for coffee. Losing track of time, the two talk for hours.

Practice 8

# Review

## MY WRITER'S JOURNAL

Work with a classmate to give and receive feedback about your narrative paragraphs. Use the following form to record your thinking about your writing process for your narrative paragraph. Use the writer's journal on page 93 as a model for your own journal. Discuss the decisions you made as you wrote, and describe what you have learned by writing. Also, ask for advice about how to improve your paragraph.

MAIN IDEA: ........................................................................................................................................

.........................................................................................................................................................

.........................................................................................................................................................

.........................................................................................................................................................

LOGICAL ORDER: ...............................................................................................................................

.........................................................................................................................................................

.........................................................................................................................................................

.........................................................................................................................................................

RELEVANT DETAILS: ...........................................................................................................................

.........................................................................................................................................................

.........................................................................................................................................................

.........................................................................................................................................................

EFFECTIVE EXPRESSION: ....................................................................................................................

.........................................................................................................................................................

.........................................................................................................................................................

.........................................................................................................................................................

# Writing Assignments

## Considering Audience and Purpose

Study the sequence of photographs of Jennifer Hudson at the beginning of the chapter. Assume the pictures are to be used to document her achievements on a website designed to promote her career. Write a narrative that will be recorded as a voice-over and heard as the pictures flash on the screen.

## Writing for Everyday Life

Assume you or someone you know recently took action in an emergency situation. Write a paragraph for a letter to a friend relaying the event as it unfolded. Choose words that reflect one of the following: (1) approval of a courageous act or (2) concern for a foolish act.

## Writing for College Life

Assume you have witnessed an important historical event such as the invention of the wheel, the first flight into space, landing on the moon, the last battle fought in the Civil War, or 9/11. Write a paragraph for a local paper documenting the event as it occurred.

## Writing for Working Life

Assume you are filing for worker's compensation for an injury that occurred on the job. Write a paragraph for a report to your supervisor in which you record the events as they occurred.

**PEARSON**
**mywritinglab**
**WANT A BETTER GRADE?**
For more practice with narration, go to
**www.mywritinglab.com**
> Using Patterns of Organization to Develop Paragraphs > The Narrative Paragraph.

# 6

# The Process Paragraph

A process is a series of steps, occurring in chronological order.

Every day we repeat countless processes, from cooking a meal to flossing our teeth. Effective use of processes allows us to perform efficiently in every aspect of our lives. In our personal lives, we follow specific processes to file our taxes or enhance our health. In our professional lives, most of us go through an interview process to secure a job and an evaluation process to get a raise. In our academic lives, we follow set procedures to enroll in classes, learn, and achieve high GPAs.

A process may describe the steps necessary to complete a task such as changing a tire, activating an iPod, or creating a web page. A process may also describe the phases, stages, or cycle of a recurring event such as the phases of the moon, the stages of human development, or the cycle of grief. To write a process paragraph, a writer identifies and explains the logical time order of the individual steps or stages in the task or cycle. An effective process paragraph also relies heavily on concrete descriptive details and vivid images so the reader can mentally see the process as it unfolds.

# What's the Point of Process?

Visualizing a process helps a writer discover his or her point about the procedure. The following sequence of photographs documents a series of steps in a set of Pilates exercises called "spine stretch and roll like a ball." Study each photograph in the timeline. Write a caption that briefly describes each picture. Then answer the question "What's the point?" with a one-sentence statement of the overall main idea.

**PHOTOGRAPHIC ORGANIZER: PROCESS**

STEP ONE

What is happening?

_____

_____

_____

STEP TWO

What is happening?

_____

_____

_____

STEP THREE

What is happening?

_____

_____

_____

STEP FOUR

What is happening?

_____

_____

_____

**What's the point?**

_____

_____

_____

## My First Thoughts: A Prewriting Activity

Set a time limit, such as five minutes, and write in your notebook about the images you just studied. Do not let your pen or pencil stop. Even if you must repeat ideas, keep writing until the time limit is up. Let the ideas flow freely. Getting your first thoughts about a topic on paper is one excellent way to overcome writer's block and set your mind to thinking.

# Making a Point Using Process: One Student Writer's Response

The following paragraph offers one writer's point about the set of exercises depicted in the photographs. Read the process and the explanations; complete the activities in **bold type** in the annotations. Then read the writer's journal entry that records decisions made during the writing process.

**Main Idea:**
The main idea is the point the author is making about the topic. The topic is "an exercise sequence." **Underline the author's point about this topic.**

**Chronological Order:**
The transition "First" signals time order. **Circle four more time order signal words.**

**Effective Expression:**
Vivid details such as "sitting tall and straight … as if you were sitting next to a wall" creates a mental picture for the reader. **Double underline three more vivid descriptive details.**

**Relevant Details:**
Relevant details explain specific steps that build strength and flexibility. Strength is required to curve the spine and pull in the stomach. **Draw a box around a step in the process that builds flexibility.**

Spine Stretch and Roll Like a Ball

(1) "Spine stretch and roll like a ball" is an exercise sequence that builds strength and flexibility in the core area of your body supported by the spine. (2) First, assume the proper starting position. (3) Begin by sitting tall and straight on your mat as if you were sitting next to a wall. (4) Open your legs slightly wider than hip-width apart, placing your heels on the outside edges of the mat. (5) Pull your navel up and in. (6) Extend your arms at shoulder height parallel to your legs and flex your feet, pressing through your heels and pointing your toes toward the ceiling. (7) Next, tighten your buttocks and round your torso up and over. (8) Continually press your lower back behind you and scoop in your abdominals. (9) As you deepen the curve of your spine, press your navel further in as if it could kiss your spine. (10) Imagine your body forming a U-shape. (11) Once you are fully extended, hang your head between your shoulders, and hold the stretch. (12) To roll like a ball from this position, bend your knees and draw both ankles toward the core of your body and balance on your sit bones. (13) Grasp an ankle in each hand; pull your feet close to your buttocks, and place your head snugly between your knees. (14) Imagine your body taking the shape of a small, tight C. (15) Then, inhale and roll back. (16) As you roll, keep your feet close to your body and your head tucked between your knees. (17) Roll until you are balanced on your shoulder blades, but do not roll onto your neck. (18) Throughout the roll, maintain your C-shape and keep your navel pressed into your spine. (19) Finally, exhale as you roll back into your starting position.

# The Writer's Journal

**PEER EDITING**

The student writer of "Spine Stretch and Roll Like a Ball" completed the following reflection to record his thinking through the writing process. Read his writer's journal that describes a few key choices he made as he wrote. Then, in the given space, answer his question about the main idea of his paragraph. Work with a peer or a small group of classmates.

MAIN IDEA: *Even though I really like this topic, I know a lot of people just aren't into exercise. As I reread the paragraph, it sounds like I am only talking to people who already care about exercise, but I really want to inspire everyone to exercise. How can I make my topic interesting to people who need to exercise but don't?*

# Developing Your Point Using Process

A process shows how to do something or how something works. To describe a process, a writer uses chronological order (also called time order), relevant concrete descriptive details, and vivid images.

## The Point: The Main Idea

When you write a process paragraph, you limit your topic to a specific set of details based on time order. Most likely, you also have an opinion or point of view about the process, and this opinion or attitude is your point or main idea. A topic sentence states the point or purpose of the steps, directions, or phases.

For example, the following topic sentence contains (1) the topic, (2) the writer's opinion about the topic, and (3) the pattern of organization used to organize details.

The topic is "grief." The writer's opinion is stated with the phrase "emotional work" and time order is established with the phrases "the six phases" and "in progress."

The six phases | of grief | represent an emotional work | in progress.

PATTERN OF
ORGANIZATION:
TIME ORDER

TOPIC

AUTHOR'S OPINION

PATTERN OF
ORGANIZATION:
TIME ORDER

This example illustrates the relationships of the topic, the author's opinion, and the pattern of organization in this particular topic sentence. Note that the phrase "the six phases of grief" combines the topic and the pattern of organization.

**TOPIC SENTENCES**

Practice creating topic sentences. The following items present a topic, an opinion, and time order signal word(s). Combine the ideas in each group to create a topic sentence for a process.

1. TOPIC: *Test-taking anxiety*

OPINION: *can be overcome*

TIME ORDER SIGNAL WORDS: *in several steps*

TOPIC SENTENCE: ...........................................................

2. TOPIC: *Checking the oil and changing the oil in a car*

OPINION: *easy and quick*

TIME ORDER SIGNAL WORDS: *process*

TOPIC SENTENCE: ...........................................................

# Logical Order

A process describes the individual actions that make up each step or phase within the process. Just as time order words in the topic sentence signal a process, time order transition words show the flow of events as the process unfolds. Strong transitions establish coherence, a clear and understandable flow of ideas.

## Transition Words Used to Show Time Order

| | | | | | |
|---|---|---|---|---|---|
| after | currently | last | now | since | until |
| afterward | eventually | later | often | soon | when |
| as | finally | meanwhile | previously | then | while |
| before | first | next | second | ultimately | |

---

**TIME ORDER**

The following information appears in the safety publication *How to Survive a Submerging Car* sponsored by the Florida Highway Patrol. Determine the logical order of the sentences. *Hint:* Underline the time order transition words. Then answer the question "What's the point?"

_____ Then, while the car is still floating, **get out**; crawl through the opened window and swim to shore.

_____ The first thing to do in a floating car is to **push** the button to unbuckle your seatbelt.

_____ Next, **open** the window; electric windows should still work while the car is floating.

_____ When a car plunges into a lake or river, it should float for about three minutes, giving you enough time to safely exit the car before it sinks.

_____ P.O.G.O. stands for Push, Open, and Get Out.

_____ Once the car sinks, the P.O.G.O. method still works.

_____ In a submerged car, first **push** the button that releases your seatbelt.

_____ Finally, **get out**; push yourself out of the car and quickly swim to the surface.

_____ Then, **open** your car door.

**What's the point?**

_____

# Relevant Details

As a writer narrows a topic into a focused main idea about a process, the thinking process brings to mind many details of time and space. A writer evaluates the relevance of each detail and uses only those that illustrate the main idea. Some relevant details show the action of the process; other details explain the author's opinion about the process. Relevant details also include vivid descriptive and sensory details. These details work together to create a vivid mental image of the author's main point about the process. During the prewriting phase, a timeline can help a writer organize ideas as they are generated. Study the following timeline that was used to generate details about the phases of grief.

**The Six Phases of Grief**

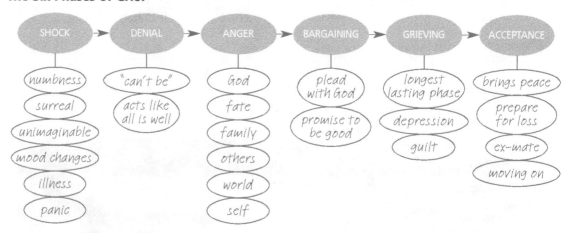

Practice 4

**RELEVANT DETAILS**

Assume you are going to write about the major stages of the human life cycle for a college psychology course. Create a timeline similar to the one above for the stages of grief. Compare your timeline with that of a peer or a small group of classmates.

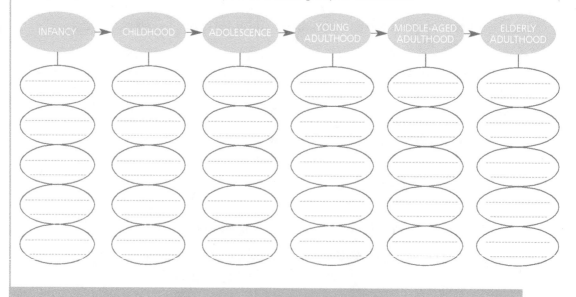

During the prewriting phase, a writer naturally generates irrelevant details. In fact, an effective writer often produces far more details than can be used to make a specific point. Irrelevant details do not explain, support, or illustrate the focused point of the paragraph. A careful writer uses the revision process to double check details for relevance and to eliminate irrelevant details.

The following paragraph develops the ideas recorded in the brainstorming list about the six phases of grief. Circle the main idea. Underline at least three concrete details. Cross out the two details that are not relevant to the main idea.

1. Shock    2. Denial    3. Anger    4. Bargaining    5. Grief    6. Acceptance

### The Phases of Grief

(1) In her book, *On Death and Dying*, Dr. Elizabeth Kübler-Ross explains the phases of grief we experience when we learn that a loved one is terminally ill. (2) The six phases of grief represent an emotional work in progress. (3) The first phase is shock. (4) During this initial phase, we experience a fog of numbness; life seems surreal as it crumbles around us, and the chore ahead of us seems unimaginable. (5) Throughout the second phase, denial, we work hard to erect the illusion that recovery is possible or that life is still normal. (6) We simply think, "This can't be happening to me." (7) Once we move past denial, we then grapple with the third phase of grief—anger. (8) We aim our anger at God, fate, doctors, family, the world, or even ourselves. (9) Thoughts such as "If only I had…" or "How can others just go on with their lives?" occupy our minds. (10) During traumas such as divorce, we often become angry with our ex-mate. (11) During the fourth phase, known as bargaining, we negotiate with God to cure the problem in exchange for our good behavior. (12) The fifth phase, usually the longest lasting, is grieving. (13) We often labor in mourning for months or years. (14) Chipping away at depression, guilt, physical illness, loneliness, panic, and abrupt mood changes employs all our energies. (15) The final phase of grief occurs as acceptance. (16) Often, for those of us facing our own death, acceptance brings the wage of peace. (17) As survivors of loss, such as divorce, we usually find ourselves working to re-build our lives and move on.

# Effective Expression: Vivid Images

Show, don't tell! Create vivid word pictures that deepen your reader's understanding of your point. Two figures of speech create vivid images: simile and metaphor.

A **simile** is an indirect comparison between two different ideas or things that uses *like, as, as if,* or *as though.*

### Example:

> As Robin crossed the finish line, his legs pumped like pistons.

A **metaphor** is a direct comparison between two different ideas or things that does *not* use *like, as, as if,* or *as though.* Often a metaphor uses words such as *is, are,* or *were* to make the direct comparison between the two ideas.

### Example:

> As Robin crossed the finish line, his legs were pumping pistons.

## VIVID IMAGES

Revise each of the following sentences to create vivid images by using similes and metaphors suggested by the photos. Discuss your work with your class or in a small group of your peers.

**1.** To ensure a healthful serving size, limit meat portions to 3 ounces.

**2.** Adolescence is a stage of human development made up of great change leading to adulthood.

# Using Process in Your Academic Courses

Many college courses in subjects such as biology, ecology, history, political science, psychology, and composition use process in their discussions. As you study these subjects, you will learn about processes involving the physical world, mental health, government, and writing. In addition, you will record processes to learn or demonstrate what you have learned. For example, a science lab may require you to conduct an experiment, record the steps you took, and evaluate the process. Some college writing assignments ask you to reflect upon your personal writing process so you can strengthen your writing skills.

**USING PROCESS IN A COMPOSITION ASSIGNMENT**

During a composition class, a student wrote the following paragraph in her writer's journal to reflect upon the effectiveness of her writing process. Assume you are her peer editor, and, based on what you have learned in this chapter about writing a process paragraph and in Chapter 2, offer her some advice.

> Kristen Elizabeth Spengler
>
> Writing 101
>
> September 27, 2010
>
>
> My Writer's Journal: My Writing Process
>
> (1) I start my writing process by mapping. (2) I make what is like a spider web with one basic idea in the middle of the page and supporting ideas branching off all around it. (3) After brainstorming for a while, I go on the computer and put the ideas I came up with into sentences. (4) Usually, I like to lay it all out on the computer and print it out because it is easier for me to see it while I'm typing my draft. (5) After I type up all the ideas I brainstormed, I print it out and turn it in.

Practice 7

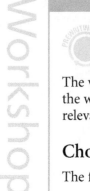

Workshop

# Workshop: Writing a Process Paragraph Step by Step

PREWRITING

## Prewrite Your Paragraph

The various activities below will walk you through the steps of the prewriting stage of the writing process: choosing a topic, focusing your point, and generating and organizing relevant details.

### Choose Your Topic

The following activities are designed to help you choose a topic.

1. Create a bank of topics. Use the following headings and brainstorm or list as many processes about each topic as you possibly can. Don't criticize your thoughts; just get as many relevant processes written down as quickly as possible. Compare your bank of topics with those of your classmates.

    - Recycling Trash
    - Auditioning
    - Studying
    - Training an Animal

2. Generate ideas with a freewrite. Choose one of the topics from your topic bank and think of the steps necessary to complete the process. Write about the process for ten minutes without stopping.

3. Select a photograph or series of photographs that illustrates a process. Write captions; brainstorm steps, directions, or phases; and freewrite about the photograph(s). Remember to ask "What is happening?" and "What's the point?" as you generate ideas.

### Focus Your Point

Read a freewrite you have generated for a process. Underline words that suggest your values, opinions, or attitudes about the process. Use a thesaurus and choose several vivid words to express your thoughts. Think about why the steps are important. Identify your audience and purpose. Create a list of concrete details and vivid images that show the actions that occur during the process. State in one sentence the point of the process.

AUDIENCE: ........................................................................................................

PURPOSE: ..........................................................................................................

........................................................................................................................

LIST OF CONCRETE DETAILS: ...............................................................................

........................................................................................................................

WHAT'S THE POINT? ...........................................................................................

........................................................................................................................

## Generate and Organize Relevant Details

Using ideas you have recorded so far and the process flowchart, generate and organize details that support your point.

**What's the point?**

TOPIC SENTENCE: ..........................................................................................................

..........................................................................................................

..........................................................................................................

**What is happening?**

| First Step |
| --- |
|  |

↓

| Second Step |
| --- |
|  |

↓

| Third Step |
| --- |
|  |

↓

| Fourth Step |
| --- |
|  |

 # Write a Draft of Your Paragraph

Using the ideas you generated during the prewriting phase, compose a draft of your process paragraph. Return to the prewriting process at any time to generate additional details as needed. Use your own paper.

 # Revise Your Draft

Once you have created a draft of a process, read the draft to answer the questions in the "Questions for Revising a Process Paragraph" box that follows. Indicate your answers by annotating your paper. If you answer "yes" to a question, underline, check, or circle examples. If you answer "no" to a question, write needed information in margins and draw lines to indicate placement of additional details. Revise your paragraph based on your reflection. (*Hint:* Experienced writers create several drafts as they focus on one or two questions per draft.)

## Questions for Revising a Process Paragraph:

☐ Have I stated or implied a focused main idea? Have I created a strong impression? Can I state my point in one sentence?

☐ Is the order of the steps, directions, or phases within the process clear? Have I used strong transitions?

☐ Have I made my point with adequate details?

☐ Have I included only the details that are relevant to my topic sentence?

☐ Have I used vivid images to make the process clear to my readers?

☐ Have I used concrete details to make my point?

## Proofread Your Draft

Once you have made any revisions to your paragraph that may be needed, proofread your paragraph to eliminate careless errors such as fused sentences.

### Grammar in Action: Eliminating Fused Sentences

A **fused sentence** occurs when two or more independent clauses are punctuated as one sentence. Correct a fused sentence by applying any of the following four edits: (1) separate independent clauses with a period and capital letter; (2) insert a coordinating conjunction (*for, and, nor, but, or, yet*, or *so*) and a comma between independent clauses; (3) insert a semicolon between the independent clauses; or (4) insert a semicolon with an appropriate transition between independent clauses.

- **A fused sentence:**

   Plants take in water through their roots they take in the gas carbon dioxide through their foliage plants use sunlight to turn water and carbon dioxide into food through the process of photosynthesis.

- **Two ways to correct the above fused sentence:**

   *ADDED COMMA AND COORDINATING CONJUNCTION "AND" TO SEPARATE INDEPENDENT CLAUSES*

   1. Plants take in water through their roots, and they take in the gas carbon dioxide through their foliage; plants use sunlight to turn water and carbon dioxide into food through the process of photosynthesis.

   *ADDED SEMICOLON TO SEPARATE INDEPENDENT CLAUSES*

Workshop

*ADDED PERIOD TO SEPARATE INDEPENDENT CLAUSES; THE FIRST LETTER OF THE SECOND INDEPENDENT CLAUSE IS NOW CAPITALIZED*

**2.** Plants take in water through their roots. In addition, they take in the gas carbon dioxide through their foliage; then, plants use sunlight to turn water and carbon dioxide into food through the process of photosynthesis.

*ADDED SEMICOLON AND TRANSITION WORD "THEN" TO SEPARATE INDEPENDENT CLAUSES*

---

### ELIMINATING FUSED SENTENCES

Edit to eliminate fused sentences.

**1.** Using anabolic steroids is a fast way to increase body size some athletes are willing to cheat at a sport they take these steroids to increase body mass beyond what hard work alone could produce.

-------------------------------------------------

-------------------------------------------------

-------------------------------------------------

**2.** Effective questioning occurs in an order that draws out the exact information needed questions should focus on easy-to-answer factual information that puts the person at ease then the interviewer can move to ideas that can't be stated as a fact.

-------------------------------------------------

-------------------------------------------------

-------------------------------------------------

# Review

**MY WRITER'S JOURNAL**

Work with a classmate to give and receive feedback about your process paragraphs. Use the following form to record your thinking about your writing process for your process paragraph. Use the writer's journal on page 109 as a model for your own journal. Discuss the decisions you made as you wrote, and describe what you have learned by writing. Also, ask for advice about how to improve your paragraph.

MAIN IDEA: ..........................................................................................................................................

..........................................................................................................................................................

..........................................................................................................................................................

..........................................................................................................................................................

LOGICAL ORDER: ...............................................................................................................................

..........................................................................................................................................................

..........................................................................................................................................................

..........................................................................................................................................................

RELEVANT DETAILS: ..........................................................................................................................

..........................................................................................................................................................

..........................................................................................................................................................

..........................................................................................................................................................

EFFECTIVE EXPRESSION: ....................................................................................................................

..........................................................................................................................................................

..........................................................................................................................................................

..........................................................................................................................................................

# Writing Assignments

## Considering Audience and Purpose

Study the sequence of photographs about the set of Pilates exercises at the beginning of the chapter. Draft a process paragraph based on one of the following two writing situations:

Assume you are keeping a personal exercise journal. Write a paragraph in which you describe the steps in your exercise sequence. Include the challenges you might face in each phase of the process.

Assume you are an instructor of an exercise class for an elderly group. Think about specific movements in each step of the exercise that might have to be adapted due to poor balance or stiffness of joints. Write a paragraph for the Senior Citizens' Health Club Newsletter that describes these adapted exercises.

## Writing for Everyday Life

Assume that a friend or family member has asked you for advice about how to open a bank account; write a paragraph that explains how to do so. Be sure to include information about necessary personal identification and available banking services. Choose words that reflect one of the following: (1) endorsement of the banking services or (2) warning against possible problems.

## Writing for College Life

Assume you are in a college course called Student Success, and you have been assigned to write a brief oral report about how to study. Write a paragraph that records the text for your speech in which you describe the most effective way to take notes during class.

## Writing for Working Life

Assume you are the director of the Human Resources department for a corporation, and you are volunteering your services at a job fair designed to help unemployed citizens secure jobs. You have agreed to teach participants how to handle the interviewing process. Write a paragraph as part of your handout that describes the steps necessary to prepare for an interview.

**mywritinglab**
**WANT A BETTER GRADE?**
For more practice with process, go to
www.mywritinglab.com
> Using Patterns of Organization to Develop Paragraphs > The Process Paragraph.

# 7

## The Example Paragraph

An example, also called an exemplification, is a specific illustration of a more general idea.

When we communicate—with family members, employers, teachers, or friends—we often use examples to clarify a point we want to make. Think of a situation you were in recently where you used examples to make a point. What makes an example effective?

In everyday life, we illustrate our decorating ideas with paint chips and swatches of fabric. In working life, we offer examples of our hard work and successes when we apply for jobs and promotions. In college life, professors and textbook authors use examples to teach concepts in every discipline.

To write an example paragraph, a writer moves from a general idea to specific examples that support and clarify the main point. Sometimes, as in a science lab report, a writer may present the specific examples first and then come to a general conclusion based on the examples. An effective example paragraph also relies heavily on concrete details, the logical order of importance, and, often, parallel expression.

# What's the Point of Examples?

Generating and organizing examples help a writer to discover his or her point about a particular topic. The following photographs offer three examples of a thrifty lifestyle. Study each photograph. Write a caption that briefly describes each example of thrifty living. Then, answer the question, "What's the point?" with a one-sentence statement of the overall main idea.

**PHOTOGRAPHIC ORGANIZER: EXAMPLES**

EXAMPLES OF A THRIFTY LIFESTYLE

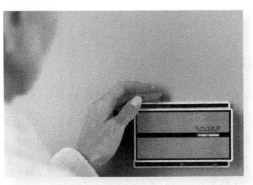

**Example 1:**

What is this?

--------------------------------

--------------------------------

**Example 2:**

What is this?

--------------------------------

--------------------------------

**Example 3:**

What is this?

--------------------------------

--------------------------------

**What's the point?**

--------------------------------

## My First Thoughts: A Prewriting Activity

Set a time limit, perhaps five minutes, and write in your notebook about the images you just studied. Do not let your pen or pencil stop. Even if you must repeat ideas, keep writing until the time limit is up. Let ideas flow freely. Getting your first thoughts about a topic on paper is one excellent way to kick start your writing process.

# Making a Point Using Examples: One Student Writer's Response

The following paragraph offers one writer's point about what the people in the photographs exemplify on the previous page. Read the exemplification and the explanations; complete the activities in **bold type** in the annotations. Then read the writer's journal entry that records decisions made during the writing process.

**Main Idea:**
The main idea is the point the author is making about the topic. The topic is "A thrifty lifestyle." **Underline the author's point about this topic.**

**Listing Order:**
The transitional phrase "for example" signals that the paragraph is developed by examples. **Circle two more transitional phrases that indicate a list of examples.**

**Effective Expression:**
Parallelism refers to the way ideas of equal importance are worded. To achieve parallelism, a writer uses the same form of wording for a set, series, or list of ideas or details. Repeating a form of wording or type of phrase makes your ideas easier to follow. **Double underline two more ideas with –ing phrasing.**

**Relevant Details:**
Concrete details list specific minor details for each major example of "a thrifty lifestyle." **Draw boxes around two more concrete minor details that support a major example.**

## Be Thrifty: Save Money

(1) When hard times hit the economy, most of us get back to the basics. (2) That old saying "a penny saved is a penny earned" states some good basic advice. (3) A thrifty lifestyle saves money. (4) For example, adjusting our thermostats can lower our energy bill up to 10% a month. (5) In the winter, we should set the thermostat to 68°F while we're awake and even lower while we're asleep or away from home. (6) In the summer, we should set the thermostat to 78°F. (7) If we usually pay $300.00 a month for energy, we could save $30.00 a month. (8) A second example of thrifty living is saving loose change. (9) Most of us have tons of change in our wallets, at the bottom of our purses and backpacks, in our cars, and even in our sofas and chairs. (10) We can put that money to good use by rolling loose change and depositing the rolls into a savings account. (11) Saving 50 cents a day in loose change adds up to $15 a month. (12) Another example of thriftiness is packing a lunch. (13) Typically, each of us spends $6 to $12 every time we eat out during a work or school day. (14) If one person packed a lunch every day, he or she would save $60 to $120 a week! (15) That means we could save as much as $480 a month, and that's just for one person. (16) Think of what a family could save by packing lunches. (17) As these three examples prove, living a thrifty lifestyle can save each of us thousands of dollars in just one year.

# The Writer's Journal

LEARNING OUTCOMES
READING AND WRITING

**PEER EDITING**

The student writer of "Be Thrifty: Save Money" completed the following reflection to record some of her thinking about her writing process. Read her writer's journal that describes a few key choices she made as she wrote. Then, in the given space, answer her questions about her use of details in her paragraph. Work with a peer or a small group of classmates.

RELEVANT DETAILS: My first draft was way too long. Once I had a topic, I did a freewrite about it, and within 5 minutes, I had filled two pages with lots of examples for saving money by being thrifty. It was kind of hard to figure out what to cut. For example, I wanted to give some hints about rolling coins (like how often, where to get supplies, etc.) and packing lunches (like nutrition, variety, and weight loss/gain). Do you think I should include some of these details? Why or why not? If so, which details and where?

# Developing Your Point Using Examples

An exemplification illustrates a main point with one or more examples. To exemplify a point, a writer lists the examples, often according to the order of importance; explains each example with relevant concrete details; and often uses parallel expression.

## The Point: The Main Idea

When you write an exemplification, you limit your topic to a set of specific examples, instances, or cases. Most likely, you also have an opinion or point of view about the examples, and this opinion or attitude is your point or main idea. You may reveal your opinion by listing the examples in a particular order of importance. A topic sentence states the point or purpose of the examples.

For example, the following topic sentence contains (1) the topic; (2) the writer's opinion about the topic; and (3) the pattern of organization used to organize details.

The topic is "body art." The pattern of organization is established with the phrase "such as tattooing and piercing" and the verb "exemplifies." The writer's opinion is stated with the phrase "self-expression."

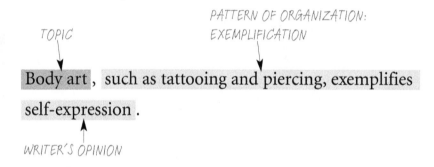

Sometimes in an example paragraph, a topic sentence only implies the pattern of organization as in the following version.

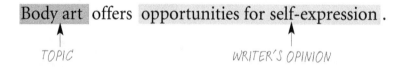

When the example pattern of organization is only implied by the topic sentence, then transitions that signal and list examples establish the pattern of organization within the body of the paragraph. Notice in the following example that the two major detail sentences state the topic, pattern of organization, and writer's opinion.

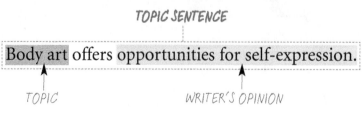

Tattooing is one example of body art as self-expression.

PATTERN OF ORGANIZATION:     TOPIC     WRITER'S OPINION
EXEMPLIFICATION

MAJOR DETAIL SENTENCE #2

Piercing is another example of artistic self-expression.

PATTERN OF ORGANIZATION:     TOPIC     WRITER'S OPINION
EXEMPLIFICATION

**TOPIC SENTENCES**

The items below present a topic, an opinion, and example signal word(s). Combine the ideas in each group to create a topic sentence for an example paragraph.

**1.** TOPIC: *Foods*     OPINION: *inflame the condition diverticulitis*

EXAMPLE (OR LISTING) SIGNAL WORDS: *Certain*

TOPIC SENTENCE: _____

_____

**2.** TOPIC: *A good friend*     OPINION: *compassion and honesty*

EXAMPLE (OR LISTING) SIGNAL WORDS: *illustrates*

TOPIC SENTENCE: _____

_____

**3.** TOPIC: *Solar energy*     OPINION: *is versatile and cheap*

EXAMPLE (OR LISTING) SIGNAL WORDS: *not included; only implied*

TOPIC SENTENCE: _____

_____

**4.** TOPIC: *SUV drivers*     OPINION: *rugged, aggressive*

EXAMPLE (OR LISTING) SIGNAL WORDS: _____

TOPIC SENTENCE: _____

_____

Practice 2

# Logical Order

Once you have selected your topic and focused on a main idea, you are ready to generate additional details and list your ideas based on their order of importance. To use examples to illustrate a main point, a writer moves from a general idea to a major support to a minor support. To signal the movement between these levels of ideas, a writer uses transitions to signal or list examples. Strong transitions establish coherence, a clear and understandable flow of ideas.

## Transitions Used to Signal Examples

| | | | |
|---|---|---|---|
| an illustration | for instance | once | to illustrate |
| for example | including | such as | typically |

## Transitions Used to List Examples

| | | | | |
|---|---|---|---|---|
| also | final | for one thing | last of all | second |
| and | finally | furthermore | moreover | third |
| another | first | in addition | next | |
| besides | first of all | last | one | |

**LOGICAL ORDER**

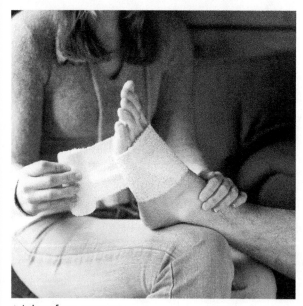

▲ Injury from overuse

Fill in the blank with appropriate transitions to signal or list examples.

In the drive to become physically fit, many risk injury by overtraining. Overuse injuries develop through the daily stresses placed on various parts of the body (1) _____ tendons, muscles, (2) _____ joints. Plantar Fasciitis is (3) _____ of an overuse injury from walking, jogging, (4) _____ running. This injury is an inflammation of the band of tissue that stretches across the sole of the foot. (5) _____, the foot is tender from the ball to the heel, making it painful to walk.

The following information was published on a government website for consumer protection. Determine the logical order of the sentences. Complete the exercise by answering the question "What's the point?" Discuss your answers with your class or with a small group of peers.

**Consumer Beware!**

_____ The third and most common example of fraud is phishing.

_____ Phishing is an email message that lures a consumer to a phony website.

_____ The email sender pretends to be from a legitimate government organization, bank, or retailer.

_____ The phishy email stated, "We recently reviewed your account, and we need more information to help us provide you with secure service."

_____ The message also directed the receiver "to visit the Resolution Center and complete the 'Steps to Remove Limitations.'"

_____ A recent instance of phishing came from a phony PayPal site.

_____ A second example of fraud is the phone scam; a caller pretends to represent a trusted organization or company.

_____ In one instance, a caller claims to work for the court and says the listener has been called for jury duty.

_____ The caller then demands personal information such as a social security number, birth date, and credit card numbers.

_____ The first and least common example of fraud is the handyman sting.

_____ The handyman offers to fix the problem, such as replacing a roof or removing a fallen tree, for a cash fee lower than any reputable company could offer.

_____ The handyman shows up on the doorstep of a home in obvious need of repair, usually after severe weather such as a tornado or hurricane.

_____ Most often, the money is paid upfront, and the work is never completed.

**What's the point?**

---------------------------------------------------------------------------

---------------------------------------------------------------------------

---------------------------------------------------------------------------

# Relevant Details

As a writer narrows a topic into a focused main idea, the thinking process brings to mind many details that answer the questions *who, what, when, where, why,* and *how.* A writer evaluates the relevance of each detail and uses only those that exemplify the main idea. Some relevant details express major examples of the main point; minor details may further illustrate major examples. Some major and minor details may explain the author's opinion about the examples. During the prewriting phase, a list can help a writer organize ideas as they are generated. Study the following list generated about the topic "Examples of State Gun Laws."

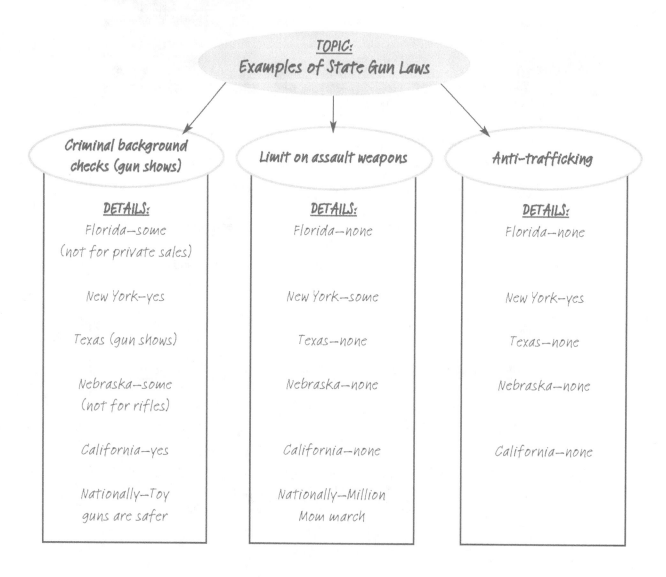

During the prewriting phase, a writer naturally generates irrelevant details. In fact, an effective writer often produces far more details than can be used to make a specific point. Irrelevant details do not exemplify, explain, or support the focused point of the paragraph. A careful writer uses the revision process to double check details for relevance and to eliminate irrelevant ones.

The following paragraph, adapted from the *stategunlaws.org* website, develops the ideas recorded in the brainstorming list about state gun laws. Circle the main idea. Underline three concrete major examples. Cross out the two details that are not relevant to the main point.

## State Gun Laws

(1) New York, Florida, Texas, Nebraska, and California gun control laws vary greatly from state to state. (2) For example, of the five states—New York, Florida, Texas, Nebraska, and California—only New York has an anti-trafficking law that places a one-handgun-per-month limit on gun sales. (3) In the other four states, anyone can easily traffic guns to criminals by buying as many handguns as they want from gun stores and turning them over for profit on the streets. (4) Unbelievably, toy guns face stricter safety regulations than do real guns. (5) In addition, only two states, California and New York, require criminal background checks at gun shows. (6) Florida and Nebraska require partial background checks; for example, Florida requires a criminal background check for handguns, but no background check is necessary to purchase an assault rifle such as AK47. (7) Alarmingly, Texas does not require background checks at gun shows. (8) Perhaps the most alarming example of our uneven approach to gun control is the overall lack of limits on assault weapons. (9) Of the five states, only California bans the sale of semiautomatic assault weapons such as the Uzi. (10) New York has a partial limit on such sales; for example, the state does not ban the sale of "rapid fire ammunition magazines that hold up to 100 rounds." (11) Texas, Nebraska, and Florida have no limits on assault weapons and magazines. (12) A national network of volunteers known as the Million Mom March works to strengthen and unify gun laws.

# Effective Expression: Parallel Language

Parallel language is the use of similar and balanced expressions in a pair or series of words, phrases, or clauses. Parallelism makes a piece of writing more enjoyable, more powerful, and more readable. Study the following examples from a student's first thoughts about the seasons of the year.

**Non-Parallel Words:**

Summer time is ideal for swimming, boating, and a picnic.

**Revised Words for Parallelism:**

Summer time is ideal for swimming, boating, and picnicking.

*THIS SERIES OF WORDS (NOUNS) ALL END IN –ING.*

**Non-Parallel Phrases:**

The seasons can go from the fire of summer to the freezing winter.

**Revised Phrases for Parallelism:**

The seasons can go from the fire of summer, to the chill of fall, to the freeze of winter, to the breeze of spring.

*THIS SET OF IDEAS REPEATS A PATTERN OF PREPOSITIONAL PHRASES.*

**Non-Parallel Clauses:**

I love the fall because the leaves turn colors, and it's football season.

**Revised Clauses for Parallelism:**

I love the fall because the leaves turn colors, and television programming turns to football.

*THESE CLAUSES ARE NOW BOTH DEPENDENT CLAUSES THAT BEGIN WITH THE SAME SUBORDINATING CONJUNCTION ("BECAUSE") AND USE THE SAME VERB ("TO TURN").*

Practice 6

**PARALLEL EXPRESSION**

Revise the following sentences so ideas are expressed in parallel language. Discuss your work with your class or with a small group of your peers.

**1.** Examples of activities that strengthen the heart include jogging, swimming, and jump rope.

**2.** A healthy heart lifestyle includes the following: getting plenty of sleep, eating a balanced diet, and regular exercise.

# Using Examples in Your Academic Courses

Every college course uses examples to clarify ideas. As you study these subjects, you will learn about examples of governments, important historical figures, psychological concepts, scientific principles, effective speeches, and so on. In addition, you will prove what you have learned by providing examples of the concepts and skills you have studied.

---

**USING EXAMPLES IN A SHORT-ANSWER COMMUNICATION ESSAY EXAM**

Assume you are taking a college class in communication. Your professor has given your class a set of study questions to help you prepare for an upcoming exam. A peer in your study group started the following prewrite to one of the study questions. Study her notes; then fill in the blank with a one-sentence answer to the study question. Finally, on your own paper, write a draft of a paragraph. Include appropriate example transition words. Work with a peer or in a small group.

**Study Question:** What is the purpose of listening?

**Answer to Study Question** *Listening serves several purposes.*

**Example**

We learn from others.

We learn from parents, teachers, and others.

We learn about others, the world, and ourselves.

**Example**

We relate to others.

We develop long-lasting relationships.

We increase understanding.

We avoid conflict.

**Example**

We influence others.

We respect others.

We earn the respect and trust of others.

# Workshop: Writing an Example Paragraph Step by Step

## Prewrite Your Paragraph

The various activities that follow will walk you through the steps of the prewriting stage of the writing process: choosing a topic, focusing your point, and generating and organizing relevant details.

### Choose Your Topic

The following activities are designed to help you choose a topic.

1. Create a bank of topics. Use the following headings to brainstorm or list as many examples about each topic as you possibly can. Don't criticize your thoughts; just get as many relevant examples written down as quickly as possible. Add more topics and examples as they occur to you. Compare your bank of topics with those of your classmates.

   - Pollution
   - Job Skills
   - Effective Teachers
   - Alternative Energy Supplies

2. Generate ideas with a freewrite. Choose one of the topics from your topic bank and think of examples that illustrate the topic. Write about the topic and examples for ten minutes without stopping.

3. Select a photograph or series of photographs that illustrates a topic. Write captions, brainstorm examples, and freewrite about the photograph(s). Remember to ask "What do(es) the picture(s) illustrate?" and "What's the point?"

### Focus Your Point

Read a prewrite you have generated for an exemplification. Underline words that suggest your values, opinions, or attitudes about the topic and the examples. Think about why the details are important. Identify your audience and purpose. Write a list of additional concrete examples that illustrate your point. State in one sentence the point of the examples.

AUDIENCE: _____

PURPOSE: _____

LIST OF CONCRETE DETAILS: _____

_____

WHAT'S THE POINT? _____

_____

## Generate and Organize Relevant Details

Using ideas you have recorded so far and the following idea map, generate and organize details that support your point.

**Example: Illustrations of an Idea**

What's the point?

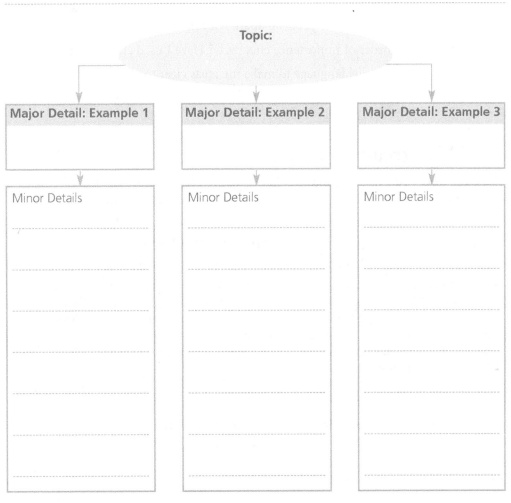

Topic: _____

| Major Detail: Example 1 | Major Detail: Example 2 | Major Detail: Example 3 |
| --- | --- | --- |
| Minor Details | Minor Details | Minor Details |

 # Write a Draft of Your Paragraph

Using the ideas you generated during the prewriting phase, compose a draft of your example paragraph. Return to the prewriting process at any time to generate additional details as needed. Use your own paper.

 # Revise Your Draft

Once you have created a draft of an example paragraph, read the draft and answer the questions in the "Questions for Revising an Example Paragraph" box that follows. Indicate your answers by annotating your paper. If you answer "yes" to a question, underline, check, or circle examples. If you answer "no" to a question, write the additional details in the margin and draw lines to indicate their placement. Revise your paragraph based on your reflection. (*Hint:* Experienced writers create several drafts as they focus on one or two questions per draft.)

# Questions for Revising an Example Paragraph:

☐ Have I stated or implied a main idea? Have I made my point? Can I state my point in one sentence?

☐ Have I used concrete details to make my point?

☐ Have I included only the details that are relevant to my point?

☐ Have I used order of importance effectively? Have I used strong transitions?

☐ Have I used parallel language to make my ideas clear to my readers?

## Proofread Your Draft

Once you have made any revisions to your paragraph that may be needed, proofread your paragraph for proper usage and punctuation, such as using commas in a series.

### Grammar in Action: Using Commas in a Series

Use commas to separate three or more words, phrases, or clauses in a series. One of the following conjunctions is used between the last two items of a series: *for, and, nor, but, or, yet,* or *so*; for example, sending, receiving, *and* forwarding emails. Some experts state that the comma before the conjunction is optional. However, leaving the last comma of the series out may cause confusion, so many experts advise including it. In writing for college, we suggest you include it. Study the following examples:

- **Using Commas to Separate Three or More Words:**

  Dave Chappelle is candid, creative, and comical.

  *Coordinating conjunction*

- **Using Commas to Separate Three or More Phrases:**

  Texas offers vacation experiences that are enjoyable and educational: exploring Big Ben National Park, visiting The Alamo, and touring the NASA Space Center.

  *Coordinating conjunction*

- **Using Commas to Separate Three or More Clauses:**

  Our company is looking for employees who can find solutions, who can work as a team, and who can excel in their roles.

  *Coordinating conjunction*

Edit these sentences for proper use of commas in a series. Rewrite them on the lines below.

**1.** I only need three pairs of shoes—running shoes low-heeled pumps and reef sandals.

_____

_____

**2.** The study of psychology includes units such as the biology of the brain the development of the mind and the social behaviors of a human being.

_____

_____

**3.** Those who snore are those who are more likely to have heart attacks who are more likely to be in an automobile accident and who are more likely to suffer from daytime fatigue.

_____

_____

_____

**4.** Heart disease is linked to diet exercise and genetics.

_____

_____

**5.** You need better fitting shoes if you have to dig the corner of your toenail from under your skin if you have a build-up of dead skin such as corns or calluses or if you have tired aching feet at the end of a long hard day.

_____

_____

_____

**6.** Snoring can be caused by a variety of factors such as alcohol consumption nasal problems sleep apnea and the structure of your mouth.

_____

_____

# Review

Work with a classmate to give and receive feedback about your example paragraphs. Use the following form to record your thinking about your writing process for your example paragraph. Use the writer's journal on page 125 as a model for your own journal. Discuss the decisions you made as you wrote, and describe what you have learned by writing. Also, ask for advice about how to improve your paragraph.

MAIN IDEA: ..........................................................................................................................................

LOGICAL ORDER: ..................................................................................................................................

RELEVANT DETAILS: ..............................................................................................................................

EFFECTIVE EXPRESSION: ........................................................................................................................

# Writing Assignments

## Considering Audience and Purpose

Study the set of photographs of examples of thrifty living at the beginning of the chapter. Assume you are a volunteer working with HOPE, a nonprofit group that assists families. Your task this month is to write a column for the group's newsletter. Write a paragraph that identifies and explains additional examples of money-saving ideas for family life.

## Writing for Everyday Life

Assume that you are keeping a personal journal and you want to capture the essence of your daily life so your children and grandchildren will know about the customs, fashions, or nature of this time in your life and our society. Use examples to make your point. Choose words that reflect one of the following attitudes: (1) realistic, (2) idealistic.

## Writing for College Life

Assume you are a member of the Student Government Association, and you are helping with freshman orientation. Identify two or three aspects of college life about which new students should be aware. Use examples to make your point.

## Writing for Working Life

Assume a peer is applying for a job as a supervisor of a sales team at Best Buy or Radio Shack (or some other job that requires leadership and commitment) and has asked you for a recommendation. Interview the peer; then write a one-paragraph recommendation in which you use examples to support your recommendation.

# 8

# The Classification Paragraph

A classification is a division of a topic into one or more subgroups.

Whether we are grocery shopping, studying, job hunting, or searching for that special someone, we often gather and group information based on types. For example, most of us have experienced or observed the social cliques that form in high schools, neighborhoods, and on the job.

A writer uses classification to sort, group, and label items and ideas based on shared traits or types. In everyday life, we fulfill various social roles such as life-partner, parent, sibling, friend, employee, or student. In working life, we promote people to higher levels of responsibility and pay based on particular types of skills and attitudes. In college life, each of us probably prefers certain kinds of courses, likes certain types of teachers, and does better on certain types of tests.

To write a classification paragraph, a writer divides a topic into subgroups based on shared traits or qualities. The writer lists and often labels each subgroup, describes its traits, and offers examples that best represent the group. Because groups and subgroups are listed, transitions are often used to signal logical order and ensure coherence. An effective classification paragraph uses details of description and examples, logical order, and (as in any effective paragraph) sentence variety.

# What's the Point of Classification?

Identifying and labeling groups or types helps a writer to discover his or her point about a particular topic. Study the following set of photographs. In the space provided, (1) identify the types of music represented by the three photographs; (2) list the traits of each subgroup; (3) describe specific examples based on the photographs; and (4) answer the question "What's the point?" with a one-sentence statement of the overall main idea.

PHOTOGRAPHIC ORGANIZER: CLASSIFICATION

TOPIC: TYPES OF MUSIC

| 1ST TYPE | 2ND TYPE | 3RD TYPE |

▲ Garth Brooks

▲ Ludacris and Queen Latifah

▲ Marc Anthony

**1.** What type of music does each artist in the photographs represent?

**2.** Traits:                     Traits:                     Traits:

**3.** Examples:                 Examples:                 Examples:

**What's the point?**

## My First Thoughts: A Prewriting Activity

Brainstorm about the images you just studied. Set a time limit, such as five minutes, and write in your notebook about the images and the details you generated. Write as quickly as you can without stopping. Let the ideas flow freely. Getting your first thoughts about a topic on paper is one excellent way to overcome writer's block and set your mind to thinking.

LEARNING OUTCOMES
STRUCTURE

# Making a Point Using Classification: One Student Writer's Response

**Effective Expression:**
Parallelism refers to the similarity in the way ideas are worded. To achieve parallelism in this sentence, the writer repeats the subject "music" and uses the same form to express each verb. **Double underline three other expressions that repeat a pattern of wording.**

The following paragraph offers one writer's point about the types of music illustrated by the photographs. Read the classification paragraph below and the explanations; complete the activities in **bold type** given in the annotations. Then read the writer's journal that records decisions made during the writing process.

### Music's Variety Is Music's Power

(1) Music expresses our individuality; music connects us to one another; music carries our culture. (2) The power of music comes from the variety of the lives it expresses. (3) Three major types of popular music illustrate the powerful variety of music. (4) The first major type of music is country music. (5) Country music is based on the traditional folk music of the rural South and the cowboy music of the West. (6) Country songs express strong personal emotions about topics such as mother, home, love, hard work, prison, the rambling man, and religion. (7) Country musicians like Garth Brooks typically play such instruments as the guitar and fiddle. (8) The second major type of music that reveals the diversity of music is Hip Hop or rap music. (9) Rap music is a form of music that came about in African American urban communities. (10) Rap is characterized by beat-driven rhymes spoken over instruments or mixed recordings. (11) Rappers like Queen Latifah and Ludacris often express strong political and social views. (12) A third major type that illustrates the powerful variety in music is Salsa music. (13) Salsa, with its origin in Cuba, is a popular form of Latin-American dance music. (14) Salsa is characterized by Afro-Caribbean rhythms; its fast, energetic tempo stirs the urge to dance. (15) Performers like Marc Anthony use percussion instruments such as claves, congas, and cowbells.

**Main Idea:**
The main idea is the point the author is making about the topic. The topic is "popular music." **Underline the author's point about this topic.**

**Listing Order:**
The transitional phrase "first major type" signals that the paragraph is developed based on classification. **Circle two more phrases that signal a list of types.**

**Relevant Details:**
Relevant details use descriptive details of traits and examples. Descriptive details include sensory details such as "fast, energetic tempo stirs the urge to dance." **Draw a box around two more details that appeal to the senses.**

# The Writer's Journal

## PEER EDITING

The student writer of "Music's Variety Is Music's Power" completed the following reflection to record her thinking through the writing process. Read her writer's journal that describes a few key choices she made as she wrote. Then, in the given space, answer her questions about the main idea for her paragraph. Work with a peer or a small group of classmates.

MAIN IDEA: Getting started was really hard for me. I spent a lot of time staring at a blank page, unable to come up with a way to get started. I knew what to say about each type of music, I just couldn't figure out how to word the beginning. Finally, I gave up and just started writing the body of the paragraph, so I think the title and introduction are weak, and there isn't a conclusion. Could you suggest a better title? What would you do to make the opening more interesting? And is the conclusion okay as it is? Or do I need to add something? If so, what?

# Developing Your Point Using Classification

A classification makes a main point by grouping or sorting ideas. To support a point through classification, a writer divides a topic into subgroups based on common traits or principles. Writers offer relevant concrete details of descriptions and examples, and (as in every piece of writing) control sentence structure.

## The Point: The Main Idea

When you write a classification, you limit your topic to a set of ideas or groups based on types, shared traits, and common principles. Most likely, you also have an opinion or point of view about the groups, traits, or common principles. This opinion or attitude is your point or main idea. You also reveal your opinion by discussing the groups or traits in a particular order of importance. A topic sentence states the point or purpose of the groups, types, or traits.

For example, the following topic sentence contains (1) the topic; (2) the writer's opinion about the topic; and (3) the pattern of organization used to organize details.

The topic is "friendship." The pattern of organization is established with the phrase "three types of." The writer's opinion is stated with the phrase "equally important interpersonal relationships."

TOPIC        PATTERN OF ORGANIZATION: CLASSIFICATION SIGNAL WORDS

Friendships offer three types of equally ◄—— WRITER'S OPINION

important interpersonal relationships. ◄

The example above illustrates the relationship of the topic, the writer's opinion, and the pattern of organization in this particular topic sentence.

### TOPIC SENTENCES

Practice creating topic sentences. You are given a topic, an opinion, and classification signal word(s). Combine the ideas in each group to create a topic sentence for a classification.

**1.** TOPIC: *leisure activities*    OPINION: *relaxing and inexpensive, strengthen*

*family ties*

CLASSIFICATION SIGNAL WORDS: *two types of*

TOPIC SENTENCE: ....................................................................

**2.** TOPIC: *diet*    OPINION: *healthful*

CLASSIFICATION SIGNAL WORDS: *several traits*

TOPIC SENTENCE: ....................................................................

# Logical Order

Once you have divided a topic into groups, types, or traits and focused on a main idea, you are ready to generate additional details and list your ideas in their order of importance. To make a point using classification, a writer moves from a general idea (the group) to a major support (a particular trait of the group) to a minor support (an example of the trait). To signal the movement between these levels of ideas, a writer uses transitions to signal or list groups, types, or traits. Strong transitions establish coherence, a clear and understandable flow of ideas.

## Words That Are Used to Signal Groups, Types, or Traits

| | | | | |
|---|---|---|---|---|
| aspect | classify | group | quality | style |
| attribute | classification | ideal | rank | trait |
| branch | collection | kind | section | type |
| brand | division | level | set | typical |
| categories | element | order | sort | variety |
| characteristic | feature | part | status | |
| class | form | principle | stratum | |

## Transitions That Combine with Signal Words to List Groups, Types, or Traits

| | | | | |
|---|---|---|---|---|
| also | final | for one thing | last of all | second |
| and | finally | furthermore | moreover | third |
| another | first | in addition | next | |
| besides | first of all | last | one | |

---

**LOGICAL ORDER**

Based on the logical order of ideas, fill in the blanks with the appropriate classification signal words. Compare and discuss your answers with a peer or in a small group of your classmates.

I write in support of Henry William's promotion in _____ and pay. Mr. William has several _____ that will make him an effective manager. _____ of these _____ are his communication _____ and his _____ of commitment. He is the _____ who listens and learns. He is the _____ who works for the success of his whole _____.

# Relevant Details

As a writer narrows a topic into a focused main idea, the thinking process brings to mind many details that answer the questions such as *who, what, when, where, why,* and *how.* A writer evaluates the relevance of each detail and uses only those that clarify or support the main idea based on classification. Some relevant details identify subgroups, types, or traits of the main point. Minor details may offer examples of subgroups, types, or traits. Some major and minor details may explain the writer's opinion about the topic and how it is being classified. During the prewriting phase, a list can help a writer organize ideas as they are generated. Study the following concept map that was used to generate ideas about the topic "Two types of comedy that dominate television."

**Concept Map**

| Topic: Two types of comedy that dominate television | | |
|---|---|---|
| **Traits** | **Type 1:** Sketch comedy | **Type 2:** Situation comedy |
| Length: | Short scenes or sketches (1–10 mins.) | 30 min. story line |
| Material: | Actors improvise/write scripts Avoids violence, uses bad language | Writers create scripts Avoids violence and bad language |
| Focus: | Politics, current events, issues, ensemble acting | Social relationships at home and work, ensemble acting |
| Examples: | Colgate Comedy Hour, Monty Python's Flying Circus, SNL, Mad TV, Chappelle's Show, Ed Sullivan (best show of all) | I Love Lucy, Friends, Seinfeld, Everybody Hates Chris |

During the prewriting phase, a writer naturally generates irrelevant details. In fact, an effective writer often produces far more details than can be used to make a specific point. Irrelevant details do not explain or support the focused point of the paragraph. A careful writer uses the revision process to double check details for relevance and to eliminate irrelevant ones.

The following paragraph develops the ideas recorded in the brainstorming list about comedy. Circle the main idea. Underline a trait for each group. Cross out the two details that are not relevant to the main point.

### Television Comedy: Sketches and Sitcoms

(1) Two types of comedy have long dominated television. (2) One type is sketch comedy. (3) Sketch comedy is a series of short comedy scenes that typically range from one to ten minutes. (4) Often the actors improvise the sketch, making it up as they go; then they write the script based on their improvisation. (5) This kind of humor avoids violence, often uses offensive language, and focuses on politics, issues, and current events. (6) Well-known examples of sketch comedy include *Monty Python's Flying Circus, Saturday Night Live, Mad TV,* and *Chappelle's Show.* (7) However, *The Ed Sullivan Show* remains the all time best variety show to have appeared on television. (8) A second type of comedy dominating television is the sitcom or situation comedy, also an ensemble routine. (9) Sitcoms are usually set in a specific location such as a home or office, and they present amusing story lines about a group of characters such as a family, friends, or co-workers in an office. (10) Often episodes are self-contained stories that are resolved in less than 30 minutes; some sitcoms do use ongoing story lines based on developing relationships between characters. (11) This type of humor avoids violence, rarely uses offensive language, and focuses on social relationships. (12) Well-known examples of situation comedy include *I Love Lucy, Friends, Seinfeld,* and *Everybody Hates Chris.* (13) Overall, sitcoms are more appropriate for family viewing than sketch comedy.

# Effective Expression: Controlled Sentence Structure

Control of sentence structure enhances effective expression. You can express ideas through the use of four sentence types: simple, compound, complex, and compound-complex. Study the following definitions and examples of these four types of sentences.

**1**. A **simple sentence** contains one independent clause.

INDEPENDENT CLAUSE

The food pyramid classifies food into six groups.

**2**. A **compound sentence** contains two or more independent clauses. These clauses can be joined with:

**a.** A comma and a coordinating conjunction (*for, and, nor, but, or, yet, so*: FANBOYS),

INDEPENDENT CLAUSES

We must eat healthfully, and we must exercise regularly.

**b.** A semicolon,

INDEPENDENT CLAUSES

The food pyramid has two roles; it classifies food and features physical activity.

OR

**c.** A semicolon with a conjunctive adverb.

INDEPENDENT CLAUSES

MyPyramid.gov is helpful; for example, experts explain calorie values.

**3**. A **complex sentence** contains one independent clause and one or more dependent clauses. A dependent clause begins with a subordinating conjunction (such as *although, because, when, who, which,* and *that*) placed immediately before a subject and verb. Sometimes, the subordinating conjunction also serves as the subject of the verb in the dependent clause.

INDEPENDENT CLAUSE          DEPENDENT CLAUSE

Physical activity means movement of the body that uses energy.

**4**. A **compound-complex** sentence contains two or more independent clauses and one or more dependent clauses. This sentence type combines the traits of the compound and complex sentences.

DEPENDENT CLAUSE          INDEPENDENT CLAUSES

When we eat well and move often, we feel better, and we do more.

▲ Food Pyramid poster to promote healthy eating

Label each of the following sentences as a simple, compound, complex, or compound-complex sentence. Revise each sentence into the new type of sentence indicated. Discuss your work with your class or with a small group of your peers.

_____ **1.** Foods from wheat, rice, oats, cornmeal, barley, or another cereal grain are grain products. Bread, pasta, oatmeal, breakfast cereals, tortillas, and grits are examples of grain products.

REVISE INTO A COMPOUND SENTENCE: _____

_____

_____

_____ **2.** Oils are fats that are liquid at room temperature, like canola, olive, and other vegetable oils used in cooking.

REVISE INTO A COMPOUND-COMPLEX SENTENCE: _____

_____

_____

# Using Classification in Your Academic Courses

Classification plays two roles in most academic courses: (1) to narrow a topic and (2) to research a topic. First, any academic topic can be narrowed by breaking a larger topic into subgroups. For example, the following concept map was created for a paper about leadership in a sociology class.

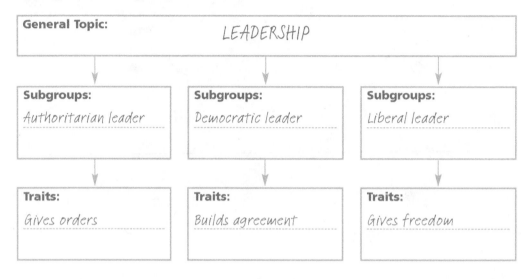

| General Topic: | LEADERSHIP | |
|---|---|---|
| **Subgroups:** Authoritarian leader | **Subgroups:** Democratic leader | **Subgroups:** Liberal leader |
| **Traits:** Gives orders | **Traits:** Builds agreement | **Traits:** Gives freedom |

**USING CLASSIFICATION TO NARROW AN ACADEMIC TOPIC**

Use the following classification concept map to narrow a topic for a history class. Work with a peer or small group of classmates.

| General Topic: | TYPES OF GOVERNMENT | |
|---|---|---|
| **Subgroups:** | **Subgroups:** Democracy | **Subgroups:** |
| **Traits:** | **Traits:** | **Traits:** Power is seized by an individual or group. |

Second, classification plays a key role in research because information is organized based on types. Two well-known methods of classifying information are the Dewey Decimal System and the Library of Congress System. Your college library uses one of these two types to arrange books on the shelves by labeling them with a system of letters and numbers. When you are assigned a research topic, you will use classification to find the information you need.

Practice 6

Listed below are the letters and titles of the main classes and one subgroup of the Library of Congress Classification. Study the list and answer the questions.

A – GENERAL WORKS
B – PHILOSOPHY. PSYCHOLOGY. RELIGION
C – AUXILIARY SCIENCES OF HISTORY
D – WORLD HISTORY AND HISTORY OF EUROPE, ASIA, AFRICA, AUSTRALIA, NEW ZEALAND, ETC.
E – HISTORY OF THE AMERICAS
F – HISTORY OF THE AMERICAS
G – GEOGRAPHY. ANTHROPOLOGY. RECREATION
H – SOCIAL SCIENCES
    H – Social Sciences (General)
    HA – Statistics
    HB – Economic theory. Demography
    HC – Economic history and conditions
    HD – Industries. Land use. Labor
    HE – Transportation and communications
    HF – Commerce
    HG – Finance
    HJ – Public finance
    HM – Sociology (General)
    HN – Social history and conditions. Social problems. Social reform

HQ – The family. Marriage. Women
HS – Societies: secret, benevolent, etc.
HT – Communities. Classes. Races
HV – Social pathology. Social and public welfare. Criminology
HX – Socialism. Communism Anarchism
J – POLITICAL SCIENCE
K – LAW
L – EDUCATION
M – MUSIC AND BOOKS ON MUSIC
N – FINE ARTS
P – LANGUAGE AND LITERATURE
Q – SCIENCE
R – MEDICINE
S – AGRICULTURE
T – TECHNOLOGY
U – MILITARY SCIENCE
V – NAVAL SCIENCE
Z – BIBLIOGRAPHY. LIBRARY SCIENCE. INFORMATION RESOURCES (GENERAL)

—"Library of Congress Classification Outline."
*Library of Congress* 5 July 2005. 14 August 2009
http://www.loc.gov/catdir/cpso/lcco/lcco.html

**1.** Write the letter of the group that would contain the following book titles:

..............  *Dealing with Relatives (—even if you can't stand them): Bringing Out the Best in Families at Their Worst* by Rick Brinkman and Rick Kirschner

..............  *Encyclopedia of Family Health*

**2.** Write the letter of the group that you would search for the following information:

..............  The principles of Islam

..............  The author Toni Morrison, winner of the Nobel Prize for Literature

# Workshop: Writing a Classification Paragraph Step by Step

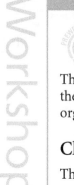

## Prewrite Your Paragraph

The various activities below will walk you through the steps of the prewriting stage of the writing process: choosing a topic, focusing your point, and generating and organizing relevant details.

### Choose Your Topic

The following activities are designed to help you choose a topic.

1. Create a bank of topics. Use the following headings to brainstorm or list as many categories and subgroups about each topic as you possibly can.
   Don't analyze your thoughts; just get as many relevant categories written down as quickly as possible. Add more topics and categories as they occur to you. Compare your bank of topics with those of your classmates.

   • Birth Order (traits of oldest, middle, youngest, only child)
   • Music
   • Technology
   • Vehicles
   • Life Roles

2. Generate ideas with a freewrite. Choose one of the topics from your topic bank and think of the traits that set a group or subgroup apart. Write about the traits of the group and subgroups for ten minutes without stopping.

   OR

   Select a photograph or series of photographs that illustrates a group or subgroup. Write captions, brainstorm traits, and freewrite about the photograph(s). Remember to ask "What is the group or subgroup represented by this picture(s)?" and "What's the point?"

### Focus Your Point

Read a freewrite you have generated for a classification. Underline words that suggest your values, opinions, or attitudes about the topic and its subgroups or categories. Think about why the traits are important. Think about what examples best represent the group, categories, or subgroups. Identify your audience and purpose. Write a list of additional concrete traits and examples that explain your point. State in one sentence the point of the groups, traits, and examples.

AUDIENCE: _____

PURPOSE: _____

LIST OF TRAITS: _____

WHAT'S THE POINT? _____

## Generate and Organize Relevant Details

Use the graphic organizer below to either organize the ideas you have already created or to generate details to support your point.

| Types (groups) of | | |
| --- | --- | --- |

| 1st Type/group | 2nd Type/group | 3rd Type/group |
| --- | --- | --- |

| Traits: | Traits: | Traits: |
| --- | --- | --- |

| Examples: | Examples: | Examples: |
| --- | --- | --- |

**What's the point?**

_____

_____

## Write a Draft of Your Paragraph

Using the ideas you generated during the prewriting phase, compose a draft of your classification paragraph. Return to the prewriting process at any time to generate additional details as needed. Use your own paper.

Workshop

# Revise Your Draft

Once you have created a draft of a classification paragraph, read the draft and answer the questions in the "Questions for Revising a Classification Paragraph" box. Indicate your answers by annotating your paper. If you answer "yes" to a question, underline, check, or circle examples. If you answer "no" to a question, write the additional details in the margin and draw lines to indicate their placement. Revise your paragraph based on your reflection. (*Hint:* Experienced writers create several drafts as they focus on one or two questions per draft.)

## Questions for Revising a Classification Paragraph:

☐ Have I made my point? Can I state my point in one sentence?

☐ Have I divided my topic into types, groups, or categories? Have I clearly labeled each group? Have I discussed the common traits and examples of each group?

☐ Have I used strong transitions of classification?

☐ Have I used concrete details to make my point?

☐ Have I included only the details that are relevant to my topic sentence?

☐ Have I used the following to make my ideas clear to my readers: vivid verbs and images, parallel language, controlled sentence structure?

# Proofread Your Draft

Once you have made any revisions to your paragraph that may be needed, proofread your paper to eliminate distracting errors such as comma splices.

For more information on eliminating comma splices, see pages 452–463.

### Grammar in Action: Eliminating Comma Splices

Comma splices and fused sentences have been categorized as two of the most common errors in student writing. Both the comma splice and the fused sentence occur when writers join ideas without the proper punctuation.

A **comma splice** occurs when a writer uses *only a comma* to join two or more independent clauses.

COMMA SPLICE

Americans enjoy many vacation options, some choose family bonding activities such as trips to family reunions or theme parks, others choose special-interest activities such as Bike Week in Daytona Beach or spring break in Cancun.

COMMA SPLICE

A **comma splice** can be corrected in three different ways.

---

**Three Rules for Properly Joining Two or More Independent Clauses**

A writer can properly join two or more independent clauses in several ways:
**1.** Use a comma AND a coordinating conjunction (*for, and, nor, but, or, yet, so*: FANBOYS).
**2.** Use a semicolon.
**3.** Use a semicolon with a transition (*for example, in addition, however, therefore, thus*, etc.).

---

Study the following examples:

**1.** Americans enjoy many vacation options; some choose family bonding activities such as trips to family reunions or theme parks, but others choose special-interest activities such as Bike Week in Daytona Beach or spring break in Cancun.

**2.** Some choose family bonding activities such as trips to family reunions or theme parks; others choose special-interest activities such as Bike Week in Daytona Beach or spring break in Cancun.

**3.** Americans enjoy many vacation options; for example, some choose family bonding activities such as trips to family reunions or theme parks.

---

### ELIMINATING COMMA SPLICES

Edit these sentences to eliminate comma splices. *Hint:* Underline subjects once and verbs twice to identify independent clauses.

**1.** My car matches my personality, we are both dependable and conservative.

**2.** Both of us are dependable, for example, I have perfect attendance, put in long hours, and meet my goals.

**3.** I have perfect attendance, put in long study hours, and maintain a high GPA, my Toyota Camry has a perfect maintenance record, gets great gas mileage, and lives up to its reputation.

# Review

Work with a classmate to give and receive feedback about your classification paragraphs. Use the following form to record your thinking about your writing process for your classification paragraph. Use the writer's journal on page 196 as a model for your own journal. Discuss the decisions you made as you wrote, and describe what you have learned by writing. Also, ask for advice about how to improve your paragraph.

MAIN IDEA: .................................................................................................................................

...............................................................................................................................................

...............................................................................................................................................

...............................................................................................................................................

LOGICAL ORDER: .........................................................................................................................

...............................................................................................................................................

...............................................................................................................................................

...............................................................................................................................................

RELEVANT DETAILS: ......................................................................................................................

...............................................................................................................................................

...............................................................................................................................................

...............................................................................................................................................

EFFECTIVE EXPRESSION: ..............................................................................................................

...............................................................................................................................................

...............................................................................................................................................

...............................................................................................................................................

## Considering Audience and Purpose

Study the set of photographs about the types of music at the beginning of the chapter. Assume you are a mentor to a young person who is just becoming interested in music. You have decided to start a collection of music for him or her. First, identify the type(s) of music you want to include in this gift collection. Create a list of specific artists and songs for the type or types of music you have chosen. Then, write a note to go with the gift; write a paragraph that explains the type(s) of music in the collection.

## Writing for Everyday Life

Assume you have just experienced an event as an invited guest, and you would like to follow up with a written thank you note. Write a one-paragraph thank you note in which you include the following information: the type of event, the quality of your experience, the most vivid aspects of the event, and the traits of your host that you appreciate. Choose words that reflect one of the following: (1) polite and reserved or (2) warm and enthusiastic.

## Writing for College Life

Assume you are in a college psychology class. Your teacher has assigned a chapter on "The Six Basic Emotions and Their Combinations" as the basis of discussion for your next class meeting. The teacher also requires you to keep a learning log. You have decided to record in your learning log what you currently know about these ideas before you begin your reading assignment. Write one paragraph in which you identify, describe, and classify six basic types of emotions you have observed or experienced.

## Writing for Working Life

Assume you are compiling information for a résumé for a position as manager trainee at a business such as Target, Best Buy, or Olive Garden. Use the following categories to create your résumé.

**Personal Information:** Name, address, phone number, and e-mail address

**Objective:** Manager Trainee position with <u>name of business</u>

**Education:**

**Work Experience:**

**Activities:**

# 9

# The Comparison and Contrast Paragraph

A comparison examines how two or more things are similar. A contrast looks at how two or more things are different.

Comparing and contrasting ideas is an essential part of critical thinking. When we choose between Subway and McDonald's or Apple and Dell computers, we are weighing the similarities or differences of products and services and making a choice by comparison shopping. What are some basic comparable points for any consumer to consider when shopping? What are some other situations in which we use comparable points as the basis of our thinking or actions?

In everyday life, we compare or contrast the neighborhoods we want to live in and the prices of homes we want to buy, or the honesty and policies of political candidates as we decide for whom we will vote. In working life, we compare or contrast the salaries, benefits, and working conditions among several career opportunities. In college life, we compare and contrast leaders, governments, cultures, literature, technology, writers, or philosophies in a wide range of courses.

To write a comparison or a contrast paragraph, identify the comparable points between two (or more) topics. Once you identify the points of comparison, brainstorm a list of similarities and differences for each one. Then, list and explain examples of each similarity or difference.

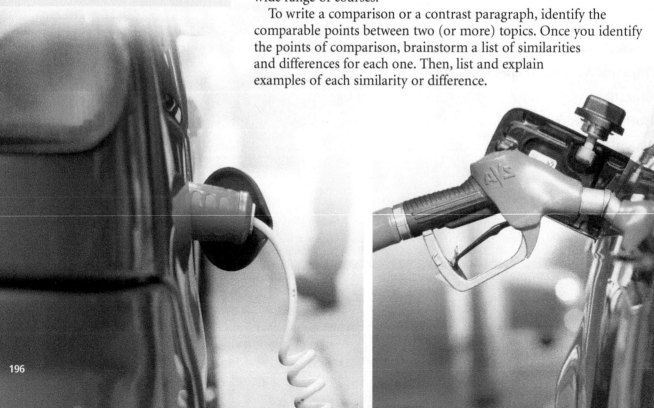

# What's the Point of Comparison and Contrast?

Often ideas become clearer when they are analyzed based on how they relate to one another. The comparison and contrast patterns of organization allow a writer to explore the ways in which ideas are related. The following set of photographs document some similarities and differences between electric and gas vehicles. Study the sets of images. Answer the following questions about each comparable point. Then answer the question "What's the point?" with a one-sentence statement of the overall main idea.

**PHOTOGRAPHIC ORGANIZER: COMPARE AND CONTRAST**

SIMILAR TO OR DIFFERENT FROM

GAS VEHICLES
(DODGE CHALLENGER)

ELECTRIC VEHICLES
(DODGE CIRCUIT EV)

What is the **1st** comparable point?

SIMILAR TO OR DIFFERENT FROM

What is the **2nd** comparable point?

SIMILAR TO OR DIFFERENT FROM

What is the **3rd** comparable point?

ELECTRIC VEHICLE
CHARGING STATION

**What's the point?**

Brainstorm about the images you just studied. Set a time limit, such as five minutes, and write in your notebook about the images and the details you generated. Write as quickly as you can without stopping. Let the ideas flow freely. Getting your first thoughts about a topic on paper is one excellent way to kick-start your writing process.

# Making a Point Using Comparison and Contrast: One Student Writer's Response

The following paragraph offers one writer's point about the similarities and differences between electric and gas vehicles as illustrated by the photographs. Read the comparison and contrast paragraph below and the explanations; complete the activities in **bold type** in the annotations. Then read the writer's journal entry that records decisions made during the writing process.

**LOGICAL ORDER:**
Words of comparison or contrast signal similarities or differences. **Circle two more signal words or phrases for comparison or contrast.**

**MAIN IDEA:**
The main idea is the point the author is making about the topic. **Underline the two topics being compared and contrasted and underline the author's point about the two topics.**

**RELEVANT DETAILS:**
Relevant details include descriptive details about similarities or differences between comparable points. **Draw a box around two more details of similarities or differences.**

**EFFECTIVE EXPRESSION:**
This sentence gives equal weight to both types of vehicles. **Double underline another sentence that expresses equal ideas with the use of semicolon.**

### Electric or Gas Vehicles?

(1) Pollution, global warming, and the price of fuel pose real problems for an auto industry churning out gas vehicles. (2) However, electric vehicles offer hope for the future. (3) A comparison between electric vehicles and gas vehicles shows pleasing similarities and differences. (4) Most electric vehicles look just like a gas vehicle. (5) For example, the electric-powered Dodge Circuit EV resembles the gas-powered Dodge Challenger. (6) Both sport the bold look of a muscle car, and both have all the standard features. (7) They even perform similarly; both go from 0 to 60 mph in 6 seconds. (8) Although these similarities promise to please, many drivers will really like the differences between electric and gas vehicles. (9) For example, the lithium-ion battery of the Circuit EV uses far less energy than the gas guzzling V8 engine used by the Challenger. (10) The Circuit EV can go 150 to 200 miles between charges and costs about $6 to $12 a week in electricity; in contrast, the Challenger averages 14 miles per gallon in the city and 22 on the highway. (11) Plus, based on the price of oil, gasoline can cost as much as $5 a gallon, and those dollars add up with the miles. (12) The final difference is convenience. (13) Many people and much energy must be used to refuel a gas vehicle. (14) Oil has to be refined into gasoline, stored, transported, and pumped. (15) However, to recharge an electric vehicle, all one has to do is plug it into a standard household outlet or a socket on a charging station.

# The Writer's Journal

## PEER EDITING

The student writer of "Electric or Gas Vehicles?" completed the following reflection to record his thinking through the writing process. Read his writer's journal that describes a few key choices he made as he wrote. Then, in the given space, answer his questions about his use of effective expression in his paragraph. Work with a peer or a small group of classmates.

EFFECTIVE EXPRESSION: *I used coordination to state most of my ideas because I wanted to be sure to cover each point equally, like in sentences 6, 7, and 10. Does the repeated use of signal words for comparison and contrast make my paragraph boring or interesting? Why? I also had trouble with some of my word choices. I really support electric vehicles, but I couldn't find the right words to get my support across. For example, I am not really satisfied with the word "pleasing" in sentence 3. Should I leave it out, or could you suggest another word? Is it important to give my opinion, or should I stick with just the facts?*

ELECTRIC VEHICLE
CHARGING STATION

# Developing Your Point Using Comparison and Contrast

A **comparison** makes a point by discussing the *similarities* between two or more topics. A **contrast** makes a point by discussing the *differences* between two or more topics. To support a point through comparison or contrast, a writer identifies the comparable points of the topic, offers relevant and concrete descriptions and examples for each comparable point, and effectively uses coordination and subordination of ideas.

## The Point: The Main Idea

When you write a comparison or a contrast piece, you limit your thoughts to a set of topics based on their relationship to each other. Most likely you have an opinion or belief about the two topics and their comparable points. Your opinion is your point or main idea. In a comparison or contrast paragraph, you also reveal your opinion by discussing the topics and their points of similarities or differences in the order of your own choosing. A topic sentence states the overall point of the comparison or the contrast between the two topics.

For example, the following topic sentence contains (1) the comparable topics, (2) the writer's opinion about the topic, and (3) the pattern of organization used to organize details.

The comparable topics are "Giada De Laurentiis" and "Rachael Ray, celebrity chefs." The pattern of organization is established with words "even though" and "differ." The writer's opinion is stated with the clause "styles differ greatly."

*PATTERN OF ORGANIZATION: TRANSITION WORDS THAT SIGNAL CONTRAST*

*TOPIC*

Even though Giada De Laurentiis and Rachael Ray are both celebrity chefs, their styles differ greatly. ◄——*WRITER'S OPINION*

---

### TOPIC SENTENCES

Practice creating topic sentences. The first two items present a topic, an opinion, and comparison and contrast signal word(s). Combine the ideas to create a topic sentence for a comparison or a contrast. Then, complete the practice by making your own topic sentences.

1. TOPIC: *the communication styles of men and women*

OPINION: *significant*

COMPARISON OR CONTRAST SIGNAL WORDS: *differ three ways*

TOPIC SENTENCE:

*Practice 2*

# Logical Order

Once you have identified the comparable points between your topics and have focused on a main idea, you are ready to generate and organize additional details. To make a point using comparison or contrast, a writer moves from a general idea (the comparison or contrast of two or more topics) to a major support (a comparable point about the topics) to minor supports (details or examples of the comparable point about the topics). To signal the movement among these levels of ideas, a writer uses transitions to signal similarities or differences and examples. Strong transitions establish coherence, a clear and understandable flow of ideas.

## Words That Signal Comparison

| | | | | |
|---|---|---|---|---|
| alike | equally | in the same way | likewise | similarity |
| as | in a similar fashion | just as | resemble | similarly |
| as well as | in a similar way | just like | same | |
| equal | in like manner | like | similar | |

## Words That Signal Contrast

| | | | | |
|---|---|---|---|---|
| although | conversely | differently | more | on the other hand |
| as opposed to | despite | even though | most | still |
| at the same time | difference | in contrast | nevertheless | to the contrary |
| but | different | in spite of | on the contrary | unlike |
| by contrast | different from | instead | on the one hand | yet |

---

**LOGICAL ORDER**

Based on the logical order of ideas, fill in the blanks with the appropriate comparison or contrast signal words. Compare and discuss your answers with a peer or in a small group of your classmates.

If you could build your ideal mate, he or she would probably look, act, and think very much _____ you. By being attracted to people _____ yourself, you validate yourself. You tell yourself that you're worthy of being liked. _____ there are exceptions, the _____ factor probably means that you will be attracted to your own mirror image. You will be attracted to people who are _____ to you in nationality, race, ability, physical traits, intelligence, attitudes, and so on. If you were to ask a group of friends, "To whom are you _____ attracted?" they would probably name the _____ attractive people they know. _____ if you were to watch these friends, you would find that they have relationships with people who are about _____ in attractiveness.

--adapted from DeVito, Joseph A. *The Interpersonal Communication Book,* 11th ed., 2007. p. 236.

Practice 3

# Relevant Details

As a writer narrows a topic into a focused main idea, the thinking process brings to mind many details that answer the questions *who, what, when, where, why,* and *how.* A writer evaluates the relevance of each detail and uses only those that clarify or support the main idea. In a comparison or contrast paragraph, some relevant major details include those that identify comparable topics or points. Relevant minor details offer examples and explanations of the similarities or differences between comparable points. Relevant details include descriptions, explanations, and examples of similarities or differences between two or more topics. Details are logically ordered to best support the point.

**Comparable Topics in a Venn Diagram**

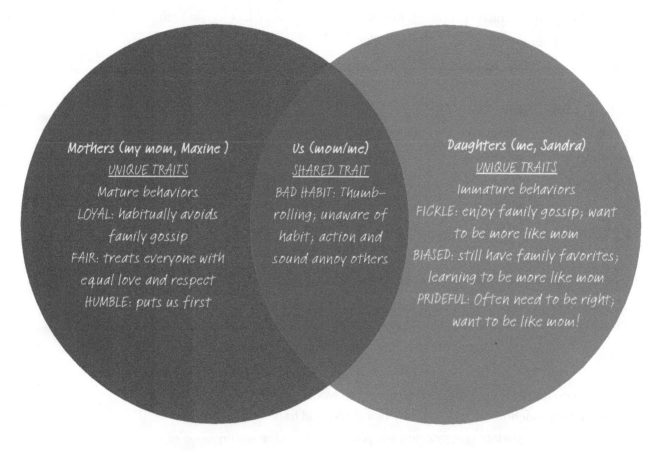

During the prewriting phase, a writer naturally generates irrelevant details. In fact, an effective writer often produces far more details than can be used to make a specific point. Irrelevant details do not explain or support the focused point of the paragraph. A careful writer uses the revision process to double check details for relevance and to eliminate irrelevant ones.

The following paragraph explains and illustrates the ideas generated using the Venn diagram. Circle the main idea. Underline the words that signal similarities or differences and double underline three supporting points of similarities discussed in the paragraph. Cross out two details that are not relevant to the main point.

### Bonds of Habits Tie Us Together

(1) I never realized how similar parents and their children can be. (2) My mother, Maxine, has a habit of rolling her thumbs. (3) She sits with her hands clasped, fingers laced, and thumbs rolling. (4) The action creates a soft rhythmic swish as the pad of one thumb brushes the top of her other thumb. (5) I don't know why, but the sight and sound of mother's thumb-rolling drives me to distraction. (6) Sometimes, I can hardly concentrate on my thoughts. (7) She remains completely unaware of the habit or how much it bothers me. (8) The one time I mentioned the behavior, she was embarrassed, and she tried for a while to break herself of the habit. (9) Although I vowed never to develop any such quirk, I recently caught myself in the middle of my own mother-like thumb roll. (10) As my husband described his golf swing, his eyes kept darting to my hands in the same way my own eyes react to Mom's thumb roll. (11) Suddenly he fell silent mid-sentence. (12) We heard a sound just like the one made by mother's thumb roll. (13) Just like my mother, I sat with my hands clasped, fingers laced, and thumbs rolling. (14) My husband asked, "Maxine," (he called me by mother's name instead of my name!) "Maxine, are you aware that you are a thumb-roller? (15) And that, for some reason, it gets on my nerves?" (16) My habit of leaving lids loose on containers also drives my husband nuts. (17) Now I know just how maddeningly similar parents and their children can be.

# Effective Expression: Use of Coordination and Subordination

Effective expression reflects a writer's thoughtful match of ideas to words and structure. Two types of sentence structures enable effective expression of comparison or contrast: coordination and subordination.

**Coordination** expresses an **equal** relationship between **similarities** with words such as: *and, likewise, similarly, also.* Coordination expresses an **equal** relationship between **differences** with words such as *but, yet, or, however, in contrast.*

A **compound sentence** is an example of **coordination**.

**Example**

An athlete trains the body for competitions; *likewise,* a student trains the mind for final exams.

**Subordination** expresses an **unequal** relationship between **similarities** with words such as: *as, just as, just like, like.* **Subordination** expresses an **unequal** relationship between **differences** with words such as *although, even though, while.*

A **complex sentence** is an example of **subordination**.

**Example**

*Just as* an athlete trains the body for competitions, a student trains the mind for final exams.

For more information on coordination and subordination, see pages 411–412.

## USING COORDINATION AND SUBORDINATION

Label each of the following sentences as a compound or a complex sentence. Identify the pattern of organization expressed by each sentence as comparison, contrast, or both.

**1.** Although the pessimist and the optimist face many of the same challenges in life, they differ greatly in their actions, words, and thoughts.

SENTENCE TYPE: ........................................................................................

PATTERN OF ORGANIZATION: ........................................................................

**2.** Just as the pessimist faces rejection and disappointments, the optimist endures those same hardships common to all humans.

SENTENCE TYPE: ........................................................................................

PATTERN OF ORGANIZATION: ........................................................................

**3.** The pessimist focuses on problems and remains passive; in contrast, the optimist focuses on solutions and takes action.

SENTENCE TYPE: ........................................................................................

PATTERN OF ORGANIZATION: ........................................................................

*Practice 5*

# Using Comparison and Contrast in Your Academic Courses

College writing assignments are often based on information gathered through class lectures, textbook reading assignments, and research. For example, essay exams often test students on material given in class or assigned in readings. Note-taking is an excellent pretest and prewriting activity. When you take or revise notes, set up a graphic organizer into which you can plug information from your class notes or reading assignments. A popular note-taking graphic divides an 11-inch by 8.5-inch page into three sections: a 8-inch by 3-inch left margin for key terms; a 8-inch by 5-inch right margin for notes; and a 3-inch by 8.5-inch wide bottom margin for a summary. This format allows you to write, reflect, and write for understanding as you study.

| Key Terms | Notes |
|---|---|
| | |
| | |
| | |
| Summary | |

## USING COMPARISON AND CONTRAST IN AN ART APPRECIATION COURSE: TAKING NOTES

Study the following set of notes taken during a lecture in a college art appreciation class. In the bottom margin, write a short paragraph that states and supports the main idea of the notes.

| Tragic hero | Virtuous, admirable, rich, powerful, and male, but flawed; inner conflict and guilt; accepts responsibility for suffering; loses all. |
|---|---|
| Example | 5th Century BCE: In Oedipus the King, Oedipus loses power, wealth, family, and independence due to his limited wisdom and great pride. |
| Melodramatic hero | A symbol of good, male or female, a stereotype of courage and honesty, etc. No flaws; no inner conflict or guilt; fights against and defeats evil; all ends well. |
| Example | Pauline, the heroine of Perils of Pauline, is a "damsel in distress" who escapes many life-threatening, thrilling perils (dangers) due to her courage and ingenuity. |

Summary: What are the differences between a tragic hero and a melodramatic hero?

# Workshop: Writing a Comparison and Contrast Paragraph Step by Step

 ## Choose Your Topic

The following activities are designed to help you choose a topic.

1. Create a bank of topics. Use the headings given below to brainstorm, or list as many similarities or differences about sets of topics as you possibly can. Don't criticize your thoughts. Add more topics, similarities, or differences as they occur to you. Revisit topic banks created during your study of previous chapters and identify comparable topics. Compare your bank of topics with those of your classmates.

   - Family Members
   - Natural Disasters
   - Neighborhoods
   - Movies

2. Generate ideas with a freewrite. Choose one of the topics from your topic bank and think about the points of similarities or differences. Write about the similarities or differences for ten minutes without stopping.

   OR

   Select a set of photographs that illustrates the similarities or differences between two topics. Write a caption, brainstorm comparable points, and freewrite about the photograph(s). Remember to ask, "What are the similarities or differences represented by these images?" and "What's the point?"

## Focus Your Point

Read a prewrite you have generated for a comparison or contrast paragraph. Identify your audience and purpose. Annotate the text: Underline or insert words that suggest your values, opinions, or attitudes about the topics and their points of similarity or difference. State in a sentence or two the importance of each similarity or difference between the comparable topics. Generate one or more concrete examples for each comparable point. Finally, state the point of the comparison or contrast paragraph in one sentence.

AUDIENCE: 

PURPOSE: 

LIST OF CONCRETE EXAMPLES: 

WHAT'S THE POINT?

# Generate and Organize Relevant Details

Using ideas you have recorded so far and the concept chart below, generate and organize details that support your point.

| Concept Chart: Comparison/Contrast | | | |
|---|---|---|---|
| COMPARABLE TOPICS: | TOPIC A | LIKE OR UNLIKE | TOPIC B |
| **1st** attribute, point, basis of comparison | | Like or unlike | |
| **2nd** attribute, point, basis of comparison | | Like or unlike | |
| **3rd** attribute, point, basis of comparison | | Like or unlike | |

What's the point?

------------------------------------------------

------------------------------------------------

------------------------------------------------

------------------------------------------------

# Write a Draft of Your Paragraph

Using the ideas you generated during the prewriting phase, compose a draft of your comparison or contrast paragraph. Return to the prewriting process at any time to generate additional details as needed. Use your own paper.

# Revise Your Draft

Once you have created a draft of your comparison or contrast paragraph, read the draft and answer the questions in the "Questions for Revising a Comparison and Contrast" box that follows. Indicate your answers by annotating your paper. If you answer "yes" to a question, underline, check, or circle examples. If you answer "no" to a question, write the additional details in the margins and draw lines to indicate their placement. Revise your paragraph based on your reflection.

## Questions for Revising a Comparison and Contrast Paragraph:

☐ Have I chosen appropriately comparable topics? Have I clearly labeled each comparable point as a similarity or a difference?

☐ Have I made my point? Can I state my point in one sentence?

☐ Are my ideas logically and clearly ordered? Have I used strong transitions of comparison or contrast?

☐ Have I used concrete details to make my point?

☐ Have I included only the details that are relevant to my topic sentence?

☐ Have I used the following to make my ideas clear and interesting to my readers: vivid verbs and images, parallel language, controlled sentence structure, coordination, or subordination?

# Proofread Your Draft

Once you have revised your paragraph, proofread to ensure precise usage and grammar, such as editing for proper use of a comma after introductory elements.

## Grammar in Action: Commas after Introductory Elements

Commas are used after introductory elements: a word, phrase, or dependent clause that comes before an independent clause.

A dependent clause—an incomplete thought containing a subject and a verb—is signaled by a subordinating conjunction (*although, because, while…*) or a relative pronoun (*who, which, that…*).

An independent clause is a complete thought containing a subject and a verb.

- **Introductory word used with independent clause**

  Similarly, Sandra twiddles her thumbs.

- **Introductory phrase used with independent clause**

  In contrast, comedy's main purpose is to entertain.

- **Introductory dependent clause used with independent clause**

  Although Bob and Tom are both baby boomers, they differ greatly in values and lifestyles.

### COMMAS AND INTRODUCTORY ELEMENTS

Edit the following sentences for proper use of a comma after an introductory element. Identify the type of introductory element used in each sentence.

*Hint:* To identify a dependent clause, look for subordinating conjunctions and relative pronouns immediately in front of a subject and verb. To identify an independent clause, underline subjects once and verbs twice; then check to be sure a subordinating conjunction or relative pronoun does not come first.

............... 1. Unlike those who are habitually late  Consuelo has received three merit raises for prompt, efficient work.

............... 2. Like a fire hydrant opened full force  Deborah poured out her grief.

............... 3. However  the traveling nurse program offers better pay and greater mobility.

............... 4. The oldest child enjoyed the full attention of her parents; in contrast  the youngest child always had to share her parents' attention with her siblings.

# Review

Work with a classmate to give and receive feedback about your comparison and contrast paragraphs. Use the following form to record your thinking about your writing process for your comparison and contrast paragraph. Use the writer's journal on page 161 as a model for your own journal. Discuss the decisions you made as you wrote, and describe what you have learned by writing. Also, ask for advice about how to improve your paragraph.

MAIN IDEA: ................................................................................................................

LOGICAL ORDER: ........................................................................................................

RELEVANT DETAILS: ....................................................................................................

EFFECTIVE EXPRESSION: ..............................................................................................

## Considering Audience and Purpose

Study the set of photographs that show the similarities and differences between electric and gas vehicles. Write a letter to your United States Senator or to the editor of your local newspaper. In your letter call for support for either the electric or the gas vehicle. Explain the points of comparison that prove one better than the other.

## Writing for Everyday Life

Assume that you have just experienced a life-altering event, such as a near-death experience, a graduation, a marriage, the birth of a child, a severe loss, or the breaking of a bad habit. You have been asked to talk about "Change" to a specific audience such as the Rotary Club, a civic group. Identify your audience and write a short speech in which you discuss three before-and-after comparable points. Allow your tone through word choice to reflect either sadness and regret or pride and encouragement.

## Writing for College Life

Assume you are in a biology class and you read the following textbook question on the study guide for the final exam: "In what ways did the human skeleton change as upright posture and bipedalism evolved? Describe the changes by comparing the human skeleton and the skeleton of a quadruped such as a baboon." – Campbell, Mitchell, and Reece. *Biology: Concepts and Connections*, 5th ed. 2005 Longman. p. 620.

Test what you already know about the subject by writing a paragraph. Identify the comparable points of similarities and/or differences between the two topics. Look up words in your dictionary as needed.

## Writing for Working Life

Assume that you are applying for a management position at a local business or mid-sized company. You had the following positions and experiences, which are listed on your résumé: Treasurer, Student Government Association; Certified in various computer programs and software; Member of Toastmasters, a public-speaking organization. Write a paragraph in which you compare the skills you've developed with the skills needed at the job for which you are applying.

---

**PEARSON**
**mywritinglab**

**WANT A BETTER GRADE?**
For more practice with comparison and contrast, go to **www.mywritinglab.com** > Using Patterns of Organization to Develop Paragraphs > The Comparison and Contrast Paragraph.

# 10

# The Definition Paragraph

A definition explains what a word or concept means.

We are all familiar with the word *definition*. In fact, we apply or create definitions in every aspect of life. Call to mind what you already know about a definition. Answer the following questions: How would you define "a good life"? What are the traits and examples of "a good life"? What information should be included in a definition?

The definition pattern of organization is helpful in all areas of life. In personal life, you rely upon a doctor's definition of your symptoms when you seek medical treatment. In working life, you define your job duties to ensure your best performance. In college life, you will define the specialized meanings and examples of words in each content area.

To write a definition paragraph, the writer names a concept, explains its traits, describes the concept using similar terms, and offers examples of the concept. Often a contrast clarifies meaning; thus, a writer may also include an example and explanation of what the term or concept is *not*.

# What's the Point of a Definition?

The following definition-concept chart shows three visual examples of a concept and one visual example of what the concept is not. Study the chart and the visual examples. Then, write answers to the questions asked in the chart. Consider these questions as you write your answers: What is the concept being defined? What are some examples? What traits does each example represent? Then, answer the question "What's the point?" with a one-sentence statement of the overall main idea.

PHOTOGRAPHIC ORGANIZER: DEFINITION

**Definition Concept Chart**

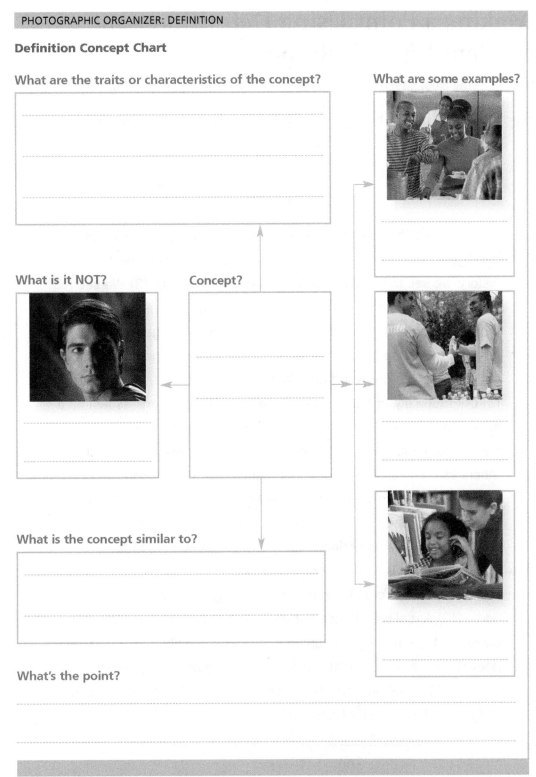

*Concept map adapted from following sources:*

Frayer, D., Frederick, W. C., and Klausmeier, H. J. (1969). *A Schema for Testing the Level of Cognitive Mastery.* Madison, WI: Wisconsin Center for Education Research.

Schwartz, R., & Raphael, T. (1985). "Concept of definition: A Key to Improving Student's Vocabulary." *The Reading Teacher,* 39, 198-205.

Brainstorm about the images you just studied. Set a time limit, such as five minutes, and write in your notebook about the images and the details you generated. Write as quickly as you can without stopping. Let the ideas flow freely. Getting your first thoughts about a topic on paper is one excellent way to overcome writer's block and set your mind to thinking.

# Making a Point Using Definition: One Student Writer's Response

The following paragraph offers one writer's point about the concept depicted in the photographs. Read the definition and the explanations; complete the activities in **bold type** in the annotations. Then read the writer's journal entry that records decisions made during the writing process.

## An Everyday Hero

**EFFECTIVE EXPRESSION:**
Vivid images make your point interesting and memorable. This phrase paints a vivid picture in the reader's mind.
**Double underline three more vivid images.**

**RELEVANT DETAILS:**
Relevant details include descriptive details about traits and examples.
**Draw boxes around two additional traits of a hero.**

**LISTING ORDER:**
The transition "third" indicates that a list of at least three traits are listed.
**Circle two other transitions that introduce supporting details.**

**MAIN IDEA:**
The main idea states the author's point about a concept. The concept being defined is "hero."
**Underline the writer's point about the concept.**

(1) Every evening, the news reminds us that times are difficult and our needs are great. (2) Even in this nation, one of the wealthiest in history, we see too many who are hungry or homeless. (3) We see too many suffering with diseases such as AIDS and cancer. (4) We see too many who don't have the literacy skills needed to get and hold a job. (5) It would be great if life were like the movies, and a superhero could swoop into our world and defeat hunger, disease, and illiteracy. (6) Unfortunately, in the real world, we can't find solutions as fast as a speeding bullet. (7) In the real world, we need real-life everyday heroes. (8) First, we need compassionate people who care about others as much as they care about themselves. (9) Second, we need humble people who want to serve others without looking for a reward. (10) Third, we need dedicated people who won't quit no matter what. (11) A real hero is an ordinary person who makes a significant difference in the lives of others. (12) A real hero seeks out the hungry and homeless to serve them hot meals and give them safe, warm beds. (13) A real hero hands out water at a charity walk to defeat disease. (14) A real hero volunteers to read to a child. (15) A real hero doesn't have x-ray eyesight, superhuman strength, or supersonic speed. (16) A real hero has better gifts--a vision of hope, the strength of faith, and the speed of good-will.

# The Writer's Journal

## PEER EDITING

The student writer of "An Everyday Hero" completed the following reflection to record her thinking through the writing process. Read her writer's journal that describes a few key choices she made as she wrote. Then, in the given space, answer her questions about her use of main idea, relevant details, and effective expression in her paragraph. Work with a peer or a small group of classmates.

MAIN IDEA: *I didn't state my main idea until sentence 11. Should I have stated it earlier in the paragraph? Why or why not?*

RELEVANT DETAILS: *Sentences 8–10 give examples of a real hero. Are these examples specific enough? Or should I have named names and told little stories about each example?*

EFFECTIVE EXPRESSION: *I tried to use vivid images to make my paragraph interesting. For example, I used words like "swoop" and "defeat" and "as fast as a speeding bullet." And I rewrote the last two sentences a lot just for vivid images; I want to show the difference between a make-believe hero and a real hero. Do these vivid images help make my point? Why or why not? Do you have any suggestions to improve my wording? Also does my paragraph sound choppy? If so, where?*

# Developing Your Point Using Definition

A definition clarifies the meaning of a concept. A definition makes a point by classifying a concept, describing its traits, describing what it is *like*, describing what it is *not like*, and illustrating it with examples. To support a point by definition, a writer may also use figurative language.

## The Point: The Main Idea

When you write a definition paragraph, most likely, you have an opinion or belief about the concept, characteristics, or examples. Your opinion is your point or main idea. A topic sentence states the overall point of the definition. Often a definition topic sentence emphasizes one aspect of the definition: its class, its traits, what it is like, or what it is not like.

For example, each of the following two topic sentences contains (1) a concept, (2) the writer's attitude about the concept, and (3) the pattern of organization used to organize details.

### Definition by Classification: Group or Traits

TOPIC

PATTERN OF ORGANIZATION:
DEFINITION SIGNAL WORDS

WRITER'S OPINION

A classical hero is a male character who suffers due to his pride.

### Definition by Comparison: Synonyms or Analogies

TOPIC

PATTERN OF ORGANIZATION:
DEFINITION SIGNAL WORDS

Faith is like a tree. ◄── WRITER'S OPINION

---

**Practice 2**

### TOPIC SENTENCES

The items present a topic, an opinion, and definition signal words. Combine the ideas in each group to create a topic sentence for a definition.

**1.** TOPIC: *depression*

OPINION: *treatable illness that affects the body and mind*

DEFINITION SIGNAL WORDS: *is a*

TOPIC SENTENCE: _____

**2.** TOPIC: *a hypocrite*

OPINION: *a spy or traitor*

DEFINITION SIGNAL WORDS: *is*

TOPIC SENTENCE: _____

# Logical Order

Once you have narrowed your topic into a focused subject, you are ready to generate and organize additional details. To make a point using definition, a writer moves from a general idea (the concept to be defined) to major and minor supporting details. These include traits and examples of *what it is, what it is like,* or *what it is not like.* To signal the relationship between these levels of ideas, a writer often uses the following pattern of wording: "A concept is…"; "A term means…"; "for example."   Strong signal words establish coherence, a clear and understandable flow of ideas.

## Key Words and Transition Words That Signal Definition

| | | | |
|---|---|---|---|
| also | constitutes | in particular | means |
| another trait | defined as | indicates | one trait |
| are | denotes | is | specifically |
| connotes | for example | is not | such as |
| consists of | in addition | like | suggests |

---

**RELATIONSHIP OF DETAILS**

Fill in the blanks with the appropriate transition or signal words for definition. Work with a peer or in a small group of your classmates.

### Sexual Harassment

Sexual harassment _____ a form of sex discrimination. _____, unwelcome sexual advances, requests for sexual favors, and other verbal or physical conduct of a sexual nature is sexual harassment when submission to or rejection of this conduct affects an individual's employment, interferes with an individual's work performance, or creates a hostile or offensive work environment. Sexual harassment can occur in a variety of situations, _____ the following. _____, the victim as well as the harasser may be a woman or a man. The victim does not have to be of the opposite sex. Second, the harasser can be the victim's supervisor, an agent of the employer, a supervisor in another area, a co-worker, or a non-employee. _____, the victim does not have to be the person harassed but could be anyone affected by the offensive conduct. _____, unlawful sexual harassment may occur without economic injury to or discharge of the victim. _____, the harasser's conduct must be unwelcome. An example is a co-worker who regularly tells sexually explicit jokes and makes demeaning comments about male coworkers and clients.

—Adapted from United States Equal Employment Opportunity Commission. *"Facts about Sexual Harassment."* 15 April 2009

# Relevant Details

As a writer narrows a topic into a focused main idea, the thinking process brings to mind many details that answer questions such as *who, what, when, where, why,* and *how.* A writer evaluates the relevance of each detail and uses only those that clarify or support the main idea. In a definition paragraph, some relevant major details include those that classify and describe the traits of a term or concept. Relevant minor details offer examples and illustrations of the term or concept as defined. Some major and minor details may explain the writer's opinion about the concept. Relevant details include types, traits, descriptions, and examples of the concept being defined.

During the prewriting phase, a concept chart can help a writer organize ideas. Study the following Definition Concept Chart about the topic "graffiti."

**Definition Concept Chart**

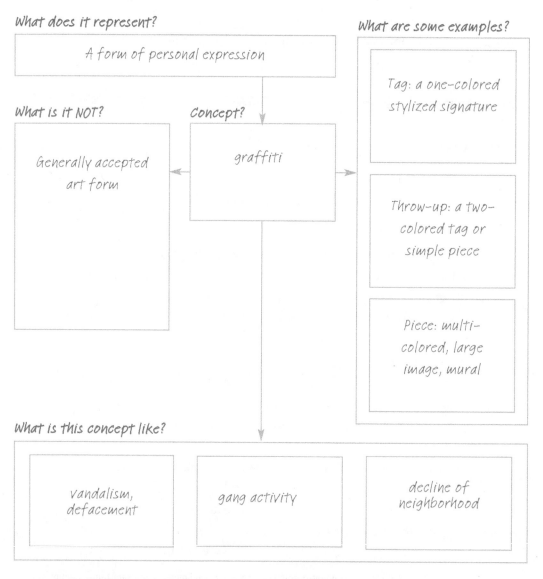

What does it represent?

A form of personal expression

What are some examples?

Tag: a one-colored stylized signature

Throw-up: a two-colored tag or simple piece

Piece: multi-colored, large image, mural

What is it NOT?

Generally accepted art form

Concept?

graffiti

What is this concept like?

vandalism, defacement

gang activity

decline of neighborhood

During the prewriting phase, a writer naturally generates irrelevant details. In fact, an effective writer often produces far more details than can be used to make a specific point. Irrelevant details do not explain or support the focused point of the paragraph. A careful writer uses the revision process to double check details for relevance and to eliminate irrelevant ones.

The following paragraph develops the ideas generated about graffiti during the brainstorming and prewriting phases. Circle the main idea. Underline the three major details. Cross out two details that are not relevant to the main point.

### Graffiti

(1) Although graffiti is a common sight, many do not understand its true nature: vandalism. (2) Graffiti, a form of personal expression, is the unlawful markings of an individual or group on private and public surfaces. (3) One type of graffiti is known as a tag, a stylized signature of a tagger or writer. (4) A tag is quickly created with one color that starkly contrasts with the background upon which it is written. (5) Tags can be written with spray paint, fat-tipped markers, etching tools, or pre-tagged stickers. (6) Another kind of graffiti is the throw-up, a two-dimensional image made with large bubble letters that are outlined in black or white and filled in with another color. (7) A writer often uses throw-ups to bomb an area in a short amount of time. (8) A third type of graffiti, similar to a mural, is the piece, short for masterpiece. (9) Time-consuming to create, a piece is a large, colorful, and complex image that usually reflects a political or social issue. (10) Piecing demonstrates a high level of aerosol paint control. (11) Unlike more widely accepted forms of art, graffiti is not generally regarded as aesthetically pleasing, nor is it thought of as a means to explore or enhance the appreciation of beauty. (12) Graffiti is much more likely to be labeled as vandalism and defacement, and seen as evidence of a gang or a neighborhood in decline. (13) Instances of graffiti are evident in both urban and suburban public areas such as parks, restrooms, buildings, and trains. (14) Graffiti can be removed by scraping, power washing, chemically treating, or painting the affected surface. (15) Many communities fight graffiti by offering legal walls as concrete canvases for graffiti writers.

▲ An example of "throw-up" graffiti

▲ Mural-style graffiti

▲ An example of tagging

# Effective Expression: Sound Structure and Vivid Images

Effective expression reflects a writer's thoughtful match of ideas to words and structure. Writers rely heavily on the various forms of the *to be* verb (such as *is*) to write a definition. Often the use of *is* leads to nonstandard phrasing or bland expressions. To add interest and maintain clarity, consider the following hints.

**Hint 1:** Avoid *is when* and *is where* to construct your definition. One way to eliminate *is when* and *is where* is to follow the verb with a synonym that renames the subject of the sentence.

**Nonstandard**

Addiction is when a person has a compulsive need for a habit-forming substance such as alcohol.

**Revised**

Addiction is a compulsive need for a habit-forming substance such as alcohol.

**Hint 2:** Use *is* to create a vivid image. A vivid image often allows the writer to express a point about the concept being defined.

Addiction is a self-made prison of compulsive need.

**Hint 3:** Replace *is* with an action verb. An action verb often allows the writer to express a point about the concept being defined.

Addiction imprisons a person in the compulsive need for habit-forming substances such as alcohol.

---

### SOUND STRUCTURE AND VIVID IMAGES

Revise the following sentences to avoid nonstandard phrasing or bland expressions. Discuss your work with your class or with a small group of your peers.

**1.** An input device is where a machine feeds data into a computer, such as a keyboard.

REVISED: ............................................................................

............................................................................

**2.** A character is when any symbol requires a byte of memory or storage in computer software.

REVISED: ............................................................................

............................................................................

▲ Input device

*Practice 5*

220

# Using Definition in Your Academic Courses

The definition paragraph serves as an excellent way to write for understanding. By defining key concepts and specialized vocabulary in your content courses, you will deepen your learning.

**USING DEFINITION IN A COMMUNICATIONS ASSIGNMENT: DEFINING SPECIALIZED VOCABULARY**

The following definition concept chart is based on information taken from a college communications textbook. Demonstrate your understanding of the concept and the relationship among the details in the definition. Using your own words, write a definition of the concept in the space below.

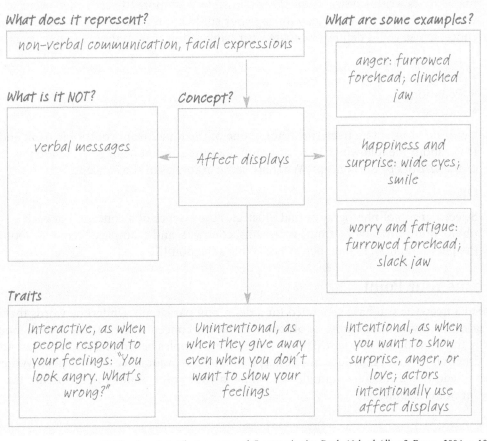

**What does it represent?**

non-verbal communication, facial expressions

**What is it NOT?**

verbal messages

**Concept?**

Affect displays

**What are some examples?**

anger: furrowed forehead; clinched jaw

happiness and surprise: wide eyes; smile

worry and fatigue: furrowed forehead; slack jaw

**Traits**

Interactive, as when people respond to your feelings: "You look angry. What's wrong?"

Unintentional, as when they give away even when you don't want to show your feelings

Intentional, as when you want to show surprise, anger, or love; actors intentionally use affect displays

—DeVito, Joseph A. *The Interpersonal Communication Book, 10th ed.* Allyn & Bacon, 2004, p. 182.

# Workshop: Writing a Definition Paragraph Step by Step

### Choose Your Topic

The following activities are designed to help you choose a topic.

1. Create a bank of topics. Use the headings below to brainstorm or list as many concepts to be defined as you possibly can. Don't analyze your thoughts; just get as many topics written down as quickly as possible. Add more topics as they occur to you. Revisit topic banks created during your study of previous chapters for terms or concepts you could define. Compare your bank of topics with those of your peers.

   - Hip Hop Music
   - Role Models
   - Pollution
   - Success

2. Generate ideas with a freewrite. Choose one of the topics from your topic bank and think about the following: To what group does the concept belong? What are the characteristics of the concept? What are some examples of the concept?

   OR

   Select a group of photographs that illustrates the essence of a concept. For each photo: brainstorm types, traits, synonyms, contrasts, and examples. Freewrite about the photograph(s). Remember to ask "What's the point?"

## Focus Your Point

Read a freewrite you have generated for a definition paragraph. Underline words that suggest your values, opinions, or attitudes about the concept and its traits. Think about why the concept is important. Think about what examples best represent each trait and a situation that best illustrates the concept. Identify your audience and purpose. Write a list of additional concrete examples that explain your point. State in one sentence the point of the definition.

AUDIENCE: ......................................................................................................................................

PURPOSE: ........................................................................................................................................

...........................................................................................................................................................

LIST OF DETAILS AND EXAMPLES: ...................................................................................................

...........................................................................................................................................................

WHAT'S THE POINT? ......................................................................................................................

...........................................................................................................................................................

# Generate and Organize Relevant Details

Using ideas you have recorded so far and the following definition concept chart, generate and organize details that support your point.

**Definition Concept Chart**

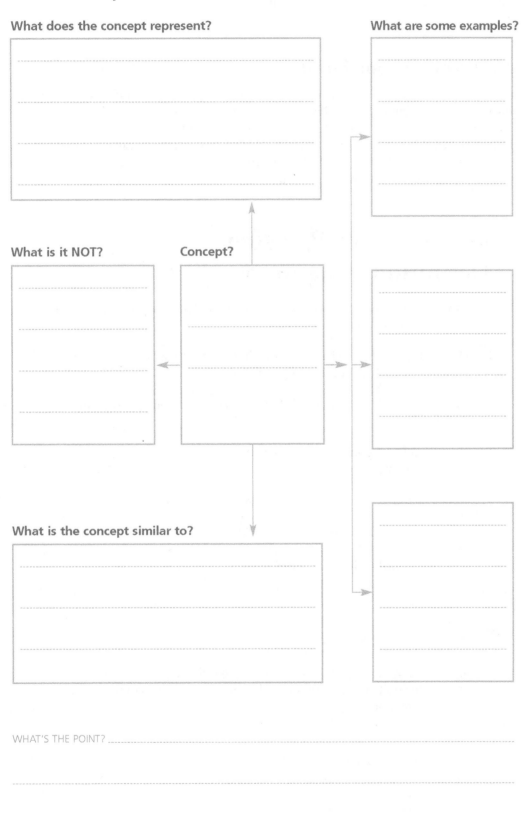

**What does the concept represent?**

**What are some examples?**

**What is it NOT?**

**Concept?**

**What is the concept similar to?**

WHAT'S THE POINT?

223

# Write a Draft of Your Paragraph

Using the ideas you generated during the prewriting phase, compose a draft of your definition paragraph. Return to the prewriting process at any time to generate additional details as needed. Use your own paper.

# Revise Your Draft

Once you have created a draft of a definition paragraph, read the draft and answer the questions in the "Questions for Revising a Definition Paragraph" box that follows. Indicate your answers by annotating your paper. If you answer "yes" to a question, underline, check, or circle examples. If you answer "no" to a question, write the additional details in the margins and draw lines to indicate their placement. Revise your paragraph based on your reflection.

## Questions for Revising a Definition Paragraph:

- ☐ Have I chosen an important concept to define? Have I clearly classified and illustrated the concept?

- ☐ Have I stated or implied a focused main idea? Can I state my point in one sentence? Have I created a strong impression?

- ☐ Have I effectively used order of importance? Have I used strong transitions of definition?

- ☐ Have I made my point with adequate details? Have I used concrete details to make my point?

- ☐ Have I included only the details that are relevant to my topic sentence?

- ☐ Have I used the following to make my ideas clear and interesting to my readers: vivid verbs and images, parallel language, controlled sentence structure, coordination, or subordination?

# Proofread Your Draft

Once you have made any revisions to your paragraph that may be needed, proofread your paragraph for proper usage and punctuation, such as using commas to set off nonessential information.

# Grammar in Action: Proper Use of Commas with Nonessential Information

In a sentence, some information that describes or modifies a word is nonessential. Nonessential information doesn't restrict the meaning of the word being described or modified. Nonessential information can be words, phrases, or clauses. If you can leave the information out of the sentence without changing the meaning of the sentence, then the information is nonessential. Use **commas before** and **after** nonessential words, phrases, and clauses. Use commas after nonessential words, phrases, and clauses that introduce a sentence.

- **Nonessential Word:**

Regular physical activity, moreover, promotes health, psychological well-being, and a healthy body weight.

My husband, Bob, runs six miles every other day.

- **Nonessential Phrase:**

A healthful diet, for example, includes a variety of fruits and vegetables each day.

Janine, eating a healthful diet and exercising, has lost 25 pounds.

- **Nonessential Clause:**

My great-grandmother, who is nearly 90 years old, goes bowling every week.

Sandra's diet, which is laden with high-fat, high-calorie foods, must change to ensure her good health.

---

## PROPER COMMA USE WITH NONESSENTIAL INFORMATION

Edit these sentences for proper use of commas before and after nonessential words, phrases, or clauses. Underline the nonessential information and insert the commas as needed.

**1.** Patience, however, is not tolerance of harmful wrongdoing.

**2.** Jerome, who has been my friend since childhood, does not tolerate gossip.

**3.** Jerome, wanting to stand on his principles, broke up with a girl who was a gossip.

**4.** Patience is, on the other hand, acceptance based on forgiveness.

**5.** Once Iva, who was a gossip until Jerome broke up with her, changed her ways, Jerome asked her out again.

# Review

Work with a classmate to give and receive feedback about your definition paragraphs. Use the following form to record your thinking about your writing process for your definition paragraph. Use the writer's journal on page 215 as a model for your own journal. Discuss the decisions you made as you wrote, and describe what you have learned by writing. Also, ask for advice about how to improve your paragraph.

MAIN IDEA: ........................................................................................................................

..........................................................................................................................................

..........................................................................................................................................

..........................................................................................................................................

LOGICAL ORDER: ...............................................................................................................

..........................................................................................................................................

..........................................................................................................................................

..........................................................................................................................................

RELEVANT DETAILS: ...........................................................................................................

..........................................................................................................................................

..........................................................................................................................................

..........................................................................................................................................

EFFECTIVE EXPRESSION: .....................................................................................................

..........................................................................................................................................

..........................................................................................................................................

..........................................................................................................................................

..........................................................................................................................................

# Writing Assignments

## Considering Audience and Purpose

Study the set of photographs about the people and situations at the beginning of the chapter. Assume you have benefited personally from the efforts of one of the people depicted in the images. Brainstorm a list of attributes of this person. Write a one-paragraph thank you letter to this person in which you define what he or she means to you.

## Writing for Everyday Life

Assume that you have agreed to seek counseling to improve a relationship with a family member or coworker. The counselor has asked you to define your role in the relationship. Identify the type of relationship you have with your family member or coworker, the major traits of the relationship, and examples or incidents that illustrate the nature of your relationship. Allow your tone—through your word choice—to reflect one of the following: (1) concern or (2) resentment.

## Writing for College Life

Assume you are a first-semester college student who is enrolled in a study skills class, and you have been assigned to write a paragraph that defines student success. Based on your experience and observations, write a definition of student success that addresses attitudes, behaviors, and skills.

## Writing for Working Life

Assume that you work in a retail store that sells clothes, electronics, or some other specialized merchandise. Also assume that sales and morale are down. Write a one-paragraph memo to your supervisor in which you define the morale problem.

# 11

# The Cause and Effect Paragraph

A cause is the reason an event took place. An effect is the result of an event. Cause leads to effect.

Understanding the relationship between cause and effect is a vital critical thinking skill used in all aspects of life. For example, when an illness strikes us, our physician must correctly identify the cause of our symptoms in order to treat us. In addition, the side effects of any medication to treat the illness must be taken into account. What are some other instances in which we consider causes and effects?

Thinking about cause and effect points out the relationship between events based on reasons and results. For example, in your personal life, you may have identified that stress causes you to eat for comfort. In working life, you may have identified the need to master certain software programs to be competitive in the job market. In college life, you may have identified how logical causes and effects play a role in the study of history, science, or economics. To write a cause and effect paragraph, identify a set of related events, objects, or factors. Then, label each event, object, or factor within the group as either a cause or an effect. Be sure to test each event as a true cause. Events that occur at or near the same time may be coincidental and unrelated. Then, present your details in a logical order that explains why each cause leads to a specific effect.

# What's the Point of Cause and Effect?

Often ideas become clearer when they are analyzed based on how they relate to one another. The cause and effect pattern of organization allows a writer to explore the ways in which ideas are related based on reasons and results. The following set of photographs documents a set of causes and effects. Study the images and write captions that identify the appropriate causes and effects illustrated. Answer the following questions: What is this? Why did it happen? What is this further effect? Answer the question "What's the point?" with a one-sentence statement of the overall main idea.

PHOTOGRAPHIC ORGANIZER: CAUSE AND EFFECT

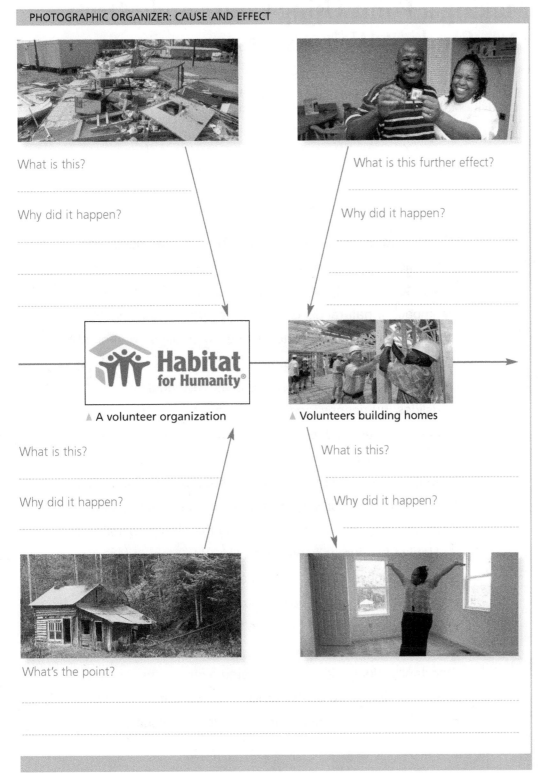

What is this?

Why did it happen?

What is this further effect?

Why did it happen?

▲ A volunteer organization

▲ Volunteers building homes

What is this?

Why did it happen?

What is this?

Why did it happen?

What's the point?

## My First Thoughts: A Prewriting Activity

Brainstorm about the images you just studied. Set a time limit, such as five minutes, and write in your notebook about the images and the details you generated. Write as quickly as you can without stopping. Let the ideas flow freely. Getting your first thoughts about a topic on paper is one excellent way to kick-start your writing process.

# Making a Point Using Cause and Effect: One Student Writer's Response

The following paragraph offers one writer's point about the causes and effects illustrated by the photographs. Read the cause and effect paragraph and the explanations; complete the activities in **bold type** in the annotations. Then read the writer's journal entry that records decisions made during the writing process.

**EFFECTIVE EXPRESSION:**
Precise word choice makes your point credible. Writers often confuse the word "affect," a verb that means to influence with "effect," a noun which means result. **Double underline a verb that can be replaced with "affects." Double underline two nouns that can be replaced with "effect."**

**STRONG TRANSITIONS:**
The transitional word "because" signals that "natural disasters and poverty" occur as causes before "Habitat for Humanity calls for volunteers." **Circle two more transitional words or phrases that signal cause or effect.**

**RELEVANT DETAILS:**
Relevant details include descriptive details that describe the qualities of a cause or effect. "Quality and affordable" are important traits of the homes built by Habitat for Humanity. These traits become the effect or goals. **Draw boxes around three more relevant details that describe a cause or effect.**

**MAIN IDEA:**
The main idea is the point the author is making about the topic. The topic is Habitat for Humanity. **Underline the author's point about this topic.**

A Noble Response: A Joyous Result

(1) Volunteer work is a noble response to human need, and one basic human need is safe and comfortable shelter. (2) Habitat for Humanity affects this basic need. (3) Because of the impact of natural disasters and poverty on housing, Habitat for Humanity calls for volunteers to build quality and affordable houses that results in home ownership for those in need. (4) In recent years, natural disasters such as earthquakes, mudslides, hurricanes, and tsunamis have caused countless homes to be reduced to rubble or obliterated. (5) As a result, hundreds of thousands of people are left homeless and without resources to rebuild. (6) Currently, poverty influences many around the world by causing families to live in shoddy structures with little hope of improving their living conditions. (7) Habitat for Humanity was established to meet these very needs. (8) Consequently, strangers voluntarily come together to accomplish one goal: to build a house for a family. (9) The end results are obvious. (10) First, the family, who also helped build their home, owns their home. (11) In addition, and just as importantly, along with home ownership comes the joy and pride of an improved quality of life. (12) Habitat for Humanity is a noble response to human need with joyous results.

# The Writer's Journal

**PEER EDITING**

The student writer of "A Noble Response: A Joyous Result" completed the following reflection to record his thinking through the writing process. Read his writer's journal that describes a few key choices he made as he wrote. Then, in the given space, answer his questions about his use of relevant details and effective expression in his paragraph. Work with a peer or a small group of classmates.

RELEVANT DETAILS: Once I decided on my topic, the graphic organizer really helped me think of details. I divided my details into two groups. I gave two reasons Habitat for Humanity was created, and I gave a few of the effects HH has had on people. Do you think I gave enough details? Should I have mentioned specific disasters like Hurricane Katrina? Why or why not?

EFFECTIVE EXPRESSION: I proofread several times to make sure I used "effect" and "affect" correctly. Could you proofread it one more time? Did I use these words correctly? Should I have used these two words more often, since this is a cause and effect paragraph? For example in sentence 8, I used the word "goal." Should I have used "effect" or "affect" here? Or is "goal" more effective? Why? Do you see other words that should be replaced to make my point?

# Developing Your Point Using Cause and Effect

A cause and effect paragraph makes a point by discussing the reasons and results among a set of events, objects, or factors. To support a point through cause and effect, a writer identifies a set of events, objects, or factors. A writer then identifies the specific details of cause and effect between each of the events, objects, or factors. The writer tests each reason and result to weed out true causes and effects from coincidence. The writer discusses the specific details in the order that reflects the logical relationship among causes and effects. In addition, the writer uses precise word choice for effective expression.

## The Point: The Main Idea

When you write a cause and effect paragraph, you limit your thoughts to a set of topics based on their relationship to each other. Most likely you have an opinion or belief about the topics and their causes and effects; your opinion is your point or main idea. A topic sentence states the overall point of the causes and effects.

For example, the following topic sentence contains (1) the topic, (2) the writer's opinion about the topic, and (3) the pattern of organization used to organize details.

*TOPIC*

*WRITER'S OPINION*

Addiction to television has led to several negative effects on American students.

*PATTERN OF ORGANIZATION: CAUSE AND EFFECT SIGNAL WORDS*

The topic is the "addiction to television [of] American students." The pattern of organization is established with the signal words "led to several effects." The writer's opinion is stated with the modifier "negative."

---

**Practice 2**

**TOPIC SENTENCES**

The items present a topic, an opinion, and cause or effect signal word(s). Combine the ideas in each group to create a topic sentence for a cause and effect.

1. TOPIC: *smoking cigarettes*     OPINION: *adverse*

CAUSE OR EFFECT SIGNAL WORDS: *leads to physical effects*

TOPIC SENTENCE: _____

2. TOPIC: *bullying*     OPINION: *low self-esteem and anger*

CAUSE OR EFFECT SIGNAL WORDS: *stems from*

TOPIC SENTENCE: _____

# Logical Order

Once you have identified a topic, a set of factors, their relationships based on cause and effect, and have focused on a main idea, you are ready to generate and organize additional details. To make a point using cause or effect, a writer moves from a general idea (the overall causal relationship) to a major support (a specific cause or effect of the topic) to minor supports (details or examples of a specific cause or effect). To signal the movement among these levels of ideas, a writer uses transitions to signal causes, effects, and examples. Strong transitions establish coherence, a clear and understandable flow of ideas.

## Transitions That Signal Cause and Effect

| | | | | |
|---|---|---|---|---|
| accordingly | consequently | hence | on account of | so |
| as a result | due to | if…then | results in | therefore |
| because of | for that reason | leads to | since | thus |

## Verbs That Signal Cause and Effect (sample list)

| | | | | | |
|---|---|---|---|---|---|
| affect | constitute | create | force | institute | restrain |
| cause | construct | determine | induce | preclude | stop |
| compose | contribute | facilitate | initiate | prevent | |

## Nouns That Signal Cause and Effect (sample list)

| | | | | |
|---|---|---|---|---|
| actor | consequence | end | influence | product |
| agent | creation | event | issue | result |
| author | creator | grounds | outcome | source |
| condition | effect | impact | outgrowth | |

---

**CAUSE AND EFFECT**

Fill in the blanks with the appropriate transition or signal words for cause and effect. Work with a peer or in a small group of your classmates.

### How Is Stroke Prevented?

A stroke is the _____ of a disease of the blood vessels in the brain, and underlying health conditions can _____ a stroke. For example, heart disease, high blood pressure, high cholesterol, and diabetes can _____ to a stroke. _____ you have any of these conditions, _____ take your medication as prescribed by your health care provider. Second, a healthful diet lowers your risk for a stroke. _____, eat a diet low in saturated fat and rich in fruits, vegetables, and whole grains. For example, eating too much meat and whole milk dairy products can _____ in high cholesterol, which raises your risk for a stroke.

Practice 3

# Relevant Details

As a writer narrows a topic into a focused main idea, the thinking process brings to mind many details that answer questions such as *who*, *what*, *when*, *where*, *why*, and *how*. A writer evaluates the relevance of each detail and uses only those that clarify or support the main idea. In a cause and effect paragraph, some relevant major details include those that identify a specific cause or effect. Relevant minor details offer examples and explanations of the cause or effect. Relevant details include descriptions, examples, and explanations of the causal relationship between a set of events, situations, objects, or factors.

One writer generated these ideas while brainstorming using a fishbone cause and effect concept map.

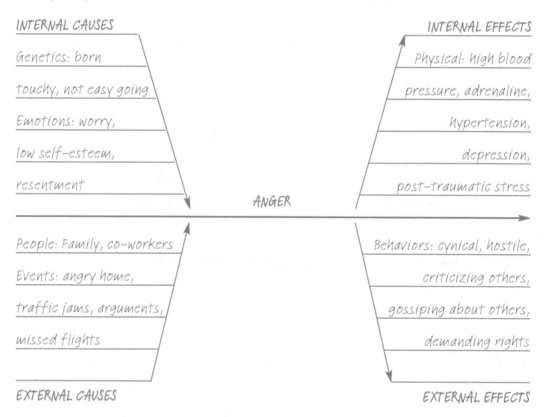

INTERNAL CAUSES

Genetics: born

touchy, not easy going

Emotions: worry,

low self-esteem,

resentment

ANGER

INTERNAL EFFECTS

Physical: high blood

pressure, adrenaline,

hypertension,

depression,

post-traumatic stress

People: Family, co-workers

Events: angry home,

traffic jams, arguments,

missed flights

EXTERNAL CAUSES

Behaviors: cynical, hostile,

criticizing others,

gossiping about others,

demanding rights

EXTERNAL EFFECTS

During the prewriting phase, a writer naturally generates irrelevant details. In fact, an effective writer often produces far more details than can be used to make a specific point. Irrelevant details do not explain or support the focused point of the paragraph. A careful writer uses the revision process to double check details for relevance and to eliminate irrelevant ones.

Baseball manager argues with home plate umpire ▶

The following paragraph develops the ideas generated about anger during the brainstorming phase using the fishbone cause and effect concept map shown on page 201. Circle the main idea. Underline two causes and two effects. Cross out two details that are not relevant to the main point.

### Anger Inside and Out

(1) Anger can be a normal, healthy emotion, yet anger can also spiral out of our control and lead to problems that affect our work, our families, and our lives. (2) To control anger, we need to understand its causes and effects. (3) Basically, anger is the result of both internal and external forces. (4) Genetics and emotions are two internal forces that give rise to anger. (5) According to experts, some people are born innately touchy and easily angered. (6) Others of us are born with mild, easy-going tendencies. (7) Another internal force is the complex mixture of our emotions. (8) Worry, low self-esteem, anxiety, or resentment can cause anger to flare. (9) In addition, external forces such as people and events can trigger anger. (10) For example, if we have been raised in an environment of anger without learning how to cope with negative feelings, we are much more likely to be easily angered. (11) As a result, a disagreement with a family member or coworker, a traffic jam, or a cancelled airline flight ignites angry feelings. (12) Not only does our anger arise from internal and external forces, but also our anger has internal and external effects. (13) Anger has immediate physical effects: it causes our heart rate, blood pressure, and adrenaline to rise. (14) Ultimately, chronic anger can lead to hypertension or depression. (15) Post-traumatic stress syndrome also leads to depression. (16) Chronic anger also may result in cynical and hostile behavior towards others. (17) When we feel angry, we may act out our hostility by criticizing others, gossiping about them, or rudely demanding our rights. (18) Ultimately, uncontrolled anger damages our relationships with others and diminishes our quality of life. (19) We need to understand the reasons and results of our anger before we can hope to control this volatile emotion.

# Effective Expression: Correct Use of Words

Effective expression reflects a writer's thoughtful choice of words for impact on the reader. Some words, such as *affect* and *effect*, seem closely related because they are similar in their sounds and spellings. These similarities often cause confusion and lead to the misuse of the words. However, their meanings are clearly distinct, so thoughtful writers use the correct word for effective expression.

*Affect* is a verb that means **to influence.**

**Example**

Video games **affect** learning by improving concentration and visual skills.

*Effect* is a noun that means **result.**

**Example**

Video games have a positive **effect** on learning by improving concentration and visual skills.

*Effect* is a verb that means **to bring about.**

**Example**

The new law will **effect** a change in the sentencing of sex offenders.

---

### CORRECT USE OF AFFECT AND EFFECT

Complete the following sentences with the correct use of the words *affect* and *effect*. (*Hint:* Substitute the words *influence* or *result* as a test for exact meaning in the context of the sentence.)

1. The lack of bright light during winter months produces an ..................... known as Seasonal Affective Disorder (SAD), a form of depression.

2. The long, dark hours of winter ..................... as much as 6 percent of the population.

3. The ..................... of SAD include loss of energy, social withdrawal, overeating, weight gain, and difficulty concentrating.

4. Researchers believe that reduced sunlight ..................... the biological rhythms that control the body's internal clock.

5. Researchers also believe that heredity, age, and the body's chemical balance ..................... the onset of SAD.

6. Exposure to sun and sun lamps for one to three hours a day ..................... a positive change in the mood of one who suffers from SAD.

# Using Cause and Effect in Your Academic Courses

Often college writing assignments require that you combine information you learn from your textbooks with your observations about how that information applies to real-world situations. Textbooks may provide graphic organizers to emphasize key concepts and make them easy to understand. Use these graphic organizers to learn and apply the concept. A good way to review your textbook notes is to add examples you have observed in life to the concept you are studying.

**USING CAUSE AND EFFECT IN A SOCIOLOGY ASSIGNMENT**

Study the following graphic taken from a college sociology textbook. In a small group or with a classmate, add examples of each concept that you and your classmate(s) have observed. Then, write a paragraph in answer to the question at the end of the practice. Use a dictionary as necessary.

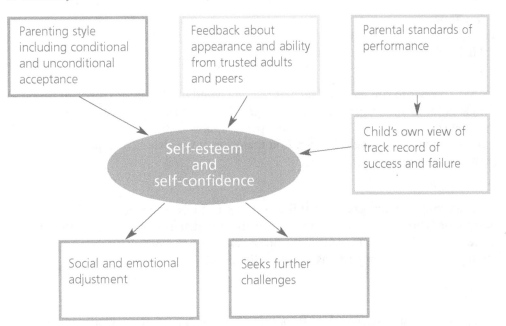

—Jaffe, Michael L. *Understanding Parenting, 2nd Ed.* Allyn & Bacon. 1997 p. 241.

EXAMPLE OF PARENTAL STANDARD: ......................................................................................

EXAMPLE OF CHILD'S VIEW OF SUCCESS AND FAILURE: ....................................................

EXAMPLE OF FEEDBACK: ..............................................................................................................

EXAMPLE OF PARENTING STYLE: ................................................................................................

EXAMPLE OF FURTHER CHALLENGE: .........................................................................................

EXAMPLE OF ADJUSTMENT: .........................................................................................................

On a separate sheet of paper, answer the following question:
What factors influence children's self-esteem and self-confidence?

# Workshop: Writing a Cause and Effect Paragraph Step by Step

### Choose Your Topic

The following activities are designed to help you choose a topic.

1. Create a bank of topics: Use the following headings to brainstorm or list as many causes and effects as you possibly can. Don't criticize your thoughts; just get as many relevant causes and effects written down as quickly as possible. Add more topics, causes, or effects as they occur to you. Revisit topic banks created during your study of previous chapters; identify causes and effects. Compare your bank of topics with those of your peers.

   - YouTube
   - Friendship
   - Fuel-efficient Cars
   - Romance

2. Reread a freewrite you created (such as the one based on the photographs of the people in the chapter opening or the one generated in Practice 4). Underline ideas that you could use for a cause and effect paragraph. Number the points you recorded to indicate a logical order. Add major or minor details of explanation and examples as needed.

   OR

   Select a group of photographs that illustrate a set of related events, situations, objects, or factors. Generate a list that identifies the details of each event, situation, object, or factor as either a cause (reason) or an effect (result). Freewrite about the photograph(s). Remember to ask "What's the point?"

## Clarify Your Point

Read a prewrite you have generated for a cause and effect paragraph. Underline words that suggest your values, opinions, or attitudes about the events. Think about why the information is important. Think about what examples best represent each cause or effect. Think about a situation that best illustrates the concept. Identify your audience and purpose. Write a list of additional concrete examples that explain your point. In one sentence, state the point of the cause and effect paragraph.

AUDIENCE: .............................................................................................................................

PURPOSE: ...............................................................................................................................

LIST OF CONCRETE DETAILS: ...........................................................................................

WHAT'S THE POINT? .........................................................................................................

.............................................................................................................................................

## Generate and Organize Relevant Details

Use the graphic organizer below to either organize the ideas you have already created or to generate details to support your point.

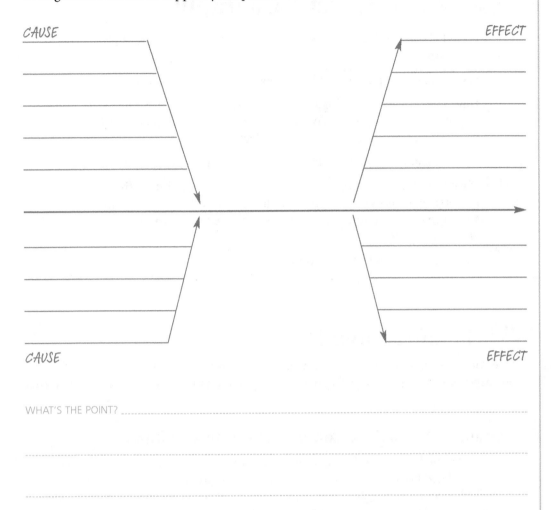

CAUSE           EFFECT

CAUSE           EFFECT

WHAT'S THE POINT? .......................................................................................

## Write a Draft of Your Paragraph

Using the ideas you generated during the prewriting phase, compose a draft of your cause and effect paragraph. Return to the prewriting process at any time to generate additional details as needed. Use your own paper.

## Revise Your Draft

Once you have created a draft of your cause and effect paragraph, read the draft and answer the questions in the "Questions for Revising a Cause and Effect Paragraph" box that follows. Indicate your answers by annotating your paper. If you answer "yes" to a question, underline, check, or circle examples. If you answer "no" to a question, write the additional details in the margins and draw lines to indicate their placement. Revise your paragraph based on your reflection.

# Questions for Revising a Cause and Effect Paragraph:

☐ Have I chosen an important set of related events, situations, objects, or factors?

☐ Have I made my point? Can I state my point in one sentence?

☐ Have I effectively used a logical order based on short-term, long-term, most important, least important, obvious, or subtle causes and effects? Have I used strong transitions of cause and effect?

☐ Have I included only the details that are relevant to my topic sentence?

☐ Have I used the following to make my ideas clear and interesting to my readers: vivid verbs and images, parallel language, controlled sentence structure, coordination, subordination, precise use of words such as *affect* and *effect*?

☐ Have I used concrete details to make my point?

## Proofread Your Draft

Once you have made any revisions to your paragraph that may be needed, proofread your paper to eliminate unnecessary errors, such as editing for commonly confused words.

### Grammar in Action: Commonly Confused Words

As you learned earlier in this chapter, some words, such as *affect* and *effect*, seem closely related because they are similar in their sounds and spellings. The similarities often cause these words to be confused with one another and lead to their misuse. However, their meanings are clearly distinct, so thoughtful writers choose the precise word for effective expression. The following list presents a group of words that are commonly confused. Memorize this list of words and their meanings so you can use each one precisely in your writing.

| | |
|---|---|
| **its, it's** | **its** (possessive form of it); **it's** (contraction of *it is* or *it has*) |
| **their, they're, there** | **their** (possessive of they); **they're** (contraction of *they are*); **there** (points to a place) |
| **to, two, too** | **to** (suggests movement or direction); **two** (a number); **too** (also) |
| **whose, who's** | **whose** (possessive form of *who*); **who's** (contraction of *who is* or *who has*) |
| **your, you're** | **your** (possessive form of *you*); **you're** (contraction of *you are*) |

Edit the following rough draft of a paragraph written by student Seiko Kaneyama about the effects of stress due to a language barrier. Cross out the words used incorrectly and insert the correct word.

### The Main Cause of My Stress: The Language Barrier

(1) For me, the language barrier is the biggest source of stress. (2) Four years ago, I lost my husband to heart failure. (3) He passed away in the hospital. (4) Because I could not express myself in English, no matter how I tried, no one could understand me or what I wanted. (5) The stress reached too the point that I was shaking and collapsed in tears. (6) Its still one of the most difficult and frustrating memories of my life. (7) Today, my stress is from language problems at work with some co-workers. (8) For example, when a mistake is made, someone always blames me. (9) They say, "Your two hard too understand." (10) Or they say that I do not understand what there saying. (11) As a result, I have to do my job better than anyone else. (12) Some people try to take advantage of me because there sure that I would not complain because of my imperfect English.(13) Its very difficult their. (14) School causes me stress, to. (15) I speak and write Chinese, Japanese, and Korean. English is very difficult; its a very frustrating language. (16) One of the most stressful moments is when I ask questions at school. (17) Most professors interrupt me before I can fully express myself; I feel miserable, and it keeps me from asking questions at school. (18) This language problem at work, at school, and in everyday life causes me great stress. (19) In the past, I have had headaches, and I have become irritable. (20) However, I feel that I have become a person whose able to handle these stressful situations better, and as my language skills improve, I feel more confident and less and less stressful.

# Review

Work with a classmate to give and receive feedback about your cause and effect paragraphs. Use the following form to record your thinking about your writing process for your cause and effect paragraph. Use the writer's journal on page 193 as a model for your own journal. Discuss the decisions you made as you wrote, and describe what you have learned by writing. Also, ask for advice about how to improve your paragraph.

MAIN IDEA:

LOGICAL ORDER:

RELEVANT DETAILS:

EFFECTIVE EXPRESSION:

# Writing Assignments

## Considering Audience and Purpose

Study the set of photographs at the beginning of the chapter. Assume you are the one who now owns the home built by Habitat for Humanity. Assume that as you worked beside the volunteers to build your home, you became friendly with the project director, Wilma Weindmyer. Write a one-paragraph thank you letter to Ms. Weindmyer that explains the impact of building and owning your own home.

## Writing for Everyday Life

Assume that you are the mentor of a young person who is a member of your family or community. Assume the young person is making some choices that can have lasting negative consequences. Perhaps the youth is hanging out with the wrong crowd, or skipping school, or experimenting with drugs. Write a one-paragraph letter that explains the dangers of the wrong choices or the benefits of mature choices. Choose your words to reflect one of the following: (1) stern warning or (2) warm encouragement.

## Writing for College Life

Assume you are applying for a scholarship set up to aid a person currently enrolled as a full-time college student with at least a 3.0 GPA. Assume you must compete with other students to win the scholarship by writing a one-paragraph essay on the topic "Education Matters." Write a paragraph that explains one or both of the following: (1) the impact the education has had and will have on you or (2) the impact you hope to have as an educated member of society.

## Writing for Working Life

Assume that you are applying for a job with a company or organization. Perhaps you are applying for a job as a health care provider, teacher, office manager, or computer programmer. Write a one-paragraph cover letter that explains the impact you can have on the job due to your skills, work ethic, and character.

PEARSON
**mywritinglab**

**WANT A
BETTER GRADE?**
For more practice with cause and effect, go to
**www.mywritinglab.com**
> Using Patterns of Organization to Develop Paragraphs > The Cause and Effect Paragraph.

# 12

# The Persuasive Paragraph

A persuasive claim is a strong stand on a debatable topic supported by facts, examples, and opinions.

In almost every area of our lives, we engage in some form of persuasion. Whether convincing a friend to see a particular movie or proving we are the right candidate for a particular job, we use reasons, logic, and emotion to get others to agree with our views. What are some other situations that use persuasion to influence our beliefs and behaviors? Why are certain arguments or points of view so persuasive?

To be persuasive, a writer asserts a strong stand on one side of a debatable issue. Then the writer supports that stand by offering convincing evidence such as reasons, facts, examples, and expert opinions. In everyday life, our court system is based on proving claims of guilt or innocence. In working life, we use reasons to resolve workplace disputes. In college life, we encounter debatable claims in every discipline. In addition to asserting a claim and supporting it with evidence, a persuasive writer acknowledges and rebuts (disproves, challenges) the opposition.

# What's the Point of Persuasion?

The purpose of persuasion is to convince the reader to agree with a particular claim about a debatable topic. Persuasion is a call to action or a call to a change of mind. The following photos represent several reasons against building a Target store in the location of a popular neighborhood park. Study the photographs. In the space provided, identify the claim, reasons, and an opposing point of view about removing the park to build a Target store. Answer the question "What's the point?" with a one-sentence statement of the overall main idea.

**PHOTOGRAPHIC ORGANIZER: PERSUASION**

What is the issue?

-----------------

-----------------

SUPPORTING POINTS          OPPOSING POINT

What is this reason?                                    What is this point?

-----------------

-----------------

What is this reason?       SUPPORT THAT REFUTES OPPOSING POINT

                                                       What is this reason?

-----------------

-----------------

What is this reason?

-----------------

-----------------

**What's the point?**

-----------------

-----------------

-----------------

245

## My First Thoughts: A Prewriting Activity

Brainstorm about the images you just studied. Set a time limit, such as five minutes, and write in your notebook about the images and the details you generated. Write as quickly as you can without stopping. Let the ideas flow freely. Getting your first thoughts about a topic on paper is one excellent way to overcome writer's block and set your mind to thinking.

LEARNING OUTCOMES
STRUCTURE

# Making a Point Using Persuasion: One Student Writer's Response

The following paragraph offers one writer's point that argues against building a new Target store in her neighborhood, as illustrated by the photographs. Read the persuasive paragraph and the explanations; complete the activities in **bold type** in the annotations. Then read the writer's journal entry that records decisions made during the writing process.

**MAIN IDEA:**
The main idea is the point the author is claiming about the topic. **Underline the topic and circle the writer's claim about this topic.**

**EFFECTIVE EXPRESSION:**
To persuade a reader, an author uses subjective words that express opinions, attitudes, and values. **Double underline at least three more subjective words or phrases.**

**STRONG TRANSITION:**
The transition phrase "First of all" signals that the author is offering a reason in support of her claim. **Circle three more transitional words or phrases that signal a reason of support.**

**RELEVANT DETAILS:**
In persuasion, relevant details not only include facts and consequences, but also refute opposing points. Here, the writer offers another location better suited to a retail store. **Draw a box around one other opposing point and the writer's counter point.**

### Let the Children Play: No Target

Dear Mayor and Commissioners:

(1) I strongly oppose relocating our community's invaluable recreational center at the corner of Nova Road and Main Trail to make space for a Target store. (2) I am outraged and shocked that you even think moving our playground so it sits on top of a land field behind a new Target is an option. (3) Most likely, you think a Target will stimulate the economy, but a Target in this location is not worth the money it would generate. (4) First of all, the intersection will not be able to sustain the kind of traffic that a Target will draw. (5) This type of traffic will create added dangers for the children commuting to their "relocated" park. (6) Secondly, the development will destroy one of the few remaining ecological parks; Nova Park is not only a natural habitat, but also a shady oasis for the many families that live nearby. (7) Why pave over this natural refuge when there is so much bare land out Williamson and US 1? (8) Those roads can better bear the added traffic. (9) Thirdly, a park at the edge of the neighborhood adds more value to the neighborhood than a Target. (10) I am an expectant mother and have planned on walking my child to this park just as my parents did with me. (11) I grew up playing on those monkey bars and swinging under the beautiful canopy of oaks that you now threaten to destroy with a lame, hot parking lot and an unattractive, square building. (12) I do not wish to take my child to the back of a Target store to play. (13) Finally, this type of mega-retail store often increases crime in the surrounding area. (14) This nearsightedness is not the kind of leadership I will vote for. Respectfully, A Concerned Citizen

# The Writer's Journal

## PEER EDITING

The student writer of "Let the Children Play: No Target" completed the following reflection to record her thinking through the writing process. Read her writer's journal that describes a few key choices she made as she wrote. Then, in the given space, answer her questions about her use of logical order and effective expression in her paragraph. Work with a peer or a small group of classmates.

LOGICAL ORDER: I wanted to use an order that would make my argument sound strong and smart. So rather than just telling them I was angry about the issue, I also included three examples of why their consideration of this development made me upset. Once I had recorded my three major ideas that began with "First of all, Secondly, and Thirdly" I saw that each of those ideas needed support to be more effective. So I added an additional sentence after each major idea to help explain how I felt. Do you agree with the order of my ideas? Why or why not? How could I improve on the order of my ideas?

EFFECTIVE EXPRESSION: When I first sat down to write my city officials about why a Target store should not relocate my neighborhood park, I was angry. I just wanted them to know I was disappointed with them. But as I wrote, I became anxious. The longer I thought about the issue, more and more points against the development flooded my mind. I wanted to address them all without sounding boring. Is my tone okay? Do I come across too strong? How could I improve my tone?

# Developing Your Point Using Persuasion

A persuasive paragraph makes a point by supporting one side of a debatable topic and refuting the opposing side. The details that support and refute the point include reasons based on facts, examples, effects, and expert opinions on the topic. In addition, a writer uses effective expression to qualify ideas and control the point of view.

## The Point: The Main Idea

A persuasive paragraph gives your opinion or stand on an issue. A topic sentence states the debatable topic, the writer's persuasive opinion, and, possibly, a pattern of organization. Because persuasion is a purpose, the writer may choose any particular pattern of organization to support a claim. In addition, the writer's persuasive opinion is often signaled by the following types of subjective words or phrases: *all, always, only, must, must not, should, should not,* or *too.*

For example, the following topic sentence contains (1) the debatable topic, (2) the writer's persuasive opinion, and (3) a pattern of organization used to organize details.

*DEBATABLE TOPIC*  *WRITER'S OPINION*  *DEBATABLE TOPIC*

Colleges and universities should provide substance free housing for students for several reasons.

*PATTERN OF ORGANIZATION: PERSUASION SIGNAL WORDS*

---

**TOPIC SENTENCES**

The items present a debatable topic, the writer's opinion, and a pattern of organization. Combine the ideas in each group to create a topic sentence for a persuasive paragraph.

**1.** TOPIC: *education about crystal meth*

OPINION: *horrific, is our best hope to end this plague*

PATTERN OF ORGANIZATION: *the consequences of*

TOPIC SENTENCE: _____

_____

**2.** TOPIC: *procrastination by students, academic*

OPINION: *is the leading, failure*

PATTERN OF ORGANIZATION: *cause of*

TOPIC SENTENCE: _____

_____

248

# Logical Order

Once you have identified a debatable topic, you are ready to generate and organize the details. To make a persuasive point, a writer moves from a general idea (the claim) to a major support (a reason, fact, example, expert opinion, or reason against the opposing view) to a minor support (also a reason, fact, example, expert opinion, or argument against the opposing view). Transitions and signal words indicate the importance and movement among details. Strong transitions and signal words establish coherence, a clear and understandable flow of ideas.

## Transitions That Signal Persuasion

| | | | | |
|---|---|---|---|---|
| accordingly | even so | however | nonetheless | therefore |
| admittedly | finally | in conclusion | obviously | thus |
| although | first (second, | indeed | of course | to be sure |
| because |     third, etc.) | in fact, in truth | on the one hand | truly |
| but | for | in summary | on the other hand | undoubtedly |
| certainly | furthermore | last | since | |
| consequently | granted | meanwhile | some believe | |
| despite | hence | nevertheless | some may say | |

## Signal Words That Qualify an Idea as Persuasive (sample list)

| | | | | | |
|---|---|---|---|---|---|
| all | every | may | often | probably, probable | think |
| always | has/have to | might | only | seem | too |
| believe | it is believed | must | ought to | should | usually |
| could | likely | never | possibly, possible | sometimes | |

---

**LOGICAL ORDER**

Fill in the blanks with the appropriate transition or signal words for persuasion. Work with a peer or in a small group of your classmates.

### For the Sake of the Children

For their safety and well-being, children ............ be removed from homes that house meth labs. According to John W. Gillis, the director of the Office for Victims of Crime, "children who live at or visit home-based meth labs face acute health and safety risks." A few of these risks include fire hazards, chemical explosions, physical and sexual abuse, and medical neglect. In addition, because of the hand to mouth behavior of young children, they are ............ to ingest toxic chemicals used to make the drug. ..................... , removal of a child from his or her home is a traumatic experience. However, the dangers posed by the "meth" lifestyle ............ outweigh the risks posed by removing the child from these chaotic homes.

—Swetlow, Karen. *"Children at Clandestine Methamphetamine Labs: Helping Meth's Youngest Victims."* OVC Bulletin. Office for Victims of Crime. U.S. Department of Justice. June 2003. 3 April 2006. <http://www.ojp.usdoj.gov/ovc/publications/bulletins/children/197590.pdf>.

Practice 3

# Relevant Details

As a writer narrows a topic into a focused main idea, he or she generates supporting details that answer the questions such as *who*, *what*, *when*, *where*, *why*, and *how*. A writer evaluates the relevance of each detail and uses only those that clarify or support the main idea. The supports of a persuasive claim are reasons, facts, examples, effects, expert opinions, and details that refute the opposing view.

Compare the following chart of Persuasive Supporting Details with the ideas in the Persuasive Thinking Map about metal detectors in public schools.

| **Persuasive Supporting Details** | |
|---|---|
| REASON | A cause of an event or action. An explanation. A basis or foundation of an idea. |
| FACT | A specific detail that is true based on objective proof. Objective proof can be physical evidence, an eyewitness account, or the result of accepted scientific investigation. |
| EXAMPLE | An illustration or instance of a general idea. |
| EFFECT | A result or consequence of an event or action. Consider positive effects of claim and negative effects of opposing views. |
| EXPERT OPINION | A view based on much training and extensive knowledge in a given field. Be sure to stay with opinions of experts in the field of the topic that is being debated. For example, a physician, an expert in medicine, is not an expert in criminal justice. |
| SUPPORTS THAT REFUTE | To refute is to disprove or counter an opposing point; supports include reasons, facts, effects, examples, and expert opinions. |

**Persuasive Thinking Map**

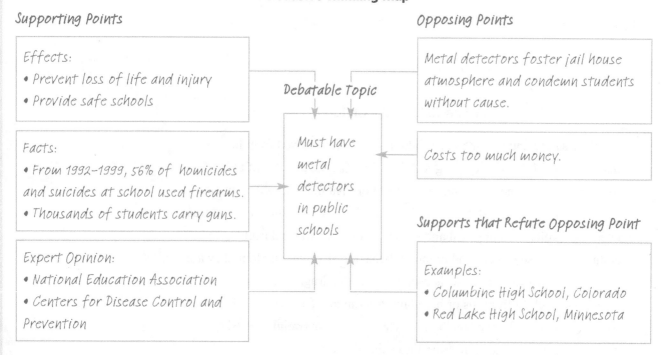

During the prewriting phase, a writer naturally generates irrelevant details. In fact, an effective writer often produces far more details than can be used to make a specific point. Irrelevant details do not explain or support the focused point of the paragraph. A careful writer uses the revision process to double check details for relevance and to eliminate irrelevant ones.

The following paragraph develops the ideas about metal detectors in public schools generated using the persuasive thinking map. Circle the main idea. Underline one example of each of the following: fact, example, effect, and a support that refutes the opposing view. Cross out the detail that is not relevant to the main point.

## Pay the Price: Stop the Shootings

(1) Public school officials should use metal detectors to screen students for possession of firearms in order to reduce the numbers of injuries and deaths. (2) The use of metal detectors signals students that safety measures are in place and that violence will not be tolerated. (3) Some oppose the use of metal detectors as a step that fosters a jail house atmosphere and condemns students as guilty without cause. (4) These opponents to metal detectors also decry the economic cost of screening students for possession of firearms. (5) Unfortunately, evidence indicates that the need to provide a safe school and the right to a safe school far outweigh these concerns. (6) According to the Centers for Disease Control and Prevention, from 1992 to 1999, 56% of homicides and suicides occurring at school involved firearms. (7) In addition, the National Education Association estimates that "on a daily basis, 100,000 students carry guns to school, 160,000 miss classes due to fear of physical harm, and 40 are injured or killed by firearms." (8) Tragic school shootings have already occurred and signal that the danger is clear and present. (9) For example, in 1999 at Columbine High School, in Colorado, two students massacred 12 fellow students and a teacher, injured 24 other people, and then committed suicide. (10) As recently as 2005, at Red Lake High School in Minnesota, a student killed five students and injured seven others after he had killed his grandfather and his grandfather's girlfriend at home. (11) He also shot himself. (12) All of these shooters obviously suffered mental health problems. (13) Though these incidents are extreme, they are not isolated. (14) These incidents show that public schools must screen students for weapons. (15) The cost of not doing so is too high!

## Works Cited

Centers for Disease Control and Prevention. "Source of Firearms Used by Students
    in School-Associated Violent Deaths—United States, 1992–1999." *Morbidity*
    *and Mortality Weekly Report* 52(09): 169-72. 7 March 2003. Web. 14 Aug. 2009.
"School Violence." National Education Association. Washington, D.C.: 1993.

# Effective Expression: Use of Subjective Words to Persuade

Effective expression is the result of a writer's thoughtful choice of words for impact on the reader. Subjective words reflect a strong stand because they express opinions, emotions, value judgments, and interpretations. Because subjective words express personal opinions, they can bring meanings and stir reactions in the reader not intended by the writer. Therefore, a thoughtful writer carefully chooses subjective words for effective expression. Note the differences between the neutral words and the subjective words in the following list:

| Neutral Words | Subjective Words |
| --- | --- |
| injury | wound, gash |
| perpetrator | criminal, delinquent, achiever |
| shelter | haven, hut |

## EFFECTIVE EXPRESSION: USE OF SUBJECTIVE WORDS TO PERSUADE

Use your dictionary and thesaurus to find an effective biased word to fill in the blank in each sentence. In the spaces after each sentence, describe the impact you intend to have on your reader through your choice of words. Discuss your work with your class or small group.

**1.** Spanking is a .............................................................................................................

...........................................................................................................................................

**2.** Laws that require cyclists to wear helmets are .............................................

...........................................................................................................................................

**3.** Completion of a college education requires ....................................................

...........................................................................................................................................

**4.** Burning the United States flag is an act of ......................................................

...........................................................................................................................................

**5.** President Barack Obama is ...................................................................................

...........................................................................................................................................

# Using Persuasion in Your Academic Courses

Often college textbooks present situations to help you think critically and come to your own conclusions about a debatable topic. An excellent study technique is to write a paragraph in response to the information and questions. Many professors of these courses will also ask you to write an essay in which you explain your understanding of a controversial issue. You may find that you can use the information from the textbook as a resource for your writing assignment.

USING PERSUASION IN A COLLEGE BUSINESS ASSIGNMENT: RESPONDING TO A CONTROVERSIAL ISSUE

Read the following study prompt about an ethical issue based on a college business textbook lesson. Then follow the directions given in the section "The Dilemma."

## Taking a Stance: Ethics in Business

### The Situation

An on-going debate revolves around the roles and activities of business owners in contributing to the greater social good. Promoting a proactive stance, some people argue that business should be socially responsible. In a proactive stance, businesses should seek opportunities to benefit the community in which they do business. Others say that businesses exist to make profits for owners, so they have no further obligation to society than that (the defensive stance). The defensive stance gives credit to businesses because they create jobs and pay taxes.

### The Dilemma

Pair up with a classmate. Choose one side of this debate. On your own sheet of paper, create a persuasive thinking map to support the side you have chosen. Then, take the opposite side of the debate and create a persuasive thinking map to support that side of the issue. Use the persuasive thinking map on page 212 as a model.

--Adapted from Griffin and Ebert. *Business.* Prentice Hall 2006, p. 86.

Practice 6

# Workshop: Writing a Persuasive Paragraph Step by Step

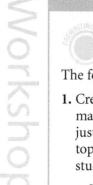

### Choose Your Topic

The following activities are designed to help you choose a topic.

1. Create a bank of topics: Use the following debatable topics to brainstorm or list as many facts, effects, and examples as you possibly can. Don't analyze your thoughts; just get as many ideas written down as quickly as possible. Add more debatable topics and examples as they occur to you. Revisit topic banks created during your study of previous chapters. Compare your bank of topics with those of your peers.

   - Violence in Cartoons
   - Sex Education
   - Teenage Drivers
   - Conserving Energy

2. Choose a list of topics from Activity 1. Brainstorm possible points the opposition could use to challenge your ideas. Identify relevant expert opinions you will need to include. Determine where you could locate those opinions. For example, can you interview an expert? Locate an expert opinion on the Internet? Read a newspaper or magazine article?

   OR

   Select a group of photographs that illustrate a debatable topic. Generate a list that includes facts, effects, examples, and opposing points. Search for expert opinions to include. Freewrite about the photograph(s). Remember to ask "What's the point?"

## Focus Your Point

Read a prewrite you have generated for a persuasive paragraph. Underline words that suggest your values, opinions, or attitudes about the events, situations, objects, or factors. Why is the subject important? Think about the reasons, facts, effects, and examples that best represent your claim. Identify your audience. Think about what specific reaction you want from your audience. Do you want to change your audience's mind about an issue, raise your audience's awareness about an issue, or call your audience to take a specific action? In one sentence, state the claim of your persuasion.

AUDIENCE: ................................................................................

PURPOSE—AUDIENCE REACTION: ...................................................

..................................................................................................

CONCRETE EXAMPLES: ...................................................................

..................................................................................................

WHAT'S THE POINT? STATE YOUR CLAIM: ..........................................

## Generate and Organize Relevant Details

Use the persuasive thinking map below to either organize the ideas you have already created or to generate details that support your point.

**Persuasive Thinking Map**

The Debatable Topic: What is the issue? .................................................................

................................................................................................................................

**Supporting Points**

Reason 1: ..........................................................................

..........................................................................................

Reason 2: ..........................................................................

..........................................................................................

Reason 3: ..........................................................................

..........................................................................................

**Opposing Point**

..........................................................................................

..........................................................................................

**Support that Refutes Opposing Point**

..........................................................................................

..........................................................................................

**What's the point?**

................................................................................................................................

................................................................................................................................

 # Write a Draft of Your Paragraph

Using the ideas you generated during the prewriting phase, compose a draft of your persuasive paragraph. Return to the prewriting process at any time to generate additional details as needed. Use your own paper.

 # Revise Your Draft

Once you have created a draft of a persuasive paragraph, read the draft and answer the questions in the "Questions for Revising a Persuasive Paragraph" box that follows. Indicate your answers by annotating your paper. If you answer "yes" to a question, underline, check, or circle examples. If you answer "no" to a question, write the additional details in the margins and draw lines to indicate their placement. Revise your paragraph based on your reflection.

PORTFOLIO

Workshop

# Questions for Revising a Persuasive Paragraph:

- ☐ Have I chosen an important debatable topic?
- ☐ Have I made my point? Can I state my point in one sentence?
- ☐ Have I effectively used reasons, facts, effects, examples? Have I used strong signal words of persuasion?
- ☐ Have I used concrete details to make my point?
- ☐ Have I included only the details that are relevant to my topic sentence? Have I used effective and relevant expert opinions? Have I addressed important opposing points effectively? Have I documented my sources properly?
- ☐ Have I used the following to make my ideas clear and interesting to my readers: vivid verbs and images, parallel language, controlled sentence structure, coordination, subordination, precise use of words such as *affect* and *effect*, and thoughtful use of biased words?
- ☐ Have I used subjective words to persuade my reader?

## Proofread Your Draft

Once you have made any revisions to your paragraph that may be needed, proofread you paper to ensure appropriate usage and grammar, such as the consistent use of point of view.

### Grammar in Action: Consistent Use of Point of View

Point of view is established with the use of personal pronouns. Personal pronouns identify three points of view: first person, second person, and third person.

**Personal Pronouns and Points of View**

- **First Person** (informal tone)
  I, me, mine, myself, my
  we, us, ours, our, ourselves

- **Second Person** (informal tone)
  you, your, yours, yourselves

- **Third Person** (formal tone)
  he, him, his, himself
  she, her, hers, herself
  it, its, itself
  they, them, their, theirs, themselves

Common sense tells us that we cannot shift between several individuals' points of view. However, often, we shift point of view carelessly, as in the following sentence.

> Television addiction contributes to our obesity. When you choose to sit in front of a television from the minute you get home until you go to bed, you leave no time for exercise.

Consistent use of point of view strengthens coherence or the clear flow of ideas. Therefore, carefully edit your writing to ensure consistent use of point of view, as in the following edited version of the sentence above.

> Television addiction contributes to our obesity. When we choose to sit in front of a television from the minute we get home until we go to bed, we leave no time for exercise.

### CONSISTENT USE OF POINT OF VIEW

Edit these sentences for consistent use of point of view. Cross out the pronoun that causes a shift in point of view and insert a noun or pronoun that establishes consistent use of point of view. Discuss your answers with a small group of peers or with your class.

**1.** A parent must monitor children's access to the Internet because you are vulnerable to predators in chat rooms and virtual communities like MySpace.com.

**2.** Some people believe that abstinence is the only way you can prevent unwanted pregnancies and the spread of sexually transmitted diseases.

**3.** People should not talk on the cell phone and drive at the same time. I was run off the road by a man who was obviously having an intense cell phone conversation while he was driving.

**4.** Getting enough sleep is crucial to a person's long-term health. When you deprive yourself of sleep, you deprive the body of its ability to repair itself through rest.

**5.** Women should limit their intake of alcohol to one serving of red wine per day; keep in mind that one serving is five ounces.

# Review

Work with a classmate to give and receive feedback about your persuasive paragraphs. Use the following form to record your thinking about your writing process for your persuasive paragraph. Use the writer's journal on page 209 as a model for your own journal. Discuss the decisions you made as you wrote, and describe what you have learned by writing. Also, ask for advice about how to improve your paragraph.

MAIN IDEA:

LOGICAL ORDER:

RELEVANT DETAILS:

EFFECTIVE EXPRESSION:

# Writing Assignments

## Considering Audience and Purpose

Study the set of photographs at the beginning of the chapter. Assume you are the mayor or a commissioner who has received this letter from "A Concerned Citizen." Write a one-paragraph response that states your official stand on the issue. Or assume you are a representative for Target. Write a one-paragraph response to support the building of a Target at the Nova Park location.

## Writing for Everyday Life

Assume that you and your family, or you and a group of your friends, have decided to take a vacation together. Each of you has a different destination and activity in mind. Write a one-paragraph e-mail to your family or group of friends in which you convince them to travel to your choice of destinations. Be sure to include facts, effects, examples, expert opinions, and reasons that counter any opposition to your choice. Allow your word choice and tone to reflect your enthusiasm.

## Writing for College Life

Assume that you disagree with a grade you have received for a course or an assignment. Write a one-paragraph letter to your professor in which you argue for the grade you believe you have earned. Be sure to include facts that prove what you have learned, examples of what you have learned, and explanations of the benefits of what you have learned. As part of your proof, include ideas and concepts you have learned from your professor (as an expert in the field). Allow your word choice and tone to reflect both respect for the professor and self-confidence in your abilities.

## Writing for Working Life

Assume that you are a supervisor of a shift of workers at a fast food restaurant or department store. Assume that you are short of staff, and the busy season is approaching: You need more workers. Write a one-paragraph memo to your district manager, Derwood Kuntz, persuading him to authorize you to hire three additional workers. Be sure to include reasons, facts, examples, effects, and points that will counter any opposition he may pose.

mywritinglab

**WANT A BETTER GRADE?**
For more practice with persuasion, go to **www.mywritinglab.com** > Using Patterns of Organization to Develop Paragraphs > The Persuasive Paragraph.

# 13

## Subjects, Verbs, and Simple Sentences

A simple sentence, also called an *independent clause*, includes a subject and a verb and expresses a complete thought.

Communicating about a real-life situation helps us to understand the purpose of subjects, verbs, and simple sentences. The photographs on these pages show a boat built for the future. Read the statements given in Practice 1 about this amazing boat, and answer the question "What's the point of subjects, verbs, and simple sentences?"

# What's the Point of Subjects, Verbs, and Simple Sentences?

PHOTOGRAPHIC ORGANIZER: SUBJECTS, VERBS, AND SIMPLE SENTENCES

Read the following set of statements. Circle the one that makes the most sense. Discuss why the statement you chose makes sense and why the other two do not.

▲ **Earthrace**

Earthrace, a wave-piercing speedboat.

Fueled by plant oils races across the world.

Earthrace, a wave-piercing speedboat fueled by plant oils, races across the world.

**What's the point of subjects, verbs, and simple sentences?**

------------------------------------------------------------

------------------------------------------------------------

# Understanding the Point of Subjects, Verbs, and Simple Sentences: One Student Writer's Response

The following paragraph offers one writer's reaction to the statements about Earthrace and the importance of subjects, verbs, and simple sentences.

*The last statement is the only one that made sense to me. The first statement gives a topic, and the second statement describes a topic and includes a verb "races." Both statements sound like parts of an idea instead of complete thoughts.*

# Applying the Point: Subjects, Verbs, and Simple Sentences

A subject and a verb unite to state a focused and complete thought in a sentence.

## Subjects

A **subject** is the person, place, object, or topic about which a writer expresses a focused thought or makes an assertion. To identify a subject, ask: Who or what did this? Alternatively, ask: Who or what is this?

### Types of Subjects

A subject is expressed in a variety of ways based on the focus of the writer's thought or point. Two common types of subjects include the **simple subject** and the **compound subject**.

**Simple Subjects: Three Types**

- **Simple Subject, Type 1:** A single person, place, object, or topic is the focus of thought.

SUBJECT
↓
Biodiesel is a renewable fuel produced from plants or animal fat.

- **Simple Subject, Type 2:** A group of words expresses the focus of thought.

SUBJECT
↓
Using renewable fuel reduces pollution.

- **Simple Subject, Type 3:** A suggestion, command, or order is the focus of thought.

Support the use of renewable fuels.
↑
"YOU" IS UNDERSTOOD, BUT NOT STATED, AS THE
SUBJECT OF THE SENTENCE, WHICH IS A COMMAND.

**Compound Subject**

- **Compound Subject:** Two or more people, places, objects, or topics are the subjects of a focused thought.

*COMPOUND SUBJECTS*

The sun, wind, and water are renewable energy sources.

*COMPOUND SUBJECTS ARE OFTEN JOINED BY THE COORDINATE CONJUNCTION "AND."*

**SUBJECTS**

Underline the <u>subject</u> once in each of the following sentences. Then, identify each subject by its type, writing *simple* or *compound* in the blanks. Share and discuss your responses in a small group or with your class.

........................... **1.** Ferry boats and military crafts also use wave-piercing technology.

........................... **2.** Wave-piercers have a very narrow bow.

........................... **3.** Narrowing the bow reduces the up and down bounce of the boat's bow.

........................... **4.** The narrow hull pierces through the water rather than riding over the top.

........................... **5.** Waste cooking oil, soya oil, and canola oil are the sources of the fuel for Earthrace.

........................... **6.** In 1998, the "Cable & Wireless Adventurer," a British boat, raced around the world in 75 days.

........................... **7.** Monsoon conditions and large waves have challenged the Earthrace crew during the last legs of their race around the world.

........................... **8.** Consider the accomplishment of Pete Bethune, the skipper of Earthrace, and his crew.

_____

**9.** Write a sentence using a simple subject. Suggested topic: A useful invention.

_____

**10.** Write a sentence using a compound subject. Suggested topic: Energy sources.

_____

For more information on verbs, see <www.mywritinglab.com>

# Verbs

A **verb** makes an assertion about a subject. A verb states an occurrence (*occur, happen*), a state of being (*is, seems*), or an action (*run, talk*) of the subject. Three basic types of verbs include **linking verbs, action verbs,** and **helping verbs.**

## Linking Verbs

A **linking verb** connects the subject to a word that renames, describes, or defines the subject. Linking verbs often describe a state of being.

## Commonly Used Linking Verbs

- *am, is, are, was, were, am being, has been…*

SUBJECT      LINKING VERB

Renewable power is natural power.

- *appear, become, look, seem, turn*

SUBJECT     LINKING VERB

Water turns into energy or hydro power.

- *feel, smell, sound, taste*

SUBJECT     LINKING VERBS

The engine feels hot and smells like burning oil.

---

**Practice 3**

**LINKING VERBS**

Fill in each blank with a linking verb that best completes the meaning of the sentence. Discuss your responses in a small group or with your class.

**1.** Energy ........................ the ability to do work.

**2.** We ........................ the warmth of the sun's energy.

## Action Verbs

An **action verb** shows the behavior of the subject.

SUBJECT     ACTION VERB

Sport utility vehicles guzzle gas.

---

**ACTION VERBS**

Underline the action verb twice in each of the following sentences.

**1.** Shontel exercises to burn energy.

**2.** Michael jogs for an hour to burn around 700 calories.

**3.** Shantel jumps rope for 10 minutes every day.

**4.** She also climbs the 100 steps in the football stadium.

**5.** After jogging, Michael swims a half mile in the ocean.

**6.** Finally, he bikes for five miles.

**7.** Shantel and Michael win many physical fitness competitions.

---

## Helping Verbs

A **helping verb** is used with a main verb to create a verb phrase. Helping verbs are also used to form questions. The verbs *be*, *do*, and *have* can be used alone or as helping verbs.

VERB PHRASE

HELPING VERB     MAIN VERB

I will begin a routine of regular exercise and healthful eating.

VERB PHRASE

HELPING VERB     MAIN VERB

Have you lost weight?

| Common Helping Verbs | | | | | | |
|---|---|---|---|---|---|---|
| be<br>being<br>been<br>am<br>are<br>is<br>was<br>were | do<br>does<br>did | have<br>had<br>has | may<br>might<br>must | could<br>should<br>would | can<br>shall<br>will | have to<br>have got to<br>ought to<br>supposed to<br>used to |

Practice 5

**HELPING VERBS**

Underline the <u>verb phrase</u> twice in each of the following sentences.

1. Hurricanes, ice storms, and tonadoes can be devastating natural disasters.

2. Due to lack of road access, emergency services may be delayed for up to 72 hours after a major disaster.

3. Citizens must be prepared before any major storm.

4. Lack of preparation can cause loss of property and even life.

5. One should have plenty of canned food, bottled water, and candles or oil lamps.

6. Buying a generator as an alternative power source would be wise.

7. Citizens ought to heed severe weather warnings.

Practice 6

**HELPING VERBS**

Underline the <u>subject</u> once and the <u>verb phrase</u> twice in each of the following sentences.

1. Everyone should exercise at least three times a week.

2. Most people do not get enough exercise in their daily routine.

3. Has Eugene lost weight?

4. Lifting weights and walking will build muscle and increase bone density.

5. Fruits and vegetables taste good and are good for you.

For more practice
with verbs:
<www.mywritinglab.com>

▲ **Exercise class**

---

**SUBJECTS AND VERBS**

Follow the directions to create five sentences. Suggested topic for your sentences: Exercise: Barriers or Benefits.

**1.** Write a sentence with a simple subject: ........................................................................

........................................................................................................................................

**2.** Write a sentence with a compound subject: ..................................................................

........................................................................................................................................

**3.** Write a sentence using a linking verb: ........................................................................

........................................................................................................................................

**4.** Write a sentence with an action verb: ........................................................................

........................................................................................................................................

**5.** Write a sentence with a helping verb: ........................................................................

........................................................................................................................................

# The Simple Sentence

A **simple sentence** is a group of related words that includes a subject and a verb and expresses a complete thought. A simple sentence is also known as an **independent clause**. An idea that is missing a subject or a verb is a fragment or an incomplete thought.

## Distinguishing Between a Fragment and the Simple Sentence

**Fragment with missing subject:**

VERB

Became the first female to win a major auto race.

**Fragment with missing verb:**

SUBJECT

Danica Patrick becoming the first female to win a major auto race.

**Simple Sentence:**

SUBJECT          VERB

Danica Patrick became the first female to win a major auto race.

**Practice 8**

### SIMPLE SENTENCES

Create a simple sentence from each of the following fragments. From the box below, fill in the blank with a subject or a verb that best completes each thought.

| Verbs | Subjects |
|---|---|
| is | competitors |
| provide | Danica Patrick |
| made | |

**Danica Patrick at 2005 Indianapolis 500 race** ▶

**1.** Indy racing the most extreme form of auto racing.

Indy racing ................... the most extreme form of auto racing.

**2.** Losing the first 49 races of her career her desire to win stronger.

Losing the first 49 races of her career ................... her desire to win stronger.

**3.** Determined, took the lead from Helio Castrneves on the 198th lap in a 200-lap race.

Determined, ................... took the lead from Helio Castrneves on the 198th lap in a 200-lap race.

**4.** Her were forced to pit for fuel in the final laps.

Her ................... were forced to pit for fuel in the final laps.

**5.** Heroes like Danica hope to female competitors in sports and beyond.

Heroes like Danica ................... hope to female competitors in sports and beyond.

# Locating Subjects and Verbs to Identify Complete Thoughts

To avoid fragments and to state ideas as complete thoughts, proofread to identify the subjects and verbs of each sentence. Identifying prepositional phrases as you proofread will help you locate the subject of the sentence.

## Understand the Prepositional Phrase

A **preposition** is a word that has a noun or pronoun as its object and states a relationship between its object and another word. A prepositional phrase begins with a preposition and ends with the object of the preposition.

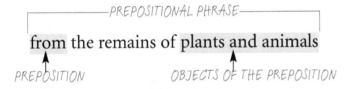

PREPOSITIONAL PHRASE

from the remains of plants and animals

PREPOSITION          OBJECTS OF THE PREPOSITION

The following chart lists a few common prepositions and examples of their objects.

| Common Prepositions with Possible Objects | | | |
| --- | --- | --- | --- |
| **Preposition** | **Object** | **Preposition** | **Object** |
| about | the house | for | Texas |
| after | the movie | from | the past |
| along | the street | in/into | a wallet |
| as/like | the parent | of | the boys |
| below | the surface | on | the chair |
| by | evening | to | the college |
| during | the storm | with | patience |

# Find the Prepositional Phrases

The object of the preposition can never be the subject or the verb of a sentence. Since subjects and verbs are often surrounded by prepositional phrases, you need to identify these phrases. Identifying prepositional phrases keeps you from confusing them with the subject of the sentence. And often, once these phrases are identified, the subject and the verb—or lack of either—becomes easier to recognize.

---

**IDENTIFYING PREPOSITIONAL PHRASES**

Place parentheses around all (prepositional phrases) in the following simple sentences.

1. The United States of America consumes about 882 million gallons of petroleum products each day.

2. After millions of years, some organic remains of animals and plants turn into crude oil.

3. The refining process of crude oil creates products like gasoline, diesel fuel, heating oil, and jet fuel.

4. The characteristics of gasoline depend on the type of crude oil.

5. The cost of crude oil acts as the main contributor to the record high gasoline prices of 2008.

---

## The FIL Process

To identify subjects and verbs, follow these three simple steps:

1. **F**ind Prepositional Phrases:  Place parentheses around (prepositional phrases).

2. **I**dentify the Verb:  Underline the <u>verb</u> (action or linking) twice.

3. **L**ocate the Subject:  Ask: Who or what did this or who or what is this? The answer is the subject. Underline the <u>subject</u> once.


SUBJECT          PREPOSITIONAL PHRASE                          VERB

Gasoline prices (in the United States) typically increase

(during the spring and summer) (due to an increase) (in demand).

PREPOSITIONAL PHRASE

## IDENTIFYING SUBJECTS AND VERBS

Identify the subjects and verbs in the following simple sentences. Annotate each sentence: Place (prepositional phrases) in parentheses, underline the <u>verb</u> twice, underline the <u>subject</u> once.

**1.** The retail price of gasoline is affected by several factors.

**2.** In addition to the cost of crude, taxes from federal, state, and local governments are the largest part of the retail price of gasoline.

**3.** The level of supply in relationship to demand also affects the retail price of gasoline.

**4.** Problems at refineries and interruption of the supply of gasoline affect its cost at the pump.

**5.** The price on the pump includes the retailer's cost of buying gasoline and operating the service station.

## SUBJECTS, VERBS, AND SIMPLE SENTENCES REVIEW

Read the following paragraph written by a student. In each sentence, underline the <u>subject</u> once, underline the <u>verb</u> twice, and place parentheses around the (prepositional phrase). *Hint:* Some sentences use the understood subject *you*. Then, write three simple sentences of your own.

(1) For each gallon of gas used by driving, twenty pounds of carbon dioxide pollute the air. (2) We, as residents in a large city, can take action to reduce our use of fuel-based pollution. (3) First of all, our bus system runs on electronic and hybrid fuel and deserves our support. (4) Our use of mass transit will reduce pollution. (5) Obviously, a bus full of people, as opposed to the average car with one or two people, is a much more efficient use of fuel. (6) Secondly, many of us could carpool with our coworkers. (7) Think about it. One car with four people on the road is better than four people in four cars on the road. (8) Finally, we of able bodies should walk and bike more often. (9) Using our own energy for transportation causes no pollution at all. (10) In addition to the benefits of less pollution, these changes in our behavior are going to save us money at the gas pump.

Write three simple sentences. Suggested topic:  Transportation issues.

**1.** ...................................................................................................................

...................................................................................................................

**2.** ...................................................................................................................

...................................................................................................................

**3.** ...................................................................................................................

...................................................................................................................

# Writing Assignments

## Writing for Everyday Life

Read the following letter to the editor of a newspaper. In each sentence, underline the <u>subject</u> once, underline the <u>verb</u> twice, and place parentheses around the (prepositional phrase).

Dear Editor:

An article about building solar power plants in our community appeared on Monday in the business section of your paper. Many of us in the area are excited about the benefits of solar energy. The uses for solar energy include heating water for domestic use and the space heating of buildings. The energy from one solar power plant will offer enough electricity to run hundreds of homes. The source of solar power is renewable. And the energy from the sun does not harm the quality of our air. The Chief Officer of The State Power and Light Company has earned our thanks.

## Writing for College Life

Read the following paragraph written for a college economics class. In each sentence, underline the <u>subject</u> once, underline the <u>verb</u> twice, and place parentheses around the (prepositional phrase).

The relationship between supply and demand sets the price in the market place. Demand is the purchase of specific quantities of a good or service at different prices in a given time. Supply is the creation and delivery of specific quantities of a good or service at different prices in a given time. For a demand to exist, someone must be willing to pay for the goods. Often, a product in high demand but short in supply will have a high price. In contrast, a product in low demand but high in supply will have a lower price.

# Writing for Working Life

Read the following memo sent from a director to her staff. Identify subjects, verbs, and prepositional phrases. Underline <u>subjects</u> once, <u><u>verbs</u></u> twice, and place parentheses around (prepositional phrases). *Hint:* Some sentences use the understood subject *you*.

> TO:        The Accounting Staff
> FROM:      Maya Berry, Director of Accounting
> SUBJECT:   Going Green
>
> Dear Staff:
> In compliance with our company's new energy policies, our department is making the following changes. All of the lights are to remain off in unoccupied rooms. On your way out of a room, remember to shut off the lights. Recycling bins for paper, aluminum, and plastic waste have been placed near each of your cubicles. Paper cups for coffee and water are no longer being provided in the break room. You must supply your own coffee mug or glass. I appreciate your cooperation in this matter.
>
> Best Regards,
> Maya Berry

## WHAT HAVE I LEARNED?

To test and track your understanding, complete the following sentences. Use several sentences as needed for each response.

**1.** A subject is ..............................................................................................

..............................................................................................

..............................................................................................

**2.** The two types of subjects are ..............................................................

**3.** A verb ..................................................................................................

The three basic types of verbs are .........................................................

**4.** A simple sentence is ...........................................................................

..............................................................................................

**5. How will I use what I have learned?**
In your notebook, discuss how you will apply to your own writing what you have learned about subjects and verbs.

**6. What do I still need to study about subjects and verbs?**
In your notebook, describe your ongoing study needs by describing what, when, and how you will continue studying subjects and verbs.

Academic Learning Log

LEARNING OUTCOMES
SELF-EVALUATION

PORTFOLIO

# 14

# Compound and Complex Sentences

A compound sentence joins together two or more independent clauses. A complex sentence combines one independent or main clause and one or more dependent clauses.

Communicating about a real-life situation helps us to understand the purpose of compound and complex sentences. The photographs of Marc Anthony, Dayanara Torres, and Jennifer Lopez on these pages illustrate a blended family. Read the statements given in Practice 1, complete the activities, and answer the question "What's the point of compound and complex sentences?"

◀ Marc Anthony and his pregnant wife Dayanara Torres

# What's the Point of Compound and Complex Sentences?

## PHOTOGRAPHIC ORGANIZER: COMPOUND AND COMPLEX SENTENCES

The following ideas are stated using four types of sentences: (1) simple, (2) compound, (3) complex, and (4) compound-complex. Discuss with a small group of peers in what ways these sentences differ from each other.

1. in 2008, Marc Anthony and Jennifer Lopez became the proud parents of twins Marc and Emme.

2. The twins are the first children of Jennifer Lopez, but Marc Anthony has three other children.

3. Children who are in a blended family often struggle with the changes in their lifestyles.

4. At least one-third of all children in the U.S. will live in a stepfamily before they reach age 18; fortunately, most blended families work out their problems.

**What's the point of compound and complex sentences?**

▲ Marc Anthony and his wife Jennifer Lopez with their twins

_____

_____

_____

_____

_____

_____

_____

# Understanding the Point of Compound and Complex Sentences: One Student Writer's Response

The following paragraph offers one writer's thoughts about the differences among sentence types.

First, I found the subjects and verbs in each sentence. In the first sentence, a compound subject states one idea. The second sentence gives two different ideas. Third sentence mixes two ideas about one subject. The fourth sentence is made up of several ideas. I want to know why the commas and semicolons are used in sentences 2 and 4. The four types of sentences are four different ways to say something.

# Applying the Point: Compound and Complex Sentences

A **clause** is a group of related words that includes a subject and a verb. Two types of clauses provide the basis of all sentences: the (1) **independent clause** and the (2) **dependent clause**.

**1.** The Independent Clause

A focused and complete thought expressed with a subject and a verb; also known as a *main clause* or **simple sentence**.

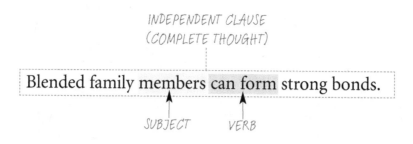

INDEPENDENT CLAUSE
(COMPLETE THOUGHT)

Blended family members can form strong bonds.

SUBJECT    VERB

## 2. The Dependent Clause

For more about subordinating conjunctions, see page 281.

(1) An incomplete thought expressed with a subject and a verb marked by a subordinating conjunction such as *after*, *before*, or *when*.

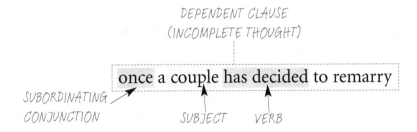

For more about relative pronouns, see page 282.

(2) An incomplete thought marked by a relative pronoun, such as *who* or *which*, acting as the subject of the verb.

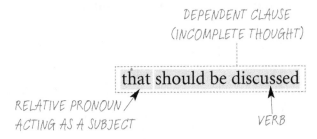

---

### TYPES OF CLAUSES

Identify each of the following clauses as **I** for independent or **D** for dependent. *Hint:* Circle subordinating conjunctions and relative pronouns.

_____ **1.** Older children may feel left out.

_____ **2.** When a new baby comes into a blended family.

_____ **3.** Children who live in blended families.

_____ **4.** If they can be with both biological parents.

_____ **5.** Children of blended families can adjust and thrive.

Practice 2

© Pearson Education, Inc.

# A Compound Sentence

A compound sentence is made up of two or more independent clauses. A **compound sentence** links two or more independent clauses together as **equally important** ideas through one of three methods.

## Three Ways to Combine Independent Clauses into a Compound Sentence

1. **A comma and a coordinating conjunction**: The coordinating conjunction serves as a transition that shows the relationship of ideas within the sentence. Use the acronym FANBOYS to help you remember the seven coordinating conjunctions—*for, and, nor, but, or, yet,* or *so.*

*[Independent clause,] and [independent clause.]*

| Coordinating Conjunctions (FANBOYS) and Meanings | | | | | | | |
|---|---|---|---|---|---|---|---|
| **Coordinating Conjunction** | For | And | Nor | But | Or | Yet | So |
| **Meaning** | Result | Addition | Negation | Contrast | Choice | Contrast | Result |

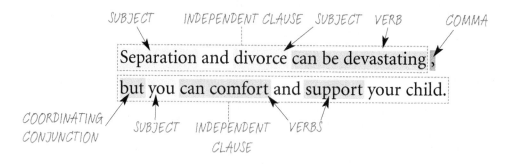

2. **A semicolon, conjunctive adverb, and a comma:** The conjunction shows the relationship of ideas within the sentence. In addition, the conjunctive adverb introduces the next clause. A comma follows the conjunctive adverb since it is an introductory element of the next clause:

*[Independent clause;] therefore, [independent clause.]*

| Common Conjunctive Adverbs and the Relationships They Express | | | | | |
|---|---|---|---|---|---|
| **Addition** | **Cause or Effect** | **Comparison or Contrast** | **Example** | **Emphasis** | **Time** |
| also | accordingly | however | for example | certainly | finally |
| besides | as a result | in comparison | for instance | indeed | meanwhile |
| further | consequently | in contrast | | in fact | next |
| furthermore | hence | instead | | still | then |
| in addition | therefore | likewise | | undoubtedly | thereafter |
| incidentally | thus | nevertheless | | | |
| moreover | | nonetheless | | | |
| | | otherwise | | | |
| | | similarly | | | |

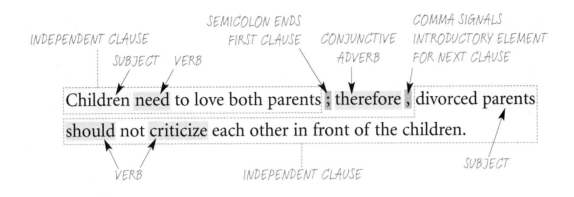

**3. A semicolon:** A semicolon joins two closely related independent clauses.

*[Independent clause.] [independent clause.]*

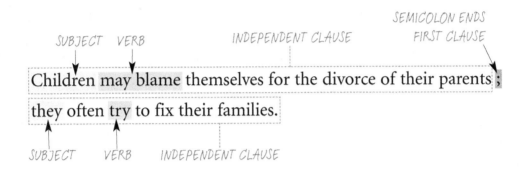

---

**COMPOUND SENTENCES**

Insert the proper punctuation in each of the following compound sentences. **Hint:** Identify the subjects and verbs. Place parentheses around (prepositional phrases); underline the <u>subject</u> once; underline the <u>verb</u> twice.

**1.** A divorce creates a painful loss for everyone parents and children need time to mourn the loss of the family.

**2.** Parents should sit down together and talk with their children so both parents can comfort them and promise to be there for them.

**3.** Eventually, a divorced parent will likely remarry as a result a new blended family faces several challenges.

**4.** Only the biological parent should discipline his or her children, and the same rules apply to all the children of the same age.

**5.** A blended family of biological and step children is a new start for everyone; therefore, the new family should create new family traditions such as a family movie night once a month.

**6.** Write a compound sentence. Suggested topic: Family traditions.

---

For more information on how to identify subjects, verbs, and prepositional phrases, see page 270.

## COMPOUND SENTENCES

Create compound sentences by combining the following sets of simple sentences. Vary the ways in which you join ideas. Use appropriate conjunctions and punctuation to show the relationship between ideas within each new sentence.

**1.** In the 1900s, Americans thought of marriage as a holy and life-long vow. Divorce was seen as wrong and harmful.

------------------------------------------

------------------------------------------

**2.** Slowly, people's views about marriage changed. They began to see marriage as short-term and based on feelings instead of duty.

------------------------------------------

------------------------------------------

**3.** The meaning of divorce also changed. It was no longer a symbol of failure but of freedom and new beginnings.

------------------------------------------

------------------------------------------

**4.** The roles of men and women in a marriage also changed. The changes forced couples to figure out how to divide duties of work, home, and children.

------------------------------------------

------------------------------------------

**5.** In the past, men earned the wages. Women took care of the children and the home.

------------------------------------------

**6.** Many are thankful for these changes in marriage. These changes have made divorce more common.

------------------------------------------

------------------------------------------

**7.** Write a compound sentence. Suggested topic: Advice to a young couple.

------------------------------------------

------------------------------------------

Adapted from Henslin, James M. *Essentials of Sociology: A Down-to-Earth-Approach,* 7th ed., 2008. p. 15.

# A Complex Sentence

A **complex sentence** contains one independent or main clause and one or more dependent clauses. A **dependent clause** expresses a **subordinate** or minor detail about an idea in the independent clause. A complex sentence joins independent and dependent clauses by placing a subordinating conjunction at the beginning of the dependent clause. **Subordinating conjunctions** state the relationship between the main clause and the subordinate clause.

| Subordinating Conjunctions and the Relationships They Express | | | | |
|---|---|---|---|---|
| **Cause** | **Contrast** | **Time** | **Place** | **Condition** |
| as | although | after | where | even if |
| because | as if | as | wherever | how |
| in order that | even though | as long as | | if |
| now that | though | before | | only if |
| since | whereas | once | | that |
| so | while | since | | unless |
| | | until | | what |
| | | when | | when |
| | | whenever | | whether or not |
| | | while | | |

INDEPENDENT CLAUSE              DEPENDENT CLAUSE

Your role in society is set before you are born.

SUBJECT          VERB     SUBORDINATING CONJUNCTION

---

**COMPLEX SENTENCES**

Underline the dependent clauses in each sentence. In the blank after each sentence, state the relationship between the dependent clause and the main clause.

**1.** Society was waiting to teach you how you are to act as a boy or a girl. _____

**2.** Whether you were born rich, poor, or middle-class, your status also affects your role in society. _____

**3.** Although you occupy a status or a position, you play a role. _____

**4.** A father fulfills his role by providing food, shelter, and love because of his status as a parent. _____

**5.** Write a complex sentence using a subordinating conjunction. State the relationship between your dependent and main clauses. Suggested topic: Traits of a good father.

_____

_____

Practice 5

A special kind of subordinating conjunction is the relative pronoun. A **relative pronoun** connects the dependent clause to a noun in the main clause. The choice of a relative pronoun indicates whether the dependent clause is describing a person or thing.

| Relative Pronouns and What They Indicate | | |
| --- | --- | --- |
| **People** | **Things** | **People or Things** |
| who | which | that |
| whom | | |
| whose | | |

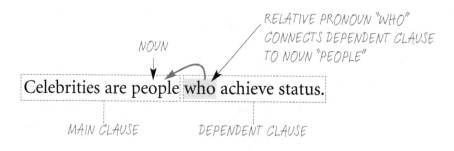

RELATIVE PRONOUN "WHO"
CONNECTS DEPENDENT CLAUSE
TO NOUN "PEOPLE"

NOUN

Celebrities are people who achieve status.

MAIN CLAUSE          DEPENDENT CLAUSE

### COMPLEX SENTENCES

Insert the relative pronoun that best completes each sentence. Circle the nouns described by the relative pronoun.

**1.** An ascribed status is something ............... you are born into.

**2.** A female ............... is born into a wealthy family did not choose the status of female or wealth.

**3.** An achieved status is a position ............... you achieve or earn.

**4.** Both a college president and a bank robber are examples of those ............... have achieved a status.

**5.** Write a complex sentence using a relative pronoun. Suggested topic: The status of women in society.

............................................................................................................

............................................................................................................

282

## Placement and Punctuation of a Dependent Clause within a Complex Sentence

1. **Before the main clause:** A dependent clause at the beginning of a sentence acts as an introductory element and must be set off with a comma.

*Subordinating conjunction dependent clause*, **main clause**.

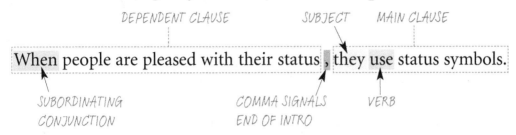

2. **In the middle of the main clause:** The context of the clause controls the use of commas. Many dependent clauses in the middle of a sentence are **relative clauses.** Relative clauses are either essential or nonessential.

(a) If the dependent clause adds information **essential** to the meaning of the sentence, no commas are needed. Most often, essential information limits or restricts the meaning of a common noun such as *man* or *woman*.

**Main** *relative pronoun dependent clause* **clause**.

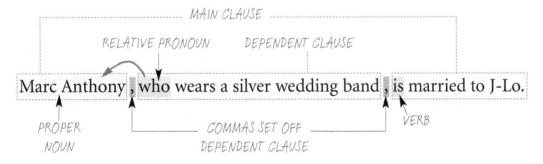

(b) If the dependent clause adds information that is **nonessential** to the meaning of the main clause, insert commas before and after the dependent clause. Usually a nonessential clause describes a proper noun.

**3. After the main clause:** The context of the clause controls the use of commas in these instances:

(a) If the dependent clause begins with a **subordinating conjunction**, no comma is needed.

**Main clause** *subordinating conjunction dependent clause.*

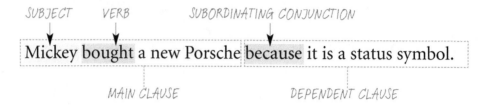

(b) If the dependent clause begins with a relative pronoun, determine if the information is essential or nonessential. An **essential** dependent clause does not need a comma.

**Main clause** *dependent clause.*

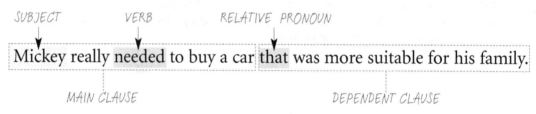

(c) Insert a comma before a dependent clause that is **nonessential**.

**Main clause,** *relative pronoun dependent clause.*

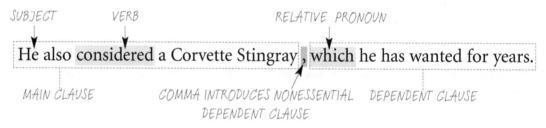

---

**COMPLEX SENTENCES**

Edit each of the following complex sentences for proper punctuation.

1. Roxanne attends the community college, that is close to her home.

2. Roxanne who is majoring in music and dance wants to be like Jennifer Lopez.

3. Few people, who train in music and dance, achieve the status of Lopez.

## COMPLEX SENTENCES

Create five complex sentences by combining the following sets of simple sentences. Use appropriate subordinating conjunctions, relative pronouns, and punctuation to show the relationship between ideas within each new sentence.

**1.** Angelina Jolie and Brad Pitt use their status to help others. They have achieved world-wide stardom.

---------------------------------

---------------------------------

---------------------------------

**2.** Pitt and Jolie are favorite targets of the press. They bring world attention to worthy causes.

---------------------------------

---------------------------------

**3.** Angelina Jolie has traveled to 20 countries. She is a United Nations Goodwill Ambassador.

---------------------------------

---------------------------------

**4.** Brad Pitt visited the Lower 9th Ward right after Hurricane Katrina. He was shocked by what he saw.

---------------------------------

---------------------------------

**5.** Pitt started the Make It Right Foundation to build new homes in the 9th Ward. The new homes will be eco-friendly and sturdy.

---------------------------------

---------------------------------

**6.** In 2006, Pitt and Jolie spent Christmas Day with a Colombian refugee family in Costa Rica. Costa Rica has over ten thousand Colombian refugees.

---------------------------------

---------------------------------

# A Compound-Complex Sentence

A **compound-complex sentence** is two or more independent clauses and one or more dependent clauses. A compound-complex sentence joins coordinate and subordinate ideas into a single sentence. All the punctuation rules for both compound and complex sentences apply to the compound-complex sentence.

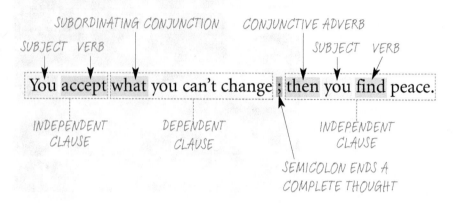

Practice 9

## COMPOUND-COMPLEX SENTENCES

Create and properly punctuate four compound-complex sentences by combining the following simple sentences. Discuss your work with a classmate or with a small group of peers.

**1.** Deidra needs to understand. She can only change herself. She can't change other people.

**2.** Deidra doesn't like her job. She must be the one to make a change. She could look for another job or learn how to cope with conflict.

**3.** Deidra is afraid. She is afraid of failure and rejection. She doesn't take chances. She doesn't trust others easily.

**4.** Her distrust makes her seem unfriendly. Her attitude offends others. She has achieved the status of disgruntled employee.

## FOUR SENTENCE TYPES REVIEW

Write and properly punctuate four different types of sentences. Suggested topic: Traits of an effective employee.

1. Simple ____________________

2. Compound ____________________

3. Complex ____________________

4. Compound-Complex ____________________

Practice 10

# Writing Assignments

## Writing for Everyday Life

In the following letter to her friend, a young woman shares her thoughts about meeting her future in-laws. Edit the paragraph for correct punctuation of sentence types. Use your own paper.

Dear Billie Jean:

I just met my future in-laws. We are so different. You know. That I come from a single parent family. My mom was a career woman who made her own way and she taught me to do the same My mom and I are more like best friends than mother and daughter. Manuel's mother is different. She enjoys the status of a stay-at-home mom she loves cooking, cleaning, and controlling everyone. I hope she likes me. Because I like her.

## Writing for College Life

Read the following paragraph about the term "social class" from the college textbook *Essentials of Sociology: A Down-to-Earth-Approach,* 7th ed. by James Henslin. Edit the paragraph for correct punctuation of sentence types. Use your own paper.

To understand people, we must examine the social locations that they hold in life. Especially significant is social class which is based on income, education, and occupational prestige. Large numbers of people who have similar amounts of income and education and who work at jobs that are roughly equal in prestige make up a social class. Our social class affects our behavior it even affects our ideas and attitudes.

## Writing for Working Life

Read the following memo written from a supervisor to an employee. Edit the paragraph for correct punctuation of sentence types. Use your own paper.

To:     Eugene Beltz
From:   Amanda Ortiz, Manager
RE:     · Employee training

As I indicated in your yearly evaluation you are required to attend a series of training sessions. That will build your skills as a team member. Because you need to improve your public speaking skills you will join Toastmasters. You will also enroll in the workshop for conflict resolution it is scheduled for next month and it will last for six weeks. Once you have completed this training we will review your eligibility for promotion.

PEARSON
mywritinglab
**WANT A
BETTER GRADE?**
For more practice and writing assignments on compound and complex sentences, go to
**www.mywritinglab.com >
The Basic Sentence >
Compound and Complex
Sentences.**

**WHAT HAVE I LEARNED?**

To test and track your understanding, answer the following questions.

**1.** What is a clause, and what are the two types of clauses?

**2.** What is a simple sentence?

**3.** What is a compound sentence?

**4.** What is a complex sentence?

**5.** What is a complex-compound sentence?

**6. How will I use what I have learned?**
In your notebook, discuss how you will apply to your own writing what you have learned about sentence types. When will you apply this knowledge during the writing process?

**7. What do I still need to study about sentence types?**
In your notebook, describe your ongoing study needs by describing what, when, and how you will continue studying sentence types.

## Coordination

| | | |
|---|---|---|
| **Option 1**<br>Independent clause | ⎧ , for<br>⎪ , and<br>⎪ , nor<br>⎨ , but<br>⎪ , or<br>⎪ , yet<br>⎩ , so ⎫⎬⎭ | independent clause. |

| | | |
|---|---|---|
| **Option 2**<br>Independent clause | { ; (semicolon only) } | independent clause. |

| | | |
|---|---|---|
| **Option 3**<br>Independent clause | ⎧ ; also,<br>; anyway,<br>; as a result,<br>; besides,<br>; certainly,<br>; consequently,<br>; finally,<br>; furthermore,<br>; however,<br>; incidentally,<br>; in addition,<br>; in fact,<br>; indeed,<br>; instead,<br>; likewise,<br>; meanwhile,<br>; moreover,<br>; nevertheless,<br>; next<br>; now<br>; on the other hand,<br>; otherwise,<br>; similarly,<br>; still<br>; then<br>; therefore,<br>; thus<br>⎩ ; undoubtedly, ⎫⎬⎭ | independent clause. |

## Subordination

| | | |
|---|---|---|
| **Option 4** | After<br>Although<br>As<br>As if<br>Because<br>Before<br>Even though<br>If<br>In order that<br>Since<br>So that<br>Though<br>Unless<br>Until<br>When<br>Whenever<br>Where<br>Whereas<br>Whether<br>While | dependent clause, independent clause. (When you begin with a dependent clause, put a comma at the end of the dependent clause.) |
| **Option 5**<br>Independent clause | after<br>although<br>as<br>as if<br>because<br>before<br>even though<br>if<br>in order that<br>since<br>so that<br>though<br>unless<br>until<br>when<br>whenever<br>where<br>whereas<br>whether<br>while | dependent clause |

**Note:** In Option 4, words are capitalized because the dependent clause will begin your complete sentence.

# 15 Sentence Variety

Sentence variety is the use of sentences of different lengths, types, and purposes.

Communicating about a real-life situation helps us to understand the purpose of sentence variety. The photograph on the facing page illustrates a family day trip to a local landmark. Read the accompanying short paragraph about the landmark in Practice 1, complete the activities, and answer the question "What's the point of sentence variety?"

# What's the Point of Sentence Variety?

**PHOTOGRAPHIC ORGANIZER: SENTENCE VARIETY**

Read the following short paragraph. What do all the sentences have in common? Describe the overall effect of the paragraph.

The Ponce de Leon Inlet Lighthouse was built in 1884. The lighthouse is 175 feet tall. The lighthouse is the second highest lighthouse on the East Coast. The lighthouse is a very highly visited site. It has many resources. It has lots of old photographs. It has a visitor's video about its history.

**What is the point of sentence variety?**

----------------------------------------

----------------------------------------

----------------------------------------

----------------------------------------

----------------------------------------

# Understanding the Point of Sentence Variety: One Student Writer's Response

The following paragraph records one writer's thoughts about the point of sentence variety in the paragraph in Practice 1.

> In the paragraph about the lighthouse, every sentence starts with the words "the lighthouse" or the pronoun "it," and most of the sentences use the same verbs "is" and "has." In addition, the sentences are all simple and about the same length, using four to ten-words. The paragraph seems flat and dull.

# Applying the Point: Sentence Variety

**Sentence variety** adds interest and power to your writing. You can achieve sentence variety by varying the purposes, types, and openings of your sentences.

## Vary Sentence Purpose

Every sentence expresses a purpose.

**1. Declarative sentences** make a statement to share information and are punctuated with a period. Declarative sentences are often used to state a main idea and supporting details.

A mayday call signals a life-threatening emergency.

**2. Interrogative sentences** ask a question and are punctuated with a question mark. Usually, the writer also provides an answer to the question. An interrogative sentence may be used to introduce a topic and lead into a topic sentence.

What is your emergency?

**3. Imperative sentences** give a command that demands an action and are punctuated with a period. Imperative sentences are often used to give directions to complete a process or persuade a reader to take action.

You must tell us your position.

**4. Exclamatory sentences** express a strong emotion and are punctuated with an exclamation point. Exclamatory sentences emphasize a significant point.

Mayday, mayday, our boat is flooding!

Most often, you will rely upon the declarative sentence to share information with your reader. However, thoughtful use of a question, command, or exclamation gives your writing variety and adds interest to your ideas.

Read the following paragraph, adapted from "Disaster by the Late Storm: Awful Shipwreck at Minot's Ledge," an 1849 newspaper article. Identify the purpose of each sentence.

### Awful Shipwreck at Minot's Ledge

(1) Who can imagine such a tragedy? (2) When the Saint John struck, her small boat was got ready, but was swamped by a large number jumping into her. (3) Shortly after, the long boat broke her fastening and floated off. (4) After the ship struck the rocks, she thumped awhile. (5) But shortly she went to pieces, holding together not more than sixty minutes. (6) Seven women and three men came ashore on pieces of the wreck, alive, but very much exhausted. (7) Towards nightfall, the bodies began to come ashore, and quite a number were taken from the surf, all, however, dead. (8) Dead bodies would be thrown upon the rocks, but before they could be reached, the sea would carry them back again. (9) Ninety-nine people perished! (10) We must honor the loss of these poor souls; we must never forget this tragedy.

Sentence 1. _____    Sentence 6. _____

Sentence 2. _____    Sentence 7. _____

Sentence 3. _____    Sentence 8. _____

Sentence 4. _____    Sentence 9. _____

Sentence 5. _____    Sentence 10. _____

# Vary Sentence Types

You learned in Chapters 13 and 14 about the four types of sentences: simple, compound, complex, and compound-complex. When writers rely on one type of sentence more than the others, their work becomes dull and flat, like a speaker delivering a speech in a monotone. As writers combine sentences, they must decide if the combined ideas are equal in importance, or if one idea is more important than another.

**Coordinating ideas** makes each idea equal in importance. To combine coordinate ideas, use a comma and a coordinating conjunction (FANBOYS: *for, and, nor, but, or, yet,* or *so*).

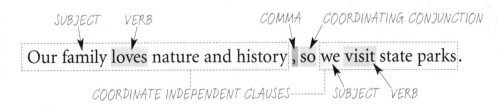

**Subordinating ideas** makes one idea dependent on (and less important than) another idea. To make an idea subordinate, use a subordinating conjunction (*after, although, as, because, before, since, unless,* etc.). If the new subordinate clause begins the sentence as an introductory element, include a comma at the end of that clause to set it off from the main independent clause.

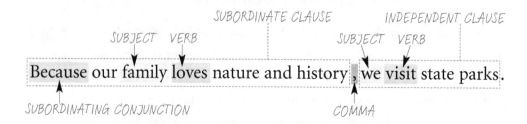

As you study methods of combining sentences, you will learn how to coordinate or subordinate ideas. To add interest and emphasis to your writing, vary the type of your sentences. Many writers use the revision process to combine sentences to achieve variety and interest.

## Combine Two or More Simple Sentences into One Simple Sentence

A series of short simple sentences often creates a choppy flow of ideas. Combining closely related short simple sentences into one simple sentence creates a smooth flow of ideas. Short simple sentences can be combined in several ways.

### COMBINE SENTENCES WITH A COMPOUND SUBJECT

When two separate simple sentences possess the same verb, they can become one sentence with a compound subject. A **compound subject** is two or more nouns or pronouns joined by the coordinating conjunction **and.** Note that the verb form of a compound subject must be plural. This method of coordinating ideas places equal emphasis on each subject.

**Original Sentences:**

SUBJECT  VERB                                          SUBJECT  REPEATED VERB

Hiking is one fun activity at a state park. Kayaking is another fun

activity. Visiting museums at a state park is also fun.
        SUBJECT                           REPEATED VERB

**Sentences Combined with a Compound Subject:**

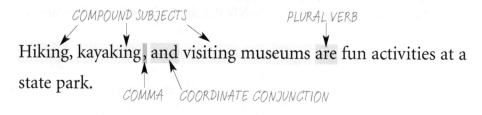

Combine the following simple sentences into a new simple sentence using compound subjects. *Hint:* Delete words or reword ideas as needed to create a smooth flow of ideas.

**1.** The Fairchild Oak is located in Bulow State Park. The ruins of a sugar cane plantation are also in the park.

-------------------------------------------------------------------

**2.** The 400-year-old Fairchild Oak is impressive. The Bulow ruins are also remarkable.

-------------------------------------------------------------------

## COMBINE SENTENCES WITH A COMPOUND VERB

When two separate simple sentences possess the same subject, they can become one sentence with a **compound verb**, two or more verbs joined by a coordinating conjunction of addition or contrast: *and, or, but,* or *yet.* When only two verbs are joined, no comma is needed before the conjunction. This method of coordinating ideas places equal emphasis on each verb.

**Original Sentences:**

SUBJECT    VERB                              SUBJECT    VERB

Stephen Crane wrote powerful stories. Stephen Crane lived a

dramatic life.

**Sentences Combined with a Compound Verb:**

SUBJECT                    COMPOUND VERBS

Stephen Crane wrote powerful stories and lived a dramatic life.

Combine the following simple sentences into a new simple sentence using compound verbs.

**1.** Crane was a journalist. Crane really wanted to report on the freedom fighters in Cuba.

-------------------------------------------------------------------

**2.** Smugglers used the steam tug Commodore to run guns to the Cuban freedom fighters. They hired Crane as an able seaman.

-------------------------------------------------------------------

-------------------------------------------------------------------

## COMBINE SENTENCES WITH A PHRASE

A phrase is a group of related words that lacks both a subject and a verb. Because it lacks a subject and a verb, it cannot act as a sentence. A phrase acts as a single part of speech in a sentence; for example, a phrase can function as an adjective. The use of commas depends upon where the phrase appears. This sentence combination subordinates an idea by placing less emphasis on the idea in the phrase.

**Original Sentences:**

SUBJECT  VERB  REPEATED SUBJECT  VERB

Stephen Crane remains a much admired novelist. He is the author of *The Red Badge of Courage*.

**Revised with phrase at the beginning of sentence:**

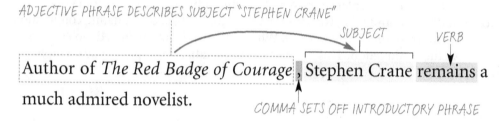

ADJECTIVE PHRASE DESCRIBES SUBJECT "STEPHEN CRANE"

SUBJECT  VERB

Author of *The Red Badge of Courage*, Stephen Crane remains a much admired novelist.

COMMA SETS OFF INTRODUCTORY PHRASE

**Revised with phrase in the middle of sentence:**

ADJECTIVE PHRASE DESCRIBES SUBJECT "STEPHEN CRANE"

SUBJECT  VERB

Stephen Crane, a much admired novelist, is the author of *The Red Badge of Courage*.

COMMAS SET OFF PHRASE IN MIDDLE OF SENTENCE

**Revised with phrase at the end of sentence:**

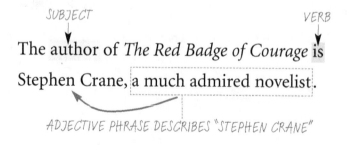

SUBJECT  VERB

The author of *The Red Badge of Courage* is Stephen Crane, a much admired novelist.

ADJECTIVE PHRASE DESCRIBES "STEPHEN CRANE"

In each of the items below, combine the given simple sentences into one new sentence using a phrase. In your answers, follow the placement of the phrase suggested in parentheses at the end of each item. Use appropriate punctuation.

Lighthouse staircase ▶

**1.** The earliest lighthouses were simply bonfires. These bonfires were built on hillsides to guide ships. (end of sentence).

-------------------------------------------------------------------

-------------------------------------------------------------------

**2.** The first lighthouse was built in 285 BCE. It was serving the old world city of Alexandria. (beginning of sentence)

-------------------------------------------------------------------

-------------------------------------------------------------------

**3.** The first American lighthouse came into service in 1716. It was at Boston Harbor. (end of sentence)

-------------------------------------------------------------------

-------------------------------------------------------------------

**4.** The lantern was typically a round, square, octagonal, or decagonal-shaped cast-iron house for a lens. It was surrounded by an exterior stone or cast iron gallery with railing. (beginning of sentence)

-------------------------------------------------------------------

-------------------------------------------------------------------

**5.** Stairs gave access to the lantern at the top of the tower. The stairs were winding around a central column or spiral inside the tower wall. (middle of sentence)

-------------------------------------------------------------------

-------------------------------------------------------------------

For information on how to create compound and complex sentences, see pages 274–289.

# Combine Ideas Using Compound and Complex Sentence Types

Combine ideas of equal importance using **coordination**, joining independent clauses into a **compound sentence**. Combine ideas of unequal importance—a main idea and a subordinate, or minor, idea—using **subordination**, joining an independent clause with a dependent clause into a **complex sentence**.

**VARY SIMPLE SENTENCES**

Use subordination and coordination to logically combine the ideas in the twelve sentences below into five sentences. Punctuate properly. (*Note:* For more help on how to create compound and complex sentences and punctuate them correctly, see Chapter 14.)

(1) We have been fighting a war in Iraq. (2) I have been deployed several times. (3) I am in the Army. (4) I have gone through a lot of emotions and experiences because of the war. (5) I read Stephen Crane's novel *The Red Badge of Courage*. (6) *The Red Badge of Courage* is about the Civil War. (7) It is supposed to be a realistic view of war. (8) I read with great interest. (9) I compared my experiences to the experiences of Henry Fleming. (10) He is the main character. (11) The novel makes a good point. (12) Youths must quickly mature in order to survive.

# Vary Sentence Openings

Most often, we begin our sentences with the subject followed by the verb. To add interest and to shift the emphasis of an idea, you can vary the ways in which you begin a sentence. You have already worked with two types of sentence openings: phrases and dependent clauses. Two additional ways to begin a sentence include using adverbs and prepositional phrases. As introductory elements in a sentence, both an adverb and a prepositional phrase are set off with a comma.

### ADVERB

• Describes or modifies another adverb, a verb, or an adjective

• Answers the questions: *How? How often? How much? When? Where?* and *Why?*

• Usually ends in *-ly: angrily, beautifully, frequently*

*ADVERB*     *COMMA SETS OFF INTRODUCTORY ELEMENT*

Patiently , Liza listened to the speaker.

## PREPOSITIONAL PHRASE

- Begins with a preposition and ends with a noun or pronoun, the object of the preposition
- Object of the preposition describes or modifies another word in the sentence
- Common prepositions and objects: *about the yard, at the store, by the door, in the house, on the way, to the corner, with you*

*PREPOSITIONAL PHRASE*     *COMMA SETS OFF INTRODUCTORY ELEMENT*

After the lecture , Liza recopied her notes.

### VARY SENTENCE OPENINGS

Revise the openings of the sentences to vary emphasis and expression. Move the position of the adverb or prepositional phrase to the beginning of a sentence as appropriate.

Angel Oak Tree ▶

**1.** Angel Oak, outside Charleston, South Carolina, is the oldest thing east of the Rockies.

----------

**2.** Angel Oak is apparently around 1,500 years old.

----------

**3.** Angel Oak, over 65 feet high, sprouted 1,000 years before Columbus came to the New World.

----------

**4.** Angel Oak, in modern times, has become a popular tourist attraction.

----------

**5.** It has impressively survived hurricanes, floods, and earthquakes.

----------

*Practice 7*

# Writing Assignments

## Writing for Everyday Life

Revise the following letter to create a variety of purposes, types, patterns, openings, and lengths of sentences. Use your own paper.

Dear Maxine,

It was so good to be with you during our family vacation. We enjoyed all the activities that you planned for us. We were surprised by the Fairchild Oak. We were impressed with its size and beauty. Your Uncle Adolph is still talking about the Ponce de Leon Lighthouse. He is a history buff. He was fascinated. He especially liked learning about the shipwreck experiences of the author Stephen Crane. We enjoyed the sightseeing. We enjoyed reconnecting with family most of all.  Thank you so much for all you did for us. You now need to come see us.

All our love, Aunt Frances

## Writing for College Life

Assume your humanities teacher has assigned a short response paper about the significance of a local landmark. Assume you have composed the following piece of writing. Revise the draft to create a variety of purposes, types, patterns, openings, and lengths of sentences. Use your own paper.

The Alamo is located in San Antonio, Texas. The Alamo was originally called Mission San Antonio de Valero. It was the home of Native Americans. They had been converted to Christianity. The Spanish military set up a station there. They were stationed there in the early 1800s. The Alamo, in time, became a place for Mexican Revolutionaries. Mexican Revolutionaries fought for Mexico's independence from Spain. Texan and Tejano volunteers fought Mexican troops during the Texas Revolution. A group of volunteers took over the Alamo. They took it over in 1835.  They defended the Alamo against Santa Ana's army. They would not surrender. They were defeated. The year was 1836. The Alamo honors the struggle against overwhelming odds. The Alamo honors the love for liberty.

# Writing for Working Life

Revise the following draft of a letter of application to create a variety of purposes, types, patterns, openings, and lengths of sentences. Use your own paper.

> To Whom It May Concern:
>
> I am applying for the position of front office manager in your organization. I received my Master of Business Administration from the University of Sindh Jamshoro, Pakistan. I worked as a travel guide with Waljis Travel. Waljis Travel is a well-known tour company in Pakistan. I also worked in media management with Spanish television in Pakistan. I also worked as an administrative officer with Snow Land Trek and Tour at Skardu. I am ready to take a challenging job. I am eager to take a job where my skills and knowledge will benefit the company.
>
> Best Regards,
>
> Shamshad Hussain

**mywritinglab**

**WANT A BETTER GRADE?**
For more practice and writing assignments on sentence variety, go to **www.mywritinglab.com > Writing Clear Sentences > Sentence Variety.**

---

## WHAT HAVE I LEARNED?

To test and track your understanding of sentence variety, answer the following questions.

**1.** What are the four purposes for sentences? _____,

_____, _____, _____

**2.** What are the four ways to combine simple sentences? _____,

_____, _____

**3.** What are four ways to vary sentence openings? _____,

_____, _____

**4.** Why is it important to vary sentence length? _____

**5. How will I use what I have learned?**
In your notebook, discuss how you will apply to your own writing what you have learned about sentence variety. When will you apply this knowledge during the writing process?

**6. What do I still need to study about sentence types?**
In your notebook, discuss your ongoing study needs by describing what, when, and how you will continue studying and using sentence variety.

Academic Learning Log

LEARNING OUTCOMES SELF-EVALUATION

PORTFOLIO

# 16

# Sentence Clarity: Point of View, Number, and Tense

Sentence clarity creates a logical flow of ideas through consistency in person, point of view, number, and tense.

Communicating about a real-life situation helps us to understand the purpose of sentence clarity. The photograph on the facing page captures two young men break dancing. Read the accompanying original and revised sentences about the young men in Practice 1, complete the activities, and answer the question "What's the point of sentence clarity?"

# What's the Point of Sentence Clarity?

▲ Hip-hop Dancers

What do you think the following sentence means? How could the sentence seem confusing to some readers?

**Original Sentence:** Anthony and Kadeem often listened to Hip-hop music and practice his dance moves.

Is the above sentence describing a current or a past event? Whose dance moves are being discussed—Anthony's, Kadeem's, or both?

Below, the sentence has been revised for clarity. Circle the words that have been revised. How do these revised words clarify the meaning of the sentence?

**Revised Sentence:** Anthony and Kadeem often listen to Hip-hop music and practice their dance moves.

**What is the point of sentence clarity?**

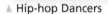

# Understanding the Point of Sentence Clarity: One Student Writer's Response

The following paragraph offers one writer's reaction to the clarity of the sentence about the break dancers.

> I was confused by the first sentence. I didn't know when the action took place. Did the men get together in the past or is this something they do now? Also, the wording made me wonder who was practicing dance moves. The revised sentence answered my questions by changing two words. Changing "listened" to "listen" made it clear that this takes place in the present. And changing "his" to "their" made it clear that both of them practice dance moves.

# Applying the Point: Sentence Clarity

**Sentence clarity** is the precise choice of the form and arrangement of words and groups of words within a sentence. A clearly stated sentence is consistent in person, point of view, number, and tense. As a result, sentence clarity creates a coherent flow of ideas within and among sentences. Often, sentence and paragraph clarity emerge during the revision process. As you study the sentence clarity techniques in this chapter, revise pieces of your own writing and peer edit for a classmate. Apply and track what you are learning as you go.

## Use Consistent Person and Point of View

The term **person** refers to the use of pronouns to identify the difference between the writer or speaker, the one being written or spoken to, and the one being written about or spoken of. **Point of view** is the position from which something is considered, evaluated, or discussed; point of view is identified as first person, second person, or third person. Person and point of view also communicate tone.

### Three Points of View

| Person | Traits | Pronouns |
| --- | --- | --- |
| **First Person** | The writer or speaker; informal, conversational tone | singular: *I, me*<br>plural: *we, our* |
| **Second Person** | The one being written or spoken to; can remain unstated; informal, conversational tone | singular: *you*<br>plural: *you* |
| **Third Person** | The one being written about or spoken of;<br>formal, academic tone | singular: *he, she, it, one*<br>plural: *they* |

## Illogical Shift in Person

An abrupt or **unnecessary shift in person or point of view** causes a break in the logical flow of ideas. The key is to use the same phrasing throughout a paragraph.

**Illogical Shift in Person:**

Anyone can learn to dance despite your age.

THIRD PERSON             SECOND PERSON

**Revisions:**

Anyone can learn to dance despite his or her age.

THIRD PERSON             THIRD PERSON

You can learn to dance despite your age.

SECOND PERSON           SECOND PERSON

---

### CONSISTENT PERSON AND POINT OF VIEW

Edit the following statements to ensure consistent use of person in each sentence.

**1.** Dancers develop self-confidence; therefore, you are more outgoing.

**2.** A dancer can truly reflect your feelings through your body movements.

**3.** Dancing helps your circulatory system as it makes one's heart pump blood faster.

**4.** One can control their weight and improve your overall fitness by burning off calories while dancing.

**5.** For many people, dance becomes more than your hobby; it provides you with a new lifestyle based on confidence and fitness.

Practice 2

# Use Consistent Number

The term *number* refers to the difference between a singular noun or pronoun and plural nouns and pronouns. Once you choose a point of view, carefully edit your writing to ensure **consistent use of number**: singular pronouns refer to singular nouns, and plural pronouns refer to plural nouns.

|  | **Singular** | **Plural** |
|---|---|---|
| **First Person** | *I, me, my, mine*<br>*myself* | *we, our, ours*<br>*ourselves* |
| **Second Person** | *you, yours, yourself* | *you, yours, yourselves* |
| **Third Person** | *he, she, it*<br>*him, his, her, hers, its*<br>*himself, herself, itself*<br>*one, everyone, none* | *they, them,*<br>*theirs,*<br>*themselves* |

## Illogical Shift in Number

When pronouns act as the subject of a verb, they, too, must agree in number. An abrupt or **unnecessary shift in number** causes a break in the logical flow of ideas.

**Illogical Shift in Number:**

*PLURAL, THIRD PERSON PRONOUN*

*SINGULAR NOUN* —→ Hip-hop is a form of urban youth culture; they include rap music, graffiti, and break dancing. *PLURAL VERB*

**Revision:**

*SINGULAR, THIRD PERSON PRONOUN*

*SINGULAR NOUN* —→ Hip-hop is a form of urban youth culture; it includes rap music, graffiti, and break dancing. *SINGULAR VERB*

---

**CONSISTENT NUMBER**

Edit the following statements to ensure consistency in number within each sentence.

**1.** Break dancing has four basic elements; it is toprock, downrock, power moves, and freezes.

**2.** A male break dancer is called a b-boy because they can express themselves through the four elements of break dancing.

**3.** A b-boy uses toprock moves to show their ability to rock the beat while they are standing up.

**4.** B-boys use downrock to show off its speed and agility by using his hands and feet on the floor.

**5.** Power moves are borrowed from gymnastics; it requires upper body strength and momentum.

**6.** A freeze halts all movement in a freestanding pose; they are often handstands or pikes.

Revise the following paragraph to change the point of view from third person to second person. Change nouns, pronouns, and verbs as needed for consistency in point of view and number.

### How to Break Dance Using the 6-Step

(1) Roxanne practices these six steps to master the basic footwork of break dancing. (2) Starting in a push-up position with her legs spread apart shoulder width, she lifts her right hand and puts her left leg where her right hand was. (3) Next, she brings her right leg behind her left knee and points her right hand to the sky. (4) Then, she steps her left foot out and brings her right hand back down to the floor. (5) At this point, her back is facing the floor, and both of her knees are bent. (6) Her fourth move is to put her right foot in front of her left foot. (7) Then, she steps her left foot away while she shifts her weight onto her right arm and left foot. (8) Finally, she brings her right foot under her left foot as she brings her left hand back to the ground in front of her so she is back into the push-up position.

# Use Consistent Tense

**Consistent tense** expresses the logical sequence of events or existence. Verb *tense* expresses the time or duration of an action or state of being. Primary tenses include three timeframes: The **past** *was*; the **present** *is*; the **future** *will be*. The following chart offers definitions, examples, and possible signal words for the three primary tenses of verbs in English.

| Primary Verb Tenses | | |
|---|---|---|
| **Past** | **Present** | **Future** |
| Action or state of being ended at a certain point in the past | Action or state of being exists or is repeated | Action or state of being occurs in the future |
| **danced** | **dance/dances** | **will dance** |
| Past Tense Signal Words | Present Tense Signal Words | Future Tense Signal Words |
| • before<br>• for several days, weeks, etc.<br>• last week, month, year<br>• one hour, day, week, year ago<br>• yesterday | • always<br>• every day, week, month, year<br>• frequently<br>• now<br>• sometimes<br>• usually | • in the future<br>• later<br>• next week, month, year, etc.<br>• soon<br>• tomorrow<br>• tonight |

## Illogical Shift in Tense

An abrupt change from one verb tense to another without a logical reason, also called an **illogical shift in tense**, breaks the logical flow of ideas and causes confusion.

**Illogical Shift in Tense:**

PRESENT TENSE

Music **exerts** a powerful influence on her physically; soothing music lowered her blood pressure.

PAST TENSE

**Revisions:**

PRESENT TENSE

Music **exerts** a powerful influence on her physically; soothing music lowers her blood pressure.

PRESENT TENSE

PAST TENSE

Music **exerted** a powerful influence on her physically; soothing music lowered her blood pressure.

PAST TENSE

**CONSISTENT TENSE**

Edit the following sentences to ensure consistency in tense.

**1.** Before Shannon passes the final exam, her heart rate raced with stress.

**2.** Every time she takes a test, she feared it.

**3.** Shannon learned that music helps her older sister to relax before taking an exam.

**4.** After Shannon learns about her sister's experience, she listened to music before the exam.

**5.** From now on, Shannon will not only study but also listens to classical music before an exam.

---

## Logical Shift in Tenses

**Frequently, a writer states the logical movement from one tense to another tense. Often signal words indicate this logical shift in tense.**

**Past to Present Tense:** Jay-Z and Beyoncé dated for years; they are now a married couple.

**Present to Future Tense:** They are a power couple who will only become richer in the future.

Jay-Z and Beyoncé ▶

---

**CONSISTENT TENSE**

Edit the following paragraph to ensure consistency in tense.

(1) Jay-Z co-owns The 40/40 Club. (2) The club started in New York City as a high-end sports bar, and today it opened another location in Atlantic City, New Jersey. (3) In the future, Jay-Z opens 40/40 Clubs in Los Angeles, Las Vegas, and Singapore. (4) Currently, Jay-Z was also in the process of making a deal with concert promoter Live Nation for $150 million; the upcoming deal awards the most money contracted by a musician.

Revise the following student paragraph for consistent use of point of view, number, and tense.

# RAPPING: THE TRUTH HURTS

(1) Many people cry out against Hip-hop music. (2) Critics say that Hip-hop music passed on the wrong message to young people. (3) One of the reasons people opposed Hip-hop was because of the curse words used by many rap artists. (4) But rappers used these words to capture the anger and frustration of people in their neighborhoods. (5) Critics also complain about the graphic sexual content of lyrics, and many lyrics put women down through the use of crude names. (6) Rapper David Banner says that the words are honest. (7) The lyrics only describe a certain type of women, and other women should not be offended. (8) He also point out that sex sells. (9) Hip-hop musicians see himselves as artists. (10) He sees his job is to capture the reality of the society as they see it. (11) They expect to offend you if you don't want to know the truth.

Revise the following student paragraph for consistent use of point of view, number, and tense.

# IT'S A WOMAN'S WORLD, TOO

(1) Hip-hop is often seen as a man's world. (2) But three women prove that Hip-hop is a woman's world, too. (3) Ciara dreams of being a famous singer. (4) Then in 2004, she burst on the music scene with her hit single *Goodies*. (5) The album sold millions worldwide and earns her several awards. (6) Her breathy vocals and athletic dance moves make her fun to watch. (7) You may not think that Rihanna is as good as she can be, but her single *S.O.S.* delivers a powerful beat and makes good use of her deep voice. (8) In the future, she only improves. (9) In fact, since the release of her debut album *Music of the Sun* in 2005, Rihanna has turned out a dozen hit singles in the United States. (10) Finally, Beyoncé is the queen of Hip-hop. (11) First, she rose to fame as the lead singer of Destiny's Child; then she starts a successful solo career. (12) You have to admire her sex appeal and amazing voice. (13) In 2008, she is named one of the most powerful celebrities in the world. (14) These women rock!

# Writing Assignments

## Writing for Everyday Life

Revise the following paragraph, written as a posting to a Facebook blog, for sentence clarity. Use your own paper.

Over the past three months, I have gotten in shape and reduced my stress, and I now wanted to help someone else do the same in their lives. I used *Hip-hop Cardio and Strength Building* videos and got fantastic results. Each video was a 45 minute workout routine. There are five DVDs. First you learned the basic six-step. They develop your balance and strengthens your core. Then over the course of several weeks, you learned the hottest dance moves. Soon, you are dancing like a pro. The hard-driving beat of the music is a great outlet for all my pent up frustration and worries. Since the DVDs help me, I know they help someone else.

## Writing for College Life

Edit the following paragraph, written in response to a short-answer question on a college humanities exam, for sentence clarity. Use your own paper.

**Test Question:** What is the difference between Rap and Hip-hop?

**Student Answer:** Rap is something you do; Hip-hop is something you live. Hip-hop is a label for a lifestyle. They include DJing, music, break dancing, graffiti, and clothing. This lifestyle is based on the belief that a person has the right to live their lives in any way they choose. Hip-hop will celebrate emotional release and fully living every moment. Rap is the musical element of the Hip-hop culture. Rap began in the urban setting of the Bronx. During the 1970s, DJs and emcees give toasts; they half-sang, half spoke rhymes in a rapid-fire beat. Rap reflected the values of the Hip-hop lifestyle. Sometimes, rap is a social protest; other times it was an honest picture of urban life; often it is bitter and angry.

# Writing for Working Life

The following letter requests permission to use a song in a fundraising presentation. Edit the letter for sentence clarity. Use your own paper.

Dear Mr. Smith:

I work for the non-profit organization "Youth Rock." We sponsored urban centers that provide computers, tutoring, and counseling to urban youth. We are putting together a multimedia presentation to raise funds. We understand that you are the owner of the copyright in the musical composition "Rock On," and we want to use the entire song in the presentation. Since we was on a limited budget, we hoped that you will allow us this use without any charge. If a fee was required, please let us know the amount. Your signature below, under "confirmed by," will indicate that you agreed to permit this use without payment of a fee. Thank you for your help with this matter, and we look forward to hearing from you.

Sincerely,
Wayne Scroggins

## WHAT HAVE I LEARNED ABOUT SENTENCE CLARITY?

To test and track your understanding of sentence clarity, answer the following questions. Use several sentences as needed for each response.

**1.** What is sentence clarity? .................................................................................................

.................................................................................................................................................

**2.** What are three techniques used to achieve sentence clarity?

(a) .......................................................................................... ,

(b) .......................................................................................... , and

(c) .......................................................................................... .

**3. How will I use what I have learned?** In your notebook, discuss how you will apply to your own writing what you have learned about sentence clarity. When will you apply this knowledge during the writing process?

**4. What do I still need to study about sentence types?** In your notebook, describe your ongoing study needs by describing what, when, and how you will continue studying and using sentence clarity.

LEARNING OUTCOMES
SELF-EVALUATION

Academic Learning Log

PORTFOLIO

# 17 Parallelism

Parallelism is the expression of equal ideas—similar words, phrases, or clauses—in a sentence in the same, matching grammatical form.

Memorable quotations can help us to understand the purpose of parallelism. The photographs on the next page represent well-known public figures who made powerful statements. Read the quotations, complete the activities, and answer the question "What's the point of parallelism?"

"You can fool all the people some of the time, and some of the people all the time, but you cannot fool all the people all the time."

—ABRAHAM LINCOLN

# What's the Point of Parallelism?

**PHOTOGRAPHIC ORGANIZER: PARALLELISM**

Each of the following well-known quotations uses parallelism to make an idea memorable and powerful. What do these statements have in common?

"To be or not to be,
that is the question."

—*HAMLET,* ACT III, SCENE I

"Free at last, free at last
Thank God almighty
We are free at last."

—MARTIN LUTHER KING, JR

"I think,
therefore I am."

—RENÉ DESCARTES

**What is the point of parallelism?**

-------------------------------------------------------------

-------------------------------------------------------------

-------------------------------------------------------------

# Understanding the Point of Parallelism: One Student Writer's Response

The following paragraph records one writer's definition of parallelism based on the traits of the example quotations.

> *Each sentence repeats a word or a group of words such as "to be," "free at last," and "I." The repeated ideas are about the same length, too. By repeating words, the writers made their points kind of catchy. I think parallelism creates rhythm, like a song or a poem, by repeating the same or similar words in similar ways.*

# Applying the Point: Parallelism

**Parallelism** refers to the balance of equal ideas expressed in the same grammatical form. Parallel expressions bring clarity, interest, and power to a piece of writing. You can achieve parallelism by emphasizing equal ideas using similar structures and patterns of words, phrases, or clauses. You can also use certain types of conjunctions and punctuation to signal parallel structures.

## Parallel Words

Parallel structure uses a pair or series of closely related compound words to emphasize a point. Parallel words often, but not always, use similar **suffixes** (word endings).

**Nonparallel:**

NOUN        ADJECTIVE

César Chávez was a migrant worker and heroic.

**Revised for Parallelism:**

NOUNS

César Chávez was a migrant worker and a hero.

**Nonparallel:**

ADJECTIVE     ADVERB

César Chávez brave yet peacefully sought equality.

**Revised for Parallelism:**

ADVERBS

César Chávez bravely yet peacefully sought equality.

**Nonparallel:**

NONPARALLEL VERBS

Migrant workers labored hard, earned little, and suffering abuse.

**Revised for Parallelism:**

PARALLEL VERBS

Migrant workers labored hard, earned little, and suffered abuse.

▲ César Chavez

Revise the following sentences to achieve emphasis through parallel words.

**1.** As migrant workers, Chávez's family picked fruits and vegetables, lived in migrant camps, and sometimes sleeping in their car.

-------------------------------------------------------------------------------

-------------------------------------------------------------------------------

**2.** Chávez attended 30 different schools and finally quits after the eighth grade.

-------------------------------------------------------------------------------

-------------------------------------------------------------------------------

**3.** Chávez encouraged workers to protest, to strike, to fast, with the use of nonviolence, changing their world.

-------------------------------------------------------------------------------

-------------------------------------------------------------------------------

**4.** Write a sentence that uses parallel words. Suggested topic: The traits of a hero.

-------------------------------------------------------------------------------

-------------------------------------------------------------------------------

# Parallel Phrases

Parallel structure uses a pair or series of closely related compound phrases to emphasize a point. Parallel phrases repeat similar word patterns or groups.

**Nonparallel:**

*PREPOSITIONAL PHRASE*    *GERUND PHRASE*

Fannie Lou Hamer believed in justice and speaking powerfully.

**Revised for Parallelism:**

*PARALLEL PREPOSITIONAL PHRASES*

Fannie Lou Hamer believed in justice and spoke with power.

*PARALLEL VERBS*

**Nonparallel:**

*PRESENT PARTICIPLE PHRASE*    *PAST PARTICIPLE PHRASE*

Living in Mississippi and worked as a sharecropper, Hamer became a civil rights leader.

**Revised for Parallelism:**

*PARALLEL PRESENT PARTICIPLE PHRASES*

Living in Mississippi and working as a sharecropper, Hamer became a civil rights leader.

**Nonparallel:**

*INFINITIVE PHRASE*    *GERUND PHRASE*

Fannie Lou Hamer worked to register voters and helping the poor.

**Revised for Parallelism:**

*PARALLEL INFINITIVE PHRASES*

Fannie Lou Hamer worked to register voters and to help the poor.

◄ Fanny Hamer Speaking

Revise the following sentences to achieve emphasis through parallel phrases.

**1.** The youngest of 20 children and having had polio, six-year-old Fannie Lou Hamer began working in the fields.

-------------------------------------------------------------------

-------------------------------------------------------------------

**2.** She always prayed for the chance to better her life and helping her race, but she didn't know how.

-------------------------------------------------------------------

-------------------------------------------------------------------

**3.** As a civil rights leader, she helped herself and others by registering voters and to give speeches.

-------------------------------------------------------------------

-------------------------------------------------------------------

**4.** Her faith in God, love for people, and sensing purpose shaped the life of Fannie Lou Hamer.

-------------------------------------------------------------------

-------------------------------------------------------------------

**5.** Write a sentence that uses parallel phrases. Suggested topic: Reasons to vote.

-------------------------------------------------------------------

-------------------------------------------------------------------

For more information on sentence types and sentence elements, see pages 260–273, "Subjects, Verbs, and Simple Sentences," and pages 274–289, "Compound and Complex Sentences."

# Parallel Clauses

Parallel structure uses a set of closely related clauses to emphasize a point. Parallel structure begins with a clause and continues with clauses to create a balanced, logical statement. Parallel structure establishes a pattern of similarly structured clauses to express closely related ideas. Use parallel words and phrases within clauses.

*INDEPENDENT CLAUSE*

**Nonparallel:**

The Cherokee Nation had always been ruled by men, but Wilma Pearl Mankiller who became the nation's first female Chief.

*DEPENDENT CLAUSE (ILLOGICAL MIXED STRUCTURE)*

**Revised for Parallelism:**

The Cherokee Nation had always been ruled by men, but

Wilma Pearl Mankiller became the nation's first female Chief.

*PARALLEL INDEPENDENT CLAUSES*

*INDEPENDENT CLAUSE*

**Nonparallel:**

Mankiller raised the typical women's issues of education and health care; in fact, deeming them tribal priorities.

*PHRASE*

**Revised for Parallelism:**

Mankiller raised the typical women's issues of education and health care; in fact, she deemed them the main priorities of the tribe.

*PARALLEL INDEPENDENT CLAUSES*

◄ Wilma Mankiller,
Cherokee Chief

Revise the following sentences to achieve emphasis through parallel clauses.

**1.** A people who control the education of their children are a people in control of their future.

_____

_____

**2.** Under her leadership, the Cherokee people trusted their own thinking, solving their own problems, believing in their own abilities.

_____

_____

**3.** Mankiller built health clinics, and she was responsible for bringing water and electricity to poor communities, also supporting small businesses and serving her people well.

_____

_____

**4.** Gender has nothing to do with leadership, and leadership is not about gender.

_____

_____

**5.** Write a sentence that uses parallel clauses. Suggested Topic: A personal hero.

_____

_____

# Punctuation for Parallelism

The comma and the semicolon (sometimes along with coordinating conjunctions), and numbered, lettered, or bulleted items in a list signal ideas of equal importance. Ideas marked by these pieces of punctuation are best expressed with parallelism.

**Coordinating conjunctions** always signal an equal relationship among words, phrases, and clauses. Use commas between parallel items in a series. Use a comma with a coordinating conjunction to join independent clauses.

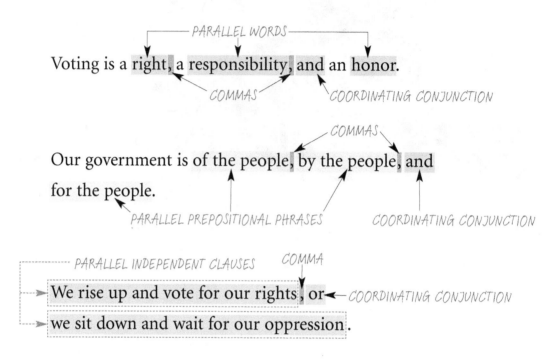

**Semicolons** signal two or more closely related independent clauses.

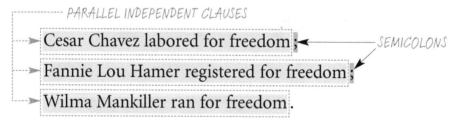

**Numbers, letters, or bullets** signal items in a list. Lists are often used in résumés, business letters, and presentations. Note that colons can introduce a list, and semicolons can separate items.

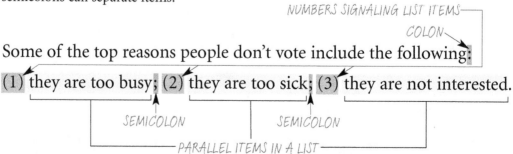

## PARALLELISM

Edit the following sentences for proper use of punctuation for parallel expression.

**1.** The Declaration of Independence of the United States was written to ensure life liberty and the pursuit of happiness.

**2.** The Voting Rights Act of 1965 banned literacy tests poll taxes and methods used to prevent people from voting.

**3.** No citizen shall be denied the right to vote in any federal state or local election.

**4.** Write a sentence using parallelism. Suggested topic: The importance of voting.

-------------------------------------------------------------

-------------------------------------------------------------

-------------------------------------------------------------

-------------------------------------------------------------

## PARALLELISM REVIEW

Edit and revise the following paragraph for parallel expression and proper punctuation of parallel expressions.

### Interpersonal Silence

(1) If I could meet anyone in the world, I would want to meet Martin Luther King, Jr. (2) He was a man of great wisdom, courage, and generous. (3) He could have sat in his quiet life as a Baptist preacher; raising his children; he could have grown old with his wife. (4) Instead, he chose to stand. (5) He stood for righteousness, fighting against injustice, and opposing violence. (6) His earnest face and his moving speeches even now stir my heart. (7) I think he knew that his work would cost him his life, yet still he stood and still he spoke. (8) In his spirit, now I rise and take my own stand for justice now lifting my voice, I say "let freedom ring."

# Writing Assignments

## Writing for Everyday Life

Assume you are in charge of a drive to register voters. Edit the following flyer that you plan to post on community bulletin boards. Use your own paper.

> The next election will set the country's course for civil rights, health care, welfare, jobs, taxes, support for the arts, and saving the environment.
>
> •
>
> Exercising your rights
>
> •
>
> Speak out on how you want your taxes spent.
>
> •
>
> Your vote counts.
>
> •
>
> You really don't want to delay.
>
> •
>
> **REGISTER NOW**.

## Writing for College Life

Assume you are giving a PowerPoint presentation in your government class. Edit the following outline of your PowerPoint slides so that each element is parallel. Use your own paper.

**Title Slide:**

The Branches of Government and Examples of Duties

**Slide Two:**

The Executive Branch

- Carries out Law
- Commander and Chief of the Armed Forces

**Slide One:**

The Legislative Branch

- Creates law
- Regulates commerce

**Slide Three:**

The Judiciary

- Interprets the law
- Settles disputes between states

# Writing for Working Life

Edit the following portion of a résumé to ensure parallel expression.
Use your own paper.

> OBJECTIVE
> - To secure the position of Staff Assistant for Congresswoman Jane Doe
> - Helping Congresswoman Jane Doe fulfill her mission in Washington
>
> WORK EXPERIENCE
> **BARACK OBAMA FOR PRESIDENT OF THE UNITED STATES,**
> **Volunteer, 2007-2008**
> - Assisted on a part time basis with the campaign in the 6th District
> - Staffed the campaign office, greeted visitors, and providing them with information on Obama and his stands on the issues.
> - Leading a team delivering campaign literature door to door.
> - Determined routes and organizing volunteers

**mywritinglab**

**WANT A BETTER GRADE?**
For more practice and writing assignments on parallelism, go to **www.mywritinglab.com > Writing Clear Sentences > Parallelism.**

---

## WHAT HAVE I LEARNED ABOUT PARALLELISM?

To test and track your understanding, answer the following questions. Use several sentences as needed for each response.

**1.** What is parallelism? .........................................................................

.........................................................................................................

**2.** Parallel ................................ often, but not always, use similar suffixes (word endings).

**3.** Parallel phrases repeat similar ................................................................

**4.** Repeat parallel patterns of ................................ to pace ideas through the thoughtful arrangement and sequence of sentence types.

**5.** What types of punctuation signal parallelism? (a) ................................ ;

(b) ................................ ; and (c) ................................ .

**6. How will I use what I have learned?** In your notebook, discuss how you will apply to your own writing what you have learned about parallelism. When will you apply this knowledge during the writing process?

**7. What do I still need to study about sentence types?** In your notebook, describe your ongoing study needs by describing what, when, and how you will continue studying and using parallelism.

Academic Learning Log

LEARNING OUTCOMES
SELF-EVALUATION

PORTFOLIO

# 18

# Run-ons: Comma Splices and Fused Sentences

A comma splice is an error that occurs when a comma is used by itself to join two sentences. A fused sentence is an error that occurs when two sentences are joined without any punctuation.

According to research, comma splices and fused sentences are two of the most common errors made by student writers. The photograph on the next page shows an exercise program. Read about this exercise and then answer the question "What's the point of learning about correcting comma splices and fused sentences?"

# What's the Point of Correcting Run-ons— Comma Splices and Fused Sentences?

PHOTOGRAPHIC ORGANIZER: COMMA SPLICES AND FUSED SENTENCES

Read the following short description of CrossFit, a unique approach to physical fitness. The paragraph contains 2 comma splices and 4 fused sentences. How do these errors affect the reading of the paragraph?

### CrossFit

CrossFit builds fitness through strength training, gymnastics, and sprinting. A trainee gains control, endurance, and flexibility CrossFit promotes a broad and general physical fitness for everyone the workouts are based on functional movements they copy the natural actions carried out by the body in everyday life, for example, a squat is the action of standing from a seated position a dead-lift is the action of picking up an object off the ground, both are functional movements. A typical workout uses these kinds of movements in short, intense sessions.

**What's the point of learning about correcting comma splices and fused sentences?**

-------------------------------------------------------------------

-------------------------------------------------------------------

-------------------------------------------------------------------

-------------------------------------------------------------------

-------------------------------------------------------------------

# Understanding the Point of Correcting Run-ons—Comma Splices and Fused Sentences: One Student Writer's Response

The following paragraph offers one writer's response to the opening paragraph about CrossFit.

*Reading this paragraph was kind of frustrating. There were no real pauses in the ideas, so it was hard to figure out where an idea ended or began. The paragraph needs punctuation (like periods) so the ideas are clear and easy to follow.*

# Applying the Point: Correcting Run-ons—Comma Splices and Fused Sentences

Comma splices and fused sentences are punctuation errors that occur where independent clauses are improperly joined to form a compound sentence. To properly combine clauses into a compound sentence, the end of each independent clause must be signaled by appropriate punctuation, such as a semicolon, a comma followed by a coordinating conjunction, or a period at the end of the sentence.

## Comma Splice

A **comma splice** occurs when a comma is used by itself (without a coordinating conjunction) to join two independent clauses.

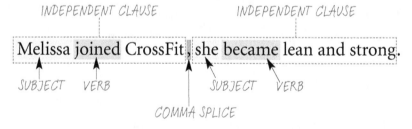

## Fused Sentence

A **fused sentence** occurs when two independent clauses are joined without any punctuation.

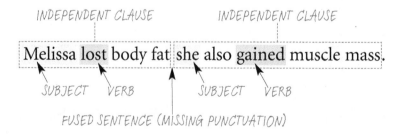

Test your ability to identify comma splices, fused sentences, and properly combined clauses. In each blank, write **CS** for comma splice, **FS** for fused sentence, or **C** for correctly punctuated.

........... **1.** I want to pass on to you my appreciation for your CrossFit workouts, your program really works.

........... **2.** I am an Army Major, I have been doing this for about three months, boy, I really saw the results today.

........... **3.** We are required to pass a physical fitness test in the Army, today I achieved the highest results in all areas.

........... **4.** I completed 77 push-ups in 2 minutes, 80 sit-ups in 2 minutes, and a 2 mile run in 13 minutes I got the perfect score of 300 points I credit all my success to CrossFit.

........... **5.** I am in the best shape of my life lighter, stronger, faster, and way healthier I no longer have joint pain.

........... **6.** I look forward to these workouts, and my staff and I have made them a part of our daily physical training.

........... **7.** CrossFit works for my wife, too, she was never active, but now she can do pull-ups, push-ups, sprints, and many other physically demanding exercises.

........... **8.** My friends, family, and colleagues want to know more about CrossFit so I would appreciate some information to share with them.

........... **9.** Scott, your kind remarks about CrossFit mean a lot to me, and I am pleased that you are seeing results from your hard work.

........... **10.** CrossFit is a core strength and conditioning program this exercise program is not a specialized fitness program.

........... **11.** CrossFit builds physical competence in each of ten recognized areas of fitness they are cardiovascular and respiratory endurance, stamina, strength, flexibility, power, speed, coordination, agility, balance, and accuracy.

........... **12.** We train our clients in gymnastics from basic to advanced movements, so they gain the ability to control their bodies through strength and flexibility.

........... **13.** We emphasize Olympic Weightlifting this sport has the unique ability to develop an athlete's explosive power, control of external objects, and mastery of key motor recruitment patterns.

........... **14.** CrossFit improves the natural ability of the body to function, our exercises are based on natural movements.

........... **15.** For example, the squat is essential to your well-being, the squat can both greatly improve your athleticism, the squat keeps your hips, back, and knees sound and functioning in your senior years.

........... **16.** The squat does not harm the knees, in fact, squats rehabilitate damaged or delicate knees.

........... **17.** The squat, in the bottom position, is nature's intended sitting posture, and the rise from the bottom to a standing position is a natural movement.

........... **18.** We encourage and assist our athletes to explore a variety of sports for they need to find ways to express and apply their fitness.

........... **19.** This program can be adapted to everyone's level of fitness so no one should feel intimidated or afraid to try.

........... **20.** CrossFit is not just for elite athletes anybody can succeed with CrossFit.

# Five Ways to Correct Comma Splices and Fused Sentences

As a writer, you have the choice of several ways to correct or avoid comma splices and fused sentences. Each method creates a specific effect. Most experts recommend using a variety of these methods, rather than always relying on the same one.

## 1. Separate sentences using a period and capital letter

Punctuating the independent clauses as separate sentences is a method often used to correct comma splices and fused sentences.

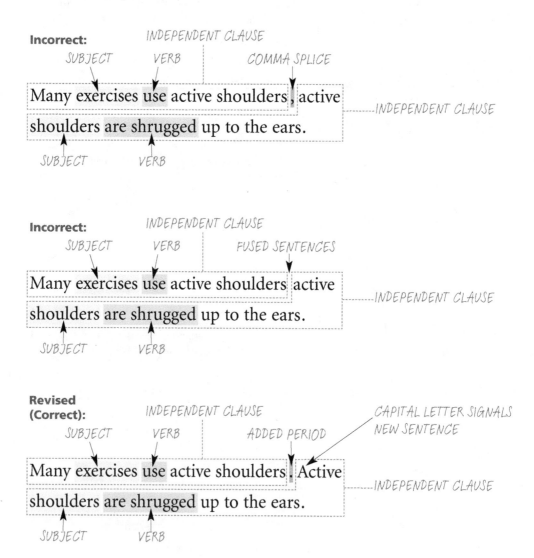

Practice 3

▲ L-pull-up in lower position

▲ L-pull-up in top position

Edit the following sentences to eliminate comma splices and fused sentences. Separate clauses by inserting a period and capital letter as needed.

1. Robert hangs from the bar he flexes at the hips, his legs are parallel to the ground and at right angles to his body.

2. He keeps his legs parallel to the ground in addition, his legs are at right angles to his body.

3. He does not jerk his torso, instead he pulls until his head is over the bar.

4. He does as many repetitions as possible without dropping his feet below his bottom throughout the entire set he maintains this L-shape.

5. Robert found the L-pull-up very challenging, at first, he had to keep his legs straight or tucked up under him.

6. Robert is able to complete 100 L-pull-ups at a time he maintains perfect form.

7. Yesterday, Robert did 100 L-pull-ups, then he did 50 air squats.

8. Write a compound sentence. Suggested topic: The benefits of an L-pull-up.

## 2. Join sentences with a comma followed by a coordinating conjunction

Sentences can be properly joined by inserting a comma followed by a coordinating conjunction between the independent clauses. The acronym FANBOYS stands for each of the coordinating conjunctions: *for, and, nor, but, or, yet, so*. This method of combining sentences states the relationship between ideas of equal importance.

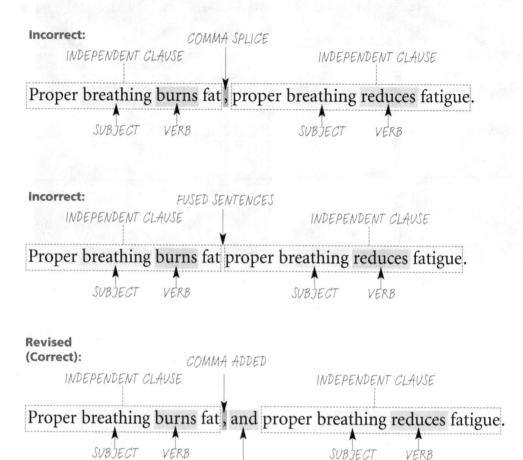

**Woman Doing Sit-ups** ▶

Edit the following sentences to eliminate comma splices and fused sentences. Join independent clauses with a comma and a coordinating conjunction.

1. One should never hold one's breath during an exercise holding one's breath raises blood pressure.

2. Breath-holding deprives the body of oxygen, it reduces blood flow to the brain and increases the pressure in the chest.

3. Before exercising, Shawna practices proper breathing she sits straight in a firm chair with her fingertips gently resting on her stomach.

4. She inhales deeply through her nostrils; she feels her abdomen expand her diaphragm her chest rises as her lungs expand with air.

5. To exhale deeply, Shawna relaxes her chest and diaphragm she pulls her stomach toward her spine.

6. Shawna repeats this breathing pattern, she can notice how the air moves in and out of her body.

7. During exercise Shawna breathes deeply and fully, she inhales and exhales in a steady rhythm.

8. Shawna inhales during the exertion stage of the exercise she exhales during the recovery stage of the exercise.

9. Write a compound sentence using a comma and a coordinating conjunction. Suggested topic: Reducing stress through proper breathing.

--------------------------------------------------------------------------------

--------------------------------------------------------------------------------

### 3. Join sentences with a semicolon

Use a semicolon to join independent clauses when no conjunction is present. A semicolon indicates that the two sentences of equal importance are so closely related that they can be stated as one sentence; however, a semicolon alone does not state the relationship between the two clauses. The relationship between clauses may be one of the following: *time, space, order of importance, general to specific, addition, cause, effect, comparison,* or *contrast.*

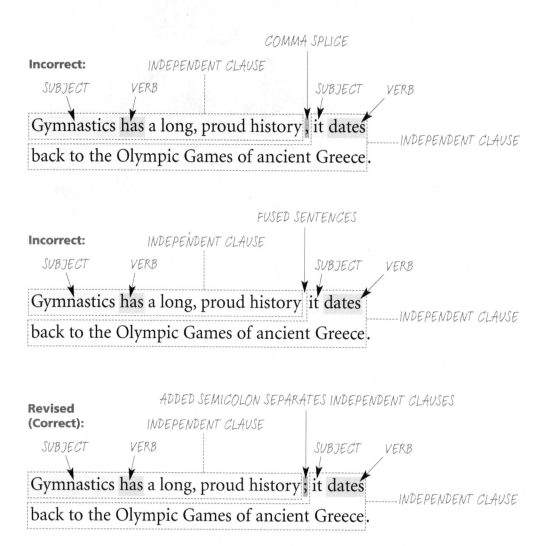

Artistic Gymnastics -
US Olympic Trials ▶

Edit the following sentences by inserting
semicolons as needed to correct comma
splices and fused sentences.

**1.** Shawn Johnson was only 16 years old she won a spot on the 2008 U.S. Olympic team.

**2.** Shawn Johnson is able to perform the toughest of gymnastic skills she became the All-Around
World Champion during her first year competing in the Senior Division.

**3.** She does a standing full this move is a back flip with a full twist on a beam.

**4.** She also has mastered a tucked double-double to do this move, she completes two flips with
two twists on the floor.

**5.** She is also able to complete a double-twisting double layout off of the uneven bars this is
probably her weakest event!

**6.** In awarding points to gymnasts, skills are arranged in different levels "A" skills are rated as
basic skills "G" skills are rated the most difficult.

**7.** Shawn performs three "G" level elements on three different events most likely she is the only
athlete in the world with three "G" level elements.

**8.** Most gymnasts practice 40 hours a week Shawn only practices 20-25 hours each week.

**9.** Write a compound sentence using a semicolon. Suggested topic: A well-known athlete.

Practice 5

### 4. Join sentences with a semicolon followed by a conjunctive adverb

For more information about joining ideas of equal importance, see pages 274–289, "Compound and Complex Sentences."

Use a semicolon with a conjunctive adverb to join independent clauses. Conjunctive adverbs are transition words that state the relationships between ideas of equal importance. A few common examples include *also, consequently, for example, furthermore, however, then, meanwhile, therefore,* and *thus.*

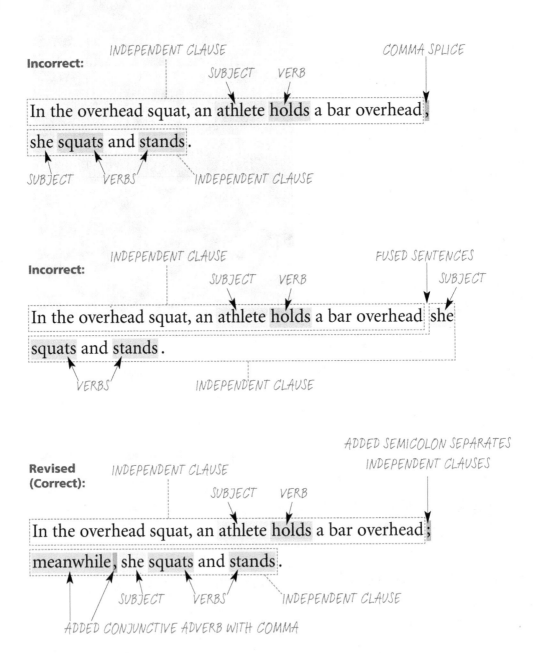

**Incorrect:**

INDEPENDENT CLAUSE    COMMA SPLICE
SUBJECT    VERB

In the overhead squat, an athlete holds a bar overhead, she squats and stands.

SUBJECT    VERBS    INDEPENDENT CLAUSE

**Incorrect:**

INDEPENDENT CLAUSE    FUSED SENTENCES
SUBJECT    VERB    SUBJECT

In the overhead squat, an athlete holds a bar overhead she squats and stands.

VERBS    INDEPENDENT CLAUSE

**Revised (Correct):**

ADDED SEMICOLON SEPARATES INDEPENDENT CLAUSES
INDEPENDENT CLAUSE
SUBJECT    VERB

In the overhead squat, an athlete holds a bar overhead; meanwhile, she squats and stands.

SUBJECT    VERBS    INDEPENDENT CLAUSE
ADDED CONJUNCTIVE ADVERB WITH COMMA

Not only do these transitions state the relationship between ideas, but also they introduce an independent clause and must be set off with a comma.

340

▲ **Tara Nott of the United States**

Edit and revise the following sentences to correct comma splices and fused sentences. Join independent clauses with a semicolon and one of the following transitions: *consequently, for example, furthermore, however, in addition,* or *therefore.*

**1.** Tara Nott won an Olympic gold medal in weight lifting in 2000, she became the first U.S. athlete in 40 years to win an Olympic gold medal in weight lifting.

**2.** Tara Nott was 28 years old, 5 feet and 1 inch tall, and 105 pounds she was a tough and talented athlete.

**3.** Weightlifting was not her first choice as a sport, she is the only athlete to have ever trained in three Olympic sports.

**4.** She trained first as a gymnast she became an All-American soccer player.

**5.** She lifted 225 pounds, more than twice her body weight she won the gold medal.

**6.** Lifting depends more on technique than on bulk, a lifter relies on quickness and timing.

**7.** Tara Nott shattered the myth of massive, bulky lifters more women are now interested in weight lifting.

**8.** Her performance in the 2000 Olympics was inspirational it has been posted on YouTube.

**9.** Write a compound sentence using a semicolon and conjunctive adverb. Suggested topic: Going to the gym.

.................................................................................................................

.................................................................................................................

## 5. Join sentences using a subordinating conjunction

For more information on complex sentences, see pages 274–289, "Compound and Complex Sentences."

Not all ideas are of equal importance. Frequently, writers choose to join ideas in a complex sentence made up of an independent clause and one or more dependent clauses. A subordinating conjunction signals the beginning of a dependent clause and states its subordinate relationship to the independent clause. Some examples of subordinating conjunctions include *although, as, because, if,* and *when*. Relative pronouns also connect a dependent clause to an independent clause. Examples of relative pronouns include *that, which,* and *who*.

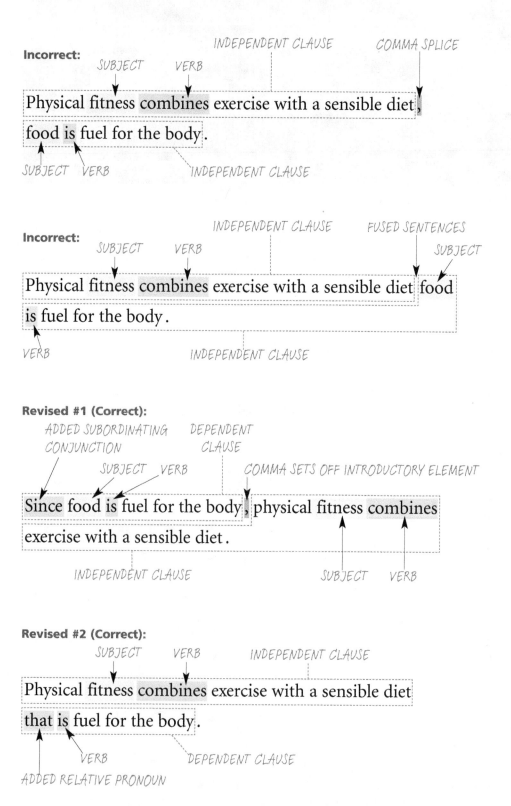

342

Bowl of beef stew
(Zone Diet) ▶

Revise the following compound sentences into complex sentences to correct comma splices and fused sentences. Use the following subordinating conjunctions: *although, because, that, which,* and *when.*

**1.** The Zone diet is an ideal diet, it reduces the risk of disease and improves athletic ability.

-------------------------------------------------

-------------------------------------------------

**2.** The Zone is more than a diet the Zone is a state of being refreshed, alert, and energized.

-------------------------------------------------

-------------------------------------------------

**3.** Your metabolism improves with this diet it is 30% protein, 30% fat, and 40% carbohydrates.

-------------------------------------------------

-------------------------------------------------

**4.** You adopt the Zone diet you reduce the causes and effects of heart disease, high blood pressure, and diabetes.

-------------------------------------------------

-------------------------------------------------

**5.** The Zone diet recommends a small amount of protein at every meal and for two snacks a day this is around the size of your palm.

-------------------------------------------------

-------------------------------------------------

# Writing Assignments

## Writing for Everyday Life

Read the following e-mail appeal written to a friend. Edit to correct comma splices and fused sentences. Use your own paper.

Dear Lara,

I am sending you this email as a written plea to get you in the gym and working out I know we have talked a lot about your wanting to lose those growing inches and becoming healthier and stronger talk is only talk and will not help you become the person you envision it is very easy to keep putting off you will feel so much better after just one workout. You will not be worrying about your weight gain, you will be doing something about it. I am ready to go to the gym with you any time. --Heather

## Writing for College Life

The following paragraph was written as an analysis of two popular diets for a health class. Edit to correct comma splices and fused sentences. Use your own paper.

Two popular diets differ in several ways these diets are the Zone and Weight Watchers. The Zone focuses on wellness it recommends small portions of protein and fat and larger portions of fruits and vegetables in contrast Weight Watchers focuses on weight goals it recommends eating what you want you control portions. On the one hand, the Zone balances fat, protein, and carbohydrates for health on the other hand Weight Watchers focuses on calories in, calories out it includes exercise and social support. The Zone diet is debated by experts they say the diet's science is not proven. However, Weight Watchers has the support of most national organizations it is the most highly recommended diet.

## Writing for Working Life

Read the following information which was written to future clients and posted on the homepage of a local gym. Edit to correct comma splices and fused sentences. Use your own paper.

Contact us and schedule your first session there is no charge for the first session it's on us. This first session will be used to determine your goals and establish your current fitness level you will then be put through a brief and intense workout. This will give you a taste of what we do and it will provide us with valuable information about you. The first session ends we will sit down and discuss what we learned about you and what you learned about us. You want to continue from there the next step is signing up for our Fundamentals Course.

**mywritinglab**

**WANT A BETTER GRADE?**

For more practice and writing assignments on run-ons, go to **www.mywritinglab.com > Recognizing and Avoiding Errors > Run-ons: Comma Splices and Fused Sentences.**

## WHAT HAVE I LEARNED ABOUT CORRECTING COMMA SPLICES AND FUSED SENTENCES?

To test and track your understanding, complete the following ideas. Use several sentences as needed for each response.

**1.** A comma splice is

**2.** A fused sentence is

**3.** What are the five ways to eliminate comma splices and fused sentences?

**4. How will I use what I have learned about correcting comma splices and fused sentences?**
In your notebook, discuss how you will apply to your own writing what you have learned about comma splices and fused sentences.

**5. What do I still need to study about correcting comma splices and fused sentences?**
In your notebook, describe your ongoing study needs by describing what, when, and how you will continue studying comma splices and fused sentences.

# 19

# Fragments

A fragment is an incomplete thought.

Thinking about a real-life situation helps us to understand the impact of fragments on our ability to communicate. The photo illustrates a couple talking about plans for home improvements. Read about the situation and answer the question "What's the point of learning about fragments?"

# What's the Point of Correcting Fragments?

PHOTOGRAPHIC ORGANIZER: FRAGMENTS

▲ **Kitchen under construction**

Suppose you are remodeling your kitchen. You ask two contractors the same questions. Below are their replies.

**Contractor A:**
"One month maybe…need a deposit…for materials…discounts at area dealers…guaranteeing work for five years…"

**Contractor B:**
"We can begin work on the kitchen in one month and finish in another month. Before we begin work, we need a deposit for materials. We have agreements with area dealers for discounts on your appliances. We guarantee our work for five years. Let's make an appointment to draw up plans and sign an agreement."

With which contractor will you be able to communicate easily and clearly if you hire one of them?

_____

**What's the point of learning about fragments?**

_____

_____

_____

_____

_____

# Understanding the Point of Correcting Fragments: One Student Writer's Response

The following paragraph offers one writer's reaction to the statements about the kitchen renovations given by the contractors.

> Contractor A is hard to understand. Before he finishes one idea, he begins another one. It sounds like he has a hard time staying focused or paying attention. His ideas are all over the place. In contrast, contractor B makes his ideas clear and easy to follow. He finished his ideas and gave much more information.
>
> The difference between contractor A and contractor B favors contractor B. He seems more professional and trustworthy. The contrast between these responses shows me that it is important to communicate in complete sentences. The way we express ourselves has an effect on our image and could even affect our ability to get a job.

# Applying the Point: Correcting Fragments

The ability to write ideas in complete thoughts or sentences is an important tool in building coherent paragraphs and essays. A sentence has two traits.

**SENTENCE: Complete Thought-Complete Information**

   **TRAIT ONE:** A sentence states a complete and independent thought.

   **TRAIT TWO:** A sentence contains a subject and a verb.

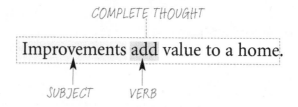

A **sentence** contains all the information needed to clearly express a complete thought. In contrast, a fragment is often recognized by what is missing from the thought. A **fragment** is an incomplete thought.

### FRAGMENT: Incomplete Thought-Missing Information

A **fragment** is missing one of the following: a subject, a verb, or both subject and verb.

| | |
|---|---|
| Missing Subject: | Happens before and after a paint job. |
| Missing Verb: | Renee not using primer paint. |
| Missing Subject and Verb: | To properly paint a wall. |

Even when a group of words includes both a subject and a verb, it still can be a fragment. A subordinating conjunction signals a fragment that has both a subject and a verb. These types of fragments are missing an independent clause.

**Fragment (Missing an Independent Clause):**

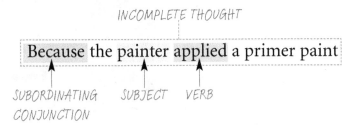

To identify a fragment, ask the following questions:

- Does the idea have a verb?
- What is the subject of the verb?
- Does the idea express a complete thought?

---

**IDENTIFYING FRAGMENTS**

Identify fragments and sentences. Write **F** for *fragment* next to the incomplete thoughts. Write **S** for *sentence* next to the complete thoughts.

_____ **1.** Painting the interior is the least costly way to improve a home.

_____ **2.** Selecting the type and color of the paint and using the proper tools.

_____ **3.** Save money by doing the painting yourself.

_____ **4.** Painting tools include masking tape, paint rollers, buckets, drop cloths, and sandpaper.

_____ **5.** A container that holds paint when using a paint roller.

Practice 2

# Types of Fragments

Sentences can be broken into smaller pieces or fragments. Often these fragments are either phrases or dependent clauses punctuated as if they are complete sentences. An effective writer understands fragments and how they are used to build complete sentences. The following examples illustrate the difference between a phrase, a dependent clause, and a sentence.

**Phrase: Incomplete Thought**

Moving in the new house tomorrow

*MISSING SUBJECT AND VERB*

**Dependent Clause: Incomplete Thought**

which is a dream come true

*VERB*

*RELATIVE PRONOUN/SUBJECT*

▲ Couple moving home

**A Sentence: Complete Thought**

We are moving in the new house tomorrow, which is a dream come true.

This section discusses seven common types of fragments: (1) prepositional phrase, (2) appositive phrase, (3) infinitive phrase, (4) gerund phrase, (5) participle phrase, (6) dependent clause, and (7) relative clause, and techniques you can use to revise fragments into sentences. A writer may use two techniques to revise fragments into sentences:

- Combine existing ideas
- Add missing ideas

## Phrase Fragments

A **phrase** is a group of words that acts as a single unit. A phrase is a fragment because it does not contain both a subject and a verb. To create a sentence, add information (such as a subject, a verb, or both) to the phrase, or join the phrase to an existing sentence.

## 1. PREPOSITIONAL PHRASE

A **prepositional phrase** begins with a preposition (such as *at, or, in, to, toward, for, since,* and *of*) and ends with the object of the preposition. A prepositional phrase adds information about direction, manner, space, and time such as *in the house* or *after the game.*

COMPLETE THOUGHT          PREPOSITIONAL PHRASE

Sue Ling was confident. About remodeling a house.

SUBJECT   VERB          PREPOSITION          OBJECT OF THE PREPOSITION

**Revised to Combine Ideas:**

COMPLETE THOUGHT

Sue Ling was confident about remodeling a house.

**Revised to Add Ideas:**

COMPLETE THOUGHT               COMPLETE THOUGHT

Sue Ling was confident. She knew about remodeling a house.

SUBJECT   VERB   ADDED SUBJECT   ADDED VERB

---

### PREPOSITIONAL PHRASE FRAGMENTS

Build two new sentences using the prepositional phrase. First, combine the existing sentence with the prepositional phrase to create a new sentence. Then, create another new sentence by adding missing information to the prepositional phrase.

**prepositional phrase:**

for his family

**sentence:**

Cia Lin has been working to provide a home.

**1.** COMBINE IDEAS: _____

_____

**2.** ADD IDEAS: _____

_____

Practice 3

## 2. APPOSITIVE PHRASE

An **appositive phrase** contains a noun that renames or describes another noun in the same sentence. An appositive phrase combines with an complete thought to add detail. Place an appositive phrase next to the noun it renames.

APPOSITIVE PHRASE FRAGMENT          COMPLETE THOUGHT

A talented handy person . Jeri enjoys fixing up her home.

SUBJECT   VERB

**Revised to Combine Ideas:**

COMPLETE THOUGHT

A talented handy person, Jeri enjoys fixing up her home.

INTRODUCTORY PHRASE SET OFF WITH A COMMA

**Revised to Add Ideas:**

COMPLETE THOUGHT

Jeri is a talented handy person who enjoys fixing up her home.

ADDED VERB          ADDED RELATIVE PRONOUN/SUBJECT
                    OF NEW DEPENDENT CLAUSE

---

**Practice 4**

### APPOSITIVE PHRASE FRAGMENTS

Build two new sentences using the appositive phrase. First, combine the existing sentence with the appositive phrase to create a new sentence. Then, create another new sentence by adding missing information to the appositive phrase.

**Appositive phrase:**

A low-cost, energy-saving step.

**Sentence:**

Fixing a leaky faucet lowers your water bill.

▲ Handy person

**1.** COMBINE IDEAS: ............................................................

..............................................................................................

**2.** ADD IDEAS: ...................................................................

..............................................................................................

## 3. INFINITIVE PHRASE

An infinitive is a form of a verb, but it is not a verb. Combining *to* with a verb forms an **infinitive** as in the following: *to go, to talk,* and *to think.* An **infinitive phrase** is made up of an infinitive and the object of the infinitive such as *to quit smoking* or *to run a mile.* An infinitive phrase can act as a noun, adjective, or adverb.

COMPLETE THOUGHT                    INFINITIVE PHRASE

Jeri crawled into her attic. To inspect the insulation.

SUBJECT   VERB

**Revised to Combine Ideas:**

COMPLETE THOUGHT

Jeri crawled into her attic to inspect the insulation.

**Revised to Add Ideas:**

COMPLETE THOUGHT                    COMPLETE THOUGHT

Jeri crawled into her attic. She needed to inspect the insulation.

ADDED SUBJECT   ADDED VERB

---

### INFINITIVE PHRASE FRAGMENTS

Build two new sentences using the infinitive phrase. First, combine the existing sentence with the infinitive phrase to create a new sentence. Then, create another new sentence by adding missing information to the infinitive phrase.

**Infinitive phrase:**

To install on your roof.

**Sentence:**

Solar water heaters are green and easy.

▲ Solar water heater

1. COMBINE IDEAS: _____

_____

2. ADD IDEAS: _____

_____

_____

Practice 5

# *-ing* Phrases: Gerunds and Participles

An *-ing* phrase can function as either a noun or an adjective. An *-ing* phrase used as a **noun** is called a **gerund**. An *-ing* phrase used as an **adjective** is called a **participle**.

## 4. GERUND PHRASE

A gerund is a form of a verb, but it is not a verb. A **gerund** is a **noun** that ends in *-ing*, such as *going, talking,* and *thinking*. A **gerund phrase** is made up of a gerund and the object of the gerund such as *quitting smoking* or *running three miles*. A gerund phrase functions as a **noun.** For example, a gerund phrase can be the subject of a sentence or an object of a verb or preposition.

COMPLETE THOUGHT — —ING PHRASE FRAGMENT (GERUND)

Jeri saved thousands of dollars. Doing her own home repairs.

SUBJECT VERB

**Revised to Combine Ideas:**

COMPLETE THOUGHT

Jeri saved thousands of dollars by doing her own home repairs.

ADDED PREPOSITION · ACTS AS OBJECT OF THE PREPOSITION "BY"

**Revised to Add Ideas:**

ADDED VERB · COMPLETE THOUGHT

She enjoys doing her own home repairs.

ADDED SUBJECT · ACTS AS A NOUN AS OBJECT OF THE VERB "ENJOYS"

---

### *-ing* FRAGMENTS

Build two new sentences using the gerund phrase. First, combine the existing sentence with the *-ing* phrase to create a new sentence. Then, create another new sentence by adding missing information to the gerund phrase.

**-ing phrase:**

Owning a home

**Sentence:**

We have worked to fulfill our dream for years.

**1.** COMBINE IDEAS: ........................................................................

..................................................................................................

**2.** ADD IDEAS: ...........................................................................

..................................................................................................

## 5. PARTICIPLE PHRASE

A participle is a form of a verb, but it is not a verb. A **participle** is an **adjective** that ends in *-ing*, such as *going, talking,* and *thinking*. A **participle phrase** is made up of a participle and the object of the participle such as *quitting smoking*, or *running a mile*. A participle phrase functions as an **adjective;** it describes nouns and other adjectives.

-ING PHRASE FRAGMENT (PARTICIPLE)  COMPLETE THOUGHT

Hammering a nail . Lou smashed his thumb.

SUBJECT  VERB

**Revised to Combine Ideas:**

COMPLETE THOUGHT

Hammering a nail , Lou smashed his thumb.

COMMA SETS OFF PHRASE AS INTRODUCTORY ELEMENT

ACTS AS AN ADJECTIVE; DESCRIBES THE SUBJECT "LOU"

**Revised to Add Ideas:**

COMPLETE THOUGHT

Lou was hammering a nail when he smashed his thumb.

OBJECT OF VERB

THE PARTICIPLE "HAMMERING" BECOMES PART OF THE VERB

### *-ING* FRAGMENTS

Build two new sentences using the participle phrase. First, combine the existing sentence with the participle phrase to create a new sentence. Then, create another new sentence by adding missing words to the participle phrase.

**Participle phrase:**

Moving out of his parent's house.

**Sentence:**

Keyshawn will be on his own for the first time.

**1.** COMBINE IDEAS: ----------------------------------------------------------------

------------------------------------------------------------------------------------

**2.** ADD IDEAS: ----------------------------------------------------------------------

------------------------------------------------------------------------------------

Practice 7

# Clause Fragments

A **clause** is a set of words that contains a subject and a verb. An **independent clause** states a complete thought in a sentence that begins with a capital letter and ends with punctuation such as a period or a semicolon. In contrast, a **dependent clause** expresses an incomplete thought or fragment.

**6.** DEPENDENT CLAUSE

A **dependent clause**, also known as a **subordinate clause**, does not make sense on its own. A dependent clause is formed by placing a subordinating conjunction in front of a subject and a verb.

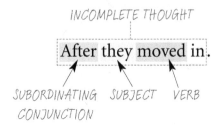

A **subordinating conjunction** states the relationship between two clauses.

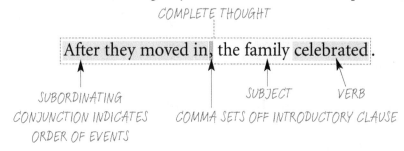

The following chart lists common subordinating conjunctions based on the relationships they express.

| Subordinating Conjunctions and the Relationships They Express | | | | |
|---|---|---|---|---|
| **Cause** | **Contrast** | **Time** | **Place** | **Condition** |
| as | although | after | where | even if |
| because | as if | as | wherever | if |
| in order that | even though | as long as | | only if |
| now that | though | before | | unless |
| since | whereas | once | | when |
| that | while | since | | whether or not |
| so | | until | | |
| so that | | when | | |
| | | whenever | | |
| | | while | | |

To create a sentence, combine a dependent clause with an independent clause. Or revise the dependent clause into an independent clause by dropping the subordinating conjunction.

*COMPLETE THOUGHT*       *DEPENDENT CLAUSE FRAGMENT*

They hung the tire swing. Before they unpacked.

*SUBJECT*   *VERB*       *SUBORDINATING CONJUNCTION*

**Revised to Combine Ideas:**

*COMPLETE THOUGHT*

They hung the tire swing then they unpacked.

*INDEPENDENT CLAUSE*       *DEPENDENT CLAUSE*

**Revised to Add Ideas:**

*COMPLETE THOUGHT*

They hung the tire swing; then they unpacked.

*SEMICOLON JOINS TWO INDEPENDENT CLAUSES*

---

**DEPENDENT CLAUSE FRAGMENTS**

Build two new sentences using the infinitive phrase. First, combine the existing sentence with the infinitive phrase to create a new sentence. Then, create another new sentence by adding missing information to the dependent clause.

**Dependent clause:**

That even adults can enjoy.

**Sentence:**

A tire swing is an easy, thrifty, old-fashioned addition to the yard.

▲ **Tire swing**

**1.** COMBINE IDEAS: ................................................

........................................................................

**2.** ADD IDEAS: ....................................................

........................................................................

Practice 8

© Pearson Education, Inc.

### 7. RELATIVE CLAUSE

A **relative clause** describes a noun or pronoun in an independent clause. A **relative pronoun** introduces the relative clause and relates it to the noun or pronoun it describes.

| Relative Pronouns | | | | |
|---|---|---|---|---|
| who | whom | whose | which | that |

Join the relative clause to the independent clause that contains the word it describes. Or revise the relative clause into an independent clause by replacing the relative pronoun with a noun.

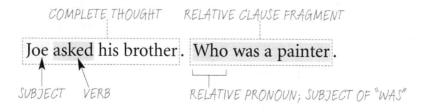

COMPLETE THOUGHT    RELATIVE CLAUSE FRAGMENT

Joe asked his brother. Who was a painter.

SUBJECT   VERB       RELATIVE PRONOUN; SUBJECT OF "WAS"

**Revised to Combine Ideas:**

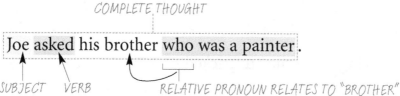

COMPLETE THOUGHT

Joe asked his brother who was a painter.

SUBJECT   VERB       RELATIVE PRONOUN RELATES TO "BROTHER"

**Revised to Add Ideas:**

COMPLETE THOUGHT

Dan was a painter.

NOUN REPLACES RELATIVE PRONOUN "WHO"

With the following sets of ideas, build four new sentences using the relative clause. In each set, combine the existing sentence with the relative clause to create a new sentence. Then, create another new sentence by revising the relative clause into an independent clause.

**Relative Clause:**

that needed extensive repairs.

**Sentence:**

Heather and John bought an historic home.

▲ **Home in need of repair**

**1.** COMBINE IDEAS: ......................................................................................................................

........................................................................................................................................................

**2.** ADD IDEAS: ............................................................................................................................

........................................................................................................................................................

**Relative Clause:**

who had prior experience in restoring historic homes.

**Sentence:**

Heather and John hired a contractor.

**3.** COMBINE IDEAS: ......................................................................................................................

........................................................................................................................................................

**4.** ADD IDEAS: ............................................................................................................................

........................................................................................................................................................

**Digital image of Hurricane Mitch** ▶

Revise the ideas to eliminate fragments by combining or adding ideas.

**1.** After a storm hits. Homeowners can lessen the chance of further damage by taking a few simple steps.

--------------------------------------------------

--------------------------------------------------

**2.** Instead of waiting for insurance to kick in. Homeowners can help themselves with simple repairs to roofs and windows. That can prevent further water damage to their homes.

--------------------------------------------------

--------------------------------------------------

**3.** By putting up tarps. And boarding up broken windows with plywood. You can help prevent more serious repair work.

--------------------------------------------------

--------------------------------------------------

**4.** Getting a tarp over a hole in a leaky roof can prevent water from doing additional damage. To drywall, electrical systems, and flooring.

--------------------------------------------------

--------------------------------------------------

**5.** Homeowners have to use common sense. Not doing anything too risky and making sure the storm is over. Before going on the roof.

--------------------------------------------------

--------------------------------------------------

Proofread the following paragraph for fragments. Revise to eliminate fragments by combining or adding ideas.

## Storm Shutters

(1) To protect a home from damage in wind storms. (2) Install impact-resistant shutters over all large windows and glass doors. (3) Not only do they protect doors and windows from wind-borne objects, but they can reduce damage. (4) Caused by sudden pressure changes when a window or door is broken. (5) Laminated windows (plastic bonded to glass) are another option. (6) And are a very good choice. (7) For either building a new home or adding to an old one. (8) The easiest shutters to install are those that simply cover the opening with plywood. (9) In past hurricanes, many homeowners have seen their temporary plywood shutters blown off. (10) Because they were not properly fastened. (11) If you have a wood-frame house, use strong fasteners to attach the panels over windows. (12) Have these temporary shutters stored and ready to use. (13) Since building supply stores often sell out of these materials quickly during a storm warning. (14) If your home is made with concrete blocks. (15) You will have to install anchors well in advance.

—Adapted from National Hurricane Center. "Shutters." Hurricane Preparedness Week. Aug. 2008. <http://www.nhc.noaa.gov/HAW2/english/retrofit/shutters.shtml>.

▲ **Virginia Beach residents prepare for the arrival of Hurricane Isabel**

# Writing Assignments

## Writing for Everyday Life

Assume you have been asked to give your feedback about a recent purchase you made. Edit to eliminate fragments. Use your own paper.

> To the Sales Manager at Best Buy:
>
> Dusty Parrish assisted me today with purchasing a dishwasher. That I wanted at the best price offered in the area! Answering all of my questions about appliances and helping me in every way he can to make the best decisions. Happy to have bought my dishwasher from such a thoughtful person!
>
> Sincerely,
> Beth Agassi

## Writing for College Life

Read the following paragraph written for a sociology class. Edit to eliminate fragments. Use your own paper.

> Social class is based on three areas. Property, prestige, and power. For example, property is one way to determine a person's standing in society. However, ownership is not the only important aspect of property For example, some powerful people control property. Such as managers of corporations. Although they do not own the property. If managers can control property for their own benefit. Awarding themselves big bonuses and large perks. It doesn't matter that they don't own the property. That they use for themselves.

## Writing for Working Life

Read the following memo from an employee requesting a raise. Edit to eliminate fragments. Use your own paper.

> To:     Serita Delgado
> From:   Latoya Williams
> RE:     Annual Evaluation
>
> As you requested. I am writing to document my efforts. That qualify me for my yearly raise. Always willing to come in early or stay late. I have worked above expectations. When new team members are hired. I conduct their initial training. And follow up with them as a mentor. In addition, I have taken part in all available training sessions. Including those that are not required. Clients and coworkers writing me letters and emails of gratitude.

To test and track your understanding of correcting fragments, complete the following ideas. Use several sentences as needed for each response.

**1.** What are the two traits of a sentence?

......................................................................................................................................................

......................................................................................................................................................

**2.** A fragment is ................................................................................................................................

......................................................................................................................................................

**3.** A phrase is ....................................................................................................................................

......................................................................................................................................................

**4.** A clause is ....................................................................................................................................

......................................................................................................................................................

**5.** Two types of clauses are ............................................ and ............................................ clauses.

**6.** The five types of phrases discussed in this chapter include the ............................................,

............................................, ............................................, ............................................, and ............................................

**7.** Two ways to eliminate fragments include ........................ ideas or ........................ ideas.

**8. How will I use what I have learned?** In your notebook, discuss how you will apply to your own writing what you have learned about correcting fragments.

**9. What do I still need to study about fragments?** In your notebook, describe your ongoing study needs by describing what, when, and how you will continue studying fragments.

*Academic Learning Log*

LEARNING OUTCOMES
SELF-EVALUATION

PORTFOLIO

# 20

# Nouns and Pronouns

A noun names a person, animal, place, or thing. A pronoun stands in the place of a noun that has been clearly identified earlier in the text.

Thinking about a real-life situation helps us to understand the purpose of nouns and pronouns in our communication. The following photographs are still shots from the megahit movie *The Dark Knight*. Study the picture, complete the activity, and answer the question "What's the point of learning about nouns and pronouns?"

# What's the Point of Learning About Nouns and Pronouns?

**PHOTOGRAPHIC ORGANIZER: NOUNS AND PRONOUNS**

Read the following short review of *The Dark Knight*, the second film in the Batman series by director Christopher Nolan. Work with a small group of your peers; fill in the blanks with the nouns and pronouns that have been omitted from each sentence. Answer the question "What's the point of learning about nouns and pronouns?"

**Review of *The Dark Knight***

_____ is more than

just a comic _____ turned

into a _____ . _____

is a _____ of the struggle

between _____ and

_____ . _____

gives one of _____ best

_____ as a flawed

_____ _____

struggles to remain moral. As the

wicked Joker, _____

creates a creepy _____

_____ relishes in

_____ and _____ .

▲ Batman and the Joker

**What's the point of learning about nouns and pronouns?**

_____

_____

# Understanding the Point of Learning About Nouns and Pronouns: One Student Writer's Response

The following paragraph offers one writer's reaction to the activity based on "Review of *The Dark Knight*."

*This was a challenging activity, like putting together a puzzle with missing pieces. It was fun trying to figure it out with a group. We all came up with so many different ways to fill in each blank. We really had to study the words around each blank for clues. The activity taught me that we use nouns or pronouns in every statement we make, and without them, our ideas don't make sense.*

# Applying the Point: Nouns

Often, nouns are the first words we learn to speak as we hear the names of people and things that we want or need. The word "noun" comes from the Latin word *nomen*, which means "name." A **noun** names a person, animal, place, object, element, action, or concept.

One type of noun is the proper noun. A **proper noun** names an individual person, place, or thing. A proper noun is always capitalized. The second type of noun is the common noun. A **common noun** is a general name for any member of a group or class. A common noun is not capitalized.

## TYPES OF NOUNS

Complete the following chart. Use appropriate capitalization. Share your answers with a small group of peers or your class.

| WHAT A NOUN NAMES | COMMON NOUNS | PROPER NOUN |
|---|---|---|
| Person | politician | |
| Animal | | Lassie |
| Place | city | |
| Object | vehicle | |
| Element | | none |
| Action | | none |
| Concept | religion | |

Practice 2

366

A proper or common noun can function in a sentence as a subject, an object of a verb, an object of a preposition, or an appositive (which describes another noun).

## Uses of a Noun

| Function in Sentence | Example |
|---|---|

**• Subject**

*PROPER NOUN AS SUBJECT*

Roberto has arrived.

**• Object of a verb**

*VERB*    *PROPER NOUN AS OBJECT OF VERB "ORDERED"*

Maria ordered a Coca-Cola.

**• Object of a preposition**

*PREPOSITION*    *COMMON NOUN AS OBJECT OF THE PREPOSITION "AT"*

We were at the theatre.

**• Appositive (describes another noun)**

*SUBJECT (PROPER NOUN)*    *COMMON NOUN AS APPOSITIVE DESCRIBING "CHRIS"*

Chris is my hero.

---

### USES OF A NOUN

Locate the nouns in the following sentences. Then identify the type and use of each noun by completing the charts below each sentence.

**1.** A superhero has superhuman powers and usually fights evil or crime.

| NOUN | TYPE | FUNCTION |
|---|---|---|
| | | |
| | | |
| | | |
| | | |

**2.** Superman, also known as Clark Kent, can fly, shoot beams of energy, move at supersonic speeds, and lift incredible amounts of weight.

| NOUN | TYPE | FUNCTION |
|---|---|---|
| | | |
| | | |
| | | |
| | | |
| | | |
| | | |
| | | |

Practice 3

# Count and Noncount Nouns

**Count nouns** name distinct individual units of a group or category. Count nouns usually refer to what we can see, hear, or touch. Count nouns are typically common nouns and can be singular or plural. Most plural count nouns are formed by adding *-s* or *-es*. However, many singular count nouns use irregular spellings in their plural form.

| Examples of Count Nouns | | |
| --- | --- | --- |
| | **Singular** | **Plural** |
| **Regular** | character, story | characters, stories |
| **Irregular** | child, woman | children, women |

**Noncount nouns** name a nonspecific member of a group or category. Noncount nouns, which are typically common nouns, do not have plural forms. Noncount nouns name things that cannot be divided into smaller parts. Often, noncount nouns represent a group of count nouns. The following chart illustrates the differences between noncount and count nouns.

| Examples of Noncount and Corresponding Count Nouns | |
| --- | --- |
| **Noncount Noun** | **Count Noun** |
| money | pennies, nickles, dimes, coins, dollars, bills |
| time | days, weeks, months, years, eras |

## PAST PARTICIPLE OF REGULAR VERBS

Read the following sentences. Identify the **boldfaced** nouns as a count or noncount noun.

**1.** In X-men, the **series** of **movies**, Mystique is a dangerous **villain.**

_____

**2.** She has scaly blue **skin** and yellow reptilian **eyes.**

_____

**3.** She is a **shapeshifter** who can take on the form of other **humans** or **objects.**

_____

_____

**4.** She is also a **nudist** who loathes **clothing.**

_____

**5.** Mystique's exact **age** remains unknown, but her own **words** indicate she is over 100 years old.

_____

▲ *X-men: The Last Stand*

# Articles and Nouns

An **article** is an adjective that describes a noun as general or specific. An article indicates the noun's relationship to a larger group. The following chart illustrates the general guidelines for use of an article before a noun.

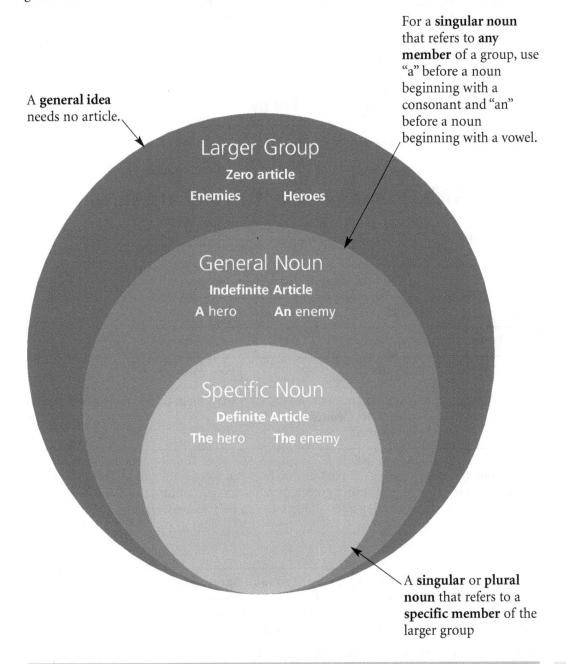

A **general idea** needs no article.

For a **singular noun** that refers to **any member** of a group, use "a" before a noun beginning with a consonant and "an" before a noun beginning with a vowel.

## Larger Group
**Zero article**

Enemies    Heroes

## General Noun
**Indefinite Article**

**A** hero    **An** enemy

## Specific Noun
**Definite Article**

**The** hero    **The** enemy

A **singular** or **plural noun** that refers to a **specific member** of the larger group

---

**NOUNS AND ARTICLES**

Read the sentences below. Insert the correct article (*a, an,* or *the*) in the spaces in front of each noun. If zero article is required, leave the space blank.

Of all (1) ............... movies, Justine loves (2) ............... action movies best. She enjoys (3) ............... special effects and (4) ............... action scenes. (5) ............... chase scene puts her on (6) ............... edge of her seat. (7) ............... example of (8) ............... good movie, according to her, (9) is ............... oldie-goldie, (10) ............... *Terminator.*

Practice 5

# Applying the Point: Pronouns

**Pronouns and antecedents** work closely together to communicate an idea. A **pronoun** refers to or stands in the place of a noun that has been clearly identified earlier in the discussion. An **antecedent** is the noun to which a pronoun refers. Every pronoun should refer clearly and specifically to one particular antecedent.

ANTECEDENT OF PRONOUN "HE"     PRONOUN "HE" REFERS TO ANTECEDENT "SUPERHERO"

The modern superhero is a symbol of the culture from which he comes.

In the preceding example, the pronoun clearly refers to the antecedent.

> For more information on using precision in drafting sentences, see pages 306–317, "Sentence Clarity: Point of View, Number, and Tense."

## How to Make Pronouns and Antecedents Agree

A pronoun and its antecedent must agree with each other in three ways: person, number, and gender. The following chart presents pronouns based on these traits.

| Pronouns: Person, Number, and Gender | | |
|---|---|---|
| | **Singular** | **Plural** |
| **First Person** | I, me, my, mine | we, us, ours |
| **Second Person** | you, yours | you, yours |
| **Third Person** | he, him, his (**masculine**) she, her, hers (**feminine**) it, its (**neutral**) | they, their, theirs (**neutral**) |

**Pronoun agreement** makes the relationship between a pronoun and its antecedent obvious and clear. **Faulty pronoun agreement** reflects vague wording and results in reader confusion. Remembering a few guidelines can help you establish pronoun agreement.

| Guidelines for Clear Pronoun Agreement |
|---|
| • Pronoun choice establishes consistent use of the person of pronouns. |
| • Singular pronouns refer to or replace singular nouns. |
| • Plural pronouns refer to or replace plural nouns. |
| • Feminine pronouns refer to or replace feminine nouns. |
| • Masculine pronouns refer to or replace masculine nouns. |
| • Use gender-neutral plural pronouns and antecedents to make statements that could apply to women or men. |

▲ Marlon Brando in *Superman*

Underline the antecedent of each pronoun in the following sentences. Then fill in the blank with a pronoun that agrees with its antecedent. Refer to the chart on page 370.

**1.** The concept of the hero, along with ............. distinct traits, is found in almost every culture.

**2.** In ancient stories, the hero is someone of noble birth; ............. parents are divine or royal, wealthy, and highly respected.

**3.** Likewise, the modern superheroes Superman and Batman are of noble birth; ............. both have powerful, wealthy, well-respected parents.

**4.** Superman is born to noble parents; ............. is Kal-El, the son of Jor-El, a senior statesman of the planet Krypton.

**5.** Batman, also known as Bruce Wayne, is born to a family with a billion-dollar business; ............. is a vast and powerful company.

**6.** The classical hero is often separated from or abandoned by ............. parents.

**7.** Jor-El foresees the destruction of ............. home planet, so ............. seals ............. son in a space-basket and sends ............. across the galaxy to Earth.

**8.** When ............. is just a boy, Batman is also separated from ............. parents; ............. are murdered before ............. eyes.

**9.** The modern superhero shares another trait with the classical hero; ............. is the rescue or adoption of the hero by surrogate parents.

**10.** For example, the loyal butler Alfred of Bruce Wayne (Batman) becomes ............. father figure, and the childless *Kents* find and adopt Kal-El (Superman) as ............. son.

# How to Correct Faulty Pronoun Agreement

Faulty pronoun agreement usually occurs when the guidelines for clear agreement are ignored. Once you understand why faulty pronoun agreement occurs and how it can be corrected, you can avoid vague agreements in your writing; then you can create pronoun agreement based on person, number, and gender.

## Faulty Pronoun Agreement due to Shift in Person

**PROBLEM:** When the person of the pronoun differs from the person of the antecedent, it is called a faulty **shift in person**. In the example below, the faulty shift is from third person to second person.

*THIRD-PERSON ANTECEDENT "PERSON" DOES NOT AGREE WITH SECOND-PERSON PRONOUN "YOUR"*

A person's thoughts lead to your actions.

**CORRECTION #1:** Correct the shift in person by changing the antecedent to agree with the pronoun.

*REVISED SECOND-PERSON ANTECEDENT AGREES WITH SECOND-PERSON PRONOUN*

Your thoughts lead to your actions.

**CORRECTION #2:** Correct by changing the pronoun to agree with the antecedent.

*THIRD-PERSON ANTECEDENT AGREES WITH REVISED THIRD-PERSON PRONOUN*

A person's thoughts lead to her actions.

---

**Practice 7**

### PRONOUN AGREEMENT BASED ON PERSON

Edit the following two sentences for pronoun agreement based on person.

**1.** The behaviors we choose are influenced by your attitude about the behavior.

**2.** For example, if you don't like or value math, one is less likely to study the subject.

# Faulty Pronoun Agreement due to Shift in Number

**PROBLEM:** In a sentence with a faulty **shift in number,** the pronoun is a different number than the number of the antecedent. In the two examples below, the faulty shift is from singular to plural; the revised sentences show two different ways to correct the same problem.

*SINGULAR ANTECEDENT DOES NOT AGREE WITH PLURAL PRONOUN*

An individual is able to change their attitudes.

**CORRECTION #1:** Correct by making the antecedent the same number as the pronoun.

*SINGULAR ANTECEDENT AGREES WITH SINGULAR PRONOUN*

An individual is able to change her attitudes.

**CORRECTION #2:** Correct by making the pronoun the same number as the antecedent.

*PLURAL ANTECEDENT AGREES WITH PLURAL PRONOUN*

Individuals are able to change their attitudes.

*VERB REVISED TO PLURAL TO AGREE WITH PLURAL SUBJECT "INDIVIDUALS"*

**PRONOUN AGREEMENT BASED ON NUMBER**

▲ Michael Phelps at Beijing 2008 Olympics

Edit the following two sentences for pronoun agreement based on number.

**1.** If a person thinks he can accomplish a task, then usually they do.

**2.** For example, athletes like Michael Phelps break records because he believes he can.

# Faulty Pronoun Agreement due to Shift in Gender

**PROBLEM:** In a sentence with a faulty **shift in gender,** the pronoun is a different gender than the gender of the antecedent. Most often, gender agreement problems are due to using the masculine pronoun to refer to antecedents that could apply to either men or women.

*SINGULAR ANTECEDENT IS NEUTRAL (COULD BE MASCULINE OR FEMININE)*

A person expands his thoughts through reading.

*MASCULINE PRONOUN DOES NOT AGREE WITH NEUTRAL ANTECEDENT*

**CORRECTION #1:** Correct by rewording to make the pronoun the same gender as the antecedent.

*NEUTRAL, SINGULAR ANTECEDENT AGREES WITH NEUTRAL, SINGULAR PRONOUN "HIS OR HER"*

A person expands his or her thoughts through reading.

If you reword the sentence by making the pronoun and its antecedent (neutral and) plural, make sure all other parts of the sentence are plural as necessary.

*NEUTRAL, PLURAL ANTECEDENT AGREES WITH NEUTRAL, PLURAL PRONOUN*

People expand their thoughts through reading.

**CORRECTION #2:** Correct by rewording to make the antecedent the same gender as the pronoun. In the instance below, this requires adding a feminine proper noun ("Juanita") to match the feminine pronoun.

*ADDED SINGULAR FEMININE ANTECEDENT TO AGREE WITH SINGULAR FEMININE PRONOUN*

Juanita expands her mind through reading.

## PRONOUN AGREEMENT BASED ON GENDER

Edit the following two sentences for pronoun agreement based on gender.

**1.** Readers come into contact with ideas that differ from his or her own values.

**2.** For example, by reading stories about strong, independent women, a reader may begin to question his stereotypical beliefs about women.

## PRONOUN AGREEMENT REVIEW

Edit the following paragraph for pronoun agreement based on person, number, and gender.

When the hero of a story is a woman, their mission differs from the quest of a male hero. In addition, your typical heroine is quite different from the female hero. For example, a heroine exists as the object of a male's desire. In contrast, the female hero has their own journey. Female heroes often fight against what society expects of her. In contrast, the quest of a male hero gives them the chance to live up to what society expects of you. Male and female heroes reflect or challenge the values of your culture.

▲ Angelina Jolie as Lara Croft

# How to Use Pronoun Case Clearly

**Pronoun case** identifies the function of a pronoun in a sentence. The definitions and examples of the three cases of pronouns are shown in the following chart.

| Pronoun Case | | | | | | |
|---|---|---|---|---|---|---|
| | **Subjective Case** | | **Objective Case** | | **Possessive Case** | |
| | **Singular** | **Plural** | **Singular** | **Plural** | **Singular** | **Plural** |
| **1ˢᵗ Person** | I | we | me | us | my, mine | our, ours |
| **2ⁿᵈ Person** | you | you | you | you | your, yours | your, yours |
| **3ʳᵈ Person** | he, she, it<br><br>who<br>whoever | they, those | him, her, it<br><br>whom<br>whomever | them | his, her, hers its, whose | their, theirs |

**Subjective case** pronouns act as subjects or predicate nouns. A **predicate noun** restates the subject, usually by completing a linking verb such as *is*.

*SUBJECTIVE CASE PRONOUN ACTS AS SUBJECT OF VERB "ADMIRE"*

I admire Heath Ledger's portrayal of the Joker.

*SUBJECT IS RENAMED BY SUBJECTIVE CASE PRONOUN*

If anyone deserved an Oscar, it was he.

**Objective case** pronouns act as an object of a verb or preposition. The **object** of a sentence is a noun or pronoun to which the action of a verb is directed or to which the verb's action is done.

*VERB      OBJECT OF VERB*

The movie held us spellbound.

*PREPOSITION      OBJECT OF THE PREPOSITION*

The movie ticket is for whom?

**Possessive case** pronouns show ownership.

*POSSESSIVE CASE PRONOUN INDICATES OWNERSHIP OF "SEAT"*

His seat had gum on it.

Complete the following two sentences with the proper case of each missing pronoun. Discuss your answers with a small group of your peers.

**1.** ............ are looking for powerful moral figures ............ are above ............ and ............ will come to rescue ............ when ............ need ............ .

**2.** People tend to read about heroes with ............ ............ can identify.

# How to Correct Faulty Use of Pronoun Case in Comparisons Using "as" or "than"

Pronouns in comparisons using "as" or "than" can be in the subjective, objective, or possessive case. Writers often confuse the subjective and objective cases because they think it sounds more formal.

**PROBLEM:** The objective case pronoun is being used as the subject of a clause.

INCORRECT USE OF OBJECTIVE CASE PRONOUN

Laura is as strong as him. ------ DEPENDENT CLAUSE WITH IMPLIED VERB "IS"

**CORRECTION:**

SUBJECTIVE CASE PRONOUN ACTS AS SUBJECT OF IMPLIED VERB "IS"

Laura is as strong as he [is].

**PROBLEM:** The subjective case pronoun is being used as the object of a verb.

INCORRECT USE OF SUBJECTIVE CASE PRONOUN

The movie affected Marion as much as I. ------ DEPENDENT CLAUSE WITH IMPLIED SUBJECT AND VERB

**CORRECTION:**

THE IMPLIED VERB "AFFECTED" REQUIRES THE OBJECTIVE CASE PRONOUN

The movie affected Marion as much as [it affected] me.

Complete the following two sentences with the proper case of each missing pronoun. Discuss your answers with a small group of your peers.

**1.** Molly is a better athlete than ............ even though Molly doesn't train as many hours as ............ .

**2.** Injuries don't afflict Molly as much as ............ .

# Faulty Use of Case in Compound Constructions

In some instances, a pronoun is joined with a noun or another pronoun to form a **compound**.

- **Joseph and I** went to a concert together.
- The mailman delivered the letter to **Joseph and me**.

To decide whether the subjective or objective case should be used for a pronoun in a compound, use the same rules that apply for a pronoun that is not in a compound. Use the subjective case for pronouns that function as subjects and the objective case for pronouns that function as objects.

**PROBLEM:** The objective case pronoun is being used in a compound subject.

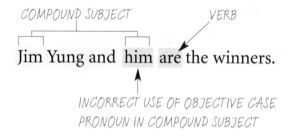

Jim Yung and him are the winners.

**CORRECTION:** Replace the pronoun with the subjective case pronoun. To identify a pronoun as part of a compound subject, delete the other part of the compound so the pronoun stands alone, and see whether the sentence still makes sense.

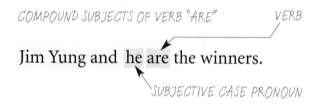

Jim Yung and he are the winners.

**PROBLEM:** The subjective case pronoun is being used in a compound object.

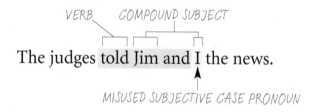

The judges told Jim and I the news.

**CORRECTION:** Replace the pronoun with the objective case pronoun. To identify a pronoun as part of a compound object, delete the other part of the compound so the pronoun stands alone, and see whether the sentence still makes sense.

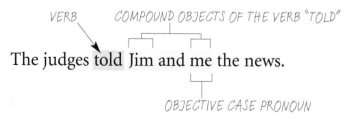

The judges told Jim and me the news.

Complete the following two sentences with the proper case of each missing pronoun.

**1.** Jamal and .................... are going to beat Justine and .................... in the triathlon.

**2.** Two other teams and .................... are trying to break the records held by last year's first place winners and .................... .

PRONOUN CASE REVIEW

Edit the following paragraph for proper pronoun case.

Many of us think of successful, modern athletes as heroes. Just as the classical hero embarks on a challenging journey, so do them who are serious athletes. Hercules, Hector, and others like they, had to prove them stronger physically and mentally than a foe. Likewise a modern athlete has to best a formidable opponent who him fears is stronger than him.

# How to Make Clear Pronoun References

Because a pronoun takes the place of a noun, careful writers make the relationship between a pronoun and its antecedent obvious and clear. Remembering a few guidelines can help you make clear pronoun references.

| Guidelines for Clear Pronoun Reference |
| --- |
| • A pronoun refers clearly and unmistakably to one antecedent. |
| • The antecedent of a pronoun is clearly stated. |
| • A pronoun appears near its antecedent. |
| • A pronoun does not make a broad or sweeping reference to an entire group of words. |

# How to Correct Faulty Pronoun References

## Faulty Pronoun Reference to More Than One Antecedent

**PROBLEM:** The pronoun does not unmistakably refer to one specific antecedent.

*PRONOUN REFERS TO*

After he twisted it, Jared put a bandage on his ankle.

**CORRECTION:** Correct by replacing the pronoun with a noun.

After he twisted his ankle, Jared put on a bandage.

*ADDED NOUN REPLACES PRONOUN WITH NO CLEAR ANTECEDENT*

## Faulty Pronoun Reference to Implied or Missing Antecedent

**PROBLEM:** The antecedent is not stated or is missing.

*ANTECEDENT?*                 *PRONOUN REFERS TO ?*

The chocolate box is empty. Who ate it?

**CORRECTION #1:** Correct by replacing the pronoun with a noun.

*ADDED NOUN REPLACES PRONOUN WITH NO CLEAR ANTECEDENT*

The chocolate box is empty. Who ate the last piece?

**CORRECTION #2:** Correct by rewording to include a clear antecedent for the pronoun.

*ANTECEDENT OF PRONOUN*          *PRONOUN REFERS TO ANTECEDENT "PIECE"*

The last piece of chocolate is gone. Who ate it?

# Faulty Pronoun Reference due to Broad Pronoun References

**PROBLEM:** The pronoun refers to a group of words, such as an entire sentence.

ANTECEDENT OF PRONOUN?        PRONOUN REFERS TO ?

Joe gripes to Teesha about the music, which annoys Teesha.

**CORRECTION:** Correct by rewording to eliminate the pronoun.

Teesha is annoyed because Joe gripes to her about the music.

---

### CLEAR PRONOUN REFERENCE

Edit the following two sentences for clear pronoun reference. Share your answers with a small group of your peers.

**1.** Angela reads books and watches movies about heroic women because she enjoys it.

**2.** Angela told her mother that she was similar to her favorite female hero.

---

### NOUN AND PRONOUN REVIEW

Write a paragraph of three to five sentences that uses nouns and pronouns properly. Exchange your paragraph with a peer and edit each other's work. Suggested topic: A definition and example of a hero.

Practice 15

Practice 16

# Writing Assignments

## Writing for Everyday Life

Assume you are writing a thank you note for a gift you have received. Edit the note to ensure proper use of nouns, articles, and pronouns. Use your own paper.

Dear Uncle Malcolm,

Matilda and me love the grill and cooking utensiles you gave us as the gifts. It was perfect, for us love to have people over and grill-out which is so much fun. Hopefully, you can join Matilda and I for one of them cookouts in near future. Thank you, again, it is unbelievable.

Sincerely,

Andre

## Writing for College Life

Assume you are writing in response to an essay prompt for a college humanities class. Edit the introduction to the essay to ensure proper use of nouns, articles, and pronouns. Use your own paper.

*Essay Prompt:* Discuss an important heroic figure in Western culture.

*Student response:* A important heroic figure in Western culture is Jesus whom is also known as The Christ. Even them whom do not believe Jesus is God in the flesh, admit that it is one of a most compelling storys. His life unfolds in the pattern similar to the classical heros. He bloodline can be traced to King David, and his claims to be the Son of God. He is separated from his father in heaven to fulfill the selfless, lethal mission on earth. After proving his spiritual power to overcome hatred and death, he is reunited with his father.

## Writing for Working Life

Assume you are the chairperson of the United Way fundraising committee at your place of work. You have composed the following e-mail to call for donations. Edit the e-mail to ensure proper use of nouns, articles, and pronouns. Use your own paper.

Dear Colleagues:

Your United Way contribution creates lasting changes right where you and me live. Local volunteers invest your contributions in an areas of education, income and health. Some of the funds support programes and services that help you with basic needs, such as childcare, emergency shelter and free health clinics. United Way also works to keep a people from needing them services in the first place. They work with a broad range of community partners. It focuses on prevention and community changes.

To test and track your understanding, answer the following questions.

1. A noun names a ......................., animal, place, object, action, or concept.

2. A ....................... noun names an individual person, place, or thing; a ....................... noun is a general name for any member of a group or class.

3. A noun can function as a ......................., object of a verb, object of a ......................., or appositive.

4. ....................... nouns name distinct individual units of a group or category; noncount nouns name a nonspecific member of a group or category.

5. An ....................... article is used before a singular noun that refers to any member of a larger group.

6. The definite article .................. is used before a singular or plural noun that refers to a specific member of a larger group.

7. A pronoun refers clearly and specifically to .................. antecedent.

8. An antecedent is the ....................... to which a pronoun refers.

9. A pronoun and its antecedent must agree with each other in three ways: ......................., ......................., and ........................

10. The three pronoun cases are ....................... case, ....................... case, and ....................... case.

11. **How will I use what I have learned about nouns and pronouns?**
    In your notebook, discuss how you will apply to your own writing what you have learned about nouns and pronouns.

12. **What do I still need to study about nouns and pronouns?**
    In your notebook, describe your ongoing study needs by describing what, when, and how you will continue studying pronouns and nouns.

# 21

## CHAPTER PREVIEW

LEARNING OUTCOMES

●━ What's the Point of Subject-Verb Agreement?

●━ Understanding the Point of Subject-Verb Agreement: One Student Writer's Response

●━ Applying the Point: Subject-Verb Agreement

●━ Writing Assignments

# Subject-Verb Agreement: Present Tense

In the present tense, subjects and verbs must agree in number. Singular subjects must take singular verbs; plural subjects must take plural verbs.

Subject-verb agreement in the present tense ranks as one of the most common errors in written standard English. For many people, subject-verb agreement reflects regional speech or the informal way we speak in daily life. For example, many Southerners say "you was" instead of "you were." It is important to understand the difference between regional speech and standard English. Then you can choose language most effective in a given situation.

# What's the Point of Subject-Verb Agreement?

PHOTOGRAPHIC ORGANIZER: SUBJECT-VERB AGREEMENT

Yearly review of an employee ▶

Complete the following activity and answer the question "What's the point of subject-verb agreement?"

Assume you are a manager, and you are completing the yearly review of the employees in your unit. You have asked each employee to submit a self-evaluation. Read the following two drafts of a self-evaluation that will be submitted by a member of your unit. Is one draft more likely to be effective in securing a raise? Why or why not?

**Draft A:**
Making good decisions are one of my strengths. When I face a decision, I think about the different choices that is possible. Each of the choices provide its own good point, and each also provide its own downside. The key to effective decisions unlock the best options.

**Draft B:**
Making good decisions is one of my strengths. When I face a decision, I think about the different choices that are possible. Each of the choices provides its own good point, and each also provides its own downside. The key to effective decisions unlocks the best options.

**What's the point of subject-verb agreement?**

_____

_____

_____

# Understanding the Point of Subject-Verb Agreement: One Student Writer's Response

The following paragraph records one writer's thoughts about the point of subject-verb agreement in the self-evaluation example.

Draft B is more likely to help the employee get a raise. This draft used singular verbs with singular subjects and plural verbs with plural subjects. As a result, Draft B sounds polished and professional. In contrast, Draft A mixed singular subjects with plural verbs or plural subjects with singular verbs. As a result, Draft A doesn't seem clear or controlled. Our group made a chart to show the differences between the two drafts.

Draft A:

| Subject | Verb |
|---|---|
| Making decisions | are |
| choices that | is |
| Each | provide |
| key | unlock |

Draft B:

| Subject | Verb |
|---|---|
| Making decisions | is |
| choices that | are |
| Each | provides |
| Key | unlocks |

As our group talked, some of us were confused by the use of the letter "s" to make a word plural. The teacher explained that the "s" is used to make many subjects plural, but the "s" is also used to make some verbs singular. So, in most cases, if there is an "s" on the subject, I now look to see if I can drop the "s" on the verb.

# Applying the Point: Subject-Verb Agreement

In the present tense, subjects and verbs must agree in number. A singular subject must have a singular verb; a plural subject must have a plural verb. The following chart uses the sample verb "write" to illustrate present tense agreement in number.

| Present Tense Agreement | | |
|---|---|---|
| | Singular **Subject** and **Verb** | Plural **Subject** and **Verb** |
| First Person | I write | We write |
| Second Person | You write | You write |
| Third Person | He She It — writes | They write |

For standard verbs, only the third-person singular verb is formed by adding -*s* or -*es*.

| Third-person singular subject | → | present tense verb ends with -*s* or -*es* |
|---|---|---|
| He<br>She<br>It | →<br>→<br>→ | watches<br>learns<br>lives |

## SUBJECT-VERB AGREEMENT

Fill in the following charts with the correct form of each subject and verb. A few blanks are completed as examples.

**1. To Work**  | Subject | Verb
First Person (singular) _____ *I* | | *work*

Second Person _____

Third Person (singular) _____

**2. To Commute** | Subject | Verb
First Person (plural) _____

Second Person _____

Third Person (plural) _____ *They* | | *commute*

**3. To Reach** | Subject | Verb
First Person (singular) _____

Second Person _____

Third Person (singular) _____

**4. To Plan** | Subject | Verb
Second Person (singular) _____

Second Person _____

Third Person (singular) _____

**5. To Agree** | Subject | Verb
First Person (plural) _____

Second Person _____

Third Person (singular) _____ *He*

Practice 2

# Key Verbs in the Present Tense:
## *To Have, To Do, To Be*

Three key verbs are used both as main verbs and as helping verbs to express a wide variety of meanings: *to have, to do,* and *to be*. Memorize their present tense singular and plural forms to ensure subject-verb agreement.

| *To Have:* **Present Tense** | | | | |
|---|---|---|---|---|
| | Singular **Subject** and **Verb** | | Plural **Subject** and **Verb** | |
| **First Person** | I | have | We | have |
| **Second Person** | You | have | You | have |
| **Third Person** | He She It | has | They | have |

Practice 3

### SUBJECT-VERB AGREEMENT: *TO HAVE*

Write the form of the verb *to have* that agrees with the subject in each of the following sentences.

**1.** Jerome_____ worked various jobs in the food industry for several years.

**2.** He and his brother _____ a plan to open their own pub.

**3.** Their passion for making craft beer and entertaining people _____ fueled their dream of owning their own pub.

**4.** They _____ saved enough money for a down payment on a building in a great location.

**5.** The location for the pub _____ a spectacular view of the river.

| *To Do:* **Present Tense** | | | | |
|---|---|---|---|---|
| | Singular **Subject** and **Verb** | | Plural **Subject** and **Verb** | |
| **First Person** | I | do | We | do |
| **Second Person** | You | do | You | do |
| **Third Person** | He She It | does | They | do |

## SUBJECT-VERB AGREEMENT: *TO DO*

Write the form of the verb *to do* that agrees with the subject in each of the following sentences.

**1.** Successful people enjoy the work they ............... .

**2.** Eric ............... his best work when he enjoys what he is doing.

**3.** However, successful people ............... face unpleasant obstacles and tasks in their work.

**4.** Too often, lack of self-confidence ............... keep us in unfulfilling jobs.

**5.** Enjoyment ............... outrank money as the main goal of a satisfying career.

The verb **to do** is often used with the adverb "not" to express a negative thought. Frequently this negative is stated in the form of the contractions *doesn't* and *don't* that combine the verb and the adverb into shorter words. The verb part of the contraction must still agree with its subject.

| *To Do* and *Not:* Contraction Form | | |
|---|---|---|
| | Singular **Subject** and **Verb** | Plural **Subject** and **Verb** |
| **First Person** | I don't agree | We don't agree |
| **Second Person** | You don't seem well | You don't seem well |
| **Third Person** | He<br>She ——doesn't care<br>It | They don't care |

## SUBJECT-VERB AGREEMENT: *TO DO* AND *NOT*

Fill in the blank with the form of the verb *to do* that agrees with the subject of each of the following sentences. Use the contractions *doesn't* and *don't* as needed.

**1.** People whose only goal is to make money, usually ............... not.

**2.** A national poll indicated that 80% of American workers ............... not enjoy their jobs.

**3.** Usually, a person ............... make a fortune in a job he or she hates.

**4.** Serena Williams ............... not play tennis only for the money; she loves the game.

**5.** In your haste to make a living, ............... forget to make a life.

The *to be* verb is unusual because it uses three forms in the present tense: *am*, *is*, and *are*.

| | Singular **Subject** and **Verb** | | Plural **Subject** and **Verb** | |
|---|---|---|---|---|
| | *To Be:* **Present Tense** | | | |
| **First Person** | I | am | We | are |
| **Second Person** | You | are | You | are |
| **Third Person** | He She It | is | They | are |

Practice 6

**SUBJECT-VERB AGREEMENT:** *TO BE*

Steve Jobs with the Apple iPhone ▶

Write the form of the verb *to be* that agrees with the subject of each of the following sentences.

1. Steve Jobs _____ working for a video gaming company when he and a computer-building friend, Steven Wozniak, started a computer business.

2. On April 1, 1976, Apple Computer Company _____ founded.

3. The iMac, the iBook, and the iPod _____ his designs.

4. Steve Jobs says, "I'm convinced that the only thing that kept me going _____ that I loved what I did. You've got to find what you love."

5. Jobs, worth $4.4 billion, _____ the picture of success.

▲ Oprah Winfrey

Write the form of *to have*, *to do*, or *to be* that agrees with the subject of each of the following sentences. Then, follow the instructions to write three sentences of your own.

**1.** Oprah Winfrey's success ............... not come easily, but ............ the result of several factors.

**2.** Oprah, who ................. goal-oriented, says, "You are where you ................. today in your life based on everything you ................. believed."

**3.** She ................. the ability to recognize an opportunity, and she ............... seize the moment.

**4.** Unlike Oprah, many people ................. have the courage to follow their passion.

**5.** Difficulties throughout her life ................. served as lessons and ................. made her wiser.

**6.** Her dedication to others and her passion for excellence ............... key aspects of her success.

**7.** Worth over $1 billion, Oprah ................. have to work; she ................. living her dream life.

**8.** Write a sentence using a form of the verb *to have*. Suggested topic: A dream or goal.

--------------------------------------------------------

--------------------------------------------------------

**9.** Write a sentence using a form of the verb *to do*. Suggested topic: A positive step toward a goal.

--------------------------------------------------------

--------------------------------------------------------

**10.** Write a sentence using a form of the verb *to be*. Suggested topic: A trait of success.

--------------------------------------------------------

--------------------------------------------------------

Practice 7

# Subjects Separated from Verbs

Subjects are often separated from their verbs by **prepositional phrases**. A **preposition** is a word that has a noun or pronoun as its object and states a relationship between its object and another word. A prepositional phrase begins with a preposition and ends with the object of the preposition. The object of the preposition can never be the subject of a sentence. Identifying prepositional phrases keeps you from confusing them with the subject of the sentence. The verb of a sentence agrees with the subject, not the object of the preposition.

**Example**

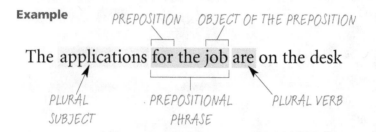

The following chart of prepositional phrases lists a few common prepositions and sample objects.

| Common Prepositional Phrases | | | |
|---|---|---|---|
| **Preposition** | **Object** | **Preposition** | **Object** |
| at | work | of | concern |
| from | home | on | the desk |
| in | the office | with | experience |

### SUBJECT-VERB AGREEMENT

Choose the verb form that agrees with the subject of each of the following sentences. Cross out prepositional phrases. Underline the subject. Circle the appropriate verb.

**1.** Demand for goods and services (affects affect) the job market.

**2.** The opportunities for healthcare occupations (has have) surged because of the fast growth in demand for health services.

**3.** The need for healthcare and social assistance (is are) going to create 4 million new jobs from now until 2016.

**4.** As more women enter the labor force, demand for childcare services (is are) expected to grow.

**5.** The longer life spans of an aging population (has have) increased the need for jobs in health care.

# Singular or Plural Subjects

To establish subject-verb agreement, first identify a subject as plural or singular. Some subjects may seem singular or plural when actually they are not. The following section identifies and discusses several of these types of subjects and the rules of their agreement with verbs.

# Indefinite Pronouns

Indefinite pronouns do not refer to specific nouns. Most indefinite pronouns are singular; a few are plural, and some can be either singular or plural. Consider the context of the indefinite pronoun to achieve subject-verb agreement.

- **Singular indefinite pronouns agree with singular verbs.**

**Example**

Each of the workers has a concern

SINGULAR INDEFINITE
PRONOUN

SINGULAR VERB "HAS" AGREES WITH
SINGULAR INDEFINITE PRONOUN "EACH"

| Singular Indefinite Pronouns | | | | | |
|---|---|---|---|---|---|
| anybody | each | everyone | neither | no one | somebody |
| anyone | either | everything | nobody | nothing | someone |
| anything | everybody | much | none | one | something |

- **Plural indefinite pronouns agree with plural verbs.**

**Example**

Few of the workers have a concern.

PLURAL INDEFINITE
PRONOUN

PLURAL VERB "HAVE" AGREES WITH
PLURAL INDEFINITE PRONOUN "FEW"

| Plural Indefinite Pronouns | | | |
|---|---|---|---|
| both | few | many | several |

| Singular or Plural Indefinite Pronouns Based on Context | | | | |
|---|---|---|---|---|
| all | any | more | most | some |

---

**SUBJECT-VERB AGREEMENT: INDEFINITE PRONOUNS**

Choose the verb form that agrees with the subject of each of the following sentences. Cross out prepositional phrases as needed. Underline the subject. Circle the appropriate verb.

1. Most of us (does do) want a fulfilling career.

2. Many (dreams dream) about starting businesses where they can enjoy a hobby all day.

3. Some of the experts (urges urge) job-seekers to "do what you love and the money will follow."

4. No one (wants want) to spend all day doing something he or she has no interest in.

5. However, few of us (realizes realize) that having to earn money at something often changes the way we feel about it.

Practice 9

## Collective Nouns

Collective nouns name a collection of people, animals, or items as a unit. The agreement between a collective noun and a verb depends on the context of the sentence.

- **When a collective noun acts as one unit, use a singular verb.**

**Example**

A board of directors makes the decision.

*SINGULAR COLLECTIVE NOUN*    *SINGULAR VERB*

- **When a collective noun represents the individuals in a group, use a plural verb.**

**Example**    *PLURAL VERB*

The board have differing opinions.

*PLURAL COLLECTIVE NOUN*

| Common Collective Nouns | | | | |
|---|---|---|---|---|
| audience | class | crowd | gang | staff |
| band | committee | faculty | group | team |
| cast | company | family | herd | troop |
| choir | crew | flock | jury | unit |

Collective vote ▶

▲ Rolling Stones – "A Bigger Bang Tour" – Shanghai

Choose the verb form that agrees with the subject of each of the following sentences. Cross out prepositional phrases as needed. Underline the subject. Circle the appropriate verb.

**1.** One mega-successful English band (is are) the Rolling Stones.

**2.** Formed in 1962, the group (is are) the longest-lived continuously active band in rock and roll history.

**3.** The crowd of fans always (screams scream) with one voice in appreciation.

**4.** In their personal lives, the band (has have) led wild lives in the past but (has have) become calmer in recent years.

**5.** A set of new songs (is are) included on their album A Bigger Bang.

**6.** The vast majority of successful musical groups (makes make) most of their money touring.

**7.** For example, The Rolling Stones band (has have) earned $92.5 million in one tour.

**8.** This cast of aging characters (is are) still going strong in their mid-sixties.

**9.** Their audience (does do) not agree on who is the most popular member of the Rolling Stones.

**10.** Write a sentence using a collective noun. Suggested topic: A successful performing group.

## Either-or/Neither-Nor

*Either or neither* often signal a singular subject that requires a singular verb.

• **To ensure subject-verb agreement, identify and cross out prepositional phrases.**

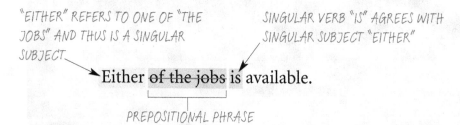

*Either-or/neither-nor* joins parts of a subject; the verb agrees with the nearer part of the subject.

• **When all parts of the subject are singular, the verb is singular.**

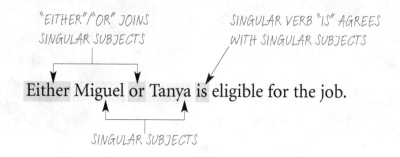

• **When all parts of the subject are plural, the verb is plural.**

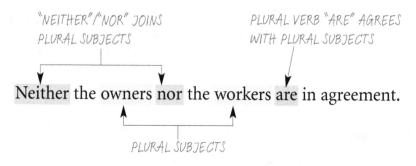

• **When one part of the subject is singular and the other part is plural, the verb agrees with the nearer part.** For smooth expression, place the plural part of the subject closer to the verb.

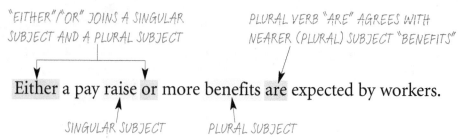

▲ Bus mechanics walk the picket line in Hollywood, CA

Choose the verb form that agrees with the subject of each of the following sentences. Cross out prepositional phrases as needed. Underline the subject. Circle the appropriate verb.

**1.** Neither family nor friends (is are) supposed to cross a picket line.

**2.** Neither the union leaders nor the company president (has have) given in on any point.

**3.** Either fringe benefits or a higher wage (is are) likely, but not both.

**4.** Either businesses or the market (has have) the right to set the minimum wage.

**5.** Neither government nor politicians (has have) the moral authority to set a worker's wage.

**6.** Neither the organizers of the strike nor the workers on strike (responds respond) to the jeers of bystanders.

**7.** Neither slander nor violence (is are) an acceptable way to negotiate working conditions.

**8.** Either Mr. Barnett or Ms. Hawkins (has have) to announce the result of the negotiations.

**9.** Either of the two offers (is are) acceptable.

**10.** Write a sentence using *either* or *neither.* Suggested topic: The ideal job.

------------------------------------------------------

------------------------------------------------------

## Subjects after Verbs

In some instances, a writer may choose to place the subject after the verb. To ensure subject-verb agreement, identify the verb, identify (and cross out) prepositional phrases, and ask who or what completes the action or state of being stated by the verb.

*There* and *Here* are never the subject of a sentence. Both of these words signal that the subject comes after the verb.

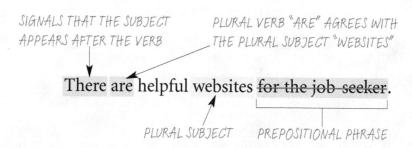

SIGNALS THAT THE SUBJECT APPEARS AFTER THE VERB

PLURAL VERB "ARE" AGREES WITH THE PLURAL SUBJECT "WEBSITES"

There are helpful websites for the job-seeker.

PLURAL SUBJECT    PREPOSITIONAL PHRASE

**Agreement in Questions** relies on understanding that the subject comes after the verb or between parts of the verb.

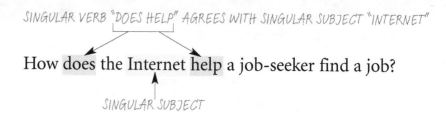

SINGULAR VERB "DOES HELP" AGREES WITH SINGULAR SUBJECT "INTERNET"

How does the Internet help a job-seeker find a job?

SINGULAR SUBJECT

Writers having difficulty determining the subject in a question can identify it by reversing the word order into a statement as in the example below.

**Example**

The Internet helps a job seeker find a job.

---

### SUBJECT-VERB AGREEMENT: SUBJECTS AFTER VERBS

Choose the verb form that agrees with the subject of each of the following sentences. Cross out prepositional phrases. Underline the subject. Circle the appropriate verb.

**1.** There (is are)) many different types of jobs described in the Occupational Outlook Handbook, 2008-09 Edition on the U.S. Department of Labor's website.

**2.** Here (is are) job search tips and information about the job market in each state.

**3.** There (is are) a search box on each page of the website to help find information about a specific occupation or topic.

**4.** (Is Are) you interested in learning more about how to use the Internet as a job-seeker?

**5.** Write a question. Suggested topic: Applying for a job.

--------------------------------------------------------------------

--------------------------------------------------------------------

# Agreement with Relative Pronouns

Agreement with relative pronouns relies on identifying the relationship among a **relative pronoun** (a pronoun such as *that, which, who,* and *whom* that introduces a dependent clause), its **antecedent** (the word the pronoun refers to), and its verb. When a relative pronoun refers to a plural antecedent, it requires a plural verb. When a relative pronoun refers to a singular antecedent, it requires a singular verb. Note that relative pronouns signal a dependent clause. The antecedent for the relative pronoun is often found in the independent clause.

INDEPENDENT CLAUSE   DEPENDENT CLAUSE

Terrell is the type of worker who does more than expected.

RELATIVE PRONOUN "WHO"  SINGULAR VERB "DOES"
REFERS TO SINGULAR    AGREES WITH SINGULAR
ANTECEDENT "WORKER"   ANTECEDENT "WORKER"

INDEPENDENT CLAUSE   DEPENDENT CLAUSE

Terrell and Jamal are the two workers who do more than expected.

RELATIVE PRONOUN "WHO"  PLURAL VERB "DO" AGREES
REFERS TO PLURAL    WITH PLURAL ANTECEDENT
ANTECEDENT "WORKERS"   "WORKERS"

| Relative Pronouns | | | |
|---|---|---|---|
| who | which | that | whoever |

**SUBJECT-VERB AGREEMENT: RELATIVE PRONOUNS**

Choose the verb form that agrees with the relative pronoun in each of the following sentences. Underline the antecedent of the relative pronoun once. Underline the relative pronoun twice. Circle the appropriate verb.

**1.** Shantel has applied for the job that (is are) posted.

**2.** Shantel has applied for all of the jobs that (has have) been posted recently.

**3.** This position requires public speaking, which (is are) one of Shantel's strengths.

**4.** Shantel is one who (does do) well in the spotlight.

**5.** Write a sentence using a relative pronoun. Suggested topic: A workforce skill.

-------------------------------------------------------------------

-------------------------------------------------------------------

Practice 13

# Writing Assignments

## Writing for Everyday Life

Read the following e-mail a parent sent to a child's teacher. Edit the paragraph to ensure subject-verb agreement. Use your own paper.

Dear Mr. Greer,

Troy's father and I thanks you for the support you has given Troy. Troy is one of the many children who has trouble learning. Being organized and staying focused is his biggest problems. However, since you has been working with him, he has improved. The thing that have helped most your website. Either I or my older children checks your website every night to see what Troy needs to do. Thank you, Mr. Greer, for being one of the teachers who cares.

## Writing for College Life

The following paragraph was written for a business communication class. Edit the paragraph to ensure subject-verb agreement. Use your own paper.

### THE EFFECTIVE HANDSHAKE

Business negotiations in America usually begins and ends with a handshake. Here is some hints for an effective handshake. Use a firm grip that show confidence, sincerity, and power. Too tight handshakes signals a power play. Fingertip handshakes or a loose grip comes across as weak or uncommitted. Use caution with people who has arthritis. An effective handshake don't yank the other person's hand. Positive words and a warm tone of voice reinforces the handshake.

## Writing for Working Life

Read the following cover letter submitted with an application for the position of an office manager for a small business. Edit the paragraph to ensure subject-verb agreement. Use your own paper.

Dear Ms. Samula:

I am applying for one of the openings that are posted on your website. There is several skills that I brings to the job. Organization and communication is necessary skills for an office manager. Both my former co-workers and my former boss has written recommendations which states my strengths in these two areas. If you needs more information, here is my home and evening phone numbers.

Sincerely,

Jordan Marsh

To test and track your understanding, answer the following questions.

**1.** What is the rule for subject-verb agreement? ........................................................

........................................................................................................................

**2.** How is the third person singular verb formed?

The third person singular is formed ..................................................................

**3.** What are the three forms of the present tense of the verb *to be*? .........................

**4.** ............................................................ separate subjects from their verbs.

**5.** Indefinite and collective pronouns are singular or plural based on the ....................

of the sentence.

**6.** When *either-or* joins part of a subject, the verb agrees with the .................... part

of the subject.

**7.** .................... and .................... are never the subject of a sentence.

**8.** In a .................... , the subject comes after the verb or between parts of

the verb.

**9.** Agreement with relative pronouns relies on identifying the relationship among a relative

pronoun, its ................................., and its verb.

**10. How will I use what I have learned about subject-verb agreement?**
In your notebook, discuss how you will apply to your own writing what you have learned
about subject-verb agreement.

**11. What do I still need to study about subject-verb agreement?**
In your notebook, describe your ongoing study needs by describing what, when,
and how you will continue studying subject-verb agreement.

# 22

# The Past Tense of Verbs

The past tense of verbs describes actions or events that have already occurred.

The past tense is one of the most commonly used verb tenses in English. Thinking about a real-life situation helps us to understand the need for the past tense as we communicate. The following photographs capture exciting moments in the 2008 Olympics. Study the pictures, complete the activity, and answer the question "What's the point of the past tense of verbs?"

# What's the Point of the Past Tense of Verbs?

PHOTOGRAPHIC ORGANIZER: THE PAST TENSE OF VERBS

As a member of a fundraising committee for local gymnasts training for the next Olympics, you are proofreading one of the letters inviting Olympic champion Shawn Johnson to a fundraising event. What do you notice about the use of past tense? How does the use of verb tense affect the message?

▲ Beijing 2008 - Artistic Gymnastics - Women's Team Finals

Dear Shawn Johnson:

Your performance at the 2008 Olympics in China was amazing. All of us at our gym hold our breath as we watched you perform. You executed every move and stick your landings with great power and energy. We also admired your team mate Nastia Lukin. Both of you soar through the air. Because of the determination and sportsmanship you both displayed even when you don't win a Gold medal, you inspire our young women. Our enrollment at the gym dramatically increase shortly after the Olympics ends. We hoped you will attend our fundraiser. Your presence will draw a crowd and help raise money to train young women to follow their dreams. Your 2008 Olympic performance bringed hope.

Best Regards,
Kimberly Ragan

What's the point of the past tense of verbs?

--------------------------------------------------------

--------------------------------------------------------

--------------------------------------------------------

# Understanding the Point of the Past Tense of Verbs: One Student Writer's Response

The following paragraph offers one writer's reaction to the fundraising invitation.

*This letter sounds awkward and makes the writer seem careless. To get someone as busy and talented as these ladies, the writer needs to sound more polished and serious. Sometimes, it seems like the action is taking place now, yet I know that this is in the past; the 2008 Olympics are obviously over. So the verbs should be in the past tense. With that in mind, I used a dictionary to double check the spelling of all the verbs I had questions about. These are the changes I would make. In sentence 2 revise "hold" to "held." In sentence 3, change "stick" to "stuck." In sentence 5, change "soar" to "soared." In sentence 6, revise "don't" to "didn't" and "inspire" to "inspired." In sentence 7, change "increase" to "increased" and "ends" to "ended." In sentence 8, "hoped" should be "hope" because it is describing a future event. Finally, the word "bringed" is a misspelling. The correct spelling for the past tense of "bring" is "brought."*

# Applying the Point: The Past Tense of Verbs

The **simple past tense** is used to describe a completed action or event. The action or event might have taken place long ago or it might have happened recently, but either way, the past tense is used to indicate that it has already occurred. The simple past tense is also often used to tell a story. Frequently, the use of the past tense is signaled by particular expressions of time: *yesterday, last night, last week, last year, three years ago,* and so on. The following time line illustrates the sequence of tenses.

Past
action/event

Present
action/event

Future
action/event

The past tense takes on different forms for regular and irregular verbs.

# Regular Verbs in the Past Tense

The following chart states the general rule for forming the past tense of regular verbs, the spelling rules for exceptions, and examples of each rule.

| Rules for Forming Past Tense of Regular Verbs | | |
|---|---|---|
| | **Base Form** | **Past Tense** |
| **General Rule:**<br>Regular verbs form the past tense by adding **-ed** to the base form of the verb. | talk ⟶ | talk**ed** |
| **Spelling Exceptions:**<br>There are several exceptions to the way in which regular verbs form the past tense: | | |
| 1. When the base form of the verb ends in **-e**, only add **-d**. | share<br>escape ⟶ | share**d**<br>escape**d** |
| 2. When the base form of the verb ends with a consonant and **-y**, delete the **-y** and add **-ied** in its place. | rely<br>marry ⟶ | rel**ied**<br>marr**ied** |
| 3. When the base form of the verb ends with **-n, -p** or **-it**, double the last letter before adding the **-ed**. | ban<br>trap ⟶<br>commit | ban**ned**<br>tra**pped**<br>commi**tted** |

---

**REGULAR VERBS IN PAST TENSE**

Fill in each blank with the past tense form of the regular verb in parentheses.

**1.** NFL quarterback Peyton Manning _____ (train) to win.

**2.** Peyton _____ (improve) his game with a challenging training routine.

**3.** He _____ (plan) on increasing his core strength and flexibility.

**4.** The routine _____ (include) fire agility drills and old-fashioned iron pumping.

**5.** He never _____ (hurry); instead he _____ (use) proper form and _____ (resist) rushing.

**6.** Manning _____ (waste) no time and _____ (skip) nothing; he _____ (want) to be on top of his game.

**7.** Write a sentence with a regular verb in the past tense. Suggested topic: An admirable athlete.

_____

_____

Colts top draft choice Peyton Manning works out ▶

**Practice 2**

# Irregular Verbs in the Past Tense

Unlike regular verbs, irregular verbs do not use *-ed* to form the past tense. Nor does the past tense of irregular verbs conform to uniform spelling rules with clear exceptions. In fact, some of the most commonly used verbs are irregular, and most writers commit these words to memory so their proper use is automatic. The chart below lists the base form and past tense form of some commonly used irregular verbs. When in doubt about the correct form of a verb, consult a dictionary to check the spelling of the past tense of an irregular verb.

## Some Common Irregular Verbs in the Past Tense

| Base Form | Past Tense | Base Form | Past Tense |
|---|---|---|---|
| become | became | lie (to recline) | lay |
| begin | began | light | lit |
| break | broke | lose | lost |
| bring | brought | make | made |
| buy | bought | mean | meant |
| choose | chose | meet | met |
| come | came | pay | paid |
| drink | drank | ride | rode |
| drive | drove | ring | rang |
| eat | ate | rise | rose |
| fall | fell | run | ran |
| feed | fed | say | said |
| feel | felt | sell | sold |
| fly | flew | send | sent |
| forget | forgot | shake | shook |
| forgive | forgave | sing | sang |
| freeze | froze | sit | sat |
| get | got | speak | spoke |
| go | went | spend | spent |
| grow | grew | swim | swam |
| hang | hung | take | took |
| have | had | teach | taught |
| hear | heard | tear | tore |
| hide | hid | think | thought |
| hold | held | throw | threw |
| keep | kept | understand | understood |
| know | knew | wake | woke (waked) |
| lay (to place) | laid | wear | wore |
| lead | led | win | won |
| leave | left | write | wrote |

IRREGULAR VERBS IN PAST TENSE

Fill in the blanks with the past tense form of the irregular verbs in the parentheses.

**1.** Written records of the Olympic Games ........................ (begin) in 776 BC in Olympia, Greece.

**2.** For the next 1200 years, the Olympic Games ........................ (take) place every four years.

**3.** In 1896, Athens, Greece, ........................ (hold) the very first modern Olympic Games.

**4.** Thousands of athletes from all over the world ........................ (come) to the 2008 Olympic Games in Beijing, China.

**5.** Write a sentence using the past tense of an irregular verb. Suggested topic: A memorable moment in sports.

--------------------------------------------------------------------

--------------------------------------------------------------------

--------------------------------------------------------------------

# Key Verbs in the Past Tense: *To Have, To Do, To Be*

Three key verbs are used both as main verbs and as helping verbs to express a wide variety of meanings: *to have, to do,* and *to be*. These three verbs are irregular verbs, so it's essential to memorize their correct forms in the past tense.

| To Have | To Do | To Be |
|---------|-------|-------|
| had | did | was (singular) |
|  |  | were (plural) |

IRREGULAR VERBS IN PAST TENSE

Fill in the blanks with the past tense form of the verbs *to have, to do,* or *to be*.

**1.** The winner ........................ the opportunity to overcome failure.

**2.** Three times, she ........................ not complete the task that ........................ before her.

**3.** Faith in her abilities and the courage to try again ........................ the keys to her final win.

**4.** She ........................ the determination to succeed.

**5.** Write a sentence using the past tense of *to have, to do,* or *to be*. Suggested topic: A past success.

--------------------------------------------------------------------

--------------------------------------------------------------------

--------------------------------------------------------------------

## Can/Could/Would

**Helping verbs** are auxiliary verbs that team up with main verbs for precise expression of an action or state of being. Three helping verbs are often confused in usage: *can, could,* and *would.* These auxiliary verbs help express the meaning of ability, opportunity, possibility, permission, and intention. The following section provides definitions and examples for each of these three helping verbs.

### Three Commonly Confused Helping Verbs: *Can, Could, Would*

- *Can* expresses physical or mental ability in the present tense.

    *"CAN" EXPRESSES A PHYSICAL ABILITY*

    I can walk for miles.

    *"CAN" EXPRESSES A MENTAL ABILITY*

    I can think clearly.

- *Could* expresses physical or mental ability, opportunity, possibility, or permission in the past tense.

    *"COULD" EXPRESSES A PHYSICAL OR MENTAL ABILITY*

    She could win a race.

    *"COULD" EXPRESSES A LOST OPPORTUNITY*

    You could have won the race.

    *"COULD" EXPRESSES POSSIBILITY*

    He could have been injured.

    *"COULD" EXPRESSES PERMISSION*

    He said that we could begin the competition.

- **Would** expresses past routine or intention in the past tense.

    *"WOULD" EXPRESSES PAST ROUTINE*

    He would practice every morning.

    *"WOULD" EXPRESSES PAST INTENTION*

    She said she would exercise later.

▲ E3 Media and Business Summit in Santa Monica

Complete each sentence with the helping verb that best completes the idea: *can, could,* or *would.*

**1.** Wii Fit _____ change how you exercise.

**2.** By playing Wii Fit every day, you, your friends, and your family _____ improve your personal health and fitness.

**3.** Before playing with Wii Fit, Beatrice _____ not exercise for more than a few minutes without stopping.

**4.** Before she played with Wii Fit, she _____ sit for hours and watch television.

**5.** Write a sentence using *can, could,* or *would* as helping verbs. Suggested topic: Benefits of exercise.

-----------------------------------------------------------

-----------------------------------------------------------

**PAST TENSE REVIEW**

Read the following passage. Edit to ensure proper use of the past tense.

Troy had ambitions to compete for a gold medal in the competition. However, two days before the meet, he fears that he had a sprained ankle. He could have given up; instead his coach and he apply the first-aid treatment called RICE: rest, ice, compression, and elevation. Immediately, he chooses to rest and does not train any more before the event. Then he could apply ice for 20 minutes every hour for the two days. In addition, he wraps his ankle with a 6-inch wide band. Finally, he keeps his foot elevated to control the swelling. He makes a quick recovery.

# Writing Assignments

## Writing for Everyday Life

Read the following letter to the editor of a local newspaper. Edit the paragraph to ensure consistent usage of the past tense. Use your own paper.

> At last night's meeting, our local school board cuts funds that support physical education. This was a terrible decision. Every year the board could cut funds, and every year our students could exercise less and less. Last year, the board promises to support physical education. They commit to funding a health program to fight the growing problem of obesity among youth. Once again, they fail our children.

## Writing for College Life

Read the following health journal assigned for credit in a college health course. Edit the paragraph to ensure consistent usage of the past tense. Use your own paper.

> I had a terrific week and make a lot of progress in making healthy decisions. I bring healthy salads for lunch at work and eat fresh vegetables, chicken, or fish for dinner. Since I would only exercise for thirty minutes each time, I choose the following activities. I run two miles every other day. On the days I did not ran, I lift weights or swim laps. I also get into a smaller clothes size for the first time in years. I feel great all week.

## Writing for Working Life

Read the following announcement sent out by management at a local business. Edit the paragraph to ensure consistent usage of the past tense. Use your own paper.

> To All Employees:
>
> Three years ago, we opened a gym on the property. We understood how important your health is to the well-being of our company. In the first year, only a few of you used the gym, and we doubted the wisdom of investing in the gym. The next year, more of you sign up and take advantage of the facility. Last year, nearly eighty percent of you work out in the gym at least once a week. Some think that the gym could be a distraction. However, your performance goes up. Therefore, we expand our hours and add more equipment. So stop by the gym to find out the new hours and see the new equipment.

**WHAT HAVE I LEARNED ABOUT THE PAST TENSE OF VERBS?**

To test and track your understanding, answer the following questions.

**1.** What is the general rule for forming the past tense of regular verbs? Give an example.

------------------------------------------

------------------------------------------

------------------------------------------

**2.** What are three exceptions to the way in which regular verbs form the past tense? Give examples.

a. ------------------------------------------

------------------------------------------

b. ------------------------------------------

------------------------------------------

c. ------------------------------------------

------------------------------------------

**3.** What are two traits of irregular verbs?

------------------------------------------

------------------------------------------

------------------------------------------

**4.** What are the correct past tense forms of the following three irregular verbs: *to be, to have,* and *to do?*

------------------------------------------

**5.** List three often-confused helping verbs.

------------------------------------------

**6. How will I use what I have learned about the past tense?**
In your notebook, discuss how you will apply to your own writing what you have learned about the past tense of regular and irregular verbs.

**7. What do I still need to study about the past tense?**
In your notebook, describe your ongoing study needs by describing what, when, and how you will continue studying the past tense of regular and irregular verbs.

Academic Learning Log

# 23

**CHAPTER PREVIEW**

- What's the Point of the Past Participle?

- Understanding the Point of the Past Participle: One Student Writer's Response

- Applying the Point: The Past Participle

- Writing Assignments

# The Past Participle

A participle is a verb form that can be used to establish tenses or voices, or it can be used as a modifier, which describes, restricts, or limits other words in a sentence.

Thinking about a real-life situation helps us to understand the purpose of the past participle in our communication. The following photograph documents polar bears in their natural habitat. Study the picture, complete the activity, and answer the question "What's the point of the past participle?"

# What's the Point of the Past Participle?

**PHOTOGRAPHIC ORGANIZER: THE PAST PARTICIPLE**

Assume you subscribe to a news blog, and that a correspondent has filed the following report, which contains misuses of the past participle. Where are the errors? What is the impact of the errors?

### The Endangered Polar Bear

The United States has list the polar bear as an endangered species. Polar bears have always depend on sea ice as a platform to hunt seals, their primary food. These bears need large and accessible seal populations and vast areas of ice from which to hunt. But sea ice has decrease throughout their Arctic range due to climate change. The most productive seal-hunting periods are during the spring and early summer before the ice has retreat. A reduction in sea ice has extended the time period during which bears cannot hunt their primary prey. Polar bears have traditionally play an important role in the culture and livelihood of Eskimos and other Native people of the North. They depend on the animals for food and clothing.

**What's the point of the past participle?**

--------------------------------------------------------

--------------------------------------------------------

# Understanding the Point of the Past Participle: One Student Writer's Response

The following paragraph offers one writer's reaction to the report on polar bears.

It was hard to pick out the errors. Sometimes, a sentence just didn't sound right, but I couldn't say why. A student in our group brought her dictionary to class, so we looked up all the verbs to see how the past participle for each one was spelled. Together, we corrected the following errors. In sentence 1, we changed "list" to "listed." In sentence 2, we changed "depend" to "depended." In sentence 4, we revised "decrease" to "decreased." In sentence 5, "retreat" became "retreated." And in sentence 7, "play" became "played." After revising, we noticed that all the verbs with a helping verb needed an "ed" added. The ideas made more sense, too.

# Applying the Point: The Past Participle

A **participle** is a verb form that can be used to establish tenses or voices, or it can be used as a modifier, which describes, restricts, or limits other words in a sentence. The **past participle** of a verb joins with helping verbs to form the present perfect and past perfect tenses and the passive voice. In addition, the past participle can act as an adjective that describes another word. Just as with the simple past tense, the past participle takes on different forms for regular and irregular verbs.

## Past Participles of Regular Verbs

In general, regular verbs form the past participle by adding *-ed* to the base form of the verb. Just as with the simple past tense, there are several spelling exceptions for the past participle of regular verbs.

| Base | Past Tense | Past Participle |
|------|-----------|-----------------|
| share | share**d** | share**d** |
| rely | rel**ied** | rel**ied** |
| commit | commit**ted** | commit**ted** |

For more about the simple past tense, see page 340.

**Practice 2**

**PAST PARTICIPLE OF REGULAR VERBS**

Complete the following chart with the proper forms of the past tense and the past participle of each verb.

| Base | | Past Tense | Past Participle |
|------|------|-----------|-----------------|
| 1. | allow | | |
| 2. | ask | | |
| 3. | believe | | |
| 4. | blot | | |
| 5. | change | | |
| 6. | listen | | |
| 7. | mug | | |
| 8. | study | | |
| 9. | try | | |
| 10. | zip | | |

# Past Participles of Irregular Verbs

As with the simple past tense, irregular verbs do not use *-ed* to form the past participle. Nor does the past participle of irregular verbs conform to uniform spelling rules with clear exceptions. In addition, the past participle forms of many irregular verbs vary from their past tense forms. Practice 3 and the chart that follows Practice 3 list the base form, past tense form, and past participle of the top 50 commonly used irregular verbs. These verbs appear in the order of the frequency of their use. As with the simple past forms of irregular verbs, when in doubt, careful writers consult a dictionary to find the form and spelling of the past participle of an irregular verb.

### PAST PARTICIPLE OF IRREGULAR VERBS

The following chart contains the top ten irregular verbs listed by frequency of use. Supply the proper forms of the past tense and the past participle of each verb. Consult a dictionary as necessary.

| Base | Past Tense | Past Participle |
|------|------------|-----------------|
| 1. say | | |
| 2. make | | |
| 3. go | | |
| 4. take | | |
| 5. come | | |
| 6. see | | |
| 7. know | | |
| 8. get | | |
| 9. give | | |
| 10. find | | |

The 10 verbs listed in Practice 3 and the following chart of 40 words represents almost 90 percent of irregular verbs that are used most often in English. Master these verbs, and you will master the majority of the verbs you have to know. These are verbs you will likely be using as you read and write for everyday, college, and working life.

## 40 Irregular Verbs Ranked by Frequency of Use

| Base Form | Past Tense | Past Participle |
| --- | --- | --- |
| think | thought | thought |
| tell | told | told |
| become | became | become |
| show | showed | shown / showed |
| leave | left | left |
| feel | felt | felt |
| put | put | put |
| bring | brought | brought |
| begin | began | begun |
| keep | kept | kept |
| hold | held | held |
| write | wrote | written |
| stand | stood | stood |
| hear | heard | heard |
| let | let | let |
| mean | meant | meant |
| set | set | set |
| meet | met | met |
| run | ran | run |
| pay | paid | paid |
| sit | sat | sat |
| speak | spoke | spoken |
| lie | lay | lain |
| lead | led | led |
| read | read | read |
| grow | grew | grown |
| lose | lost | lost |
| fall | fell | fallen |
| send | sent | sent |
| build | built | built |
| understand | understood | understood |
| draw | drew | drawn |
| break | broke | broken |
| spend | spent | spent |
| cut | cut | cut |
| rise | rose | risen |
| drive | drove | driven |
| buy | bought | bought |
| wear | wore | worn |
| choose | chose | chosen |

Grabowski, E. & D. Mindt. 1995. A corpus-based learning list of irregular verbs in English. ICAME Journal 19: 5-22. [BUC, LOB]

▲ Ocean temperatures

Test your current understanding of irregular verbs. Complete each sentence with an irregular verb from the chart "40 Irregular Verbs Ranked by Frequency of Use." Discuss your answers with a peer or your class.

**1.** Earth has _____ warmer by 1°F over the past 100 years.

**2.** Scientists _____ that human activity has _____ to global warming.

**3.** Global warming is _____ to be an average increase in the Earth's temperature, which in turn _____ to changes in climate.

**4.** Experts and politicians, such as Al Gore, have _____ about the impact of a warmer Earth.

**5.** Experts have _____ a dire picture of changes in rainfall patterns, a rise in sea level, and a wide range of impacts on plants, wildlife, and humans.

**6.** Scientists _____ that as Earth's temperature has _____ warmer, glaciers have _____ to melt and sea levels have _____.

**7.** Since the Industrial Revolution, the need for energy to use machines has steadily _____ higher and higher.

**8.** Before the Industrial Revolution, human activity _____ very few gases into the atmosphere.

**9.** But our society is _____ on burning fossil fuels, and we have _____ a mixture of gases pollute the atmosphere.

**10.** The warning has been _____ ; most of us have _____ idle in our vehicles for too long, but some of us have _____ and _____ against _____ behaviors that have _____ global warming.

# Using the Present Perfect Tense

## (*Has* or *Have* and the Past Participle)

The **present perfect tense** connects the past to the present. The present perfect tense states the relationship of a past action or situation to a current, ongoing action or situation. The present perfect tense is formed by joining the helping verbs **has** or **have** with a past participle.

### PAST PARTICIPLES

Complete the following chart with the appropriate past participle of the verbs in parentheses.

| Subject | Helping Verb | Regular Past Participle | Irregular Past Participle |
|---------|--------------|-------------------------|---------------------------|
| I | have | **1.** (accept) _____ | **6.** (tell) _____ |
| We | have | **2.** (allow) _____ | **7.** (become) _____ |
| You | have | **3.** (manage) _____ | **8.** (keep) _____ |
| He/She/It | has | **4.** (sip) _____ | **9.** (spend) _____ |
| They | have | **5.** (terrify) _____ | **10.** (wore) _____ |

**The purposes of the present perfect tense are:**

- **to express change from the past to the present.**

*PAST ACTION*

*PRESENT PERFECT "HAS CHANGED" STATES CHANGE FROM A PAST ACTION TO A PRESENT ONE*

Theo was once a litter bug, but he has changed his ways.

- **to express a situation or action that started in the past and continues to the present.**

*PRESENT PERFECT "HAVE VOLUNTEERED" STATES AN ONGOING ACTION, WHICH STARTED IN THE PAST AND IS CONTINUING NOW*

Theo and Katie have volunteered with Adopt a Highway for several years.

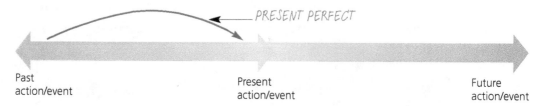

*PRESENT PERFECT*

Past action/event — Present action/event — Future action/event

▲ Barge transporting garbage near the Statue of Liberty

Fill in the blanks with the present perfect tense of the verbs in parentheses. Verbs may be either regular or irregular. Use the helping verbs *has* or *have* to form the present perfect tense.

**1.** People _____ (wrestle) with the trash problem ever since they settled in cities.

**2.** The government _____ (collect) and _____ (report) data on waste in the United States for more than 30 years.

**3.** Over the past 30 years, the waste produced in this country _____ more than _____ (double).

**4.** In recent years, Americans _____ (generate) about 250 million tons of trash each year.

**5.** During this time, Americans _____ (send) to landfills over 4 pounds of trash per person per day.

**6.** So far the average American _____ not _____ (cut) back on what he or she discards.

**7.** However, recycling _____ (meet) with more approval as the amount of waste _____ (rise).

**8.** Since the 1970s, burning trash to produce steam and electricity _____ (show) to be another effective solution.

**9.** Write a sentence using the present perfect tense of a **regular** verb. Suggested topic: Littering.

_____

_____

**10.** Write a sentence using the present perfect tense of an **irregular** verb. Suggested topic: Litter clean-up.

_____

_____

# Using the Past Perfect Tense

## (*Had* and the Past Participle)

The **past perfect** connects two past actions or situations. The past perfect is formed by joining the helping verb ***had*** with a past participle.

**PAST PERFECT TENSE**

Complete the following chart with the appropriate past participle of the verbs in parentheses.

| Subject | Helping Verb | Regular Past Participle | Irregular Past Participle |
|---|---|---|---|
| I | had | **1.** (admit) ............... | **6.** (leave) ............... |
| We | had | **2.** (cheer) ............... | **7.** (feel) ............... |
| You | had | **3.** (object) ............... | **8.** (bring) ............... |
| He/She/It | had | **4.** (try) ............... | **9.** (sit) ............... |
| They | had | **5.** (zip) ............... | **10.** (pay) ............... |

**The purposes of the past perfect tense are:**

- **to connect a previous action or event with a later action or event.**

*PAST ACTION #2*

*PAST ACTION #1: THE PAST PERFECT "HAD LEFT" SHOWS THAT THIS ACTION OCCURRED BEFORE THE OTHER PAST ACTION "SAMUEL PUT..."*

Samuel put out the trash, but the garbage truck had left.

- **to express an action or event that happened before a certain past time.**

*PAST ACTION #2*

*PAST ACTION #1: THE PAST PERFECT "HAD SORTED" SHOWS THAT THIS ACTION OCCURRED BEFORE THE OTHER PAST ACTION "HE PUT..."*

Before he put out the trash, he had sorted it for recycling.

*PAST PERFECT*

| Past action/event #1 | Past action/event #2 | Present | Future |

▲ Waste manager

Fill in the blanks with the past perfect tense of the verbs in parentheses. The verbs may be regular or irregular. Use the helping verb *had* to form the past perfect tense.

**1.** In 1989, Chad Pregracke became a commercial clammer, and by 1996 he ........................... (crawl) all over the bottom of the Mississippi River and ........................... (live) on its shorelines.

**2.** Even before Chad worked as a commercial clammer, the accumulating garbage piles littering the river ........................... (horrify) him.

**3.** In 1997, Chad began cleaning up the garbage that government officials ........................... (ignore) in the Mississippi River.

**4.** By the time he finished his first season, Chad ........................... (remove) 45,000 pounds of refuse from the river.

**5.** Chad ........................... (begin) his nonprofit organization called Living Lands and Water by the time he was 23 years old.

**6.** Before I heard about Chad Pregracke, I ........................... (gave) money to various groups to clean up waterways.

**7.** I wish I ........................... (know) about Chad's work earlier.

**8.** I ........................... (think)  only about giving money before Chad challenged us to give of our time, too.

**9.** Write a sentence using the past perfect tense of a **regular** verb: Suggested topic: Recycling.

-------------------------------------------------------------------

-------------------------------------------------------------------

**10.** Write a sentence using the past perfect tense of an **irregular** verb: Suggested topic: Littering.

-------------------------------------------------------------------

-------------------------------------------------------------------

# Using the Passive Voice
## (*To Be* and the Past Participle)

In English, verbs establish two types of voices: the active voice and the passive voice. So far, you have only worked with the active voice. Expressing what the subject of a sentence does, action verbs establish the **active voice.** When the subject of a sentence receives the action (or is acted upon), the sentence is in the **passive voice.** The passive voice is formed by joining *to be* with a past participle. In addition, the passive voice can be expressed in every tense.

**The purpose of the passive voice is to tell the reader what is done to a subject.**

**Active Voice**

*SUBJECT "WASTE MANAGEMENT" PERFORMS THE ACTION*

Waste Management serves 20 million customers.

**Passive Voice**

*SUBJECT "CUSTOMERS" RECEIVES THE ACTION*

Twenty million customers are served by Waste Management.

**Examples of the tenses of the passive voice**

**Present Tense**

*SUBJECT*    *PRESENT TENSE OF "TO BE"*    *PAST PARTICIPLE OF "BREAK"*

The compact fluorescent light bulb is broken.

**Past Tense**

*SUBJECT*    *PAST TENSE OF "TO BE"*    *PAST PARTICIPLE OF "HURT"*

Nobody was hurt.

**Present Perfect Tense**

*SUBJECT*    *PRESENT PERFECT TENSE OF "TO BE"*    *PAST PARTICIPLE OF "PICK"*

All the pieces have been picked up.

**Past Perfect Tense**

*SUBJECT*    *PAST PERFECT TENSE OF "TO BE"*    *PAST PARTICIPLE OF "PUT"*

The debris had been put in a sealed plastic bag.

▲ Plastic bag along a coral reef in Egypt

Fill in the blanks with the passive voice of the verbs in parentheses. The verbs may be regular or irregular. Use the verb *to be* to form the passive voice.

**1.** In recent years, inexpensive plastic bags ............................................ (prefer) by most stores.

**2.** Plastic bags ............................ (price) under 2 cents a bag.

**3.** Last year, an estimated 500 billion to 1 trillion plastic bags ............................ (consume) worldwide.

**4.** Hundreds of thousands of sea turtles, whales and other marine mammals ............................................ (kill) by eating discarded plastic bags that they mistook for food.

**5.** Plastic bags ............................ (find)  more often than other debris during coastal clean-ups.

**6.** Traditionally, plastic bags ............................ (see) as less harmful on the environment than paper bags.

**7.** Plastic bags ............................ (make) from natural gas or oil.

**8.** Before we went to the store, paper bags ............................ (choose) as our preference.

**9.** Write a sentence using the passive voice of a **regular** verb. Suggested topic: Reusable cloth grocery bags.

------------------------------------------------------------------------

------------------------------------------------------------------------

**10.** Write a sentence using the passive voice of an **irregular** verb. Suggested topic: Benefits or dangers of paper bags to the environment.

------------------------------------------------------------------------

------------------------------------------------------------------------

For more information on participles as adjectives see page 388.

# Using the Past Participle as an Adjective

The past participle is often used as an adjective that modifies a noun or pronoun. Both regular and irregular forms of the past participle are used as adjectives.

**The purposes of the past participle as an adjective are:**

- **to describe a noun or pronoun with a word or phrase.**

*PARTICIPLE "REUSED" DESCRIBES "WATER BOTTLES"*

Reused water bottles are not safe.

*PARTICIPLE PHRASE*

Meant for single use, water bottles should not be reused.

- **to describe the subject by completing a linking verb in the sentence.**

*LINKING VERB*

The plastic container looks worn with use.

*SUBJECT "CONTAINER" IS DESCRIBED BY PAST PARTICIPLE "WORN"*

---

**PAST PARTICIPLE AS AN ADJECTIVE**

Fill in the blanks with the past participle forms of the verbs in parentheses.

**1.** Plastic is the most widely ............................ (use) material in the United States.

**2.** ............................ (can) food and ............................ (bottle) water may contain a controversial chemical ............................ (call) bisphenol A (BPA).

**3.** Although ............................ (think) of as harmless by the plastics industry, BPA may affect the developing brains of children.

**4.** ............................ (educate) buyers avoid plastic products ............................ with the number 7, which indicates the presence of BPA.

**5.** Write a sentence using the past participle as an adjective. Suggested Topic: A harmful product.

.................................................................................................................................

.................................................................................................................................

*Practice 10*

Review what you have learned throughout this chapter by completing the following activity. Read the following paragraph. Edit to ensure use of the appropriate form of the past participle.

▲ Marine debris

# Marine Debris

(1) Marine debris has became a problem everywhere. (2) It is define as any man-made, solid material that enters our waterways. (3) Debris can enter waterways directly as dump trash. (4) Or it can simply be wash out to sea by rivers, streams, or storm drains. (5) Use and discard objects such as bottles, medical wastes, and fishing line turn into marine debris. (6) In addition to being unsightly, this litter poses a serious threat to everything with which it comes into contact.

(7) Marine debris has prove to be life-threatening to marine organisms. (8) Entangle in marine debris, millions of seabirds, sea turtles, fish, and marine mammals have suffer or died. (9) As many as 30,000 northern fur seals per year get caught in abandon fishing nets and either drown or suffocate. (10) Whales mistook plastic bags for squid, and birds may mistake plastic pellets for fish eggs. (11) Marine debris have already hurt coastal areas and the fishing industry, and the harm will continue unless we get involved.

# Writing Assignments

## Writing for Everyday Life

Read the following blog. Edit to ensure proper usage of the past participle. Use your own paper.

> Are you tire of seeing litter gum up our lakes and rivers? Are you ready to do something about it? For the past two years, our group has spend every Saturday cleaning up trash along our shores. Before we began, litter been a common sight. Since we began, we picked up broken glass, used needles, even soiled diapers. So you can imagine what it had look like before we took action. Because we have been so successful, we have been ask to expand our work. So come out and join us this Sunday for our first sweep of the East River. We need you!

## Writing for College Life

Read the following paragraph written in response to a test question on college biology exam. Edit to ensure proper usage of the past participle. Use your own paper.

> **Question:** What is the human impact on tropical rain forests?
>
> **Student Answer:** Sell for lumber or burn to clear land for ranching or farming, rain forests are being destroy at a rapid rate. Scientists has estimated that current rain forest destruction ranges from 22,000 square miles to 52,000 square miles per year. In many areas, only small fragments of forests are leave standing. These areas are too small to support many types of wildlife. At least 40% of the world's rain forests have been loss. Although the losses continue, some areas have been sit aside as protected preserves.

## Writing for Working Life

Read the following announcement to all the employees in a corporation. Edit to ensure proper usage of the past participle. Use your own paper.

> Congratulations! Your team effort has pay off. We have been award the Green Business Designation by the Environmental Protection Agency. The agency wrote in its report that we have earn the highest marks possible as an eco-friendly business. As you know before we began this process, we had not recycle paper much less use computers or office chemicals such as toner. Determine to make a difference, we now recycle everything, even ink cartridges for desk top printers. And long before we applied for this designation, we had install a solar system which supplies all our power. Even so, you been faithful to turn off lights, reset thermostats, and shut down computers. This designation make us eligible for rebates and tax breaks during this fiscal year. Thank you all for doing your part.

PEARSON
**mywritinglab**

**WANT A
BETTER GRADE?**
For more practice with the past participle, go to
**www.mywritinglab.com
> Recognizing and
Avoiding Errors > The
Past Participle.**

**WHAT HAVE I LEARNED ABOUT THE PAST PARTICIPLE?**

To test and track your understanding, answer the following questions.

**1.** The present perfect tense is formed by joining the helping verbs _____ or _____ with the past participle.

**2.** What are two purposes of the present perfect tense?

  **a.** _____

  **b.** _____

**3.** The past perfect tense is formed by joining the helping verb _____ with the past participle.

**4.** What are two purposes of the past perfect tense?

  **a.** _____

  **b.** _____

**5.** The passive voice is formed by the combination of _____ with a past participle.

**6.** The passive voice can be expressed in every _____.

**7.** What is the purpose of the passive voice?

_____

PORTFOLIO

**8.** What are two purposes of the past participle as an adjective?

  **a.** _____

  **b.** _____

**9. How will I use what I have learned about the past participle?**

In your notebook, discuss how you will apply to your own writing what you have learned about the past participle of regular and irregular verbs.

**10. What do I still need to study about the past participle?**

In your notebook, describe your ongoing study needs by describing what, when, and how you will continue studying the past participle of regular and irregular verbs.

Academic Learning Log

# 24

# Adjectives and Adverbs

An adjective describes a noun
or a pronoun. An adverb
describes a verb, an adjective,
or another adverb.

Thinking about a real-life situation helps us to understand the
purpose of adjectives and adverbs in our communication. The
following photograph captures a particular fashion statement.
Study the picture, complete the activity, and answer the question
"What's the point of learning about adjectives and adverbs?"

# What's the Point of Learning About Adjectives and Adverbs?

**PHOTOGRAPHIC ORGANIZER: ADJECTIVES AND ADVERBS**

Assume your college newspaper has called for students to submit articles about the types of fashion worn on campus. Study the photograph and fill in the blanks with adjectives and adverbs that best describe the woman's style of fashion. Work with a small group of your peers.

_____ fashion makes a _____
statement. Penciled eyebrows arch in a
_____ , _____ line
above her _____ brow line. _____ ,
_____ eyeliner encircles her eyes and
sweeps _____ her temple like
_____ feathers. _____
_____ chains, hooked from her
_____ piercing to her _____
piercings, drape across her _____
cheek. _____ hair, _____ clothes,
and _____ lipstick complete the
_____ look.

▲ Goth fashion

**What's the point of learning about adjectives and adverbs?**

_____

_____

# Understanding the Point of Learning About Adjectives and Adverbs: One Student Writer's Response

The following paragraph offers one writer's reaction to the paragraph about goth fashion.

> This was so much fun. We all think so differently, so we came up with a wide choice of words. I thought the woman looked great, but my friend was freaked out by the piercings and the chain. So we really differed in the words we chose. I learned that I can get my own point of view across based on the kinds of adjectives and adverbs I choose.

# Applying the Point: Adjectives and Adverbs

Adjectives and adverbs are descriptive words that describe, modify, or limit the meaning of other words. Adjectives and adverbs have specific functions in a sentence and thus express precise meanings. Understanding the function and purpose of adjectives and adverbs allows a writer a thoughtful and effective expression of ideas.

An **adjective** modifies—in other words, it describes—a noun or a pronoun. It answers one or more of the following questions:

- What kind?
- Which one?
- How many?

*ADJECTIVE "UNUSUAL" DESCRIBES NOUN "OUTFIT"*

Maya wore an unusual outfit.

*PRONOUN "SHE" DESCRIBED BY ADJECTIVE "BRAVE"*

She is brave.

An **adverb** modifies, or describes, a verb, an adjective, or another adverb. It answers one or more of the following questions:

- How?
- Why?
- When?
- Where?
- To what extent?

*VERB "DRESSES" DESCRIBED BY ADVERB "UNUSUALLY"*

Maya dresses unusually.

*NOUN "MAYA" DESCRIBED BY ADJECTIVE "UNUSUAL"*

Maya is bravely unusual.

*ADVERB "BRAVELY" DESCRIBES ADJECTIVE "UNUSUAL"*

▲ Hip Hop artist Nelly performs "Party People" with Fergie at the 2008 BET awards.

Identify the **boldfaced** words in each sentence as adjectives or adverbs.

**1.** Nelly is a **talented** rapper who **widely** appeals to a **large** audience.

-------------------------------------------------------------------

**2.** He **consistently** makes the **pop** chart with **smash** hits like "Hot in Herre" and "Iz U."

-------------------------------------------------------------------

**3.** Fergie is a **successful** singer with the Black Eyed Peas who has **deservedly** won the **coveted** Grammy **three** times.

-------------------------------------------------------------------

**4.** Nelly **obviously** enjoys wearing **low-riding** pants; they show off his underwear and **tattooed** torso.

-------------------------------------------------------------------

**5.** Fergie has a **constantly changing** style; it **clearly** reveals her **different** moods.

-------------------------------------------------------------------

# Participles as Adjectives

Many adjectives are formed by adding *-ed* or *-ing* to verbs. These **participle adjectives** serve two purposes: The *-ed* form describes a person's reaction or feeling; the *-ing* form describes the person or thing that causes the reaction.

*—ED PARTICIPLE ADJECTIVE DESCRIBES HOW THE "AUDIENCE" REACTS*

The amused audience laughed at the actor.

*—ING PARTICIPLE ADJECTIVE DESCRIBES THE "ACTOR" CAUSING THE REACTION*

The amusing actor made the audience laugh.

The following chart lists some of the most common participles used as adjectives.

| Common Participles Used as Adjectives | | | |
|---|---|---|---|
| alarmed | alarming | exhausted | exhausting |
| amused | amusing | fascinated | fascinating |
| annoyed | annoying | frightened | frightening |
| bored | boring | horrified | horrifying |
| concerned | concerning | irritated | irritating |
| confused | confusing | pleased | pleasing |
| depressed | depressing | satisfied | satisfying |
| discouraged | discouraging | shocked | shocking |
| encouraged | encouraging | stimulated | stimulating |
| engaged | engaging | terrified | terrifying |
| excited | exciting | worried | worrying |

## PARTICIPLES AS ADJECTIVES

Complete the following ideas by filling in the blanks with the proper participle adjective.

**1.** Some _____ parents protest the influence of pop stars.

**2.** _____ youth often adopt the styles of their pop heroes.

**3.** Many of these _____ stars wear _____ outfits.

**4.** The _____ trend of sexy clothing for preteens is one of their concerns.

**5.** Too many pop stars send _____ messages to young people.

# Nouns and Verbs Formed as Adjectives

In addition to the *-ed* and *-ing* word endings or suffix, many adjectives are formed by other types of word endings. Just as a suffix transforms a verb into a specific type of adjective or adverb, a suffix can also create adjectives out of nouns. Adjectives come in so many forms that using a few carefully chosen adjectives can add power and interest to your writing. For your reference, the following chart lists a few frequently used adjectives by some of their word endings.

| | | | | | | | | |
|---|---|---|---|---|---|---|---|---|
| **Common Adjectives** | | | | | | | | |
| **Word Endings** | *-able* *-ible* | *-ful* | *-ic* | *-ish* | *-ive* | *-less* | *-ly* *-y* | *-ous* |
| **Examples** | acceptable | bashful | alcoholic | boorish | abusive | cheerless | actually | ambiguous |
| | accessible | cheerful | aquatic | oafish | combative | jobless | cagy | auspicious |
| | capable | forgetful | dramatic | devilish | decisive | mindless | daffy | courageous |
| | honorable | graceful | erratic | elfish | instinctive | needless | earthy | glamorous |
| | laughable | joyful | gigantic | lavish | receptive | noiseless | lively | industrious |
| | obtainable | merciful | majestic | skittish | reflective | pointless | manly | malicious |
| | plausible | peaceful | melodic | snobbish | secretive | senseless | seemly | nervous |
| | tangible | rightful | organic | squeamish | selective | useless | smelly | righteous |

## NOUNS AND VERBS FORMED AS ADJECTIVES

Complete the following ideas by filling in the blanks with the proper adjective formed from a noun or verb in the chart "Common Adjectives." Work with a small group of your peers. Use a dictionary to look up unfamiliar words.

**1.** Fashion industry leaders are sometimes accused of ........................ practices.

**2.** Some say ........................ clothing is ........................ mostly because of the cheap labor of sweat shops.

**3.** Critics also think the use of animal skin for clothing is ........................ .

**4.** Others say that most people in the fashion industry are ........................ and ........................ .

**5.** And many would be ........................ if not for the fashion industry.

**6.** Write a sentence using an adjective formed from a verb from the charts "Common Adjectives" and "Participles as Adjectives." Suggested topic: Labor Rights.

......................................................................................................................

......................................................................................................................

**7.** Write a sentence using an adjective formed from a noun from the chart "Common Adjectives." Suggested topic: Sweatshops.

......................................................................................................................

......................................................................................................................

......................................................................................................................

# Placement of Adjectives

A careful writer not only chooses the precise word for impact, but also arranges words in the most effective order for the greatest impact on the reader. As you work with adjectives, be aware that the placement of an adjective varies based on its relationship to other words.

Adjectives can appear before a noun.

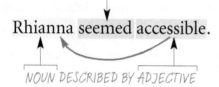

*ADJECTIVE DESCRIBES NOUN "FAN"*

The bashful fan approached Rihanna.

Adjectives can appear after **linking verbs** such as *is, are, were, seems,* and *appears.*

*LINKING VERB*

Rhianna seemed accessible.

*NOUN DESCRIBED BY ADJECTIVE*

Adjectives can appear after **sensory verbs**—those that describe physical senses—such as *look, smell, feel, taste,* and *sound.*

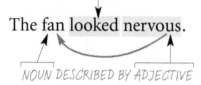

*SENSORY VERB*

The fan looked nervous.

*NOUN DESCRIBED BY ADJECTIVE*

Practice 5

## PLACEMENT OF ADJECTIVES

Fill in the blanks by choosing the phrase that best completes the sentence's idea by appropriate placement of adjectives.

**1.** Serena and Venus Williams have had _____ on sports fashion.

**a.** a dramatic impact          **b.** impact a dramatic          **c.** a impact dramatic

**2.** They courageously _____ of dress on the tennis court.

**a.** ignored rules senseless          **b.** ignored senseless rules          **c.** rules senseless ignored

**3.** The Williams _____ as businesswomen and athletes.

**a.** capable are sisters          **b.** are sisters capable          **c.** sisters are capable

**4.** _____ as trailblazers.

**a.** Admired they are          **b.** They are admired          **c.** Are they admired

**5.** They are examples of the rewards _____ .

**a.** of desires rightful          **b.** desires of rightful          **c.** of rightful desires

# Order of Adjectives

Adjectives that appear before a noun follow a particular order. Effective writers use adjectives sparingly. Rarely are more than two or three used in one sequence. The chart below outlines the preferred order of adjectives in English arranged by common types and includes three examples of expressions that follow that order. Notice that the order moves from the subjective description of *opinion* to objective descriptions such as *material* and *purpose*.

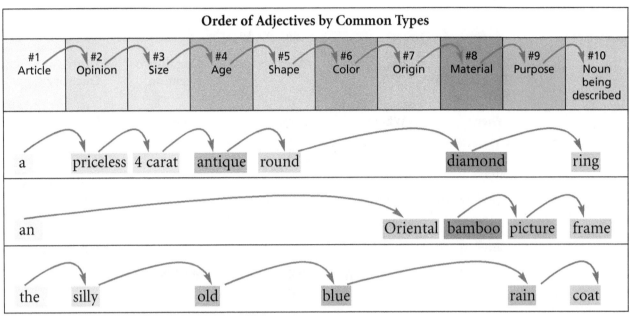

## ORDER OF ADJECTIVES

**A.** Choose the option that best completes the idea by listing adjectives in the proper order.

**1.** _____ cat sleeps all day.

**a.** The sick, 16-year-old, black    **b.** The black, sick, 16-year-old    **c.** The 16-year-old, sick, black

**2.** For many, _____ kitchen is a top priority.

**a.** a modern, roomy, attractive    **b.** attractive, an, modern, roomy    **c.** an attractive, roomy, modern

**B.** Describe each noun with a set of two or more adjectives. List adjectives in proper order.

**1.** _____ computer

**2.** _____ car

**3.** _____ song

*Practice 6*

# Adverbs

The most common use of adverbs is to describe verbs. In addition, adverbs modify other types of words such as adjectives and other adverbs. In purpose, adverbs answer the reporter's questions *When? Where?* and *How?*

Many adverbs are derived from adjectives, many adverbs end in -*ly*, and many adverbs are gradeable based on degree or quantity. The following chart lists some of the most frequently used adverbs based on the type of information they provide.

| Common Adverbs | | | | |
|---|---|---|---|---|
| Time, Frequency, or Sequence | Place | Manner | Certainty or Negation | Degree or Quantity |
| When? | Where? | How? | How? | How much? |
| after | everywhere | automatically | certainly | almost |
| always | here | badly | clearly | completely |
| consequently | inside | beautifully | perhaps | enough |
| during | outside | cheerfully | probably | fully |
| early | somewhere | fast | maybe | hardly |
| finally | there | happily | obviously | least |
| often | | hard | surely | less |
| next | | quickly | not | not |
| sometimes | | seriously | never | really |
| then | | slowly | | too |
| while | | well | | very |

## PLACEMENT OF ADVERBS

Complete each sentence with the most appropriate adverb.

1. Every professional .......................... needs a charcoal gray suit.

a. much  b. certainly  c. never

2. The white, long-sleeved oxford cloth shirt is .......................... a great accessory to any suit.

a. always  b. hardly  c. almost

3. The professional can .......................... do without a pair of khaki pants.

a. hardly  b. sometimes  c. almost

4. .......................... another necessity of a professional's wardrobe is the black dress shoe.

a. Consequently  b. Obviously  c. Hardly

5. .......................... , a trench coat is a practical addition to the professional's wardrobe.

a. First  b. Consequently  c. Finally

## Comparative

The comparative degree compares and makes distinctions between two people or things, usually by using the adverbs *more* or *less* or adding the suffix *-er*.

*COMPARATIVE ADJECTIVE "CUTER"*
*COMPARES "CAPRIS" WITH "CULOTTES"*

Capris are cuter than culottes.

## Superlative

The superlative degree makes distinctions among three or more people or things, usually by using the adverbs *most* or *least* or adding the suffix *-est*.

*SUPERLATIVE ADJECTIVE "CUTEST" COMPARES NOUN*
*"OUTFIT" TO ALL THE OTHER OUTFITS*

This is the cutest outfit of all.

| Degrees of Adjectives and Adverbs | | | |
|---|---|---|---|
| Degree of Comparison | Absolute: One<br><br>as _____ as | Comparative: Two<br>*-er*<br>_____ than | Superlative: Three or More<br>*-est*<br>the _____ |
| Adjectives | good | better | best |
| | bad | worse | worst |
| | much | more | most |
| Adverbs | busy | busier | busiest |
| | slowly | more slowly | most slowly |

---

**USING COMPARATIVES AND SUPERLATIVES**

Complete the following sentences with the proper comparative or superlative.

**1.** Organic fabrics are a ............................ choice than synthetic materials.

**a.** good      **b.** better      **c.** best

**2.** Cotton is a ............................ , sturdy material.

**a.** good      **b.** better      **c.** best

**3.** Cotton is ............................ cooler to wear than synthetic fibers.

**a.** much      **b.** more      **c.** most

*Practice 8*

| Spelling Guidelines Comparative and Superlative Adjectives and Adverbs | | | |
|---|---|---|---|
| NUMBER OF SYLLABLES | WORD ENDING | COMPARATIVE | SUPERLATIVE |
| **One-syllable adjectives or adverbs** | any kind | add -*er* | add -*est* |
| *Examples* | fast | faster | fastest |
| **One-syllable adjectives** | consonant-vowel-consonant | double last consonant add -*er* | double last consonant add -*est* |
| *Examples* | big | bigger | biggest |
| **Two-syllable adjectives** | ending in -*y* | change -*y* to -*i*; add -*er* | change -*y* to -*i*; add -*est* |
| *Examples* | busy | busier | busiest |
| **Two- or more syllable adjectives or adverbs** | not ending in -*y* | no change in spelling; use *more* | no change in spelling; use *most* |
| *Examples* | thrilling | more thrilling | most thrilling |

Practice 9

### SPELLING COMPARATIVES AND SUPERLATIVES

Fill in the following chart with the correct spellings of each form of the comparatives and superlatives. Use *more* and *most* as needed.

|  | Comparative | Superlative |
|---|---|---|
| **1.** hard | | |
| **2.** exciting | | |
| **3.** sad | | |

## Mastering *Good* and *Well*

Two of the most often-confused words in the English language are *good* and *well*. One reason these two words are so often confused is that *well* can be used as either an adverb or an adjective to discuss health issues.

- *Good* is an **adjective** that describes a noun or pronoun.

*NOUN IS DESCRIBED BY ADJECTIVE*

Miguel looks good in his suit.

- *Well* is an **adverb** that usually describes a **verb**.

*VERB IS DESCRIBED BY ADVERB*

Miguel did well during his interview.

- Exception *Well* is an **adjective** when used to describe a person's health issues.

*PRONOUN DESCRIBED BY ADJECTIVE*

He feels well.

---

### GOOD AND WELL

Fill in each blank with *good* or *well*.

**1.** The designer is not feeling ...................... .

**2.** Her design is a ...................... concept.

**3.** The designer finished ...................... in the competition.

---

### ADJECTIVES AND ADVERBS REVIEW

Complete the following sentences by filling in the blanks with the appropriate form or order of the adjective or adverb in parentheses.

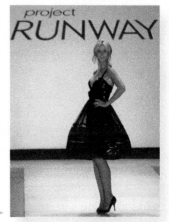

**1.** Heidi Klum is a ...................................... model.
(high-fashion, smart/smart, high-fashion)

**2.** She has done ...................... as the creator and producer of Project Runway. (good/well)

**3.** The show ...................... captured a large audience.
(quick/quickly)

Heidi Klum on the cat walk ▶

# Writing Assignments

## Writing for Everyday Life

Assume you are a parent writing to the principal of your child's school to protest the new policy about school uniforms. Edit to ensure proper use of adjectives and adverbs. Use your own paper.

> I am writing to protest the new, unfair policy that requires students to wear uniforms.
>
> School uniforms certain stifle self expression. Unfortunate, uniforms force children to find other ways to express who they are. The school has acted bad on this issue. We will do good to remember that children who wear school uniforms are more likely to use makeup early, and many resort alter their uniforms to be differently others. Wearing school uniforms may teach children that is better to conform to standard without thinking critical.

## Writing for College Life

Assume you are writing a speech in favor of school uniforms for a college speech class. Edit to ensure proper use of adjectives and adverbs. Use your own paper.

> School uniforms are a smart move for parents, students, and educators. First, uniforms get rid of gang colors in schools. They also great decrease violence due to theft of clothing and shoes. Our khaki, standardized, attractive clothing will instill order and a sense of community among students. School uniforms also reduce the distractions of unsuitably or controversially clothing. Final, school uniforms help educators identify possibly intruders who don't belong on campus.

## Writing for Working Life

Assume you are the principal of a school, and you have written a letter to send to parents and students about your school's new dress code. Edit to ensure proper use of adjectives and adverbs. Use your own paper.

> Forest High School has recent established the followed guidelines to aid parents and students in selecting the properly attire for the school. The student must be able to place his or her arms at his or her side and touch the bottom of his or her shorts or skirts with his or her longer finger. Clothing with bad chosen messages may not be worn in school. Shirts with reference to drugs, alcohol, gangs and weapons are not permitted in school. Clothing with sexual references is not suitably.

To test and track your understanding, answer the following questions.

1. An adjective modifies a ............................ or ............................ .

2. An adverb modifies a ............................, an ............................, or another ............................ .

3. Participle adjectives are formed by adding ............................ or ............................ to verbs.

4. Adjectives often appear in the following order: ............................, opinion, size, age, shape, ............................, origin, material, purpose, noun being described.

5. Adverbs answer the questions ............................, where, and ............................ .

6. Adjectives and adverbs take the form of two degrees: ............................ and ............................ .

7. The ............................ degree makes distinctions between two things, usually by using the adverbs *more* or *less* or by adding the suffix *-er*.

8. The ............................ degree makes distinctions among three or more things, usually by using the adverbs *most* or *least* or by adding the suffix *-est*.

9. *Good* is an ............................ .

10. Most often, *well* is an ............................ .

11. **How will I use what I have learned about adjectives and adverbs?**
    In your notebook, discuss how you will apply to your own writing what you have learned about adjectives and adverbs.

12. **What do I still need to study about adjectives and adverbs?**
    In your notebook, describe your ongoing study needs by describing what, when, and how you will continue studying adjectives and adverbs.

*Academic Learning Log*

# 25

# Misplaced and Dangling Modifiers

A modifier is a word or phrase that describes, clarifies, or gives more information about another word in a sentence.

A misplaced modifier is a word or phrase illogically separated from the word it describes.

Modifiers are words that describe, restrict, or limit other words in a sentence. For example, modifiers help us communicate what we see or how we feel. The photo on the next page illustrates several people experiencing intense feelings.

# What's the Point of Correcting Misplaced and Dangling Modifiers?

PHOTOGRAPHIC ORGANIZER: MISPLACED AND DANGLING MODIFIERS

Friends riding a roller coaster ▶

Read the sentence below that describes the roller coaster riders and answer the question.

WRITING FROM LIFE

Screaming with fear and joy, the roller coaster flew through the air.

**What is the point of correcting misplaced and dangling modifiers?**

---------------------------------------------------------------

---------------------------------------------------------------

---------------------------------------------------------------

---------------------------------------------------------------

# Understanding the Point of Correcting Misplaced and Dangling Modifiers: One Student Writer's Response

*The sentence made me laugh. Because of the wording, I thought of a cartoon roller coaster with a large mouth opened wide "screaming with fear and joy." Of course, the writer meant to describe the people riding the roller coaster. But the sentence doesn't include any information about the people. One way to clearly state the idea is to say, "The teenagers screamed with fear and joy as the roller coaster flew through the air."*

# Applying the Point: Correcting Misplaced and Dangling Modifiers

Sentence clarity can be achieved through appropriately placed and clearly expressed modifiers. A **modifier** is a word or phrase that describes, clarifies, or gives more information about another word in a sentence. Confusion in meaning occurs when a modifier is misplaced in the sentence or when the word being modified is not stated in the sentence. To avoid confusion, place modifiers next to the word that is being described.

## Misplaced Modifiers

A **misplaced modifier** is a word or phrase illogically separated from the word it describes. The following section offers a few examples and revisions of common types of misplaced modifiers.

### Misplaced Modifiers

**MISPLACED WORDS** A misplaced word is separated from the word it limits or restricts.

*WORD "ONLY" DESCRIBES ?*

? Denise only refused to ride the tallest roller coaster. ?

**Revision #1**

*WORD "ONLY" DESCRIBES "THE TALLEST ROLLER COASTER"*

Denise refused to ride only the tallest roller coaster.

**Revision #2**

Only Denise refused to ride the tallest roller coaster.

*WORD "ONLY" DESCRIBES "DENISE"*

**MISPLACED PHRASE** A phrase that describes a noun is placed next to the wrong noun and separated from the noun it describes.

*PHRASE "WITH A QUEASY STOMACH" DESCRIBES?*

? She got on the Ferris wheel with a queasy stomach. ?

**Revision**

*PHRASE "WITH A QUEASY STOMACH" DESCRIBES "SHE"*

With a queasy stomach, she got on the Ferris wheel.

**MISPLACED CLAUSE** A dependent clause that describes a particular word is placed next to the wrong word and is separated from the word the clause describes.

CLAUSE "WHO WAS TOO SHORT TO RIDE" DESCRIBES ?

**Example**

? ?

The little boy stood by his mother who was too short to ride.

**Revision**

CLAUSE "WHO WAS TOO SHORT TO RIDE" DESCRIBES "BOY"

The little boy who was too short to ride stood by his mother.

---

**CORRECTING MISPLACED MODIFIERS**

Coney Island
Amusement Park ▶

Revise the following student sentences to correct misplaced modifiers.

**1.** The Cyclone roller coaster thrills crowds at Coney Island which has an 85 foot drop at a 60 degree angle.

----

----

**2.** The 150 feet tall and 2000 pound Jeremy loves to ride Wonder Wheel at Coney Island.

----

**3.** Melissa only got sick at the top of the Astrotower, which is 275 feet tall.

----

**4.** Jeremy and Melissa exploding in the night sky watched the fireworks.

----

**5.** Coney Island is one of the last urban parks still open to tourists having survived since the late 1800s.

----

# Dangling Modifiers

A **dangling modifier** is a word, phrase, or clause that modifies a word not stated in the sentence. Therefore, the dangling modifier seems to describe the nearest word, yet it doesn't make sense. To revise dangling modifiers, you may need to add or rephrase ideas.

## Dangling Modifiers: Two Revision Tips

A **dangling modifier** is a phrase that describes a word not stated in the sentence.

**EXAMPLES** What do the phrases in the following sentences describe?

**Sentence #1**

When smothered in chili and cheese, we can eat dozens.

**Sentence #2**

Hungry and thirsty, my hotdog and cola disappeared quickly.

**Sentence #3**

Eating 20 hotdogs and buns in 5 minutes, my stomach inflated like a balloon.

**REVISION TIP #1** Change the dangling modifier into a logical clause with a subject and a verb.

**Revised Sentence #1**

*ADDED SUBJECT AND VERB TO CREATE DEPENDENT CLAUSE*

When hotdogs are smothered in chili and cheese, we can eat dozens.

**Revised Sentence #2**

*ADDED SUBORDINATING CONJUNCTION, SUBJECT, AND VERB TO CREATE DEPENDENT CLAUSE*

Because I was hungry and thirsty, my hotdog and cola disappeared quickly.

**Revised Sentence #3**

*ADDED SUBJECT AND VERB TO CREATE INDEPENDENT CLAUSE*

I ate 20 hotdogs and buns in 5 minutes, and my stomach inflated like a balloon.

**REVISION TIP #2** Revise the main clause to include the word being modified.

**Revised Sentence #1**

*PHRASE DESCRIBES ADDED NOUN "HOTDOGS"*

We can eat dozens of hotdogs smothered in chili and cheese.

**Revised Sentence #2**

*PHRASE DESCRIBES ADDED SUBJECT "I"*

Hungry and thirsty, I made my hotdog and cola disappear quickly.

*ADDED SUBJECT AND VERB*

**Revised Sentence #3**

*PHRASE DESCRIBES ADDED SUBJECT "I"*

Eating 20 hotdogs and buns in 5 minutes, I inflated like a balloon.

---

### CORRECTING DANGLING MODIFIERS

Revise the following student sentences to eliminate dangling modifiers.

**1.** Gaudy with bright lights and tacky signs, you must go and have fun. _____

_____

**2.** Crushed by fans and media, Nathan's Famous Restaurant begins its historic

hotdog-eating contest. _____

_____

**3.** Since beginning in 1916, Joey has created the most excitement as a contestant. _____

_____

**4.** With cheeks like a chipmunk, the last five hotdogs vanished. _____

_____

**5.** As a champion Major League Eater, 59 hotdogs in 12 minutes broke a World Record. _____

_____

Practice 4

▲ Beach near the Boardwalk

Revise to correct misplaced and dangling modifiers. Move or add ideas as needed.

**1.** On a gold leash, a woman walked by leading a toy poodle with green and pink hair.

**2.** After getting the courage, the ride took off without him.

**3.** We saw a stilt-walker on vacation roaming the boardwalk.

**4.** Laughing loudly, the gag amused the tourists.

**5.** While swimming in the ocean, something nibbled at my feet.

**6.** After surfing for hours, my body board lay on the beach.

**7.** Topped with chocolate and nuts, we enjoyed our ice cream cones.

Family looking at an
amusement park map ▶

Revise to correct misplaced or
dangling modifiers. Move or add
ideas as needed.

**1.** Taking a vacation, my stress level dropped. ....................................................

........................................................................................................................

**2.** Many of us are more likely to smoke a cigarette or drink alcohol under too much stress. ........

........................................................................................................................

**3.** Working without vacations, our health may suffer. ................................................

........................................................................................................................

**4.** Refusing to relax and get away, the heart may give out. ..........................................

........................................................................................................................

**5.** James strengthens his bond with the family on a vacation. ......................................

........................................................................................................................

**6.** Getting more hours of sleep and exercise, vacations are helpful. ..............................

........................................................................................................................

**7.** Carlos only wants to use two days of vacation this year. ........................................

........................................................................................................................

**8.** To relax and have fun, an amusement park offers low-cost thrills. ............................

........................................................................................................................

# Writing Assignments

## Writing for Everyday Life

Edit the following feedback from a guest to a resort hotel. Eliminate misplaced or dangling modifiers. Use your own paper.

I am writing to register a complaint. Tripping over a tear, the hallway carpet made me fall. I was referred to a doctor suffering from a broken ankle. Missing work as a result, my paycheck is affected. Most distressing, however, is the way your staff treated me at the time. The manager on duty only took responsibility for the torn carpet. Clumsy and avoidable, she blamed my actions. I will never again stay at your hotel, nor will I recommend it to others.

## Writing for College Life

Edit the following paragraph written for a college health class. Eliminate misplaced or dangling modifiers. Use your own paper.

Laughter has a positive physical effect. For instance, abdomen muscles get the same work out as sit-ups while laughing hard for several minutes. Laughing stimulates the heart and many body systems. Also Laughing, the immune system becomes stronger. Laughter has a positive mental effect. Less depressed and anxious, a good sense of humor helps a person. For example, many senior citizens have a sense of humor according to experts who overcome depression and suicidal thoughts. So joyfully, a vacation, a day at an amusement park, or even a roller coaster ride improves our well-being.

# Writing for Working Life

Edit the following response from a resort hotel to the feedback given by a guest. Eliminate misplaced or dangling modifiers. Use your own paper.

> We appreciate your complaint writing us about your recent stay at the Beach Front Resort. Concerned about the unfortunate events you describe, this letter outlines our response. We are conducting a full investigation of the incident. Our Executive Manager is talking to our employees looking into the matter. Reporting the incident, our insurance agent will determine liability. If you have any further questions, you may contact Mr. Cyrus Smith of concern.

**WANT A BETTER GRADE?**
For more practice with misplaced and dangling modifiers, go to www.mywritinglab.com > **Recognizing and Avoiding Errors > Misplaced and Dangling Modifiers**

---

### WHAT HAVE I LEARNED ABOUT MISPLACED AND DANGLING MODIFIERS?

To test and track your understanding, answer the following questions.

**1.** What is a misplaced modifier? _____

_____

**2.** How is a misplaced modifier corrected? _____

_____

**3.** What is a dangling modifier? _____

_____

**4.** What are two ways to correct a dangling modifier? _____

_____

_____

**5. How will I use what I have learned about misplaced and dangling modifiers?**
In your notebook, discuss how you will apply to your own writing what you have learned about misplaced and dangling modifiers. During the writing process when will you apply this knowledge?

**6. What do I still need to study about misplaced and dangling modifiers?**
In your notebook, describe your ongoing study needs by describing what, when, and how you will continue to study about misplaced and dangling modifiers.

# 26

## CHAPTER PREVIEW

● What's the Point of Effective Expression?

● Understanding the Point of Effective Expression: One Student Writer's Response

● Applying the Point: Effective Expression

● Writing Assignments

# Revising for Effective Expression

Effective expression makes language clear and interesting.

Have you ever noticed how some speakers and writers use wordy or tired and worn out expressions? Have you been confused or discouraged by a person's negative, fuzzy, or vague wording? Take a moment to think about the need for effective expression in the messages we send to others. Complete the following activity and answer the question "What's the point of effective expression?"

# What's the Point of Effective Expression?

**PHOTOGRAPHIC ORGANIZER: EFFECTIVE EXPRESSION**

Assume you received the following e-mail from a coworker. What is your impression of the person based on the language used in the e-mail?

**FROM:** Kendis Moore Kendis@ITsolutions.com

**Date:** January 15, 2010

**TO:** Dwayne <Dwayne@ITsolutions.com>

**SUBJECT:** FW: A Good Cause

To: All Employees

The reason why I am writing is to give advance notice of the fundraiser drive we will be doing in the upcoming months for the Red Cross. At this point in time, there is no doubt that we are facing a very unique situation. Terrible storms have destroyed countless in number of homes, business, and lives in the recent past years. Due to this fact, we need to raise a large in size donation for the Red Cross. Let me repeat again that in my personal opinion I believe that we have the ability to make a difference.

Please, give!

Kendis Moore
Assistant Manager
IT Solutions

**What's the point of effective expression?**

---------------------------------------------------------------

---------------------------------------------------------------

# Understanding the Point of Effective Expression: One Student Writer's Response

The following paragraph offers one writer's reaction to the e-mail from the coworker.

> This memo sounds like the writer wants to sound important. But the message comes across as empty and insincere. I most likely would not respond to this message. It's just not professional or thoughtful.

# Applying the Point: Effective Expression

Effective expression is a result of thoughtful word choice. Mark Twain once said, "The difference between the almost right word and the right word is really a large matter—it's the difference between the lightning bug and the lightning." During early drafts, writers often relate thoughts and ideas without concern for word choice. Words or phrases are needlessly repeated. Clichés (overused expressions or ideas) are sometimes included in the draft. This rush to record ideas as they occur makes good use of the writing process. However, we must take time to revise for effective expression after we have completed a draft. Effective expression involves concise, active, positive, concrete, and fresh writing. Use the revision process to achieve effective expression.

## Use Concise Language

The most effective writing is concise and to the point. Concise language avoids wordiness—the repetition of words and phrases that add nothing to the writer's meaning. The following example shows the difference between wordiness and concise writing.

**Wordy**

SUBJECT          VERB

The reason why Jamie was calling was to give advance warning about the storm.

**Concise**

SUBJECT   VERB

Jamie called to warn about the storm.

| Examples of Wordy Expressions with Revisions for Conciseness | | | |
|---|---|---|---|
| **Wordy** | **Concise** | **Wordy** | **Concise** |
| absolutely certain | certain | in this day and age | today |
| advance notice | notice | in today's world | today; currently |
| has the ability | can | personal opinion | opinion |
| he is a man who; she is a woman who | he; she | personally, I think | I think |
| | | refer back | refer |
| during the same time that | when | repeat again | repeat |
| | | summarize briefly | summarize |
| given the fact that | because | very unique | unique |
| | | whole entire | whole; entire |

## USE CONCISE LANGUAGE

Revise each sentence using concise language. Share your work with a peer or small group of classmates.

**1.** In this day and age, we need a hero who is good and inspiring.

_____

_____

**2.** In my personal opinion, we need a hero with the very unique goodness of someone like Clara Barton who was the woman who founded the Red Cross.

_____

_____

**3.** In Clara Barton's personal opinion, there are two "rules of action."

_____

_____

**4.** For one, we must have the ability to practice "control under pressure."

_____

_____

**5.** In addition, we must be able to focus on what we can do with an "unconcern for what cannot be helped."

_____

_____

Practice 2

# Use Active and Positive Language

The most effective writing uses active, positive language to state ideas. The **active voice** states what somebody or something did. The **passive voice** states what was done to someone or something. Sentences written in the active voice are more concise because the active voice uses fewer words to state an action, and it clearly states the relationship between the subject and the action. In contrast, the passive voice uses more words to state an action, and the relationship between the subject and the action is less clear. The active voice is more direct and more powerful than the passive voice.

**Active Voice**

THE SUBJECT "RED CROSS" PERFORMS THE ACTION.

The Red Cross helps millions of people.

**Passive Voice**

THE SUBJECT "MILLIONS" RECEIVES THE ACTION PERFORMED BY SOMEONE ELSE.

Millions of people are helped by the Red Cross.

---

**Practice 3**

### USE ACTIVE VOICE

Revise these sentences from passive to active voice. Share and discuss your answers with a peer or your class.

**1.** Each year in America, 70,000 disasters are responded to by the American Red Cross.

-------------------------------------------------------------------------------

**2.** Victims of house and apartment fires are helped by Red Cross volunteers.

-------------------------------------------------------------------------------

**3.** Millions of patients are given blood collected by Red Cross's blood drives.

-------------------------------------------------------------------------------

---

Effective writing also involves stating ideas in the positive, which is more powerful than stating them in the negative. Too often, the use of a negative expression makes language seem unclear. The following charts offer some tips and examples for creating positive language.

| Tips for Creating a Positive Voice |
|---|
| • Say what something **is** instead of what it **is not**.<br>*Negative:* Your actions are not funny.<br>*Positive:* Your actions are serious. |
| • Say what **can** be done instead of what **cannot** or **should not** be done.<br>*Negative:* The witness cannot lie.<br>*Positive:* The witness must tell the truth. |
| • Propose an **action** in addition to offering an **apology** or **explanation**.<br>*Negative:* Sorry, we cannot respond until our computer is online.<br>*Positive:* Sorry, we will respond as soon as our computer is online. |

The following chart lists a few negative expressions in one column and positive revisions to those expressions in the other column.

| Examples of Negative Expressions with Revisions to the Positive | |
|---|---|
| **Negative Expression** | **Positive Expression** |
| cannot lie | must tell the truth |
| cannot reconnect without | reconnect by |
| cannot waste resources | value resources |
| do not forget | remember |
| do not be late | be on time |
| do not be negative | be positive |
| never delay a response | respond quickly |
| never be rude | be polite |
| sorry, we cannot respond until | we will respond by |
| you misunderstood | let me clarify |

---

### USE POSITIVE LANGUAGE

Revise these sentences from negative statements to positive statements. Share and discuss your answers with a peer or your class.

**1.** We must not ignore those who need help.

-------------------------------------------------------------------------------

**2.** The Red Cross is not able to do its job without volunteers and donations.

-------------------------------------------------------------------------------

**3.** Joseph cannot give a donation until his next paycheck.

-------------------------------------------------------------------------------

Practice 4

# Use Concrete Language

Another key to effective writing is using **concrete language**. When writers use concrete language, they give readers vivid descriptions that can be visualized. Concrete language is the result of the thoughtful choice of nouns, verbs, adjectives, and adverbs. Your choice of words can mean the difference between writing that is **abstract** (vague, nonspecific writing) and writing that is concrete. Let's look at the difference between abstract and concrete nouns, verbs, adjectives, and adverbs.

An **abstract noun** names an emotion, feeling, idea, or trait detached from the five senses. A **concrete noun** names an animal, person, place, or object that the reader can see, touch, taste, hear, or smell (sensory details). The following chart illustrates the difference between concrete and abstract nouns.

| Abstract Noun | Concrete Noun |
|---|---|
| Justice | Judge |
| Truth | Lie detector test |

An **abstract verb** or verb phrase tells about a state of being or describes a general or nonspecific action. A **concrete verb** or verb phrase shows a specific action or creates a clear picture for the reader. The following chart illustrates the difference between abstract and concrete verbs and verb phrases.

| Abstract Verb | Concrete Verb |
|---|---|
| She is afraid. | She screams in fear. |
| He got a raise. | He earned a raise. |
| Tashika went down the road. | Tashika drove down the road. |

An **abstract adjective** is a broad and general description that is open to interpretation based on opinion. A **concrete adjective** shows a specific trait or sensory detail and is not open to interpretation. The best writing relies on the strength of concrete nouns and verbs, so use adjectives only when necessary.

| Abstract Adjective | Concrete Adjective |
|---|---|
| awesome waves | 20-foot waves |
| bad meat | rotted meat |

An **abstract adverb** is a broad and general description that is open to interpretation based on opinion. A **concrete adverb** shows a specific trait or sensory detail and is not open to interpretation. The best writing relies on the strength of concrete nouns and verbs, so use adverbs only when necessary.

| Abstract Adverb | Concrete Adverb |
|---|---|
| He has to eat a lot. | He has to eat hourly. |
| He kind of exercises. | He walks once a week. |

▲ *Destruction caused by Hurricane Ike in Galveston.*

Revise these sentences from abstract language to concrete language. Share and discuss your answers with a peer or your class.

**1.** Hurricane Ike caused a lot of damage to Galveston, Texas.

**2.** Pretty much all the buildings were really affected.

**3.** The coast of Texas got a lot of wind from Hurricane Ike.

**4.** The wind sounded awesome.

# Use Fresh Language

Effective writing also relies on using fresh language as opposed to clichés. Clichés are weak statements because they have lost their originality and forcefulness. See the example below.

**Cliché:**

You can't judge a book by its cover.

**Fresh Language:**

Outward appearance does not always provide a correct view of a person or object.

The following chart lists some popular clichés and their meanings.

| Examples of Clichés and Their Meanings | |
|---|---|
| **Cliché** | **Meaning** |
| all bent out of shape | angry, upset |
| back against the wall | no escape, no options |
| call it a day | stop working |
| doesn't have a prayer | no hope or chance for success |
| easy as A, B, C | simple, very easy |
| keep your chin up | be confident |
| missed the boat | lost opportunity |
| pain in the neck | a nuisance, a cause of trouble or concern |
| sharp as a tack | smart, witty, intelligent |
| wasted | drunk, intoxicated |

Instead of relying on clichés such as the ones presented here, use fresh language as you revise your writing. When logical, create your own similes and metaphors to express your meaning.

## USE FRESH LANGUAGE

Revise the following sentences by replacing clichés with fresh language. Share and discuss your answers with a peer or your class.

**1.** Maya is keeping her chin up as she prepares to evacuate before the storm.

_____

_____

**2.** She doesn't want to be caught with her back against the wall when the storm comes onshore.

_____

_____

Practice 6

**3.** During the last storm, she felt like she missed the boat because she waited too long to evacuate.

**4.** Evacuating is a pain in the neck, but it doesn't help to get bent out of shape about it.

### EFFECTIVE EXPRESSION REVIEW

Revise the following sentences for effective expression. Remember to use the key ingredients of effective expression—concise, active, positive, concrete, and fresh language.

**1.** In this day and age, we need leaders who are busy as bees and sharp as tacks.

**2.** Our whole, entire country is challenged by a lot of awesome natural disasters.

**3.** We must not be weak; we must not be afraid; we must not delay our action.

**4.** Given the fact that so many are in need, we cannot waste our resources.

# Writing Assignments

## Writing for Everyday Life

Assume you are writing a thank you note for a housewarming gift. Revise the note for effective expression. Use your own paper.

> Dear Aunt Jo,
>
> I just wanted to drop you a line to thank you for the very unique lamp we got from you for our porch. I have never ever before seen a lamp made from a water pump. You can bet your bottom dollar that we love the lamp. We are always delighted with your really unusual and fun gifts.

## Writing for College Life

Assume you are taking a sociology class, and you are studying the impact of a trauma, such as a natural disaster. Revise for effective expression. Use your own paper.

> To summarize briefly, there are two types of trauma: physical and mental. Physical trauma is caused by serious injury and threat. Mental trauma has the ability to cause frightening thoughts and painful feelings. They are the mind's response to very serious injury. Strong feelings can be produced by mental trauma. Extreme behavior can be caused by it, too. Trauma makes people feel like they are off their rocker as they feel intense fear or helplessness, withdrawal, lack of the ability to concentration, being irritable, sleep problems, anger, or flashbacks.

## Writing for Working Life

Assume you are applying for a job, and you have written a cover letter. Revise for effective expression. Use your own paper.

> Dear Ms. Matthews:
>
> I am writing to apply for the position of office manager. In this day and age, there is a need for very creative and hardworking employees. You better believe that I am a worker who thinks outside the box and who is willing to roll up her sleeves and get to work. I am absolutely certain that my experience and education have made me the exact right choice for this position. Don't hesitate to contact me if you need more information.

**mywritinglab**

**WANT A BETTER GRADE?**
For more practice with revising for effective expression, go to **www.mywritinglab. com > Punctuation and Mechanics > Revising for Effective Expression.**

To test and track your understanding, answer the following questions.

**1.** The most effective writing is ........................ and to the point.

**2.** ........................ avoids wordiness.

**3.** ........................ is the use of unnecessary or redundant words and phrases that add nothing to the writer's meaning.

**4.** The ........................ voice states what somebody or something did.

**5.** The ........................ voice states what was done to somebody or something.

**6.** Stating ideas in the ........................ is much more powerful than stating them in the ........................ .

**7.** ........................ language is the result of the thoughtful choice of nouns, ........................, adjectives, and adverbs.

**8.** A ........................ is a trite or overused expression.

**9. How will I use what I have learned about effective expression?**
In your notebook, discuss how you will apply to your own writing what you have learned about effective expression. When during the writing process will you apply this knowledge?

**10. What do I still need to study about effective expression?**
In your notebook, describe your ongoing study needs by describing what, when, and how you will continue studying effective expression.

# 27 The Comma

A comma is a valuable, useful punctuation device because it separates the structural elements of a sentence into manageable segments.

Misuse of the comma ranks as one of the most common errors in punctuation. The following photographs show three of the most popular pets owned by Americans. Complete the following activity about pets and answer the question "What's the point of commas?"

# What's the Point of Commas?

PHOTOGRAPHIC ORGANIZER: COMMAS

▲ Kittens with puppy

Read the following paragraph that was written to post on a website about pets. This draft does not include any commas. Where are commas needed? Why?

> More of us own a dog than any other type of pet. However we do have more fish and cats than dogs. Americans by and large keep more than one fish. Also many of us own more than one cat yet usually we own only one dog. A recent National Pet Owners Survey by the American Pet Products Manufacturer's Association broke down pet ownership in the United States. Americans own 142 million freshwater fish 88 million cats 75 million dogs 16 million birds 24 million small animals 14 million horses 13 million reptiles and 10 million saltwater fish.

**What's the point of commas?**

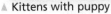

# Understanding the Point of Commas: One Student Writer's Response

The following paragraph offers one writer's reaction to the website posting about pets.

*I had to reread parts of the paragraph about pets. The ideas kept running together, or a statement didn't make sense to me. One person in our group went comma crazy and wanted to put in a comma every time she paused to take a breath as she read out loud. There were only two places that I was sure about using commas. I put commas after "However" and between each animal in the list in the last sentence. I think that commas help the reader make sense of the ideas.*

# Applying the Point: Commas

The primary purpose of the **comma** is to make a sentence easy to read by indicating a brief pause between parts of the sentence that need to be separated.

## Commas with Items in a Series

Use commas to separate a **series of items** in a list. A series of items in a list can be **three** or more words, phrases, or clauses. In addition, a series of items can be made up of subjects, verbs, adjectives, participles, and so on. Items in a series are parallel and equal in importance.

**Series of Words**

COMMAS SET OFF SERIES OF WORDS (SUBJECTS AND VERBS)

Max, Misty, and Rocky fetch, bow, and shake.

**Series of Phrases**          COMMAS SET OFF SERIES OF PHRASES

Smokey loves to chase cars, to bark loudly, and to beg for food.

**Series of Clauses**          COMMAS SET OFF SERIES OF CLAUSES

Doug is a trainer who loves dogs, who uses praise, and who gets results.

**Note:** Journalists for newspapers and magazines often omit the comma before the coordinating conjunction that joins the last item in the series; however, in academic writing, this comma, which is called the **serial comma**, is usually included.

**Chocolate Lab puppy** ▷

Edit the following sentences. Insert commas to separate a series of items in a list.

**1.** A Labrador Retriever is a dog that is gentle that gets along well with everyone and that is a good choice for a family.

**2.** The Labrador is medium sized and has an easy-to care-for dense, weather-resistant coat.

**3.** The Lab has an even temperament is outgoing and enjoys other dogs and people.

**4.** This dog is large enthusiastic and bouncy; it thrives on vigorous exercise and athletic activities.

**5.** It is peaceful with other animals is eager to please and is very responsive to training.

**6.** Labradors can be found in guide and assistance dog programs substance detection efforts and search and rescue work.

**7.** Labradors are also known for chewing objects mouthing human hands rowdiness and excited jumping.

**8.** Some Labrador Retrievers can be neurotic hyperactive dominant or aggressive.

**9.** They can suffer serious health problems from joint and bone problems to eye diseases to heart disease to cancer.

**10.** Write a sentence that lists a series of items. Suggested topic: The traits of an ideal pet.

........................................................................................

........................................................................................

# Commas with Introductory Elements

Use commas to set off the introductory element of a sentence. **Introductory elements** are ideas that appear at the beginning of a sentence. Introductory elements come before a main clause. Introductory elements can be a word, phrase, or clause.

**Introductory Word**

*COMMA SETS OFF INTRODUCTORY WORD*

Overall, living with pets provides certain health benefits.

**Introductory Phrase**

*COMMA SETS OFF INTRODUCTORY PHRASE*

In one study, pet ownership was linked to lower blood pressure.

**Introductory Dependent Clause**

*COMMA SETS OFF INTRODUCTORY CLAUSE.*

Since Maria adopted a dog, she has walked every day.

---

### COMMAS WITH INTRODUCTORY ELEMENTS

Edit the following sentences by inserting commas to set off introductory elements.

1. According to research owning a pet can help us fight heart disease and depression.

2. In one study it was found that heart patients who owned pets were more likely to be alive a year later than those who didn't own pets.

3. Additionally spending time with a pet causes the body to produce hormones that calm us down and make us feel pleasure.

4. Even if a pet is not a cuddly animal an owner still develops a strong emotional bond with it.

5. Write a sentence that uses an introductory element. Suggested topic: Disadvantages of owning a pet.

---

# Commas to Join Independent Clauses

Use a comma with a coordinating conjunction to join two or more equally important and logically related independent clauses. An **independent clause** is a complete thought or sentence. When two or more independent clauses are joined together, they form a compound sentence. To join sentences with a coordinating conjunction, place the comma before the conjunction. The acronym **FANBOYS** identifies the seven coordinating conjunctions: *for, and, nor, but, or, yet,* and *so.* The following chart lists these conjunctions and the logical relationships they establish between ideas.

*Practice 3*

| Coordinating Conjunctions and the Relationships They Establish: **FANBOYS** | | | | | | |
|---|---|---|---|---|---|---|
| For | And | Nor | But | Or | Yet | So |
| reason, result | addition | negation | contrast | choice, condition, possibility | contrast | addition, result |

# Correct Use of a Comma to Join Independent Clauses

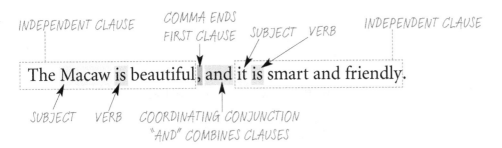

INDEPENDENT CLAUSE — COMMA ENDS FIRST CLAUSE — SUBJECT — VERB — INDEPENDENT CLAUSE

The Macaw is beautiful, and it is smart and friendly.

SUBJECT — VERB — COORDINATING CONJUNCTION "AND" COMBINES CLAUSES

**COMMAS TO JOIN INDEPENDENT CLAUSES**

Hand feeding two newly hatched Saker Falcon chicks ▶

Edit the following sentences. Insert a comma and coordinating conjunction to properly join independent clauses.

1. A baby bird can be raised to be a healthy, trusting, well-behaved companion bird a baby bird can be raised to be insecure, fearful, unsociable, and a poor eater.

2. Spoon feeding is the best way to raise a baby bird it introduces the baby to the taste of food.

3. Many owners use a syringe to feed a baby bird a syringe allows the flow of formula to match the rhythm of the baby's breathing pattern.

4. The syringe method also uses the natural feeding response it teaches the baby how to eat.

5. Write a sentence that contains two independent clauses. Properly join the clauses with a coordinating conjunction and a comma. Suggested topic: How to raise a baby animal.

# Commas with Parenthetical Ideas

Use commas to set off a parenthetical idea. A **parenthetical idea** is an idea that interrupts a sentence with information that is **nonessential** to the meaning of the sentence. Such an idea could be enclosed in parentheses. However, more often, a comma comes before and after such an idea. These interruptions can be words, phrases, or clauses.

**Parenthetical Word** — COMMAS SET OFF PARENTHETICAL WORD

A tarantula, surprisingly, can be a fun pet.

**Parenthetical Phrase** — COMMAS SET OFF PARENTHETICAL PHRASE

A tarantula, despite its reputation, is not dangerous.

**Parenthetical Clause** — COMMAS SET OFF PARENTHETICAL CLAUSE

The tarantula, which is large and hairy, is beautiful.

**Note:** Two specific types of parenthetical ideas are the **nonessential appositive** (word or phrase) and the **nonessential clause**. The uses and misuses of commas with these specific types of words, phrases, and clauses are discussed in greater detail in the next two sections.

## COMMAS WITH PARENTHETICAL IDEAS

Edit the following sentences by inserting commas to set off parenthetical ideas.

**1.** A tarantula generally is comfortable in a two and half or five gallon aquarium.

**2.** A diet of crickets along with other insects is fine for tarantulas.

**3.** A tarantula molts which is the shedding and replacing of its skin to grow larger.

**4.** Many tarantulas unfortunately are accidentally injured by their owners.

**5.** Write a sentence that contains a parenthetical idea. Suggested topic: An unusual pet.

Tarantula ▶

Practice 5

470

# Commas with Nonessential Clauses

A parenthetical idea, the **nonessential clause,** offers additional and unnecessary information that does not change the meaning of the sentence. Often nonessential information appears in a relative clause introduced by the relative pronouns *who* or *which*. A nonessential relative clause gives information about a nearby noun.

Use commas to set off a nonessential clause. Commas come before and after a nonessential clause that interrupts a sentence. A single comma sets off a nonessential clause at the end of a sentence.

*COMMAS SET OFF NONESSENTIAL CLAUSE DESCRIBING "BINDI"*

*SUBJECT*

Bindi, who is the daughter of Steve Irwin, was named after Irwin's pet crocodile.

*NONESSENTIAL CLAUSE COULD BE OMITTED WITHOUT CHANGING THE MEANING OF SENTENCE*

*COMMA SETS OFF NONESSENTIAL CLAUSE DESCRIBING "BINDI THE JUNGLE GIRL"*

*NOUN*

Bindi is the host of a Bindi the Jungle Girl, which is a 26-part wildlife documentary.

*NONESSENTIAL CLAUSE COULD BE OMITTED WITHOUT CHANGING THE MEANING OF SENTENCE*

---

**COMMAS WITH NONESSENTIAL CLAUSES**

Edit the following sentences by inserting commas to set off nonessential clauses.

**1.** Steve Irwin who was also known as the Crocodile Hunter owned the Australia Zoo.

**2.** Irwin was fatally pierced in the chest by a stingray spine at the Great Barrier Reef which is located off the coast of Queensland.

**3.** Bindi who has grown up around animals carries on her father's work.

**4.** Bindi is the youngest person to have ever appeared on the cover of *New Idea* which is an Australian magazine.

**5.** Write a sentence that contains a nonessential clause. Suggested topic: A celebrity who loves animals.

▲ Steve Irwin Memorial Service

Practice 6

# Commas with Dates and Addresses

Use commas to set off information in dates and addresses. When a date or address is made up of two or more parts, a comma separates the parts. When the parts of a date are both words or are both numbers, a comma separates the parts. And a comma follows the last item unless it is the final detail of a list or sentence.

- **Place commas after the day, date and year of a date.**

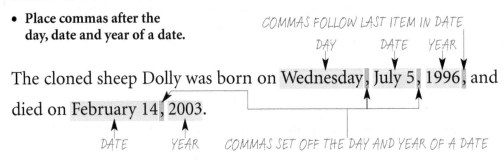

The cloned sheep Dolly was born on Wednesday, July 5, 1996, and died on February 14, 2003.

- **Place commas after the street name, town or city, and state of an address.**

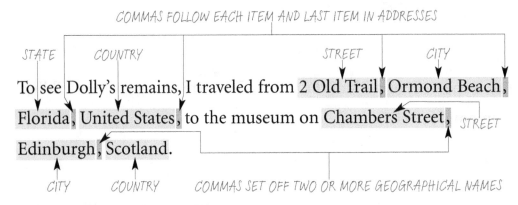

To see Dolly's remains, I traveled from 2 Old Trail, Ormond Beach, Florida, United States, to the museum on Chambers Street, Edinburgh, Scotland.

## COMMAS FOR DATES AND ADDRESSES

Edit the following sentences by inserting commas to set off dates and addresses.

1. A tabby cat named CopyCat was born on December 22 2001 and was the first cloned pet.

2. CopyCat gave birth the old-fashioned way to three kittens in September 2006 in College Station Texas.

3. Mira is the first cloned pet dog. She was born on December 5 2007 and now lives in Mill Valley California.

4. The first Jersey calf cloned in the United States Millie, was born at 400 West Main Avenue Knoxville Tennessee on August 28 2000 and died in June 2001.

5. Write a sentence that contains a date and address. Suggested topic: Your date and place of birth.

▲ First cloned cat

# Other Uses of the Comma

Commas are also used in two additional ways.

**1.** Use commas to separate consecutive **coordinate adjectives** of equal importance. **Coordinate adjectives** are a series or two or more adjectives that could be arranged in any order or could be strung together with the word *and*. They each modify the noun directly.

- **Commas between consecutive coordinate adjectives:** Use two questions to determine whether adjectives are coordinate.

  A. Can the word *and* be smoothly placed between the adjectives?

  B. Can the order of the adjectives be reversed?

If the answer is *yes* to either of these questions, then separate these coordinate adjectives with a comma.

**Commas and Coordinate Adjectives**

Cloning may have harmful, irreversible effects.

COMMA SEPARATES COORDINATE ADJECTIVES DESCRIBING NOUN "EFFECTS"

**2.** Use commas to set off direct speech.

- **Commas after a verb that introduces a quotation:** The comma is used to set off the "said" clause, called the **speech tag**, and the comma is placed before the quoted information.

COMMA SETS OFF SPEECH TAG FROM QUOTATION

Mr. Caplan said, "Pet cloning is a scam not a service."

SPEECH TAG          QUOTATION MARKS ENCLOSE SPEAKER'S EXACT WORDS

---

### OTHER USES OF THE COMMA

Edit the following sentences by inserting commas as needed to separate adjectives or to introduce a quotation.

**1.** Cloned animals can suffer unpredictable serious health issues.

**2.** Instead of cloning animal lovers should adopt one of the thousands of unwanted abandoned animals in shelters.

**3.** Miguel Lopez said "I love my frisky friendly kitty I adopted from the Humane Society."

**4.** He also said he wanted to take home a shy skinny dog that had been abused.

---

### COMMA REVIEW

Edit the following sentences by inserting commas as needed.

**1.** From the first moment I saw her I loved my small helpless puppy.

**2.** Peanut who is a mix between a Chihuahua and a poodle could fit in the palm of my hand.

**3.** She was born on August 28 1990 in Austin Texas.

**4.** She may be an old slow dog yet she loves to run bark and play.

# Writing Assignments

## Writing for Everyday Life

Assume you breed and raise potbellied pigs, and you have posted the following information on your website. Edit to ensure proper use of commas. Insert commas as needed. Use your own paper.

> I have raised Sheba who is a potbellied pig as a house pet. I wanted to make sure she had the care feeding housing and training necessary to produce a happy healthy pig. If you are interested in adopting Sheba come see her at 25 Lexington Avenue New Haven California.

## Writing for College Life

Assume you have been asked to write a short paper about cloning for a college science class. Edit to ensure proper use of commas. Insert commas as needed. Use your own paper.

> In recent years more and more animals such as sheep mice cattle goats cats rats horses and even a dog have been cloned. The first cloned dog was named Snuppy which is short for "Seoul National University puppy." Snuppy is practically identical to his cell-donor. Because cloned animals are identical to one another researchers can better study normal development reactions to drugs and the effects of pollution. Cloning might in addition keep certain species of animals from dying out. Ultimately owners may clone their beloved pets for emotional reasons.

## Writing for Working Life

Assume you are the office manager of a small business. You have composed the following memo. Edit to ensure proper use of commas. Insert commas as needed. Use your own paper.

> **To: All Employees**
> Studies have shown that pets in the workplace boost employee morale output and even sales so our company is taking part in Take Your Dog To Work Day. Make sure your dog is bathed groomed and vaccinated. If you are constantly in and out of your office you may want to bring a portable kennel for your dog's comfort. Please remember to bring treats food a bowl a leash and a favorite toy for your dog. Submit your form to participate by May 2 2010 so you can bring your dog to work. As Jonathan Swift said "Every dog must have his day."

To test and track your understanding, answer the following questions.

1. Use commas to separate a series of items in a list; a series of items in a list can be ................................ or more words, phrases, or clauses.

2. Use commas to set off the ........................... elements, ideas that appear at the beginning of a sentence.

3. Use commas in union with a coordinating conjunction to create a ........................... sentence, which is a sentence made up of two or more independent clauses.

4. Use a pair of commas to set off a ........................... idea, which is an idea that interrupts a sentence.

5. Use commas to set off a nonessential clause; often nonessential information appears in a relative clause introduced by ........................... or ............................

6. When a date or address is made up of ........................... parts, use a comma to separate the parts.

7. Use commas between ........................... adjectives.

8. Ask two questions to determine whether adjectives are coordinate:

   A. ................................................................................................................................

   B. ................................................................................................................................

9. Use a comma ........................... a verb that introduces a quotation.

10. **How will I use what I have learned about commas?**
    In your notebook, discuss how you will apply to your own writing what you have learned about commas.

11. **What do I still need to study about commas?**
    In your notebook, describe your ongoing study needs by describing what, when, and how you will continue studying commas.

# 28

# The Apostrophe

The apostrophe is used to show ownership and to form contractions by replacing omitted letters or numbers.

Thinking about a real-life situation helps us to understand the purpose of the apostrophe in our writing. Complete the following activity and answer the question "What's the point of the apostrophe?"

## The fol...
possession...

| To Show ...<br>for |
|---|
| A singula... |
| A singula...<br>ending w... |
| A regular...<br>noun end... |
| An irregul...<br>noun |
| Compoun... |
| Joint owne...<br>an item |
| Individual...<br>ownership... |
| Pronouns e...<br>with "*one*" ... |

APOSTROPHI...

Change the ph...

**1.** the promise...

**2.** the wages ...

**3.** the schedule...

**4.** the outfit of...

**5.** the ice crea...

# What's the Point of the Apostrophe?

**PHOTOGRAPHIC ORGANIZER: THE POINT OF THE APOSTROPHE**

The signs depicted in these photographs illustrate two different uses of the apostrophe. Study the signs shown in the photographs on these pages and explain why an apostrophe was used in each one.

WRITING FROM LIFE

**What's the point of apostrophes?**

New York City Law
"Don't Honk: $350 Penalty" ▶

# The Apostrophe for Contractions

An apostrophe is used to indicate the omission of letters to form a **contraction.** Most often, a contraction is formed to join two words to make one shorter word such as *don't* for *do not*. However, sometimes an apostrophe is used to form a one-word contraction such as *ma'am* for *madam* and *gov't* for *government*. An apostrophe ( ' ) takes the place of the letter or letters that are dropped to form the contraction.

The use of contractions gives a piece of writing an informal tone that records on paper the way we speak in general conversation. Writing for college courses usually requires a formal, academic tone. Thus, many professors discourage the use of contractions. Check with your professors about the required tone of your writing assignments. To ensure proper use of the apostrophe, the following chart illustrates how contracted verbs are formed.

| Apostrophe Use in Common Contractions | |
|---|---|
| The apostrophe replaces omitted letters. | |
| 'm     *APOSTROPHE REPLACES "A" IN "I AM"* <br><br> I am = I'm | 's     *APOSTROPHE REPLACES "I" IN "IT IS"* <br><br> it is = it's |
| 're     *APOSTROPHE REPLACES "A" IN "THEY ARE"* <br><br> they are = they're | 've     *APOSTROPHE REPLACES "HA" IN "I HAVE"* <br><br> I have = I've |
| n't     *APOSTROPHE REPLACES "O" IN "DO NOT"* <br><br> do not = don't | 'll     *APOSTROPHE REPLACES "WI" IN "WE WILL"* <br><br> we will = we'll |

**Practice 3**

### APOSTROPHES IN CONTRACTIONS

Use apostrophes to form contractions for the following words.

1. I am _____

2. she is _____

3. would not _____

4. let us _____

5. we are _____

6. will not _____

7. she has _____

8. it has _____

9. it will _____

10. we have _____

# Common Misuses of the Apostrophe

Quite often, the apostrophe is misused in several specific ways. The following chart lists and illustrates these common misuses of the apostrophe. Always base your use of an apostrophe on a specific rule. Proofread your writing for these common mistakes.

- **Do not use an apostrophe to form a plural noun.**

| Correct Plural | Incorrect Plural |
|---|---|
| smiles | smile's |

- **Do not use an apostrophe to form a possessive pronoun.**

| Correct | Incorrect |
|---|---|
| his<br>theirs | his'<br>their's |

- **Do not omit the apostrophe to form the possessive indefinite pronoun.**

| Correct | Incorrect |
|---|---|
| somebody's | somebodys |

- **Do not confuse contractions with similar sounding words.**

| Contraction | Possessive Pronoun |
|---|---|
| it's (it is)<br>who's (who is)<br>they're (they are) | its<br>whose<br>their |

## CORRECT USE OF THE APOSTROPHE

Underline the word that best completes each sentence.

1. Around 9 million Americans have (their / they're) identities stolen each year.

2. Identity theft occurs when (someones / someone's) using the personal identification of (other's / others) without (their / they're) permission.

3. (Your / You're / Your's) wise to protect (your / you're / yours) personal identification information, which is (your / you're / your's) name, Social Security number, or credit card number.

4. Identity thieves are crooks (who's / whose) goal is fraud, and (their / they're) hoping (your your's / you're) not paying attention.

Practice 4

▲ **Credit card thief**

Edit the paragraph to ensure correct use of the apostrophe.

(1) Junk mail and telemarketing are a waste of you're time and resources. (2) Millions of trees and billions of gallons of water are used to produce a typical years worth of junk mail in the United States. (3) In addition, its posing a greater risk to you for identity theft. (4) Each pre-approved credit offer thats sent to you opens the door for somebody to get a line of credit in you're name. (5) Heres one way to stop those pesky telemarketers' from calling. (6) Legally, telemarketers must keep a list of people whove said they dont want to be called. (7) So put you're name on the "Dont call list." (8) Confirm that youve been placed on this list each time your called by a telemarketer. (9) By doing this, in time, youll reduce all those telemarketers calls.

Write a sentence that correctly uses the apostrophe. Suggested Topic: Dangers of credit cards.

-------------------------------------------------------------

-------------------------------------------------------------

*(Side margin: Practice 5)*

▲ **Identity theft**

Edit the paragraph for correct use of the apostrophe.

(1) A person may ask that a fraud alert be placed on her's credit report. (2) Its an important step to take if she suspects shes been, or shes about to be, a victim of identity theft. (3) An alert is wise if her's wallets been stolen or if shes been taken in by a scam. (4) With a fraud alert, likely creditors must confirm hers identity before issuing credit in her name. (5) However, the creditors actions to verify ones identity may not always work. (6) When a fraud alert is placed on an individuals credit report, shes allowed to get one free credit report from each of the three nationwide consumer reporting companies. (7) And, by request, only the last four digits of a persons Social Security number will appear on her's credit reports.

Write a sentence that correctly uses the apostrophe. Suggested Topic: Identity theft.

-------------------------------------------------------------------

-------------------------------------------------------------------

# Writing Assignments

## Writing for Everyday Life

Assume you have been a victim of identity theft. You have written a letter to get information from businesses that dealt with the identity thief. Edit the body of the letter for correct use of apostrophes. Use your own paper.

> As we discussed on the phone, Im a victim of identity theft.  The thief made an illegal purchase. In addition, a fake accounts been opened at your company.  Based on federal law, Im requesting that you provide me, at no charge, copies of application and business records in youre control relating to the thiefs illegal transaction.

## Writing for College Life

Assume you are writing a response to a short-answer exam question in a college business class. Edit the paragraph for correct use of apostrophes. Use your own paper.

> **Exam Question:** What is a credit freeze?
>
> **Student Response:** Many states laws let consumers "freeze" their credit. A consumer restricts access to his' or her's credit report. A credit freezes effect is powerful. Potential creditors and other third parties will not be able to get access to the persons' credit report unless he or she temporarily lifts the freeze. This means that its unlikely that an identity thief would be able to open a new account in the victims name. In some states, anyones able to freeze they're credit file, while in other states, only identity theft victims can.

## Writing for Working Life

Assume you own a small retail business, and you have detected an illegal transaction by an identity thief. You have written a letter to the customer who has had his identity stolen. Edit the body of the letter for correct use of apostrophes. Use your own paper.

> Were contacting you about a potential problem involving identity theft. Its recommended that you place a fraud alert on you're credit file. A fraud alert tells creditor's to contact you before their to open any new accounts or change your existing accounts. Call any one of the three major credit bureaus. As soon as one credit bureau confirms you're fraud alert, the others are notified to place fraud alerts. Theyll all send they're credit reports to you, free of charge, for your review.

### WHAT HAVE I LEARNED ABOUT THE APOSTROPHE?

To test and track your understanding, answer the following questions.

**1.** What are two general purposes of an apostrophe?

   **a.** To show ......................................................................

   **b.** To form ......................................................................

**3.** What are four common misuses of the apostrophe to avoid?

   **a.** Using apostrophes to form ....................................................

   **b.** Using apostrophes to form ....................................................

   **c.** ........................................................ to form possessive indefinite pronouns

   **d.** Confusing contractions with ....................................................

#### How will I use what I have learned about the apostrophe?

In your notebook, discuss how you will apply to your own writing what you have learned about the apostrophe.

#### What do I still need to study about the apostrophe?

In your notebook, describe your ongoing study needs by describing what, when, and how you will continue studying the apostrophe.

# 29

# Quotation Marks

Quotation marks are used to set off exact words either written or spoken by other people or to set off titles of short works.

Quotation marks help us to record the ideas of other people. We have little trouble identifying who is saying what in our daily conversations. However, when we capture speech in writing, we face several challenges. The same can be said for the use of quotation marks for a title of a publication. Complete the following activity and answer the question "What's the point of quotation marks?"

# What's the Point of Quotation Marks?

### PHOTOGRAPHIC ORGANIZER: QUOTATION MARKS

Assume you are an avid fan of *The Simpsons*. You love the show so much that you have joined a blog about it, and you read the following posting on the blog. As you read the paragraph, underline the ideas that you think should be in quotation marks.

▲ An inflatable Homer Simpson dressed as Santa Claus

(1) The Simpsons may seem like a simple cartoon. (2) However, critics and educators see much more. (3) Ken Tucker of Entertainment Weekly said, The Simpson are the American family at its most complicated. (4) Homer is a prime example. (5) The Simpsons' creator Matt Goering describes Homer as a a loveable oaf. (6) But some see this cartoon father as lazy, stupid, and a poor role model for fathers. (7) The show is also famous for making fun of almost every aspect of American life. (8) For example, the episode Dial N for Nerder deals with Homer's struggle to lose weight and the effects of childish pranks. (9) Across the country, colleges offer courses that study the significance of The Simpsons. (10) To that Bart says, Holy Cow, and Homer says, D'oh!

**What's the point of quotation marks?**

_____

_____

_____

WRITING FROM LIFE

# Understanding the Point of Quotation Marks: One Student Writer's Response

The following paragraph offers one writer's reaction to the paragraph about *The Simpsons*.

> I have always had a hard time knowing when to use quotation marks and where to put them. For example, I put quotation marks around the title "The Simpsons." But someone in my group said that you aren't supposed to put quotation marks around the title of a show because it's not a short work like one episode is. So we underlined "Dial N for Nerder." We also underlined everything that came after the words "said" and "says." I need to know if periods and commas go inside or outside of quotation marks.

# Applying the Point: Quotation Marks

Use **quotation marks (" ")** to set off **direct quotes**—the exact words spoken by someone or quoted from another source—and for titles of short works. Always use quotation marks in pairs. The first quotation mark ("), also called the **opening quotation mark**, indicates the beginning of the quoted material. The second quotation mark ("), also called the **closing quotation mark**, indicates the end of the quoted material. Four general rules guide the use of quotation marks with other pieces of punctuation.

### General Guidelines for Using Quotation Marks

**1.** Place commas ( , ) and periods ( . ) inside the quotation marks ( " " ).

*QUOTATION MARKS ENCLOSE EXACT WORDS OF SPEAKER*

"You're fired," says Donald Trump.

*COMMA GOES INSIDE QUOTATION MARK*

**2.** Place semicolons ( ; ) and colons ( : ) outside the quotation marks.

*QUOTATION MARKS ENCLOSE EXACT WORDS OF SPEAKER*

Jerry said, "You complete me"; Dorothy replied, "Shut up."

*SEMICOLON GOES OUTSIDE QUOTATION MARK*

**3**. Place a question mark ( ? ) inside quotation marks when it is part of the quotation. Place a question mark outside quotation marks when the larger sentence is a question, but the quotation included in it is not.

QUOTATION MARKS ENCLOSE EXACT WORDS OF SPEAKER

Indiana Jones said, "Snakes. Why'd it hafta be snakes?"

QUESTION MARK GOES INSIDE QUOTATION MARK

QUOTATION MARKS ENCLOSE EXACT WORDS OF SPEAKER

Did he really say "I hate snakes"?

QUESTION MARK GOES OUTSIDE QUOTATION MARK BECAUSE THE SENTENCE
ITSELF IS A QUESTION, BUT THE QUOTATION INCLUDED IN IT IS NOT

**4**. Use single quotation marks for quoted information—or titles of short works—that appear within direct quotation.

DOUBLE QUOTATION MARK ENCLOSES THE WORDS POE WROTE

Edgar Allan Poe wrote, "Quoth the raven, 'Nevermore.'"

SINGLE QUOTATION MARKS ENCLOSE THE WORD STATED BY THE RAVEN

---

**QUOTATION MARKS WITH OTHER PUNCTUATION**

Insert quotation marks and other punctuation as needed.

**1**. A headline on Oprah.com about Charice Pempengco states, Teen Singing Sensation

**2**. The article goes on to report, She's never given up on her dream of something better Oprah says

**3**. When Celine Dion invited Charice to sing a duet with her at Madison Square Garden, Charice said, Thank you, idol.

**4**. Legendary producer David Foster said, A star is born.

**5**. Write a quotation that records an idea stated by someone else. Suggested Topic: An opinion about a singing star.

---

Practice 2

# Formatting and Punctuating Direct Quotations

One part of a direct quotation is the **speech tag** or the credit given to the source, the person who spoke or wrote an idea. A speech tag is formed by a subject (the speaker) and a verb that indicates the subject is speaking. A speech tag can appear at the beginning, in the middle, or at the end of a quote.

## Punctuating Direct Quotations

- **Speech tag at the beginning of quote**

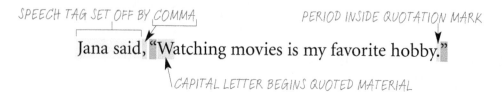

- **Speech tag in the middle of quote**

**(1) Quotation is stated in one sentence:**

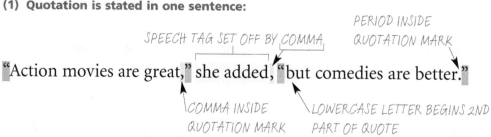

**(2) Quotation is stated in two sentences:**

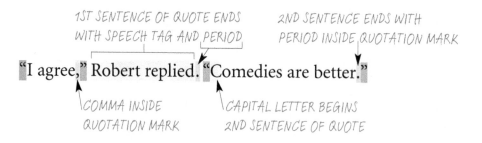

- **Speech tag at the end of quote**

QUESTION MARK INSIDE QUOTATION MARK          SPEECH TAG

"Do you want to go see a movie tonight?" Robert asked.

Edit each sentence to ensure correct punctuation of direct quotes and titles. Insert quotation marks and other punctuation as needed. Discuss your answers with your classmates.

**1.** I am Jeff McIntyre, he said to the House of Representatives  and am honored to be here to represent the American Psychological Association

**2.** He stated  The repeated exposure to violence in mass media places children at risk

**3.** One of the risks he listed was increases in aggression

**4.** A report submitted to the Senate says  James Q. Wilson, one of our foremost experts on crime, has observed  Youngsters are shooting at people at a far higher rate than at any time in recent history

**5.** Write a direct quotation to record something someone else said. Suggested topic: Advice you have received.

# Formatting and Punctuating Dialogue

Including dialogue in a piece of writing adds interest, details, and authenticity. Dialogue conveys action, time, place, and the traits and values of the speakers. Most often, dialogue is associated with creative writing, story telling, and journalism, but a well-crafted or carefully chosen piece of dialogue also can effectively support a point in an academic paper. The following chart offers a few basic tips for formatting and punctuating dialogue.

| **Tips for Formatting and Punctuating Dialogue** |
|---|
| • Use quotation marks to indicate a speaker's exact words. |
| • Use speech tags to make sure the reader knows who is speaking. |
| • Vary the placement of speech tags. |
| • Begin a new paragraph to change speakers; record each person's turn at speaking, no matter how brief, in a separate paragraph. |
| • When a speaker's speech is longer than one paragraph:<br>     Begin the speech with a quotation mark.<br>     Do not use a quotation mark at the end of the first paragraph or subsequent paragraphs.<br>     Instead, begin each new paragraph in the speech with a quotation mark.<br>     End the speech with a closing quotation mark at the end of the last paragraph. |

# Applying Appropriate Formatting

Note the ways in which Aesop's fable "The Hare and the Tortoise" applies a few of the appropriate formatting and punctuation rules for writing dialogue.

**Comment:**
New paragraphs signal changes in speaker

**Comment:**
Varied use of the speech tag

The Hare was once boasting of his speed before the other animals. "I have never yet been beaten," said he, "when I put forth my full speed. I challenge any one here to race with me."

The Tortoise said quietly, "I accept your challenge."

"That is a good joke," said the Hare; "I could dance round you all the way."

"Keep your boasting till you've beaten," answered the Tortoise. "Shall we race?"

So a course was fixed and a start was made. The Hare darted almost out of sight at once, but soon stopped and, to show his contempt for the Tortoise, lay down to have a nap. The Tortoise plodded on and plodded on, and when the Hare awoke from his nap, he saw the Tortoise just near the winning-post and could not run up in time to save the race.

Then said the Tortoise, "Plodding wins the race."

—Æsop. *Fables*, retold by Joseph Jacobs. Vol. XVII, Part 1. The Harvard Classics. New York: P.F. Collier & Son, 1909–14; Bartleby.com, 2001. www.bartleby.com/17/1/. [10 Sept. 2008].

## Practice 4

### FORMATTING AND PUNCTUATING DIALOGUE

Write out the dialogue between Blondie and Dagwood in this cartoon strip. Use appropriate formatting and punctuation.

©2008 King Features Syndicate.

# Direct and Indirect Quotations

The spoken or printed words of other people are written in two ways: as a direct quotation or as an indirect quotation. So far, you have been learning about the **direct quotation**, which uses a pair of quotation marks to indicate someone else's exact words. In contrast, an **indirect quotation** rephrases or rewords what someone said or wrote. An indirect quotation is a **paraphrase** of someone else's words. Never use quotation marks with indirect quotations. To paraphrase a direct quotation into an indirect quotation, follow these steps:

| How to Paraphrase a Direct Quote into an Indirect Quote |
| :--- |
| 1. Remove quotation marks and internal capital letters. |
| 2. Consider adding the word *that* to introduce the paraphrased idea. |
| 3. Revise verbs into past tense, except for actions continuing in the present. |
| 4. Revise verbs that command into their infinitive forms; revise speech tag for logical sense. |
| 5. Revise pronouns and signal words as needed. |

**Original Direct Quotation:**

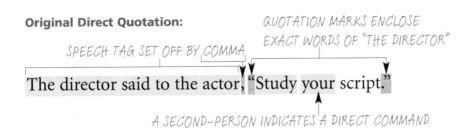

**Revised Indirect Quotation:**

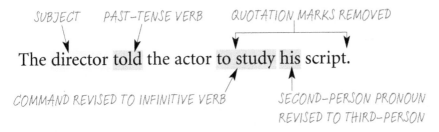

**Original Direct Quotation:**

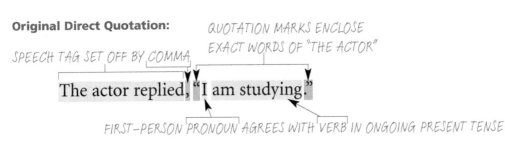

**Revised Indirect Quotation:**

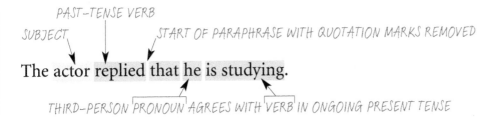

## DIRECT AND INDIRECT QUOTATIONS

Paraphrase the following direct quotes into indirect quotes. Work with a classmate or small group of peers.

**1.** Woody Allen said, "Eighty percent of success is showing up."

-------------------------------------------------------------------------------------

-------------------------------------------------------------------------------------

**2.** "Piles of gold are not as good as stores of grain," warns a Chinese proverb.

-------------------------------------------------------------------------------------

-------------------------------------------------------------------------------------

**3.** "Movies are a combination of art and mass medium," according to film critic Pauline Kael.

-------------------------------------------------------------------------------------

-------------------------------------------------------------------------------------

**4.** "Advice is what we ask for," Erica Jong said, "when we already know the answer but wish we didn't."

-------------------------------------------------------------------------------------

-------------------------------------------------------------------------------------

**5.** Actress Bridget Bardot said, "I have been very happy, very rich, very beautiful, much adulated, very famous and very unhappy."

-------------------------------------------------------------------------------------

-------------------------------------------------------------------------------------

# Titles

Quotation marks are also used to set off the titles of short works such as essays, short stories, short poems, songs, articles in magazines, TV episodes, and chapter titles in books.

- Follow the general rules for using quotation marks.
- Do not use quotation marks to set off titles of larger publications such as magazines, newspapers, and books. These larger publications are set off with italics or underlining.

**Poems**          *QUOTATION MARKS SET OFF POEM'S TITLE*

Have you read the poem "Oranges" by Gary Soto?

**Songs**                    *QUOTATION MARKS SET OFF SONG'S TITLE*

The Jonas Brothers had another hit song with "Burnin' Up."

**Television Shows**          *QUOTATION MARKS SET OFF THE TITLE OF THE EPISODE*

My favorite episode of *The Simpsons* is "All about Lisa."

*THE TITLE OF THE TV SHOW IS SET IN ITALICS*

---

### QUOTATION MARKS AND TITLES

Edit each sentence to ensure correct punctuation of titles.

1. Cinderella is a classic folk tale about a young woman rising above unjust treatment and finding her true love.

2. The song Hey Cinderella by Suzy Bogguss is about a woman's disappointment with married life.

3. The web article Cinderella Is Dead says that the modern woman no longer needs to be rescued by a prince.

4. Shel Silverstein's poem In Search of Cinderella is a witty look at the story from the prince's point of view.

5. Write a sentence that includes a title. Punctuate the title correctly. Suggested topic: Your favorite poem, song, or television show.

---

### REVIEW OF QUOTATION MARKS

Write a dialogue of four to six sentences based on a recent conversation you have had or that you have heard. Use appropriate format and punctuation. Work in pairs or with a small group of your classmates. Use your own paper.

*Practice 6*

*Practice 7*

# Writing Assignments

## Writing for Everyday Life

Assume your local community theatre is hosting an "open microphone" night, and you have written a skit. Edit the following dialogue. Use the proper format; insert quotation marks and punctuation as needed.

Nick says look I don't care what you are doing. When our daughter calls you drop everything and answer her. Justine says What? Now I'm a bad mother? Is that what you think? Nick sighs and says I didn't say that. Justine snaps You didn't have to. It's in your eyes. Nick says Really? My eyes? Are you an expert on body language? Justine says Listen, since I am such a horrible mother, do you want a divorce? Nick sighs again No I do not want a divorce. Why do you always go there?

## Writing for College Life

Assume you have written a personal response to an assigned poem for your English class. Edit the paragraph. Insert quotation marks and other punctuation as needed.

The poem Ulysses by Tennyson describes a hero returning home after a long journey and many battles. During his travels, he had become famous and honored for his deeds. However, once home, he becomes restless and unhappy. He describes his wife as aged, and he calls his subjects a savage race that hoard, and sleep, and feed and know not me. So he decides to return to a life of adventure and sets off on a new journey. His purpose is as he says, to strive, to seek, to find, and not to yield.

# Writing for Working Life

Assume you are submitting a report to your manager about a conflict between an employee and a supervisor. Edit the paragraph. Insert quotation marks and other punctuation as needed. Use your own paper.

> On July 6 at 6:30 a.m., Jordan Michaels reported a conflict with Julie Towers, his floor supervisor. Mr. Michaels says that the two of them argued about his schedule. Mr. Michaels said, Julie Towers grabbed my arm and pushed me so hard I stumbled. Ms. Towers admits, I lost control, but he said you are a dumb broad. Jordan is often rude and belligerent. Both have agreed to read the article How to Avoid Conflict in the Workplace and to see a counselor for anger management.

---

### WHAT HAVE I LEARNED ABOUT QUOTATION MARKS?

To test and track your understanding, answer the following questions.

**1.** Quotation marks are used in pairs to indicate ............................................. and

..................................................... .

**2.** ..................................... and ..................................... go inside the quotation marks.

**3.** Semicolons and colons go ..................................... the quotation marks.

**4.** Use a pair of quotation marks to set off a ..................................... , which records the exact words of another person.

**5.** A ..................................... is the credit given to the source of a quotation.

**6.** A speech tag can be placed ..................................... , ..................................... , or

..................................................... .

**7. How will I use what I have learned about quotation marks?**
In your notebook, discuss how you will apply to your own writing what you have learned about quotation marks.

**8. What do I still need to study about quotation marks?**
In your notebook, describe your ongoing study needs by describing what, when, and how you will continue studying quotation marks.

Academic Learning Log

# 30

## CHAPTER PREVIEW

LEARNING OUTCOMES

- What's the Point of End Punctuation?

- Understanding the Point of End Punctuation: One Student Writer's Response

- Applying the Point: End Punctuation

- Writing Assignments

# End Punctuation: Period, Question Mark, and Exclamation Point

End punctuation marks the end of a complete thought.

In our everyday conversations, we signal the end of complete thoughts to our listeners by our tone of voice. We pause more fully at the end of a complete thought. And our voices can go up in a question, come down in a warning, or explode with a strong feeling. Thinking about how we use our voice to express verbal ideas helps us to understand the purpose of end punctuation in our writing. Complete the following activity and answer the question "What's the point of end punctuation?"

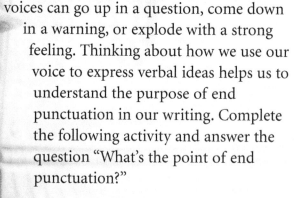

# What's the Point of End Punctuation?

**PHOTOGRAPHIC ORGANIZER: END PUNCTUATION**

Read the following transcript of a 911 call. In this draft there is no end punctuation or capital letters. Study this draft of the call. Then, insert the needed end punctuation and capitalization to show where one complete thought ends and another one begins. Use a question mark, an exclamation mark, or a period. Answers may vary, so discuss your revisions with a peer.

## 911

hello hello 911 hello can you hear me I need help my house is on fire what did you say this is Dorothea Gomez oh oh my please come quickly Princess, Princess where are you I can't find my cat

**What's the point of end punctuation?**

---------------------------------------------------------------

---------------------------------------------------------------

---------------------------------------------------------------

# Understanding the Point of End Punctuation: One Student Writer's Response

The following paragraph offers one writer's reaction to the paragraph "911."

*This activity really helped me see the real purpose of end punctuation. First of all, it's pretty clear that ideas run together and get confusing without end punctuation. And end punctuation makes the meaning of the idea clear, too. For example, "Hello!" has a different meaning than "Hello?" Our group had fun coming up with a whole bunch of different ways to say the same words by changing the end punctuation.*

# Applying the Point: End Punctuation

A **sentence** is a complete thought that begins with a capital letter and ends with a specific type of end punctuation. The **punctuation marks** that indicate the end of a sentence (called **end punctuation**) are **the period, the question mark**, and **the exclamation point.** Each of these end punctuation marks indicates the purpose or type of a sentence. The following sections present a series of charts that show the relationship among end punctuation, the type of sentence, and the purpose of the sentence. Several sections also explain common end punctuation misuses to avoid.

## The Period

| End Punctuation | Type of Sentence | Purpose of Sentence |
|---|---|---|
| The Period ( . ) | Ends a declarative statement | To inform |
| | Ends a mild imperative statement | To command without urgency |

SUBJECT    VERB       PERIOD

Many house fires begin in the kitchen.

"YOU" IS THE IMPLIED SUBJECT OF VERB

Turn off the stove. ← PERIOD ENDS IMPERATIVE STATEMENT

---

**THE PERIOD**

Edit each sentence to ensure proper use of the period and capital letters.

**1.** the biggest fire hazard in most kitchens is a grease fire it also results in the most costly damage.

**2.** kitchen fires occur for two main reasons the grease is too hot the frying food is left unattended.

**3.** two foods are most often linked to grease fires kitchen fires start most often when people are cooking fried chicken and French fries.

**4.** to prevent a kitchen fire, follow these safety tips don't let the grease get too hot don't walk away from cooking food always keep a fire extinguisher nearby.

**5.** Write a sentence that ends with a period. Suggested topic: Another possible cause of house fires.

Practice 2

# The Question Mark

| End Punctuation | Type of Sentence | Purpose of Sentence |
|---|---|---|
| The Question Mark ( ? ) | Ends an interrogative statement<br><br>May begin with *what, who,* or *how* | To ask a direct question |
| | May invert order of subject and helping verb | To question |
| | Often uses a helping verb such as *do, can, will,* or *would* | To make a request |

SUBJECT      QUESTION MARK ENDS A REQUEST

Will you turn off the stove?

VERB

Do not use a question mark at the end of an indirect question. An **indirect question** tells about or reports a question asked by someone by paraphrasing it rather than reporting the exact words used. An indirect question usually begins with phrases like *I wonder if* or *he asked.* Place a period at the end of an indirect question.

**Correct**

PHRASE INDICATES INDIRECT QUESTION        PERIOD ENDS INDIRECT QUESTION

I wonder if I turned off the stove before I left this morning.

---

### THE QUESTION MARK

Insert a period or a question mark as needed to appropriately end each idea.

**1.** Does my insurance policy cover the cost of repairing damage from a house fire

**2.** He asked his insurance agent if he had coverage for house fires

**3.** Will you please check our insurance policy to see if we are covered in case of a house fire

**4.** Write an indirect question. Suggested topic: Fire prevention

------

**5.** Write a direct question. Suggested topic: Fire prevention.

------

Practice 3

# The Exclamation Point

| End Punctuation | Type of Sentence | Purpose of Sentence |
|---|---|---|
| The Exclamation Point( ! ) | Ends an exclamatory statement | To express strong emotion |
| | Ends a strong imperative (command) | To express urgency, warning, or a forceful command |
| | Ends an interjection, a single word or phrase used as an exclamation that stands apart from the rest of a sentence | To cry out, to utter an emotion |
| | Used with interjections beginning with *how* or *what* | To emphasize an idea |

**Examples**

SUBJECT   VERB        EXCLAMATION MARK ENDS EXCLAMATORY STATEMENT

The pan is on fire!

VERB            EXCLAMATION MARK ENDS STRONG IMPERATIVE STATEMENT

Put out the fire!

EXCLAMATION MARKS SET INTERJECTIONS APART FROM MAIN SENTENCE

Wow! What a disaster! The kitchen is destroyed.

SUBJECT          VERB

---

THE EXCLAMATION POINT

Insert a period or an exclamation mark as needed to appropriately end each idea. Use capital letters as needed to make your point. Discuss your responses with your classmates.

**1.** Hey call the fire department now

**2.** I told you be careful you should never smoke in bed

**3.** Well now is not the time to point fingers just call for help

**4.** What a relief thanks for coming so quickly you saved our lives

**5.** Write a sentence of exclamation. Suggested topic: An emergency call.

Insert the appropriate end punctuation for each sentence. Capitalize words as needed.

**1.** Be prepared take a course in fire safety

**2.** Do you want to protect your property and family by purchasing Sure Safe Insurance you will

**3.** Act now before a fire occurs have an evacuation plan and practice it often

**4.** I wonder if you will buy a fire extinguisher you will good will you learn how to use it

**5.** Write a sentence with a purpose of your own choosing. Use appropriate end punctuation. Suggested topic: How to respond to a fire.

▲ Smoke alarm being tested

Practice 5

# Writing Assignments

## Writing for Everyday Life

Assume your house has been damaged by a fire. You are writing an e-mail to your insurance agent about your claim for your losses. Edit the paragraph to insert appropriate end punctuation. Capitalize words as needed. Use your own paper.

I am very unhappy with the way in which my claim has been handled I have spoken to at least six different people no one gives me a clear answer what is holding up my claim is there any additional information you need from me please contact me as soon as possible I am ready to file an official complaint

## Writing for College Life

Assume you are giving a speech about fire safety for a college speech class. Edit the paragraph to insert appropriate end punctuation. Capitalize words as needed. Use your own paper.

Is your home fire proofed you can prevent injury from fires, such as burns, and take precautions to prevent fires from starting in the first place. Follow these simple tips extinguish all cigarettes in ashtrays before you go to bed don't smoke and drink before bed don't smoke in bed anytime soak matches with water before discarding keep pads and cloths away from hot burners never spray combustible fluids in a barbeque grill keep a fire extinguisher on hand be ready be alert

## Writing for Working Life

Assume you are an insurance agent, and you are responding to a dissatisfied client. Edit to insert appropriate end punctuation. Capitalize words as needed. Use your own paper.

Dear Ms. Jones:

I am sorry to hear about your displeasure with our service I will contact our claims department and address your concerns you will hear from me as soon as possible I wonder if we have updated your contact information please check the attached form let me know of any changes or mistakes in the information hopefully we can resolve this problem to your satisfaction we appreciate your business

## WHAT HAVE I LEARNED ABOUT END PUNCTUATION?

To test and track your understanding, answer the following questions.

**1.** The _____ ends a declarative or a mild _____ statement.

**2.** The purpose of a declarative sentence is to _____; the purpose of an imperative sentence is to _____.

**3.** The question mark ends an _____; the purpose of this sentence type is to _____.

**4.** A question mark is not used at the end of an _____ question.

**5.** An exclamation point ends an _____ statement, a strong _____, and an _____.

**6.** The purpose of an exclamatory sentence is to express _____, urgency, _____, or a forceful _____.

**7. How will I use what I have learned about end punctuation?**
In your notebook, discuss how you will apply to your own writing what you have learned about end punctuation.

**8. What do I still need to study about end punctuation?**
In your notebook, describe your ongoing study needs by describing what, when, and how you will continue studying end punctuation.

# 31

## Capitalization

Capitalization clearly identifies the beginning of a new idea or the names of specific people, places, and things.

Digital media is having a clear impact on our use of capital letters. More and more often, e-mails, text messages, and websites use capital letters at random. By thinking about capitalization and the digital media, we better understand the purpose and rules in the use of capital letters. Complete the following activity and answer the question "What's the point of capitalization?"

# What's the Point of Capitalization?

### PHOTOGRAPHIC ORGANIZER: CAPITALIZATION

Study the photograph on the previous page and the following two examples of personal messages. All offer instances of the random use of capital letters in digital media. Work with a peer or small group of your classmates. Identify the edits you would make for proper use of capital letters. Discuss why the writers used capital letters as they did and the reasons for your edits.

**Computer receipt from a car rental company:**

Thank You for renting from Us. We appreciate Your Loyalty.

**Email message:**

whoa dude...WHAT HAPPENED last night After i left?  Casey did WHAT?

**What's the point of capitalization?**

# Understanding the Point of Capitalization: One Student Writer's Response

The following paragraph offers one writer's reaction to the text message.

*Our group actually debated about some of the letters. For example in the photo of the Software, we argued about the phrase "As seen On." Some of us didn't think any of those words should be in caps. Others thought the phrase was a title, so the word "seen" should be in caps. In the personal messages, it seemed like the writers used caps to stress important ideas.*

# Applying the Point: Capitalization

**Capitalization** refers to writing letters (and sometimes words) in uppercase letters. Following seven basic rules will ensure proper use of capitalization in your writing.

### RULE 1: Capitalize the first word of every sentence.

*CAPITAL LETTERS INDICATE THE START OF A SENTENCE*

People should not text message while driving. It is too dangerous.

**CAPITALIZATION**

Edit the following paragraph for proper use of capitalization.

> text messaging requires the use of a person's eyes and hands. some drivers use their knees to steer the car to free up their hands to type or read a message. they may keep one hand on the steering wheel. still, they have to take their eyes off the road to type and send the message. sending or answering a text message while driving shows a lack of common sense.

### RULE 2: Capitalize the pronoun *I*.

*ALWAYS CAPITALIZE THE FIRST-PERSON SINGULAR PRONOUN "I"*

I enjoy being online because I like chatting with friends and I like shopping.

**CAPITALIZATION**

Edit the following paragraph for proper use of capitalization.

> i get so annoyed with Joe. He is a non-stop text messager. i never see him without his iPhone. i regret buying it for him. When i try to talk with him, he ignores me because he is typing out a message. i taught him better manners than this. i am ready to cut off his phone service just so i can talk to him.

Practice 2

Practice 3

**RULE 3:** Capitalize the first letter of the first words in written greetings and salutations (for example, *Dear friends,* or *Best regards*).

*CAPITALIZE THE FIRST LETTER OF THE FIRST WORDS OF GREETINGS OR CLOSING (IN LETTERS, MEMOS, E-MAILS, ETC.)*

Dear Mr. Lin:

As you requested, I am writing to request that you stop service to account number 3284. Full payment for our current bill is enclosed. Thank you for your help in this matter.

Sincerely,

Ritu Gupta

---

**CAPITALIZATION**

Edit the following letter for proper use of capitalization.

dear Ms. Gupta:

Please accept this letter as notice of termination of services to account number 3284. Our records show that you are due a refund, so I have enclosed a check for $49.50.

best regards,

Jim Lin

Practice 4

**RULE 4:** In titles of publications, such as books, magazines, newspapers, songs, poems, plays, and articles, capitalize the first letter of the first and last words, the principal words, and the first word that comes after a semicolon or a colon.

Do not capitalize the first letters of the following in titles, unless they are the first or last word or come after a semicolon or colon: articles (*a, an, the*), prepositions (such as *in, of,* and *with*), and conjunctions (such as *and, but,* and *for*). Keep in mind that capitalization styles for titles differ in certain academic disciplines, so always check with your teacher for style guidelines.

**Article:**

CAPITALIZE THE FIRST WORD AND
PRINCIPAL WORDS IN A TITLE

"Dangerous Behaviors behind the Wheel"

UNLESS THEY ARE THE FIRST OR LAST WORD, DO NOT
CAPITALIZE THE FIRST LETTER OF MINOR WORDS, ARTICLES,
PREPOSITIONS, OR CONJUNCTIONS

**Book:**

ALWAYS CAPITALIZE THE FIRST LETTER OF THE
PRINCIPAL WORDS IN A PUBLICATION TITLE

*Privacy Lost: How Technology Is Endangering Your Privacy*

**Magazine:**

*Reader's Digest*

**Newspaper:**

*The Washington Post*

**Play or Movie:**

UNLESS THEY ARE THE FIRST OR LAST WORD, DO NOT
CAPITALIZE THE FIRST LETTER OF MINOR WORDS,
ARTICLES, PREPOSITIONS, OR CONJUNCTIONS IN TITLES

*No Exit*

**Poem or Short Story:**

"Mending Wall"

**Song:**

"Digital Man"

**Website:**

*Cellphonesafety.org*

**Note:** Digital terms, such as Internet or the World Wide Web, use initial capitalization.

---

**CAPITALIZATION**

Edit the following paragraph for proper use of capitalization in titles of publications.

(1) In 1818, the novel *frankenstein* warned about the moral dangers in the drive to advance technology. (2) That same year, the poem "ozymandias" was published; the poem is about the fall of a great king and his civilization, and it mocks human pride in human effort. (3) In 1844, the short story "rappaccini's daughter" raised the issue of corrupt medical research. (4) This ongoing concern about moral values and technology is seen today in current websites, such as the ethics center at http://ethicscenter.net/.

Write a sentence that requires the appropriate use of capitalization. Suggested topic: Your favorite movie, song, or book.

-------------------------------------------

-------------------------------------------

-------------------------------------------

## RULE 5: Capitalize the first letters in all essential words in proper nouns.

**Proper nouns** name specific people, places, things, and events. Proper nouns include people's names; certain titles of people (see Rule 6 on page 514 for details), places, and regions; organizations and associations; and publications. Each of the examples in the chart below illustrates various rules for capitalizing proper nouns.

**Note** the capitalization of initials and abbreviations. Do not capitalize common nouns.

|  | **Common Nouns** | **Proper Nouns** |
|---|---|---|
| **People** | a man or woman | Mr. Bob Jones, Ms. R. A. Grove |
|  | a professor | Professor Stevens |
|  | the name of a relative | Uncle Jeremy, Father |
|  | a believer of a religion | Muslim, Christian, Buddhist |
|  | member(s) of an organization | Democrat, Girl Scout |
| **Places** | a country | England |
|  | a street | First Avenue |
| **Things** | a language | Spanish |
|  | an academic course | Biology 101 |
|  | a sacred text | the Koran, the Torah, the Bible |
|  | a god, a religion | Christ, Christianity |
|  | a group/organization | The Jonas Brothers |
|  | a department, office, or institution | House of Representatives |
|  | a company | State Farm Insurance |
| **Events** | a day, a month | Monday, March |
| **Times** | an era | the Great Depression |
| **Periods** | a war | World War II |
|  | a holiday | Thanksgiving |

▲ *Birth Place of Dr. Martin Luther King, Jr.*

Edit the following paragraph for proper use of capitalization.

In 1776 in our declaration of independence, thomas jefferson defined the promise of america as freedom and equality for all. The words rang hollow, however, for millions of people. african americans were held in slavery prior to the civil war, and later they were denied their rights by unjust laws and social customs. The national register of historic places tells their powerful story. The long struggle of african americans to achieve the bright promise of america led to the heroic era known as the civil rights movement. The national register of historic places lists many of the places where these crucial events occurred. This list can be found on the website *we shall overcome: historic places of the civil rights movement.*

Adapted from *We Shall Overcome: Historic Places of the Civil Rights Movement.* National Parks Service. Sept. 2008. http://www.nps.gov/history/nr/travel/civilrights/intro.htm

## RULE 6: Capitalize the first letter of the title of a person when the title precedes the person's name.

Some writers capitalize the first letter of a title of very high rank even when it follows a proper name. Capitalization of the first letter of a title is also common if it appears at the end of a letter, e-mail, or other correspondence, following the person's name. Do not capitalize those titles when they appear on their own as common nouns (without modifying a particular person's name).

ALWAYS CAPITALIZE THE FIRST LETTER OF A PERSON'S TITLE WHEN IT APPEARS BEFORE THE PERSON'S NAME

D r. Mehmet Oz

WHEN A PERSON'S TITLE APPEARS AFTER THE PERSON'S NAME, THE INITIAL LETTER OF THE TITLE REMAINS LOWERCASE

Mehmet Oz, a medical doctor

CAPITALIZE THE FIRST LETTERS OF A PERSON'S TITLE

Prime Minister Harper

IN SOME CASES, IF IT'S A HIGH-RANKING TITLE, WRITERS WILL CAPITALIZE A TITLE EVEN IF IT APPEARS AFTER THE NAME

Stephen Harper, Prime Minister of Canada

---

**CAPITALIZATION**

Edit the following paragraph for proper use of capitalization.

As a woman raised in the era of the equal rights amendment, I want to live up to my potential. So I have searched for positive women role models to teach me values. First, the stories in the bible about mary the Mother of jesus christ have taught me to have faith. Second, Nurse clara barton, founder of the red cross, has taught me to take action. Third, doctor marissa sanchez, the Pediatrician I went to as a child, has taught me to break barriers. She was the first woman Doctor in our small town. And professor b.j. ocha has taught me to love learning. Finally, my Mother always teaches me by her example to be Honest and Kind.

## RULE 7: Capitalize proper adjectives. Proper adjectives are formed from proper nouns.

| Proper Noun | Proper Adjective |
|---|---|
| Africa | Africans |
| America | Americans |
| Florida | Floridian |
| Japan | Japanese |
| Spain | Spanish |
| Shakespeare | Shakespearean |

Use and capitalize brand-name trademarks as proper adjectives.

Kleenex tissue        Scotch tape

### CAPITALIZATION

Edit the following paragraph for proper use of capitalization.

Don Matthews has been all over the world. As a young soldier, he was held in a small vietnamese prison during the vietnam war. After the war, he joined the peace corps and worked as a Professor teaching english to children in china. There, he learned to love chinese food. Later, after a European tour of italy, france, and germany, he lived in the australian outback for several years.

### CAPITALIZATION

Write four sentences that require the use of capitalization. Suggested topics: Useful technology, good role models for youth, a place everyone should visit, and favorite songs. Answers may vary. Exchange your work with a peer and edit each other's sentences.

1. _____

_____

2. _____

_____

3. _____

_____

4. _____

_____

Practice 8   Practice 9

# Writing Assignments

## Writing for Everyday Life

Assume your friend has written you an e-mail about what he did last night. Edit the paragraph for proper use of capitalization. Use your own paper.

Hey Man, WHAT'S GOING ON? you won't believe what happened last night. After charles jimenez and i finished watching the movie tropic thunder, we went to club royal and listened to the new band killer bs. I had too many miller lights, so chuck had to drive me home. he was the Designated Driver!

## Writing for College Life

Assume you are writing about online relationships and technology for a college sociology class. Edit the paragraph for proper use of capitalization. Use your own paper.

online relationships are here to stay. in his book *the interpersonal communication book,* joseph devito discusses relationships and technology. the number of internet users is rapidly growing. commercial websites for meeting people are exploding in number. books currently high on the amazon.com list include titles such as *online dating for dummies.* and afternoon talk shows like *oprah, ellen,* and *dr. phil* often feature people who have met online. clearly many are turning to the internet to find a friend or romantic partner.

## Writing for Working Life

Assume you are the owner of a cab company, and you are writing a memo to your employees about the use of cell phones while driving. Edit the paragraph for proper use of capitalization. Use your own paper.

due to the accident involving one of our drivers, ahmed fahd, and the mayor of lake city, use of cell phones while driving is banned. although the accident was the fault of mayor harvey, the incident made clear the need for a formal policy on our part. the city cab employee handbook has been updated to include this policy. you can also access the entire handbook on our website citycab.com.

To test and track your understanding, answer the following questions.

**1.** Capitalize the _____ of every sentence.

**2.** Capitalize the pronoun _____ .

**3.** Capitalize the first letter of the first words of _____ and _____ .

**4.** Capitalize the first letter of _____ words in _____ .

**5.** Capitalize the first letter of the _____ of a person when the title

_____ the person's name.

**6.** Capitalize the first letter of _____ nouns. Do not capitalize

_____ nouns.

**7.** Capitalize the first letter of _____ adjectives.

**8. How will I use what I have learned about capitalization?**
In your notebook, discuss how you will apply to your own writing what you have learned about capitalization.

**9. What do I still need to study about capitalization?**
In your notebook, describe your ongoing study needs by describing what, when, and how you will continue studying capitalization.

Academic Learning Log

# 32 Understanding the Essay

## CHAPTER PREVIEW

An essay is a series of closely related ideas.

All of us of have had some experience studying, writing, or reading essays. What do you already know about essays? Where have you seen essays? What are the traits of an essay?

Perhaps the most common and flexible form of writing, an essay allows powerful personal expression. The essay is used for academic papers, business reports, business letters, newspaper and magazine articles, Web articles, and personal letters, as well as letters to the editor of a newspaper or journal. By mastering the task of writing an essay, you empower your ability to think, to reason, and to communicate.

# What's the Point of an Essay?

Like a paragraph, an **essay** is a series of closely related ideas that develop and support the writer's point about a topic. In fact, the paragraph serves as a building block for an essay since an essay is composed of two, three, or more paragraphs. Therefore, the skills you developed to write a paragraph will also help you write an effective essay.

## The Five Parts of an Essay

An essay has several basic parts: a **title**; a beginning, made up of an **introductory paragraph** that often includes a stated main idea or **thesis statement;** a middle, made up of **body paragraphs**; and an ending, often made up of a **concluding paragraph**. The following chart shows the general format of an essay.

**Hook the reader's interest. Use key words or a phrase to vividly describe your essay.** → The Title

An introduction usually consists of a brief paragraph in which you do the following: Introduce the topic. Explain the importance of the topic or give necessary background information about the topic. Hook the reader's interest. → The Introduction

State your main idea in a thesis statement—a sentence that contains your topic and your point about the topic. → Thesis Statement

The body of an essay is usually made up of a series of longer paragraphs. Most body paragraphs follow a similar pattern. Focus on one aspect of your main idea. State the focus of the paragraph in a topic sentence. Use the topic sentence to state the point you are making in the paragraph and relate the point of the paragraph to your thesis statement. Offer major details that support the topic sentence. If needed, offer minor details that support the major details. Link body paragraphs with clear transitions so your reader can easily follow your thoughts. → The Body

The conclusion restates or sums up the essay's main idea. In longer essays, the conclusion may be a separate paragraph. In shorter essays, the conclusion may be a powerful sentence or two at the end of the last body paragraph. → The Conclusion

# Making a Point Using an Essay: One Student Writer's Response

Read the following essay from the U.S. Bureau of Labor Statistics' Web site. Study the annotations and complete the activities suggested in the annotations.

**The Introduction:**
The writer begins with a bold statement designed to hook the reader's interest. The next several sentences offer important background information about an associate degree. The introduction ends with the thesis statement. Notice that the thesis statement states the topic, "associate degree," and the writer's focus, "many advantages" and "many resources."

**The Body:**
The body of this essay is made up of several paragraphs. This topic sentence states a primary support for the thesis—one advantage of an associate degree: "increased earning power." By repeating the key term "advantage," the writer ties this body paragraph to the thesis statement.

**This detail** supports the topic sentence and is introduced with the transition "First."

This sentence is a **minor detail** that supports a major detail. **Underline the phrase that introduces this detail.**

**Second major detail** that supports the topic sentence. Note the transition word "also."

**Third major detail** that supports the topic sentence is introduced with the transition "However."

**The Title:**
The writer used a phrase to appeal to the reader's desire to get a "jump start" on the future. The title introduces the topic "Associate Degree" and sums up the point of her essay in just a few words.

## Associate Degree: Two Years to a Career or a Jump Start to a Bachelor's Degree

### by Olivia Crosby

(1) In two years, you can increase your earnings, train for some of the fastest growing jobs in the economy, and pave the way for further education. (2) How? (3) Earn an associate degree. (4) An associate degree is a college degree awarded after the completion of about 20 classes. (5) It either prepares students for a career after graduation, or it allows them to transfer into a bachelor's degree program. (6) An associate degree offers many advantages, and many resources exist to help you decide upon a specific degree and college.

(7) One advantage of an associate degree is increased earning power. (8) First, people with associate degrees earn more money. (9) For example, compared with workers whose highest held degree was a high school diploma, workers with an associate degree averaged an extra $128 a week in 2001, according to the Bureau of Labor Statistics (BLS). (10) People with associate degrees are also more likely to find jobs. (11) The unemployment rate in 2001 was more than 30 percent lower for people with associate degrees compared with high school graduates. (12) And, according to several studies, advantages in the job market might be even greater for those just starting their careers. (13) However, for most people, the best part about earning an associate degree is the opportunity to enter interesting professions. (14) Training is available for those with nearly any interest, from technical fields like electronics and health care to liberal arts areas, such as design and social work. (15) And according to the BLS, careers in which workers often are required to have an associate degree are growing faster than careers that require other types of training.

(16) Another advantage of an associate degree is that it is widely available, offering a variety of experiences. (17) Degrees are available from public community colleges, private two-year colleges, for-profit technical institutes, and many four-year colleges and universities. (18) Taking classes from home is more common in associate degree programs than in any other type of educational program. (19) More than 9 percent of associate degree students used distance learning in 1998, according to the U.S. Department of Education. (20) Other students have a more traditional college experience. (21) These students choose schools that offer on-campus housing and meals. (22) And nearly all schools offer extracurricular activities—as well as academics.

(23) In addition to the many advantages of an associate degree, many resources exist to help you make the best decisions about your career. (24) First, most libraries and career centers have the Encyclopedia of Associations and the *Occupational Outlook Handbook*. (25) These books offer information about work-related associations. (26) The *Handbook* also describes hundreds of careers and how to train for them. (27) Second, counselors at colleges and career centers have information about local associate degree programs, labor markets, and financial aid. (28) Third, the easiest way to learn about specific degree programs is to request information from the schools that offer them. (29) Nearly every school provides free publications and has Web sites that describe programs and facilities. (30) For more details, consider calling, writing, or visiting prospective teachers. (31) Faculty and counselors are usually happy to speak with would-be students about courses and careers.

(32) An associate degree increases your chance for financial power and personal fulfillment—in just two years. (33) And with the many resources to help you decide on a degree and school along with the flexible paths to access, a bright future awaits you. (34) So don't delay; begin today!

—Adapted from Olivia Crosby, "Associate Degree: Two Years to a Career or a Jump Start to a Bachelor's Degree," US Department of Labor.

**This topic sentence** states another primary support for the thesis—"another advantage" of an associate degree. This phrase links this paragraph to the previous paragraph with the transition "another," and the word "advantage" ties this body paragraph to the thesis statement. Underline the words in the topic sentence that state the author's point in this paragraph.

**This topic sentence** offers another primary support for the thesis. The sentence begins with a transitional phrase "In addition to the many advantages of an associate degree." This phrase links this paragraph to the previous paragraphs and the thesis statement. Circle the words that state the author's focus in this paragraph. Underline the three major supporting details in this paragraph. Remember to look for transition words.

**The Conclusion:**
This essay ends by restating the writer's main idea and calling the reader to action. Underline the words that restate the essay's main point.

Test your understanding of the essay's structure. Read the student essay below straight through once. Complete the activities on the next page as you read the essay a second time. After reading, complete the outline with information from the essay.

Lacey Durrance
Professor Ragan
ENC 1101: Section 47
October 10, 2009

### Traits of a Successful College Student

(1) First-time college students don't realize the reality shock they will receive when they get to college. (2) High school and college atmospheres are extremely different in many ways. (3) College campuses and classes are often larger, college teachers have different expectations, and college students face many new challenges. (4) To get through college successfully, all first-time college students must be dedicated, responsible, and independent. (5) Many won't realize this until it is too late.

(6) Dedication is a primary part of being successful in college. (7) Students must work hard and take action to learn at a college level. (8) Assignments can't be left until the last minute like they might have been in high school. (9) College students must be willing to speak up in class and ask questions when they don't understand. (10) Dedication means setting priorities for success; dedication means putting off going out with friends and caring about producing the best work possible. (11) Dedicated students will do their work and do it well, spending hours reading textbooks, reviewing notes, and revising essays.

(12) For many, being responsible during high school wasn't really necessary. (13) Students might forget to do their homework and the teacher most likely would extend the deadline. (14) In contrast, college students must be responsible for their actions and accept the consequences. (15) Paying attention to what's due and when assignments should be turned in is a prime example. (16) Most college teachers stick to their deadlines and expect students to do so also. (17) Being on time to class is another example of being responsible. (18) Responsibility plays a key role in a successful college career.

(19) However, having dedication and being responsible aren't the only traits college students need to survive. (20) College students must also be independent. (21) Teachers expect students to take notes without assigning them to do so. (22) In high school, teachers often gave out notes to study from or told students where and when to take them. (23) College students must do their work without being reminded everyday. (24) However, teachers are there to help their students understand the class material. (25) They will guide their students yet not help complete their work. (26) Being independent is a skill to acquire for college success, as well as life-long success.

(27) College is hard work, and students must have these traits to be successful. (28) Most first-time college students will struggle with the new experience, yet by being dedicated, responsible, and independent, they will thrive in the college world.

**1.** Based on the title of the essay, what is the writer's topic and main point?

----------------------------------------

----------------------------------------

**2.** In the introduction, how does the writer "hook" the reader's interest?

----------------------------------------

----------------------------------------

**3.** Underline the thesis statement. Rewrite the thesis statement using your own words here.

----------------------------------------

----------------------------------------

**4.** What ideas did the writer restate in her conclusion?

----------------------------------------

----------------------------------------

**5.** The writer used a brief outline to plan and organize her ideas before she wrote her essay. Recreate her plan by completing the following outline. Fill in the blanks with her thesis statement and topic sentences.

**I.** INTRODUCTION

THESIS STATEMENT: ----------------------------------------

----------------------------------------

**II.** FIRST BODY PARAGRAPH TOPIC SENTENCE: ----------------------------------------

----------------------------------------

**III.** SECOND BODY PARAGRAPH TOPIC SENTENCE: ----------------------------------------

----------------------------------------

**IV.** THIRD BODY PARAGRAPH TOPIC SENTENCE: ----------------------------------------

----------------------------------------

**V.** CONCLUSION TOPIC SENTENCE: ----------------------------------------

----------------------------------------

----------------------------------------

Practice 1

# Developing Your Point: Writing an Essay

## The Four Levels of Information in an Essay

In addition to being made up of several parts, an essay offers several levels of information that range from general to specific. Understanding these levels of information helps a writer create and organize ideas throughout the writing process.

▲ Ladders to different levels

## Titles, Introductions, and Conclusions Express General Ideas

Titles, introductions, and conclusions introduce and summarize ideas. Chapter 14 offers helpful hints about how to effectively use titles, introductions, and conclusions.

## Thesis Statement

The thesis statement is a one-sentence summary of the main idea of the essay. All the details in the body paragraphs support the thesis statement.

## Types of Supporting Details

Two types of details are often needed to thoroughly explain a main idea: primary and secondary details. **Primary details** directly explain or support the thesis statement. **Secondary details** indirectly support the thesis statement. In an essay, topic sentences of the body paragraphs are the primary supports for the thesis statement. The examples, reasons, and facts within the body of a paragraph support the topic sentence. They serve as secondary details that support the thesis statement.

## Levels of Supporting Details

Secondary supports can also be divided into two levels: major details and minor details. A **major detail** supports a topic sentence. A **minor detail** supports a major detail. Thus, a topic sentence supports the thesis statement, and secondary supports explain a topic sentence. The following flow chart illustrates these levels of information in an essay. This chart represents a basic three-paragraph essay. This format is often expanded to include two or more body paragraphs.

# THE LEVELS OF INFORMATION IN AN ESSAY

## Introduction
Explains importance of topic and writer's point.

Offers background information about the topic.

Hooks reader's interest.

## Thesis Statement
States the main idea in a complete sentence.

Uses specific, effective wording.

Relates to all the details in the essay.

## Topic Sentence
States the main idea of the paragraph.

Offers one primary support for the thesis statement.

Relates to all the details in the paragraph.

--------------------------------------------------

## Major Detail
Supports the topic sentence.

Is a secondary support for the thesis statement.

Is more general than a minor detail.

--------------------------------------------------

## Minor Detail
Supports a major detail.

Is a secondary support for the thesis statement.

Offers the most specific details in the essay.

— **The Body**

## Conclusion
Reinforces the importance of the writer's overall point.

Read the following three-paragraph essay. Underline the thesis statement. Next, underline the three major details in the body paragraph.

## Street Luging for the Extreme Thrill

(1) Extreme sports take athletic competition to new levels of danger and excitement. (2) They often offer a combination of speed, height, danger, and mind-blowing stunts. (3) Street luging illustrates the allure of extreme sports.

(4) Street luging, like many extreme sports, involves high levels of speed, danger, and adrenaline. (5) First, street luging is all about speed. (6) A pilot lies on his or her back on a luge (a type of skateboard, eight and a half feet long) and flies through a street course at speeds of around 70 miles per hour. (7) As a result, the urethane wheels of the luge may actually flame fire and melt during a run due to the high speeds. (8) Second, street luging courses are known for their rough, hazardous road surfaces and obstacles. (9) For example, very dangerous courses are known as *bacon* while less dangerous ones are labeled *scrambled eggs*. (10) And frequently, luges snag or hook together, wobble, wipe out, or slam into barriers that mark the course. (11) Finally, the dangers of street luging are related to another important attraction of extreme sports—the thrilling rush of an adrenaline high. (12) The adrenaline rush is due to high levels of dopamine, endorphins, and serotonin produced by the body in response to the danger. (13) Adrenaline floods the body with additional surges of energy, power, and well-being so that a person can either fight or flee the danger. (14) Many extreme sports participants are called adrenaline junkies. (15) Luge pilots refer to this feeling as being "amped."

(16) Extreme sports include a wide variety of thrill-seeking sports such as wave surfing, wind surfing, BASE jumping (jumping from buildings, antennas or towers, spans or bridges, or cliffs), parachuting, and drag racing. (17) Overall, street luging offers athletes all the dangers and thrills that all extreme sports enthusiasts find so attractive.

# The Traits of an Effective Essay

The word *essay* means attempt, to make an effort to accomplish an end. An essay is a writer's attempt to share his or her unique and specific point about a specific subject to a specific audience for a specific purpose. An effective essay supports a **main idea** or **thesis statement** with **relevant details** in **logical order**, using **effective expression**.

## The Point: Main Idea or Thesis Statement

What's the point of a focused main idea? To make a clear and powerful point to your reader! An effective essay makes a clear point by focusing on a main idea. A focused main idea is the result of several thinking steps: selecting and narrowing a topic and drafting a **thesis statement**.

### Select and Narrow a Topic

Many writers break this step into two parts. First, a writer often generates a list of topics. This list serves as a bank of ideas that can be applied to a wide variety of writing situations. Second, a writer considers the writing situation.

Understanding the writing situation helps the writer narrow the topic. For example, the length of an essay often depends on your audience and purpose. A paper for an academic audience such as a history professor may have a required length of 1,000 words. In contrast, a local newspaper may limit the length of letters to the editor to 500 words. The scope of the topic needs to match the required length. For example, the 500-word letter to the editor cannot cover all the reasons one should volunteer at the local soup kitchen for the poor. Instead, you would need to narrow the topic to just two or three reasons. And you would choose only those details that are of interest to your specific audience.

---

**THE WRITING SITUATION**

The following pictures present specific writing situations. Each picture represents an audience, and each caption states the purpose for writing to that audience. First, match the audience and purpose to its appropriate topic. Then, write the letter of the topic in the appropriate space. Finally, discuss your answers with your class or in a small group.

Topics:   a. The importance of a specific lesson

b. Wisdom gained from an education

c. The proper way to discipline a child

d. Why voting is important

........ Writing Situation 1:
To Inform — to share, explain or demonstrate information

........ Writing Situation 2:
To Persuade — to change this audience's opinion or call them to action

........ Writing Situation 3:
To Express — to share personal opinions, feelings, or reactions

........ Writing Situation 4:
To Reflect — to record your understandings about what you have experienced or learned

*Practice 3*

# Draft a Thesis Statement

After choosing and narrowing a topic, a writer composes a working draft of the thesis statement. A **thesis statement** shares the same traits of a topic sentence for a paragraph. Just as the topic sentence states the main idea of a paragraph, the thesis sentence states the main idea of the essay. Both statements answer the question "What's the point?" This point is the opinion about the topic that you are explaining and supporting in the essay. In fact, your point further narrows your topic. The writer's point or opinion is often referred to as the controlling idea.

The controlling idea often includes a pattern of organization as well as the writer's opinion. You learned about patterns of organization as you studied how to develop paragraphs in Chapters 3 to 12. The following graphic illustrates an effective thesis statement.

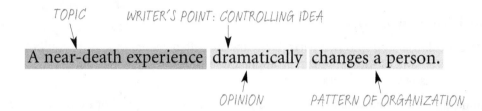

The word "dramatically" is an opinion that must be explained or supported. In addition, the word "changes" suggests a pattern of organization. This word indicates that the writer is going to compare what the person was like before the near-death experience to what the person is like after the near-death experience. The controlling idea answers the question "What's the point?" of the essay.

| **Hints for Drafting a Thesis Statement** |
|---|
| Use specific statements. Replace vague, general words with vivid, exact words. "Football is a dumb game" is too vague and general. "Football glorifies violence" is specific and vivid. |
| Always state your thesis statement as a complete sentence. |
| Avoid announcing your topic. Never say, "I am going to write about football and violence," or "My essay is about football and violence," or "My topic is football violence." |
| Review and, if necessary, revise your thesis statement after you have written a rough draft. As you think about a topic, the point you want to make often becomes clearer. |

### CREATING AND REVISING THESIS STATEMENTS

These items present a topic and a writer's point about the topic. Combine the ideas in each group to create a thesis statement. Discuss your ideas with your class or in a small group.

1. TOPIC: *workplace aggression*

WRITER'S POINT: *is on the rise and takes on several forms of behavior*

Practice 4

THESIS STATEMENT: ..............................................................................................................

...............................................................................................................................................

**2.** TOPIC: *cardiovascular disease* ................................................................................

WRITER'S POINT: *although certain factors are unavoidable, other factors* ...........

*we can influence* ..........................................................................................................

THESIS STATEMENT: ..............................................................................................................

...............................................................................................................................................

**3.** TOPIC: *major depressive disorder* ...........................................................................

WRITER'S POINT: *a common type of mood disorder with several long-term effects* .......

THESIS STATEMENT: ..............................................................................................................

...............................................................................................................................................

**4.** TOPIC: *use of chat rooms and online discussion boards* ..................................

WRITER'S POINT: *five tips for effectiveness* ....................................................................

THESIS STATEMENT: ..............................................................................................................

...............................................................................................................................................

**5.** TOPIC: *weight training machines and free weights* ...........................................

WRITER'S POINT: *similarities and differences* ................................................................

THESIS STATEMENT: ..............................................................................................................

...............................................................................................................................................

# Logical Order

In an effective essay, body paragraphs are arranged in a clear, logical order for a coherent flow of ideas. Likewise, effective writers link each paragraph to the next so that readers can follow their chain of thought.

You can achieve a coherent flow of ideas in several logical ways.

1. *Follow the order of ideas as presented in the thesis statement.* Often the controlling idea of the thesis statement divides the topic into chunks of information.

2. *Follow space order.* At times, a writer describes how something is arranged in space to develop a main idea. Description moves from top to bottom, side to side, front to back, or the reverse of these.

3. *Follow time order.* A writer may record an event or a process as it unfolds in time.

4. *Present ideas in order of importance.* Often, a writer decides upon and arranges details according to his or her opinion about the importance of the details, known as **climactic order**. Usually, climactic order moves from the least important point in the first body paragraph and builds to the essay's climax, the most important point in the final body paragraph.

## COHERENCE TECHNIQUES: THESIS STATEMENT, SPACE, TIME, AND CLIMACTIC ORDER

Complete the exercises, and share your responses with your class or in a small group.

1. **Follow space order**. Write and arrange in space order three topic sentences (primary supports) suggested by the following thesis statement. Use the photograph to generate your primary supports.

   **I.** Introduction

   THESIS STATEMENT: *Although Goth fashion varies widely, the*

   *look makes a bold, nontraditional fashion statement.*

   **II.** ..................................................................................

   **III.** ..................................................................................

   **IV.** ..................................................................................

   **V.** Conclusion

◀ Goth fashion

2. **Follow time order.** Write and arrange in time order three topic sentences (primary supports) suggested by the following thesis statement. Use the photographs to generate your primary supports.

I. Introduction

THESIS STATEMENT: *Technology plays a key role in the restoration of Sand Key Beach, Florida.*

II. _____

_____

III. _____

_____

IV. _____

_____

V. _____

_____

VI. Conclusion

▲ Before restoration

▲ During restoration

▲ After restoration

3. **Present ideas in order of importance.** Write and arrange in climactic order three topic sentences (primary supports) suggested by the following thesis statement.

I. Introduction

THESIS STATEMENT: *Stress challenges us in almost every aspect of our lives.*

II. _____

_____

III. _____

_____

IV. _____

_____

V. Conclusion

Practice 5

# Connecting Paragraphs

In addition to ordering paragraphs coherently, writers clearly connect each paragraph to the next so that readers can follow their chain of thought. The following chart lists and illustrates several options to connect paragraphs to each other.

| Connecting Paragraphs |
| --- |

**Echo or repeat important words or phrases from the thesis statement in body paragraphs.**

| | |
| --- | --- |
| I. Thesis statement: | We can *ease* the *pain* that occurs from illness or injury in several different ways. |
| II. Topic sentence: | *Pain* can be *eased* by deep breathing. |
| III. Topic sentence: | Visualization and imagery *ease pain*. |

**Refer to the main idea of the previous paragraph in the topic sentence of the present paragraph.**

| | |
| --- | --- |
| I. Thesis statement: | Applying the principles of computer ergonomics reduces the chances of injury and fatigue. |
| II. Topic sentence: | The *computer screen* should be *placed properly* to avoid painful injuries to the neck. |
| III. Topic sentence: | *Proper placement* of the *monitor* not only *reduces* the possibility of *neck injury* but also eases eye fatigue. |

**Use transitional words, phrases, or sentences.**

| | |
| --- | --- |
| I. Thesis statement: | Sleep disorders can deprive sufferers of much needed rest and complicate their lives. |
| II. Topic sentence: | *One type* of sleep disorder is known as night terrors. |
| III. Topic sentence: | *Another type* of sleep disorder, nightmares, torments many people. |
| IV. Transition sentence and topic sentence: | *At least the previous two disorders occur in the privacy of one's home.* Narcolepsy, a *third kind* of sleep disorder, can occur suddenly anywhere, and at any time without warning. |

**Tie the last idea in one paragraph to the opening of the next paragraph.**

| | |
| --- | --- |
| I. Thesis statement: | Hurricane activity is on the rise, is likely to increase, and calls for new methods of preparation. |
| II. Topic sentence and ending idea of paragraph: | Hurricane activity is on the rise because of higher ocean temperatures and lower vertical wind shear. Therefore, these *climate changes* are likely to continue for as many as 10 to 40 years. |
| III. Topic sentence: | *These shifts in climate* call for new methods of hurricane preparation. |

## CONNECTING PARAGRAPHS

Read the following essay. Underline the connections between paragraphs. Circle the key ideas that are repeated throughout the essay. Discuss with your class or in a small group the different types of connections the writer used and evaluate their effectiveness.

### A Song of Humility

(1) The neighborhood of my youth hummed with the songs of our carefree play. (2) The beat of hammers building forts and the zings of the over-ripe ammunition of our orange wars in Winter Haven, Florida, blended beautifully with the music of the times. (3) The Beatles, and all the other really far-out groups, deafened us to any world but our very own. (4) No one was more deaf than I.

(5) At that time, I was particularly deaf to the family that lived two streets over and halfway down a dusty clay side road. (6) This out of sync family lived poorer than we did. (7) They grew their own food, raised chickens, and loved loud country music. (8) Every time I passed their house, I felt sorry for them, in a smug sort of way. (9) One afternoon the mama of that family labored up the hill to our house. (10) Her son had cut a record, and she "would be obliged if we was to listen to it" and tell her what we thought. (11) I was too busy marveling at her stained clothes and dusty feet to hear how respectfully my mother responded.

(12) Mother treated everyone with respect and tried to teach her children to do so as well. (13) She insisted that the whole family listen to the twangy tune about love and shirttails, but only I took great joy in mocking it. (14) Mother told me to return the record and say she thought it "a fine tune." (15) When I objected, she said, "Consider this an avoidable duty!" (16) I stood a long time studying the rusty door of that family's dust-covered house, wondering why I hadn't the courage to do my duty.

(17) Finally, my good friend Florence appeared at the end of the alley. (18) "Florence," I cried in great relief, "come here quick." (19) I ran to meet her, and we stood a few feet away with our backs turned from the door I so dreaded. (20) In the loud, exuberant tones of an inconsiderate child, I belted out the details of my dilemma. (21) "You ought to hear this … stupid … only hicks … and I have to … Hey, wait for me," I said to her retreating back. (22) I had hoped to push my obligation into her hands. (23) "Naw," she said without looking back, "I'm already late."

(24) So, I turned to do my hated duty. (25) Then I saw the son, the singer, dart from the door into the shadows of the house. (26) I wheeled about and cried, "Florence, come back." (27) I ran to her, begging, "He heard me. (28) What should I do? (29) He heard everything I said." (30) Florence shrugged and turned away. (31) I pivoted and marched to the steps. (32) The son stepped out to meet me. (33) My words resonated in the silence that loomed between us, and I cursed the supper time desertion of the dusky streets. (34) "Young lady," he said gently. (35) I looked at him. (36) "Thank ya for bringing back my demo."

(37) To this day, the timbre of his voice shames me. (38) I had mocked him, yet he sought to soothe my soul. (39) And, now, when I feel the deafness of prejudice threaten me, I remember the song of humility I learned that day from a fine young singer.

# Relevant Details

In an effective essay, the writer provides enough relevant details to adequately or thoroughly support the essay's main idea.

## Generate Details with a Writing Plan

Most writers generate details during the prewriting stage by listing or freewriting. Once you have generated an adequate amount of details, you need to organize them into a writing plan. Many writers use clustering or outlining to help them create a plan for the essay. Clustering and outlining are excellent ways to see if you have enough details to support the point of your essay.

Some writers begin the writing process by generating details, then drafting a thesis statement, while other writers draft a working thesis statement first and then generate details. The following two practice exercises offer you an opportunity to work with both approaches. In your own writing, you should experiment to see which approach works best for you.

Often, a writer uses a prewriting technique, such as a concept map, to generate primary and secondary details. Then, the writer drafts a working thesis statement to summarize the point of the details generated with the concept map.

### GENERATE DETAILS, DRAFT A THESIS, CREATE A WRITING PLAN

Study the following list of details. Create a writing plan by filling in the concept map with groups of details from the list. Then, write a one-sentence summary (a thesis statement) of the main point that they support.

respects others

functions of effective communication on the job

builds consensus

fosters team work

diffuses confrontations

states clear expectations

seeks solutions

remains professional

encourages input from others

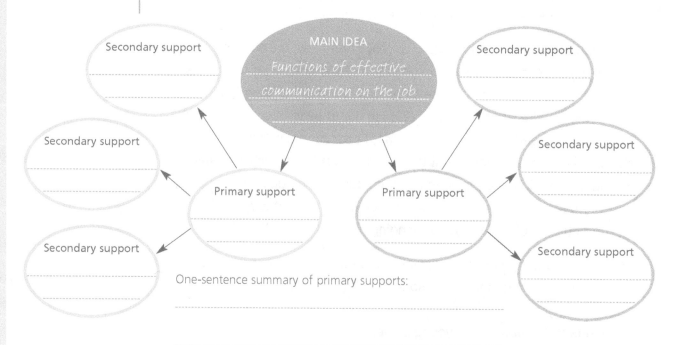

# Evaluate Details

In an effective essay, every detail supports the thesis statement. *All* the details work together as a unit to explain and support the writer's point. During the prewriting process, a writer brainstorms many details, some of which may not be related to the focus of the main idea. Therefore, as you create your writing plan, you should test the details to be sure that each one is relevant to the thesis statement. Drop those details that do not support either the thesis statement or the thesis statement's primary supports. You also may want to check details for relevance once more during the revision stage of the writing process.

**Practice 8**

---

### TESTING DETAILS FOR RELEVANCE

Study the following writing plan. Cross out details that are not relevant to the thesis statement. The following questions will help you test details for unity. Share your work with your class or in a small group of peers.

- What is the topic and controlling idea of the thesis statement? Circle the topic. Underline the controlling idea.

- Which details are the primary supporting details (the ones that will be used as topic sentences for body paragraphs)? Number the three primary supports A, B, and C.

- What are the secondary details? Number each secondary detail to correspond to a primary point: A1, A2, and so on; B1, B2, and so on; and C1, C2, and so on.

THESIS STATEMENT: *Due to the nature of lightning, you must follow lightning*

*safety guidelines to reduce risk of injury or death.*

........... Lightning is a complex event.

........... Lightning is described as having two components: leaders and strokes.

........... The leader is the probing feeler sent from the cloud.

........... The return streaks of light are a series of strokes that produce the actual lightning bolt or flash that we see.

........... Lightning is also common, unpredictable, and dangerous.

........... At any given moment, there are 1,800 thunderstorms in progress somewhere on the earth. This amounts to 16 million storms each year.

........... Lightning has been seen in volcanic eruptions, extremely intense forest fires, surface nuclear detonations, heavy snowstorms, and in large hurricanes.

........... No one can predict the location or time of the next stroke of lightning.

........... Lightning has been the second largest storm killer in the U.S. for the last 40 years, exceeded only by floods.

........... Following proven lightning safety guidelines can reduce your risk of injury or death.

........... Count the seconds between the time you see lightning and the time you hear the thunder.

........... You should already be in a safe location if that time is less than 30 seconds.

........... The safest location during lightning activity is an enclosed building.

........... Stay inside until 30 minutes after you last hear thunder.

# Effective Expression: Using a Thesaurus

One aspect of effective expression is choosing the precise word to convey your point with power and clarity. Effective writers often refer to a thesaurus to avoid repetition and to find the exact words needed to make their point. A thesaurus is a collection of words, their synonyms (words of similar meaning), and their antonyms (words of opposite meaning). Some thesauruses list words alphabetically: A–Z. Other thesauruses list words by types or groups of related words. You can find both kinds on the Internet. For example, *Roget's II: The New Thesaurus* 3rd ed. online at Bartleby.com offers both versions. You can find words by looking at the headwords as in the following two illustrations:

**Alphabetical Index:**

| A-1 | to | all right |
|-----|-----|-----------|
| all-round | to | atrocity |
| atrophy | to | big |

**Categorical Index:**

like, dislike

restraint, unrestraint

explosion, collapse

Features vary from thesaurus to thesaurus, so be sure to read the instructions on how to use a specific one. Some features include a main entry, parts of speech, a definition, a list of synonyms, a list of antonyms, field or usage labels (such as Law or slang), and a *see also* cross reference.

---

**EFFECTIVE EXPRESSION: USING A THESAURUS**

Study the two entries from *Roget's II: The New Thesaurus* 3rd ed.* Then, answer the questions.

**spew**

VERB: To send forth (confined matter) violently: belch, disgorge, eject, eruct, erupt, expel. Geology : extravasate. See EXPLOSION.

**extravasate**

VERB: Geology. To send forth (confined matter) violently: belch, disgorge, eject, eruct, erupt, expel, spew. See EXPLOSION.

1. What part of speech are these two words? _____

2. Is the word "Geology" a synonym, an antonym, or a field label? _____

3. Is the word "Explosion" in both entries a field label, a cross reference,

   or a synonym? _____

4. Insert a word from the entries that best completes the point of the following statement:
   Jeremiah's parents _____ their breath in relief as he safely completes
   his parachute jump.

*All examples from *Roget's II: The New Thesaurus* 3rd ed. Boston: Houghton Mifflin, 1995.

# Workshop: Writing an Essay Step by Step

To create an effective essay, use the complete writing process. Begin by prewriting; then, move on to drafting, revising, and editing. Writing rarely develops in a neat and orderly process. Some writers need to generate details before they can compose a working thesis statement. Others have to know exactly what their main point is before they can generate details. The following series of workshops encourages you to follow the prewriting steps in a certain order. Feel free to move between steps or to return to any step in the process as needed.

## Prewriting

During the prewriting stage, you figure out what you want to say, why you want to say it, and to whom you want to say it.

### Select and Narrow Your Topic

Select a topic on your own, pick a topic from a previous practice or workshop, or choose one of the following topics. Identify your audience and purpose.

- Movie heroes (or villains)
- Violence in sports
- Technology everyone should own
- A great achievement
- A fun activity
- Common fears

**TOPIC**
What you write

**AUDIENCE**
Who reads your writing

**PURPOSE**
Why you write

### Create a Tentative Thesis

Then, draft a tentative thesis statement.

TOPIC: .........................................................................................................................

AUDIENCE: ...................................................................................................................

PURPOSE: .....................................................................................................................

.....................................................................................................................................

THESIS STATEMENT: ....................................................................................................

.....................................................................................................................................

.....................................................................................................................................

# Generate Supporting Details with a Writing Plan

Generate primary and secondary supporting details by listing a writing plan or use the concept map to create a writing plan. Use the reporter's questions *who? what? when? where? why?* and *how?* to produce details.

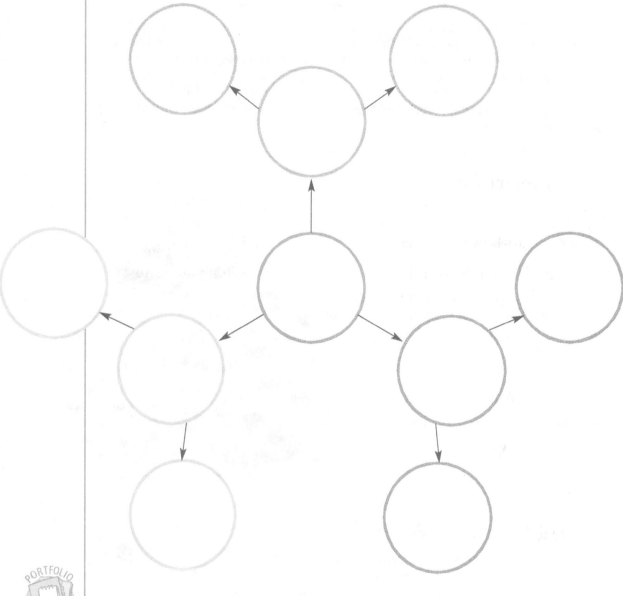

Now that you have generated some details to support your tentative thesis, you probably have a clearer sense of your controlling idea. The following thesis statement has been revised to focus the topic by including the writer's opinion and a pattern of organization.

TOPIC     WRITER'S POINT: CONTROLLING IDEA

Voter turnout remains dismal for several reasons.

OPINION     PATTERN OF ORGANIZATION (CAUSE AND EFFECT)

PORTFOLIO Workshop

## Revise Your Thesis Statement

Revise your thesis so that it includes the topic, your point about the topic, and, if appropriate, a pattern of organization.

REVISED THESIS STATEMENT:

_____

_____

## Evaluate Your Details

Use a writing plan to test your details. Complete the following outline with your revised thesis statement and details from your list or concept map. Make sure you have an adequate amount of details to convince your reader of your point. If you do not have the necessary major and minor details to support each topic sentence, brainstorm additional details. Delete details that are not related to your thesis statement or to the topic sentences (the primary supports for your thesis statement).

I.  INTRODUCTION

REVISED THESIS STATEMENT: _____

_____

_____

II. _____

_____

    A. _____

    B. _____

III. _____

_____

    A. _____

    B. _____

IV. CONCLUSION: _____

_____

PORTFOLIO

Workshop

# Write a Draft of Your Essay

Often, a writer pauses during the drafting stage of the writing process to scan what has been written so far, particularly when using a computer to write. Sometimes, while scanning, a writer may begin to make small revisions. Scanning may help a writer stay focused and can help with expression. However, you should resist the urge to spend very much time revising at this point. Your main purpose is to get a rough draft written. You can make effective revisions once you have a working draft.

Using your writing plan, write a rough draft of the body of your essay. Don't worry about the introduction and conclusion for now. Have a dictionary and thesaurus nearby just in case you get stuck trying to think of a word.

# Revise Your Essay Draft

Revision is much more than simply recopying the essay so that it is neater. A good revision requires time. So, put your essay aside for an hour or two, or even better, a day or two. You want to look at your essay with fresh eyes. Then, set aside enough time to revise your essay more than once—that way, you do not have to think of everything in one sitting. During the revising stage of your writing, think about your essay on two different levels: logic and style. The following chart offers you some helpful questions to guide you through your revision.

---

# Questions for Revising an Essay:

- ☐ Does the essay have a clearly stated thesis statement?
- ☐ Are my topic sentences clearly stated?
- ☐ Have I provided relevant support?
- ☐ Is each body paragraph fully developed with major and minor details as needed?
- ☐ Which ideas need more support?
- ☐ Is each topic sentence directly related to my thesis statement?
- ☐ Is each detail in each body paragraph related to its topic sentence?
- ☐ Have I used logical order?
- ☐ Have I provided clear connections between paragraphs?
- ☐ Have I provided clear connections between sentences within paragraphs?
- ☐ Have I used effective expression?
- ☐ Do my sentences vary in type and length?

---

Reread your essay, and as you revise, mark up your rough draft with the changes you intend to make: (1) cross out irrelevant details and vague, weak, or trite expressions, and write stronger words directly above or near them; (2) draw arrows to show where you want to move information; (3) add more details in the margin and draw a line to indicate where you will put them.

# One Student Writer's Revision Process

At the beginning of this chapter, you read the essay Lacey Durrance composed for her English class. Take a moment to reread her final draft on pages 522-523. Then, study her revisions of one draft of the essay's first two paragraphs. How does this draft differ from her final draft?

### Traits of a Successful College Student

(1) First-time college students don't realize the reality shock they will receive when they get to college. (2) High school and college atmospheres are extremely different in many ways. (3) Schools are larger; there are different teachers with different expectations, and different experiences. (4) College is a big part of growing up, and with growing up comes certain traits that you need to have to make it in college. (5) All first-time college students must have dedication, be responsible, and be independent, to get through college successfully. (6) Many won't realize this until it is too late and without these traits, they won't succeed.

(7) Dedication is the biggest part of being successful in college. (8) Students must want a good grade, and know what they need to do to achieve it. (9) Among my own personal experiences of being a first time college student, dedication has played a major part of being successful. (10) I had to change my learning process to adapt to college and so have former students. (11) Students must be hard working and take action to learn at a college level. (12) Things can't be left until the last minute like they might have been in high school. (13) College students can't only want a good grade, but must do the work to get that grade. (14) Dedication will get their work done and do it well. (15) College is very different in the sense that a lot is expected from students, and they won't be walked through anything.

# Proofreading Your Essay

Once you have revised your essay to your satisfaction, take time to carefully proofread your work. Check for the mistakes that you commonly make such as spelling errors, misplaced or missing commas, shifts in verb tense, or shifts in point of view. Publishing a clean, error-free draft proves you are committed to excellence and that you take pride in your work.

Proofread to correct spelling and grammar errors. Mark the corrections you need to make directly on the most recent draft of your essay. Create a neat, error-free draft of your essay.

---

**REVIEW:** UNDERSTANDING THE ESSAY

**1.** What are the four parts of an essay?

a. _____

b. _____

c. _____

d. _____

**2.** What are the four levels of information in an essay?

a. _____

b. _____

c. _____

d. _____

**3.** What are two types of details in an essay?

a. _____

b. _____

**4.** What are the two levels of secondary supports?

a. _____

b. _____

**5.** An effective essay supports a _____ idea with _____ details in _____ order and _____ expression.

**6.** What are the four phases of the writing process for composing an essay?

a. _____

b. _____

c. _____

d. _____

**7.** How will I use what I have learned about writing an essay? Discuss how you will apply to your own writing what you have learned about writing an essay.

-------------------------------------------------------------------

-------------------------------------------------------------------

-------------------------------------------------------------------

-------------------------------------------------------------------

-------------------------------------------------------------------

-------------------------------------------------------------------

-------------------------------------------------------------------

**8.** What do I still need to study about writing an essay? Discuss your ongoing study needs by describing what, when, and how you will continue studying about how to write an essay.

-------------------------------------------------------------------

-------------------------------------------------------------------

-------------------------------------------------------------------

-------------------------------------------------------------------

-------------------------------------------------------------------

-------------------------------------------------------------------

PORTFOLIO

Review

# Reading
# Selections

# Reading Selections

## Reading and writing are mirror reflections of the thinking process.

The connection between reading and writing is a natural one. Effective writers are often avid readers. They read and study well-written pieces by other writers as a strategy to become a better writer. To begin your thinking about the connection between reading and writing, complete the following activity.

# What's the Point of Reading to Write?

By reading, writers can learn new vocabulary, see how other writers organize ideas, add information to their bank of knowledge, and find ideas to write about.

---

**USING READING STRATEGIES TO RESPOND TO WRITING SELECTIONS**

Read the following excerpt from the selection, "Don't Call Me Middle Class: I'm a Professional" by Mark Penn (p. 591). Answer the questions that follow.

Not long ago, everyone in America wanted to be a member of the "middle class." In fact, as many as 53% of Americans described themselves that way to pollsters. 1

But with the information age and the rise of two-career incomes, being just middle class is a little old hat. The new aspiration for most Americans is to be a member of the new professional class. Rising numbers—as high as 64%—report that they consider themselves "professionals." The census shows a significant rise over the years, from 4% being professionals and skilled workers in 1910, to 36% today. The numbers have doubled since just 1980. 2

These new professionals, whose incomes were rising steadily until the financial crisis, have been at the heart of reshaping the country's economic and political life. Barack Obama more than any other president represents this shift and has uniquely appealed to these Americans. Everyone today wants to be a professional and most people believe they are. 3

1. What writing topics come to mind as you read these opening paragraphs?

2. What new words can you learn from reading this selection?

3. Based on these paragraphs, what kind of information do you need to define a concept?

*What's the point of reading to write?*

# Applying the Point: Effective Strategies for Responding to Reading Selections

The fundamental connection between reading and writing is thinking: thinking about the meaning of what you read and what you say, and thinking about the connection between what you read and what you write. To fully realize the connection between reading and writing, you need to be an active and focused thinker. Two active thinking-reading-writing tasks are annotating a text and writing a summary. The following discussions take you through several steps that show you how to think, read, think again, reread, and then write—as a strategy to improve your writing.

## How to Annotate a Text

Use your writing skills throughout the reading process to ensure that you are an active thinker. Annotate the text, take notes, and write journal entries, summaries, and critical responses to what you read. Annotating the text before and during reading is an active thinking-reading-writing strategy. You have been taught to ask questions as a prereading thinking task. When you read, annotate your text as you find the answers to your questions.

The word *annotate* suggests that you "take notes" on the page of the text. Writing notes in the margin of the page as you read focuses your attention and improves your concentration. Annotating also will improve your understanding of the writer's purpose and point. You can note questions or answers quickly where they occur, move on in your reading, and later return to those details for clarification. In addition to writing notes, you can underline, circle, or highlight important terms, definitions, examples, or other key ideas. After reading, a review of your annotations will make responding to the material easier and more efficient. The following techniques are often used to annotate a text. Use these as guidelines to develop your own system for annotating a text.

| **Annotation Techniques** |
|---|
| • Underline the main idea once. |
| • Underline major supporting details twice. |
| • Circle or highlight key words or special terms. |
| • Place small question marks above unknown words. |
| • Signal steps in a process or list by using numbers. |
| • Point out important concepts with symbols such as a star or a check. |
| • Write recall questions in the margin where the answer is found. |
| • Write a statement for an implied idea. |
| • Write a summary. |

Use your annotations to guide your written response to a piece of writing. The following selection has been annotated for you as an illustration.

## The Death of President Lincoln

### By Walt Whitman

*April 16, '65.*—I find in my notes of the time, this passage on the death of

Abraham Lincoln: He leaves for America's history and biography, so far, not only

                    *memories*

its most dramatic reminiscence—he leaves, in my opinion, the <u>greatest</u>, best, most

characteristic, artistic, <u>moral personality</u>. Not but that he had faults, and show'd

them in the Presidency; but honesty, goodness, shrewdness, conscience, and (a new

virtue, unknown to other lands, and hardly yet really known here, but the founda-

                    *Keeping the United States undivided!*

tion and tie of all, as the future will grandly develop,) UNIONISM, in its truest and

amplest sense, form'd the hard-pan of his character. These he <u>seal'd with his life</u>.

The tragic splendor of his death, purging, illuminating all, throws round his form,

        *?crown?*

his head, an aureole, that will remain and will grow brighter through time, while his-

tory lives, and love of country lasts. By many has this Union been help'd; but if one

               *legal guardian or keeper*

name, one man, must be pick'd out, he, most of all, is the <u>conservator</u> of it, to the

             *?French expression for "it will be fine"*

future. He was assassinated—but the Union is not assassinated—*ca ira!* One falls,

and another falls. The soldier drops, sinks like a wave—but the ranks of the ocean

                      *?*       *?*

eternally press on. Death does its work, obliterates, literates, a hundred, a thousand—

President, general, captain, private—but <u>the Nation is immortal</u>.

—Whitman, Walt. *Prose Works*. Philadelphia: David McKay, 1892;
Bartleby.com, 2000. www.bartleby.com/229/. 12 August 2007.

*Implied Main Idea: Lincoln preserved the UNION of the states; both he and the United States are immortal.*

---

Choose a selection from the nineteen reading selections. Annotate the text. After you have annotated the text, recall and record in your notebook what you remember about the selection.

*Practice 2*

# How to Write a Summary

A summary includes only the most important points of a text. A summary is a restatement of the main idea and the major supporting details. The length of the summary should reflect the length of the passage you are trying to understand. For example, a paragraph might be summarized in a sentence or two; an article might be summarized in a paragraph, and a much longer document may be summarized in several paragraphs.

Writing a summary by relying on the annotations you make during reading is an excellent way to check your understanding of what you read. Always use the writer's name and the title of the text in your summary. The following summary is based on the annotations of the Walt Whitman piece about Abraham Lincoln's death.

> In his short note "The Death of President Lincoln," dated April 16, 1865, Walt Whitman honors the memory of the fallen president for his devotion to "Unionism," for being a faithful keeper of the future, for ensuring that it will be fine and that the "Nation is immortal."

Write a summary based on the annotations you made for the reading selection you used in Practice 2. Use your own paper.

## A Reading Strategy for a Writer

As you read the nineteen selections included in this section, use the following reading strategy to make the connection between reading and writing. Read each selection three times. Read it once just to enjoy the writing. Then, reread the piece to annotate it for understanding. Then, read a third time to study the piece more closely to prepare for a written response. The following steps are a guide to how to get the most out of your reading.

# Reading Like a Writer

**Before Reading** Write a journal entry about the topic, title, and vocabulary. What do you already know, believe, or feel about the topic? Skim the text to identify and look up new or difficult words.

**During Reading** Annotate the text. Underline or highlight key terms, definitions, and main ideas. Generate questions to guide your thinking as you read; these questions will help you recall information after you read. Look for the answers to these questions and annotate the text when you come across the answers. Many college textbooks provide comprehension questions after a section of information. Feel free to use these after reading questions to focus your attention as you read.

**After Reading** Think, discuss, and write about what you read. Each of the nineteen reading selections has four discussion questions about the writer's main idea, relevant details, logical order, and effective expression. These directed thinking activities are called "After Reading Discussion Questions: Meaning, Structure, and Expression." Your writing will improve as you learn how other writers handle these elements.

**Discuss it** Use your annotations to compare your views about a text with those of your classmates. Be open to ideas you had not considered. Add information to your notes. Discuss possible written responses.

**Write about it** Respond in writing to the text. Each of the nineteen reading selections has two activities called "Thinking Prompts to Move from Reading to Writing."

# Twenty Reading Selections

## Description

## Snow

**JOHN HAINES**

John Haines, born in Norfolk, Virginia, in 1924, spent more than twenty years homesteading in Alaska. He is also an award-winning author of more than ten collections of poetry and has published a book of essays entitled *Fables and Distances: New and Selected Essays* (1996). The following essay is an excerpt from *The Stars, the Snow, the Fire: Twenty-five Years in the Northern Wilderness*.

**Before Reading** Write a journal entry about your experience with the outdoors. Do you enjoy being outdoors? Why or why not? What is your favorite season?

To one who lives in the snow and watches it day by day, it is a book to be read. The pages turn as the wind blows; the characters shift and the images formed by their combinations change in meaning, but the language remains the same. It is a shadow language, spoken by things that have gone by and will come again. The same text has been written there for thousands of years, though I was not here, and will not be here in winters to come, to read it. These seemingly random ways, these paths, these beds, these footprints, these hard, round pellets in the snow: they all have meaning. Dark things may be written there, news of other lives, their sorties and excursions, their terrors and deaths. The tiny feet of a shrew or a vole make a brief, erratic pattern across the snow, and here is a hole down which the animal goes. And now the track of an ermine comes this way, swift and searching, and he too goes down that white-shadow of a hole. 1

A wolverine, and the loping, toed-in track I followed uphill for two miles one spring morning, until it finally dropped away into another watershed and I gave up following it. I wanted to see where he would go and what he would do. But he just went on, certain of where he was going, and nothing came of it for me to see but that sure and steady track in the snowcrust, and the sunlight strong in my eyes. 2

Snow blows across the highway before me as I walk—little, wavering trails of it swept along like a people dispersed. The snow people—where are they 3

going? Some great danger must pursue them. They hurry and fall, the wind gives them a push, they get up and go on again.

I was walking home from Redmond Creek one morning late in January. On a divide between two watersheds I came upon the scene of a battle between a moose and three wolves. The story was written plainly in the snow at my feet. The wolves had come in from the west, following an old trail from the Salcha River, and had found the moose feeding in an open stretch of the overgrown road I was walking. 4

The sign was fresh, it must have happened the night before. The snow was torn up, with chunks of frozen moss and broken sticks scattered about; here and there, swatches of moose hair. A confusion of tracks in the trampled snow—the splayed, stabbing feet of the moose, the big, furred pads and spread toenails of the wolves. 5

I walked on, watching the snow. The moose was large and alone, almost certainly a bull. In one place he backed himself into a low, brush-hung bank to protect his rear. The wolves moved away from him—those moose feet are dangerous. The moose turned, ran on for fifty yards, and the fight began again. It became a running, broken flight that went on for nearly half a mile in the changing, rutted terrain, the red morning light coming across the hills from the sun low in the south. A pattern shifting and uncertain; the wolves relenting, running out into the brush in a wide circle, and closing again: another patch of moose hair in the trodden snow. 6

I felt that I knew those wolves. I had seen their tracks several times before during that winter, and once they had taken a marten from one of my traps. I believed them to be a female and two nearly grown pups. If I was right, she may have been teaching them how to hunt, and all that turmoil in the snow may have been the serious play of things that must kill to live. But I saw no blood sign that morning, and the moose seemed to have gotten the better of the fight. At the end of it he plunged away into thick alder brush. I saw his tracks, moving more slowly now, as he climbed through a low saddle, going north in the shallow, unbroken snow. The three wolves trotted east toward Banner Creek. 7

What might have been silence, an unwritten page, an absence, spoke to me as clearly as if I had been there to see it. I have imagined a man who might live as the coldest scholar on earth, who followed each clue in the snow, writing a book as he went. It would be the history of snow, the book of winter. A thousand-year text to be read by a people hunting these hills in a distant time. Who was here, and who has gone? What were their names? What did they kill and eat? Whom did they leave behind? 8

## Vocabulary   Before, during, and after reading the selection, annotate the text and write in your journal. Create a list of vocabulary words, along with their definitions. Give examples of their use from the selection you just read.

## After Reading Discussion Questions:   Meaning, Structure, and Expression

1. **Main Idea:** Work as a group to write a summary that answers the following questions: What purpose did John Haines have for writing this essay? Who is his intended audience? What is the main idea of the essay?
2. **Relevant Details:** Haines states "To one who lives in the snow and watches it day by day, it is a book to be read." How does the incident with the moose support this point?
3. **Logical Order:** Paragraphs 1 through 3 and paragraph 8 focus on the snow, and paragraphs 4 through 7 tell about the wolves and the moose. Would the essay be just as effective if it began with the incident about the wolves and the moose and then made the point about snow? Why or why not?

4. **Effective Expression:** According to a *Washington Post Book World* review, "Haines is a poet who crafts each sentence piece by piece . . . slowly, carefully, each word examined meticulously for rightness before being slid into place." Identify three examples of Haines's use of words that you find particularly effective. Discuss the reasons for your selections.

## Thinking Prompts to Move from Reading to Writing

1. Haines uses vivid sensory details in his descriptions of the snow, the wolves, and the moose to create strong visual images in his reader's mind. No doubt, he wrote what he had closely observed through experience. Use vivid sensory details to describe a place or event in nature that you have experienced. Choose details that make a point about the scene such as *nature soothes in times of trouble* or *nature teaches harsh lessons*.

2. Haines effectively describes the nature or temperament of the wolves and the moose based on their physical traits and behaviors. Write a description of a pet or animal that reveals its personality, temperament, or nature.

# Maya Lin's Design Submission to the Vietnam Memorial Competition

## MAYA LIN

Born in 1959 in Athens, Ohio, Maya Lin, as a senior at Yale University, submitted the winning design in a national competition for the Vietnam Veterans Memorial that now stands in Washington, D.C. Lin, a Chinese American, designs spaces that make room for individuals within the landscape.

**Before Reading** Write a journal entry about the Vietnam Memorial. What do you know about it? Have you seen it? What was its impact on you? If you have not seen it, do you want to? Why or why not? Why are monuments and memorials important?

Walking through this park-like area, the memorial appears as a rift in the earth—a long, polished black stone wall, emerging from and receding into the earth. Approaching the memorial, the ground slopes gently downward, and the low walls emerging on either side, growing out of the earth, extend and converge at a point below and ahead. Walking into the grassy site contained by the walls of the memorial we can barely make out the carved names upon the memorial's walls. These names, seemingly infinite in number, convey the sense of overwhelming numbers, while unifying those individuals into a whole. For this memorial is meant not as a monument to the individual but rather, as a memorial to the men and women who died during this war, as a whole.

The memorial is composed not as an unchanging monument, but as a moving composition, to be understood as we move into and out of it; the passage itself is gradual, the descent to the origin slow, but it is at the origin that the meaning of the memorial is to be fully understood. At the intersection of these walls, on the right side, at the wall's top, is carved the date of the first death. It is followed by the names of those who have died in the war, in chronological order. These names continue on this wall, appearing to recede into the earth at the wall's end. The names resume on the left wall, as the wall emerges from the earth, continuing back to the origin, where the date of the last death is carved, at the bottom of this wall. Thus the war's beginning and end meet; the war is "complete," coming full circle, yet

1

2

broken by the earth that bounds the angle's open side, and contained within the earth itself. As we turn to leave, we see these walls stretching into the distance, directing us to the Washington Monument, to the left, and the Lincoln Memorial, to the right, thus bringing the Vietnam Memorial into an historical context. We the living are brought to a concrete realization of these deaths.

Brought to a sharp awareness of such a loss, it is up to each individual to resolve or come to terms with this loss. For death, is in the end a personal and private matter, and the area contained with this memorial is a quiet place, meant for personal reflection and private reckoning. The black granite walls, each two hundred feet long, and ten feet below ground at their lowest point (gradually ascending toward ground level) effectively act as a sound barrier, yet are of such a height and length so as not to appear threatening or enclosing. The actual area is wide and shallow, allowing for a sense of privacy, and the sunlight from the memorial's southern exposure along with the grassy park surrounding and within its walls, contribute to the serenity of the area. Thus this memorial is for those who have died, and for us to remember them.

The memorial's origin is located approximately at the center of the site; its legs each extending two hundred feet towards the Washington Monument and the Lincoln Memorial. The walls, contained on one side by the earth, are ten feet below ground at their point of origin, gradually lessening in height, until they finally recede totally into the earth, at their ends. The walls are to be made of hard, polished black granite, with the names to be carved in simple Trajan letter. The memorial's construction involves recontouring the area within the wall's boundaries, so as to provide for an easily accessible descent, but as much of the site as possible should be left untouched. The area should remain as a park, for all to enjoy.

## Vocabulary
Before, during, and after reading the selection, annotate the text and write in your journal. Create a list of vocabulary words, along with their definitions. Give examples of their use from the selection you just read.

## After Reading Discussion Questions: Meaning, Structure, and Expression

1. **Main Idea:** Work as a group to write a summary that answers the following questions: What purpose did Maya Lin have for writing this essay? Who is her intended audience? What is the main idea of the essay?
2. **Relevant Details:** Lin writes, "For death, is in the end a personal and private matter, and the area contained with this memorial is a quiet place, meant for personal reflection and private reckoning." Based on the details in her description, how does the memorial represent this belief?
3. **Logical Order:** As Lin gives her physical description of the memorial, she explains the significance of each detail. Do her explanations help create a mental image of the memorial? Would it have been just as effective to give an uninterrupted physical description and then explain the purpose of each detail in a separate section? Why or why not?
4. **Effective Expression:** Of the 1,421 essays submitted in the design competition for the Vietnam Memorial, this essay won. In what ways did Lin use effective expression to communicate her vision? Identify three effective expressions in the essay. Discuss the reasons for your selections.

## Thinking Prompts to Move from Reading to Writing

1. Just as the memorials erected in Washington, D.C. represent people and events of historical significance, many communities build memorials to honor local individuals, groups of people, or events. Describe such a memorial in your community. Use your description to convey the significance of the memorial.
2. Identify a person, place, or event that is worthy of a memorial. Design a memorial and write an essay that describes your design and the significance of the honor.

# New Directions

## MAYA ANGELOU

An acclaimed poet, award-winning writer, activist, performer, director, and teacher, Maya Angelou was born on April 4, 1928, in St. Louis and raised in Stamps, Arkansas. Dr. Angelou has authored twelve bestselling books including *I Know Why the Caged Bird Sings* and her current bestseller *A Song Flung Up to Heaven*. In January 1993, she became only the second poet in U.S. history to have the honor of writing and reciting her original work at a Presidential Inauguration. Angelou is hailed as one of the great voices of contemporary literature. The following essay is an excerpt from her book *Wouldn't Take Nothing for My Journey Now* (1993).

**Before Reading** Write a journal entry about making a life change. Have you ever made a significant change in your life? What were the advantages or disadvantages of making the change? Was it easy? If life has not changed for you, what would you change about your life if you could?

In 1903 the late Mrs. Annie Johnson of Arkansas found herself with two toddling sons, very little money, a slight ability to read and add simple numbers. To this picture add a disastrous marriage and the burdensome fact that Mrs. Johnson was a Negro. 1

When she told her husband, Mr. William Johnson, of her dissatisfaction with their marriage, he conceded that he too found it to be less than he expected and had been secretly hoping to leave and study religion. He added that he thought God was calling him not only to preach but to do so in Enid, Oklahoma. He did not tell her that he knew a minister in Enid with whom he could study and who had a friendly, unmarried daughter. They parted amicably, Annie keeping the one-room house and William taking most of the cash to carry himself to Oklahoma. 2

Annie, over six feet tall, big-boned, decided that she would not go to work as a domestic and leave her "precious babes" to anyone else's care. There was no possibility of being hired at the town's cotton gin or lumber mill, but maybe there was a way to make the two factories work for her. In her words, "I looked up the road I was going and back the way I come, and since I wasn't satisfied, I decided to step off the road and cut me a new path." She told herself that she wasn't a fancy cook but that she could "mix groceries well enough to scare hunger away from a starving man." 3

She made her plans meticulously and in secret. One early evening to see if she was ready, she placed stones in two five gallon pails and carried them three miles to the cotton gin. She rested a little, and then, discarding some rocks, she walked in the darkness to the saw mill five miles farther along the dirt road. On her way back to her little house and her babies, she dumped the remaining rocks along the path. 4

That same night she worked into the early hours boiling chicken and frying ham. She made dough and filled the rolled-out pastry with meat. At last she went to sleep. 5

The next morning she left her house carrying the meat pies, lard, an iron brazier, and coals for a fire. Just before lunch she appeared in an empty lot behind the cotton gin. As the dinner noon bell rang, she dropped the savors into boiling fat, and the aroma rose and floated over to the workers who spilled out of the gin, covered with white lint, looking like specters. 6

Most workers had brought their lunches of pinto beans and biscuits or crackers, onions and cans of sardines, but they were tempted by the hot meat pies which Annie ladled out of the fat. She wrapped them in newspapers, which soaked up the grease, and offered them for sale at a nickel each. Although business was slow, those first days Annie was determined. She balanced her appearances between the two hours of activity. 7

So, on Monday if she offered hot fresh pies at the cotton gin and sold the remaining cooled-down pies at the lumber mill for three cents, then on Tuesday she went first to the lumber mill presenting fresh, just-cooked pies as the lumbermen covered in sawdust emerged from the mill. 8

For the next few years, on balmy spring days, blistering summer noons, and cold, wet, and wintry middays, Annie never disappointed her customers, who could count on seeing the tall, brown-skin woman bent over her brazier, carefully turning the meat pies. When she felt certain that the workers had become dependent on her, she built a stall between the two hives of industry and let the men run to her for their lunchtime provisions. 9

She had indeed stepped from the road which seemed to have been chosen for her and cut herself a brand-new path. In years that stall became a store where customers could buy cheese, meal, syrup, cookies, candy, writing tablets, pickles, canned goods, fresh fruit, soft drinks, coal, oil, and leather soles for worn-out shoes. 10

Each of us has the right and the responsibility to assess the roads which lie ahead, and those over which we have traveled, and if the future road looms ominous or unpromising, and the roads back uninviting, then we need to gather our resolve and, carrying only the necessary baggage, step off that road into another direction. If the new choice is also unpalatable, without embarrassment, we must be ready to change that as well. 11

**Vocabulary** Before, during, and after reading the selection, annotate the text and write in your journal. Create a list of vocabulary words, along with their definitions. Give examples of their use from the selection you just read.

## After Reading Discussion Questions: Meaning, Structure, and Expression

1. **Main Idea:** Work as a group to write a summary that answers the following questions: What purpose did Maya Angelou have for writing this piece? Who is her intended audience? What is the main idea of the essay? What is the significance of the title of the book from which the selection was taken? How does this piece reflect that title?

2. **Relevant Details:** Angelou captures the reality of daily life in 1903 for Annie Johnson and her community. List the details that paint this realistic picture; consider organizing your list based on sensory details. Describe the society or type of community in which Johnson lived. Are any of the details of this story similar to or different from today's society or parts of your community? In what ways?

3. **Logical Order:** Angelou ends her essay with a paragraph that explains the lesson she wants her reader to learn from Johnson's life. What is the impact of this paragraph on you as a reader? Is the concluding paragraph necessary? Why or why

not? Why do you think Angelou waits to the end of the essay to explain her point? Would the essay be as effective if she began by stating this point? Why or why not?

4. **Effective Expression:** A key statement in the essay is made by Annie Johnson, "I looked up the road I was going and back the way I come, and since I wasn't satisfied, I decided to step off the road and cut me a new path." Explain the meaning of the metaphors "road" and "path." What "road" was Johnson on? What "path" did she cut for herself? Are these metaphors effective? Why or why not?

## Thinking Prompts to Move from Reading to Writing

1. Think of an important lesson you have learned, or a truth about life that you think everyone needs to know. Write a narrative essay that illustrates this lesson or important truth about life.

2. Have you or someone you know made a decision to make a major life change? Was the change positive or negative? Was the change difficult to make? In the end, was the change worth the effort? Write a narrative that illustrates the significance of making a decision to change.

# Confessions

### AMY TAN

Born in 1952 to immigrant parents from China, Amy Tan is the award-winning author of several novels, including her widely popular and critically acclaimed novel *The Joy Luck Club*. Tragically, Tan's father and oldest brother both died of brain tumors within a year of each other, and Tan was in constant conflict with her mother. Tan's work has been translated into 35 languages, including Spanish, French, Chinese, Arabic, and Hebrew. The following selection is an excerpt from her autobiographical collection of essays *The Opposite of Fate*.

**Before Reading** Write a journal entry about the conflicts within a family. Have you ever had a terrible fight with a family member? How did it make you feel? Do mothers and daughters or fathers and sons experience a particular kind of conflict?

My mother's thoughts reach back like the winter tide, exposing the wreckage of a former shore. Often she's mired in 1967, 1968, the years my older brother and my father died.      1

1968 was also the year she took me and my little brother—Didi—across the Atlantic to Switzerland, a place so preposterously different that she knew she had to give up grieving simply to survive. That year, she remembers, she was very, very sad. I too remember. I was sixteen then, and I recall a late-night hour when my mother and I were arguing in the chalet, that tinderbox of emotion where we lived.      2

She had pushed me into the small bedroom we shared, and as she slapped me about the head, I backed into a corner, by a window that looked out on the lake, the Alps, the beautiful outside world. My mother was furious because I had a boyfriend. She was shouting that he was a drug addict, a bad man who would use me for sex and throw me away like leftover garbage.      3

"Stop seeing him!" she ordered.      4

I shook my head. The more she beat me, the more implacable I became, and this in turn fueled her outrage.  5

"You didn't love you daddy or Peter! When they die you not even sad."  6

I kept my face to the window, unmoved. What does she know about sad?  7

She sobbed and beat her chest. "I rather kill myself before see you destroy you life!"  8

Suicide. How many times had she threatened that before?  9

"I wish you the one die! Not Peter, not Daddy."  10

She had just confirmed what I had always suspected. Now she flew at me with her fists.  11

"I rather kill you! I rather see you die!"  12

And then, perhaps horrified by what she had just said, she fled the room. Thank God that was over. I wished I had a cigarette to smoke. Suddenly she was back. She slammed the door shut, latched it, then locked it with a key. I saw the flash of a meat cleaver just before she pushed me to the wall and brought the blade's edge to within an inch of my throat. Her eyes were like a wild animal's, shiny, fixated on the kill. In an excited voice she said, "First, I kill you. Then Didi and me, our whole family destroy!" She smiled, her chest heaving. "Why you don't cry?" She pressed the blade closer and I could feel her breath gusting.  13

Was she bluffing? If she did kill me, so what? Who would care? While she rambled, a voice within me was whimpering, "This is sad, this is so sad."  14

For ten minutes, fifteen, longer, I straddled these two thoughts—that it didn't matter if I died, that it would be eternally sad if I did—until all at once I felt a snap, then a rush of hope into a vacuum, and I was crying, I was babbling my confession: "I want to live. I want to live."  15

For twenty-five years I forgot that day, and when the memory of what happened surfaced unexpectedly at a writers' workshop in which we recalled our worst moments, I was shaking, wondering to myself, Did she really mean to kill me? If I had not pleaded with her, would she have pushed down on the cleaver and ended my life?  16

I wanted to go to my mother and ask. Yet I couldn't, not until much later, when she became forgetful and I learned she had Alzheimer's disease. I knew that if I didn't ask her certain questions now, I would never know the real answers.  17

So I asked.  18

"Angry? Slap you?" she said, and laughed. "No, no, *no*. You always good girl, never even need to spank, not even one time."  19

How wonderful to hear her say what was never true, yet now would be forever so.  20

## Vocabulary
Before, during, and after reading the selection, annotate the text and write in your journal. Create a list of vocabulary words, along with their definitions. Give examples of their use from the selection you just read.

## After Reading Discussion Questions: Meaning, Structure, and Expression

1. **Main Idea:** Work as a group to write a summary that answers the following questions: What purpose did Amy Tan have for writing this essay? Who is her intended audience? What is the main idea of the essay? What is the significance of the title?

2. **Relevant Details:** Tan often implies a main idea through the use of well-chosen details that draw a vivid picture. Paragraph 13 describes a shocking scene. What point is Tan making with these details? How do these details fulfill her purpose and support her main idea? Why would Tan reveal so much personal and painful information?

3. **Logical Order:** Tan sets her narrative up as a flashback to an unpleasant memory. Later, in paragraph 16, she tells us she remembered this incident in a writing workshop 25 years after it occurred. Why do you think she waited to tell us when or how she

remembered the incident? Would the essay be as effective if she had begun the narrative from the moment she recalled the incident in the workshop? Why or why not?

4. **Effective Expression:** Tan begins the essay with a simile, an indirect comparison between two things using *like* or *as*: "My mother's thoughts reach back like the winter tide, exposing the wreckage of a former shore." How are her mother's thoughts similar to the *winter tide*? To what do *wreckage* and *former shore* refer?

## Thinking Prompts to Move from Reading to Writing

1. The conflict between parent and child is age-old and universal. In her essay, Tan shows us how this timeless conflict affected her relationship with her mother. Write a narrative about a conflict between a parent and child that shows the impact of the conflict.

2. "Confessions" is a painful admission of a "worst moment" in both Amy Tan's life and her mother's life. Her confession reveals personal and potentially embarrassing information. Often, we gain wisdom and understanding through conflict and suffering. However, not every writer feels comfortable making a point through a personal confession. Find a story in the news about a "worst moment" in someone's life. Write a narrative that makes a point about the incident.

# How to Write a Personal Letter

## GARRISON KEILLOR

Born in Anoka, Minnesota, in 1942, Garrison Keillor is the host and writer of *A Prairie Home Companion* and *The Writer's Almanac* heard on public radio stations across the country and the author of more than a dozen books, including *Lake Wobegon Days, The Book of Guys, Love Me, Homegrown Democrat,* and *Pontoon: A Novel of Lake Wobegon.*

**Before Reading** Write a journal entry about letter writing. Do you or does anyone you know write letters? Why do you think letter writing is declining? How is writing a personal letter different from other kinds of writing?

We shy people need to write a letter now and then, or else we'll dry up and blow away. It's true. And I speak as one who loves to reach for the phone, dial the number, and talk. The telephone is to shyness what Hawaii is to February; it's a way out of the woods. *And yet* a letter is better. 1

Such a sweet gift—a piece of handmade writing, in an envelope that is not a bill, sitting in our friend's path when she trudges home from a long day spent among savages and wahoos, a day our words will help repair. They don't need to be immortal, just sincere. She can read them twice and again tomorrow: "You're someone I care about, Corinne, and think of often, and every time I do, you make me smile." 2

We need to write; otherwise, nobody will know who we are. They will have only a vague impression of us as "A Nice Person" because, frankly, we don't shine at conversation, we lack the confidence to thrust our faces forward and say, "Hi, I'm Heather Hooten; let me tell you about my week." Mostly we say "Uh-huh" and "Oh really." People smile and look over our shoulder, looking for someone else to meet. 3

So a shy person sits down and writes a letter. To be known by another person—to meet and talk freely on the page—to be close despite distance. To escape from anonymity and be our own sweet selves and express the music of our souls. The same thing that moves a giant rock star to sing his heart out in front of 123,000 people moves us to take ballpoint in hand and write a few lines to our dear Aunt Eleanor. *We want to be known.* We want her to know that we have fallen in love, that we have quit our job, that we're moving to New York, and we want to say a few things that might not get said in casual conversation: "Thank you for what you've meant to me. I am very happy right now." 4

The first step in writing letters is to get over the guilt of *not* writing. You don't "owe" anybody a letter. Letters are a gift. The burning shame you feel when you see unanswered mail makes it harder to pick up a pen and makes for a cheerless letter when you finally do. "I feel bad about not writing, but I've been so busy," etc. Skip this. Few letters are obligatory and they 5 are "Thanks for the wonderful gift" and "I am terribly sorry to hear about George's death" and "Yes, you're welcome to stay with us next month." Write these promptly if you want to keep your friends. Don't worry about other letters, except love letters, of course. When your true love writes, "Dear Light of My Life, Joy of My Heart, O Lovely Pulsating Core of My Sensate Life," some response is called for.

Some of the best letters are tossed off in a burst of inspiration, so keep your writing stuff in one place where you can sit down for a few minutes, and—"Dear Roy, I am in the middle of an essay but thought I'd drop you a line. Hi to your sweetie too"—dash off a note to a pal. Envelopes, stamps, address book, everything in a drawer so you can write fast when the pen is hot. A blank white 8" × 11" sheet can look as big as Montana if the pen's not so hot; try a smaller page and write boldly. Get a pen that makes a sensuous line, get a comfortable typewriter, a friendly word processor—whichever feels easy to the hand. 6

Sit for a few minutes with the blank sheet of paper in front of you, and meditate on the person you will write to; let your friend come to mind until you can almost see him or her in the room with you. Remember the last time you saw each other and how your friend looked and what you said and what perhaps was unsaid between you, and when your friend becomes real to you, start to write. Write the salutation, "Dear You," and take a deep breath and plunge in. A simple declarative sentence will do, followed by another and another. Talk about what you're doing and tell it like you were talking to us. Don't think about grammar, don't think about style, don't try to write dramatically, just give us your news. Where did you go, who did you see, what did they say, what do you think? 7

If you don't know where to begin, start with the present: "I'm sitting at the kitchen table on a rainy Saturday morning. Everyone is gone, and the house is quiet." Let your description of the present moment lead to something else; let the letter drift gently along. The toughest letter to crank out is one that is meant to impress, as we all know from writing job applications; if it's hard work to write a letter to a friend, maybe you're trying too hard to be terrific. A letter is only a report to someone who already likes you for reasons other than your brilliance. Take it easy. 8

Don't worry about form. It's not a term paper. When you come to the end of one episode, just start a new paragraph. You can go from a few lines about the sad state of pro football to the fight with your mother to your cat's urinary tract infection to a few thoughts on personal indebtedness and on to the kitchen sink and what's in it. The more you write, the easier it gets, and when you have a true friend to write to, a *compadre,* a soul sibling, then it's like driving a car; you just press on the gas. 9

Don't tear up the page and start over when you write a bad line; try to write your way out of it. Make mistakes and plunge on. Let the letter cook along and let yourself be bold. Outrage, confusion, love—whatever is in your mind, let it find a way to the page. Writing is a means of discovery, always, and when you come to the end and write "Yours ever" or "Hugs and Kisses," you'll know something that you didn't when you wrote "Dear Pal." 10

Probably your friend will put your letter away, and it'll be read again a few years from now, and it will improve with age. And forty years from now, your friend's grandkids will dig it out of the attic and read it, a sweet and precious relic that gives them a sudden clear glimpse of you and her and the world we old-timers knew. Your simple lines about where you went, who you saw, what they said, will speak to those children, and they will feel in their hearts the humanity of our times. 11

You can't pick up a phone and call the future and tell them about our times. You have to pick up a piece of paper. 12

**Vocabulary** Before, during, and after reading the selection, annotate the text and write in your journal. Create a list of vocabulary words, along with their definitions. Give examples of their use from the selection you just read.

## After Reading Discussion Questions: Meaning, Structure, and Expression

1. **Main Idea:** Work as a group to write a summary that answers the following questions: What purpose did Garrison Keillor have for writing this essay? Who is his intended audience? What is the main idea of the essay?
2. **Relevant Details:** Keillor's advice about how to write a personal letter does not begin until the fifth paragraph. How are the details in the first four paragraphs related to his main point? Would the essay be as effective without these paragraphs? Why or why not?
3. **Logical Order:** Keillor describes a step-by-step process for writing a personal letter. Map out the steps in the order he suggests them. Do you agree with his advice? Would you change the order of any of the steps? Would you add or delete any steps? Why or why not?
4. **Effective Expression:** Keillor is often praised for his light-hearted, easy-to-read style. Find three expressions that are amusing in tone. Explain the reasons for your selections.

## Thinking Prompts to Move from Reading to Writing

1. This essay offers clear instructions about how to write a letter based on Keillor's expertise in and understanding of the writing process. Think of a task or process that you understand or have mastered through experience. Write an essay that explains the significance of the task or process and the steps necessary to successfully accomplish it.
2. Keillor advises in paragraph 9, "Don't worry about form. It's not a term paper." His statement indicates differences among writing a personal letter for everyday life, writing a term paper for college life, and writing letters and reports for working life. How might the writing process change for each of these situations? Write an essay that describes how to write a term paper or a letter of application for a job. Use Keillor's essay as a model.

# How to Twitter
## JULIA ANGWIN

Julia Angwin is a mathematics major who fell in love with journalism after writing for her campus newspaper, *The Chicago Maroon*. Angwin became an award-winning journalist covering technology, media, copyright issues, and corporate corruption. She currently serves as technology editor and columnist for the *Wall Street Journal*. She has also authored the book *Stealing MySpace*, about the "swift rise and deep cultural impact" of the social networking site MySpace.

**Before Reading** Write a journal entry about your experiences with electronic communication. Do you e-mail, text, or blog? Do you use Facebook, MySpace, or Twitter? Which do you prefer and why?

When I first joined Twitter, I felt like I was in a noisy bar where everyone was shouting and nobody was listening.

Soon, I began to decode its many mysteries: how to find a flock of followers, how to talk to them in a medium that blasts to lots of people at once and how to be witty in very tiny doses.

Twitter is a mass text-messaging service that allows you to send short 140-character updates—or "tweets"—to a bunch of people at once. They are your "followers." It was designed to be read on a cellphone, though many people read it online, too.

Suddenly a lot of non-tweeters are starting to feel left out. On "The Daily Show" this week, host Jon Stewart reported on Twitter with a wink (or was it a twink?) at the narcissism of the personal broadcasting system. It has a world-wide audience of six million unique visitors a month, up from 1.2 million a year ago, according to ComScore Media Metrix.

But I have to admit I didn't understand the appeal of Twitter when I joined, at the prodding of friends, in November. One answer that explains its popularity: It's not about chatting with your friends—it's about promoting yourself.

My name was available, so I set up a profile at twitter.com/JuliaAngwin. On Twitter, however, you do not exist without followers, who subscribe to receive your messages. So I set out to follow some people in the hope that they would follow me.

I had to learn the crucial distinction between a "follower" and a "friend." On Facebook, if I'm your friend, you're my friend, and we can read all about each other. Relationships on Twitter are not reciprocal: People you follow do not have to follow you or give you permission to follow them. You just sign up and start following them. It's a bit like stalking. Heather Gold, a comedian and Twitter devotee, points out that for all its flaws, the term follower "is more honest than friend."

At first, I was the loneliest of social creatures—a leader without followers. I tried searching for my actual real-world friends using Twitter's "Find People" function, but it was down the day I joined. (Twitter is growing so fast that short outages are not unusual.)

So I asked a few colleagues for their Twitter addresses and began following them. I also searched their public lists of followers and who they followed.

Eventually, I cobbled together a mix of people I could follow: media colleagues, friends, bloggers and various people who are known as great "tweeters," such as the chief executive of online retailer Zappos.com, Tony Hsieh, who has written quite movingly on his blog about how Twitter has changed his life. He says that being forced to bear witness to his life in 140-character bursts of prose has made him more grateful for the good moments and more amused by the bad moments.

I discovered that a better way to get followers was to tweet. Every time I tweeted, I got a surge of followers.

Where were they coming from? The likely answer illuminates Twitter's greatest strength: It's easily searchable.

During the terrorist attacks in Mumbai in November, people scoured Twitter for postings from eye witnesses. When US Airways Flight 1549 landed in the Hudson River, one of the first pictures was posted as a link on Twitter.

Similar news items may have appeared on other social networks, but they were not as easy to discover. On Facebook, most people's information is viewable only by their approved friends. MySpace profile pages are searchable, but not its blogs or status updates, and it is hard to find anyone you know because most people obscure their real names.

Now, a gaggle of unknown followers were finding something in my tweets—and following me!

I quickly found that my general musings about life such as—"thank god they have wifi on jury duty"—fell like a dead weight, eliciting no response. A larger problem was that it was hard to tweet when I didn't know whom I was tweeting to. Unlike Facebook, where I know each and every one of my 287 friends, I have never met or heard of the majority of the 221 people following me on Twitter.

To understand the medium, I studied others' tweets. Former *Time* magazine writer Ana Marie Cox's tweets are a poetic mix of moments like this: "Afternoon walk. Beautiful day, I now see."

And she included wry political commentary. Forwarding a tweet from Sen. John McCain during the presidential election, she wrote: "See, if only he had sent this a year earlier . . . RT@senjohnmccain 'YEs!! I am twittering on my blackberry but not without a little help!' "

I spent a surprising amount of time trying out tweets in my head before tweeting. I aimed to tweet once a day, but often came up short. I found it difficult to fit in both news and opinion. Without a point of view, though, my updates were pretty boring. So, for instance, I changed "eating strawberries during a snowstorm." Into "eating strawberries during a snowstorm. not carbon efficient but lovely."

Another trick: including a short link to a Web site, or my own stories (using link-shrinking services like TinyURL), let me use most of the rest of the 140 characters to compose a thought.

I found a good way to get followers was to get "retweeted"—meaning that someone would pick up my tweet and send it to their followers preceded by the code "RT @juliaangwin." When I tweeted about being interviewed by Wired.com recently, two colleagues retweeted my tweet. Seven of their followers then retweeted it. As a result, I gained 22 new followers.

People also seem eager to answer questions on Twitter. I came across 25-year-old Justin Rockwell, who was spending so much time answering people's tweets about how to build better Web pages that he says he decided to try it as a business. He now makes about $350 a week scouring Twitter for people tweeting about their problems building Web pages. Using the Twitter ID ThatCSSGuy (which refers to a Web program called CSS), he offers to help solve their problems and asks for a tip in return.

But I found it difficult to acknowledge answers I received on Twitter. Twitter's reply features felt clumsy. The easiest way to reply to a tweet is to hit the @reply icon which broadcasts your answer to all your followers, essentially Twitter's equivalent of the "reply all" email function. As a result, I often didn't reply because I didn't want to spam everyone with a bunch of "thanks for your feedback" messages. So I was silent—which made me feel even more antisocial.

Twitter wasn't designed for these kinds of social interaction or conversations. As Twitter co-founder Biz Stone told me, "Twitter is fundamentally a broadcast system." The messaging features were add-ons.

Twitter is useful precisely because so many people are talking about different things at once. When he was president of Sling Media, for instance, Jason Hirschhorn constantly monitored the keyword "sling" on Twitter. "It's an up-to-the minute temperature of what people are saying about your brand," he said. He left the consumer electronics company last month.

There are more than 2,000 Twitter applications made by other people to help you sort through all the tweets. One of my favorites is Twitturly.com, which tracks the most popular URLs (or Web links) being shared across Twitter. Others such as Tweetdeck and Twhirl, help you manage and organize your tweets.

Still, the beauty of Twitter is that you don't have to commit to it; no one expects you to read all the tweets rolling in. As a result, Twitter makes for very good people watching—even if you don't go home with anyone you meet there.

**Vocabulary** Before, during, and after reading the selection, annotate the text and write in your journal. Create a list of vocabulary words, along with their definitions. Give examples of their use from the selection you just read.

## After Reading Discussion Questions: Meaning, Structure, and Expression

1. **Main Idea:** Work as a group to write a summary that answers the following questions: What purpose did Julia Angwin have for writing this essay? Who is the intended audience? What is the main idea of the essay?
2. **Relevant Details:** Angwin offers details that explain some of the difficulties she faced as she started to "tweet." Why does she offer these details? Would readers be more likely to use Twitter if she hadn't talked about the barriers she faced? Angwin also offers helpful hints about how to use Twitter. Are these hints distracting or are they effective pieces of information? Why?
3. **Logical Order:** Angwin describes the steps she took to join and use Twitter. Based on the details in her essay, create an outline guide that anyone could follow to join and use Twitter.
4. **Effective Expression:** Based on Angwin's choice of words, how would you describe the tone of this essay? Is the tone objective, humorous, critical, or supportive, or does it communicate some other attitude about Twitter? How does the tone of the essay help Angwin make her point? Explain your reasoning.

## Thinking Prompts to Move from Reading to Writing

1. According to the passage, messages on Twitter are "140-character updates—or 'tweets'". Critics of these "tweets" complain that this type of writing hurts the development of good writing skills. Supporters disagree and argue that using Twitter will actually improve writing skills. What do you think? Explain how the process of tweeting can improve or harm a person's writing style.
2. Compare or contrast "How to Write a Personal Letter" with "How to Twitter." Choose an audience and writing situation such as the following: an academic paper for a communication class, a letter to the editor of a local newspaper, an article for a magazine or newspaper's online community forum.

# My Prison Studies
**MALCOLM X with ALEX HALEY**

Malcolm X was an extraordinary leader of the black power movement in the 1960s. The son of a Baptist minister, he was born Malcolm Little in 1925 in Omaha, Nebraska. He dropped out of school in the eighth grade and moved to New York. There he became involved with drugs and was arrested and sentenced for burglary in 1946. While serving a ten-year sentence in prison, he became a member of Elijah Muhammad's Black Muslim sect, which preached that all whites are evil. Eventually he became disillusioned with Muhammad's teachings and made a pilgrimage to Mecca, Islam's holiest city. Prior to his murder in 1964, he advocated black self-help and education and began working to establish cooperative relationships between blacks and whites.

In this excerpt from his autobiography, Malcolm X describes how he taught himself to read in prison. As you read it, notice the stages involved in his processes of learning.

1    Many who today hear me somewhere in person, or on television, or those who read something I've said, will think I went to school far beyond the eighth grade. This impression is due entirely to my prison studies.

2    It had really begun back in the Charlestown Prison, when Bimbi [a prison inmate] first made me feel envy of his stock of knowledge. Bimbi had always taken charge of any conversation he was in, and I had tried to emulate him. But every book I picked up had a few sentences which didn't contain anywhere from one to nearly all of the words that might as well have been in Chinese. When I just skipped those words, of course, I really ended up with little idea of what the book said. So I had come to the Norfolk Prison Colony still going through only book-reading motions. Pretty soon, I would have quit even these motions, unless I had received the motivation that I did.

3    I saw that the best thing I could do was get hold of a dictionary—to study, to learn some words. I was lucky enough to reason also that I should try to improve my penmanship. It was sad. I couldn't even write in a straight line. It was both ideas together that moved me to request a dictionary along with some tablets and pencils from the Norfolk Prison Colony school.

4    I spent two days just riffling uncertainly through the dictionary's pages. I'd never realized so many words existed! I didn't know which words I needed to learn. Finally, to start some kind of action, I began copying.

5    In my slow, painstaking, ragged handwriting, I copied into my tablet everything printed on that first page, down to the punctuation marks.

6    I believe it took me a day. Then, aloud, I read back, to myself, everything I'd written on the tablet. Over and over, aloud, to myself, I read my own handwriting.

7    I woke up the next morning, thinking about those words—immensely proud to realize that not only had I written so much at one time, but I'd written words that I never knew were in the world. Moreover, with a little effort, I also could remember what many of these words meant. I reviewed the words whose meanings I didn't remember. Funny thing, from the dictionary first page right now, that "aardvark" springs to my mind. The dictionary had a picture of it, a long-tailed, long-eared, burrowing African mammal, which lives off termites caught by sticking out its tongue as an anteater does for ants.

8    I was so fascinated that I went on—I copied the dictionary's next page. And the same experience came when I studied that. With every succeeding page, I also learned of people and places and events from history. Actually the dictionary is like a miniature encyclopedia. Finally the dictionary's A section had filled a whole tablet—and I went on into the B's. That was the way I started copying what eventually became the entire dictionary. It went a lot faster after so much practice helped me to pick up handwriting speed. Between what I wrote in my tablet, and writing letters, during the rest of my time in prison I would guess I wrote a million words.

8

9    I suppose it was inevitable that as my word-base broadened, I could for the first time pick up a book and read and now begin to understand what the book was saying. Anyone who has read a great deal can imagine the new world that opened. Let me tell you something; from then until I left that prison, in every free moment I had, if I was not reading in the library, I was reading on my bunk. You couldn't have gotten me out of books with a wedge. Between Mr. Muhammad's teachings, my correspondence, my visitors—usually Ella and Reginald—and my reading of books, months passed without my even thinking about being imprisoned. In fact, up to then, I never had been so truly free in my life.

9

10    The Norfolk Prison Colony's library was in the school building. A variety of classes was taught by instructors who came from such places as Harvard and Boston universities. The weekly debates between inmate teams were also held in the school building. You would be astonished to know how worked up convict debaters and audiences would get over subjects like "Should babies be fed milk?"

10

11    Available on the prison library's shelves were books on just about every general subject. . . . Some of them looked ancient: covers faded, old-time parchment-looking binding. . . . Any college library would have been lucky to get that collection.

11

12    As you can imagine, especially in a prison where there was heavy emphasis on rehabilitation, an inmate was smiled upon if he demonstrated an unusually intense interest in books. There was a sizable number of well-read inmates, especially the popular debaters. Some were said by many to be practically walking encyclopedias. They were almost celebrities. No university would ask any student to devour literature as I did when this new world opened to me, of being able to read and understand.

12

13    I read more in my room than in the library itself. An inmate who was known to read a lot could check out more than the permitted maximum number of books. I preferred reading in the total isolation of my own room.

13

14    When I had progressed to really serious reading, every night at about ten P.M. I would be outraged with the "lights out." It always seemed to catch me right in the middle of something engrossing.

14

15    Fortunately, right outside my door was a corridor light that cast a glow into my room. The glow was enough to read by, once my eyes adjusted to it. So when "lights out" came, I would sit on the floor where I could continue reading in that glow.

15

16    At one-hour intervals the night guards paced past every room. Each time I heard the approaching footsteps, I jumped into bed and feigned sleep. And as soon as the guard passed, I got back out of bed onto the floor area of that light-glow, where I would read for another fifty-eight minutes—until the guard approached again. That went on until three or four every morning. Three or four hours of sleep

16

a night was enough for me. Often in the years in the streets I had slept less than that. . . .

17    I have often reflected upon the new vistas that reading opened to me. I knew right there in prison that reading had changed forever the course of my life. As I see it today, the ability to read awoke inside me some long dormant craving to be mentally alive. I certainly wasn't seeking any degree, the way a college confers a status symbol upon its students. My homemade education gave me, with every additional book that I read, a little bit more sensitivity to the deafness, dumbness, and blindness that was afflicting the black race in America. Not long ago, an English writer telephoned me from London, asking questions. One was, "What's your alma mater?" I told him, "Books." You will never catch me with a free fifteen minutes in which I'm not studying something I feel might be able to help the black man.

## Questions for Analysis

1. What is the thesis statement in the first paragraph? Underline it.

2. What, according to Malcolm X, made him decide that he had to learn to read?

3. What at first stopped Malcolm X from reading? What did he have to do before he could progress in reading?

4. How many steps or stages in the process of learning to read does Malcolm X discuss? Number them.

5. At one point he explains, "I never had been so truly free in my life." What makes him feel this way?

6. What point does Malcolm X make at the end of this excerpt?

## Suggestions for Writing

1. Malcolm X claims that college is mostly a status symbol. Do you agree or disagree? Explain your position.

2. Has anyone ever inspired you to learn something new or to achieve something difficult? Describe how the person inspired you.

3. Describe the process you went through to learn a new skill—whether in school, at home, or in some sport.

# Don't Call Me a Hot Tamale

## JUDITH ORTIZ COFER

Born in 1952 in Puerto Rico and raised in Paterson, New Jersey, Judith Ortiz Cofer is an acclaimed poet, novelist, and essayist. Her writings explore the experiences of being a minority as a Hispanic woman. She is currently the Regents' and Franklin Professor of English and Creative Writing at the University of Georgia.

**Before Reading** Write a journal entry about your experiences with stereotypes. Have you ever been stereotyped? Describe the incident. What are some common stereotypes in our culture? How are these stereotypes harmful?

On a bus to London from Oxford University, where I was earning some graduate credits one summer, a young man, obviously fresh from a pub, approached my seat. With both hands over his heart, he went down on his knees in the aisle and broke into an Irish tenor's rendition of "Maria" from *West Side Story*. I was not amused. "Maria" had followed me to London, reminding me of a prime fact of my life: You can leave the island of Puerto Rico, master the English language, and travel as far as you can, but if you're a Latina, especially one who so clearly belongs to Rita Moreno's gene pool, the island travels with you. 1

Growing up in New Jersey and wanting most of all to belong, I lived in two completely different worlds. My parents designed our life as a microcosm of their *casas* on the island—we spoke in Spanish, ate Puerto Rican food bought at the *bodega,* and practiced strict Catholicism complete with Sunday mass in Spanish. 2

I was kept under tight surveillance by my parents, since my virtue and modesty were, by their cultural equation, the same as their honor. As teenagers, my friends and I were lectured constantly on how to behave as proper *señoritas.* But it was a conflicting message we received, since our Puerto Rican mothers also encouraged us to look and act like women by dressing us in clothes our Anglo schoolmates and their mothers found too "mature" and flashy. I often felt humiliated when I appeared at an American friend's birthday party wearing a dress more suitable for a semiformal. At Puerto Rican festivities, neither the music nor the colors we wore could be too loud. 3

I remember Career Day in high school, when our teachers told us to come dressed as if for a job interview. That morning, I agonized in front of my closet, trying to figure out what a "career girl" would wear, because the only model I had was Marlo Thomas on TV. To me and my Puerto Rican girlfriends, dressing up meant wearing our mother's ornate jewelry and clothing. 4

At school that day, the teachers assailed us for wearing "everything at once"—meaning too much jewelry and too many accessories. And it was painfully obvious that the other students 5 in their tailored skirts and silk blouses thought we were hopeless and vulgar. The way they looked at us was a taste of the cultural clash that awaited us in the real world, where prospective employers and men on the street would often misinterpret our tight skirts and bright colors as a come-on.

It is custom, not chromosomes, that leads us to choose scarlet over pale pink. Our mothers had grown up on a tropical island where the natural environment was a riot of primary colors, where showing your skin was one way to keep cool as well as to look sexy. On the island, women felt freer to dress and move provocatively since they were protected by the traditions and laws of a Spanish/Catholic system of morality and machismo, the main rule of which was: *You may look at my sister, but if you touch her I will kill you.* The extended family and church structure provided them with a circle of safety on the island; if a man "wronged" a girl, everyone would close in to save her family honor. 6

Off-island, signals often get mixed. When a Puerto Rican girl who is dressed in her idea of what is attractive meets a man from the mainstream culture who has been trained to react to certain types of clothing as a sexual signal, a clash is likely to take place. She is seen as a Hot Tamale, a sexual firebrand. I learned this lesson at my first formal dance when my date leaned over and painfully planted a sloppy, overeager kiss on my mouth. When I didn't respond with sufficient passion, he said in a resentful tone: "I thought you Latin girls were supposed to mature early." It was only the first time I would feel like a fruit or vegetable—I was supposed to *ripen,* not just grow into womanhood like other girls. 7

These stereotypes, though rarer, still surface in my life. I recently stayed at a classy metropolitan hotel. After having dinner with a friend, I was returning to my room when a middle-aged man in a tuxedo stepped directly into my path. With his champagne glass extended toward me, he exclaimed, "Evita!" 8

Blocking my way, he bellowed the song "Don't Cry for Me, Argentina." Playing to the gathering crowd, he began to sing loudly a ditty to the tune of "La Bamba"—except the lyrics were about a girl named Maria whose exploits all rhymed with her name and gonorrhea. 9

I knew that this same man—probably a corporate executive, even worldly by most standards—would never have regaled a white woman with a dirty song in public. But to him, I was just a character in his universe of "others," all cartoons. 10

Still, I am one of the lucky ones. There are thousands of Latinas without the privilege of the education that my parents gave me. For them every day is a struggle against the misconceptions perpetuated by the myth of the Latina as whore, domestic worker or criminal. 11

Rather than fight these pervasive stereotypes, I try to replace them with a more interesting set of realities. I travel around the U.S. reading from my books of poetry and my novel. With the stories I tell, the dreams and fears I examine in my work, I try to get my audience past the particulars of my skin color, my accent or my clothes. 12

I once wrote a poem in which I called Latinas "God's brown daughters." It is really a prayer, of sorts, for communication and respect. In it, Latin women pray "in Spanish to an Anglo God / with a Jewish heritage," and they are "fervently hoping / that if not omnipotent, / at least He be bilingual." 13

**Vocabulary** Before, during, and after reading the selection, annotate the text and write in your journal. Create a list of vocabulary words, along with their definitions. Give examples of their use from the selection you just read.

## After Reading Discussion Questions: Meaning, Structure, and Expression

1. **Main Idea:** Work as a group to write a summary that answers the following questions: What purpose did Judith Ortiz Cofer have for writing this essay? Who is her intended audience? What is the main idea of the essay? What is the significance of the title?
2. **Relevant Details:** Cofer relies mostly on personal experience to make her point about stereotypes based on race or gender. Does she provide enough details to make her point convincingly? Would the use of facts or expert opinions strengthen her point? Why or why not?
3. **Logical Order:** Cofer opens her essay with an example from her personal life. Is this an effective opening for the essay? Why or why not? Compare the introduction of the essay to the conclusion. How does the conclusion relate to the introduction? Is this an effective conclusion? Why or why not? What other ways could Cofer have opened or closed her essay?
4. **Effective Expression:** Based on Judith Ortiz Cofer's choice of words, how would you describe the tone of this essay? Is it angry, embarrassed, disappointed, confrontational, or candid, or does it communicate some other attitude about stereotypes? Identify three expressions that illustrate the tone of the piece. Explain the reasons for your selections.

## Thinking Prompts to Move from Reading to Writing

1. Cofer makes a connection between culture and fashion. According to her description, Hispanic fashion for women is "flashy," "mature," and "sexy" with "ornate jewelry" and "tight skirts and bright colors." Write an essay in which you illustrate how fashion represents a particular culture. For example, illustrate fashion in the Hip-Hop culture.
2. Cofer's essay illustrates the stereotypes she faces as a Hispanic woman. Identify and describe a stereotype that you or someone you know has encountered. For example, what are some stereotypes that elderly people face?

# Italy! Say It Like You Eat It; or 36 Tales about the Pursuit of Pleasure
## EXCERPT FROM *EAT, PRAY, LOVE*

Elizabeth Gilbert is a noted author of short stories, novels, and nonfiction. Her most recent book is the *New York Times* #1 best-selling memoir *Eat, Pray, Love* about the year she spent traveling the world alone after a difficult divorce. Much of her writing has been optioned by Hollywood. Her *GQ* memoir about her bartending years became the Disney movie "Coyote Ugly."

**Before Reading** Write a journal entry about self-discovery and growth. How can going through difficult times make you—or anyone—stronger or wiser? If you could go anywhere, where would you go to learn more about the world and yourself? Why?

In every major city in the Western World, some things are always the same. The same African men are always selling knockoffs of the same designer handbags and sunglasses, and the same Guatemalan musicians are always playing "I'd rather be a sparrow than a snail" on their bamboo windpipes. But some things are only in Rome. Like the sandwich counterman so comfortably calling me "beautiful" every time we speak. *You want this panino grilled or*

1

*cold, bella?* Or the couples making out all over the place, like there is some contest for it, twisting into each other on benches, stroking each other's hair and crotches, nuzzling and grinding ceaselessly . . .

And then there are the fountains. Pliny the Elder wrote once: "If anyone will consider the abundance of Rome's public supply of water, for baths, cisterns, ditches, houses, gardens, villas; and take into account the distance over which it travels, the arches reared, the mountains pierced, the valleys spanned—he will admit that there never was anything more marvelous in the whole world."

A few centuries later, I already have a few contenders for my favorite fountain in Rome. One is in the Villa Borghese. In the center of this fountain is a frolicking bronze family. Dad is a faun and Mom is a regular human woman. They have a baby who enjoys eating grapes. Mom and Dad are in a strange position—facing each other, grabbing each other's wrists, both of them leaning back. It's hard to tell whether they are yanking against each other in strife or swinging around merrily, but there's lots of energy there. Either way, Junior sits perched atop their wrists, right between them, unaffected by their merriment or strife, munching on his bunch of grapes. His little cloven hoofs dangle below him as he eats. (He takes after his father.)

It is early September, 2003. The weather is warm and lazy. By this, my fourth day in Rome, my shadow has still not darkened the doorway of a church or a museum, nor have I even looked at a guidebook. But I have been walking endlessly and aimlessly, and I did finally find a tiny little place that a friendly bus driver informed me sells The Best Gelato in Rome. It's called "Il Gelato di San Crispino." I'm not sure, but I think this might translate as "the ice cream of the crispy saint." I tried a combination of the honey and the hazelnut. I came back later that same day for the grapefruit and the melon. Then, after dinner that same night, I walked all the way back over there one last time, just to sample a cup of the cinnamon-ginger.

I've been trying to read through one newspaper article every day, no matter how long it takes. I look up approximately every third word in my dictionary. Today's news was fascinating. Hard to imagine a more dramatic headline than *"Obesita! I Bambini Italiani Sana i Piu Grassi d'Europa!"* Good God! Obesity! The article, I think, is declaring that Italian babies are the fattest babies in Europe! Reading on, I learn that Italian babies are significantly fatter than German babies and very significantly fatter than French babies. (Mercifully, there was no mention of how they measure up against American babies.) Older Italian children are dangerously obese these days, too, says the article. (The pasta industry defended itself.) These alarming statistics on Italian child fatness were unveiled yesterday by—no need to translate here—*"una task force internazionale"* It took me almost an hour to decipher this whole article. The entire time, I was eating a pizza and listening to one of Italy's children play the accordion across the street. The kid didn't look very fat to me, but that may have been because he was a gypsy. I'm not sure if I misread the last line of the article, but it seemed there was some talk from the government that the only way to deal with the obesity crisis in Italy was to implement a tax on the overweight . . .? Could this be true? After a few months of eating like this, will they come after me?

It's also important to read the newspaper every day to see how the pope is doing. Here in Rome, the pope's health is recorded daily in the newspaper, very much like weather, or the TV schedule. Today the pope is tired. Yesterday, the pope was less tired than he is today. Tomorrow, we expect that the pope will not be quite so tired as he was today.

It's kind of a fairyland of language for me here. For someone who has always wanted to speak Italian, what could be better than Rome? It's like somebody invented a city just to suit my specifications, where everyone (even the children, even the taxi drivers, even the actors on the commercials!) speaks this magical language. It's like the whole society is conspiring to

2

3

4

5

6

7

teach me Italian. They'll even print their newspapers in Italian while I'm here; they don't mind! They have bookstores here *that only sell books written in Italian!* I found such a bookstore yesterday morning and felt I'd entered an enchanted palace. Everything was in Italian—even Dr. Seuss. I wandered through, touching all the books, hoping that anyone watching me might think I was a native speaker. Oh, how I want Italian to open itself up to me! This feeling reminded me of when I was four years old and couldn't read yet, but was dying to learn. I remember sitting in the waiting room of a doctor's office with my mother, holding a *Good Housekeeping* magazine in front of my face, turning the pages slowly, staring at the text, and hoping the grown-ups in the waiting room would think I was actually reading. I haven't felt so starved for comprehension since then. I found some works by American poets in that bookstore, with the original English version printed on one side of the page and the Italian translation on the other. I bought a volume by Robert Lowell, another by Louise Gluck.

There are spontaneous conversation classes everywhere. Today, I was sitting on a park    8
bench when a tiny old woman in a black dress came over, roosted down beside me and started bossing me around about something. I shook my head, muted and confused. I apologized, saying in very nice Italian, "I'm sorry, but I don't speak Italian," and she looked like she would've smacked me with a wooden spoon, if she'd had one. She insisted: "You do understand!" (Interestingly, she was correct. That sentence, I *did* understand.) Now she wanted to know where I was from. I told her I was from New York, and asked where she was from. Duh—she was from Rome.

Hearing this, I clapped my hands like a baby. *Ah, Rome! Beautiful Rome! I love Rome!*    9
*Pretty Rome!* She listened to my primitive rhapsodies with skepticism. Then she got down to it and asked me if I was married. I told her I was divorced. This was the first time I'd said it to anyone, and here I was, saying it in Italian. Of course she demanded, *"Percher?"* Well . . . "why" is a hard question to answer in any language. I stammered, then finally came up with *"Tabbiamo rotto"* (We broke it).

She nodded, stood up, walked up the street to her bus stop, got on her bus and did not even    10
turn around to look at me again. Was she mad at me? Strangely, I waited for her on that park bench for twenty minutes, thinking against reason that she might come back and continue our conversation, but she never returned. Her name was Celeste, pronounced with a sharp *ch* as in *cello*.

Later in the day, I found a library. Dear me, how I love a library. Because we are in Rome,    11
this library is a beautiful old thing, and within it there is a courtyard garden which you'd never have guessed existed if you'd only looked at the place from the street. The garden is a perfect square, dotted with orange trees and, in the center, a fountain. This fountain was going to be a contender for my favorite in Rome, I could tell immediately, though it was unlike any I'd seen so far. It was not carved of imperial marble, for starters. This was a small green, mossy, organic fountain. It was like a shaggy, leaking bush of ferns. (It looked, actually, exactly like the wild foliage growing out of the head of that praying figure which the old medicine man in Indonesia had drawn for me.) The water shot up out of the center of this flowering shrub, then rained back down on the leaves, making a melancholy, lovely sound throughout the whole courtyard.

I found a seat under an orange tree and opened one of the poetry books I'd purchased yesterday.    12
Louise Gluck. I read the first poem in Italian, then in English, and stopped short at this line:

    *Dal centro delta mia vita venne una grande fontana . . .*    13

"From the center of my life, there came a great fountain . . ." I set the book down in my    14
lap, shaking with relief.

**Vocabulary** Before, during, and after reading the selection, annotate the text and write in your journal. Create a list of vocabulary words, along with their definitions. Give examples of their use from the selection you just read.

## After Reading Discussion Questions: Meaning, Structure, and Expression

1. **Main Idea:** Work as a group to write a summary that answers the following questions: What purpose did Elizabeth Gilbert have for writing this essay? Who is the intended audience? What is the main idea of the essay?
2. **Relevant Details:** Elizabeth Gilbert uses the power of descriptive details to give life to her examples and illustrations. Find examples of her use of the following descriptive details: sight, sound, taste, smell, and touch or physical sensations. How do these details help her make her point?
3. **Logical Order:** Elizabeth Gilbert does not state the main idea of this selection in a thesis sentence. Instead, she makes her point by describing examples of her favorite fountains and illustrating her attempts to learn Italian. Then, she concludes the selection by inferring her main idea in the last two sentences. Do you think the selection would have been more effective if she had stated her main idea? Why or why not?
4. **Effective Expression:** Some have described Gilbert's tone in this selection as poetic. Do you agree or disagree? How would you describe Gilbert's tone? Give examples to support your views.

## Thinking Prompts to Move from Reading to Writing

1. Throughout literature, authors use fountains to illustrate certain key principles or values in the human experience. In paragraphs 3 and 11, Elizabeth Gilbert describes two examples of fountains in Rome. What does each fountain represent to her? What life principle(s) does each one illustrate? Why do you think she was so affected by the line from Louise Gluck's poem "From the center of my life, there came a great fountain . . ."?
2. In paragraph 7, Elizabeth Gilbert describes herself as "starved for comprehension." What examples does she give from her life to illustrate her hunger to learn? Discuss the relationship between the desire to understand and learning. What causes the desire to understand?

# Classification

# Michelle Obama

## OPRAH WINFREY

"Through the power of media, Oprah Winfrey has created an unparalleled connection with people around the world. As supervising producer and host of the top-rated, award-winning *The Oprah Winfrey Show*, she has entertained, enlightened and uplifted millions of viewers for the past two decades. Her accomplishments as a global media leader and philanthropist have established her as one of the most respected and admired public figures today" (Oprah.com). Winfrey wrote the following article for *Time* magazine's annual *Time 100* issue, which names the people who most affect our world.

**Before Reading** Write a journal entry about an influential person. Whom do you think has most affected our world? Why?

1. Michelle Obama doesn't just inspire us. She affirms us with her intelligence, authenticity, depth and compassion. We see the best of ourselves in her and marvel that no matter what she's doing, she brings 100% of herself to the experience.

2. I first met Michelle almost five years ago, shortly after Senator Barack Obama's riveting 2004 DNC speech. Long before there was serious talk of a campaign for the presidency, I remember going to the Obamas' house for dinner. I figured there would be takeout since I knew that, like me, Michelle had worked all day. But no, there she was in the kitchen, calm and organized, preparing linguine with shrimp and vegetables.

3. The woman I witnessed five years ago, with her graciousness, care and attention to detail, is the same woman I visited in the White House in February. Her very presence makes you feel welcome. Her political power is secondary to her heart power, and I salute her for that. I trust her. I know that whatever she gives her attention to, the truth will always be present. She doesn't make false moves.

4. The joy Michelle, 45, brings to her roles as First Mother and First Lady is what makes her so intoxicating. We want that joy in the roles we inhabit as mothers, wives, workers, daughters and friends. And while we admire those arms and applaud her fashion choices (from J. Crew to top designers), her greatest influence is that she makes us want to be our own best selves— and maybe lift a few weights too.

5. Watching her on the global stage greeting the Queen and chatting with dignitaries and representing us the way we imagine presenting ourselves on our best day, I was reminded of lines from Maya Angelou's poem "Phenomenal Woman": "It's the fire in my eyes, / And the flash of my teeth, / The swing in my waist, / And the joy in my feet. / I'm a woman / Phenomenally."

6. How sweet it is that America has a First Lady who embodies the vibrancy and confidence of a seriously prepared 21st century woman. A phenomenal woman indeed.

**Vocabulary** Before, during, and after reading the selection, annotate the text and write in your journal. Create a list of vocabulary words, along with their definitions. Give examples of their use from the selection you just read.

## After Reading Discussion Questions: Meaning, Structure, and Expression

1. **Main Idea:** Work as a group to write a summary that answers the following questions: What purpose did Oprah Winfrey have for writing this essay? Who is the intended audience? What is the main idea of the essay?

2. **Relevant Details:** Do you think Oprah Winfrey gave enough details to convince the reader that Michelle Obama is a hero or icon of great influence? Which details are the most convincing to you? What additional details would you add to strengthen the point of the essay? What would you have liked to have learned about Michelle Obama from someone who knows her as well as Winfrey does? Where in the tribute would you place this additional information?

3. **Logical Order:** Why did Oprah Winfrey choose to use the lines from Maya Angelou's poem "Phenomenal Woman" as part of her conclusion? Would her essay have been more effective if she had used the lines from the poem in the introduction to grab our attention? Why or why not?

4. **Effective Expression:** In her article, Oprah Winfrey uses words such as "marvel," "intoxicating," "vibrancy," and "phenomenal." How would you describe the tone set by these words? Is Oprah Winfrey expressing just her personal opinion or does she speak for a majority? If she speaks for a majority, does she speak for women, men, or both? Explain your reasoning.

## Thinking Prompts to Move from Reading to Writing

1. In her tribute to Michelle Obama, Oprah Winfrey uses the phrases "the best of ourselves" and "our own best selves." What do you think she means by these phrases? What are the traits of "our best selves"? Do these traits vary from person to person or are they universal traits common to everyone? Who makes you want to be your own best self? How do you encourage others to be their best selves? Assume you are writing an essay for a college psychology course. Describe the traits of a role model who inspires others to be their "best selves," such as a teacher or a parent.

2. *Time* magazine divides its list of most influential people into four categories: Builders & Titans; Artists & Entertainers; Heroes & Icons; Scientists & Thinkers. Oprah Winfrey wrote about Michelle Obama as a Hero & Icon. Whom would you nominate to the annual *Time 100*? In which group does your nominee belong? What role does this person play in society? What admirable traits does this person possess? Assume you are writing for the 2010 *Time 100* issue. Write a tribute about a person who has most affected our world.

# The Truth about Lying

## JUDITH VIORST

Judith Viorst was born in Newark, New Jersey, in 1931. As the author of several works of fiction and nonfiction, for children as well as adults, she has been honored with various awards for her journalism and psychological writings.

**Before Reading** Write a journal entry about your experiences with lying. Have you ever told a lie or been lied to? Why was the lie told? How do you feel when you lie or are lied to? Is lying necessary sometimes? If so, when?

I've been wanting to write on a subject that intrigues and challenges me: the subject of lying. I've found it very difficult to do. Everyone I've talked to has a quite intense and personal but often rather intolerant point of view about what we can—and can never *never*—tell lies about. I've finally reached the conclusion that I can't present any ultimate conclusions, for too many people would promptly disagree. Instead, I'd like to present a series of moral puzzles, all concerned with lying. I'll tell you what I think about them. Do you agree?

### Social Lies

Most of the people I've talked with say that they find social lying acceptable and necessary. They think it's the civilized way for folks to behave. Without these little white lies, they say, our relationships would be short and brutish and nasty. It's arrogant, they say, to insist on being so incorruptible and so brave that you cause other people unnecessary embarrassment or pain by compulsively assailing them with your honesty. I basically agree. What about you?

Will you say to people, when it simply isn't true, "I like your new hairdo," "You're looking much better," "It's so nice to see you," "I had a wonderful time"?

Will you praise hideous presents and homely kids?

Will you decline invitations with "We're busy that night—so sorry we can't come," when the truth is you'd rather stay home than dine with the So-and-sos?

And even though, as I do, you may prefer the polite evasion of "You really cooked up a storm" instead of "The soup"—which tastes like warmed-over coffee—"is wonderful," will you, if you must, proclaim it wonderful?

There's one man I know who absolutely refuses to tell social lies. "I can't play that game," he says; "I'm simply not made that way." And his answer to the argument that saying nice things to someone doesn't cost anything is, "Yes, it does—it destroys your credibility." Now, he won't, unsolicited, offer his views on the painting you just bought, but you don't ask his frank opinion unless you want *frank,* and his silence at those moments when the rest of us liars are muttering, "Isn't it lovely?" is, for the most part, eloquent enough. My friend does not indulge in what he calls "flattery, false praise, and mellifluous comments." When others tell fibs, he will not go along. He says that social lying is lying, that little white lies are still lies. And he feels that telling lies is morally wrong. What about you?

### Peace-Keeping Lies

Many people tell peace-keeping lies; lies designed to avoid irritation or argument; lies designed to shelter the liar from possible blame or pain; lies (or so it is rationalized) designed to keep trouble at bay without hurting anyone.

I tell these lies at times, and yet I always feel they're wrong. I understand why we tell them, but still they feel wrong. And whenever I lie so that someone won't disapprove of me or think less of me or holler at me, I feel I'm a bit of a coward, I feel I'm dodging responsibility, I feel . . . guilty. What about you?

Do you, when you're late for a date because you overslept, say that you're late because you got caught in a traffic jam?

Do you, when you forget to call a friend, say that you called several times but the line was busy?

Do you, when you didn't remember that it was your father's birthday, say that his present must be delayed in the mail?

And when you're planning a weekend in New York City and you're not in the mood to visit your mother, who lives there, do you conceal—with a lie, if you must—the fact that you'll be in New York? Or do you have the courage—or is it the cruelty?—to say, "I'll be in New York, but sorry—I don't plan on seeing you"?

(Dave and his wife Elaine have two quite different points of view on this very subject. He calls her a coward. She says she's being wise. He says she must assert her right to visit New York sometimes and not see her mother. To which she always patiently replies: "Why should we have useless fights? My mother's too old to change. We get along much better when I lie to her.")

Finally, do you keep the peace by telling your husband lies on the subject of money? Do you reduce what you really paid for your shoes? And in general do you find yourself ready, willing, and able to lie to him when you make absurd mistakes or lose or break things?

"I used to have a romantic idea that part of intimacy was confessing every dumb thing that you did to your husband. But after a couple of years of that," says Laura, "have I changed my mind!"

And having changed her mind, she finds herself telling peace-keeping lies. And yes, I tell them too. What about you?

### Protective Lies

Protective lies are lies folks tell—often quite serious lies—because they're convinced that the truth would be too damaging. They lie because they feel there are certain human values that supersede the wrong of having lied. They lie, not for personal gain, but because they believe it's for the good of the person they're lying to. They lie to those they love, to those who trust them most of all, on the grounds that breaking this trust is justified.

They may lie to their children on money or marital matters.

They may lie to the dying about the state of their health.

They may lie about adultery, and not—or so they insist—to save their own hide, but to save the heart and the pride of the men they are married to.

They may lie to their closest friend because the truth about her talents or son or psyche would be—or so they insist—utterly devastating.

I sometimes tell such lies, but I'm aware that it's quite presumptuous to claim I know what's best for others to know. That's called playing God. That's called manipulation and control. And we never can be sure, once we start to juggle lies, just where they'll land, exactly where they'll roll.

And furthermore, we may find ourselves lying in order to back up the lies that are backing up the lie we initially told.

And furthermore—let's be honest—if conditions were reversed, we certainly wouldn't want anyone lying to us.

Yet, having said all that, I still believe that there are times when protective lies must nonetheless be told. What about you?

If your Dad had a very bad heart and you had to tell him some bad family news, which would you choose: to tell him the truth or lie?

If your former husband failed to send his monthly child-support check and in other ways behaved like a total rat, would you allow your children—who believed he was simply wonderful—to continue to believe that he was wonderful?

If your dearly beloved brother selected a wife whom you deeply disliked, would you reveal your feelings or would you fake it?

And if you were asked, after making love, "And how was that for you?" would you reply, if it wasn't too good, "Not too good"?

Now, some would call a sex lie unimportant, little more than social lying, a simple act of courtesy that makes all human intercourse run smoothly. And some would say all sex lies are bad news and unacceptably protective. Because, says Ruth, "a man with an ego that fragile

14

15

16

17

18

19

20

21

22

23

24

25

26

27

28

29

30

31

doesn't need your lies—he needs a psychiatrist." Still others feel that sex lies are indeed protective lies, more serious than simple social lying, and yet at times they tell them on the grounds that when it comes to matters sexual, everybody's ego is somewhat fragile.

"If most of the time things go well in sex," says Sue, "I think you're allowed to dissemble when they don't. I can't believe it's good to say, 'Last night was four stars, darling, but tonight's performance rates only a half.'" 32

I'm inclined to agree with Sue. What about you? 33

### Trust-Keeping Lies

Another group of lies are trust-keeping lies, lies that involve triangulation, with *A* (that's you) telling lies to *B* on behalf of *C* (whose trust you'd promised to keep). Most people concede that once you've agreed not to betray a friend's confidence, you can't betray it, even if you must lie. But I've talked with people who don't want you telling them anything that they might be called on to lie about. 34

"I don't tell lies for myself," says Fran, "and I don't want to have to tell them for other people." Which means, she agrees, that if her best friend is having an affair, she absolutely doesn't want to know about it. 35

"Are you saying," her best friend asks, "that if I went off with a lover and I asked you to tell my husband I'd been with you, that you wouldn't lie for me, that you'd betray me?" 36

Fran is very pained but very adamant. "I wouldn't want to betray you, so . . . don't ask me." 37

Fran's best friend is shocked. What about you? 38

Do you believe you can have close friends if you're not prepared to receive their deepest secrets? 39

Do you believe you must always lie for your friends? 40

Do you believe, if your friend tells a secret that turns out to be quite immoral or illegal, that once you've promised to keep it, you must keep it? 41

And what if your friend were your boss—if you were perhaps one of the President's men— would you betray or lie for him over, say, Watergate? 42

As you can see, these issues get terribly sticky. 43

It's my belief that once we've promised to keep a trust, we must tell lies to keep it. I also believe that we can't tell Watergate lies. And if these two statements strike you as quite contradictory, you're right—they're quite contradictory. But for now they're the best I can do. What about you? 44

Some say that truth will out and thus you might as well tell the truth. Some say you can't regain the trust that lies lose. Some say that even though the truth may never be revealed, our lies pervert and damage our relationships. Some say . . . well, here's what some of them have to say. 45

"I'm a coward," says Grace, "about telling close people important, difficult truths. I find that I'm unable to carry it off. And so if something is bothering me, it keeps building up inside till I end up just not seeing them any more." 46

"I lie to my husband on sexual things, but I'm furious," says Joyce, "that he's too insensitive to know I'm lying." 47

"I suffer most from the misconception that children can't take the truth," says Emily. "But I'm starting to see that what's harder and more damaging for them is being told lies, is *not* being told the truth." 48

"I'm afraid," says Joan, "that we often wind up feeling a bit of contempt for the people we lie to." 49

And then there are those who have no talent for lying. 50

"Over the years, I tried to lie," a friend of mine explained, "but I always got found out and I 51
always got punished. I guess I gave myself away because I feel guilty about any kind of lying.
It looks as if I'm stuck with telling the truth."

For those of us, however, who are good at telling lies, for those of us who lie and don't get 52
caught, the question of whether or not to lie can be a hard and serious moral problem. I liked
the remark of a friend of mine who said, "I'm willing to lie. But just as a last resort—the
truth's always better."

"Because," he explained, "though others may completely accept the lie I'm telling, I don't." 53
I tend to feel that way too. 54
What about you? 55

## Vocabulary
Before, during, and after reading the selection, annotate the text and write
in your journal. Create a list of vocabulary words, along with their definitions. Give
examples of their use from the selection you just read.

## After Reading Discussion Questions: Meaning, Structure, and Expression

1. **Main Idea:** Work as a group to write a summary that answers the following questions:
   What purpose did Judith Viorst have for writing this essay? Who is her intended
   audience? What is the main idea of the essay? What is the significance of the title?
2. **Relevant Details:** Viorst describes four types of lies. Examine the examples she gives for
   each type of lie. Do you agree that she chose the best examples? Why or why not?
3. **Logical Order:** Throughout the essay, Viorst poses questions directly to the audience.
   Locate those questions. Why did she place these questions where she did? What impact
   do the questions have on the effectiveness of the essay?
4. **Effective Expression:** Based on her word choice, who is the intended audience for this
   essay? Identify several expressions that you used as clues to identify the audience. Does
   the point of the essay have meaning for other audiences? What changes in words or
   examples would you recommend to make this essay appealing to a specific audience that
   is different from the one Viorst intended?

## Thinking Prompts to Move from Reading to Writing

1. Throughout the essay, Viorst asks her readers if they agree with her. Discuss your views
   about these four types of lies. Write a classification essay that answers the questions she
   poses to the reader.
2. Lying is an act that leads to a variety of emotional reactions for both the one who lies
   and the one who is lied to. How do you feel when you lie? How do you feel when you
   know you have been lied to? Write an essay that classifies and explains the types of
   reactions people have in response to lying.

# The Talk of the Sandbox; How Johnny and Suzy's Playground Chatter Prepares Them for Life at the Office

### DEBORAH TANNEN

Deborah Tannen is best known as the author of *You Just Don't Understand*, which was on the *New York Times* bestseller list for nearly four years, including eight months as #1, and has been translated into 30 languages. Professor Tannen serves on the linguistics department faculty at Georgetown University. She has published twenty-one books and over 100 articles, and is the recipient of five honorary doctorates. The following article first appeared in the "Outlook" section of the *Washington Post.*

**Before Reading**  Write a journal entry about the differences between men and women. For example, do men and women differ in the ways they fight, apologize, compete, or learn? How so?

Bob Hoover of the Pittsburgh *Post-Gazette* was interviewing me when he remarked that after years of coaching boys' softball teams, he was now coaching girls and they were very different. I immediately whipped out my yellow pad and began interviewing him—and discovered that his observations about how girls and boys play softball parallel mine about how women and men talk at work.

Hoover told me that boys' teams always had one or two stars whom the other boys treated with deference. So when he started coaching a girls' team, he began by looking for the leader. He couldn't find one. "The girls who are better athletes don't lord it over the others," he said. "You get the feeling that everyone's the same." When a girl got the ball, she didn't try to throw it all the way home as a strong-armed boy would; instead, she'd throw it to another team member, so they all became better catchers and throwers. He went on, "If a girl makes an error, she's not in the doghouse for a long time, as a boy would be."

"But wait," I interrupted. "I've heard that when girls make a mistake at sports, they often say 'I'm sorry,' whereas boys don't."

That's true, he said, but then the girl forgets it—and so do her teammates. "For boys, sports is a performance art. They're concerned with how they look." When they make an error, they sulk because they've let their teammates down. Girls want to win, but if they lose, they're still all in it together—so the mistake isn't as dreadful for the individual or the team.

What Hoover described in these youngsters were the seeds of behavior I have observed among women and men at work.

The girls who are the best athletes don't "lord it over" the others—just the ethic I found among women in positions of authority. Women managers frequently told me they were good managers because they did not act in an authoritarian manner. They said they did not flaunt their

1

2

3

4

5

6

power, or behave as though they were better than their subordinates. Similarly, linguist Elisabeth Kuhn found that women professors in her study informed students of course requirements as if they had magically appeared on the syllabus ("There are two papers. The first paper, ah, let's see, is due. . . . It's back here [referring to the syllabus] at the beginning"), whereas the men professors made it clear that they had set the requirements ("I have two midterms and a final").

A woman manager might say to her secretary, "Could you do me a favor and type this letter right away?" knowing that her secretary is going to type the letter. But her male boss, on hearing this, might conclude she doesn't feel she deserves the authority she has, just as a boys' coach might think the star athlete doesn't realize how good he is if he doesn't expect his teammates to treat him with deference.

7

I was especially delighted by Hoover's observation that, although girls are more likely to say, "I'm sorry," they are actually far less sorry when they make a mistake than boys who don't say it, but are "in the doghouse" for a long time. This dramatizes the ritual nature of many women's apologies. How often is a woman who is "always apologizing" seen as weak and lacking in confidence? In fact, for many women, saying "I'm sorry" often doesn't mean "I apologize." It means "I'm sorry that happened."

8

Like many of the rituals common among women, it's a way of speaking that takes into account the other person's point of view. It can even be an automatic conversational smoother. For example, you left your pad in someone's office; you knock on the door and say, "Excuse me, I left my pad on your desk," and the person whose office it is might reply, "Oh, I'm sorry. Here it is." She knows it is not her fault that you left your pad on her desk; she's just letting you know it's okay.

9

Finally, I was intrigued by Hoover's remark that boys regard sports as "a performance art" and worry about "how they look." There, perhaps, is the rub, the key to why so many women feel they don't get credit for what they do. From childhood, many boys learn something that is very adaptive to the workplace: Raises and promotions are based on "performance" evaluations and these depend, in large measure, on how you appear in other people's eyes. In other words, you have to worry not only about getting your job done but also about getting credit for what you do.

10

Getting credit often depends on the way you talk. For example, a woman told me she was given a poor evaluation because her supervisor felt she knew less than her male peers. Her boss, it turned out, reached this conclusion because the woman asked more questions: She was seeking information without regard to how her queries would make her look.

11

The same principle applies to apologizing. Whereas some women seem to be taking undeserved blame by saying "I'm sorry," some men seem to evade deserved blame. I observed this when a man disconnected a conference call by accidentally elbowing the speaker-phone. When his secretary re-connected the call, I expected him to say, "I'm sorry; I knocked the phone by mistake." Instead he said, "Hey, what happened?! One minute you were there, the next minute you were gone!" Annoying as this might be, there are certainly instances in which people improve their fortunes by covering up mistakes. If Hoover's observations about girls' and boys' athletic styles are fascinating, it is even more revealing to see actual transcripts of children at play and how they mirror the adult workplace. Amy Sheldon, a linguist at the University of Minnesota who studies children talking at play in a day care center, compared the conflicts of pre-school girls and boys. She found that boys who fought with one another tended to pursue their own goal. Girls tended to balance their own interests with those of the other girls through complex verbal negotiations.

12

Look how different the negotiations were:

13

Two boys fought over a toy telephone: Tony had it; Charlie wanted it. Tony was sitting on a foam chair with the base of the phone in his lap and the receiver lying beside him. Charlie

14

picked up the receiver, and Tony protested, "No, that's my phone!" He grabbed the telephone cord and tried to pull the receiver away from Charlie, saying, "No, that—uh, it's on MY couch. It's on MY couch, Charlie. It's on MY couch. It's on MY couch." It seems he had only one point to make, so he made it repeatedly as he used physical force to get the phone back.

Charlie ignored Tony and held onto the receiver. Tony then got off the couch, set the phone base on the floor and tried to keep possession of it by overturning the chair on top of it. Charlie managed to push the chair off, get the telephone and win the fight.

This might seem like a typical kids' fight until you compare it with a fight Sheldon videotaped among girls. Here the contested objects were toy medical instruments: Elaine had them; Arlene wanted them. But she didn't just grab for them; she argued her case. Elaine, in turn, balanced her own desire to keep them with Arlene's desire to get them. Elaine lost ground gradually, by compromising.

Arlene began not by grabbing but by asking and giving a reason: "Can I have that, that thing? I'm going to take my baby's temperature." Elaine was agreeable, but cautious: "You can use it—you can use my temperature. Just make sure you can't use anything else unless you can ask." Arlene did just that; she asked for the toy syringe: "May I?" Elaine at first resisted, but gave a reason: "No, I'm gonna need to use the shot in a couple of minutes." Arlene reached for the syringe anyway, explaining in a "beseeching" tone, "But I—I need this though."

Elaine capitulated, but again tried to set limits: "Okay, just use it once." She even gave Arlene permission to give "just a couple of shots."

Arlene then pressed her advantage, and became possessive of her property: "Now don't touch the baby until I get back, because it IS MY BABY! I'll check her ears, okay?" (Even when being demanding, she asked for agreement: "okay?")

Elaine tried to regain some rights through compromise: "Well, let's pretend it's another day, that we have to look in her ears together." Elaine also tried another approach that would give Arlene something she wanted: "I'll have to shot her after, after, after you listen—after you look in her ears," suggested Elaine. Arlene, however, was adamant: "Now don't shot her at all!" What happened next will sound familiar to anyone who has ever been a little girl or overheard one. Elaine could no longer abide Arlene's selfish behavior and applied the ultimate sanction: "Well, then, you can't come to my birthday!" Arlene uttered the predictable retort: "I don't want to come to your birthday!"

The boys and girls followed different rituals for fighting. Each boy went after what he wanted; they slugged it out; one won. But the girls enacted a complex negotiation, trying to get what they wanted while taking into account what the other wanted.

Here is an example of how women and men at work used comparable strategies.

Maureen and Harold, two managers at a medium-size company, were assigned to hire a human-resources coordinator for their division. Each favored a different candidate, and both felt strongly about their preferences. They traded arguments for some time, neither convincing the other. Then Harold said that hiring the candidate Maureen wanted would make him so uncomfortable that he would have to consider resigning. Maureen respected Harold. What's more, she liked him and considered him a friend. So she said what seemed to her the only thing she could say under the circumstances: "Well, I certainly don't want you to feel uncomfortable here. You're one of the pillars of the place." Harold's choice was hired.

What was crucial was not Maureen's and Harold's individual styles in isolation but how they played in concert with each other's style. Harold's threat to quit ensured his triumph—when used with someone for whom it was a trump card. If he had been arguing with someone who regarded this threat as simply another move in the negotiation rather than a non-

15

16

17

18

19

20

21

22

23

24

negotiable expression of deep feelings, the result might have been different. For example, had she said, "That's ridiculous; of course you're not going to quit!" or matched it ("Well, I'd be tempted to quit if we hired your guy"), the decision might well have gone the other way.

Like the girls at play, Maureen was balancing her perspective with those of her colleague and expected him to do the same. Harold was simply going for what he wanted and trusted Maureen to do likewise.   25

This is not to say that all women and all men, or all boys and girls, behave any one way. Many factors influence our styles, including regional and ethnic backgrounds, family experience and individual personality. But gender is a key factor, and understanding its influence can help clarify what happens when we talk.   26

Understanding the ritual nature of communication gives you the flexibility to consider different approaches if you're not happy with the reaction you're getting. Someone who tends to avoid expressing disagreement might learn to play "devil's advocate" without taking it as a personal attack. Someone who tends to avoid admitting fault might find it is effective to say "I'm sorry"—that the loss of face is outweighed by a gain in credibility.   27

There is no one way of talking that will always work best. But understanding how conversational rituals work allows individuals to have more control over their own lives.   28

**Vocabulary** Before, during, and after reading the selection, annotate the text and write in your journal. Create a list of vocabulary words, along with their definitions. Give examples of their use from the selection you just read.

## After Reading Discussion Questions: Meaning, Structure, and Expression

1. **Main Idea:** Work as a group to write a summary that answers the following questions: What purpose did Deborah Tannen have for writing this essay? Who is the intended audience? What is the main idea of the essay?
2. **Relevant Details:** The details of this passage explain the similarities and differences in the conversation styles of four groups of people. What are those four groups? Which groups are compared to each other? Which groups are contrasted with each other? Tannen uses several comparable points such as playing sports, fighting, and apologizing. Why do you think she chose these three specific activities to make her comparisons?
3. **Logical Order:** How does Deborah Tannen organize her ideas? Does she talk about the similarities and differences between men and women point by point? Or does she organize her comparison and contrast by presenting one block of ideas (the communication styles of males) and then another (the communication styles of females)? Do you think she chose the more effective method for ordering her details? Why or why not?
4. **Effective Expression:** Deborah Tannen uses transitional words and phrases to clearly identify her specific points of comparison. For example, reread the first sentence in paragraph 6. Circle the phrase that connects the topic "girl athletes" to "women in positions of authority." Does this transitional phrase indicate a comparison or a contrast between the two groups of females? Find two additional transitional words or phrases that identify comparable points in the passage. What are the comparable points or topics? Based on the transitional words or phrases, are these topics being compared, contrasted, or both? Discuss the importance of transitional expressions in a piece of writing.

## Thinking Prompts to Move from Reading to Writing

1. In this essay, Deborah Tannen reports her observation and study of human behavior. For example, reread paragraphs 13 through 28. This section objectively reports the differences between the communication styles of boys and girls—like a case study. First she narrates fight between the boys; then she narrates girls' fight. Simply by recording their behaviors, she illustrates their differences. Use this method of reporting to compare two topics of your choosing. For example, for a college health class report about the differences between effective and ineffective reactions to stress.

2. Deborah Tannen illustrates the differences between males and females by comparing and contrasting their communication styles as children and adults. What other differences between men and women have you observed? For example, do men and women prefer different types of movies, sports, books, cars? Do they differ in the way they act in their roles as parents, siblings, children, or friends? Write an essay using your own set of comparable points that discusses other important differences between men and women. Choose an audience and writing situation such as the following: an academic paper for a social science class or an article for the college newspaper.

# A Fable for Tomorrow
## RACHEL CARSON

Born in Springfield, Pennsylvania, in 1902, Rachel Carson lived the rugged life of a farmer's daughter. A biologist, environmentalist, and nature writer, Carson became a foreleader in the environmental movement. Her book *Silent Spring* raised the alarm and instigated change in national attitudes and policies about pesticides. She was awarded the Presidential Medal of Freedom.

**Before Reading** Write a journal entry about your views about the environment. Are you concerned about the environment? Why or why not? What do you think is the greatest threat to our environment? Why? What should be done?

There was once a town in the heart of America where all life seemed to live in harmony 1
with its surroundings. The town lay in the midst of a checkerboard of prosperous farms, with fields of grain and hillsides of orchards where, in spring, white clouds of bloom drifted above the green fields. In autumn, oak and maple and birch set up a blaze of color that flamed and flickered across a backdrop of pines. Then foxes barked in the hills and deer silently crossed the fields, half hidden in the mists of the fall mornings.

Along the roads, laurel, viburnum and alder, great ferns and wildflowers delighted the 2
traveler's eye through much of the year. Even in winter the roadsides were places of beauty, where countless birds came to feed on the berries and on the seed heads of the dried weeds rising above the snow. The countryside was, in fact, famous for the abundance and variety of its bird life, and when the flood of migrants was pouring through in spring and fall people traveled from great distances to observe them. Others came to fish the streams, which flowed clear and cold out of the hills and contained shady pools where trout lay. So it had been from the days many years ago when the first settlers raised their houses, sank their wells, and built their barns.

Then a strange blight crept over the area and everything began to change. Some evil spell 3
had settled on the community: mysterious maladies swept the flocks of chickens; the cattle

and sheep sickened and died. Everywhere was a shadow of death. The farmers spoke of much illness among their families. In the town the doctors had become more and more puzzled by new kinds of sickness appearing among their patients. There had been several sudden and unexplained deaths, not only among adults but even among children, who would be stricken suddenly while at play and die within a few hours.

There was a strange stillness. The birds, for example—where had they gone? Many people spoke of them, puzzled and disturbed. The feeding stations in the backyards were deserted. The few birds seen anywhere were moribund; they trembled violently and could not fly. It was a spring without voices. On the mornings that had once throbbed with the dawn chorus of robins, catbirds, doves, jays, wrens, and scores of other bird voices there was now no sound; only silence lay over the fields and woods and marsh.  4

On the farms the hens brooded, but no chicks hatched. The farmers complained that they were unable to raise any pigs—the litters were small and the young survived only a few days. The apple trees were coming into bloom but no bees droned among the blossoms, so there was no pollination and there would be no fruit.  5

The roadsides, once so attractive, were now lined with browned and withered vegetation as though swept by fire. These, too, were silent, deserted by all living things. Even the streams were now lifeless. Anglers no longer visited them, for all the fish had died.  6

In the gutters under the eaves and between the shingles of the roofs, a white granular powder still showed a few patches; some weeks before it had fallen like snow upon the roofs and the lawns, the fields and streams.  7

No witchcraft, no enemy action had silenced the rebirth of new life in this stricken world. The people had done it themselves.  8

This town does not actually exist, but it might easily have a thousand counterparts in America or elsewhere in the world. I know of no community that has experienced all the misfortunes I describe. Yet every one of these disasters has actually happened somewhere, and many real communities have already suffered a substantial number of them. A grim specter has crept upon us almost unnoticed, and this imagined tragedy may easily become a stark reality we all shall know.  9

**Vocabulary** Before, during, and after reading the selection, annotate the text and write in your journal. Create a list of vocabulary words, along with their definitions. Give examples of their use from the selection you just read.

## After Reading Discussion Questions: Meaning, Structure, and Expression

1. **Main Idea:** Work as a group to write a summary that answers the following questions: What purpose did Rachel Carson have for writing this essay? Who is her intended audience? What is the main idea of the essay? What is the significance of the title?
2. **Relevant Details:** When Carson begins her concluding paragraph by stating, "This town does not actually exist," she admits that she has used a fictitious example to make her point. Does she provide enough details to make her point convincingly? Would the use of facts or expert opinions strengthen her point? Why or why not? What is the effect of her sudden admission of using a fictitious example?
3. **Logical Order:** Carson contrasts two descriptions of a fictional place: what the place was like before it was damaged by pesticides and what the place looked like after the damage occurred. Does she organize these contrasting views point by point or by presenting one block of ideas (description of the place before it was damaged) and then another (description of the place after it was damaged)? Do you think she chose the more effective method for ordering her details? Why or why not?

**4. Effective Expression:** To make her point, Carson describes sensory details of sights and sounds to create vivid mental images in the reader's mind. Identify four sensory details: two that depict the town before it changed and two that depict the town after it changed. What impact do these details have on the reader?

## Thinking Prompts to Move from Reading to Writing

1. Carson uses sensory details to describe the change of seasons in this fictitious town, such as "in spring, white clouds of bloom drifted above the green fields." Write an essay that contrasts the seasons as they occur in a particular place. Use sensory details to depict the contrast of sights, sounds, aromas, or textures among the seasons.

2. "A Fable for Tomorrow" is a story that warns the reader about the negative effects of pesticide by contrasting before and after images. Identify a specific problem such as gangs, graffiti, drug abuse, alcoholism, an eating disorder, or obesity. Write a fable that warns against this problem by contrasting before and after situations.

# What is Poverty?

## JO GOODWIN-PARKER

The following selection was published in *America's Other Children: Public Schools Outside Suburbs,* by George Henderson in 1971 by the University of Oklahoma Press. The author specifically requests the right to her privacy and offers no additional information about herself for public use. In her essay, a personal testimony about living in poverty, she speaks directly to the reader.

**Before Reading** Write a journal entry about your response to poverty. How would you define poverty? Why are people poor? How does society react to the poor? Do you think our government does enough to help poor people? What can be done to fight poverty?

You ask me what is poverty? Listen to me. Here I am, dirty, smelly, and with no "proper" underwear on and with the stench of my rotting teeth near you. I will tell you. Listen to me. Listen without pity. I cannot use your pity. Listen with understanding. Put yourself in my dirty, worn out, ill-fitting shoes, and hear me. 1

Poverty is getting up every morning from a dirt- and illness-stained mattress. The sheets have long since been used for diapers. Poverty is living in a smell that never leaves. This is a smell of urine, sour milk, and spoiling food sometimes joined with the strong smell of long-cooked onions. Onions are cheap. If you have smelled this smell, you did not know how it came. It is the smell of the outdoor privy. It is the smell of young children who cannot walk the long dark way in the night. It is the smell of the mattresses where years of "accidents" have happened. It is the smell of the milk which has gone sour because the refrigerator long has not worked, and it costs money to get it fixed. It is the smell of rotting garbage. I could bury it, but where is the shovel? Shovels cost money. 2

Poverty is being tired. I have always been tired. They told me at the hospital when the last baby came that I had chronic anemia caused from poor diet, a bad case of worms, and that I needed a corrective operation. I listened politely—the poor are always polite. The poor always listen. They don't say that there is no money for iron pills, or better food, or worm medicine. The idea of an operation is frightening and costs so much that, if I had dared, I would have laughed. Who takes care of my children? Recovery from an operation takes a long time. I have three children. When I left them with "Granny" the last time I had a job, I came home to find the baby covered with fly specks, and a diaper that had not been changed since I left. When the dried diaper came off, bits of my baby's flesh came with it. My other child was playing with a sharp bit of broken glass, and my oldest was playing alone at the edge of a lake. I made twenty-two dollars a week, and a good nursery school costs twenty dollars a week for three children. I quit my job. 3

Poverty is dirt. You can say in your clean clothes coming from your clean house, "Anybody can be clean." Let me explain about housekeeping with no money. For breakfast I give my 4 children grits with no oleo or cornbread without eggs and oleo. This does not use up many dishes. What dishes there are, I wash in cold water and with no soap. Even the cheapest soap has to be saved for the baby's diapers. Look at my hands, so cracked and red. Once I saved for two months to buy a jar of Vaseline for my hands and the baby's diaper rash. When I had saved enough, I went to buy it and the price had gone up two cents. The baby and I suffered on. I have to decide every day if I can bear to put my cracked sore hands into the cold water and strong soap. But you ask, why not hot water? Fuel costs money. If you have a wood fire it costs money. If you burn electricity, it costs money. Hot water is a luxury. I do not have luxuries. I know you will be surprised when I tell you how young I am. I look so much older. My back has been bent over the wash tubs every day for so long, I cannot remember when I ever did anything else. Every night I wash every stitch my school age child has on and just hope her clothes will be dry by morning.

Poverty is staying up all night on cold nights to watch the fire knowing one spark on the newspaper covering the walls means your sleeping child dies in flames. In summer poverty is watching gnats and flies devour your baby's tears when he cries. The screens are torn and you pay so little rent you know they will never be fixed. Poverty means insects in your food, in your nose, in your eyes, and crawling over you when you sleep. Poverty is hoping it never rains because diapers won't dry when it rains and soon you are using newspapers. Poverty is seeing your children forever with runny noses. Paper handkerchiefs cost money and all your rags you need for other things. Even more costly are antihistamines. Poverty is cooking without food and cleaning without soap.     5

Poverty is asking for help. Have you ever had to ask for help, knowing your children will suffer unless you get it? Think about asking for a loan from a relative, if this is the only way you can imagine asking for help. I will tell you how it feels. You find out where the office is that you are supposed to visit. You circle that block four or five times. Thinking of your children, you go in. Everyone is very busy. Finally, someone comes out and you tell her that you need help. That never is the person you need to see. You go see another person, and after spilling the whole shame of your poverty all over the desk between you, you find that this isn't the right office after all—you must repeat the whole process, and it never is any easier at the next place.     6

You have asked for help, and after all it has a cost. You are again told to wait. You are told why, but you don't really hear because of the red cloud of shame and the rising cloud of despair.     7

Poverty is remembering. It is remembering quitting school in junior high because "nice" children had been so cruel about my clothes and my smell. The attendance officer came. My mother told him I was pregnant. I wasn't, but she thought that I could get a job and help out. I had jobs off and on, but never long enough to learn anything. Mostly I remember being married. I was so young then. I am still young. For a time, we had all the things you have. There was a little house in another town, with hot water and everything. Then my husband lost his job. There was unemployment insurance for a while and what few jobs I could get. Soon, all our nice things were repossessed and we moved back here. I was pregnant then. This house didn't look so bad when we first moved in. Every week it gets worse. Nothing is ever fixed. We now had no money. There were a few odd jobs for my husband, but everything went for food then, as it does now. I don't know how we lived through three years and three babies, but we did. I'll tell you something, after the last baby I destroyed my marriage. It had been a good one, but could you keep on bringing children in this dirt? Did you ever think how much it costs for any kind of birth control? I knew my husband was leaving the day he left, but there were no goodbye between us. I hope he has been able to climb out of this mess somewhere. He never could hope with us to drag him down.     8

That's when I asked for help. When I got it, you know how much it was? It was, and is, seventy-eight dollars a month for the four of us; that is all I ever can get. Now you know why there is no soap, no needles and thread, no hot water, no aspirin, no worm medicine, no hand cream, no shampoo. None of these things forever and ever and ever. So that you can see clearly, I pay twenty dollars a month rent, and most of the rest goes for food. For grits and cornmeal, and rice and milk and beans. I try my best to use only the minimum electricity. If I use more, there is that much less for food.

Poverty is looking into a black future. Your children won't play with my boys. They will turn to other boys who steal to get what they want. I can already see them behind the bars of their prison instead of behind the bars of my poverty. Or they will turn to the freedom of alcohol or drugs, and find themselves enslaved. And my daughter? At best, there is for her a life like mine.

But you say to me, there are schools. Yes, there are schools. My children have no extra books, no magazines, no extra pencils, or crayons, or paper and most important of all, they do not have health. They have worms, they have infections, they have pink-eye all summer. They do not sleep well on the floor, or with me in my one bed. They do not suffer from hunger, my seventy-eight dollars keeps us alive, but they do suffer from malnutrition. Oh yes, I do remember what I was taught about health in school. It doesn't do much good.

In some places there is a surplus commodities program. Not here. The country said it cost too much. There is a school lunch program. But I have two children who will already be damaged by the time they get to school.

But, you say to me, there are health clinics. Yes, there are health clinics and they are in the towns. I live out here eight miles from town. I can walk that far (even if it is sixteen miles both ways), but can my little children? My neighbor will take me when he goes; but he expects to get paid, one way or another. I bet you know my neighbor. He is that large man who spends his time at the gas station, the barbershop, and the corner store complaining about the government spending money on the immoral mothers of illegitimate children.

Poverty is an acid that drips on pride until all pride is worn away. Poverty is a chisel that chips on honor until honor is worn away. Some of you say that you would do something in my situation, and maybe you would, for the first week or the first month, but for year after year after year?

Even the poor can dream. A dream of a time when there is money. Money for the right kinds of food, for worm medicine, for iron pills, for toothbrushes, for hand cream, for a hammer and nails and a bit of screening, for a shovel, for a bit of paint, for some sheeting, for needles and thread. Money to pay in money for a trip to town. And, oh, money for hot water and money for soap. A dream of when asking for help does not eat away the last bit of pride. When the office you visit is as nice as the offices of other governmental agencies, when there are enough workers to help you quickly, when workers do not quit in defeat and despair. When you have to tell your story to only one person, and that person can send you for other help and you don't have to prove your poverty over and over and over again.

I have come out of my despair to tell you this. Remember I did not come from another place or another time. Others like me are all around you. Look at us with an angry heart, anger that will help.

9

10

11

12

13

14

15

16

**Vocabulary** Before, during, and after reading the selection, annotate the text and write in your journal. Create a list of vocabulary words, along with their definitions. Give examples of their use from the selection you just read.

## After Reading Discussion Questions: Meaning, Structure, and Expression

1. **Main Idea:** Work as a group to write a summary that answers the following questions: What purpose did Jo Goodwin-Parker have for writing this essay? Who is her intended audience? What is the main idea of the essay?
2. **Relevant Details:** Parker offers her own life experiences to define poverty. Does she provide enough details to make her point convincingly? Would the use of facts or expert opinions strengthen her point? Why or why not?
3. **Logical Order:** Parker defines poverty with a series of seven statements that begin with "Poverty is." Summarize her definition of poverty using these seven statements. Do you agree with the order in which she presents these statements? Why or why not?
4. **Effective Expression:** Based on Parker's choice of words, how would you describe the tone of this essay? Is it angry, embarrassed, disappointed, reflective, sad, or optimistic, or does it communicate some other attitude about poverty? Identify three expressions that illustrate the tone of the piece. Explain the reasons for your selections.

## Thinking Prompts to Move from Reading to Writing

1. Often, people do not understand what they have not experienced. Parker defines poverty for people who have never experienced it. In the last sentence in the first paragraph, she commands her readers to step into her shoes so they can learn from her experiences. Assume the view of one who understands an issue such as depression, addiction, or prejudice based on experience. Write an essay that defines the issue so that someone who has not experienced it can better understand the problem.
2. In her essay, Parker defines the problem of poverty, but she does not offer a solution, other than to say "look at us with an angry heart, anger that will help." What kind of anger will help this situation? Respond to Parker by writing an essay that defines this kind of anger. Consider using a phrase like "Anger that will help is" to reply to specific points she raises in her essay.

# Don't Call Me Middle Class: I'm a Professional

## MARK PENN

Mark Penn is the worldwide CEO of the public relations firm Burson-Marsteller, president of the polling firm Penn, Schoen and Berland Associates, and author of *Microtrends: The Small Forces Behind Tomorrow's Big Changes*. Penn has helped to elect over twenty-five leaders in the United States, Asia, Latin America, and Europe in addition to serving as chief adviser to President Bill Clinton in the 1996 presidential election and to Hillary Rodham Clinton through her Senate and presidential races. The following article appeared in the *Wall Street Journal*.

**Before Reading** Write a journal entry about your understanding of "class" in America. For example, what does it mean to be "middle class"? What does it mean to be "blue collar"? What does it mean to be a "professional"?

Not long ago, everyone in America wanted to be a member of the "middle class." In fact, as many as 53% of Americans described themselves that way to pollsters.

But with the information age and the rise of two-career incomes, being just middle class is a little old hat. The new aspiration for most Americans is to be a member of the new professional class. Rising numbers—as high as 64%—report that they consider themselves "professionals." The census shows a significant rise over the years, from 4% being professionals and skilled workers in 1910, to 36% today. The numbers have doubled since just 1980.

These new professionals, whose incomes were rising steadily until the financial crisis, have been at the heart of reshaping the country's economic and political life. Barack Obama more than any other president represents this shift and has uniquely appealed to these Americans. Everyone today wants to be a professional and most people believe they are.

The seeds of this surging class were in the new economy. As President Clinton used to point out all the time, 24 million new jobs were created during his eight-year tenure. None, however, were in the manufacturing sector, which now covers less than one in 10 jobs overall.

The traditional definition of a professional still applies: people with an advanced degree in areas like law, medicine or divinity. They have reached record numbers, approaching 100,000 a year. There are about 43,000 law degrees awarded annually, a 20% increase in the past decade. Even larger professions today are those of teachers and nurses, who number just over 6.5 million.

But the definition of professional has expanded. Most people in the fields of advertising, communications, health care and computer science consider themselves professionals. Often they even have new titles to convey this—for example what used to be called "headhunters" are now Career Management Professionals.

A look at the fastest-growing jobs shows how new-information professionals are emerging in high numbers. Network engineers are projected to be the fastest growing group in America, with computer software engineers also high on the list. Other groups with record numbers: home health aides for aging baby boomers, and veterinarians, for all the animals affected by the growing humanization of pets.

An analysis of the last election showed the emergence of this new class. Exit polls showed that in 1996, just 9% of households earned over $100,000. In last year's election, one in four (26%) earned over $100,000. And the fabled 1% earning over $200,000 in income were actually 6% of the voters. The lowest economic class over the same period saw its numbers fall nearly in half. (Of course inflation accounts for some of the change, but not all of it.)

In the past, the $100,000+ earners voted solidly Republican. In the last election, they were evenly split, with the $200,000+ voters picking Obama over McCain by 52/46. This was a sea change in political behavior for this group, now dominated by the emergence of the new professional class.

But while these political numbers are surprising, they depict a change that is much wider than the last presidential election or just politics. In the past the $100,000+ earners were dominated by small business owners and corporate executives—people who ran organizations and were strongly antigovernment—viewing government action as an intrusion into their freedom.

Today's new professional is better educated, better read, more plugged-in, more socially tolerant, more environmentally conscious—and while they like individuality in how they dress and act, they are much more open to having government solve our problems. Jobs like "network" engineer are all about improving collaboration.

But if "new professionals" were the "soccer moms" of the last election, how will this spill over into commercial life? Soccer moms needed minivans. What do new professionals need?

Clearly they are the heart of the marketplace for high-end technology. Apple marketing and pricing goes right to the core of this group. More than anything else, smart phones are the SUVs of the new professional class. Currently one in 10 phones in the U.S. is a smart phone, but that is growing at 35% a year. The Amazon Kindle would be attractive to technology-savvy professionals who like to read.

13

The titles of young professionals may be loftier and more formal—everyone these days is "chief" of something, from "chief talent officer" to "chief of creativity." But their clothing, of course, is more casual—neat, modern and green. And while hybrids are just 2.5% of all car purchases, 42% of hybrid drivers are in this class. Toyota and Lexus hit the sweet spot of these buyers over the last few years while Audi is making a comeback. Mercedes lost ground with them.

14

Younger professionals are pouring into the cities, creating unexpected revivals there while older professionals are retiring to the Sunbelt, creating new stresses in those communities.

15

In many ways, we are catching up to Europe. Those societies made the transition away from manufacturing earlier, producing professionals who wanted more stable lives with state-provided healthcare, longer maternity leaves and social help for raising children. And so the convergence of these attitudes and the collapse of the Republican Party are tied to the growth of the new professional voter and their changed outlook.

16

In the 1950s it was Levittown and the middle class that changed our society by creating the suburbs and a renewed focus on individual opportunity as the key to success. Today it's the professional class that is reshaping where and how we live, and its emphasis on the network, teamwork and collaboration is spearheading a new outlook on everything from technology to government intervention.

17

## Vocabulary

Before, during, and after reading the selection, annotate the text and write in your journal. Create a list of vocabulary words, along with their definitions. Give examples of their use from the selection you just read.

## After Reading Discussion Questions: Meaning, Structure, and Expression

1. **Main Idea:** Work as a group to write a summary that answers the following questions: What purpose did Mark Penn have for writing this essay? Who is the intended audience? What is the main idea of the essay?
2. **Relevant Details:** Mark Penn describes the traits and gives examples of the "new professional." Identify three traits of the new professional. Then, identify at least one example of each trait.
3. **Logical Order:** Mark Penn waits until paragraphs 5 and 6 to clearly define the term "professional." Should he have defined this term earlier in the article? Why or why not?
4. **Effective Expression:** At times, Mark Penn uses slang such as "old hat," "plugged-in," and "sweet spot." Other times, he uses the jargon of a market researcher such as "the humanization of pets" and "political numbers . . . predict a change." Is this mixture of informal and formal tones effective? Why or why not?

## Thinking Prompts to Move from Reading to Writing

1. In paragraph 13, Mark Penn states that high-end technology is as important to the new professional as the minivan was to a soccer mom. What is high-end technology? Why is high-end technology so important to the new professional? Assume you are a new professional such as a personal trainer, lawyer, or Web page designer. You are writing a business plan to submit to the Small Business Association for a start-up loan. Define

your profession, and describe the kind of technology you need to purchase to succeed in your profession.

2. In his essay, Mark Penn claims that the professional class has changed our society. Based on his article, in what ways has the professional class reshaped society? What other cultures have had an impact on American life? Define a culture of your choice, such as the Hip-hop culture. In your definition, discuss the influence this culture has had—or is having—on American society. Assume you are writing an academic paper for a humanities class or a posting for a blog about diversity and tolerance.

# Through Young Eyes

## MICHAEL S. MALONE

Michael S. Malone is the author of a dozen best-selling business books including *The Virtual Corporation, Going Public, Infinite Loop* (the Apple story), and *Virtual Selling*. In addition, Malone writes *The Silicon Insider*, a popular weekly technology column for ABCNews.com. He also contributes regularly to the *Wall Street Journal*, *Wired*, and *Fast Company*. Currently, Malone serves as Editor-in-Chief of Edgelings.com, a news and features website founded by a team of prominent Silicon Valley media and technology executives. The following article appeared in Edgelings.com in the Consumer Electronics and Lifestyle/Culture section.

**Before Reading**  Write a journal entry about your experiences with technology. Does technology—such as social networks, smart phones, the Web, instant messaging, online gaming—improve a person's life? In what ways? Can these forms of technology be harmful? In what ways? Does the good of technology outweigh the bad? Why or why not?

1    Technology in all of its forms—social networks, smart phones, the Web, instant messaging, on-line gaming—is a net loss for today's young people. At least according to one group of Silicon Valley 8th graders.

2    "It's bad for us, but it sure is fun," says Eric Bautista, 13, one of the students in Sister Jolene Schmitz's junior high school class at Resurrection School in Sunnyvale, California.

3    Admittedly, this informal survey offers, at best, only anecdotal evidence. Still, it is pretty shocking that a group of young teenagers, all of them technologically very astute, and living in the very heart of Silicon Valley, would come to such a conclusion.

4    These kids, born about the time the Internet became widely adopted, live within blocks of where the Intel microprocessor, the Apple computer and the Atari video game were all invented. They spend their days (and nights) surfing the web, playing on-line games and instant messaging. Most have cell phones in their backpacks. And many have at least one parent who works in the electronics industry.

5    Yet, when asked to weigh the benefits of having high technology in their lives versus the costs—intellectually, emotionally, socially—of that technology, the class voted 31–3 negative . . . a ratio so extreme that it argues against an aberration and towards a larger question about the overall impact of technology on the lives of our young people.

6    "We try to find the happy medium," says Stephanie Abreu, 13, "But we don't know where it is."

7    This isn't to say that the 8th graders, all of them heading off to top-tier Silicon Valley high schools, don't love their tech toys and tools. On the contrary, when asked to list all of the positives about tech, they weren't short of answers: access to information with unprecedented scope, the ability to socialize with large groups over vast distances, 24/7 multi-media communication, and perhaps best of all, whole new worlds of entertainment.

Moreover, this brave new digital world has always been part of their lives and, perhaps a bit jaded by it all, they find the idea of world without computers and cell phones surprisingly appealing: in a class vote, one-third of the students said they would prefer to have lived in the long-ago, pre-tech world of the late 1950s. 8

When asked what they find wrong with living in our modern Wired Web World, the students had no shortage of answers, most of which fell into a half-dozen categories. I'll let the students largely speak for themselves—voices describing the dark side of the tech revolution with a sincerity few of us adults have ever heard before: 9

- *Time-waster*: "Technology is the key to procrastination," says Kenny Kobetsky, 14. Eighty percent of the class said they had missed sleep due to playing on the Internet, fifty percent said they had forgotten to do homework for the same reason. "The Internet is just so tantalizing," says Nick Gregov, 14. "I actually think McDonalds is healthier than my computer," adds Blake Billiet, 13. Though the students did admit that the Web and cellphone can save time that used to be burned up driving to the store or library, few felt that these gains exceeded the many hours wasted on text or web surfing. 10

- *Loss of motivation*: "With all of these toys, it's hard to get out of the house," says Sybile Moser, 14. Many of the students said that while technology makes it easier to access information and learn new things, the lack of interaction with others often makes that learning biased and distorted—you only learn what you want to learn. "The students miss the give and take, the debate of learning together when they are on the Web," says Sister Jolene. Because of this, the students say, it's hard for them to keep their attention fixed on any one topic, but prefer instead to drift along in the information flow, letting it take them wherever it leads. 11

- *Addictive*: "The Internet is like a gateway drug," says Christine Doan, 13. Alex Nguyen, 13, compared the experience to eating ice cream—you love it even though it's bad for you. Even at their young age, many of the students already have Facebook pages and spend as much time there as watching television. Not surprisingly then, when asked if, despite all of their worries about the cost of technology in their lives, if any of them would give up their laptop or their cellphone, almost no one raised a hand. 12

- *Second Hand Knowledge*: This answer was probably the biggest surprise. The eighth graders seemed to intuitively appreciate that the experiences and information they received from the Web and other digital sources was essentially a simulacrum of reality—a re-creation on a glowing flat screen of the three dimensional natural world . . . and that something was being lost in the translation. "We don't get as much out of things if we don't experience them ourselves," says Lauren Fahey, B. We seem to spend a lot of our lives as bystanders," adds Katherine Wu, 13. 13

- *Exposure*: The news is regularly filled with stories of Internet predators preying on naïve young people, or about the easy availability to adolescents of on-line pornography and other vices. But these eighth graders were anything but innocents about the dark side of the Web—and indeed, showed surprising maturity in their strategies for coping with threats all-but unknown to previous generations. "Look, when you're talking to a 'friend', you don't really know if it's really them—especially if they are introduced by someone else," says Peyton Yniguez, 14. "The nature of friendship changes," says Jonathon Robbins, 14. But the most astute, and disturbing, comment belonged to Jenna Kunz, 14: "You have to develop your own special conscience for the Internet." 14

- *Disturbed Values*: All of these forces can't help but affect a young person's sense of values. The eighth graders, in some ways sophisticated beyond their years, instinctively understand that. "We can't respect anything anymore," says Eric Bautista. Adds Jenna Kunz, "You don't care about things as much; you aren't as passionate as you should be." And yet, that said, these are still kids who are excited about graduation and the prospects of the impending four years of high school. And world-weary as they might sound, each one of the above comments provoked conversation so loud and lively that Sister Jolene spent most of the time just trying to keep the noise down to a dull roar. 15

In the end, if the news is surprising to us adults that teenagers believe technology is a net loss in their lives, there is consolation in knowing that these young people —themselves creations of the digital age—are not starry-eyed acolytes of the latest computer game or web site. Rather, technology is the world they casually operate within and they have a deep understanding of its rewards and its costs, what it gives and takes away. And for all of our fears for them, they themselves show an extraordinary sense of perspective. 16

Stephanie Abreu said it best: "Technology is like family. Sometimes it's good, sometimes bad. But you love it all the same." 17

*Special thanks to Sr. Jolene's 8th grade class at Resurrection School, Sunnyvale, California for its assistance in the preparation of this article.* 18

## Vocabulary
Before, during, and after reading the selection, annotate the text and write in your journal. Create a list of vocabulary words, along with their definitions. Give examples of their use from the selection you just read.

## After Reading Discussion Questions: Meaning, Structure, and Expression

1. **Main Idea:** Work as a group to write a summary that answers the following questions: What purpose did Michael S. Malone have for writing this essay? Who is the intended audience? What is the main idea of the essay?
2. **Relevant Details:** In paragraph 9, Malone states "I'll let the students largely speak for themselves—" to signal his use of direct quotes as supporting details. Why does he use so many direct quotes? Does he use too many? Would the essay be more effective if he had paraphrased the students' ideas? Why or why not? Are these students a good source of information? Why or why not?
3. **Logical Order:** In paragraphs 10 through 15, Malone lists the things these young people think is wrong with technology—a list of six harmful effects arising from the "dark side of the tech revolution." Do you think Michael Malone presented the list in a particular order of importance? For example, is "time waster" less harmful than "disturbed values"? Are all these effects equally harmful? Assume Malone did list the effects from least to most significant. Do you agree with the given order? Would you reorder these effects based on their significance? How and why?
4. **Effective Expression:** Reread paragraph 14. In the last sentence of the paragraph, Jenna Kunz, 14, states "You have to develop your own special conscience for the Internet." Malone describes her statement as "the most astute, and disturbing." What does she imply in her use of the word "conscience" in her statement? What kind of "special conscience" is needed for the Internet? Do you agree with Malone's assessment about her comment? Why or why not?

## Thinking Prompts to Move from Reading to Writing

1. "Through Young Eyes" generated some online comments from readers. One reader criticized the article by writing, "Interview 'normal' teens at a non-Catholic school and

you will get a different answer." Do the students' views as expressed in this article represent the views of "normal" youth? Would most youth agree that technology is harmful? Work with a group of your peers and conduct your own research into this topic. Create a survey based on the information in this article. Ask students in your classes to fill out the survey. Then, write a report on your findings based on the anecdotal evidence you gather from the survey. Assume you are writing an academic paper for a sociology class.

2. Michael Malone introduces his topic in the first sentence as "technology in all of its forms." His article explores the effects of technology on a general level. Narrow this line of thought by focusing on a specific type of technology. For example, think about the views expressed in the reading selections "How to Write a Personal Letter" by Garrison Keillor and "How to Twitter" by Julia Angwin. Write an essay that explains how technology has impacted written communication for better or worse. Assume you will post your writing as a comment to Malone's article "Through Young Eyes" on Edgelings.com. Or write an academic paper for a humanities course that explains how technology in transportation has affected society for better or worse.

# Why We Crave Horror Movies
## STEPHEN KING

Stephen King, born in Portland, Maine in 1947, has been writing full-time since the 1973 publication of his novel *Carrie*. He has since published over 40 books and has become one of the world's most successful writers.

**Before Reading**  Write a journal entry about your reaction to horror movies. Do you enjoy horror movies? Why or why not? Why do you think horror movies are so popular? Do graphically violent horror movies have a harmful effect on society? Explain your reasons.

I think that we're all mentally ill: those of us outside the asylums only hide it a little  1
better—and maybe not all that much better, after all. We've all known people who talk to themselves, people who sometimes squinch their faces into horrible grimaces when they believe no one is watching, people who have some hysterical fear—of snakes, the dark, the tight place, the long drop . . . and, of course, those final worms and grubs that are waiting so patiently underground.

When we pay our four or five bucks and seat ourselves at tenth-row center in a theater  2
showing a horror movie, we are daring the nightmare.

Why? Some of the reasons are simple and obvious. To show that we can, that we are not afraid,  3
that we can ride this roller coaster. Which is not to say that a really good horror movie may not surprise a scream out of us at some point, the way we may scream when the roller coaster twists through a complete 360 or plows through a lake at the bottom of the drop. And horror movies, like roller coasters, have always been the special province of the young; by the time one turns 40 or 50, one's appetite for double twists or 360-degree loops may be considerably depleted.

We also go to re-establish our feelings of essential normality; the horror movie is innately  4
conservative, even reactionary. Freda Jackson as the horrible melting woman in *Die, Monster, Die!* confirms for us that no matter how far we may be removed from the beauty of a Robert Redford or a Diana Ross, we are still light-years from true ugliness.

And we go to have fun.  5

Ah, but this is where the ground starts to slope away, isn't it? Because this is a very peculiar sort of fun indeed. The fun comes from seeing others menaced—sometimes killed. One critic has suggested that if pro football has become the voyeur's version of combat, then the horror film has become the modern version of the public lynching.

It is true that the mythic, "fairytale" horror film intends to take away the shades of gray. . . . It urges us to put away our more civilized and adult penchant for analysis and to become children again, seeing things in pure blacks and whites. It may be that horror movies provide psychic relief on this level because this invitation to lapse into simplicity, irrationality and even outright madness is extended so rarely. We are told we may allow our emotions a free rein . . . or no rein at all.

If we are all insane, then sanity becomes a matter of degree. If your insanity leads you to carve up women like Jack the Ripper or the Cleveland Torso Murderer, we clap you away in the funny farm (but neither of those two amateur-night surgeons was ever caught, heh-heh-heh); if, on the other hand your insanity leads you only to talk to yourself when you're under stress or to pick your nose on the morning bus, then you are left alone to go about your business . . . though it is doubtful that you will ever be invited to the best parties.

The potential lyncher is in almost all of us (excluding saints, past and present; but then, most saints have been crazy in their own ways), and every now and then, he has to be let loose to scream and roll around in the grass. Our emotions and our fears form their own body, and we recognize that it demands its own exercise to maintain proper muscle tone. Certain of these emotional muscles are accepted—even exalted—in civilized society; they are, of course, the emotions that tend to maintain the status quo of civilization itself. Love, friendship, loyalty, kindness—these are all the emotions that we applaud, emotions that have been immortalized in the couplets of Hallmark cards. . . .

When we exhibit these emotions, society showers us with positive reinforcement; we learn this even before we get out of diapers. When, as children, we hug our rotten little puke of a sister and give her a kiss, all the aunts and uncles smile and twit and cry, "Isn't he the sweetest little thing?" Such coveted treats as chocolate-covered graham crackers often follow. But if we deliberately slam the rotten little puke of a sister's fingers in the door, sanctions follow—angry remonstrance from parents, aunts and uncles; instead of a chocolate-covered graham cracker, a spanking.

But anticivilization emotions don't go away, and they demand periodic exercise. We have such "sick" jokes as, "What's the difference between a truckload of bowling balls and a truckload of dead babies?" (You can't unload a truckload of bowling balls with a pitchfork . . . a joke, by the way, that I heard originally from a ten-year-old.) Such a joke may surprise a laugh or a grin out of us even as we recoil, a possibility that confirms the thesis: If we share a brotherhood of man, then we also share an insanity of man. None of which is intended as a defense of either the sick joke or insanity but merely as an explanation of why the best horror films, like the best fairy tales, manage to be reactionary, anarchistic, and revolutionary all at the same time.

The mythic horror movie, like the sick joke, has a dirty job to do. It deliberately appeals to all that is worst in us. It is morbidity unchained, our most base instincts let free, our nastiest fantasies realized . . . and it all happens, fittingly enough, in the dark. For those reasons, good liberals often shy away from horror films. For myself, I like to see the most aggressive of them—*Dawn of the Dead,* for instance—as lifting a trap door in the civilized forebrain and throwing a basket of raw meat to the hungry alligators swimming around in that subterranean river beneath.

Why bother? Because it keeps them from getting out, man. It keeps them down there and me up here. It was Lennon and McCartney who said that all you need is love, and I would agree with that.

As long as you keep the gators fed.

**Vocabulary** Before, during, and after reading the selection, annotate the text and write in your journal. Create a list of vocabulary words, along with their definitions. Give examples of their use from the selection you just read.

## After Reading Discussion Questions: Meaning, Structure, and Expression

1. **Main Idea:** Work as a group to write a summary that answers the following questions: What purpose did Stephen King have for writing this essay? Who is his intended audience? What is the essay's main idea?

2. **Relevant Details:** In paragraphs 10 and 11, King uses children as examples to support his point. Why do you think he uses these examples? Do you think these examples are typical of most children? Do you agree that these examples effectively support his point? Why or why not?

3. **Logical Order:** King declares his thesis in paragraph 11. Locate his thesis statement. Why do you think King waited until this late in the essay to state his thesis? Reread his introduction. What is his opening point? Why do you think he opened his essay with this idea? How would the impact of the essay change if King had stated his thesis in the opening paragraph?

4. **Effective Expression:** To make his point, King appeals to our senses and prior experiences with references to roller coasters, Jack the Ripper, lynching, and alligators. Discuss how each of these images supports his point.

## Thinking Prompts to Move from Reading to Writing

1. King offers reasons that explain the positive effects of horror movies. However, many disagree with this view and see the violence in horror movies as a negative factor in our society. Write an essay that explains the negative impact of horror movies.

2. King claims that we are "all mentally ill" and that horror movies appeal to the "worst in us." However, many believe that humans are basically good. The famous American essayist Emerson once encouraged us "to look into yourselves and do good because you are good." Write an essay that illustrates the goodness and positive impact of human nature. Consider, for example, the reasons and effects of Habitat for Humanity or other charities or volunteer organizations.

# Let's Tell the Story of All America's Cultures

## YUH JI-YEON

Yuh Ji-Yeon, born in 1965, immigrated with her parents to Chicago from Seoul, Korea. She is best known for her book *Beyond the Shadow of Camptown* that examines the experiences of Korean women who immigrated to this country as brides of U.S. soldiers. She currently teaches history at Northwestern University.

**Before Reading** Write a journal entry about the positive contributions of minorities to the culture of the United States. For example, how have African Americans, Asians, or Latinos affected music, movies, fashion, or politics? Identify a particular person who has made a specific contribution. Do you think history books adequately record the contributions made by minorities? Explain your reasons.

I grew up hearing, seeing and almost believing that America was white—albeit with a little black tinge here and there—and that white was best. 1

The white people were everywhere in my 1970s Chicago childhood: Founding Fathers, Lewis and Clark, Lincoln, Daniel Boone, Carnegie, presidents, explorers and industrialists galore. The only black people were slaves. The only Indians were scalpers. 2

I never heard one word about how Benjamin Franklin was so impressed by the Iroquois federation of nations that he adapted that model into our system of state and federal government. Or that the Indian tribes were systematically betrayed and massacred by a greedy young nation that stole their land and called it the United States. 3

I never heard one word about how Asian immigrants were among the first to turn California's desert into fields of plenty. Or about Chinese immigrant Ah Bing, who bred the cherry now on sale in groceries across the nation. Or that plantation owners in Hawaii imported labor from China, Japan, Korea and the Philippines to work the sugar cane fields. I never learned that Asian immigrants were the only immigrants denied U.S. citizenship, even though they served honorably in World War I. All the immigrants in my textbook were white. 4

I never learned about Frederick Douglass, the runaway slave who became a leading abolitionist and statesman, or about black scholar W.E.B. Du Bois. I never learned that black people rose up in arms against slavery. Nat Turner wasn't one of the heroes in my childhood history class. 5

I never learned that the American Southwest and California were already settled by Mexicans when they were annexed after the Mexican-American War. I never learned that Mexico once had a problem keeping land-hungry white men on the U.S. side of the border. 6

So when other children called me a slant-eyed chink and told me to go back where I came from, I was ready to believe that I wasn't really an American because I wasn't white. 7

America's bittersweet legacy of struggling and failing and getting another step closer to democratic ideals of liberty and equality and justice for all wasn't for the likes of me, an immigrant child from Korea. The history books said so. 8

Well, the history books were wrong.                                                      9

Educators around the country are finally realizing what I realized as a teenager in the    10
library, looking up the history I wasn't getting in school. America is a multicultural nation,
composed of many people with varying histories and varying traditions who have little in
common except their humanity, a belief in democracy and a desire for freedom.

America changed them, but they changed America too.                                      11

A committee of scholars and teachers gathered by the New York State Department of        12
Education recognizes this in their recent report, "One Nation, Many Peoples: A Declaration of
Cultural Interdependence."

They recommend that public schools provide a "multicultural education, anchored to the     13
shared principles of a liberal democracy."

What that means, according to the report, is recognizing that America was shaped and       14
continues to be shaped by people of diverse backgrounds. It calls for students to be taught that
history is an ongoing process of discovery and interpretation of the past, and that there is
more than one way of viewing the world.

Thus, the westward migration of white Americans is not just a heroic settling of an         15
untamed wild, but also the conquest of indigenous peoples. Immigrants were not just white,
but Asian as well. Blacks were not merely passive slaves freed by northern whites, but active
fighters for their own liberation.

In particular, according to the report, the curriculum should help children "to assess       16
critically the reasons for the inconsistencies between the ideals of the U.S. and social realities.
It should provide information and intellectual tools that can permit them to contribute to
bringing reality closer to the ideals."

In other words, show children the good with the bad, and give them the skills to help       17
improve their country. What could be more patriotic?

Several dissenting members of the New York committee publicly worry that America will      18
splinter into ethnic fragments if this multicultural curriculum is adopted. They argue that the
committee's report puts the focus on ethnicity at the expense of national unity.

But downplaying ethnicity will not bolster national unity. The history of America is the story   19
of how and why people from all over the world came to the United States, and how in
struggling to make a better life for themselves, they changed each other, they changed the
country, and they all came to call themselves Americans.

*E pluribus unum.* Out of many, one.                                                      20

This is why I, with my Korean background, and my childhood tormentors, with their lost-     21
in-the-mist-of-time European backgrounds, are all Americans.

It is the unique beauty of this country. It is high time we let all our children gaze upon it.    22

**Vocabulary** Before, during, and after reading the selection, annotate the text and
write in your journal. Create a list of vocabulary words, along with their definitions. Give
examples of their use from the selection you just read.

## After Reading Discussion Questions: Meaning, Structure, and Expression

1. **Main Idea:** Work as a group to write a summary that answers the following questions:
   What purpose did Yuh Ji-Yeon have for writing this essay? Who is her intended
   audience? What is the essay's main idea?
2. **Relevant Details:** Yuh blends details from her personal experiences with expert
   opinions. Identify the details based on her experiences. Are the personal details she

provides convincing enough to persuade her reader to agree with her? Identify the details based on expert opinions. Does Yuh provide enough expert opinions and factual details to make her point? Why did she choose to include both personal experiences and expert opinions? Is the mixture persuasive? Why or why not?

3. **Logical Order:** An effective persuasive technique is to answer the concerns of the opposing view. Yuh waits to address the opposing view until paragraph 18. Why did she choose to do so at this point in her essay? Would her point be better made if she addressed the opposing view earlier in the essay? Why or why not?

4. **Effective Expression:** In paragraphs 1 through 6, Yuh repeats the parallel phrases "I never heard" or "I never learned." What is the impact of repeating these phrases and other parallel expressions on the essay's effectiveness? Explain your answer.

## Thinking Prompts to Move from Reading to Writing

1. Yuh identifies and argues against one problem in education that she sees as particularly troubling. What problems have you noticed in our country's educational system or at your institution? For example, some suggest school uniforms as a solution to behavior problems and underachievement in public education. Another example is the acute problem of binge drinking on college campuses. Identify a problem or a solution to a problem in education. Take a stand on the issue. Write an essay that convinces others to agree with your stand; be sure to answer the opposing view.

2. Yuh calls for educators to "tell the story of all America's cultures," and she offers several examples of important historical figures that she never learned about in school. Identify a person, place, or event that students should study. Write an essay to convince your teacher, school board, or community to include this person, place, or event in the curriculum. Anticipate and answer the opposing view.

# I Have a Dream
## MARTIN LUTHER KING, JR.

Dr. Martin Luther King, Jr., born in Atlanta, Georgia, became a Baptist minister and one of the greatest civil rights leaders of the twentieth century. Influenced by Henry David Thoreau and Mahatma Gandhi, King transformed the civil rights movement of the 1950s and 1960s with his message of nonviolent civil disobedience as a means to achieve racial equality. He received the Nobel Peace Prize in 1964. King was assassinated on April 4, 1968, at the age of 39. The following passage is considered one of his most memorable speeches, delivered on the occasion of the March on Washington, a demonstration in the nation's capital in support of equal rights, on August 28, 1963. Dr. King spoke to more than 200,000 marchers from the steps of the Lincoln Memorial that day.

**Before Reading** Write a journal entry about Dr. Martin Luther King, Jr. and the civil rights movement. What do you know about what happened? What impact has Dr. King had on our society?

I am happy to join with you today in what will go down in history as the greatest demonstration for freedom in the history of our nation.

Five score years ago, a great American, in whose symbolic shadow we stand today, signed the Emancipation Proclamation. This momentous decree came as a great beacon light of hope to millions of Negro slaves who had been seared in the flames of withering injustice. It came as a joyous daybreak to end the long night of their captivity. But one hundred years later, the Negro still is not free. One hundred years later, the life of the Negro is still sadly crippled by the manacles of segregation and the chains of discrimination. One hundred years later, the Negro lives on a lonely island of poverty in the midst of a vast ocean of material prosperity. One hundred years later, the Negro is still languished in the corners of American society and finds himself an exile in his own land. And so we've come here today to dramatize a shameful condition.

In a sense we've come to our nation's capital to cash a check. When the architects of our republic wrote the magnificent words of the Constitution and the Declaration of Independence, they were signing a promissory note to which every American was to fall heir. This note was a promise that all men, yes, black men as well as white men, would be guaranteed the "unalienable Rights" of "Life, Liberty and the pursuit of Happiness." It is obvious today that America has defaulted on this promissory note, insofar as her citizens of color are concerned. Instead of honoring this sacred obligation, America has given the Negro people a bad check, a check which has come back marked "insufficient funds."

But we refuse to believe that the bank of justice is bankrupt. We refuse to believe that there are insufficient funds in the great vaults of opportunity of this nation. And so, we've come to cash this check, a check that will give us upon demand the riches of freedom and the security of justice.

We have also come to this hallowed spot to remind America of the fierce urgency of Now. This is no time to engage in the luxury of cooling off or to take the tranquilizing drug of gradualism. Now is the time to make real the promises of democracy. Now is the time to rise from the dark and desolate valley of segregation to the sunlit path of racial justice. Now is the time to lift our nation from the quicksands of racial injustice to the solid rock of brotherhood. Now is the time to make justice a reality for all of God's children.

It would be fatal for the nation to overlook the urgency of the moment. This sweltering summer of the Negro's legitimate discontent will not pass until there is an invigorating autumn of freedom and equality. Nineteen sixty-three is not an end, but a beginning. And those who hope that the Negro needed to blow off steam and will now be content will have a rude awakening if the nation returns to business as usual. And there will be neither rest nor tranquility in America until the Negro is granted his citizenship rights. The whirlwinds of revolt will continue to shake the foundations of our nation until the bright day of justice emerges.

But there is something that I must say to my people, who stand on the warm threshold which leads into the palace of justice: In the process of gaining our rightful place, we must not be guilty of wrongful deeds. Let us not seek to satisfy our thirst for freedom by drinking from the cup of bitterness and hatred. We must forever conduct our struggle on the high plane of dignity and discipline. We must not allow our creative protest to degenerate into physical violence. Again and again, we must rise to the majestic heights of meeting physical force with soul force.

The marvelous new militancy which has engulfed the Negro community must not lead us to a distrust of all white people, for many of our white brothers, as evidenced by their presence here today, have come to realize that their destiny is tied up with our destiny. And they have come to realize that their freedom is inextricably bound to our freedom.

We cannot walk alone. 9

And as we walk, we must make the pledge that we shall always march ahead. 10

We cannot turn back. 11

There are those who are asking the devotees of civil rights, "When will you be satisfied?" We 12
can never be satisfied as long as the Negro is the victim of the unspeakable horrors of police
brutality. We can never be satisfied as long as our bodies, heavy with the fatigue of travel,
cannot gain lodging in the motels of the highways and the hotels of the cities. We cannot be
satisfied as long as the Negro's basic mobility is from a smaller ghetto to a larger one. We can
never be satisfied as long as our children are stripped of their self-hood and robbed of their
dignity by signs stating: "For Whites Only." We cannot be satisfied as long as a Negro in
Mississippi cannot vote and a Negro in New York believes he has nothing for which to vote.
No, no, we are not satisfied, and we will not be satisfied until "justice rolls down like waters,
and righteousness like a mighty stream."

I am not unmindful that some of you have come here out of great trials and tribulations. 13
Some of you have come fresh from narrow jail cells. And some of you have come from areas
of persecution and staggered by the winds of police brutality. You have been the veterans of
creative suffering. Continue to work with the faith that unearned suffering is redemptive. Go
back to Mississippi, go back to Alabama, go back to South Carolina, go back to Georgia, go
back to Louisiana, go back to the slums and ghettos of our northern cities, knowing that
somehow this situation can and will be changed.

Let us not wallow in the valley of despair, I say to you today, my friends. 14

And so even though we face the difficulties of today and tomorrow, I still have a dream. It is 15
a dream deeply rooted in the American dream.

I have a dream that one day this nation will rise up and live out the true meaning of its 16
creed: "We hold these truths to be self-evident, that all men are created equal."

I have a dream that one day on the red hills of Georgia, the sons of former slaves and the 17
sons of former slave owners will be able to sit down together at the table of brotherhood.

I have a dream that one day even the state of Mississippi, a state sweltering with the heat of 18
injustice, sweltering with the heat of oppression, will be transformed into an oasis of freedom
and justice.

I have a dream that my four little children will one day live in a nation where they will not 19
be judged by the color of their skin but by the content of their character.

I have a *dream* today! 20

I have a dream that one day, down in Alabama, with its vicious racists, with its governor 21
having his lips dripping with the words of "interposition" and "nullification"—one day right
there in Alabama little black boys and black girls will be able to join hands with little white
boys and white girls as sisters and brothers.

I have a *dream* today! 22

I have a dream that one day every valley shall be exalted, and every hill and mountain 23
shall be made low, the rough places will be made plain, and the crooked places will be made
straight; "and the glory of the Lord shall be revealed and all flesh shall see it together."

This is our hope, and this is the faith that I go back to the South with. 24

With this faith, we will be able to hew out of the mountain of despair a stone of hope. With this 25
faith, we will be able to transform the jangling discords of our nation into a beautiful symphony of
brotherhood. With this faith, we will be able to work together, to pray together, to struggle together,
to go to jail together, to stand up for freedom together, knowing that we will be free one day.

And this will be the day—this will be the day when all of God's children will be able to sing 26
with new meaning:

*My country 'tis of thee, sweet land of liberty, of thee I sing.* 27

*Land where my fathers died, land of the Pilgrim's pride,* 28

*From every mountainside, let freedom ring!* 29

And if America is to be a great nation, this must become true. 30

And so let freedom ring from the prodigious hilltops of New Hampshire. 31

Let freedom ring from the mighty mountains of New York. 32

Let freedom ring from the heightening Alleghenies of Pennsylvania. 33

Let freedom ring from the snow-capped Rockies of Colorado. 34

Let freedom ring from the curvaceous slopes of California. 35

But not only that: 36

Let freedom ring from Stone Mountain of Georgia. 37

Let freedom ring from Lookout Mountain of Tennessee. 38

Let freedom ring from every hill and molehill of Mississippi. 39

From every mountainside, let freedom ring. 40

And when this happens, when we allow freedom ring, when we let it ring from every village 41
and every hamlet, from every state and every city, we will be able to speed up that day when
*all* of God's children, black men and white men, Jews and Gentiles, Protestants and Catholics,
will be able to join hands and sing in the words of the old Negro spiritual:

*Free at last! Free at last!* 42

*Thank God Almighty, we are free at last!* 43

## Vocabulary

**Vocabulary**  Before, during, and after reading the selection, annotate the text and write in your journal. Create a list of vocabulary words, along with their definitions. Give examples of their use from the selection you just read.

## After Reading Discussion Questions:  Meaning, Structure, and Expression

1. **Main Idea:** Work as a group to write a summary that answers the following questions: What purpose did Martin Luther King, Jr. have for giving this speech? Who is the intended audience? What is the main idea of the speech?

2. **Relevant Details:** Martin Luther King, Jr. is known for his powerful style. At times, he draws on sensory details such as "an invigorating autumn of freedom and equality" (paragraph 6). He also creates word pictures as in "the manacles of segregation" (paragraph 2). These figures of speech create vivid mental images that support his point and set the tone. Find at least three additional powerful figures of speech in this reading. What is Dr. King describing in these figures of speech—historical facts, emotions, ideals?

3. **Logical Order:** Martin Luther King, Jr. presents his argument for change in three phases or sections. The first section, paragraphs 1 through 6, describes the social conditions surrounding the speech. The second section, paragraphs 7 through 14, calls for action. The third section, paragraphs 15 through 43, describes his "dream." Why did he choose this order for his ideas?

4. **Effective Expression:** Martin Luther King, Jr. skillfully phrases his ideas. His use of parallelism and certain repeated phrases adds drama and emphasis to his words. For example, in paragraph 25 every sentence is parallel; each is a simple sentence that begins with a prepositional phrase that is followed by a subject and verb. In fact, King creates this parallelism by repeating the wording in certain phrases such as "with this faith" and "we will be able to." Search the entire speech for other examples of parallelism and repeated phrases. Discuss the impact of each example. How do parallelism and repeated phrasing affect the pace of the speech?

## Thinking Prompts to Move from Reading to Writing

**1.** In this speech, Dr. King confronted prejudice and shared his dream of a world where all people enjoy justice and peace. What is a current problem that we must confront to improve our society? How would Dr. King respond to a major issue we face today, such as drug abuse, global warming, or human trafficking? Write about a dream you have for making the world a better place. Assume you are competing in a "Freedom of Expression" writing contest sponsored by local merchants in honor of Black History month. Winners will receive $200 in cash, and the winning essay will be read on the local radio station throughout the month of February.

**2.** Identify one problem in your local community. Explain why the problem is significant and discuss the steps necessary to correct it. Assume you are writing a letter to the editor of your newspaper.

# Remarks by the President at the Holocaust Days of Remembrance Ceremony

## BARACK OBAMA

The Holocaust was the systematic, state-sponsored persecution and murder of approximately six million Jews by the Nazi regime and its partners. *Holocaust* is a word of Greek origin meaning "sacrifice by fire." The United States Congress established the Days of Remembrance as our nation's annual commemoration of the Holocaust. Congress also created the United States Holocaust Memorial Museum. The museum is a lasting living memorial to the victims. On Tuesday, April 21, 2009, President Barack Obama gave the following speech at the Holocaust Remembrance Day in Washington, D.C. The Museum chose *Never Again: What You Do Matters* as the theme for the 2009 observance. President Obama spoke to that theme.

**Before Reading**   Write a journal entry about what you know about the Holocaust. Also, respond to the theme the museum chose for the 2009 Days of Remembrance. What do you think is meant by Never Again: What You Do Matters? How could this theme apply to current events around the world or in our country?

We gather today to mourn the loss of so many lives, and celebrate those who saved them; honor those who survived, and contemplate the obligations of the living. 1

It is the grimmest of ironies that one of the most savage, barbaric acts of evil in history began in one of the most modernized societies of its time, where so many markers of human progress became tools of human depravity: science that can heal used to kill; education that can enlighten used to rationalize away basic moral impulses; the bureaucracy that sustains modern life used as the machinery of mass death—a ruthless, chillingly efficient system where many were responsible for the killing, but few got actual blood on their hands. 2

While the uniqueness of the Holocaust in scope and in method is truly astounding, the Holocaust was driven by many of the same forces that have fueled atrocities throughout history: the scapegoating that leads to hatred and blinds us to our common humanity; the justifications that replace conscience and allow cruelty to spread; the willingness of those who are neither perpetrators nor victims to accept the assigned role of bystander, believing the lie that good people are ever powerless or alone, the fiction that we do not have a choice. 3

But while we are here today to bear witness to the human capacity to destroy, we are also here to pay tribute to the human impulse to save. In the moral accounting of the Holocaust, as we reckon with numbers like 6 million, as we recall the horror of numbers etched into arms, we also factor in numbers like these: 7,200—the number of Danish Jews ferried to safety, many of whom later returned home to find the neighbors who rescued them had also faithfully tended their homes and businesses and belongings while they were gone.

We remember the number five—the five righteous men and women who join us today from Poland. We are awed by your acts of courage and conscience. And your presence today compels each of us to ask ourselves whether we would have done what you did. We can only hope that the answer is yes.

We also remember the number 5,000—the number of Jews rescued by the villagers of Le Chambon, France—one life saved for each of its 5,000 residents. Not a single Jew who came there was turned away, or turned in. But it was not until decades later that the villagers spoke of what they had done—and even then, only reluctantly. The author of a book on the rescue found that those he interviewed were baffled by his interest. "How could you call us 'good'?" they said. "We were doing what had to be done."

That is the question of the righteous—those who would do extraordinary good at extraordinary risk not for affirmation or acclaim or to advance their own interests, but because it is what must be done. They remind us that no one is born a savior or a murderer—these are choices we each have the power to make. They teach us that no one can make us into bystanders without our consent, and that we are never truly alone—that if we have the courage to heed that "still, small voice" within us, we can form a minyan for righteousness that can span a village, even a nation.

Their legacy is our inheritance. And the question is, how do we honor and preserve it? How do we ensure that "never again" isn't an empty slogan, or merely an aspiration, but also a call to action?

I believe we start by doing what we are doing today—by bearing witness, by fighting the silence that is evil's greatest co-conspirator.

In the face of horrors that defy comprehension, the impulse to silence is understandable. My own great uncle returned from his service in World War II in a state of shock, saying little, alone with painful memories that would not leave his head. He went up into the attic, according to the stories that I've heard, and wouldn't come down for six months. He was one of the liberators—someone who at a very tender age had seen the unimaginable. And so some of the liberators who are here today honor us with their presence—all of whom we honor for their extraordinary service. My great uncle was part of the 89th Infantry Division—the first Americans to reach a Nazi concentration camp. And they liberated Ohrdruf, part of Buchenwald, where tens of thousands had perished.

The story goes that when the Americans marched in, they discovered the starving survivors and the piles of dead bodies. And General Eisenhower made a decision. He ordered Germans from the nearby town to tour the camp, so they could see what had been done in their name. And he ordered American troops to tour the camp, so they could see the evil they were fighting against. Then he invited congressmen and journalists to bear witness. And he ordered that photographs and films be made. Some of us have seen those same images, whether in the Holocaust Museum or when I visited Yad Vashem, and they never leave you. Eisenhower said that he wanted "to be in a position to give firsthand evidence of these things, if ever, in the future, there develops a tendency to charge these allegations merely to propaganda."

Eisenhower understood the danger of silence. He understood that if no one knew what had happened, that would be yet another atrocity—and it would be the perpetrators' ultimate triumph.

What Eisenhower did to record these crimes for history is what we are doing here today. That's what Elie Wiesel and the survivors we honor here do by fighting to make their memories part of our collective memory. That's what the Holocaust Museum does every day on our National Mall, the place where we display for the world our triumphs and failures and the lessons we've learned from our history. It's the very opposite of silence.

But we must also remember that bearing witness is not the end of our obligation—it's just the beginning. We know that evil has yet to run its course on Earth. We've seen it in this century in the mass graves and the ashes of villages burned to the ground, and children used as soldiers and rape used as a weapon of war. To this day, there are those who insist the Holocaust never happened; who perpetrate every form of intolerance—racism and anti-Semitism, homophobia, xenophobia, sexism, and more—hatred that degrades its victim and diminishes us all.

Today, and every day, we have an opportunity, as well as an obligation, to confront these scourges—to fight the impulse to turn the channel when we see images that disturb us, or wrap ourselves in the false comfort that others' sufferings are not our own. Instead we have the opportunity to make a habit of empathy; to recognize ourselves in each other; to commit ourselves to resisting injustice and intolerance and indifference in whatever forms they may take—whether confronting those who tell lies about history, or doing everything we can to prevent and end atrocities like those that took place in Rwanda, those taking place in Darfur. That is my commitment as President. I hope that is yours, as well.

It will not be easy. At times, fulfilling these obligations require self-reflection. But in the final analysis, I believe history gives us cause for hope rather than despair—the hope of a chosen people who have overcome oppression since the days of Exodus; of the nation of Israel rising from the destruction of the Holocaust; of the strong and enduring bonds between our nations. It is the hope, too, of those who not only survived, but chose to live, teaching us the meaning of courage and resilience and dignity. I'm thinking today of a study conducted after the war that found that Holocaust survivors living in America actually had a higher birthrate than American Jews. What a stunning act of faith—to bring a child in a world that has shown you so much cruelty; to believe that no matter what you have endured, or how much you have lost, in the end, you have a duty to life.

We find cause for hope as well in Protestant and Catholic children attending school together in Northern Ireland; in Hutus and Tutsis living side by side, forgiving neighbors who have done the unforgivable; in a movement to save Darfur that has thousands of high school and college chapters in 25 countries, and brought 70,000 people to the Washington Mall—people of every age and faith and background and race united in common cause with suffering brothers and sisters halfway around the world.

Those numbers can be our future—our fellow citizens of the world showing us how to make the journey from oppression to survival, from witness to resistance, and ultimately to reconciliation. That is what we mean when we say "never again."

So today, during this season when we celebrate liberation, resurrection, and the possibility of redemption, may each of us renew our resolve to do what must be done. And may we strive each day, both individually and as a nation, to be among the righteous.

Thank you, God bless you, and God bless the United States of America.

**Vocabulary** Before, during, and after reading the selection, annotate the text and write in your journal. Create a list of vocabulary words, along with their definitions. Give examples of their use from the selection you just read.

## After Reading Discussion Questions: Meaning, Structure, and Expression

**1. Main Idea:** Work as a group to write a summary that answers the following questions: What purpose did President Obama want to fulfill by giving this speech? Who is the intended audience? What is the main idea of the speech?

**2. Relevant Details:** In paragraph 5, President Obama refers to "the five righteous men and women who join us today from Poland." Does President Obama give us enough information about these people? Who are they and what did they do? What clues does President Obama give us about the actions of these people? Why did he include paragraph 5? Should he have given us more information? Why or why not?

**3. Logical Order:** In paragraph 10 President Obama shares with the audience the personal experience of his great uncle as a soldier and returning veteran of World War II. Why did he include this personal example? And why did he choose to place it where he did in the speech? Would this information have been more effective as part of the introduction or conclusion instead of its current location? Why or why not?

**4. Effective Expression:** How would you describe the overall tone or mood of the speech? What tone does President Obama take in paragraphs 1 through 3? What tone does he use in paragraphs 4 through 6? What is his attitude in paragraphs 11 through 16? What is the relationship between his tone and the event at which he is speaking? What impact does he want to have on his audience? Give examples of specific words to support your interpretation of his tone.

## Thinking Prompts to Move from Reading to Writing

**1.** In paragraph 14, President Obama condemns those "who perpetrate every form of intolerance—racism and anti-Semitism, homophobia, xenophobia, sexism, and more—hatred that degrades its victim and diminishes us all." Assume you are writing an essay for a college sociology class. Choose one of the forms of intolerance listed by President Obama. Define the term you chose and explain how this form of intolerance "degrades its victim and diminishes us all." Then, suggest ways to confront or resist this form of intolerance.

**2.** In his speech, President Obama calls us to "bear witness" against injustice by "fighting the silence that is evil's greatest co-conspirator." Assume you are an officer of your college's Student Government Association (SGA). SGA is organizing a Holocaust Remembrance Day at your college. As the SGA representative, you are asked to give a speech of remembrance. Also assume a copy of your speech will be printed in the college newspaper. Go to the homepage of the Holocaust Museum at <http://www.ushmm.org/>. Browse the site for information for your speech. Use the following MLA format to document your information.

United States Holocaust Memorial Museum. "Title of Article." *Title of Page or Resource within Museum's Webpage.* [Date of access in the following form: day month year.] <URL>.

**Example of a Citation:**

United States Holocaust Memorial Museum. "The Holocaust." *Holocaust Encyclopedia.* 18 Oct. 2009 <http://www.ushmm.org/wlc/en/index.php?ModuleId=10005143>.

# Text Credits

Angelou, Maya. "New Directions," from *Wouldn't Take Nothing for My Journey Now*, copyright © 1993 by Maya Angelou. Used by permission of Random House, Inc. For on-line information about Random House, Inc. and authors, see the Internet web site at http://www.randomhouse.com.

Angwin, Julia. "How to Twitter" by Julia Angwin from *The Wall Street Journal*, March 13, 2009. Reprinted by permission of *The Wall Street Journal*, Copyright © 2009 Dow Jones & Company, Inc. All Rights Reserved Worldwide. License numbers 2313140683745 (print) and 2313140765339 (ebook).

Ashwell, Rachel. "Don't Leave School Just Yet" from *What I Know Now: Letters to My Younger Self*, edited by Ellyn Spragins. Copyright © 2006 by Ellyn Spragins. Afterword copyright © 2008 by Ellyn Spragins. Used by permission of Broadway Books, a division of Random House, Inc.

Brady, Judy. "Why I Want a Wife." Originally published in *Ms. Magazine*, Spring 1971. Reprinted by permission of the author.

Carson, Rachel. "A Fable for Tomorrow" from *Silent Spring*. Copyright © 1962 by Rachel L. Carson, copyright © renewed 1990 by Roger Christie. Reprinted by permission of Frances Collin, Trustee. All copying including electronic and/or re-distribution of this text is expressly forbidden.

Cofer, Judith Ortiz. "Don't Call Me a Hot Tamale!" or "The Myth of the Latin Woman: I Just Met a Girl Named Maria," from *The Latin Deli: Prose and Poetry*. Reprinted by permission of The University of Georgia Press.

De Vito, Joseph. *Interpersonal Communication Book*. © 2009. Reproduced by permission of Pearson Education, Inc.

Farrell, Warren. "Are Women Earning More Than Men?" from Forbes.com, May 12, 2006. Reprinted by Permission of *Forbes Magazine* © 2009 Forbes LLC.

Franklin, Benjamin. "The Whistle." Brander Matthews, ed. *The Oxford Book of American Essays*. New York: Oxford University Press, 1914; Bartleby.com, 2000. www.bartleby.com/109/. (Dec. 22, 2008)

From *The Autobiography of Malcolm X* by Malcolm X and Alex Haley. Copyright © 1964 by Alex Haley and Malcolm X. Copyright © 1965 by Alex Haley and Betty Shabazz. Used by permission of Random House, Inc.

Gilbert, Elizabeth. "Book One: Italy," from *Eat, Pray, Love*, copyright © 2006 by Elizabeth Gilbert. Used by permission of Viking Penguin, a division of Penguin Group (USA) Inc.

Goodwin-Parker, Jo. "What is Poverty?" in *America's Other Children: Public Schools Outside Suburbia*, by George Henderson. Copyright © 1971 by University of Oklahoma Press, Norman. Reprinted by permission of the publisher. All rights reserved.

Haines, John. "Snow" from *The Stars, The Snow, The Fire: Twenty-Five Years in the Alaska Wilderness*. Copyright © 1989 by John Haines. Reprinted by permission of Graywolf Press, Minneapolis, Minnesota, www.Graywolf Press.org.

Hasselstrom, Linda M. "Why One Peaceful Woman Carries a Pistol," in *Land Circle*, Fulcrum, Inc., 1991. Used by permission of Fulcrum Inc.

Henslin, James A. *Essentials of Sociology: A Down-to-Earth Approach*, 7th ed. Boston: Allyn & Bacon, 2008.

Hospice Council of Metropolitan Washington. "A Guide to Grief" from www.nhpco.org/marketplace. Copyright © 2006 National Hospice and Palliative Care Organization, Alexandria, Virginia. All rights reserved. http://iweb.nhpco.org/iweb/Purchase/ProductDetail.sapx?Product_code=713461. Reprinted with permission.

Hughes, Robert. *Running With Walker: A Memoir*. Copyright © Robert Hughes. Reprinted by permission of Jessica Kingsley Publishers.

Jaffe, Michael L. *Understanding Parenting*, © 1997 Allyn and Bacon, Boston, MA. Reproduced by permission of Pearson Education, Inc.

Keillor, Garrison. "How to Write a Personal Letter," from *We Are Still Married*. (Originally written for "Power of The Printed Word" series by the International Paper Company.) Copyright © 1989 by International Paper Company. Reprinted by permission of Garrison Keillor.

King, Martin Luther, Jr. "I Have a Dream," speech delivered 28 of August 1963 at the Lincoln Memorial, Washington, DC. Reprinted by arrangement with The Heirs to the Estate of Martin Luther King Jr., c/o Writers House as agent for the proprietor New York, NY. Copyright 1963 Dr. Martin Luther King Jr.; copyright renewed 1991 Coretta Scott King.

King, Stephen. "Why We Crave Horror Movies." Reprinted With Permission. © Stephen King. All rights reserved. Originally appeared in *Playboy* (1982).

Leman, Dr. Kevin. "Birth Order—Does It Really Make Any Sense?" from *The Birth Order Book*, published by Revell, a division of Baker Publishing Group. Copyright © 1985, 1998 Kevin Leman. Reprinted with permission.

Lubell, Sam. "Block That Ringtone!" Copyright © 2004 by the New York Times Co. Reprinted by permission of PARS for New York Times.

Madden, John. "My Favorite Guys" from *One Knee Equals Two Feet* by John Madden and Dave Anderson, copyright © 1986 by John Madden, Inc. Used with permission of Villard Books, a division of Random House, Inc. Copyright © 1986 John Madden, Inc. For on-line information about other Random House, Inc. books and authors, see the Internet web site at http://www.randomhouse.com.

Malone, Michael S. "Through Young Eyes." Posted by Edgelings on May 14, 2009, © 2009 PJM Tech: Edgelings. Reprinted by permission.

Michigan State Board of Education. (1994). Graphics from *Assessment Frameworks for the Michigan High School Proficiency Test in Communication Arts. Part I: Writing*. Lansing, MI: Michigan Department of Education. Reprinted with permission.

# Photo Credits

Rob Melnychuk/Corbis: 2; Pelene Rogers/Alamy: 3 top; ©fotofresh/Alamy: 3 top center; Hans Neleman/Zefa/Corbis: 14; Tom Stewart/Surf/Corbis: 15 top left; Ronnie Kaufman/Corbis: 15 top right; Matthew Cavanaugh/epa/Corbis: 15 bottom left; JGI/Getty Images: 15 bottom right; Randy Faris/Corbis: 18 top left; Getty Images: 18 top right; Ramin Talaife/Corbis: 18 bottom left; Dex Images/Corbis: 18 bottom right; Richard Hutchings/Terra/Corbis: 20 left; Charles Gullung/Corbis: 20 right; Comstock/Corbis: 21 left; AFP/Getty Images: 21 right; Richard Hutchings/Terra/Corbis: 22 left; AFP/Getty Images: 22 right; Richard Hutchings/Terra/Corbis: 22 bottom left; Charles Gullung/Corbis: 22 center left; Constock/Corbis: 22 center right; ©Mike Baldwin/www.CartoonStock.com: 26; Mark Peterson/Corbis: 28; Corbis: 30; Turbo/Corbis: 32; Julian Stratenschulte/epa/Corbis: 38; ©Trains and Planes/Alamy: 50; Gideon Mendel/Corbis: 52 top; Flame/Corbis: 52 center; Brand X/Corbis: 52 bottom; Bloomimage/Corbis: 54 top; Andrew Fox/Corbis: 54 center; Gabe Palmer/Corbis: 54 bottom; © 81A Productions/Corbis: Ed Quinn/Corbis: 57 top; Heiko Wolfraum/epa/Corbis: 57 center; 57 bottom; Henry Diltz/Corbis: 64 left; JP Laffont/Sygma/Corbis: 64 right; 330; Daniel Martinez/Somos Images/ Corbis: 331; Edward Bock/Corbis: 337; Rick Rickman/ NewSport/Corbis: 339; Clive Brunskill/Allsport/Getty Images: 341; Envision/Corbis: 343; Jose L. Pelaez/Corbis: 346; Ed Bock/Corbis: 347; Floresco Productions/Corbis RF: 350; John Lund/Drew Kelly/Blend Images/Corbis: 352; Alex Bartel/ Arcaid/Corbis: 353; Solus-Veer/Corbis: 357; Alison Wright/ Corbis: 358; Warren Faidley/Corbis: 360; Paul Buck/epa/ Corbis: 361; Richard Cummins/Corbis: 444; Bill Varie/Corbis: 445; James Leynse/Corbis: 447; Bob Krist/Corbis: 450; Ken Seet/Corbis RF: 451; Steve Cole/Getty Images RF: 384; Image Source/Corbis: 385; Peer Grimm/epa/Corbis: 390; Bjorn Sigurdson/epa/Corbis: 391; moodboard/Alamy RF: 394; Liu song/epa/Corbis: 395; Robert Galbraith/Reuters/Corbis: 397; Rick Rickman/NewSport/Corbis: 402; Ren Long/Xinhua Press/Corbis: 403; Brent Smith/Reuters/Corbis: 405; Mario Anzuoni/Reuters/Corbis: 409; Daniel J. Cox/Corbis: 412; Hans Strand/Corbis: 413; NASA/Corbis: 417; Louie Psihoyos/Corbis: 419; Layne Kennedy/Corbis: 421; Mike Nelson/epa/Corbis: 423; Peter Hulme/Ecoscene/Corbis: 425; Archives du 7eme Art/Photos12/Alamy: 364; Archives du 7eme Art/Photos12/Alamy: 365; 20th Century Fox/ZUMA/Corbis: 368; Bettmann/Corbis: 371; Fei Maohua/Xinhua Press/Corbis: 373; Pictorial Press Ltd./Alamy: 375; Patrick Giardino/Corbis: 379; Klaus-Dietmar Gabbert/epa/Corbis: 428; Klaus-Dietmar Gabbert/epa/Corbis: 429; Mario Anzuoni/Reuters/Corbis: 431; Brendan McDermid/Reuters/Corbis: 439; Yoshio Tomii/amanaimages/Corbis: 464; DLILLC/Corbis: 465; Jim Craigmyle/Corbis: 467; Vivianne Moos/Corbis: 469; Christine Kokot/dpa/Corbis: 470; Steve Holland/Reuters/Corbis: 471; Corbis: 471; Richard Cummins/Corbis: 476; Jerry Arcieri/Corbis: 477; Jim Craigmyle/Corbis: 478; Paul Barton/Corbis: 482; Paul Barton/Corbis: 483; Pam Gardner/Frank Lane Picture Agency/Corbis: 485; Douglas Kirkland/Corbis: 418; Barry Lewis/Corbis: 487; ©2008 King Features Syndicate, Inc. World rights reserved: 492; Robert Landau/Terra/Corbis: 494; J. Emilio Flores/Corbis: 498; Digital Vision/Alamy: 503; Andrew Holbrooke/Corbis: 506; David Arky/Corbis: 507;

James Leynse/Corbis: 512; Bob Krist/Corbis: 513; Ken Seet/Corbis: 452; Larry W. Smith/epa/Corbis: 459; Paul A. Souders/Corbis: 110; Corbis/ Bettmann: 111; Corbis/Bettmann: 112 (all); Corbis/ Bettmann: 113 (all); Corbis/Bettmann: 115; Joseph Sohm/Corbis: 121; Douglas Kirkland/Corbis: 142 (all); Frank Micelotta/Getty Images: 143 (top); Mike Blake/Corbis: 143 (center); Frank Polich/Reuters/ Corbis: 143 (bottom); © Rebecca Emery/Corbis: 144; Dorling Kindersley Media Library: 145 (all); Dorling Kindersley Media Library: 147 (all); Richard Hutchings/PhotoEdit, Inc.: 149. Page 151 (top to bottom): David Young-Wolff/PhotoEdit, Inc., Image100/Corbis RF, Michael Newman/PhotoEdit, Inc., Jeff Greenberg/Alamy, Elizabeth Lippman, Image100/Corbis RF. Gregor Schuster/zefa/Corbis: 152 (top); Ray Coleman/Photo Researchers, Inc: 152 (bottom);. Richard Drury/The Image Bank/Getty Images: 160; Sean Justice/Corbis RF: 161 (top) Fancy/Veer/Corbis RF: 161 (center); Image Source/ Corbis: 161 (bottom); Sean Justice/Corbis RF: 163 (top); Fancy/Veer/Corbis RF: 163 (center); Image Source/Corbis: 163 (bottom) DInspirestock/Corbis: 166; Blend Images/Alamy: 167 (left); George Shelley/ Corbis: 167 (center); David Young-Wolff/PhotoEdit, Inc.: 167 (right): Radius Images/Alamy: 170; ©Envision/Corbis: 167; Hans Neleman/Corbis: 178; John Atashian/Corbis: 179 (left); Jessica Rinaldi/ Reuters/Corbis: 179 (center); Chad Batka/Corbis: 179 (right); John Atashian/Corbis: 181 (top); Jessica Rinaldi/Reuters/Corbis: 181 (center); Chad Batka/ Corbis: 181 (bottom); Jon Ragel/Corbis: 185; mypyramid.com: 187; Dorling Kindersley Media Library: 196 (left); Klaus Hackenberg/Corbis: 196 (right); Alan Look/Corbis: 197 (top left); Alan Look/ Corbis: 197 (top right); Transtock/Corbis: 197 (center left); Car Culture/Corbis: 197 (center right); Robert Llewellyn/zefa/Corbis: 197 (bottom left); Ashley Cooper/Corbis: 197 (bottom right). Page 199 (top to bottom): Alan Look/Corbis, Alan Look/ Corbis, Transtock/Corbis, Car Culture/Corbis, Robert Llewellyn/zefa/Corbis, Ashley Cooper/Corbis. ©Robert W. Ginn/PhotoEdit, Inc.: 204 (top); ©Richard M. Abarno/Corbis: 204 (bottom); Chloe Johnson/Alamy: 210; David James/Warner Bros/ ZUMA/Corbis: 211 (left); SW Productions/BrandX/ Corbis: 211 (top right); Simon Jarratt/Corbis: 211 (center right); Gabe Palmer/Corbis: 211 (bottom right); ©Thunderdog Studios, Inc./Thunderdog Collective/Corbis: 219 (left); Art Kowalsky/Alamy: 219 (center); Chloe Johnson/Alamy: 219 (right); Gene Blevins/La Daly News/Corbis: 220; George Diebold/Corbis: 228; Courtesy Habitat for Humanity: 229 (all except top left); Joseph Sohm, ChromoSohm Inc./Corbis: 229 (top left); Courtesy Habitat for Humanity 231 (all except 231 top); Joseph Sohm, ChromoSohm Inc./Corbis: 231 (top); Tim Shaffer/Reuters/Corbis: 234; Michael Newman/ PhotoEdit, Inc.: 235 (both); John Lund/Nevada Wier/ Blend Images/Corbis RF: 241; Hill Street Studios/ Blend Images/Corbis: 244; Alan Shein Photography/ Corbis: 245 (top); Benelux/zefa/Corbis: 245 (second row left); James Leynse/Corbis: 245 (second row right); Lisa B./Corbis: 245 (third row left); Fancy/ Veer/Corbis: 245 (third row right); Ariel Skelley/ Corbis:

# Index